Do

FINANCIAL MARKETS IN HONG KONG
Law and Practice

FINANCIAL MARKETS IN HONG KONG

Law and Practice

BERRY FONG-CHUNG HSU
DOUGLAS W. ARNER
MAURICE KWOK-SANG TSE
SYREN JOHNSTONE

Consulting Editors
LAURENCE LU-JEN LI
PAUL LEJOT

OXFORD
UNIVERSITY PRESS

OXFORD

UNIVERSITY PRESS

Great Clarendon Street, Oxford OX2 6DP

Oxford University Press is a department of the University of Oxford.
It furthers the University's objective of excellence in research, scholarship,
and education by publishing worldwide in

Oxford New York

Auckland Cape Town Dar es Salaam Hong Kong Karachi
Kuala Lumpur Madrid Melbourne Mexico City Nairobi
New Delhi Shanghai Taipei Toronto

With offices in

Argentina Austria Brazil Chile Czech Republic France Greece
Guatemala Hungary Italy Japan Poland Portugal Singapore
South Korea Switzerland Thailand Turkey Ukraine Vietnam

Oxford is a registered trade mark of Oxford University Press
in the UK and in certain other countries

Published in the United States
by Oxford University Press Inc., New York

British Library Cataloguing in Publication Data

Data available

Library of Congress Cataloging-in-Publication Data

Financial markets in Hong Kong : law and practice / Berry Fong-Chung Hsu ... [et al.]
    p. cm.
Includes bibliographical references and index.
ISBN–13: 978–0–19–929078–9 (alk. paper)
ISBN–10: 0–19–929078–4 (alk. paper)
1. Financial services industry—Law and legislation—China—Hong Kong.
2. Financial institutions—Law and legislation—China—Hong Kong.
3. Financial services—China—Hong Kong. 4. Corporate governance—Law and
legislation—China—Hong Kong. 5. Securities—China—Hong Kong. I. Hsu,
Berry Fong-Chung, 1950–
    KNQ9323.6.F56 2006
    346.5125'082—dc22
                            2006002378

Typeset by RefineCatch Limited, Bungay, Suffolk
Printed in Great Britain
on acid-free paper by
Biddles Ltd., King's Lynn

ISBN 0–19–929078–4   978–0–19–929078–9

1 3 5 7 9 10 8 6 4 2

FOREWORD

The past 25 years has been a time of profound, indeed revolutionary, change in the financial markets and institutions of the world. The hallmarks of that change were innovation, globalization, governance, and regulatory engagement. Since 1994, those forces have actually gathered more strength, and the financial landscape continues to undergo large and visible changes around the globe.

This book offers a comprehensive exploration of the developments occurring in Hong Kong's financial markets and institutions—ie innovation, globalization, governance, and regulatory engagement—with a focus on Hong Kong's unique role in the economic emergence and financial reforms in China's transitional economy. The actual practices of financial institutions, investors, and financial instruments are appropriately given extensive coverage.

The book's coverage of institutions, investors, and instruments is as current and up-to-date as can be produced in the face of frequent and significant change both in Hong Kong and across Asia. The authors have made a major effort to get the latest information and data on the players in the financial game and the legal and regulatory rules by which it is played. The focus on the actual practices of financial institutions is particularly beneficial to students and practitioners who will inevitably have to respond to changes in those institutions and their environment.

The discussion of corporate and market conduct, a topic of great interest today, is timely and useful. The attempt to anchor such discussions in Hong Kong's proper role as helping China's eventual emergence as an economic and financial power and to shape that emergence through actively supporting China's engagement with the global system is particularly helpful.

The authors' commitment to giving the readers a substantial amount of information and analysis regarding international and regional issues in finance that impact on Hong Kong's financial markets and system makes the book a particularly valuable text. Their discussions range across a wide field, encompassing markets for currencies, bonds, and stocks as well as derivative securities. The text gives some detailed explanations about the operations, structure, and regulation of these major markets and institutions. Just a glance at the table of contents shows that this book covers many relevant topics, which today's students and practitioners must know in order to function in the increasingly integrated international financial system in which they are working. The authors have done all those interested in this topic a great service.

Professor Richard YC Wong
Deputy Vice-Chancellor
The University of Hong Kong

FOREWORD

Despite the fact that Hong Kong is the second largest financial market in Asia ex-Japan, with a stock market capitalization of US$ 900 billion and daily turnover exceeding US$ 2.6 billion, there are not many books on its financial markets and regulatory framework.

Hong Kong is truly one of the most international of financial centres, with institutional investors accounting for 40 per cent of exchange turnover and foreign investors comprising roughly one third. It is the major fund-raising centre for Mainland Chinese enterprises with Chinese companies accounting for half of recent initial public offerings (IPOs). Most of the top global banks, investment banks, insurance companies, securities houses, and fund managers are represented in Hong Kong, mainly because of Hong Kong's low tax regime, free market orientation, free media, and rule of law. It has the highest concentration of international firms of lawyers and accountants in East Asia as well as global standard financial infrastructure, such as payment and stock trading and clearing systems.

Fortunately, a group of academics and financial markets experts of the University of Hong Kong's Asian Institute of International Financial Law (AIIFL) have decided to meet this gap in text and reference books on Hong Kong's law, rules and practice of regulation in respect of financial markets. This book will be a valuable point of reference for practitioners, students, and researchers alike.

Many observers of financial markets marvel at how the institutions of investors, issuers, intermediaries, and regulators operate together to produce information, prices and exchange property rights efficiently and transparently. This conglomerate of systems—legal, economic, and social—manage to deal with speculation, greed, and even misconduct, managing volatility over time and geography. Much of this needs to be explained to neighbouring financial markets in Asia, particularly those in transition, so that they too can benefit from the efficiency and robustness of free markets, surely one of the wonders of social invention in recent history. The deeper appreciation of the need for efficient and robust property rights infrastructure will help improve resource allocation in Asia and eventually help the integration of markets in Asia to global standards.

I congratulate the team and AIIFL for producing a landmark effort in helping us understand how the marvel of financial markets work in Hong Kong.

Andrew Sheng
Chairman
Hong Kong Securities and
Futures Commission
(1998–2005)

CONTENTS—SUMMARY

CONTENTS

II REGULATION OF INTERMEDIARIES, PRODUCTS, AND SERVICES

3. Regulation of Financial Intermediaries, Products, and Services

IV THE INTERNATIONAL DIMENSION

TABLE OF CASES

TABLES OF LEGISLATION AND REGULATORY RULES

LIST OF ABBREVIATIONS

ABC	Agricultural Bank of China
ABS	Asset-backed security
AG	Aktiengesellschaft
AI	Authorized Institutions
AIIFL	Asian Institute of International Financial Law
AMC	Asset Management Company
APEC	Asia-Pacific Economic Cooperation
ATS	Automated trading services
BAO	Banking (Amendment) Ordinance 2005
BCC(HK)	Bank of Credit and Commerce (Hong Kong) Limited
BCCI	Bank of Credit and Commerce International SA
BIS	Bank for International Settlements
bn	billion(s)
BO	Banking Ordnance (Cap 155)
BOC	Bank of China
CAMEL	Capital, asset quality, management, earnings, and liquidity
Cap	Chapter
CAR	Capital adequacy ratio
CART	Capital Adequacy Review Tribunal
CBP	Code of Banking Practice
CBRC	China Banking Regulatory Commission
CCASS	Central Clearing and Settlement System
CCB	China Construction Bank
CDO	Collateralized debt obligation
CDS	Credit default swap
CEO	Chief executive officer
CEPA	Closer Economic Partnership Agreement
CFG Report Rules	Rules on Corporate Governance Report
CG Code	Code on Corporate Governance
CIRC	China Insurance Regulatory Commission
CIS	Collective Investment Scheme
CLN	Credit-linked note
CMU	Central Money-markets Unit
CO	Companies Ordinance (Cap 32)
c/p	Counterparty

CPSS	Core Principles for Systemically Important Payment Systems
CSRC	China Securities Regulatory Commission
CSSO	Clearing and Settlement Systems Ordinance (Cap 584)
DCASS	Derivative Clearing and Settlement System
DPSO	Deposit Protection Scheme Ordinance (Cap 581)
DTC	Deposit-taking company
DTCA	Deposit Taking Company Association
EBA	Exchange Banks Association
EBRD	European Bank for Reconstruction and Development
EFAC	Exchange Fund Advisory Committee
EFN	Exchange Fund Note
EFO	Exchange Fund Ordinance (Cap 66)
EU	European Union
FATF	Financial Action Task Force on Money Laundering
FDI	Foreign direct investment
FDIC	Federal Deposit Insurance Corporation
FIE	Foreign-invested enterprise
FI-FMC	Foreign investors' fund management company
FRA	Forward rate agreement
FRR	Securities and Futures (Financial Resources) Rules (Cap 571N)
FSA	Financial Services Authority
FSAP	Financial Sector Assessment Programme
FSMA	Financial Markets and Services Act 2000
FSSA	Financial System Stability Assessment
FSTB	Financial Services and the Treasury Bureau
FTA	Free trade agreement
GAAP	Generally Accepted Accounting Principles
GATS	General Agreement on Trade in Services
GATT	General Agreement on Tariffs and Trade
GDP	Gross domestic product
GEM	Growth Enterprise Market
GEMLR	GEM Listing Rules
HIBOR	Hong Kong interbank offered rate
HKAB	Hong Kong Association of Banks
HKABO	Hong Kong Association of Banks Ordinance (Cap 364)
HKATS	Hong Kong Automated Trading System
HKEx	Hong Kong Exchanges and Clearing Limited
HKFE	Hong Kong Futures Exchange
HKFI	Hong Kong Federation of Insurers
HKICL	Hong Kong Interbank Clearing Limited (1995)

HKICPA	Hong Kong Institute of Certified Public Accountants
HKIEBS	Hong Kong Institute of Economics and Business Strategy
HKMA	Hong Kong Monetary Authority
HKMC	Hong Kong Mortgage Corporation Limited
HKSAR	Hong Kong Special Autonomous Region
HKSCC	Hong Kong Securities Clearing Company Limited
IAIS	International Association of Insurance Supervisors
IARB	Insurance Agents Registration Board
IAS	International Accounting Standards
IASB	International Accounting Standards Board
ICAC	Independent Commission Against Corruption
ICBC	Industrial and Commercial Bank of China
ICCB	Insurance Claims Complaints Bureau
ICF	Investor Compensation Fund
ICO	Insurance Companies Ordinance (Cap 41)
IDS	International Disclosure Standards
IDT	Insider Dealing Tribunal
IFRS	International Financial Reporting Standards
IMF	International Monetary Fund
IOSCO	International Organization of Securities Commissions
IPO	Initial public offering
ISDA	International Swaps and Derivatives Association Inc
IT	Information technology
ITS	Provisional Regulations for the Administration of the Issuance and Trading of Stock
JVSC	Joint venture securities company
LIBOR	London interbank offered rate
LR	Listing Rules
LSE	London Stock Exchange
LTCM	Long-Term Capital Management LLP
MCO	Money Changers Ordinance (Cap 34)
MFN	Most favoured nation
MLO	Money Lenders Ordinance (Cap 163)
MMT	Market Misconduct Tribunal
MNC	Multinational corporation
MOFTEC	Ministry of Foreign Trade and Economic Cooperation
MPF	Mandatory Provident Fund
MPFA	Mandatory Provident Fund Schemes Authority
MPFO	Mandatory Provident Fund Schemes Ordnance (Cap 485)
MRC	Market risk charge
MTN	Medium-term note

NDRC	National Development and Reform Commission
NPC	National People's Congress
NPL	Non-performing loan
OCC	Office of the Comptroller of the Currency
OCI	Office of the Commissioner of Insurance
OECD	Organization for Economic Cooperation and Development
ORSO	Occupational Retirement Schemes Ordinance (Cap 426)
OTC	Over-the-counter
OTS	Office of Thrift Supervision
PBOC	People's Bank of China
PN	Practice note
PR	Percentage ratio
PRC	People's Republic of China
PRiME	Portfolio Risk Margining System
QFII	Qualified Foreign Institutional Investor
REIT	Real estate investment trust
RI	Registered institution
RLB	Restricted licence bank
RMB	Renminbi
RTGS	Real-Time Gross Settlement
SA	Société Anonyme
SAFE	State Administration of Foreign Exchange
SAIC	State Administration for Industry and Commerce
SAR	Special Administrative Region
SASAC	State-owned Assets Supervision and Administration Commission
SAT	State Administration of Taxation
SCCLR	Standing Committee on Company Law Reform
SCEFI	Steering Committee on the Enhancement of Financial Infrastructure
SEC	Securities and Exchange Commission
SEHK	The Stock Exchange of Hong Kong Limited
SFAT	Securities and Futures Appeals Tribunal
SFC	Securities and Futures Commission
SFO	Securities and Futures Ordinance (Cap 571)
SIC	Standing Interpretation Committee
SMLR	Securities and Futures (Stock Market Listing) Rules (Cap 571V)
SOCB	State-owned commercial bank
SOE	State-owned enterprise
SPE	Special purpose entity

SRO	Self-regulatory organization
TA	Telecommunications Authority
TAC	Takeovers Appeal Committee
TRS	Total return swap
UK	United Kingdom
UNCITRAL	United Nations Commission on International Trade Law
US	United States
USTR	US Trade Representative
VAR	Value-at-risk
VSA	Very substantial acquisition
VSD	Very substantial disposal
WFE	World Federation of Exchanges
WTO	World Trade Organization

AUTHORS AND CONSULTING EDITORS

Authors

Berry FC Hsu, BSc, LLM (Alberta), MA (Oregon), PhD (London), Barrister and Solicitor (Supreme Court of Victoria), is an Associate Professor of Law in the Department of Real Estate and Construction, and Deputy Director of the Asian Institute of International Financial Law of the Faculty of Law of the University of Hong Kong. He is the author of several books on the common law system, banking and finance, and taxation.

Douglas W Arner, BA (Drury), JD (SMU), LLM Banking & Finance, PhD (London), is an Associate Professor, Director of the Asian Institute of International Financial Law, and Director of the LLM (Corporate & Financial Law) Programme at the Faculty of Law of the University of Hong Kong. He has published widely and been involved in financial markets reform in Asia, Europe, and Africa with, among others, the World Bank, Asian Development Bank, APEC, European Bank for Reconstruction and Development, and Development Bank of Southern Africa.

Maurice KS Tse, BSc (HKU), MBA, MSc, PhD (Michigan State), ASA (Society of Actuaries), is an Associate Professor of Finance, Associate Dean of the Faculty of Business and Economics, and Director of the Centre for Asian Entrepreneurship and Business Values of the University of Hong Kong. He is also a Director of Ajia Partners Asia Absolute Return Master Fund and Absolute Return Fund. He taught previously at Indiana University (Bloomington/Indianapolis) in the USA. His research areas include the effects of government regulations on financial markets, corporate finance, real estate finance, and risk management.

Syren Johnstone, BA (Hons 1) (Sydney), MSc (Oxon), Dip. Law, MA (Law), is a Visiting Fellow of the Asian Institute of International Financial Law of the Faculty of Law of the University of Hong Kong. He was previously a transactional and corporate lawyer in his roles with Linklaters as Senior Solicitor, with BSCH as Regional Head (Asia) of Legal and Compliance, and with Société Générale as Regional Head (Asia) of Transaction Management where he was the SFC registered Investment Adviser for Equity Corporate Finance.

Consulting Editors

Laurence LJ Li, BA (Yale), JD (Harvard), PCLL (HKU), is a member of the New York Bar and an Honorary Fellow of the Asian Institute of International Financial Law of the Faculty of Law of the University of Hong Kong. He was with a major US firm before returning to Hong Kong to join the Securities and Futures Commission. He left the Commission as Director of Corporate Finance in 2005 to become a barrister.

Paul Lejot, BSc (Econ) (London), is a Visiting Fellow of the Asian Institute of International Financial Law of the Faculty of Law of the University of Hong Kong, and a Visiting Research Fellow of the ICMA Centre, University of Reading. He has extensive coverage and product management experience in debt markets, structured finance, and corporate finance with ABN Amro Bank, Bank of America, and Security Pacific Bank, among others, in Hong Kong, London, and Singapore.

INTRODUCTION

Once a semi-respectable, lightly regulated offshore trading and financial centre, Hong Kong has become a major hub for financial services. Since the late 1970s, growth in the Hong Kong economy and its financial services sector has been spurred by the gradual opening of China's economy to trade and market forces, and the resources that it gathers and offers as a modern financial entrepôt. An essential element of Hong Kong's success in responding to such opportunities and becoming a leading financial centre is the legal and regulatory architecture that govern the territory's financial markets. That architecture has evolved to a level of sophistication at least equal to that of Hong Kong's regional competitors.

The framework and functioning of law and regulation underpinning Hong Kong's financial markets and institutions is the central subject of this volume. It is clear that the system has developed under unusually heterogeneous influences; part transplanted from a former colonial power, in part influenced by a non-interventionist laissez-faire ethic, and partly the product of Asian commercial and cultural practices. It is also increasingly influenced by trends toward global harmonization of financial sector regulation.

Trends in globalization and continual advances in technology have revolution-ized the world's financial markets. With widening dispersal of information and a prevailing general liberalization and deregulation of financial markets, invest-ments shift to markets that are liquid, efficient, and which present favourable risk–return profiles. The speed of innovation in financial products and transac-tions has also supported growth in cross-border trading of instruments of all kinds. All financial hubs thus require a forward-looking regulatory framework, not only to safeguard stability and to protect the investing public, but also to support competitiveness, market development, and economic growth. In this regard, Hong Kong's regulatory system has undergone significant developments in recent years.

Hong Kong's increasing institutional sophistication has also begun to influ-ence financial market reform in Mainland China. The on-going transformation of China's centrally planned economy to a socialist market model, and its accession to the World Trade Organization (WTO) in 2001 require extensive reform in the regulatory framework of markets, legal institutions, and economic structure, as well as new popular attitudes that reflect a nation with a con-temporary world perspective. While Hong Kong's financial markets may pro-vide valuable guidance in this regard, potential stresses in the operation of the financial sector in Hong Kong need to be managed from a broadly informed approach to regulation. Continued development will not only be a prerequisite for the prosperity of Hong Kong, but essential if Hong Kong is to participate constructively in the reformation of the financial markets and economic system of Mainland China.

This book has four parts.

Part I considers the framework of Hong Kong's financial markets. Chapter 1 provides an overview of the financial markets in Hong Kong and indicates today's challenges for Hong Kong as a leading Asian financial centre, while Chapter 2 outlines the territory's framework of financial law and regulation.

Part II is a comprehensive analysis of financial law and regulation. Chapter 3 focuses on the regulation of financial institutions, products, and services. It explains the law's implication and requirements for specific financial services and products, including banking, investment, insurance, and pensions. In add-ition, it discusses regulation of financial intermediaries, including their licensing and authorization, and on-going requirements for compliance by financial institutions, notably banks, securities firms, and insurers. Chapter 4 describes Hong Kong's listing rules and other procedures governing public offerings. It discusses the listing process, specific requirements for prospectuses and making public offers, and the responsibilities and potential liabilities of the company offering securities as well as those of its directors and the financial advisers involved in any transaction. Chapter 5 discusses financial derivatives in Hong Kong from the perspective of investors, users, and regulators.

Part III deals with corporate governance and market conduct, and highlights the issues and problems with the prevailing disciplinary regime for companies, securities firms, and other market participants. Chapter 6 shows why corporate governance is important in the financial marketplace and in doing so shows how corporate behaviour is regulated through common law and equity, statute, each company's constitutional documents, and regulations that specifically address governance issues. Chapter 7 examines regulations promoting fairness, transpar-ency, and efficiency in the mergers and acquisitions market and in particular reviews the operation of the Code on Takeovers and Mergers. Chapter 8 deals with the legal framework regulating market misconduct, with particular regard to insider transactions, market manipulation, fraud, and deception.

Part IV puts the analysis of Hong Kong's financial regulatory architecture in an international perspective, covering issues and reforms extending beyond a mainly domestic orientation. Chapter 9 describes China's current financial markets and developing regulatory framework with specific focus on banking, securities, and insurance. Finally, Chapter 10 discusses challenges to Hong Kong's continued development as an international financial centre serving China and the Asian region, focusing on regulatory changes to support financial stability and enhance competitiveness, in the context of a value system relevant to Hong Kong's prevailing corporate culture.

In producing a book of this nature, we have been supported by many others. In particular, we would like to thank the following:

- Rachel Mullaly, Wendy Lynch, Faye Judges, Geraldine Mangley, Caroline Quinnell, and the Law Delegate at Oxford University Press for their support and expertise, as well as eleven anonymous referees for their comments;
- Richard YC Wong, Andrew Sheng, and Alan Siu, for their comments and support;
- Georg Lienke, Lusong Zhang, Wei Wang, Albrecht von Bernuth, and Lilia Qun Wan, for research assistance;
- the Asian Institute of Financial Law (AIIFL) of the University of Hong Kong, especially Charles Booth and Flora Leung. This work was partially supported by a grant from the University Research Committee (URC) of the University of Hong Kong to AIIFL to support the URC Strategic Research Area of corporate and financial law and policy;
- the Hong Kong Institute of Economics and Business Strategy (HIEBS) of the University of Hong Kong, for financial support: This work was partially supported by a grant from the University Grants Committee (UGC) of the Hong Kong Special Administrative Region, China (Project No AoE/H-05/99) to the HIEBS;
- the Research Grants Committee (RGC) of the UGC. This work was partially supported by a grant from the RGC of the HKSAR, China (Project No HKU 7401/05H).

Without their support and that of our partners and families, the production of this volume would not have been possible.

Berry FC Hsu
Douglas W Arner
Maurice KS Tse
Syren Johnstone
Laurence LJ Li
Paul Lejot

PART I

THE FRAMEWORK OF HONG KONG'S FINANCIAL MARKETS

1

HONG KONG'S FINANCIAL MARKETS

This chapter provides background to the development and configuration of **1.01**
Hong Kong's financial markets and institutions. It describes the main elements
of current financial sector activity in the territory, and the conditions under
which they function. It identifies the characteristics of modern financial markets, discussing the historical growth of the sector in Hong Kong. The chapter
then shows how economic behaviour shapes financial market activity. Hong
Kong's markets reflect the business structure, trade practices, and culture of its
companies and people.

The success of any market-orientated economy depends on effective compe- **1.02**
tition, and in particular to a system that fairly treats all participants, without
excessively favouring interest groups or individual organizations. Without equal
treatment and transparency, the investing public risk being disadvantaged while
the system works quietly to protect the interests of the few. Hong Kong's
financial markets have long been characterized by a short-term outlook and

quasi-gambling nature, characteristics supported by the historical absence of a sound regulatory framework. This chapter argues that such a framework is vital in balancing deleterious aspects of this tendency, especially in terms of effective competition and investor protection. It first discusses theories of regulation and explores their socio-economic implications. Finally, it examines the structure and operations of Hong Kong's enforcement and adjudicative bodies in enforcing financial regulations.

A. Overview of Financial Markets in Hong Kong

1.03 The development of the regulatory framework of financial markets in Hong Kong owes much to a series of financial crises. Successive governments were reluctant to reform or strengthen the financial regulatory framework or were dissuaded from doing so by commercial interests. The former British colonial government's only declared policy was of positive non-intervention, famously espoused by Philip Haddon-Cave, an influential 1970s Financial Secretary. Most investors are not financial experts and thus rely upon the influence of the government to help protect their savings. The territory's constitutional Basic Law provides for the economy to retain its capitalist nature for 50 years after 30 June 1997. Since the first securities exchange was established in 1891, the common law doctrine of caveat emptor has applied to its fullest extent in the financial markets and they remained very lightly regulated until the mid-1970s. However, the fortunes of a laissez-faire economy depend on efficiency and effective competition, which in turn demands the free flow of information among all market participants. Inasmuch as financial markets facilitate resource allocation, whether through dealings in shares, providing a price mechanism for financial assets and a means of risk sharing, or in mitigating conflicts of interest between corporate managers and shareholders, a prerequisite is an effective regulatory framework to protect investors' rights. The deceived investor will not invest.

1.04 Before analysing regulatory issues in Hong Kong's financial markets, this section reviews the territory's banking, equity, fixed income, insurance, and derivatives sectors. In particular, it identifies the challenges facing each of these markets, all of which are addressed in later sectoral chapters.

(1) Linked exchange rate

1.05 Fiscal policy is made and monitored by the Financial Secretary and the Chief Executive of the Hong Kong Special Administrative Region (SAR). Yet an independent monetary policy cannot properly exist under the territory's linked exchange rate system, which resembles a conventional currency board. The power to issue legal tender is devolved under the Legal Tender Notes Issue Ordinance (Cap. 65) to three commercial banks, Bank of China (Hong Kong) Limited, The Hongkong and Shanghai Banking Corporation Limited (HSBC) and Standard Chartered Bank (Hong Kong) Limited, although the government issues coins and certain low denomination notes.

The former colonial government established a linked exchange rate system in **1.06** 1983 to help restore confidence after abrupt property market losses and political uncertainty. The Hong Kong dollar had been fixed to sterling for long periods before and after 1941–5, and the post-sterling, post-Bretton Woods floating rate world was thought too volatile for the stability of a small, open economy. The new system involved pegging the local currency at a fixed rate to the US dollar. Many commentators have seen the arrangement as crucial to Hong Kong's position as a trading and financial entrepôt, not least during the approach to the 1997 handover of sovereignty. However, while the peg reduces foreign exchange risks for trading companies and investors it leaves Hong Kong largely bereft of independent monetary policy and exposed to changes in US interest rates, which has been significant at times of high nominal interest rates given the importance of the interest rate sensitive property sector in the domestic economy.

The exchange rate system requires both the domestic monetary base and **1.07** changes in the monetary base to be matched by foreign currency reserves. These reserves consist mainly of foreign currency cash and OECD government securities, the greater share denominated in US dollars.[1] Hong Kong's determination to maintain its currency system was made most clear by the scale of government intervention during the first months of the Asian financial crisis. In August and October 1997 the HK dollar came under severe selling pressure, with speculators encouraged by profits from previous forward sales of southeast Asian and Korean currencies. Only Hong Kong and Mainland China had failed to fall, and China's substantial 1994 devaluation (and extensive capital controls) made it less susceptible to selling. The attack was made in two markets, using spot and forward sales of the HK dollar and short positions in the stock market (because of its comparative liquidity) in expectation of forced rises in interest rates. The traders' view appeared to be that if they failed to dislodge the peg, they would cause interest rates to rise under the linked exchange rate system, which would drive down the equity markets and allow profits to be taken in at least one of the two markets. The all-share index dropped by over 23 per cent from 20 to 23 October, and the government withdrew liquidity from the money markets

---

[1] Subject to the broad provisions of the Exchange Fund Ordinance (Cap. 66), esp. s 3.

to force overnight rates from single figures to as high as 300 per cent.[2] The government's response was unusual and controversial. As well as using reserves in large amounts to buy HK dollars, it entered the stock market as a share buyer of last resort, quickly becoming owner of around 5 per cent of the capitalization of the leading Hang Seng Index constituents. Speculative attacks duly eased and order returned within weeks to the money and stock markets.

1.08 The government was later able to realize profits on its unorthodox and unpredictable share purchases, but the existence of the currency board with an overvalued exchange rate then prevented any easing in monetary policy, leading to prolonged deflation and output losses until early 2004. Furthermore, regardless of the success of government tactics, the extent of monetary intervention in 1997 questions the basis of the currency regime. Such action would be technically impossible with a conventional currency board: Hong Kong wishes the world to accept its commitment to maintain the peg (and has resources easily sufficient to do so) but intervention means that the commitment is based upon confidence, not the system itself. Research has suggested that the confidence effect attributed to the peg can be empirically identified with an assembly of continuing factors, of which the totemic pegged currency is most visible, but that a history of conservative fiscal policies, at least until 1998, has as important an impact on financial stability.[3]

1.09 It would seem that stability carries costs and advantages that shift over time. In the long-run, structural changes in Hong Kong's currency policy may become likelier following the beginning of a freer currency regime in Beijing in July 2005.

1.10 The HK dollar was first pegged at HK$7.80/US$1.00 and allowed to appreciate to HK$7.75/US$1.00 in 1998–2000. The Hong Kong Monetary Authority (HKMA)—responsible for managing the system—modified the system in May 2005 by introducing a 'strong-side' undertaking to buy US dollars from the market at HK$7.75/US$1.00, and announced the shifting of the existing 'weak-side' undertaking from HK$7.80/US$1.00 to HK$7.85/US$1.00. As at end-May 2005, the monetary base totalled HK$ 280.6 billion (US$ 36.2 billion) and Exchange Fund foreign currency reserves were US$ 122.4 billion, the world's fifth largest holding and in excess of three times the resources theoretically needed to sustain the peg.

---

[2] *The Economist*, 23 October 1997; HKEx. The most comprehensive account of these events is given in C Goodhart and Lu Dai, *Intervention to Save Hong Kong: the Authorities' Counter-Speculation in Financial Markets* (Oxford: Oxford University Press, 2003).
[3] eg YK Kwan & F Lui, 'How well has the Currency Board performed? Evidence from Hong Kong', Hong Kong University of Science and Technology, mimeo, 1999.

(2) Banking and foreign exchange

Hong Kong's growth as a financial services hub has been supported by the rule **1.11**
of law and is largely based on the banking sector, both domestic and foreign
owned, which began heavily to finance overseas trade in the 1950s, and
expanded in the 1970s and beyond into a sizeable interbank and offshore lending market. End-2004 Bank for International Settlements (BIS) data show
Hong Kong to be the second largest offshore banking centre measured by size
of reporting banks' aggregate claims, and Asia's second largest international
banking centre after Japan.[4] Interbank lending consistently accounts for around
80 per cent of these totals. Hong Kong is the third largest foreign exchange
market in Asia measured by average daily turnover and the sixth largest in the
world, with average daily turnover of foreign exchange transactions reaching
US$ 102 billion in April 2004.[5] As at end-July 2005, 202 authorized banks
operated in Hong Kong, together with 84 other overseas banks with representative offices in the territory. While this physical presence is far smaller than in the
early 1990s prior to several waves of consolidation among banks in many parts
of the world, it remains comparable only to London and New York.

Hong Kong introduced a US dollar payments clearing system in 2000, admitted **1.12**
the euro to the system in 2003 and in the same year the People's Bank of China
(PBOC) appointed Bank of China's Hong Kong subsidiary to clear renminbi
payments.[6] This was the first foreign use of its currency permitted by China,
and includes deposit-taking, money exchange, remittances, and credit and debit
card issuance.[7] One consequent challenge for Hong Kong is to prevent its
efficient financial markets from becoming active in renminbi money-laundering
for Chinese entities. This and similar issues are addressed in subsequent chapters.

(3) Equity

Hong Kong overtook London and Tokyo in 2004 to become the world's fifth **1.13**
largest stock market measured by annual new capital raised and Asia's most
important securities fund raising hub: total capital raised amounted to US$ 36
billion in 2004.[8] At end of March 2005 the Hong Kong Stock Exchange's
(HKEx) capitalization totalled US$ 843 billion, the second largest in Asia after

---

[4] Available at <http://www.bis.org/statistics/bankstats.htm>. Measured respectively by consolidated claims of reporting banks on individual countries, and total external positions of banks
in individual reporting countries in all currencies.

[5] BIS Triennial Central Bank Survey of Foreign Exchange and Derivatives Market Activity
(April 2004), available at <http://www.bis.org>.

[6] HKMA press release, 24 December 2004.

[7] There are transaction limits in each case. Source: HKMA press release, 18 November 2003.

[8] Source: <http://www.hkex.com.hk/data/markstat>.

Japan, and the ninth globally. Table 1.1 shows the capitalization of HKEx listed companies as at end-July 2004 and end-July 2005.[9]

Table 1.1 Capitalization of HKEx companies as at end-July 2004 and end-July 2005

Market capitalization	July 2005	July 2004
Main board:		
Listed companies	906	873
Market capitalization	US$ 928 bn	US$ 705 bn
Growth Enterprise Market:		
Listed companies	202	201
Market capitalization	US$ 8 bn	US$ 9 bn

At the end of July 2005, 1,108 companies were listed on the stock exchange, including 202 companies listed on the smaller Growth Enterprise Market (GEM), and represented a total market capitalization of US$ 935.8 billion.[10] Hong Kong is also an important hub for venture capital and direct investment in Asia, currently managing more than 25 per cent of the total capital pool in the region.

1.14 The Stock Exchange of Hong Kong, owned and operated by Hong Kong Exchanges and Clearing (HKEx) may now be the most liquid overseas market for mainland China enterprises. Capital movements into and from the territory are unrestricted and neither capital gains nor dividends are taxable. Since the early 1990s, Hong Kong's equity capital market has been a powerful funding source for China's state-owned enterprises, accounting for more than 80 per cent of the offshore capital raised by mainland companies.[11] As of December 2004, 301 mainland companies (comprising H-share, red-chip, and private mainland companies) were listed in Hong Kong, their market capitalization amounting to US$ 256 billion, or 30 per cent of HKEx's total.[12] Four new issues in June 2005 raised a total of US$ 7.4 billion, the largest monthly amount yet achieved through new Hong Kong listings. It is generally expected that Hong Kong's securities sector will enjoy further benefits as a result of the Closer Economic Partnership Agreement (CEPA) taking full effect.

1.15 Since 1990 participation by international institutional investors has grown steadily and may now be the major single force in determining the share market's performance. However, few non-Chinese foreign companies are listed in Hong Kong, which may be a function of current HKEx listing rules that favour

---

[9] Sources: <http://www.hkex.com.hk/data> and <http:// www.hkgem.com/statistics/>.
[10] Sources: <http://www.hkex.com.hk/data/> and <http://www.hkgem.com/statistics/>.
[11] International Monetary Fund report on China and Hong Kong (June 2003).
[12] Source: Hong Kong Stock Exchange 2005.

local and China companies and those registered in offshore domiciles popular among Hong Kong corporate groups. At the end of 2004 as many as 766 organizations offered equity trading services. Total employment in the trading services sector was 12,495.[13] The principal underwriters for initial public offerings in the primary market are international banks but retail participants are served mainly by locally owned brokers and banks.

Later chapters will show that Hong Kong has sought to establish an effective regulatory framework, which it sees as essential for success as a financial centre. However, recent years have seen examples of the illegal diversion of cash within securities firms, and governance and regulatory standards for newly listed companies often appear inadequate to investors. Several prominent cases emerged in 2004 and 2005 of fraudulent practice by the owners and management of listed companies. These examples hamper the effectiveness of an equity market. Many investors ask how effective is the quality control of newly listed companies or those awaiting listing? How effective are HKEx rules in screening listing applicants?[14]   **1.16**

None of these examples will shock an experienced local investor. They may be a permanent feature of the Hong Kong securities market because the narratives are often similar. A major shareholder director of a company pledges shares to a bank as security for a personal loan. The director then defaults on the loan or the bank becomes nervous about the company's credit risk, leading it to call the loan, sell the pledged shares into the market to recoup the proceeds, and produce a crash in the company's share price and causing its demise. Those most at risk are outside investors who have no knowledge of the personal borrowing activity of the major shareholder.   **1.17**

A further problem for some newly (and indeed many) listed companies is relatively small capitalization, which makes price manipulation easy to effect. Market manipulation intends to mislead investors into believing that a company is performing better (or worse) than in reality with continuous share transactions aimed at influencing the stock price. Research has shown that even uninformed investors profit through trade-based manipulation, which can entail no more than falsely driving up a stock price prior to taking profits. The equilibrium amount of manipulation can exist under very natural market conditions.[15]   **1.18**

Certain brokers function as dealers for listed companies, maintaining 'order' in   **1.19**

---

[13] Source: Census & Statistics Department of the HKSAR government.
[14] The corresponding regulatory issues are addressed in Chapter 4.
[15] F Allen & G Gorton, 'Stock price manipulation, market microstructure and asymmetric information' (1992) 36 *European Economic Review* 624–30.

the client's stock price, a simple form of manipulation. The major shareholder of a listed company lends his shares of a company to its dealer, who trades in the stock so as to maintain an upward trend for the company's stock price and make the return pattern seem positive. When the price reaches a certain level and with trading volumes increasing, the major shareholders of the company announce a share offering or sell into the rising trend. Small investors unaware of the scam may be fooled into investing. Chapter 8 explains the regulatory framework dealing with all facets of market misconduct.

(4) Debt

1.20 In the past fifteen years a market has emerged in the issuance and trading of HK dollar public debt instruments that now has the characteristics, unusual among its peers, of being both highly sophisticated and materially underused. While both the private sector and government have been attracted to business development and bond market reform, the result is gleaming but yet to be stress-tested. It is ironic that two of Asia's leading financial hubs—Hong Kong and Singapore—were the last of the region's major economies to sanction local currency bond markets of any kind and now both share the features of being well developed in terms of system and investor infrastructure, but used far less by home or overseas issuers than their potential would suggest.[16]

1.21 Hong Kong's debt market accommodates issuance as complex as any in non-Japan Asia, so that both local and offshore borrowers regularly issue structured HK dollar notes under medium-term note (MTN) programmes, but the general level of liquidity lacks depth and breadth. At end-2004 the nominal value of the market in domestic debt securities of more than 12 months' remaining tenor was US$ 46.5 billion, the second smallest in non-Japan Asia (ahead of the Philippines, with far more primitive domestic markets) and the amount of similar government debt outstanding was the smallest of all at US$ 15.8 billion.[17] The net amount of new HK dollar debt issued in 2004 was no more than US$ 1.7 billion, compared to US$ 50.2 billion and US$ 39.5 billion in the Korean and Australian domestic markets, respectively. Australia's 2004 national income was a multiple of 3.7 times that of Hong Kong but its domestic bond market was 7.7 times as large; Korea's bond market reached a capitalization 12.2 times that of Hong Kong, despite its 2004 GDP measuring

---

[16] Hong Kong and Singapore each permitted public issuance in the mid-1970s, some forty years after Thailand and the Philippines. See P Lejot, D Arner, & Liu Qiao, 'Asia's bond markets: reforms to promote activity and lessen financial contagion', Hong Kong Institute of Economics and Business Strategy working paper 1090, 2004, available at <http://www.hiebs.hku.hk/working_papers.asp>.

[17] BIS data, available at <http://www.bis.org/statistics/secstats.htm>.

only 4.1 times as great as that of the territory.[18] Not uncommonly in East Asia, the HK dollar bond market ranks well behind its local equity and bank loan cousins.

The major reason for illiquidity and ill-use is best expressed as cultural: Hong **1.22** Kong lacks no resources for deal structuring but has no tradition of traded debt, and corporate governance practice has historically been insufficient to support issues by large companies. The result of a largely outsourced monetary policy makes it difficult for outstanding money market instruments and longer-term bonds to leave the relatively closed circle of the HKMA and eligible banks, so that bonds in issue are either held to maturity for lack of alternatives, or trade within a restricted set. Furthermore, a history of persistent general government surpluses prevented the development of a meaningful benchmark risk-free yield curve until recently. Other limiting factors are addressed elsewhere in this volume: the equity markets have a strong gambling orientation that is not associated with debt instruments unless highly liquid; and bank lending to major borrowers has been highly competitive and often cross-subsidized by income from banking products that were for many years protected by an officially sanctioned cartel.

The HKMA's attitude to market reform is now generally supportive. It seems to **1.23** wish to leave the private sector to develop activity in conventional traded bonds and more complex derivative-linked issues, but has proven unwilling to date to 'overfund' by itself issuing debt substantially surplus to any government or infrastructural borrowing requirement, arguing that the mechanics of the currency board militate against this tactic in a way not present in, for example, Singapore.[19] Its promotional focus since 2000 has attached to two particular developments, first, to encourage the use of securitization techniques, especially with the government-sponsored Hong Kong Mortgage Corporation (HKMC), and to encourage the issuance of retail targeted bonds, for example, by securitizing government revenue streams, through issues for real estate investment trusts (REITs) or the Asian Bond Fund, a regional central bank plan begun in 2005 to create small denomination exchange-traded bond funds. These preferences also accord with other official or regulatory objectives, for example, to encourage commercial lenders to diversify in the composition of their local lending, so that the authorities have from time-to-time dissuaded banks from holding more than a certain proportion of risk assets in commercial or residential mortgage loans. Retail bonds have the 'advantage' of being relatively low in volatility but they fail to generate any of the wider risk management features associated with

---

[18] GDP data for 2004, source Economist Intelligence Unit.
[19] Although the Exchange Fund Ordinance allows substantial borrowing.

major debt capital market instruments, nor a back-up to the banking sector in times of crisis.

1.24 There are relatively few restrictions specific to foreign borrowers wishing to issue in HK dollars. HKEx debt instrument listing rules have been modified in recent years to allow for shelf registration[20] and international investors may freely invest in debt instruments issued in Hong Kong, although many potential investors face a tax disadvantage in acquiring corporate debt issues. The clearing and settlement facility for handling transactions in Exchange Fund Bills and Notes, and eligible private debt issues is the HKMA's Central Moneymarkets Unit (CMU) which is a computerized Real-Time Gross Settlement (RTGS) system created in 1996 to handle both real-time and end-of-day delivery. As elsewhere, non-retail trading is conducted through an over-the-counter (OTC) market among major banks, and institutional investors can also trade on a number of electronic bond platforms.

(5) Insurance

1.25 Hong Kong's insurance industry operates in a regulated, open market. Insurance companies from any jurisdiction can offer products in or from Hong Kong providing they meet the requirements of the industry regulator, the Office of the Commissioner of Insurance under the Insurance Companies Ordinance.[21]

1.26 Judged by size and product variety, the Hong Kong insurance market is among the most developed in Asia, and in 2004 represented the second largest by per capita insurance premiums in the region after Japan. The range of insurance products available in Hong Kong spans from general insurance including both direct business and reinsurance, to specific segments, including property damage, general liability, accident, health, vehicle, and long-term insurance including individual life insurance, group life insurance, and retirement schemes. The long-term insurance business has experienced double-digit growth for ten consecutive years since 1993, supported in part by the introduction of the Mandatory Provident Fund (MPF) scheme in the early 1990s. Table 1.2 presents a snapshot of the Hong Kong insurance market in 2002–3.

1.27 As at end-December 2005, 175 insurers were licensed to operate in the territory, divded among 110 engaged solely in general insurance, 46 in long-term insurance, and the remainder classed as composite insurers. Of the total, 89 were locally-incorporated insurers, one was a Mainland firm, and 41 were based in

---

[20] Listing Rules Ch 37 as at 1 January 2005, available at <http://www.hkex.com.hk/rule/listrules/vol1_4.htm>.
[21] OECD, *Insurance Regulation and Supervision in Asia*, p 121.

Table 1.2 The Hong Kong insurance market 2002–3

Insurance market	2002	2003
Total premium income (US$ million)	11,406	13,076
Long-term business	8,400	9,901
General business	3,006	3,175
Insurance penetration (premium income as % of GDP)	7.1	8.4
Long-term business	5.2	6.0
General business	1.8	1.9
Insurance density (per capita expenditure, US$)	1,681	1,922
Long-term premium per capita	1,238	1,455
General business per capita	443	467
Population Covered by Life Policies (%)	77	82

Source: Office of the Commissioner of Insurance

Bermuda, Britain, or the US.[22] Economies of scale are important in the dominant presence of some insurers. In 2002 the top 10 insurers held about 74 per cent of the long-term insurance market in Hong Kong and about 38 per cent of the general insurance market.

Foreign insurers and reinsurers have expanded their regional operations in Hong Kong in anticipation of an expansion of regional demand and of China's accession to the WTO.[23] This phenomenon may partly be attributed to changes in domestic US regulation in 1999 allowing banks to engage in traditional insurance once dominated by specialist groups. Standardized life insurance, vehicle insurance, and product categories such as annuities are increasingly easily reproduced, which has forced encouraged insurance companies to choose between offering a broader scope in financial services, pursuing a niche segment such as financial guarantee provision, or seek opportunities overseas. With the opening of China's insurance sector and expansion elsewhere in Asia, it is likely that the presence of foreign firms in the region will grow. **1.28**

A more recent development that has helped push the growth of Hong Kong's insurance sector is the signing of CEPA between the HKSAR and the mainland in 2003 under which the mainland government grants favourable treatment to a specific list of industries in Hong Kong to enter and to gain access to the China market. It took effect in January 2004. In August 2004 the HKSAR and Mainland China agreed under the CEPA framework to CEPA II, the second **1.29**

---

[22] Source: Office of the Commissioner of Insurance 2004.
[23] China's WTO obligations have begun to open its insurance market to qualified foreign insurers. In particular, a foreign insurer may seek a licence if it has more than 30 years of experience in a WTO member country, has a representative office established in China for two consecutive years, and has global assets of over US$ 5 billion. Qualified foreign insurers and insurance brokers may now operate in 15 provinces and may acquire up to 50% of local insurers.

phase of liberalization measures to relax further access to the Mainland market, adding among others eight new areas for Hong Kong service providers, while further relaxing the business scope for some of the 18 service sectors already open under CEPA. It is generally expected that Hong Kong's insurance sector and professionals will benefit.[24]

1.30 Closer economic integration between Hong Kong and the mainland will increase both growth and development opportunities for insurers in Hong Kong and challenges to the cross-border regulatory environment. Currently, Mainland citizens may freely buy Hong Kong life insurance in Hong Kong but local insurance agents may not transact in China.[25] It would be unlawful under China's insurance laws for Hong Kong agents even to give business cards and explain to Mainland clients the content of Hong Kong polices.[26] However, China's enormous life insurance market induces many local agents secretly to sell to Mainland citizens, typically inviting potential clients to visit the territory as tourists to finalize and sign policy agreements. This practice may explain the fast recent growth of the life sector in Hong Kong. It also raises concern in the China Insurance Regulatory Commission that such underground practices could become a vehicle for money-laundering.[27]

(6) Derivatives

1.31 Growth in Hong Kong's derivatives markets makes it host to an important centre for risk management in East Asia. HKEx lists covered (derivative) warrants on its main board, and equity, interest rate and fixed income futures and options contracts on its Hong Kong Futures Exchange (HKFE) subsidiary. Covered warrant issuance and trading has become notably prominent, for reasons explained in Chapter 5.

---

[24] Under CEPA, groups formed by Hong Kong insurance companies, rather than any individual company, may apply to enter the Mainland market, if (1) their global assets exceed US$ 5 bn, (2) a Hong Kong insurance company in the group has more than 30 years of operations, and (3) a Hong Kong group company has maintained at least one representative office in the Mainland for 2 consecutive years. Moreover, the maximum permitted shareholding of a Hong Kong insurer in a Mainland insurance company was raised from 10% to 24.9%. CEPA also provides a more formal and well-defined channel to Hong Kong insurance professionals to enter the Mainland market. In particular, Hong Kong insurance professionals can enjoy the following privileges: (1) After obtaining the Mainland's professional qualifications in actuarial science, Hong Kong residents with Chinese citizenship are permitted to practice in the Mainland without prior approval, and (2) After obtaining the Mainland's insurance qualifications, Hong Kong residents are permitted to practice in the Mainland.

[25] To be a licensed insurance agent in China, an insurance agent must attain and satisfy all professional and practice requirements as prescribed under China's Insurance Law and China Insurance Regulatory Commission (CIRC).

[26] Source: CIRC-Beijing Practice Qualifications for Insurance Intermediary (<http://www.circ.gov.cn/circbj/>).

[27] Source: CIRC website, March 2005.

Four equity index products are listed and traded through HKEx, namely,   **1.32**
FTSE/Xinhua China 25 Index (FXI China 25) Futures and Index Options,
Hang Seng Index Futures and Options, H-shares Index Futures and Options,
and Mini-Hang Seng Index Futures and Options. Equity index products are
traded on a margin basis so that capital requirements are much less than
those required to buy the underlying constituent stocks of the index. The HKEx
interest rate and fixed income products are HIBOR Futures and Three-year
Exchange Fund Note (EFN) Futures. All these products, if applied properly, help
investors to manage risks inherent in stocks, broad-based market fluctuations,
and interest rates.

Covered, or derivative warrants in Hong Kong have become one of the   **1.33**
world's most heavily traded exchange-listed derivative instruments in recent
years. In 2004 low trading volume exceeded that in Germany, Italy, or Switzerland to become the most active market. Chapter 5 shows how growth in covered
warrant issuance and trading can be attributed to relatively favourable listing
rules, a collapse in 'penny stocks' in 2002, restricted opportunities for legalized
gambling, and intense mass-media coverage and marketing.

Although the payoffs of covered warrants on expiry represent a zero-sum game   **1.34**
between the issuer and investors, the market may not favour the many small
investors in covered warrants compared to the issuer. There are three principal
concerns for the covered warrant market in Hong Kong. First, HKEx's Listing
Rules freely permit further tranches of existing issues. Second, trading may
increase the volatility of underlying stocks. Third, there may be gaps in the
regulatory framework that leave too much of the scrutiny for this market to the
HKEx.

Further issues are especially likely when the underlying stock price is rising and   **1.35**
the issuer's holding of the listed warrant is no more than 20 per cent of the
existing issue, because the issuer has to keep an adequate holding in order
to maintain an orderly market and to provide trading liquidity. The number of
warrants outstanding in the market keeps rising through further issues, the
issuer hedges its exposure by transacting in both warrants and the underlying
stock.

The question then is whether trading in covered warrants typically increases the   **1.36**
volatility of the underlying stocks. For example, a 301-point drop in the Hang
Seng Index on 18 August 2005 revived a debate over the inherent volatility of
warrants and their ability to transform an orderly retreat into a chaotic rout.
Some brokers unconnected with covered warrant issuance claim that heavy
warrant trading and related hedging activity accentuated the day's sell-off in the
cash equity market. The rationale behind this argument can be understood
with the concept of the 'delta' of a warrant. The price sensitivity of a warrant

(delta) indicates how much the value of a warrant will change as a result of a small change in the underlying stock price. The delta value of a call warrant is positive because the market value of a call warrant increases with the underlying stock price. The issuer will often trade the underlying stock in order to hedge a short position in warrants after issuance. For risk management purposes, the issuer would minimize the price risk of its position by keeping the delta of the short warrant position as small or close to zero as possible by buying and selling the underlying stock when its price shifts. Since the value of delta also shifts with the change in the stock price level, the long position in the underlying stock will have to be rebalanced when there is a change in the underlying stock price so as to maintain the hedged position. As the stock price increases, the delta value increases, which forces the issuer to hedge its short warrant position by buying the underlying stock amid a rising price. On the other hand, as the stock price falls, the delta value will fall and the issuer will have to sell the underlying stock. Such hedging activity is often blamed for causing excessive volatility in the stock market.

1.37   The typical point of view of issuers is that warrant trading and corresponding hedging activities provide liquidity for the market. On the other hand, however, critics are concerned that heavy volumes of outstanding warrants become more important than the fundamentals behind the underlying stocks, causing ultimately irrational trading patterns and prices. How well protected are small market participants in general? The issues with respect to derivatives and investor protection are addressed in Chapter 5.

B. Development and Characteristics of Hong Kong's Financial Markets and Institutions

1.38   Once a small fishing village, Hong Kong has developed into a major international financial centre,[28] hosting more than 140 licensed banks and over 40 restricted licence banks, including representatives from 110 of the largest international banks ranked by total assets.[29] With a market capitalization of US$

---

[28] Hong Kong has the world's second highest per capita holding of foreign exchange, Asia's second largest source of foreign direct investment, Asia's second least corrupt economy, Asia's highest concentration of fund managers, Asia's second largest venture capital centre, Asia's second most developed insurance market in terms of per capita insurance premium, Asia's third and the world's 10th largest stock market, the world's fifth largest equity fund raising centre and the largest in Asia, Asia's third largest international banking centre, and the world's sixth largest foreign exchange market. See <http://finance.tdctrade.com/>.

[29] See Hong Kong Monetary Authority, *Annual Report* (Hong Kong: HKMA, 2004), pp 139–43.

740,799 million as at March 2004, its equities market is ranked eighth globally and second in Asia.[30] The maintenance of the rule of law in Hong Kong arguably provided the stability necessary for this economic and social progression. The government is unusually mandated under the Basic Law to provide 'an appropriate economic and legal environment for the maintenance of the status of Hong Kong as an international financial centre'.[31] What then is a financial market?

(1) The nature of financial markets

The term 'financial market' is defined neither in case law nor legislation in Hong Kong. From a layman's perspective, it has been said to be 'a market in which financial assets are traded'[32] that is, where sellers and buyers deal with each other. A properly constituted market operates under a set of rules within an institutional framework. Financial assets are intangible, including securities, certificates, or bank balances, as compared to tangible assets.[33] In other words, a financial market is the place where capital in the economy is exchanged through financial intermediaries. The assets traded in a financial market include stocks, bonds, commodities, foreign exchange, and related derivative instruments. Accordingly, a financial market is often known as a centre for the exchange of capital. As a matter of practice, a financial market includes both money markets and capital markets. The former concentrate on short-term claims and debt instruments and the latter trade in long-term debt and equity instruments. **1.39**

The money market deals in short-term claims and debt instruments, which may include acceptances, commercial paper, certificates of deposit, and government bills. Conventional returns are low but the investments are usually low risk and liquid. On the other hand, the capital market is the trading forum for long-term **1.40**

---

[30] 'Domestic Market Capitalization', *Statistics* (Paris: World Federation of Exchanges, 2004) <http://www.fibv.com/publications/EQU1104.XLS>.

[31] Basic Law of the Hong Kong Special Administrative Region, art 109.

[32] P Moles & N Terry, *The Handbook of International Financial Terms* (Oxford: Oxford University Press, 1997), p 220.

[33] At common law, property is divided into two types. One is movable property (or personal property/personality), and the other is immovable property (or real property/realty). With one exception, all interests in land are immovable property. Personal property can be classified as either 'tangible' or 'intangible'. A person can enforce their legal right to tangible personal property by obtaining physical possession of it without taking legal proceedings in a court of law. In some cases, the property right may well not be capable of being physically possessed, because it may exist only in the form of a right or an interest over the property, such as a gold certificate which entitles a person to claim two kilograms of gold. This property right itself is intangible in nature, as all that a person has is a document, which entitles the holder to claim two kilograms of gold. That person may not take possession of the gold and has rights enforceable only through a court of law by a court action. The right over the two kilograms of gold is therefore a right of action and not a right of possession.

debt and equity instruments. The boundary between equity and debt is becoming more and more blurred as more products derived from these instruments appear. The most important aspect of these markets is that they assume the economic function of creating liquidity. The transfer of property rights of financial assets ostensibly operates in an uncertain environment, as unexpected risks arise that influence prevailing prices, whether in relation to credit, operational, legal, payment, or market risks. An optimal financial market is thus also a forum for the exchange of information.

1.41   Segments of the financial market are normally provided and maintained by an organization or association of intermediaries for trading some or all the above instruments, typically called an exchange. In Hong Kong, there is now one equity and derivatives exchange, the Hong Kong Exchange and Clearing House Ltd or HKEx, as a result of an enactment arising from financial crises and historical developments.

(2) Evolution of Hong Kong's financial markets

1.42   This section discusses the development of Hong Kong's markets and examines details of regulatory control and the adequacy of its regulatory framework. The financial markets in Hong Kong have undergone three stages of development that here are described as the dark, medieval, and modern ages.

The dark age

1.43   The 'dark age' is the period prior to a financial market crash in 1973. During this period, there was virtually no regulatory supervision of the financial markets.[34] There were no statutory requirements regulating the listing of securities beyond general prospectus requirements for companies and limited provisions under other statutes. The securities industry was loosely regulated under the relevant provisions of the Companies Ordinance,[35] the Stamp Duty Ordinance,[36] and the Stock Exchange Control Ordinance. Anyone could operate a financial exchange market. In 1891, the first Hong Kong Stock Exchange was established. In 1969 the Far East Stock Exchange was established to suit the interests of small companies. The only commodities trading in Hong Kong from 1910 to 1977 was at the Chinese Gold and Silver Exchange Society, a self-regulated organization.[37] Several stock exchanges were established in the early 1970s and

---

[34] BAK Rider & HL French, *The Regulation of Insider Trading* (London: Macmillan, 1979), pp 329–31.

[35] Cap. 32.   [36] Cap. 117.

[37] *Report of the Securities Review Committee* (Hong Kong: Securities Review Committee, May 1988), p 399.

several collapsed during the market crash in 1973, when the Hang Seng Index lost over 90 per cent of its value.

These unregulated markets could not serve the proper interests of the investing public. Most investors were uninformed and unsophisticated individuals, and securities prices were excessively determined by demand as compared to their value.[38] According to the then Commissioner of Banking, '[t]here was very little real investing going on in Hong Kong; it was sheer gambling'.[39] The problems were aggravated by a lack of expertise in this area.[40] During this period, some interested parties even argued that regulatory control of the financial markets was unnecessary.[41] They suggested that since there were few public companies, capital did not have to move through the financial markets.[42]   **1.44**

In April 1962 the Companies Law Revision Committee was commissioned, and published its first report in June 1971. However, few of its recommendations were enacted into law.[43] In 1972 the Companies (Amendment) Ordinance was enacted to govern company prospectuses. It was the first legislative attempt in Hong Kong to control the financial market. The Stock Exchange Control Ordinance of 1973 restricted the number of stock exchanges to four, Hong Kong Stock Exchange (1891), Far East Stock Exchange (1969), Kam Ngan Stock Exchange (1971), and Kowloon Stock Exchange (1973). In the same year, the Commodity Exchange (Prohibition) Ordinance was also enacted, restricting the establishment and operation of commodities exchanges.[44] However, regulatory control was still far from adequate. Withholding relevant information, misrepresentation, forgery, and fraud were prevalent in the financial markets. There was no regulatory control over investment advisers and dealers save for the ineffective anti-fraud and anti-theft provisions of the criminal law statutes.[45]   **1.45**

The medieval age

As a result of the financial market crash in 1973, thousands of people lost their life savings. The government then began to enact piecemeal legislation regulating the financial markets. In 1974 the Securities Ordinance[46] was enacted establishing a watchdog body for financial markets, the Securities Commission, and   **1.46**

---

[38] Higgins, above, p 21.

[39] WD Hartley, 'Where the Action Is', *The Wall Street Journal*, 29 March 1973, p 34.

[40] T Ujejski, 'Securities Regulation', in R Wacks (ed), *The Law in Hong Kong 1969–1989* (Hong Kong: Oxford University Press, 1989), p 283.

[41] MF Higgins, *Securities Regulation in Hong Kong 1972–1977* (The Netherlands: Sijthoff & Noordhoff, 1978), pp 1–16.

[42] ibid, p 3.   [43] ibid, p 31.

[44] *Report of the Securities Review Committee*, above, p 429.   [45] Ujejski, above, pp 285–8.

[46] Cap. 333.

providing a regulatory framework for the operation of the stock exchanges. The Securities Commission was vested with investigative powers. The ordinance classified market professionals as dealers, investment advisers, or representatives and required them to register with the Securities Commission. The ordinance also established a Stock Exchange Compensation Fund to partially compensate clients of defaulting securities firms. At the same time, the Protection of Investors Ordinance[47] was enacted. This ordinance intended to protect investors by ensuring that accurate information was provided to them. It prohibited fraudulent and reckless advertisements. In 1976 the Commodities Trading Ordinance was enacted making provisions for establishing a commodities exchange and controlling trading in commodities futures contracts. This ordinance also established a Commodities Trading Commission with functions similar to those of the Securities Commission.[48]

1.47 This series of ordinances did provide some form of stability in the securities and futures markets. Critics argued that an effective regulatory framework could not arise from these ordinances due to the general philosophy of non-intervention by the government and the lack of resources.[49] In the 1970s and 1980s all financial markets underwent rapid growth but the regulatory framework of the financial markets in Hong Kong remained static. A number of new financial products were introduced into the financial markets, with increasing sophistication. As a result, the regulatory framework had to catch up with international trends. The four private stock exchanges continued to operate under their own listing rules and procedures. In consolidating their management and control, the Stock Exchanges Unification Ordinance[50] was enacted in 1980. This ordinance provided a mechanism to merge the four stock exchanges into the Stock Exchange of Hong Kong Limited (SEHK), with the principals and traders of the constituent stock exchanges maintaining their rights to trade in the new exchange. The merger was completed in 1986. Under this ordinance, the trading activities of the SEHK were regulated by the Commissioner of Securities.

1.48 In October 1987 there was a worldwide stock markets crash and Hong Kong was not immune. Immediately after the crash, the SEHK was shut down for four working days. Many individual investors lost their life savings as they had to meet payments for margin calls and settle previous purchases but could not realize the value of their shares. In the meantime, large investors continued to trade over-the-counter (OTC) or on a private basis. After the stock exchange resumed business, the Hang Seng Index fell to 2,242 points from its all-time high of 3,950 points.[51] The Hong Kong government had no legal authority

---

[47] Cap. 335.   [48] *Report of the Securities Review Committee*, above, pp 429–30.
[49] Ujejski, above, pp 292–4.   [50] Cap. 361.
[51] *Report of the Securities Review Committee*, above, p 352.

to take any action during this crisis. According to the Financial Secretary at that time:[52]

> The question of government approval does not arise since the exchange has the power to take such action under its own rules. The Government was, however, informed in advance of the proposed action, which it regards as a sensible response to the situation . . . The exchange considers that it will take four days to clear the backlog . . . I think it is preferable for self-regulatory bodies such as the exchange to make use of their own powers where these are available instead of resorting to government intervention. This is in line with our general philosophy towards the financial markets in Hong Kong.

In a short time, this closure adversely affected Hong Kong's international repu- **1.49** tation and eroded confidence in its already fragile financial market.[53] On a positive note, the 1987 crash prompted the government to reform the financial markets in line with international standards. In November 1987 the Securities Review Committee was formed and its conclusions are the source of the modern financial regulatory framework in Hong Kong. In 1989 the Securities and Futures Commission Ordinance[54] was enacted in accordance to the Review Committee's recommendations of creating a new and more effective regulatory agency to supervise the financial industry. The Securities and Futures Commission (SFC) was thus created with new powers of supervision, intervention, investigation, prosecution, and even adjudication.[55]

The modern market

The SFC has been implementing the recommendations of the Securities **1.50** Review Committee in restructuring the regulatory framework of the financial markets.[56] It is invested with the task of overhauling the existing laws regulating the securities markets. It was the driving force of a number of enactments regulating the securities markets. In 1991 the Securities (Insider Dealing) Ordinance[57] was enacted replacing the relevant provisions in the Securities Ordinance of 1974 with more detailed and comprehensive provisions. The Securities (Disclosure of Interests) Ordinance[58] was enacted in the same year imposing mandatory disclosure on those who acquire more than 10 per cent of a company's shares. This was a new approach in preventing fraud and improper practices in the financial markets. In 1992 the Securities and Futures

---

[52] *Proceedings of the Council* (Hong Kong: Hong Kong Legislative Council (21 October, 1987)), p 138.
[53] *Report of the Securities Review Committee*, above, 27n.   [54] Cap. 24.
[55] Ujejski, above, pp 299–300.
[56] *The Securities and Futures Commission* (Hong Kong: Securities and Futures Commission, 1986), p 15.
[57] Cap. 395.   [58] Cap. 396.

(Clearing Houses) Ordinance was enacted, which empowered the SFC to declare which clearing houses were to be recognized and make rules and procedures for their operation. However, the SFC did not normally intervene in the management and governance of the Stock Exchange of Hong Kong or the Hong Kong Futures Exchange. As a result of the 1987 crash, these exchanges voluntarily made significant reforms in their settlement, risk management, and trading systems.[59]

Recent developments

1.51 Prior to the enactment of the composite Securities and Futures Ordinance,[60] the regulatory framework of the financial markets was scattered across some twelve ordinances, including the Companies Ordinance.[61] As a result of the recommendation by the Securities Review Committee, in April 1996, the SFC published *A Consultation Paper on a draft for a composite Securities and Futures Bill* which proposed consolidating and rationalizing eight of these ordinances, as well as updating certain other provisions.[62] The objective was to provide a modern, simplified, and user-friendly ordinance. As expected, the Securities and Futures Bill met resistance from the financial sector and listed companies[63] but finally was enacted in March 2002.

(3) How sophisticated a market is Hong Kong?

1.52 Regulatory reforms of Hong Kong's financial markets have typically been implemented after financial crises resulting from market failure. From an economic perspective, there are transaction costs in providing adequate information. The gaming aspect of the financial markets in Hong Kong demands a paternalistic approach of the government to regulate the behaviour of market participants in enhancing the efficiency of the financial markets, so that the dependence upon skill and knowledge in investment decisions is maximized. Within most financial systems, a central regulatory objective is to protect small investors, who commonly lack market leverage or political bargaining power. Therefore, free market forces cannot operate to allocate resources efficiently. Accordingly, regulations are essential to ensure that resources are efficiently allocated, for example, insider dealing prohibitions and prospectus requirements.

---

[59] *The Securities and Futures Commission* (Hong Kong: Securities and Futures Commission, 1986), p 15.
[60] Cap. 571.   [61] Cap. 32.
[62] Hong Kong: Securities and Futures Commission, 1996.
[63] E Yiu, 'Securities law still in grip of bitter bickering', *South China Morning Post*, 9 December 2000; E Yiu, 'SFC calls for reform to battle coming challenges', *South China Morning Post*, 28 December 2000.

In this era of globalization, funds enter and leave national jurisdictions in split **1.53** seconds and as multi-billion dollar financial transactions. Financial technology advances at such a speed that regulators cannot realistically grasp the new products in the financial markets, so that regulating transactions and institutions is becoming more difficult. With lucrative compensation, the financial sector attracts more innovation than do regulatory agencies. Like other jurisdictions, the regulatory framework of finance in Hong Kong is a product of various attempts by regulators to address the deficiencies of the financial markets learned from each financial crisis, after compromising with market participants. The currency board was established in 1983 to help restore confidence after foreign exchange and banking crises. The SFC (formerly a government department) was established in 1989 as a result of the market crash of 1987. The HKMA (formerly two government departments) was created in 1993 following the collapse of the Bank of Credit and Commerce International (BCCI). The demutualization and merger of the stock and futures exchange took place after the Asian financial crisis of 1997. The Securities and Futures Ordinance was belatedly and reluctantly enacted after this crisis as a result of the review following the 1987 market crash and also in response to the events of 1997–8.

A sound regulatory framework is vital for long-term stability. Hong Kong's **1.54** prosperity depends on its success as a centre for trade and finance. The question is what system should Hong Kong adopt and to what extent should the financial markets be regulated? As in other common law jurisdictions, Hong Kong has developed a number of regulatory agencies, each with its own specific jurisdiction, to enforce specific financial regulations. These are discussed in Chapter 2.

Theories of regulation

In Hong Kong, apathy towards the financial markets by legislators has helped to **1.55** maintain a regulatory framework supportive of the interests of major financial institutions. The delays in enacting the composite Securities and Futures Ordinance is only one example. There has always been a close relationship between the government and major commercial interests in Hong Kong. Senior executives from the financial sector[64] have always been appointed as members of the Executive Council directly or Legislative Council indirectly as of de facto right.[65] The Basic Law makes provision for functional constituencies, which

---

[64] Three members of the HKEx Board of Directors were sitting members of the influential Executive Council appointed by the Chief Executive as at 1 December 2005. During the colonial era, the chairman of Hongkong and Shanghai Banking Corporation (HSBC) had a de facto seat on the Executive Council.

[65] B Hsu, *Laws of Banking and Finance in the Hong Kong SAR* (Hong Kong: Hong Kong University Press), p 190.

assures representatives from the banking and financial, insurance, real estate, commercial, and industrial sectors of seats in the Legislative Council.[66] Civil servants who monitor banking and financial institutions report to these Councils. Banks and the large family controlled conglomerates that are their clients historically have formed a close circle. Similarly, the stock exchange has until recently been dominated by a small number of corporate groups, offering minority stakes to the public. Under this circumstance, the regulatory framework of finance in Hong Kong is a result of compromise among its influential economic, political, and social elites.

1.56 The capture theory states that regulators are not concerned with the public interest, but rather collude with interest groups that control the regulators in maximizing their own wealth.[67] It holds that the regulatory framework is the product of interest groups struggling among themselves in maximizing their benefits.[68] This theory explains the regulatory framework of the financial market in Hong Kong where the coalition of powerful business and financial interests is influential over financial regulations. This was not only successful in delaying the enactment of the Securities and Futures Ordinance, but instrumental in shelving the proposal of the SFC to take over the frontline regulatory role over the HKEx. The regulatory process in Hong Kong is more likely an outcome of negotiation between the coalition of interested market participants and the financial regulators. When regulations promote the interest of investors, it is more likely the result of public pressure arising from financial crisis. This draws a complementary 'public interest' theory, holding that regulation is an outcome of public demand in addressing inefficient or inequitable market practices.

1.57 The public interest theory, which considers regulation as a natural regulatory response to market failure, is applicable to Hong Kong, as market failures can always be explained by the inadequate regulatory framework. The imperfections of the financial markets in Hong Kong have justified and continue to justify government intervention. However, there is a cost attached to such regulation, which is imposed upon financial market participants in Hong Kong. Ultimately, it is the investing public who bear this transaction cost. The public interest would not be properly served if financial regulators only pay lip service to an efficient and equitable market while supporting the interests of entrenched elites. Regulators should have to adhere to strict conflict of interest rules and should not be allowed to deal with the institutions they contact in the

---

[66] Basic Law, Annex II; Legislative Council Ordinance (Cap. 542), s 20.
[67] R Ho, 'The Regulatory Framework of the Banking Sector', in R Ho, R Scott, & KA Wong (eds), *The Hong Kong Financial System* (Hong Kong: Oxford University Press, 1996).
[68] RA Posner, 'Theories of Economic Regulation' (1974) 5 *Bell Journal of Economics* 335–6.

course of their duties for at least a period of time, say a 'cooling off' period of two years. The present Civil Service Regulations on outside employment are far from satisfactory as they apply only to retired civil servants.[69] Most officials in the HKMA and SFC are appointed on contract terms and are not bound by these regulations. Indeed, there was serious public criticism when a very senior former executive of the SFC joined the very firm he had investigated.[70]

The political economy of financial regulation

One of the main reasons why the regulatory framework is inadequate in address-   **1.58**
ing financial crime is the failure to enforce a strong system of criminal justice in dealing with financial offences (or white-collar crimes). Criminologists have suggested that power issues may suggest why financial offences have been mar-ginalized.[71] Large corporations have to depend on the financial sector to raise money to finance their business. Some of these corporations actually dominate the economic life of Hong Kong, from grocery stores and telecommunications to real estate. Constitutionally, the executive Government of the HKSAR is accountable to the Legislative Council, which has the power to impeach the Chief Executive.[72] When the symbiotic relationship between the powerful tycoon and the political leader is an issue, legislators would be loth to question it.[73] Nevertheless, financial misconduct is more serious than other types of fraud as not only investors suffer, the entire economy may be placed in crisis as a result.

According to one study, a major obstacle to rigorous enforcement of white-   **1.59**
collar crimes in the financial markets is attributed to the moral ambivalence of market participants.[74] There is evidence that white-collar crimes are more tolerated with little stigma, if any, attached (though this may be changing post-Enron). The profit-making objectives of a business are often in conflict with its social responsibilities.[75] Accordingly, a strong regulatory framework is required in ensuring compliance.

(4) The gaming nature of financial markets

From the outset, financial markets are not balanced in terms of fairness. If all   **1.60**
things are equal, financial intermediaries and insiders possess an advantageous

---

[69] Civil Service Regulations, reg 13.6.
[70] D Tsang, 'Reshuffle sees ex-SFC boss joining Sun Hung Kai board', *South China Morning Post*, 21 June 1997; C Buddle, 'Police part in Allied probe hidden, court told', *South China Morning Post*, 4 May 2000.
[71] Gilligan, above, p 14.   [72] Basic Law, art 73(9).
[73] P Bowring, 'Hong Kong's judicial system: the last defender of the people', *South China Morning Post*, 19 May 2003.
[74] Gilligan, above, pp 74–5.   [75] ibid, pp 74–5.

edge in terms of information resources. A large number of investors have little knowledge regarding the risks they face. However, it is doubtful whether investors will read financial information such as prospectuses even when written in plain language.[76] Most investors in Hong Kong do not analyse the markets before making their investment decisions but rather run with the crowd. Some may analyse the markets, but their approach is technical rather than fundamental or portfolio oriented. A survey by the SFC has determined that two-thirds of investors in Hong Kong consider their knowledge and skill in investment to be insufficient.[77] They are informationally impaired, either because they do not have the necessary information or lack the skill to analyse the information.

1.61   In addition, the volatility of the financial markets in Hong Kong is a concern which cannot be ignored. The controversies surrounding the implementation of minimum share prices illustrate unfair practices in the financial markets. In this episode, the HKEx released *Consultation Papers on Proposed Amendments to the Listing Rules relating to Initial Listing and Continuing Listing Eligibility and Cancellation of Listing Procedures*[78] in July 2002, proposing the adoption of a minimum share price requirement of HK$ 0.5 (or less than US$ 0.065). This led to a sell-off of 'penny stocks' and the plan has now been shelved.[79]   Those who invest at such price levels tend to be gambling although a small number of blue chip stocks in Hong Kong trade at low nominal price levels because of poor corporate governance. A proper listed company can always use share consolidation to meet the listing criteria. If the playing field is level, the regulatory framework should protect participants who have poorly informed behavioural impulses. This is not the case in Hong Kong where gambling has always been a way of life,[80] and the financial markets facilitate this habit.

1.62   Economists may claim that the efficient capital market hypothesis drives financial markets. This assumes that traders in the financial markets make rational use of all available information. Therefore, any errors about future price movements will offset each other, and contribute to the restoration of appropriate equilibrium prices. On the practical side, rational decisions are not always made, as some financial market participants have a narcotic attraction to

---

[76] *Joint Announcement on the Use of Plain Language in Prospectuses and Application Forms* (Hong Kong: Securities and Futures Commission and the Stock Exchange of Hong Kong Ltd, 23 March 1998).

[77] *Retail Investor Survey* (Hong Kong: Securities and Futures Commission, October 2001), p 2. <http://www.hksfc.org.hk/eng/search/html/index.html>.

[78] (Hong Kong: Hong Kong Exchanges and Clearing House Ltd, July 2002), pp 82–3.

[79] E Yiu, 'Exchange black flips on penny stocks', *South China Morning Post*, 29 July 2002.

[80] MH Bond, *Beyond the Chinese Face* (Hong Kong: Oxford University Press, 1991), p 91.

gambling.[81] The securities market may fulfil the psychological needs of many people who lack long-term investment interests. It has been observed that financial markets are casinos for those players who wish to treat them as such.[82] Realistically, the confidence in these intangible financial assets is affected by many uncertain factors, including the behaviour of market players, their culture, and their background.

As in certain other jurisdictions, the Hong Kong financial markets have many elements of gaming, in fact if not in law. The Gambling Ordinance prohibits gambling save for certain defined exceptions.[83] 'Gaming' is the playing of or at any game for winnings in money or other property whether or not any person playing the game is at risk of losing any money or other property.[84] Under the ordinance, 'game' means, inter alia, a game of chance or a game of chance and skill combined.[85] An element of chance may not suffice as there should be present a high probability of chance. To avoid an activity being a game of chance, skill must play a predominant role in its outcome.[86] The issue is whether in the long run the actions of the players affect the observed outcome.[87] As investors in the financial markets make profits contingent upon a future event, which cannot be accurately predicted, there is a risk that all securities and futures contracts are void by reason of their illegality under the Gambling Ordinance.[88] Accordingly, the Securities and Futures Ordinance expressly excludes the operation of the Gambling Ordinance to any transaction which it regulates, unless the SFC specifically provides otherwise.[89] This saves elements of the financial markets, for example, the trading of derivatives, from being illegal gambling. In the context of ensuring financial and management stability of the markets, the ethical aspects of the game have to be first addressed. **1.63**

(5) Ethical issues

The HKSAR government claims that Hong Kong is an international financial centre and its Securities and Futures Ordinance has the regulatory objectives of maintaining and promoting the fairness, efficiency, competitiveness, transparency, and orderliness of the securities and futures industry.[90] However, the **1.64**

---

[81] GP Gilligan, *Regulating the Financial Services Sector* (London: Kluwer Law International, 1999), p 83.

[82] ibid.   [83] Gambling Ordinance (Cap. 148), s 3.   [84] Gambling Ordinance, s 2.

[85] ibid.

[86] H Solomon, 'Jurimetrics', in FN David (ed), *Research Papers in Statistics* (New York: Wiley, 1966), p 319.

[87] WA Wagenaar, *Paradoxes of Gambling Behaviour* (London: Lawrence Erlbaum Associates, 1988), p 79.

[88] Cap. 148.   [89] Securities and Futures Ordinance (Cap. 571) ('SFO'), s 404(2).

[90] SFO, s 4(a).

regulatory framework of the financial markets is not consumer protection legislation in that it imposes no implied conditions or warranties on financial institutions which deal with investors, although such institutions are subject to codes of conduct in the manner in which they deal with investors.

1.65   The relevant ordinances attempt to ensure that there is fair play in the financial markets. Naturally, if the market is fair, risk is reduced. One of the risks is that one party has an unfair advantage over another party or parties and benefits from such unfair advantage. Fairness in the financial markets demands that the players, stakeholders, and participants should observe ethical standards. The relationship between financial institutions and their clients is fiduciary in nature. The former are expected to operate with utmost good faith. As such, the regulatory framework of finance should be based on ethical standards. However, there is always a gap between the law of finance and the ethical standards expected from financial market participants.

1.66   The decisions taken by actors in the financial markets have a far-reaching impact on society and the economy as a whole. The management of a financial institution has a duty to maximize profits for its shareholders, and the manager of a trust fund has a similar duty to maximize income for its beneficiaries. Accordingly, insofar as they operate within the limit of the law to achieve these objectives, to them the ethical issues are secondary. In other words, social responsibility is often ignored. An example can be shown by the speculative attack on the HK dollar amidst the Asian financial crisis in August 1998.[91] As described above, in that episode there were speculators double playing the equity, currency market, and the futures market.[92] An attack on the currency market would force up interest rates, and this would be followed by profit-taking through short-selling of the futures index. The aim of these speculative attacks was to make quick profits in the futures market[93] but it might also result in the melt-down of the entire financial system. During the crisis, share prices, interest levels, and interest rates in Hong Kong were dictated wholly by manipulators,[94] yet regulators and the government were unable to identify the manipulators, being disguised as they were by many different channels.[95] On 15 August

---

[91]   B Hsu, 'Are Hong Kong's Economic Fundamentals Really Sound? A Call for Reform and Transparency', in D Arner, M Yokoi-Arai, & Z Zhou (eds), *Financial Crises in the 1990s: A Global Perspective* (London: The British Institute of International and Comparative Law, 2001), pp 344–7.

[92]   ibid; 'LCQ13: Gov't move aims to frustrate "double play" strategy', *Press Release*, Financial Services Bureau, 14 October 1998.

[93]   'Transcript of Financial Secretary's press briefing', *Daily Information Bulletin*, Hong Kong: Government Information Services, 14 August 1998.

[94]   'Financial Secretary's transcript', *Daily Information Bulletin*, Hong Kong: Government Information Services, 8 September 1998.

[95]   *LC Paper No. CB(1) 534/98–99*, Hong Kong: Legislative Council, 7 September 1998, p 6.

1998 the HKSAR government intervened in a counterattack by deploying its Exchange Fund to deal with this very exceptional circumstance.[96]

The nature and the suddenness of the government's action took many by surprise.[97] The intervention drew the wrath of the financial sector, as most of the major investment banks and funds were counting on the success of the attack on the Hong Kong currency to take quick profits. Three years after the intervention, George Soros, whose Quantum Fund had taken sizable positions against the HK dollar and the stock markets in the speculative attack, suggested that the HKSAR government did a good job by preventing the collapse of Hong Kong's financial markets.[98] From the perspective of investment professionals, it was merely a legitimate venture to maximize profits. The calculated consequence to the livelihoods of the people of Hong Kong was irrelevant. Some even criticized the measures of the HKSAR government as illegal manipulation of the stock market.[99] On the other hand, the HKSAR government argued that it was merely maintaining financial stability and a level playing field.

1.67

The attitude of the investment community as discussed in the foregoing paragraphs illustrates the importance of its professional culture. In this context, culture is defined as the set of deep-rooted values, attitudes, and beliefs that affect the way a profession, community, or firm perceive and behave. Hong Kong is a place where people come to make a fortune, then leave for more relaxing environs. Most people in Hong Kong, whether Chinese or otherwise, consider wealth the most important objective.[100] Therefore, unethical behaviour should be prohibited by legislation rather than by social censure. Prior to the enactment of the Securities and Futures Ordinance, insider dealing offences resulted only in civil penalties, and were more cost effective than speculative attacks on the HK dollar. While this carried no risk to the wrongdoer, harm was done to others due to the unfair use of information. The failure to criminalize this conduct in the past meant that insiders ignored the legal prohibition if the benefits outweighed the penalties. Those who want inside information are financial professionals, listed companies, and investors. In Hong Kong, vested interests formed an unstable coalition against public interests by opposing

1.68

---

[96] ibid.

[97] 'Hong Kong Investors Play Guessing Game', *The Asian Wall Street Journal*, 19 August 1998.

[98] 'Three Years On, Soros Praises Government over Intervention', *South China Morning Post*, 23 September 2001, p N-3.

[99] K Lynch, 'The temptation to intervene: Problems created by the Government's intervention in the Hong Kong stock market', paper presented in Challenges for the New International Financial Architecture: Lessons from East Asia, Hong Kong: Asian Institute of International Financial Law, June 1999, p 13. See also Goodhart Lu (*op. cit.*).

[100] SL Wong, 'Modernization and Chinese Culture in Hong Kong', 106 (1986) *The China Quarterly* 322–3.

regulatory control over insider dealing.[101] The ethical issues relating to market misconduct are discussed in detail in Chapter 8.

1.69   In a free market system the dominant consideration is to maximize profits. From an economic perspective, profit should be maximized through rationality by making the most efficient use of all available resources.[102] In the competitive world of finance, when a firm earns less than its competitors, it loses its ability to attract high-quality employees. As human resources are the most important asset of financial firms, the consequence is that underperforming institutions will be edged out. The measurement of success of a financial institution is inevitably the profits it generates, and this is the case even for firms with an ethically oriented mandate, such as environmental funds. Observing ethical standards beyond what is mandated is irrelevant and may be an obstacle to success when there is a cost attached in doing so. The view has been expressed that a firm's ethical behaviour would be inversely correlated to income gener-ated.[103] An ethical dilemma is undoubtedly present. A financial institution which sets high ethical standards among its employees may be subject to higher expenditure than those competitors that observe the regulatory minimum. In ensuring that the playing field is level, the regulatory framework cannot rely upon financial institutions to regulate their ethical conduct voluntarily without legal sanction.

(6)   Elements of fairness

1.70   In Hong Kong, there never has been any real application of the notion of fairness in the financial markets. The goal of a 'level playing field' has become fashion-able in Hong Kong only in recent years, after decades of recurring financial crises, and began to be central in the rhetoric used, particularly in statements by its financial regulatory agencies.[104] Nevertheless, the concept of a level playing field has never been discussed. It is uncertain what constitutes a level playing field in Hong Kong's context, as it has different meanings for different interests. An understanding of the regulatory framework requires a common acknowledge-ment of the goal of a level playing field from the perceptions of the regulators

---

[101] J Moir, 'Plan to criminalize inside trade blasted', *South China Morning Post*, 10 October 2000; J van der Kamp, 'Case for abolishing insider rules', *South China Morning Post*, 11 October 2000; E Yiu, 'Banks say bill "too tough" on disclosure', *South China Morning Post*, 22 May 2001.

[102] JH Michelman, 'Some Ethical Consequences of Economic Competition', 2 (1983) *Journal of Business Ethics* 82–5.

[103] ibid, pp 85–6.

[104] eg an internet search of the Securities and Futures Commission's website has shown that this phrase has been used extensively since 2001 and has appeared in no less than 157 speeches and press releases, etc. See <http://www.hksfc.org.hk/eng/search/html/index.html>.

and stakeholders of the financial markets. Historically, the powerful financial cartel in Hong Kong devised market rules in its own way with the blessing of the law. In any event, this does not mean that there is no shared value of the level playing field in Hong Kong. It has been suggested that the perimeter of the level playing field can be defined by the four basic elements of fairness.[105] An understanding of the financial markets in Hong Kong is demonstrated by analysing these four basic elements.

This first element is that all players must start equally.[106] This is not the case in Hong Kong. For example, the Hong Kong Association of Banks (HKAB) was incorporated by the Hong Kong Association of Banks Ordinance.[107] All licensed banks are statutory members of the Association.[108] The three leading banks[109] in Hong Kong are statutory members of the powerful Committee of the Association.[110] This ordinance empowers the Association 'from time to time to make such rules relating to the conduct of the business of banking after consultation with the Financial Secretary', and the Association is empowered to discipline members who violate any rule relating to the conduct of the business of banking.[111] Therefore, what is conceived as a level playing field in Hong Kong's context may not necessarily be followed in other jurisdictions or cultures.

1.71

The second element of fairness is that it is the outcome that counts.[112] Accordingly, if market participants are disadvantaged, fairness requires that there should be no restriction for competition.[113] The goal of regulatory competition among different regulatory agencies should encourage innovation and result in the implementation of the most efficient regulatory framework.[114] Prior to the enactment of the Securities and Futures Ordinance, an exempted person (eg a bank) was not required to register as a securities dealer or adviser.[115] The SFC only had to be satisfied that an applicant for exemption dealt with securities as part of its ordinary business, which was unlikely to pose an undue risk to investors.[116] This gave special consideration to banking institutions that provided investment advice to their clients. The SFC could also exempt from the licensing requirements those who only advised financial institutions or overseas clients.[117] Further, it could declare any licensed bank or trustee company an

1.72

---

[105] HA Garten, *U.S. Financial Regulation and the Level Playing Field* (New York: Palgrave, 2001), p 7.

[106] ibid, pp 7–10.   [107] Cap. 364.

[108] Hong Kong Association of Banks Ordinance (Cap. 364) (HKABO), s 7(1).

[109] The Hong Kong and Shanghai Banking Corporation (HSBC), Standard Chartered Bank, and the Bank of China.

[110] HKABO, s 8(1)(a).   [111] HKABO, ss 12(1) & 17(1).

[112] Garten, above, pp 10–11.   [113] ibid.   [114] ibid.

[115] SFO, s 47.   [116] Securities Ordinance (Cap. 333), ss 60 & 61.

[117] Securities Ordinance, ss 60(4) & 61(1).

exempt dealer without consideration.[118] The grant of exempt dealer and exempt investment adviser status to banking institutions was an abdication of power by the SFC, on the assumption that they fell under the jurisdiction of the HKMA. This acted against the principle of regulatory competition. Although the Securities and Futures Bill originally retained such exemption, it was eventually replaced in the Securities and Futures Ordinance with a system of dual regulation—with the HKMA regulating the securities activities of banks, albeit under identical rules to the SFO and related subsidiary legislation. The levelling of this playing field in Hong Kong met with opposition from banking institutions.[119]

1.73 The third element of fairness is that fair play is demanded.[120] Notwithstanding that Hong Kong is a free market economy, a level playing field requires the protection of market participants that have lesser bargaining power. Accordingly, the regulatory framework should ensure such market participants that the financial markets are fair by equalizing bargaining power.[121] The introduction of the Mandatory Provident Fund in Hong Kong means that all employers and employees make contributions to the funds administered by financial institutions.[122] As employers do not have a vested interest in the returns of the investment funds, they are more interested in cost effectiveness, ie what each financial institution offers rather than with the fairness of the trust conditions of each fund. The upshot is that some financial institutions impose onerous terms in the trust within statutory limits while offering lower costs to the employers. Employees have no bargaining power in the selection of the financial institution. There is thus a conflict of interest between employers and employees. What employers perceive as fair is their ability to choose the financial institutions in an open market. Therefore, the regulatory framework should protect employees without bargaining power by removing onerous the trust conditions and enhancing the transparency and accountability of the investment funds as if the employees can choose them with fair bargaining power in the open market.

1.74 The fourth element of fairness is that the market rather than government should pick winners and losers.[123] Accordingly, market participants should be free to reap the gains and bear the losses and the government should not distort the outcome.[124] The financial markets in Hong Kong suffer the worst form of

---

[118] Securities Ordinance, s 60(4).
[119] E Yiu, 'Bankers and brokers do battle over two new bills', *South China Morning Post*, 8 December 2000.
[120] Garten, above, p 11.   [121] ibid.
[122] Mandatory Provident Fund Schemes Ordinance (Cap. 485).
[123] Garten, above, pp 11–12.   [124] ibid.

moral hazard problem as demonstrated by the events in the case of CA Pacific Securities in 1998. In that case, the government gave in to the demands of investors and politicians to pay greater compensation from the Securities Compensation Fund.[125] Many investors in this episode were reckless as to the nature of the documents they had signed. There is no level playing field in using taxpayers' money to raise the compensation paid to market losers as a result of regulatory deficiencies. As another example, the enactments of the Hang Lung Bank (Acquisition) Ordinance 1983 and the Overseas Trust Bank (Acquisition) Ordinance 1984 to rescue two failing banks with resources from the Exchange Fund distorted general monetary policy. As yet another example, with the real estate market decline in Hong Kong after the Asian financial crisis in 1997, the HKSAR government took a series of measures to rescue the real estate markets.[126] The ostensible motive was to bail out both banking institutions (from increasing negative equity assets)[127] and politically influential real estate developers. These measures distort the level playing field and the objectives of a free market economy.

(7) Unfair bargaining in financial markets

Although the Securities and Futures Ordinance harmonized laws relating to securities and futures markets, the regulatory structure is still scattered across numerous agencies that regulate financial institutions in accordance to the activities they undertake. Accordingly, a financial institution may be regulated by at least four agencies.[128] Each such agency is vying for resources from the HKSAR government. An example is that while Hong Kong claims to be an international financial centre, there is no prudential rule requiring financial institutions to be accountable to beneficiaries of pension funds they manage. The financial institution may be exploiting the indifference of the employers who select it, the apathy of the relevant regulatory agency, which has its own agenda, and the lack of knowledge and sophistication of employees. This is not fair play as financial institutions that voluntarily choose to be accountable to the beneficiaries of

1.75

---

[125] 'Editorial', *Ming Pao Daily*, 24 January 1998, p A2; 'HK failed companies' liquidators say no', *Wall Street Journal*, 25 February 1998.

[126] B Hsu, 'Is the Financial Crisis over in the Hong Kong Special Administrative Region?: An Evaluation of the HKSAR's Banking Framework', 16:2 (2001) *Banking & Finance Law Review* 285–6; *A Statement on Housing Policy by the Secretary for Housing, Planning and Lands* (Hong Kong: Housing, Planning & Lands Bureau, Government of the Hong Kong Special Administrative Region, 13 November 2002).

[127] *Residential mortgage loans in negative equity March quarter* (Hong Kong: Hong Kong Monetary Authority, May 2003). <http://www.info.gov.hk/hkma/eng/press/category/resident_index.htm>.

[128] HKMA, Office of the Commissioner of Insurance, Mandatory Provident Fund Schemes Authority, and SFC.

their pension funds have to incur additional costs and they have to compete with the ones who choose the regulatory minimum.

1.76   When the playing field is level, competition should safeguard against conflicts of interest and abusive behaviour of financial institutions.[129] This only operates well when consumers in the financial markets have the bargaining power freely to choose the financial institutions they wish to deal with and that they are competent to choose. In Hong Kong, consumers have no bargaining power as the financial institutions are free to collude among themselves for unfair contractual terms within the regulatory framework in the absence of competition or anti-trust legislation. The confidence of the public in the financial markets is crucial to economic and political stability. Therefore, it could be argued that a comprehensive regulatory framework of the financial markets should prevail over market competition. Hong Kong has never had any long-term planning of its regulatory framework (despite support for this in the Basic Law) and, as with many other financial centres, its regulatory structure has grown in response to financial crises.

1.77   There is no doubt that there are transaction costs attached to compliance with rules of fair play.[130] While these costs would ultimately be passed to the consumers it should also bring the benefit of risk reduction and enhanced market development. Not all these rules achieve efficiency and fairness to all market participants. To the extent such rules are inefficient, such rules may result in more competitive inequalities among financial institutions,[131] thus rendering the playing field even less level. Therefore a balance has to be struck. It should always be the responsibility of the regulators to review and adjust the rules of fair play to ensure that they are efficient and fair to all market participants.

C. Hong Kong as Asia's Financial Centre

1.78   How international is Hong Kong's financial services industry? Few would say it is not, at the very least. When Hong Kong sneezes, markets around the world certainly notice. A recent study shares this view.[132] According to its findings, during the Asian financial crisis between October 1997 and March 1998, contagion from the real estate market in Hong Kong contributed around 53 per cent of the volatility to the Australian real estate securities market, 40 per cent to the Japanese market, and 45 per cent to the US market. Thus, equity market contagion from Hong Kong had comparable impact on those markets. The

---

[129] Garten, above, p 145.   [130] ibid, p 155.   [131] ibid, p 156.
[132] S Bond, M Dungey, & R Fry, 'A Web of Shocks: Crises Across Asian Real Estate Markets', Cambridge University, working paper, February 2004.

financial markets around the world are so integrated that it takes very little time for the butterfly effect to travel across continents.

(1) The financial services industry in Hong Kong

To evaluate the international-orientation of Hong Kong's financial services industry, this section examines five key areas of financial services, namely, products for investing and saving, raising capital and extending credit, transferring funds, managing risk, and offering financial advice. **1.79**

First, Hong Kong allows the freest flows of capital in the region. In terms of choice of financial products and services, Hong Kong is international not only at the wholesale level, but perhaps also for retail participants at the retail level. For example, there is a spectrum of equity funds available for local and foreign investors to invest in any major equities market in the world. Although the debt market is small by international standards and relative to the local equity market, banks in Hong Kong offer various services that allow investors to invest in fixed income securities outside Hong Kong through swap arrangements, bond funds with returns linked to US Treasuries or corporate yield spreads, or structured products that mimic fixed income securities in the US and Europe. **1.80**

Hong Kong is a regional centre for fund management, with 172 companies providing fund management and advisory services. They manage more than 2,000 authorized funds. About 60 per cent of institutional and 25 per cent of pension funds are managed by international financial managers. About 70 per cent of assets in authorized funds belong to foreign investors. **1.81**

The Hong Kong stock market has channelled from local and foreign investors more than 80 per cent of the capital that companies in China raised from overseas. However, international company listings in Hong Kong from other sources have become minimal in recent years. Bank loans are still the mainstay of debt financing for companies in Hong Kong. Banks in Hong Kong also provide to the corporate sector various kinds of structured loans and those with embedded derivative features. **1.82**

Hong Kong is a major centre for non-life reinsurance in the region. Risk management tools in Hong Kong include traded stock options, futures, and warrants. Interest-rate linked instruments and currency derivatives are actively traded in Hong Kong's wholesale money, currency, and other over-the-counter derivatives markets, although the size and scope of the overall exchange-traded derivatives market is smaller than that of Singapore. **1.83**

It is beyond doubt that the financial services industry has managed to do all that it should in each area in order to stay competitive internationally within the confine of the existing market infrastructure and socio-politico-economic environment. **1.84**

Although there is room for growth and improvement in certain areas, the international orientation of Hong Kong's financial services industry is clear.

(2) China's international financial centre

1.85 Competition among financial centres is unending and Hong Kong is facing a potential threat from Shanghai as the leading financial centre in China. In fact, Shanghai surpassed Hong Kong in terms of stock market capitalization and domestic bonds outstanding in 2001, though this has subsequently been reversed.

1.86 The experience of London mirrors what Hong Kong should do to maintain its competitive edge as a leading international financial centre. Since the launch of the euro, Frankfurt has been competing against London to be the leading international financial centre in Europe. The hard fact is that not only has Frankfurt failed to get anywhere close to that aim, it has even fallen further behind London as a centre for foreign exchange transactions and in attracting international company listings, except for exchange-traded derivatives transactions.

1.87 The factors underlying the success of London are seemingly obvious, namely, a well-established infrastructure with many multinational companies (MNCs) and foreign headquarters, a highly open and transparent legal system for financial transactions, the use of English (the global language), an open door policy to foreign talent, efficient free flow of information, and the competitiveness of the banks and brokers relative to their rivals in Europe.[133] All these factors combine to make it difficult for a strong rival like Frankfurt to gain ground.

1.88 As a financial centre in China, Hong Kong has unique features. Hong Kong has always practised a laissez faire market economy; it has its own independent but imported English common law system which is transparent; it has a simple tax system with low tax rates; culturally, it is a melting pot of Chinese and Western traditions; there is no foreign exchange control; it has a liberal regime toward foreign bank and equity ownership and a free port policy to foreign professionals; and it is an integral part of China's economy. All these factors have culminated in making Hong Kong the window to the international capital markets for China.

1.89 Under CEPA, banks in Hong Kong will be allowed to open branches in the mainland if they have total assets of US$ 6 billion or more.[134] This is a significantly

---

[133] MKS Tse, 'How International is Hong Kong Financial Services Industry', *Hong Kong: The Servicing Economy* (September 2004), p 4.

[134] CEPA provisions on Financial Services Cooperation: Banking sector under CEPA I service sectors with further liberalization under CEPA II, implemented from 1 January 2004.

lower entrance requirement than under China's WTO commitments. The relaxation of restrictions for conducting renminbi business will allow the medium-sized banks in Hong Kong to enter the Mainland market, and for those who have already established branches there to expand their network nation-wide. It will certainly further strengthen the position of those Hong Kong banks that operate on the Mainland to have better access to renminbi business. Furthermore, the second-phase of liberalization measures under CEPA will allow Mainland branches of Hong Kong banks to conduct insurance agency business.

The benefits of CEPA will go beyond opening the Mainland door for Hong **1.90** Kong's small and medium-sized banks. Banks in the Mainland are encouraged to relocate their international treasury and foreign exchange trading centres to Hong Kong as well as to develop networks in Hong Kong through acquisition. The 'Financial Services Cooperation' provisions of CEPA will enable Hong Kong to reinforce its function and status as an international banking centre.

(3) Hong Kong and finance in Asia

Hong Kong's financial market is one of the most advanced financial centres in **1.91** Asia. Its status in the region is built on relatively high standards of market transparency, disclosure, and prudentially supervised financial institutions. These factors, together with non-discriminatory low tax policy, a well-developed financial infrastructure, and the sophistication of its financial professionals, mean that Hong Kong has the potential to become the most prominent financial centre in the region.

With the continuous increase in trade and business activities between China **1.92** and the region, Hong Kong, as a major financial centre in China, will certainly play a very important role in providing financial services for trade and investment in the region.

(4) Global financial markets and the role of Hong Kong

In recent years, Hong Kong has been a high scorer in several of the international **1.93** rankings, which serves as an indication of how well Hong Kong is recognized internationally. For example, in terms of economic freedom Hong Kong is ranked first out of 155 countries;[135] in terms of competitiveness Hong Kong is second out of 60 economies;[136] in press freedom Hong Kong is ranked 34th out of 167 countries;[137] in terms of quality of life, Hong Kong is 18th out of 111

---

[135] *Heritage Foundation/The Wall Street Journal*: 2005 Index of Economic Freedom.
[136] *IMD International*: (countries and regions): World Competitiveness Yearbook 2005.
[137] *Reporters without borders*: Third annual worldwide press freedom index (2004).

countries;[138] in terms of corruption, Hong Kong is ranked 16th most favourably out of 146;[139] in human development Hong Kong is 23rd out of 177 countries;[140] in competitiveness, Hong Kong is 21st out of 104 countries.[141] Few would say that Hong Kong is not international. However, the international orientation of Hong Kong's financial services hinges on whether Hong Kong can continue to offer something unique to the global financial markets and how well Hong Kong links to the global financial markets.

1.94 For the financial services industry in Hong Kong to remain international, Hong Kong must maintain its status as a regional and international hub by attracting more foreign and Mainland corporations to open their regional headquarters in Hong Kong.

1.95 To enhance Hong Kong's financial stability with better protection against external shocks, Hong Kong needs to further develop its small debt market. Increased economic integration with the Mainland is a challenge, but it will create cross-border opportunities for Hong Kong's financial service sector to develop. The lack of risk management tools and derivative products in China has left room for Hong Kong to develop into a convenient centre for risk management for multinational corporations operating in China. Presently, confidence in Hong Kong's financial markets is high, but this confidence is nevertheless fragile. Frequent scandals at Mainland companies have tarnished the image of such companies and will make it more costly for many state-owned enterprises to raise capital through share offerings in Hong Kong and abroad.

1.96 Being at the gateway to China and a free port open to the rest of the world, the role of the Hong Kong financial market should be more than just to help Mainland companies to raise capital and list in Hong Kong. Rather, by listing in Hong Kong, it should aim at adding value in governance. Value added ensues from better corporate governance compared to Parent Companies in the Mainland, higher transparency in relation to the company's operations, higher accountability to stakeholders, and enhanced access to international sources of capital. To restore investors' confidence in such firms, Hong Kong needs to tighten enforcement of its listing rules and strengthen scrutiny of listing applicants. These and other matters are addressed in subsequent chapters.

---

[138] *The Economist*: The World in 2005—Worldwide quality-of-life index, 2005.
[139] *Transparency International*: Corruption Perceptions Index 2004.
[140] *United Nations Development Programme*: Human Development Index 2004.
[141] *World Economic Forum*: Global Competitiveness Report 2004–2005—Growth Competitiveness Index Ranking.

2

FINANCIAL LAW AND REGULATION

Following the introduction to financial markets in Hong Kong and their devel- **2.01**
opment in Chapter 1, this chapter presents an overview of the legal and institutional framework for finance in Hong Kong. In approaching financial law and
regulation in Hong Kong, it is useful to have a framework of analysis from
which to proceed. In this regard, this chapter is based upon a framework derived
from international standards and financial markets research. Building on this
framework, Parts II and III then address individual aspects in detail.

While Hong Kong has not always had effective systems of financial regulation, it **2.02**
has been steadily strengthening its regulatory framework both for financial markets and institutions.[1] The increasing effectiveness of its legal and institutional
regulatory framework has enhanced its development as an international financial
centre over the past decade and will be vital to its continued success in the future.

Chapter 1 showed how public financial law in Hong Kong has undergone three **2.03**
stages of development.[2] In particular, the period from 1986 has been one of

---

[1] See generally I Tokley, *Hong Kong Banking Law and Practice* (Butterworths, 1996); R Ho,
R Scott, & K Wong (eds), *The Hong Kong Financial System* 381 (Hong Kong: OUP, 1991);
T Ghose, *The Banking System of Hong Kong* (1987).
[2] See B Hsu, *Laws of Banking and Finance in the Hong Kong SAR* (Hong Kong: Open
University of Hong Kong, 1998), pp 152–70, 235–43.

strengthening of regulation and supervision of financial institutions and markets, with the overriding goal of achieving 'international standards'. Further, the period from 1986 to 1995 was a time of modernization and a search for standards of best practice, not only in Hong Kong but globally. Following the financial crises of recent years associated with Mexico, East Asia, Russia, Argentina, and elsewhere attention has focused on the importance of developing such standards and upon their implementation into domestic legal systems and supervisory practice.[3] This is an ongoing process that is likely to shape the development of public financial law in both Hong Kong and throughout China.

2.04   Financial regulation in Hong Kong prior to the 1990s developed as post-hoc responses to serious financial crises. Indeed, prior to the mid-1980s, Hong Kong had no public financial law; rather, cartels of financial sector corporations largely regulated themselves, mainly avoiding official interest and functioning as an informal club.[4] According to one leading scholar, '[t]he banking crisis of 1982–1986 and the near bankruptcy of the futures market during the world stock market crash of October 1987, forced the authorities to undertake a far-ranging reform of the regulatory framework'.[5]

2.05   At the base of financial markets are Hong Kong's economic, governance, legal, and taxation systems. Upon that base, financial markets in Hong Kong are underpinned by legal and institutional arrangements addressing: company law and corporate governance;[6] property and collateral; insolvency;[7] financial information (accounting[8] and auditing[9]); market integrity;[10] and financial regulation (structure, banking[11] and payment and settlement,[12] securities,[13] insurance,[14] pensions, and conglomerates).

---

[3] See D Arner, *Law, Financial Stability and Economic Development* (New York: Cambridge University Press, 2006 forthcoming).

[4] For a description of a similar system in the UK prior to 1979, see C Hadjiemmanuil, *Banking Regulation and the Bank of England* (London: LLP, 1996).

[5] YC Jao, *Hong Kong as an International Financial Centre: Evolution, Prospects and Policies* (Hong Kong: City University of Hong Kong, 1997), p 26.

[6] OECD, Principles of Corporate Governance.

[7] World Bank, Principles and Guidelines for Insolvency and Creditor Rights System (April 2001); UNCITRAL, Legislative Guide on Insolvency Law (forthcoming). At present, the IMF, World Bank, and UNCITRAL are cooperating to produce a single standard but no agreement has yet been reached.

[8] IASB, International Financial Reporting Standards (IFRS).

[9] IFA, International Standards on Auditing.   [10] FATF, 40+8 Recommendations.

[11] Basel Committee, Core Principles of Effective Banking Supervision.

[12] CPSS, Core Principles for Systemically Important Payment Systems; CPSS/IOSCO, Recommendations for Securities Settlement Systems.

[13] IOSCO, Objectives and Principles for Securities Regulation.

[14] IAIS, Insurance Supervisory Principles.

A. Foundations of Hong Kong's Financial Markets

Hong Kong's legal and institutional framework is an interesting case: under   **2.06**
British rule, it developed as a laissez-faire capitalist system based on English
common law and imported British statutes, with a largely administrative government with few democratic features reporting to the colonial government in
London. Since the 1997 transfer of sovereignty to the People's Republic of
China, Hong Kong has continued to operate a capitalist system based upon
common law and existing statutes but in the context of the socialist market
economy and civil law legal system of the PRC (discussed further in Chapter 9),
still with a largely administrative government now reporting to the central
government in Beijing, though with some democratic features. As such, it is
perhaps unique in terms of its economic, governmental, and legal foundations.

Historically, Hong Kong has been known for its laissez-faire system of capital-   **2.07**
ism; however, this has never been a completely accurate picture. While Hong
Kong has lacked the sort of linked financial and governmental systems of
other Asian economies (eg South Korea, Japan, and Singapore), there has
historically been a close working relationship between leading businesses and
the government, with business typically assuming self-regulatory responsibility,
largely as a result of government dependence on a property-based revenue
system. This has changed over the past two decades with the relationship
between government, business, and the financial system becoming increasingly
rule-based and transparent though with continuing influence by dominant
economic elites.

Following the reversion of Hong Kong to the PRC, Hong Kong remains largely   **2.08**
legally and administratively separate under the principle of 'one country, two
systems'. As a corollary in respect to financial systems, there exist 'two markets,
two monetary systems and two responsible monetary authorities', one for the
Mainland and one for Hong Kong. This suggests that the financial systems of
the two will remain administratively separate, while becoming increasingly
interlinked.

(1) Economic, governance, and legal systems

From 1 July 1997 Hong Kong became a Special Administrative Region (SAR) of   **2.09**
the PRC enjoying a high degree of autonomy. The Basic Law, enacted by the
PRC National People's Congress, is the constitutional document of post-
colonial Hong Kong and the blueprint for its future development. Specific
provisions have been laid down in the Basic Law on the changes brought about
by its new status and on the implementation of the concept of 'one country,

two systems'. The Basic Law is thus a PRC law establishing the framework for the SAR of Hong Kong.

Basic Law and Common Law

2.10   The fundamental legal framework of Hong Kong is the 'Basic Law'. It sets out the general principle of 'one country, two systems', with the capitalist system of Hong Kong and the socialist market system of Mainland China coexisting side by side for a minimum of 50 years. The Basic Law grants Hong Kong a high degree of autonomy and executive, legislative and independent judicial powers and guarantees the existence of its current political, economical, and financial system until at least 2047.

2.11   In anticipation of the resumption of exercise of sovereignty over Hong Kong, the Basic Law was adopted by the PRC National People's Congress on 4 April 1990. Article 8 of the Basic Law provides that the

> laws previously in force in Hong Kong, that is, the common law, rules of equity, ordinances, subordinate legislation and customary law shall be maintained, except for any that contravene this Law, and subject to any amendment by the legislature of the Hong Kong Special Administrative Region.

Article 18 of the Basic Law provides that the

> laws in force in the Hong Kong Special Administrative Region shall be this Law, the laws previously in force in Hong Kong as provided for in Article 8 of this Law, and the laws enacted by the legislature of the Region.

2.12   English statutes and judicial decisions are the primary source of existing Hong Kong law prior to the 1997 handover. The pre-existing legal framework continues under the Basic Law. As a former British colony governed by common law, judicial precedent has served to develop most aspects of financial law. English judicial decisions are no longer binding, but carry persuasive weight, as do decisions from other common law jurisdictions.

2.13   Because of the importance of the Hong Kong economy to both Hong Kong and the Mainland, 70 of the Basic Law's 160 Articles are related to economic matters.[15] For instance, Articles 109, 112, 114, and 116 determine that Hong Kong remains a free port, a separate customs territory and an international financial centre, with its markets for foreign exchange, gold, and securities and futures remaining in place. According to Article 115, Hong Kong shall pursue a policy of free trade and safeguard the free movement of goods, intangible assets and capital. Hong Kong shall also have independent finances and use its financial

---

[15] HKMA, *Hong Kong—Pacific Powerhouse*, (*Hong Kong—The Next Century* by Donald Tsang (former Financial Secretary)), p 13.

revenues exclusively for its own purposes.[16] Under Article 105, rights of individuals and legal persons to the acquisition, use, and inheritance of property remain protected in Hong Kong.

It is, therefore, clear that the pre-existing laws relating to banking and finance in Hong Kong remain in force after 30 June 1997 and until changed by the legislature. **2.14**

This section first discusses the legislative process in enacting financial regulations and the legal framework under which they are administered and adjudicated. Then, it mentions the relevant provisions of the Basic Law which provide a constitutional framework in promoting Hong Kong as a financial centre. **2.15**

Legislative process and administrative framework

The law-making body in Hong Kong is the Legislative Council. The Basic Law spells out the authority and composition of the Legislative Council.[17] The Basic Law also regulates the exercise of legislative power, in that it defines what is law-making power and who has the authority to enact legislation (ordinances).[18] The Legislative Council with the assent of the Chief Executive enacts ordinances. The Basic Law provides that members of the Legislative Council may introduce bills, other than those relating to public expenditure, political structure, or operation of government.[19] Drafting of legislation is the function of the Department of Justice (though in practice in the financial field a draft will be produced by the relevant government agency) and a bill is then submitted to the legislative process. In the financial sphere, the Financial Services and Treasury Bureau have also made an important contribution to the reform process. The written consent of the Chief Executive is required before bills relating to government policies are introduced. This applies to most of the ordinances relating to banking and finance. In any event, the Legislative Councils of the Hong Kong SAR and former British Hong Kong have traditionally taken a passive role in financial matters. Like other jurisdictions, legal reforms in financial markets tend to come from regulatory agencies rather than legislators. There is an active programme of law reform: the Law Reform Commission of Hong Kong was established in 1980, and considers aspects of the law referred to it by the Secretary for Justice or the Chief Justice but does not prepare draft legislation. **2.16**

---

[16] Basic Law, art 106.   [17] Basic Law, chap IV & art 3.

[18] Ordinances in Hong Kong are typically referred to by their respective chapter number of the Laws of Hong Kong, available at <http://www.legislation.gov.hk>, eg Companies Ordinance, Chapter 32, Laws of Hong Kong. This is typically shortened to 'Cap.' neg Companies Ordinance (Cap. 32). Subsidiary legislation—essentially regulations—typically is numbered with the primary number, followed by a letter, eg Companies (Requirements for Documents) Regulation (Cap. 32A). Subsidiary legislation requires a simpler legislative approval process than primary legislation.

[19] Basic Law, art 74.

2.17 The Basic Law provides the ambit of executive and legislative powers by enumerating the power of the Chief Executive and the government, respectively.[20] These powers conform to the traditional common law view that the executive function involves performing particular acts or issuing particular orders in accordance with the law. It also enumerates the powers of the Legislative Council.[21] Such powers fall within the traditional common law view that the legislative function involves formulating rules for general application. The administration and enforcement of ordinances relating to banking and finance is vested in the Hong Kong Monetary Authority (HKMA), Securities and Futures Commission (SFC), Office of the Commissioner of Insurance (OCI), and the Mandatory Provident Fund Schemes Authority (MPFA). In addition, there is a variety of self-regulatory organizations that take varying roles, including the Hong Kong Association of Banks (HKAB) and Hong Kong Exchanges and Clearing (HKEx). There is a complicated separation of authority among these agencies, each with its own investigative styles and enforcement priorities.

Legal framework

2.18 Adjudicative power is vested in the judiciary in accordance with the provisions of the relevant ordinances and the inherent power of the court on judicial review. As a major banking and finance centre, Hong Kong requires a sound system of adjudication, to provide international investors with confidence. In case of disputes in enforcing the provisions of an ordinance, there should be internal mechanisms for their resolution. If a citizen is still aggrieved after going through all such internal panels, there are further channels available for redress, eg taking up the grievance to a court of law. The judiciary in Hong Kong is independent from other branches of government. Article 2 of the Basic Law provides:

> The National People's Congress authorizes the Hong Kong Special Administrative Region to exercise a high degree of autonomy and enjoy executive, legislative and independent judicial power, including that of final adjudication, in accordance with the provisions of this Law.

Separation of powers

2.19 The Basic Law entrenches the doctrine of separation of powers by providing that the executive, legislative, and judicial powers are to be vested in the Chief Executive and Government, the Legislative Council, and the judiciary respectively.[22] Part IV of the Basic Law spells out the ambit of judicial power. Article 80 of the Basic Law provides that the 'courts of the Hong Kong Special Administrative Region at all levels shall be the judiciary of the Region, exercising the

---

[20] Basic Law, arts 48 & 62.   [21] Basic Law, arts 72 & 73.
[22] Basic Law, arts 48, 62, 72, 73, & 80.

judicial power of the Region'. The Basic Law does not expressly define judicial power. Article 83 of the Basic Law, however, provides that the structure, powers, and functions of the courts of Hong Kong shall be prescribed by law. Article 84 of the Basic Law provides that precedents of other common law jurisdictions may be referred to by the courts of Hong Kong. Therefore, Australian and Canadian sources, for example, are relevant, in addition to English sources.[23] According to *Brandy v Human Rights and Equal Opportunity Commission*,[24] the Australian High Court said:

> Difficulty arises in attempting to formulate a comprehensive definition of judicial power not so much because it consists of a number of factors as because the combination is not always the same. It is hard to point to any essential or constant characteristic. Moreover, there are functions which, when performed by a court, constitute the exercise of judicial power but, when performed by some other body, do not.

> One is tempted to say that, in the end, judicial power is the power exercised by courts and can only be defined by reference to what courts do and the way in which they do it, rather than by recourse to any other classification of functions. But that would be to place reliance upon the elements of history and policy, which, whilst they are legitimate considerations, cannot be conclusive.

The Basic Law only invests the courts with judicial power. Accordingly, Article **2.20** 80 of the Basic Law intends that only judges can exercise the judicial power of Hong Kong. Article 85 of the Basic Law provides that:

> The courts of the Hong Kong Special Administrative Region shall exercise judicial power independently, free from any interference. Members of the judiciary shall be immune from legal action in the performance of their judicial functions.

This provision is possible only if judges can only exercise judicial power and **2.21** powers incidental to it. They must be separated and not be meddled with by any other branch of the government in the performance of their functions. In ensuring their independence, judges should not perform any executive or legislative function unless it is necessary and essential in the performance of their judicial functions. They should not be polluted by being required to consider political issues. The separation of judicial power implies that the legislature cannot dictate to the judiciary as to the manner and outcome of the exercise of its jurisdiction. It is within the ambit of the legislative power to grant or withhold substantive rights. However, it will be an encroachment of judicial power if the legislature makes law to interfere with the judicial process itself,[25]

---

[23] Most of the litigation involving separation of powers in British Commonwealth countries arises from the interpretation of the Australian Commonwealth Constitution, because the Australian Constitution expressly provides for the separation of judicial powers from the two other branches of government (Commonwealth of Australia Constitution Act 1900, s 71).

[24] (1995) 183 CLR 245, 267.

[25] *Lim v Minister for Immigration* (1992) 176 CLR 1, 36–7.

as this would be considered as an exercise of judicial power by the legislative branch.

The constitutional framework of financial markets

2.22 The current banking and finance framework in Hong Kong is derived from a capitalist market-based model. The Basic Law expressly states that the socialist system and policies shall not be practised in Hong Kong, and the established capitalist system and way of life shall remain unchanged for 50 years.[26] The Basic Law provides constitutional protection for holders of Hong Kong currency. It provides that Hong Kong shall have its own legal tender.[27] All laws regulating the issue of currency must abide by Article 111 of the Basic Law, which also provides that:

> The authority to issue Hong Kong currency shall be vested in the Government of the Hong Kong Special Administrative Region. The issue of Hong Kong currency must be backed up by a 100 per cent reserve fund. The system regarding the issue of Hong Kong currency and the reserve fund system shall be preserved by law.

2.23 The Basic Law ensures the continuation of the financial markets in Hong Kong by providing, inter alia, that the markets for foreign exchange, gold, securities, futures, and the like shall continue in Hong Kong. In ensuring that the SAR remains a centre of trade, commerce, and finance, it also provides that there will be free flow of capital within, into, and out of Hong Kong.[28] Exchange control policies shall not be applied in Hong Kong. The Basic Law provides that Hong Kong shall manage and control its own exchange fund and that it shall pursue a policy of free trade and safeguard the free movement of goods, intangible assets and capital.[29] Article 110 of the Basic Law provides that:

> The monetary and financial systems of the Hong Kong Special Administrative Region shall be prescribed by law.
> The government of the Hong Kong Special Administrative Region shall, on its own, formulate monetary and financial business and financial markets, and regulate and supervise them in accordance with law.

(2) Company law and corporate governance

2.24 The Companies Ordinance (Cap. 32) is the primary piece of legislation governing companies and their activities, from incorporation to winding up. 'Company'

---

[26] Basic Law, art 5.
[27] Basic Law, art 111. The HKSAR government may authorize designated banks to issue or continue to issue Hong Kong currency under statutory authority, after satisfying itself that any issue of currency will be soundly based and that the arrangements for such issue are consistent with the object of maintaining the stability of the currency.
[28] Basic Law, art 112.   [29] Basic Law, arts 113 & 115.

means any company incorporated under the Companies Ordinance or one of its predecessors.[30] As an international financial centre, Hong Kong and its markets host many non-Hong Kong companies. The Companies Ordinance also deals with non-Hong Kong companies, that is, companies incorporated outside Hong Kong but which have established a place of business in Hong Kong.[31]

The other significant bodies of company law applicable in Hong Kong are, first, **2.25** those developed under common law and equity, and second, those imposed through statute (the most important of which is the Securities and Futures Ordinance or SFO) and rules (especially the Listing Rules of HKEx). The latter are discussed further below and in subsequent chapters. In regard to the former, in broad terms this aspect of Hong Kong company law follows that which has developed in the English courts, although decisions taken since 1 July 1997 are no longer of binding precedent for the Hong Kong courts.[32]

The Companies Ordinance comprises 367 sections and 20 schedules. It is **2.26** divided into nineteen parts, addressing the following issues: (1) incorporation of companies and matters incidental thereto (sections 4 to 36);[33] (2) share capital and debentures (sections 37 to 79);[34] (3) distribution of profits and assets (sections 79A to 79P);[35] (4) registration of charges (sections 80 to

---

[30] CO s 2.   [31] CO s 332.

[32] Since the resumption of Chinese sovereignty on 1 July 1997, the Basic Law of the Hong Kong Special Administrative Region of the People's Republic of China is the main constitutional document for Hong Kong. Basic Law, art 8 states:

> The laws previously in force in Hong Kong, that is, the common law, rules of equity, ordinances, subordinate legislation and customary law shall be maintained, except for any that contravene [the Basic Law], and subject to any amendment by the legislature of the Hong Kong Special Administrative Region.

[33] Part I includes the following divisions: (1) memorandum of association (ss 4–8); (2) articles of association (ss 9–13); (3) form of memorandum and articles (s 14); (4) registration (ss 15–19); (5) provisions with respect to names of companies (ss 20–22C); (6) general provisions with respect to memorandum and articles (ss 23–27); (7) membership of company (ss 28–28A); (8) private companies (ss 29–31); (9) contracts etc (ss 32–35); and (10) authentication of documents (s 36).

[34] Part II includes the following divisions: (1) prospectus (ss 37–41A); (2) allotment (ss 42–45); (3) commissions and discounts (ss 46–47); (4) financial assistance by a company for acquisition of its own shares: provisions applying to all companies (ss 47A–47C), listed companies (s 47D), and unlisted companies (ss 47E–48); (5) construction of references to offering shares or debentures to the public (s 48A); (6) issue of shares at premium, redeemable preference shares, and shares at a discount (s 48B); (7) merger relief (ss 48C–48F); (8) redeemable shares and purchase by company of its own shares: redemption and purchase generally (ss 49–49H), redemption or purchase of own shares out of capital—private companies only (ss 49I–49O), and supplementary (ss 49P–50); (9) miscellaneous provisions as to share capital (ss 51–57C); (10) reduction of share capital (ss 58–63); (11) variation of shareholders' rights (ss 63A–64A); (12) transfer of shares and debentures, evidence of title (ss 65–74); and (13) special provisions as to debentures (ss 74A–79).

[35] Part IIA includes the following divisions: (1) relevant accounts (ss 79F–79L); and (2) supplementary (ss 79M–79P).

91);[36] (5) management and administration (sections 92 to 168B);[37] (6) statutory derivative action (sections 168BA to 168BK); (7) disqualification of directors (sections 168C to 168T); (8) winding-up (sections 169 to 296);[38] (9) receivers and managers (sections 297 to 302A); (10) general provisions as to registration (sections 303 to 306); (11) application to companies formed or registered under former Ordinances (sections 307 to 309); (12) companies not formed under the Companies Ordinance but authorized to register thereunder (sections 310 to 325); (13) winding-up of unregistered companies (sections 326 to 331A); (14) companies incorporated outside Hong Kong (sections 332 to 341); (15) restrictions on sale of shares and offers of shares for sale (sections 342 to 344); (16) dormant companies (section 344A); (17) miscellaneous (sections 345 to 360);[39] (18) prevention of evasion of the Societies Ordinance (sections 360A to 360N); and (19) savings (sections 361 to 367).

---

[36] Part III includes the following divisions: (1) registration of charges with Registrar of Companies (ss 80–87); (2) provisions as to company's register of charges and as to copies of instruments creating charges (ss 88–90); and (3) application of Part III to companies incorporated outside Hong Kong (s 91).

[37] Part IV includes the following divisions: (1) registered office and name (ss 92–94); (2) register of members (ss 95–102); (3) branch register (ss 103–106); (4) annual return (ss 107–110); (5) meetings and proceedings (ss 111–120); (6) accounts and audit (ss 121–141C); (7) summary financial reports of listed companies (ss 141CA–141CG); (8) relevant financial documents and summary financial reports on computer networks (s 141CH); (9) accounts of certain private companies (s 141D); (10) inspection (ss 142–152); (11) inspection of companies' books and papers (ss 152A–152F); (12) inspection of specified corporations' records by members (ss 152FA–152FE); (13) directors and other officers (ss 153–164); (14) avoidance of provisions in articles or contracts relieving officers from liability (s 165); (15) arrangements and reconstructions (ss 166–168); and (16) minorities (ss 168A–168B).

[38] Part V includes the following divisions: (1) preliminary: modes of winding up (s 169), and contributories (ss 170–175); (2) winding-up by the court: jurisdiction (s 176), cases in which company may be wound up by court (ss 177–178), petition for winding-up and effects thereof (ss 179–183), commencement of winding-up (s 184), consequences of winding-up order (ss 185–187), Official Receiver and liquidators (ss 188–205), committee of inspection (ss 206–208), general power of court in case of winding-up by court (ss 209–227); (3) winding-up by court with a regulating order (ss 227A–227E); (4) winding up by court by way of summary procedure (s 227F); (5) voluntary winding-up: resolutions for and commencement of voluntary winding-up (ss 228–230), consequences of voluntary winding-up (ss 231–232), certificate of solvency (s 233), provisions applicable to a members' voluntary winding-up (ss 234–239A), provisions applicable to a creditors' voluntary winding-up (ss 240–248), and provisions applicable to every voluntary winding-up (ss 249–257); and (6) provisions applicable to every mode of winding-up: proof and ranking of claims (ss 263–265), effect of winding-up on antecedent and other transactions (ss 266–270), offences antecedent to or in course of winding up (ss 271–277), supplement provisions as to winding-up (ss 278–286), supplementary powers of court (ss 287–289), provisions as to dissolution (ss 290–292A), central accounts (ss 293–295), and rules and fees (s 296).

[39] Part XIII includes the following divisions: (1) prohibition of partnerships with more than 20 members (s 345); (2) provisions related to documents and disposal thereof (ss 346–348B); (3) form of registers etc (ss 348C–348D); (4) miscellaneous offences (ss 349–350A); (5) injunctions (s 350B); (6) general provisions as to offences (ss 351–355); (7) service of documents and legal proceedings (ss 356–359); and (8) general provisions as to Chief Executive in Council (ss 359A–360).

The schedules address the following matters: (1) table A; (2) form of statement **2.27** in lieu of prospectus to be delivered to Registrar by a private company on becoming a public company and reports to be set out therein; (3) matters to be specified in prospectus and reports to be set out therein; (4) form of statement in lieu of prospectus to be delivered to Registrar by a company which does not issue a prospectus or which does not go to allotment on a prospectus issued, and reports to be set out therein; (5) powers; (6) table of fees to be paid to the Registrar of Companies; (7) provisions relating to acquisition of minority shares after successful takeover offer; (8) accounts; (9) accounts of certain private companies under section 14D; (10) punishment of offences under the Ordinance; (11) provisions relating to acquisition of minority shares after successful buy out by share repurchase; (12) table of fees to be paid to a company; (13) matters for determining unfitness of directors; (14) companies to which section 291AA or 344A of the Companies Ordinance does not apply; (15) offers specified for the purposes of paragraph (b)(ii) of the definition of 'prospectus' in section 2(1) of the Companies Ordinance; (16) warning, etc, statements to be contained in certain documents; (17) contents and publication requirements of advertisements mentioned in section 388(2)(e) of the Companies Ordinance; (18) amendment of prospectus consisting of one document; (19) provisions in accordance with which a prospectus may consist of more than one document; and (20) persons specified for the purposes of section 40 of the Companies Ordinance.

The Companies Ordinance is supported by thirteen pieces of subsidiary **2.28** legislation:

- Companies (Requirements for Documents) Regulation (Cap. 32A)
- Companies (Forms) Regulations (Cap. 32B)
- Companies (Fees and Percentages) Order (Cap. 32C)
- Companies (Exemption from Statement of Turnover) Order (Cap. 32D)
- Companies (Specification of Names) Order (Cap. 32E)
- Companies Ordinance (Fee for Taking Affidavit, Affirmation or Declaration) Notice (Cap. 32F)
- Companies (Winding-Up) Rules (Cap. 32H)
- Companies (Disqualification Orders) Regulation (Cap. 32I)
- Companies (Reports on Conduct of Directors) Regulation (Cap. 32J)
- Companies (Disqualification of Directors) Regulation (Cap. 32K)
- Companies Ordinance (Exemption of Companies and Prospectuses from Compliance with Provisions) Notice (Cap. 32L)
- Companies (Summary of Financial Reports of Listed Companies) Regulation (Cap. 32M)

The primary administrator of the Companies Ordinance is the Companies **2.29**

Registry, supplemented by the Official Receiver for insolvency matters and the Securities and Futures Commission for certain securities matters, and HKEx for certain matters related to listed companies.

2.30 Parts of the Companies Ordinance may now be outdated. Modern company law should have sufficient transparency to instil investor confidence, minimize transaction costs, maximize efficiency in the running of a company, and place a reasonable burden on corporate management. The present version of the Companies Ordinance does not necessarily achieve these objectives. It once derived heavily from the nineteenth-century version of the British Companies Act. The Companies Law Revision Committee, appointed in 1962, made its two most significant recommendations in 1971 and 1973.[40] The Companies (Amendment) Ordinance 1984 modelled the present Companies Ordinance upon the 1948 version of the British Companies Act in implementing most of the recommendations of the Committee. Between 1973 and 1984, four new versions of the Companies Act were enacted in the UK; however, few of these developments were implemented in Hong Kong. In fact, many of the provisions of the Hong Kong Companies Ordinance at present have remained unchanged over many decades.

2.31 In addition, the Standing Committee on Company Law Reform (SCCLR) is responsible for the on-going review of the Companies Ordinance. The SCCLR was set up in 1984 by the government to advise on amendments to that Ordinance. It consists of ex-officio members (such as the Registrar of Companies and the Official Receiver), whilst non-official members come from the legal, accountancy, and banking professions.[41]

2.32 In March 1997, the *Consultancy Report on the Review of the Hong Kong Companies Ordinance*[42] was released. It provided a new direction for corporate governance. It addressed the problems of the present requirements for financial disclosure[43] and standard of care for directors,[44] as well as conflicts of interest in corporate governance.[45] It also set out new incorporation procedures[46] and a simplified share structure,[47] which would substantially reduce transaction costs. According to this report, the information required in books of account under the Companies Ordinance was outdated and no longer consistent with accounting practice.[48] It recommended the adoption of generally accepted accounting

---

[40] *First Report of the Companies Law Revision Committee—The Protection of Investors* (Hong Kong: Government Printer, 24 June 1971); *Second Report of the Companies Law Revision Committee —Company Law* (Hong Kong: Government Printer, 12 April 1973).

[41] See A Tam, 'Company Law in Hong Kong: Charting a New Course?', in R Wacks (ed), *The New Legal Order in Hong Kong* (Hong Kong: Hong Kong University Press, 1999), ch 11.

[42] (Hong Kong: Government Printer, March 1997).   [43] ibid, pp 99–105.

[44] ibid, pp 121–3.   [45] ibid, p 129.   [46] ibid, p 82.   [47] ibid, pp 88–98.

[48] ibid, pp 100–1.

principles (GAAP), which are to be set by an independent accounting standards body.[49] These recommendations, however, have yet to be substantially adopted.

(3) *Property rights*

Hong Kong's economy has historically been built on the foundations of trade **2.33** and property. In respect of property, Hong Kong is generally acknowledged to have a sophisticated system and practical application of property rights and their use, built on a nineteenth-century English framework. Interestingly, as in Mainland China, all land (with very limited exceptions) is owned by the government and released to the market through a system of leases. Historically, the greater proportion of government revenue in Hong Kong has derived from property sales and property-related levies and charges.

In preserving the capitalist system, the Basic Law stipulates that the right of **2.34** private ownership shall be protected.[50] Article 105 of the Basic Law provides that:

> The Hong Kong Special Administrative Region shall, in accordance with law, protect the right of individuals and legal persons to the acquisition, use, disposal and inheritance of property and their right to compensation for lawful deprivation of their property.
>
> Such compensation shall correspond to the real value of the property concerned at the time and shall be freely convertible and paid without undue delay.
>
> The ownership of enterprises and the investments from outside the Region shall be protected by law.

'Property' includes land and buildings, goods, choses in action, such as bank **2.35** deposits and savings certificates, and securities such as bonds, debentures, and shares.[51]

(4) *Insolvency*

Insolvency matters are addressed primarily by the Bankruptcy Ordinance and, **2.36** in respect to companies, the Companies Ordinance (discussed above).

The Bankruptcy Ordinance comprises 143 sections and two schedules. It is **2.37** divided into ten parts, addressing the following matters: (1) interpretation (sections 1 and 2); (2) proceedings from bankruptcy petition to discharge (sections 3 to 33); (3) administration of property (sections 34 to 74); (4) criminal bankruptcy (sections 74A to 74C); (5) Official Receiver (sections 75 to 78); (6) trustees in bankruptcy (sections 79 to 96); (7) constitution, procedure, and

---

[49] ibid, p 100.   [50] Basic Law, art 6.
[51] For further discussion of the interpretation of Basic Law, art 105, see A Chen, 'The Basic Law and the Protection of Property Rights', 23:1 (1993) *Hong Kong Law Journal* 55–62.

powers of court (sections 97 to 109); (8) supplemental provisions (sections 110 to 128A); (9) bankruptcy offences (sections 129 to 142); and (10) miscellaneous (section 143).

2.38   The Bankruptcy Ordinance is supported by five pieces of subsidiary legislation:

- Bankruptcy Rules (Cap. 6A)
- Bankruptcy (Forms) Rules (Cap. 6B)
- Bankruptcy (Fees and Percentages) Order (Cap. 6C)
- Meeting of Creditors Rules (Cap. 6D)
- Proof of Debts Rules (Cap. 6E)

2.39   The rules which apply to corporate insolvency are found in Parts V and X of the Companies Ordinance, and are in many respects based on the UK Companies Act of 1929.[52] The detailed rules regarding the procedures to be followed in a liquidation are in the Companies (Winding-Up) Rules. However, the Bankruptcy Ordinance, which pertains to individuals is also relevant. The Bankruptcy Ordinance was substantially reformed by the Bankruptcy (Amendment) Ordinance 1996. Its relevance to corporate insolvencies arises primarily because in some areas the bankruptcy provisions are applicable in corporate insolvencies (eg, section 34 regarding proof of debts, section 35 regarding insolvency set-off, and section 50 regarding the setting aside of unfair preferences). These statutory provisions are interpreted in a substantial body of case-law, in accordance with the common law system which continues to prevail in Hong Kong.

2.40   The primary ground for winding-up is that the company concerned is unable to pay its debts as they fall due, though there is also the provision for an order to be made on other grounds, including that the order is 'just and equitable'. If the court makes an order, the Official Receiver (who is the government officer charged with duties in respect of insolvency generally) becomes the provisional liquidator of the company, unless a provisional liquidator has already been appointed. The appointment of insolvency practitioners (partners in firms of accountants with special expertise in the field) as liquidators would normally follow. Whoever is appointed liquidator owes his or her duties to the Court that made the appointment, and which retains an overseeing role. Overall, the law favours secured creditors, who may generally realize their collateral without regard to the insolvency process.

2.41   The purpose of a liquidation is to realize the company's assets, and distribute them to creditors in the order of preference specified in the statute. It is not to preserve the company as a going concern, though a sale of the business is not

---

[52]   C Booth, 'Hong Kong Insolvency Law Reform: Preparing for the Next Millennium' [2001] *JBL* 126.

necessarily ruled out. However, it is generally accepted in Hong Kong that a failure of its corporate insolvency legislation is the lack of an effective procedure for rescuing companies in financial difficulties, and the considerable efforts to address it have not yet succeeded. The issue is dealt with separately below.

The reform of personal bankruptcy law already referred to followed a report **2.42** of the Law Reform Commission of May 1995. There have been reports on corporate rescue and insolvent trading (October 1996) and on the winding-up provisions of the Companies Ordinance (July 1999) but these have not yet been implemented. In addition to these aspects of the process, the Standing Committee on Company Law Reform (SCCLR) is responsible for the on-going review of the Companies Ordinance, and insofar as company law relates to the law of insolvency, it falls within the responsibility of the Official Receiver, who has the expertise in this regard.

Laws generally provide a structure for corporate rescue as an alternative to **2.43** liquidation, and this may include provision for temporary administration. Alternatively, as is well known, under Chapter 11 of the US Bankruptcy Code a company may continue to operate under existing management, subject to a moratorium with regard to its debts. A different model is the appointment by the court of administrators with power to continue the business shielded from creditor action (as in the case of the administration procedures in the UK Insolvency Act 1986).

The current Hong Kong Companies Ordinance does not include an effective **2.44** mechanism for corporate rescue. Schemes of arrangement are possible under section 166 of the Ordinance, but these are rarely used. Recently, corporate rescue by way of private workout has been more likely under the HKMA/HKAB *Guidelines on the Hong Kong Approach to Corporate Difficulties*, and some practical attempts have even been made through provisional liquidation. However, this cannot substitute for an effective formal corporate rescue procedure. Proposals have been made in the form of the 'Provisional Supervision' procedure, most recently in the Companies (Corporate Rescue) Bill 2001, although passage of this bill appears unlikely at this stage. (If enacted, this legislation would not apply to the rescue of certain regulated industries including banking.)

(5) Financial information

In regard to accounting and auditing rules, Hong Kong has a well-developed **2.45** system. Incorporated by the Professional Accountants Ordinance (Cap. 50) on 1 January 1973, the Hong Kong Society of Accountants (recently renamed by statute as the Hong Kong Institute of Certified Public Accountants) is the only statutory licensing body of accountants in Hong Kong responsible for regulation of the accountancy profession. Relevant procedures are detailed in the

Professional Accountants By-Laws (Cap. 50A). Rules are supplemented by the Listing Rules (discussed below and in Chapters 4 and 6) and regulatory rules of the various agencies.

2.46 At present, there is a proposed Financial Reporting Council Bill (largely following processes in the US and Europe resulting from corporate insolvencies such as that of Enron). The present version of the Bill provides for the following:

- The establishment of a Financial Reporting Council to investigate irregularities of listed company audits and financial reports and to enquire into noncompliance with legal, accounting, and regulatory requirements in financial reports;

- The establishment of an Audit Investigation Board to conduct investigations; and

- The appointment of a Financial Reporting Review Committee by the Financial Reporting Council to conduct enquiries.

2.47 If enacted, the Financial Reporting Council Bill would mark a major shift from a largely self-regulatory model of financial information to a self-regulatory model operating within an administrative framework, similar in many ways to reforms in other areas of financial markets regulation (eg banking, securities, and futures).

(6) Market integrity

2.48 The primary agencies responsible for market integrity in Hong Kong are the police, Department of Justice, and the Independent Commission Against Corruption (ICAC). In addition, the various individual regulatory agencies (eg HKMA, SFC, OCI, MPFA) all are active in addressing these issues in the context of their respective areas of responsibility (respectively banks and banking, securities, insurance, pensions). In addition, Hong Kong is a member of the Financial Action Task Force on Money Laundering (FATF), the leading international organization setting standards with respect to money laundering and terrorist financing.

(7) Taxation

2.49 Today, Hong Kong continues to have a simple, low-rate taxation system, supplemented by property related income. Under the Basic Law, Hong Kong shall take the low tax policy as a reference.[53] The Basic Law also expressly states that Hong Kong shall have its own independent finances and its revenues shall be used exclusively for its own purposes.[54] Under the Inland Revenue Ordinance

---

[53] Basic Law, art 108.   [54] Basic Law, art 106.

(Cap. 112), profits exclude profits arising from the sale of capital assets. One resulting question is whether or not the receipt is considered as capital or revenue: this is a matter for the courts to decide. The absence of a capital gains tax is conducive to the financial markets. However, it also attracts criticism that the tax base is too narrow and inequitable.

B. Financial Law and Regulation

Hong Kong's financial regulatory framework, in general, is sectoral, operating **2.50** through a 'three-tier system'. Under the first tier, the Financial Secretary is responsible for overall policy and the Financial Services and the Treasury Bureau (FSTB) is responsible for translating policies into regulation. Under the second tier, specialist regulatory agencies are in turn responsible for the regulation and supervision of financial services activities. Under the third tier, self-regulatory organizations are responsible for oversight of the activities of their members, albeit under the supervision of the relevant specialist regulatory agency and (increasingly) pursuant to legislation.

Hong Kong's sectoral regulatory structure for its financial system, which has **2.51** developed largely in response to individual crises and specific objectives (as discussed in Chapter 1) is based on separate supervisory bodies for each of the three major financial sectors, instead of there being one super regulatory body for the entire industry, as is the case in the UK with the Financial Services Authority. Today, financial services are principally regulated by the HKMA (banks and banking), the Securities and Futures Commission (SFC) (securities and futures institutions and markets), the Office of the Commissioner of Insurance (OCI) (insurance business), and the Mandatory Provident Fund Schemes Authority (MPFA) (MPF and pensions schemes). Each regulatory agency operates within the framework of one or more major ordinances and each regulatory agency is autonomous (though necessarily not independent from the government) and issues its own rules and regulations, pursuant to an increasing array of rule-making powers.

This sectoral structure has one major caveat: the HKMA regulates all activities **2.52** of banks, including activities involving securities, insurance, etc, though usually to standards identical to those of other sectoral regulators. At the same time, the SFC and HKMA have adopted a lead regulator approach to the supervision of financial groups which include both banking and securities activities, with the arrangements set out in a memorandum of understanding between the two.

In addition, a Cross-Market Surveillance Committee, comprised of representa- **2.53** tives of the FSTB, HKMA, SFC, and HKEx (and now including the OCI and

MPFA as well) was established in October 1998 to exchange market information and to formulate prompt and appropriate actions where necessary, as well as facilitate supervision of financial groups.

(1) Central banking, banking, and the HKMA and HKAB

2.54 The legal and institutional framework for banking is largely based on the Banking Ordinance, the Exchange Fund Ordinance, various ordinances derived from British sources (eg Companies Ordinance, Bills of Exchange Ordinance), and the common law. The Hong Kong Monetary Authority (HKMA) was established in 1993 and plays the roles of central bank, manager of the Exchange Fund, and regulator of the banking industry in Hong Kong. The HKMA was established through amendments to the Exchange Fund Ordinance (Cap. 66) in 1992 and commenced operations on 1 April 1993.

2.55 Overall control of the Hong Kong financial system is left to the Financial Secretary (who is a member of the cabinet of the Chief Executive) to whom the HKMA is responsible. It is an integral part of the government and supports the Financial Secretary in performing his functions under relevant ordinances. However, the HKMA enjoys a high degree of autonomy in day-to-day business, and has retained its independence, despite not being formally independent.[55] Even though the HKMA is accountable to the Financial Secretary, it is independent of the civil service.[56]

Hong Kong Monetary Authority (HKMA)

2.56 The main functions of the HKMA can be summarized as:

- Initiating and administering the official monetary policy and ensuring the stability of the Hong Kong dollar;
- Managing the Exchange Fund;
- Promoting the safety and soundness of Hong Kong's banking system; and
- Developing Hong Kong's financial infrastructure.

2.57 These functions are discharged by the ten departments of the HKMA, viz Banking Development, Banking Policy, Banking Supervision, General Counsel, Corporate Services, External, Research, Monetary Management and Infrastructure, Reserves Management, and Strategy and Risk. In addition, there is an Internal Audit division.

---

[55] See Letter from Financial Secretary to the Monetary Authority, 25 June 2005.
[56] TK Ghose, *The Banking System of Hong Kong* (Hong Kong: Butterworths, 1995, 2nd edn), 57.

Central banking and the Exchange Fund

The HKMA manages the Exchange Fund under powers delegated by the **2.58**
Financial Secretary in accordance with the Exchange Fund Ordinance (Cap.
66). In this respect, the HKMA's main obligations are to keep the HK dollar
stable and to manage the Exchange Fund in a sound and effective manner.

Exchange Fund

The Exchange Fund as a general matter forms the basis of Hong Kong's linked **2.59**
exchange rate mechanism. The Exchange Fund was created by the Currency
Ordinance 1935, later renamed the Exchange Fund Ordinance (Cap. 66) (EFO).
As its primary purpose, the Exchange Fund is to be used, inter alia, '. . . for
such purposes as the Financial Secretary thinks fit affecting, either directly or
indirectly, the exchange value of the currency of Hong Kong and for other
purposes incidental thereto'.[57] An additional purpose was added in 1992: the
Financial Secretary is entitled to use the Fund as he thinks fit to 'maintain the
stability and integrity of the monetary and financial systems of Hong Kong' and
to 'maintain Hong Kong as an international financial centre'.[58] Subject to
certain limitations, the Financial Secretary is also able to transfer money from
the Exchange Fund into the general revenue.[59] Finally, the Exchange Fund
is responsible for all related and other ancillary costs and expenditures of
the HKMA.[60]

Under section 5A of the EFO, the Financial Secretary was obliged to appoint a **2.60**
Monetary Authority to assist him in the performance of his functions under the
Exchange Fund (Amendment) Ordinance (Cap. 66). This role is now taken by
the Chief Executive of the HKMA (the 'Monetary Authority'). The powers of
the Financial Secretary under the EFO may be delegated to the HKMA on
whatever terms the Financial Secretary sees fit.[61]

In Hong Kong, note issuance is distributed between the HKMA and the note- **2.61**
issuing banks (HSBC, Standard Chartered Bank and Bank of China).[62] Details
are governed by the Legal Tender Notes Issue Ordinance (Cap. 65).

Exchange Fund Advisory Committee

The HKMA is accountable to the Financial Secretary. The Financial Secretary **2.62**
is in turn advised by the Exchange Fund Advisory Committee (EFAC), of which
the Financial Secretary is chair. The EFAC meets monthly to discuss the operations of the HKMA and to offer guidance and therefore functions much like a

---

[57] EFO s 3(1).   [58] EFO s 3(1A).   [59] EFO s 8.   [60] EFO s 6; see also s 5B.
[61] EFO s 5B.
[62] Due to the peg, the HKMA actually outsources note issuance for profit, but the three banks
maintain matching deposits at HKMA.

board of directors. The EFAC is said to 'guide' the HKMA, particularly in its management of the Exchange Fund. Members are appointed to the EFAC by the HKSAR Chief Executive and comprises nine members in addition to the Financial Secretary, including the Chief Executive of the HKMA and senior executives of Hong Kong's leading banking institutions, including each of the three note-issuing banks (HSBC, Standard Chartered Bank, and Bank of China).

Banking regulation and supervision

2.63 The Exchange Fund (Amendment) Ordinance 1992 amended the Banking Ordinance to vest the powers and duties of the Commissioner of Banking (the previous banking regulatory authority) in the HKMA with effect from 1 April 1993.[63]

2.64 Under section 7(1) of the Banking Ordinance 'the principal function of the HKMA shall be to promote the general stability and effective working of the banking system'. Under the Banking Ordinance, the HKMA (or more specifically, the 'Monetary Authority') has the following responsibilities:[64]

- Supervising compliance with the provisions of the Banking Ordinance;
- Taking all reasonable steps to ensure that the principal places of business, local branches, overseas branches, and overseas representative offices of all authorized institutions and local representative offices are operated in a responsible, honest, and business-like manner;
- Promoting and encouraging proper standards of conduct and sound and prudent business practices amongst authorized institutions;
- Suppressing or aiding in suppressing illegal, dishonourable, or improper practices in relation to the business practices of authorized institutions and money brokers;
- Cooperating with and assisting recognized financial services supervisory authorities of Hong Kong or of any place outside Hong Kong, whenever appropriate, to the extent permitted by the Banking Ordinance or any other Ordinance; and
- Considering and proposing reforms of the law relating to banking business and the business of taking deposits.

2.65 Importantly, the HKMA is responsible for banking business, defined to include only deposit-taking and cheque-related services. As a result, other forms of lending and credit creation are not addressed by the primary Banking Ordinance

---

[63] BO s 7(1).   [64] BO s 7(2).

but rather by the common law and a range of specific ordinances. At the same time, however, the HKMA regulates all activities of banks under the framework of consolidated supervision. These matters are dealt with in detail in Chapter 3.

In respect to banking business, the Banking Ordinance establishes the basic framework for three banking supervisory bodies: the HKMA,[65] the Banking Advisory Committee,[66] and the Deposit-taking Advisory Committee.[67] Together with the Exchange Fund Advisory Committee and the HKAB, these organizations carry out the most important functions of banking supervision in Hong Kong. In addition to these organizations, other bodies such as HKEx (under the Listing Rules), the SFC, and the Registrar of Companies (under the Companies Ordinance) are also involved in the supervision and regulation of the activities of banking institutions in their own areas of expertise. **2.66**

Hong Kong Association of Banks (HKAB)

The HKAB is an organization whose origin arose out of the Exchange Banks Association (EBA), which was founded in 1897 as the body representing banks in Hong Kong. The government introduced the Hong Kong Association of Banks Ordinance (Cap. 364) (HKABO) under which the HKAB took over the assets and liabilities of the EBA and also assumed its roles and functions. In addition, the HKABO established the HKAB as a body corporate.[68] **2.67**

The objects of the HKAB include:[69] **2.68**

- To further the interests of licensed banks;
- To make rules from time to time for the conduct of the business of banking;
- To consider, investigate, and enquire into all matters and questions connected with or relating to the business of banking;
- To promote, consider, support, oppose, make representations as to, and generally deal with any law affecting or likely to affect the business of banking;
- To collect, circulate, and disseminate information relating to the business of banking or otherwise likely to be of interest to members and others;
- To represent its members at and appear before any public body, committee, or inquiry or before any court or tribunal; and
- To act as an advisory body to its members and to cooperate and maintain relations with other bodies and organizations in all matters touching or concerning the business of banking.

The HKAB has the power to make by-laws, with a two-thirds majority vote and subject to approval by the Chief Executive.[70] Under the HKABO, the

---

[65] BO s 6.   [66] BO s 4.   [67] BO s 5.   [68] HKABO s 3.   [69] HKABO s 4.
[70] HKABO s 6.

Committee of the HKAB is to establish, direct, and determine the business and policies of the HKAB.[71] It comprises 12 members, with the representatives of HSBC, Standard Chartered Bank, and Bank of China being continuing members;[72] remaining members are elected every three years, with five from foreign banks and four from local banks.[73]

2.69 The Consultative Council advises the Committee on matters relating to the business of banking.[74] Its function is to advise the Committee on matters referred to it by the Committee.[75] The Committee of the HKAB has the power to make rules as to the conduct of the business of banking in Hong Kong, although in some cases this can only be done following consultation with the government.[76] Areas include:[77]

- As to the maximum rates of interest, return, discount, or other benefit which may be paid or granted by members, or by any specified category of members in respect of HK dollar deposits of their customers and specified instruments;
- As to the keeping and maintenance of clearing accounts;
- As to the imposition of deposit charges, and the minimum deposit charges to be so imposed;
- As to the payment of deposit charges by customers to members;
- As to the imposition of interest charges, and the rates of interest charges to be so imposed;
- As to the payment of interest charges by members to settlement banks, by settlement banks to the management banks, and by the management banks to the Financial Secretary for the account of the Exchange Fund;
- As to the conduct of foreign exchange business and the minimum commissions and charges to be applied therefor;
- As to the conduct of securities and safe custody business and the minimum commissions and charges to be applied therefor;
- As to the minimum charges to be applied by members for the issuance of guarantees or other documents;
- As to any other charges relating to the provision of any banking service, not being charges by way of interest or return payable on loans or advances granted by members;
- Prohibiting members from transacting any specified type of business or using any particular type of instrument.

The rules are required to be served on members in a specified manner and are

[71] HKABO ss 11, 12.
[72] HKABO s 8.
[73] HKABO s 8; HKAB By-laws (Cap. 364), s 8. [74] HKABO s 14.
[75] HKABO s 15. [76] HKABO s 12. [77] HKABO s 12.

binding on members from the moment they are served and may be amended at any time.

Advisory Committees

In addition to the HKMA and the HKAB, a Banking Advisory Committee **2.70** and a Deposit-taking Companies (DTC) Advisory Committee are established under sections 4 and 5, respectively, of the Banking Ordinance. The Banking Advisory Committee and the DTC Advisory Committee are established for the purpose of advising the Chief Executive on matters relating to the Banking Ordinance, in particular those relating to the business activities of banks, restricted licence banks (RLBs) and deposit-taking companies (DTCs). Both Committees are chaired by the Financial Secretary, with other members appointed by the Financial Secretary under the delegated authority conferred by the Chief Executive.

Legal framework for banking business

The legal framework of banking in Hong Kong is complicated by the division of **2.71** authority between the HKMA and the HKAB (see above). This is further complicated by the division of the HKMA into two key functions: the Exchange Fund and the Monetary Authority (MA),[78] governed by both the EFO and the Banking Ordinance.

The HKMA has numerous powers in relation to the legal framework: **2.72**

- consider and propose reforms of law relating to banking;[79]
- promote proper standards of conduct and sound and prudent business practices amongst authorized institutions;[80]
- issue guidelines on business practices to be followed by Authorized Institutions (AIs), which must be published in the Gazette.[81] While the guidelines do not have the force of law, they are important as they comprise one of the elements on which the HKMA relies for its general supervision: a power which is specifically granted under the EFO.

In addition to the EFO, the Banking Ordinance and related subsidiary legisla- **2.73** tion and guidance, the HKMA is also responsible for the Deposit Protection Scheme Ordinance (DPSO) (discussed in Chapter 3) and the Clearing and Settlement Systems Ordinance (Cap. 564) (discussed further below).

---

[78] Legally, the MA is an individual appointed by the Financial Secretary under EFO s 5A. The powers under the BO are personally vested in the MA. In practice, the MA heads an office known as the HKMA of which he is Chief Executive.

[79] BO s 7(2)(f).   [80] BO s 7(2)(f).   [81] BO ss 7(2) & 82.

Banking Ordinance (Cap. 155)

2.74 Hong Kong did not adopt its first ordinance regulating banking operations (the Banking Ordinance), until 1948. Revisions in 1964 provided the first regulation of banking.[82] This remained largely unchanged (and rudimentary) until 1986. Following significant bank failures during the period of 1983 to 1986, the government enacted a new Banking Ordinance (Cap. 155) intended to provide comprehensive supervision of Hong Kong's banks and deposit-taking companies for the first time. While the 1986 Ordinance largely reflected the UK Banking Act 1979 and the Banking Act 1987[83] that was then being developed in the UK, its adoption signalled the beginning of Hong Kong's search for international best practices in the area of banking regulation and supervision.

2.75 The Banking Ordinance comprises 153 sections and thirteen schedules. The Ordinance is divided into twenty-one parts, addressing the following issues: (1) preliminary matters (Part I: sections 1 to 3); (2) appointments, functions of Monetary Authority, reports by Monetary Authority and Power of Chief Executive to give directions (Part II: sections 4 to 10); (3) banking business and business of taking deposits to be carried out by authorized institutions only (Part III: sections 11 to 14A); (4) authorization (Part IV: sections 15 to 21); (5) revocation of authorization (Part V: sections 22 and 23); (6) suspension of authorization (Part VI: sections 24 to 27); (7) transfer of authorization (Part VII: sections 28 to 43); (8) local branches, local offices, local representative offices and fees (Part VIII: sections 44 to 48); (9) overseas branches, overseas representative offices, fees and overseas banking corporations (Part IX: sections 49 to 51A); (10) powers of control over authorized institutions (Part X: sections 52 to 58A); (11) audits and meetings (Part XI: sections 59 to 62); (12) disclosure of information by authorized institutions (Part XII: sections 63 to 68); (13) ownership and management of authorized institutions (Part XIII: sections 69 to 74); (14) limitations on loans by and interests of authorized institutions (Part XV: sections 79 to 91); (15) advertisements, representations, and use of title 'bank' (Part XVI: sections 92 to 97A); (16) capital adequacy ration of authorized institutions (Part XVII: sections 98 to 101); (17) liquidity ration of authorized institutions and matters affecting liquidity ratio (Part XVIII: sections 102 to 106); (18) investigations of authorized institutions (Part XX: sections 117 and 118); (19) money brokers (Part XXA: sections 118A to 118F); (20) miscellaneous matters (Part XXI: sections 119 to 137B); and (21) transitional, savings and repeal (Part XXII: sections 138 to 153).

---

[82] See SFC, *A Decade of Progress* (Hong Kong: SFC, 1999).

[83] The Banking Act 1979 itself was largely a response to the need to implement 'best practices' in the area of banking regulation and supervision as adopted by the European Community.

The thirteen schedules address the following matters: (1) specified period and **2.76** specified sums (schedule 1); (2) fees (schedule 2); (3) capital adequacy ratio (schedule 3); (4) liquidity ratio (schedule 4); (5) requirements applicable to prescribed advertisements (schedule 5); (6) specified instruments (schedule 6); (7) minimum criteria for authorization (schedule 7); (8) grounds for revocation of authorization schedule 8); (9) powers of manager of authorized institution (schedule 9); (10) minimum criteria for approval as money broker (schedule 11); (11) grounds for revocation of approval as money broker (schedule 12); (12) level of fines for offences (schedule 13); and (13) affairs or business of authorized institutions specified for purposes of definition of 'manager' (schedule 14).

In addition, the Banking Ordinance is supported by a range of subsidiary **2.77** legislation addressing a variety of matters:

- Banking Ordinance (Deposit-taking Exemptions) (Consolidation) Notice (Cap. 155A);
- Banking Ordinance (Designation of Public Statutory Corporation) Notice (Cap. 155B);
- Specification of Factors (Financial Exposure of Authorized Institutions) Notice (Cap. 155C);
- Specification of Terms for Restricted Licence Banks Notice (Cap. 155D);
- Banking (Specification of Public Sector Entities in Hong Kong) Notice (Cap. 155E);
- Banking (Specification of Class of Exempted Charges) Notice (Cap. 155F);
- Banking Ordinance (Declaration under section 2(14)(d)) (No. 2) Notice 1997 (Cap. 155G);
- Banking Ordinance (Declaration under section 2(14)(d)) (No. 3) Notice 1997 (Cap. 155H);
- Banking Ordinance (Declaration under section 2(14)(b)) Notice 1998 (Cap. 155I);
- Banking Ordinance (Declaration under section 2(14)(b)) Notice 2001 (Cap. 155J);
- Banking (Specification of Class of Exempted Charges) Notice (Cap. 155K).

Further, the HKMA has also released a *Guide to Authorization* and the *Super-* **2.78** *visory Policy Manual*. The former is discussed further in Chapter 3. The latter consolidates a wide range of guidance of various forms under the following headings: (1) introduction; (2) supervisory approach; (3) corporate governance; (4) internal controls; (5) capital adequacy (subdivided into: general, and specific capital adequacy treatment); (6) consolidated supervision; (7) credit manage-ment (subdivided into: risk management guidelines, guidelines on specific lending activities, and limitations on credit exposures); (8) interest rate risk management; (9) liquidity management; (10) operational risk management;

(11) trading activities; (12) technology risk management (subdivided into: general technology risk management, and electronic banking); (13) securities and leveraged foreign exchange business; (14) Mandatory Provident Fund; (15) money laundering; (16) financial disclosure; and (17) miscellaneous matters.

Banking (Amendment) Ordinance 2005

2.79 The Banking (Amendment) Ordinance 2005 (BAO 2005) was enacted on 6 July 2005. Its main purpose is to amend the Banking Ordinance to put in place a framework for the implementation of the Basel II capital adequacy framework in Hong Kong. The BAO 2005 comprises 15 sections and one schedule. The BAO is divided into three Parts, addressing: (1) preliminary matters (Part 1: section 1); (2) amendments to public disclosure of information and to capital adequacy ratio (Part 2: sections 2 to 7); and (3) other amendments (Part 3: sections 8 to 15). The BAO has not yet been made effective, though this will probably take place in 2007. Most importantly, it removes the specification of matters of disclosure of information and capital adequacy from the Banking Ordinance and schedules and instead makes these subject to a new rule-making power given to the HKMA. In addition, it has added a new review mechanism, the Capital Adequacy Review Tribunal (CART).

Financial infrastructure development

2.80 In addition to matters relating to the Exchange Fund and banking, the HKMA is also responsible for financial infrastructure development. To date, the HKMA has focused on two areas: (1) debt market development (discussed in Chapter 3); and (2) infrastructure and oversight (primarily payment, clearing and settlement—discussed below). In respect to the latter, the HKMA has established and supervises the following systems:

- Hong Kong Interbank Clearing Limited (1995) (HKICL)—established and jointly owned by the HKMA and the HKAB and supporting the cheque clearing, CMU, RTGS, and foreign currency systems;

- Central Moneymarkets Unit (1990) (CMU)—providing computerized clearing and settlement of Exchange Fund Bills and Notes, linkages to Euroclear and Clearstream (a subsidiary of Deutsche Borse), non-HK dollar debt securities, linkage to the RTGS (discussed below), and securities lending (repo) services;

- Real Time Gross Settlement System (1996) (RTGS)—providing a computerized interbank payment system for HK dollar payments and now extended to debt securities (via the CMU), shares (via HKEx), foreign exchange transactions, including those of Mainland China, and Hong Kong dollar cheques issued by banks in Hong Kong and presented in Shenzhen (via the Joint

Clearing Facility with the Shenzhen Branch of the People's Bank of China (PBOC)); and

- US Dollar Clearing System, Euro Clearing System, and Renminbi Clearing System—providing settlement of US dollar, euro, and renminbi transactions in Hong Kong via HSBC, Standard Chartered Bank, and Bank of China, respectively.

In support of this oversight role, Hong Kong enacted the Clearing and Settle-   **2.81** ment Systems Ordinance (Cap. 584) in 2004 to provide legislative backing. The CSSO comprises 59 sections and two schedules. The CSSO is divided into six parts, addressing the following matters: (1) preliminary matters (Part 1: sections 1 to 3); (2) designation and oversight (Part 2: sections 4 to 14);[84] (3) finality of transactions and proceedings (Part 3: sections 15 to 33);[85] (4) Appeals Tribunal (Part 4: sections 34 to 40); (5) offences (Part 5: sections 41 to 48); and (6) miscellaneous matters (Part 6: sections 49 to 59).

The two schedules address respectively: (1) provisions relating to Clearing   **2.82** and Settlement Systems Appeals Tribunal (schedule 1); and (2) clearing and settlement systems deemed to have been designated (schedule 2).[86]

In addition, a Steering Committee on the Enhancement of Financial Infra-   **2.83** structure (SCEFI) was established to examine a number of major issues in this area, including: the setting up of a single clearing arrangement for securities, stock options, and futures transactions; the enhancement of the straight-through processing across the financial markets; and the introduction of a secure, scripless securities market.

Overall, the legal and regulatory framework for banking in Hong Kong is   **2.84** comprehensive and of an international standard, though with certain caveats discussed in the final section of this chapter as well as in subsequent chapters, especially Chapter 10.

(2) Securities, the SFC, and HKEx

Prior to 1987, capital market regulation in Hong Kong was minimal, with all   **2.85** the various exchanges operating largely on the basis of self-regulation in the

---

[84] Part 2 is subdivided into the following divisions: (1) designation (ss 4–5); (2) obligations of designated systems (ss 6–8); and (3) matters pertaining to functions and powers of Monetary Authority (ss 9–14).

[85] Part 3 is subdivided into the following divisions: (1) interpretation (s 15); (2) certificate of finality (ss 16–17); (3) finality of transactions and proceedings within designated systems (ss 18–24); (4) netting of obligations of insolvent participants (s 25); and (5) miscellaneous (ss 26–33).

[86] The 'designated systems' are the CMU and the Hong Kong Dollar Clearing House Automated Transfer System.

context of the common law framework. While a Securities Commission, a Commodities Trading Commission, and a Stock Exchange Compensation Fund had been created and numerous ordinances enacted to address securities regulation during the 1970s,[87] the failure of the market in October 1987 exposed the inadequacies of the then existing system.[88] As a result of the crisis, the government commissioned the Securities Review Committee to develop a plan to upgrade Hong Kong's securities market infrastructure to international standards in November 1987. This report, known as the 'Davison Report', has served as a blueprint for the modernization of capital market regulation in Hong Kong throughout the late 1980s and the 1990s.[89]

2.86   In the area of capital market regulation, Hong Kong made a sustained effort to develop its securities legal and financial infrastructure following the world-wide market collapse of 1987.[90] Efforts in this direction prior to 1997 included the creation of the SFC and the demutualization and merger of the Stock Exchange of Hong Kong (SEHK), Hong Kong Futures Exchange (HKFE) and related clearing houses to form Hong Kong Exchanges and Clearing (HKEx). These efforts have enabled Hong Kong to become the second largest stock market in Asia after Tokyo.

2.87   Hong Kong's securities industry and regulatory framework developed rapidly since the implementation of market reforms following the October 1987 market crash.[91] Reforms undertaken in the wake of the crash included: (1) significant strengthening of the market structure within the context of the market-driven monetary and fiscal environment of the last decade, in particular changes to the constitution of the Exchanges to make them better front-line market regulators and more accountable to public interests; (2) improvement of the market technology infrastructure in respect of both trading and settlement systems, including the introduction of the electronic Central Clearing and Settlement Systems (CCASS and DCASS); and (3) the establishment of the SFC as the market-wide regulator and the introduction of international regulatory standards conducive to market transparency and fairness.

2.88   More recently, and also as a result of a Securities Review Committee recommendation, the SFC published in April 1996 a proposal to consolidate and rationalize

---

[87] eg Securities Ordinance (Cap. 333) (1974); Protection of Investors Ordinance (Cap. 335) (1974); Stock Exchange Unification Ordinance (Cap. 361) (1980).

[88] See Securities Review Committee, *The Operation and Regulation of the Hong Kong Securities Industry: Report of the Securities Review Committee* (Hong Kong: Government Printer, 1988) ('Davison Report').

[89] ibid; see Hsu, above, p 240.

[90] See K Wong, 'The Hong Kong Stock Market', in R Ho, R Scott, & K Wong, above, p 215.

[91] Government of the Hong Kong Special Administrative Region, A Policy Paper on Securities and Futures Market Reform (Hong Kong: HKSAR March 1999), p 6.

eight existing ordinances into a single ordinance, which was subsequently enacted in similar form as the Securities and Futures Ordinance.

Significantly, during the last decade the Hong Kong securities and futures mar-   **2.89**
ket has gone through a profound transformation from a largely domestic market to an international market with active trading in equity and derivative products.

Three-tier system of securities regulation

Hong Kong's securities regulatory system has three tiers: the government, the   **2.90**
SFC, and HKEx.

In relation to market surveillance, HKEx focuses on trading operations and risk   **2.91**
management, including: (1) enforcement of trading and clearing rules and detection of trading malpractices by users (liaising with the SFC as necessary in relation to those which may involve statutory offences); (2) maintenance of market transparency by monitoring price and turnover movements on a real time basis and requiring prompt disclosure of price sensitive information; (3) assisting in the risk management process by monitoring exceptional concentrations in positions and unusual price fluctuation, (4) interaction with market participants, including the handling of disputes in relation to trading matters; and (5) cross-market surveillance of HKEx's users.

The SFC, as the oversight regulator, is primarily responsible for detecting   **2.92**
market malpractices with statutory implications, and would include: (1) scrutinizing market activities to detect potential breaches of laws relating to the securities and futures market; (2) conducting investigations of possible statutory offences that fall within its jurisdiction, including those commenced on referral from HKEx, other agencies and complaints from the public; and (3) overseeing the surveillance actions undertaken by HKEx and performing cross-market surveillance of activities between HKEx markets and non-HKEx markets.

In relation to intermediaries supervision, HKEx monitors particular aspects of   **2.93**
the business of intermediaries in order to allow it to assess and manage relevant risks. The SFC is primarily responsible for routine inspections of HKEx members' businesses, for monitoring their compliance with conduct rules and liquid capital requirements and for ensuring that members have in place proper systems of management and control.

In relation to listing and corporate finance matters, HKEx remains the frontline   **2.94**
regulatory with increasing statutory support from the SFC.

Hong Kong SAR Government

The government is not involved in the day-to-day regulation of the securities   **2.95**
industry. However, the Financial Services and the Treasury Bureau facilitates

and coordinates initiatives to upgrade the overall quality in Hong Kong's financial sector. Its goal is to guarantee that Hong Kong's regulatory regime is up to date and meets the needs of investors. There is a constant dialogue between the government and the SFC about the state of regulation and the industry itself.

Securities and Futures Commission

2.96 The Securities and Futures Commission (SFC) was established on 1 May 1989 under the Securities and Futures Commission Ordinance[92] (now consolidated into the Securities and Futures Ordinance), pursuant to a recommendation by the Securities Review Committee. It is a statutory body responsible for regulating the securities and futures markets in the interests of investors through administration of the laws relating to the trading of securities, futures, and foreign exchange contracts within Hong Kong. The SFC has the duty of ensuring the enforcement of relevant provisions of the related ordinances, eg the Companies Ordinance and the Securities and Futures Ordinance (SFO).

2.97 The SFC has been active internationally. As a result, the SFC and Hong Kong have actively sought not only to implement international standards of best practice in its capital markets, but to lead the development of those standards for the rest of the world. The SFC has been active in signing memoranda of understanding and similar cooperative agreements with securities and futures regulators around the world and is actively involved in the International Organisation of Securities Commissions (IOSCO). Importantly, the SFC continues to be a full independent member of IOSCO.

2.98 The SFC is an independent non-governmental statutory body outside the civil service. Its regulatory powers cover four major fields: the Exchanges and their Affiliated Entities, Financial Intermediaries, Offers of Investment Products, and Takeovers and Mergers.[93]

2.99 According to section 5(1) of the SFO, the SFC is the regulator of the securities and futures industry. Under section 5(1) of the SFO the primary duties of the SFC are to maintain and promote the efficiency and orderliness of the securities and futures markets, to supervise all activities of market participants, to protect the investing public, and to detect and discipline illegal and improper activities within the markets.

2.100 The SFC has four operational divisions:

- the Corporate Finance division is responsible for the listing-related functions and listed companies;

---

[92] Cap. 24 (now repealed). [93] SFC, *Securities Regulation in Hong Kong*, p 395.

- the Intermediaries and Investment Products Division is in charge of licensing requirements for investment products as well as licensing and supervision of intermediaries;
- the Enforcement Division conducts market surveillance to detect market misconduct and initiates disciplinary procedures; and
- the Supervision of Markets Division oversees the activities of the exchanges and clearing houses.

Each division is supported by the Legal Services Division and the Corporate Affairs Division. The Commission itself has six Executive and seven Non-Executive Directors.

Hong Kong Exchanges and Clearing Limited (HKEx)

Hong Kong Exchanges and Clearing Ltd (HKEx) is the holding company for **2.101** the Stock Exchange of Hong Kong Ltd (SEHK) and the Hong Kong Futures Exchange Ltd (HKFE) as well as the Hong Kong Securities Clearing Company Ltd (HKSCC). HKEx is listed on the SEHK. The HKSCC clears and settles the securities transactions on the SEHK through its securities and derivatives clearing and settlement systems (CCASS and DCASS). In addition, both exchange companies each operate a further clearing house, the Stock Exchange of Hong Kong Options Clearing House Ltd, a wholly subsidiary of the SEHK that performs the function of clearing and settling standard contracts concluded on the options market operated by the SEHK. The HKFE wholly owns and operates the Hong Kong Futures Exchange Clearing Corporation Ltd which acts as clearing house for the futures transactions carried out on the futures exchange. In terms of organization, each of HKEx's subsidiaries is a separate legal entity wholly owned by HKEx, with decision-taking functions centralized with the HKEx board.

HKEx's aspirations are shaped around the fact that it is at the core of one of **2.102** Asia's few truly international financial centres. Further, it is ideally positioned to support the Mainland's immense capital and financial technology needs and possesses all the natural ingredients to become the leading 'full service' Asian market as well as the Asian pillar of the global securities and futures trading markets.[94] Under the government's strategy, HKEx is to strive for certain medium-term aspirations, namely (1) to be the Asian-time-zone pillar of the global futures and derivatives markets and one of the top five equities markets in the world, with a focus on Mainland opportunities and customers; and (2) the Asian centre of excellence for exchange-related technology, regulation

---

[94] HKSAR Government, Hong Kong Exchanges and Clearing Limited: Reinforcing Hong Kong's Position as a Global Financial Centre (Hong Kong: HKSAR, July 1999).

and services, with a focus on becoming the preferred Asian partner for other major equities and derivatives exchanges seeking to build global alliances.[95]

2.103 In respect of regulation, HKEx retains self-regulatory responsibilities as a cornerstone of its business. Priority is placed on reinforcing HKEx's 'badge of quality'.[96] All regulatory functions are housed in a single unit, separate from the exchanges and clearing houses, to provide organizational independence, with this central regulatory unit responsible for HKEx listing and listed company related rules (subject to SFC approval and review). HKEx's regulatory functions report directly to its CEO and are structured into four divisions: listings (including issuer compliance), admissions (including user compliance), surveillance, and enforcement.

2.104 The Listing Division is an organizational unit of the HKEx qua corporate group. The Listing Committee is a sub-committee of the Board of the SEHK, itself a subsidiary of HKEx. The Committee's composition is specified in the Listing Rules[97] as being 25 persons comprised of exchange participants, representatives from listed companies and market practitioners and users, and the CEO of Hong Kong Exchanges and Clearing Limited (or the Chief Executive of HKEx as his alternate).

2.105 The powers as exercised by the Listing Division are subject to review by the Listing Committee, and the powers of both the Listing Division and Listing Committee are subject to an appeal and review process by the Listing Appeals Committee. This is discussed further in Chapter 4.

2.106 The trading and clearing functions of the securities and futures markets are centralized in HKEx: it has monopolies in the operation of the exchange-based primary market, the futures exchange and all clearing operations in Hong Kong. As a result of its public functions combined with its commercial objectives, a comprehensive framework of checks and balances is necessary and is built on the basis of the SFO. In addition, there is a shareholding limit of 5 per cent to prevent control of HKEx by any individual or parties acting in concert. HKEx is regulated by the SFC to avoid conflicts of interest and to ensure a level playing field between HKEx and other listed companies subject to HKEx's listing rules and supervision.

Securities and Futures Ordinance

2.107 Under Article 109 of the Basic Law, the government is to provide an appropriate economic and legal environment for the maintenance of the status of Hong

---

[95] ibid, pp 5–6.
[96] ibid, p 13. [97] LR 2A.17.

Kong as an international financial centre. Donald Tsang, then Financial Secretary (now Hong Kong's Chief Executive), announced in his Budget Speech on
March 1999 a comprehensive market reform for the securities and futures market to enhance competitiveness in order to meet the challenge of an increasingly
globalized market place driven by the advancement of technology and the emergence of a growing population of sophisticated investors. In that respect, the
government has concluded that 'the international character of Hong Kong
necessitates a modern, flexible securities and futures regulatory framework that
will enable Hong Kong to compete effectively'.[98] The guiding principle of the
new legislation is therefore 'to provide optimal market regulation and afford
sufficient protection for investors, while at the same time encourage, not stifle,
healthy competition and market innovations'.[99]

As a result of this process (initiated by the Davison Report), the primary legisla- **2.108**
tion is now the Securities and Futures Ordinance (Cap. 571) (SFO).

The SFO serves as the legal framework for the regulation of the securities **2.109**
industry. The SFO is the largest and most detailed Ordinance in the history of
Hong Kong. In total, it is comprised of 409 sections and 10 schedules. The SFO
is divided into seventeen Parts: (1) preliminary matters (Part I); (2) Securities
and Futures Commission (Part II);[100] (3) exchange companies, clearing houses,
exchange controllers, investor compensation companies, and automated trading services (Part III);[101] (4) offers of investments (Part IV);[102] (5) licensing
and registration (Part V); (6) capital requirements, client assets, records and
audit relating to intermediaries (Part VI);[103] (7) business conduct, etc of
intermediaries (Part VII);[104] (8) supervision and investigations (Part VIII);[105]

---

[98] Financial Services Bureau, Legislative Reform for the Securities and Futures Market (HK:
FSB, June 1999), p 1. These proposals are further detailed in SFC, *Overview Guide to The
Proposed Securities and Futures Bill* (HK: SFC, July 1999) and a series of related Guides.
[99] ibid, p 1.
[100] Part II is subdivided into two divisions: (1) the Commission, and (2) accounting and
financial arrangements.
[101] Part III is subdivided into seven divisions: (1) interpretation; (2) exchange companies;
(3) clearing houses; (4) exchange controllers; (5) investor compensation companies; (6) general:
exchange companies, clearing houses, exchange controllers, and investor compensation schemes;
and (7) automated trading services.
[102] Part IV is subdivided into three divisions: (1) interpretation; (2) regulation of offers of
investments, etc; and (3) miscellaneous.
[103] Part VI is subdivided into six divisions: (1) interpretation, (2) capital requirements,
(3) client assets, (4) records, (5) audit, and (6) miscellaneous.
[104] Part VII is subdivided into five divisions: (1) interpretation; (2) business conduct;
(3) restriction on short selling, etc; (4) other requirements; and (5) miscellaneous.
[105] Part VIII is subdivided into four divisions: (1) interpretation; (2) powers to require information, etc; (3) powers of investigations; and (4) miscellaneous.

(9) discipline, etc (Part IX);[106] (10) powers of intervention and proceedings (Part X);[107] (11) Securities and Futures Appeals Tribunal (Part XI);[108] (12) investor compensation (Part XII); (13) Market Misconduct Tribunal (Part XIII);[109] (14) offences relating to dealings in securities and futures contracts, etc (Part XIV);[110] (15) disclosure of interests (Part XV);[111] (16) miscellaneous matters (Part XVI);[112] and (17) repeals and related provisions (Part XVII).

2.110 The ten schedules address: (1) interpretation and general provisions (schedule 1);[113] (2) Securities and Futures Commission (schedule 2);[114] (3) exchange companies, clearing houses, and exchange controllers (schedule 3);[115] (4) offers of investments (schedule 4);[116] (5) regulated activities (schedule 5); (6) specified titles (schedule 6); (7) offers by intermediaries or representatives for Type 1, Type 4, or Type 6 regulated activity under section 175 of the SFO

---

[106] Part IX is subdivided into three divisions: (1) interpretation; (2) discipline, etc; and (3) miscellaneous.

[107] Part X is subdivided into two divisions: (1) powers of intervention, and (2) other powers and proceedings.

[108] Part XI is subdivided into four divisions: (1) interpretation; (2) Securities and Futures Appeals Tribunal; (3) appeals; and (4) miscellaneous.

[109] Part XIII is subdivided into six divisions: (1) interpretation; (2) Market Misconduct Tribunal; (3) appeals, etc; (4) insider dealing; (5) other market misconduct; and (6) miscellaneous.

[110] Part XIV is subdivided into five divisions: (1) interpretation; (2) insider dealing offences; (3) other market misconduct offences; (4) other offences; and (5) miscellaneous.

[111] Part XV is subdivided into thirteen divisions: (1) preliminary; (2) disclosure of interests and short positions; (3) interests and short positions to be notified or disregarded; (4) requirements for giving notification; (5) listed corporation's powers to investigate ownership; (6) keeping of register; (7) disclosure of interests and short positions of directors and chief executives; (8) interests and short positions to be notified by director and chief executive or disregarded; (9) requirements for giving notification by director and chief executive; (10) keeping of register of directors' and chief executives' interests and short positions; (11) power to investigate listed corporation's ownership; (12) orders imposing restrictions on shares, etc; and (13) miscellaneous.

[112] Part XVI (miscellaneous) is subdivided into four divisions: (1) secrecy, conflict of interests, and immunity; (2) general provisions regarding proceedings and offences; (3) power to make rules, and codes or guidelines, etc; and (4) miscellaneous.

[113] Sch 1 is subdivided into five Parts: (1) interpretation, (2) specified futures exchanges; (3) specified stock exchanges; (4) multilateral agencies; (5) qualifying credit rating.

[114] Sch 2 is subdivided into two Parts: (1) constitution and proceedings of Commission, etc; and (2) non-delegable functions of Commission.

[115] Sch 3 is subdivided into eight Parts: (1) definitions; (2) specification of persons who are associated persons; (3) specification of persons who are not associated persons; (4) specification of persons who are not indirect controllers; (5) requirements for default rules of recognized clearing houses; (6) provisions applicable where there is failure to comply with notice under SFO s 59(9)(c), 61(9)(b), or 72(1) SFO; (7) specification of persons who are not minority controllers; and (8) exemption from SFO s 59(1).

[116] Sch 4 is subdivided into four Parts: (1) sum specified for purposes of SFO s 103(3)(f)(i) & (g); (2) instruments specified for purposes of SFO s 103(3)(g); (3) exempted bodies; and (4) sum specified for purposes of definition of 'relevant condition' in SFO s 103(12).

(schedule 7);[117] (8) Securities and Futures Appeals Tribunal (schedule 8);[118] (9) Market Misconduct Tribunal (schedule 9); and (10) savings, transitional, consequential, and related provisions, etc (schedule 10).[119]

Subsidiary legislation

As of August 2005, the following subsidiary legislation had been enacted pursu-　**2.111**
ant to the SFO:

- Securities and Futures (Unsolicited Calls—Exclusion) Rules (Cap. 571A)
- Securities and Futures (Recognized Counterparty) Rules (Cap. 571B)
- Securities and Futures (Registration of Commission Disciplinary Orders) Rules (Cap. 571C)
- Securities and Futures (Professional Investor) Rules (Cap. 571D)
- Securities and Futures (Leveraged Foreign Exchange Trading—Exemption) Rules (Cap. 571E)
- Securities and Futures (Leveraged Foreign Exchange Trading) (Arbitration) Rules (Cap. 571F)
- Securities and Futures (Exempted Instruments—Information) Rules (Cap. 571G)
- Securities and Futures (Client Securities) Rules (Cap. 571H)
- Securities and Futures (Client Money) Rules (Cap. 571I)
- Securities and Futures (Associated Entities—Notice) Rules (Cap. 571J)
- Securities and Futures (Registration of Appeals Tribunal Orders) Rules (Cap. 571K)
- Securities and Futures (Registration of Market Misconduct Tribunal Orders) Rules (Cap. 571L)
- Securities and Futures (Collective Investment Schemes) Notice (Cap. 571M)
- Securities and Futures (Financial Resources) Rules (Cap. 571N)
- Securities and Futures (Keeping of Records) Rules (Cap. 571O)
- Securities and Futures (Accounts and Audit) Rules (Cap. 571P)
- Securities and Futures (Contract Notes, Statements of Account and Receipts) Rules (Cap. 571Q)
- Securities and Futures (Short Selling and Securities Borrowing and Lending) (Miscellaneous) Rules (Cap. 571R)
- Securities and Futures (Licensing and Registration) (Information) Rules (Cap. 571S)

---

[117] Sch 7 is subdivided into two Parts: (1) requirements to be satisfied in relation to offers to acquire securities; and (2) requirements to be satisfied in relation to offers to dispose of securities.
[118] Sch 8 is subdivided into three Parts: (1) appointment of members and proceedings of Tribunal, etc; and (2) and (3) specified decisions.
[119] Sch 10 is subdivided into two Parts: (1) savings, transitional and supplemental arrangements; and (2) consequential and supplemental amendments.

- Securities and Futures (Investor Compensation—Claims) Rules (Cap. 571T)
- Securities and Futures (Miscellaneous) Rules (Cap. 571U)
- Securities and Futures (Stock Market Listing) Rules (Cap. 571V)
- Securities and Futures (Price Stabilizing) Rules (Cap. 571W)
- Securities and Futures (Disclosure of Interests—Securities Borrowing and Lending) Rules (Cap. 571X)
- Securities and Futures (Contracts Limits and Reportable Positions) Rules (Cap. 571Y)
- Securities and Futures (Levy) Order (Cap. 571Z)
- Securities and Futures (Levy) Rules (Cap. 571AA)
- Securities and Futures (Investor Compensation—Levy) Rules (Cap. 571AB)
- Securities and Futures (Investor Compensation—Compensation Limits) Rules (Cap. 571AC)
- Securities and Futures (Transfer of Functions—Investor Compensation Company) Order (Cap. 571AD)
- Securities and Futures (Transfer of Functions—Stock Exchange Company) Order (Cap. 571AE)
- Securities and Futures (Fees) Rules (Cap. 571AF)
- Securities and Futures (Disclosure of Interests—Exclusions) Regulation (Cap. 571AG)
- Securities and Futures (Offences and Penalties) Regulation (Cap. 571AH)
- Securities and Futures (Insurance) Rules (Cap. 571 AI)

Codes, guidelines, and circulars

2.112　The SFC has now consolidated all SFC codes, guidelines, guidance and related matters into a 'Regulatory Handbook', available in continually updated form at <http://www.sfc.hk>. The Regulatory Handbook is divided into two volumes, the first of which addresses the SFC and its role in and approach to regulation. The second contains all the various codes etc. Volume Two is divided into six sections:

- Part A—Licensing of Intermediaries and Continuing Obligations of Licensed Persons
- Part B—Specific Requirements for Regulated Activities
- Part C—Regulated Investment Products
- Part D—Corporate Finance
- Part E—Miscellaneous
- Part F—Securities and Futures Ordinance

2.113　As of August 2005, the SFC had issued the following Codes under the SFO:

- Code on Real Estate Investment Trusts (June 2005)
- Codes on Takeovers and Mergers and Share Repurchases (Apr. 2005)

- Code of Conduct for Persons Licensed by or Registered with the Securities and Futures Commission—Paragraph 16 (Mar. 2005)
- Code on Immigration-Linked Investment Schemes (Mar. 2003)
- Code on Investment-Linked Assurance Schemes (Mar. 2003)
- Code on Pooled Retirement Funds (Mar. 2003)
- Code on Unit Trusts and Mutual Funds (Mar. 2003)
- Fund Manager Code of Conduct (Mar. 2003)
- SFC Code on MPF Products (Mar. 2003)
- Code of Conduct for Corporate Finance Adviser (Mar. 2003)
- Code of Conduct for Share Registrars (Mar. 2003)
- Code of Conduct for Persons Licensed by or Registered with the Securities and Futures Commission (Mar. 2003)

As of August 2005, the SFC had issued the following guidelines: **2.114**

- Guidelines on Disclosure of Fees and Charges Relating to Securities Services (Jan. 2005)
- Guidance Note on Position Limits and Large Open Position Reporting Requirements (Apr. 2004)
- Guidelines for the Approval of Corporations as Approved Lending Agents (Mar. 2004)
- Non-Statutory Guidelines on Directors' Duties (Jan. 2004)
- Licensing Information Booklet (Aug. 2003)
- Outline of Part XV (Aug. 2003)
- Guidelines for Electronic Public Offerings (Apr. 2003)
- Investor Compensation Arrangement (Apr. 2003)
- Fit & Proper Guidelines (Mar. 2003)
- Guidance Note for Persons Advertising or Offering Collective Investment Schemes on the Internet (Mar. 2003)
- Guidance Note Issued by the SFC on Prevention of Money Laundering and Terrorist Financing (Mar. 2003)
- Guidelines on Competence (Mar. 2003)
- Guidelines on Continuous Professional Training (Mar. 2003)
- Guidelines for the Exemption of Listed Corporations from Part XV of the SFO (Disclosure of Interests) (Mar. 2003)
- Guidelines on Use of Offer Awareness and Summary Disclosure Materials in Offerings of Shares and Debentures under the Companies Ordinance (Mar. 2003)
- Guidelines on Transitional Arrangements (Mar. 2003)
- Guidelines on Waivers of Certain Licensing Fees (Mar. 2003)
- Guidance Note on Short Selling Reporting and Stock Lending Record Keeping Requirements (Mar. 2003)
- Guidelines on the Regulation of Automated Trading Services (Mar. 2003)

- Client Identity Rule Policy (Mar. 2003)
- Core Operational and Financial Risk Management Controls for Over-the-Counter Derivatives Activities of Persons Licensed by or Registered with the SFC (Mar. 2003)
- Debt Collection Guidelines for Licensed Corporations (Mar. 2003)
- Disciplinary Fining Guidelines (Mar. 2003)
- Management, Supervision and Internal Control Guidelines for Persons Licensed by or Registered with the SFC (Mar. 2003)
- Suggested Control Techniques and Procedures for Enhancing a Firm's Ability to Comply with the Securities and Futures (Client Securities) Rules and the Securities and Futures (Client Money) Rules (Mar. 2003)
- Guidelines on Applying for a Relaxation from the Procedural Formalities to be fulfilled upon Registration of a Prospectus under the Companies Ordinance (Cap. 32) (Feb. 2003)
- Guidelines on using a 'Dual Prospectus' Structure to Conduct Programme Offers of Shares or Debentures requiring a Prospectus under the Companies Ordinance (Cap. 32) (Feb. 2003)
- Guidance Note to SFC Approved Fund Management Companies—Suspension of Dealings (Nov. 2001)
- Guidelines on Exempt Fund Manager Status under the Code on Takeovers and Mergers (Apr. 2001)
- Guidelines on Exempt Principal Trader Status under the Codes on Takeovers and Mergers (Apr. 2001)
- Guidance Note on Internet Regulation (Mar. 1999)
- Project on the Use of Plain Language—How to Create a Clear Prospectus (Jan. 1998)
- How to Create Clear Announcements—Guidelines on the Use of Plain Language (July 1997)
- Guidelines for the Exemption of Listed Companies for the Securities (Disclosure of Interests) Ordinance (July 1991)

2.115 In addition to the above, the SFC has issued and continues to issue a wide range of circulars related to different aspects of the regulatory system.

Listing Rules

2.116 In addition to the above, various rules of HKEx play important roles, most especially the 'Listing Rules'. The Rules Governing the Listing of Securities on the Stock Exchange of Hong Kong Limited (Listing Rules), the application of which is considered in Chapters 4 and 6, are divided into two volumes. Volume One addresses: (1) general matters; (2) equity securities; (3) investment vehicles; (4) debt securities; (5) HKEx—Listing (Chapter 38); and (6) Guidance/Practice

Notes (covering a variety of specific matters). Volume Two includes a variety of appendices, basically including the major forms and documents required under the Listing Rules.

General matters cover the following: (1) interpretation (Chapter 1); (2) intro-   **2.117**
duction (Chapter 2); (3) composition, powers, functions, and procedures of Listing Committee, the Listing Appeals Committee, and the Listing Division (Chapter 2A); (4) review procedures (Chapter 2B); (5) authorized representative and directors (Chapter 3); (6) sponsors and compliance advisers (Chapter 3A); (7) accountants' reports and pro forma financial information (Chapter 4); (8) valuation of and information on properties (Chapter 5); and (9) suspension, cancellation, and withdrawal of listing (Chapter 6).

Equity securities matters address the following: (1) methods of listing (Chapter   **2.118**
7); (2) qualifications for listing (Chapter 8); (3) application procedures and requirements (Chapter 9); (4) restrictions on purchase and subscription (Chapter 10); (5) listing documents (Chapter 11); (6) prospectuses (Chapter 11A); (7) publication requirements (Chapter 12); (8) continuing obligations (Chapter 13); (9) notifiable transactions (Chapter 14); (10) connected transactions (Chapter 14A); (11) options, warrants, and similar rights (Chapter 15); (12) structured products (Chapter 15A); (13) convertible equity securities (Chapter 16); (14) share option schemes (Chapter 17); (15) mineral companies (Chapter 18); (16) overseas issues (Chapter 19); and (17) issuers incorporated in the PRC (Chapter 19A).

Investment vehicles matters address the following: (1) authorized collective   **2.119**
investment schemes (Chapter 20); and (2) investment companies (Chapter 21).

Debt securities matters address the following: (1) methods of listing (Chapter   **2.120**
22); (2) qualifications for listing (Chapter 23); (3) application procedures and requirements (Chapter 24); (4) listing documents (Chapter 25); (5) listing agreement (Chapter 26); (6) options, warrants, and similar rights (Chapter 27); (7) convertible debt securities (Chapter 28); (8) tap issues, debt issuance programmes, and asset-backed securities (Chapter 29); (9) mineral companies (Chapter 30); (10) states (Chapter 31); (11) supranationals (Chapter 32); (12) state corporations (Chapter 33); (13) banks (Chapter 34); (14) guarantors and guaranteed issues (Chapter 35); (15) overseas issuers (Chapter 36); and (16) selectively marketed securities (Chapter 37).

Overall, the legal and regulatory framework for securities and futures markets in   **2.121**
Hong Kong is comprehensive and of an international standard, though certain problems remain especially in the division of responsibilities between the SFC and HKEx. These are discussed in the final section of this chapter as well as in subsequent chapters.

(3) Insurance and the OCI

2.122 The legal and regulatory framework for the insurance market in Hong Kong consists of the Insurance Companies Ordinance (ICO), a statutory body called the Office of the Commissioner of Insurance ('OCI') and self-regulatory measures. These are supplemented by a large body of common law.

Office of the Commissioner of Insurance (OCI)

2.123 The OCI was established in 1992 and is the regulatory authority of the insurance industry in Hong Kong. The OCI was set up for the administration of the Insurance Companies Ordinance (Cap. 41) ('ICO') established in June 1990. It is headed by the Commissioner of Insurance who has been appointed as the Insurance Authority for administering the ICO. The Insurance Authority has five major functions, namely:

- Authorization of insurers to carry on insurance business in or from Hong Kong;
- Regulation of insurers to ensure the financial soundness and integrity of the insurance market;
- Regulation of insurance intermediaries to ensure an insurance agent is properly appointed by an insurer and registered with the Insurance Agents Registration Board (IARB) in accordance with the Code of Practice for the Administration of Insurance Agents;
- Liaison with the Insurance Industry in promoting self-regulation by the industry with the aim of enhancing the protection of policy holders; and
- Reviewing regularly the guidelines and regulations developed within the system to ensure that they are in keeping with market developments and provide adequate protection to the insuring public.

2.124 The OCI is headed by the Commissioner of Insurance. In addition, there are three Assistant Commissioners of Insurance, who are responsible for general insurance business, long-term insurance business, and policy and development respectively. Furthermore, eleven Senior Insurance Officers are responsible for a wide variety of insurance regulation related subjects ranging from authorization over intermediaries to administration.

2.125 The principal duty of the OCI is to regulate the insurance industry in order to guarantee the highest possible level of protection for policy holders in Hong Kong. This duty is framed by the general responsibility to promote the general stability of the insurance industry.

2.126 The OCI has regulatory powers in order to adequately regulate both insurers and insurance intermediaries (discussed in detail in Chapter 3).

Insurance Claims Complaints Bureau

The ICO does not provide the OCI with statutory power to intervene in case of **2.127**
a dispute between policy holders and insurers or insurance intermediaries.
Rather the ICO has established a self-regulatory system under which self-
regulatory bodies are responsible for the resolution of disputes. As one of the
self-regulatory measures, the Insurance Claims Complaints Bureau (ICCB) was
established in 1990 to handle complaints lodged by policyholders that a personal policy has not been fairly treated. In such cases, the ICCB is empowered to
make an award of up to HK$ 600,000 (US$ 77,000) per case.

The Insurance Claims Complaints Bureau handles disputes involving personal **2.128**
claims against insurers on behalf of policy holders. Complaints against insurance
intermediaries should be lodged with either the Insurance Agents Registration
Board or the Hong Kong Confederation of Insurance Brokers.

Insurance Advisory Committee

The Insurance Advisory Committee advises the Chief Executive on matters **2.129**
relating to the insurance business in Hong Kong and its regulation by the OCI.
Its current chairman is the Secretary for Financial Services and the Treasury.

Insurance Companies Ordinance (Cap. 41)

The ICO comprises 78 sections and eight schedules. The ICO is divided into **2.130**
14 parts, addressing the following issues: (1) preliminary matters (sections 1 to
5); (2) authorization (sections 6 to 14); (3) accounts and statements (sections 15
to 21); (4) long-term business (sections 22 to 25; (5) requirements for assets in
Hong Kong (sections 25A to 25C); (6) transfer of general business (sections
25D to 25F); (7) powers of intervention (sections 26 to 41); (8) insolvency
and winding-up (sections 42 to 49B); (9) special provisions relating to Lloyd's
(sections 50 to 50F); (10) exemptions (sections 51 to 53); (11) secrecy, disclosure of information, and examinations by outside authorities (sections 53A
to 53E); (12) supplementary and transitional (sections 54 to 64); (13) certain
contracts of insurance to be void (sections 64A to 64E); and (14) insurance
intermediaries (sections 65 to 78).

The eight schedules detail the following: (1) classes of insurance business; **2.131**
(2) directors and controllers; (3) accounts and statements; (4) proposed
appointment of controller within the meaning of section 13A(1) or authorized
representative under section 50B; (5) person proposing to become controller
within the meaning of section 13B(1); (6) person who has become controller of
insurer in contravention of section 13B(2); (7) powers of manager of insurer;
and (8) assets which may qualify as assets in Hong Kong.

2.132 The Insurance Companies Ordinance is supported by eight pieces of subsidiary legislation:

- Insurance Companies (Actuaries' Qualifications) Regulations (Cap. 41A)
- Insurance Companies (Register of Insurers) (Prescribed Fee) Regulations (Cap. 41B)
- Insurance Companies (Authorization and Annual Fees) Regulation (Cap. 41C)
- Insurance Companies (Miscellaneous Fees) Regulation (Cap. 41D)
- Insurance Companies (Determination of Long Term Liabilities) Regulation (Cap. 41E)
- Insurance Companies (Margin of Solvency) Regulation (Cap. 41F)
- Insurance Companies (General Business) (Valuation) Regulation (Cap. 41G)
- Insurance Companies (Actuaries' Standards) Regulation (Cap. 41H)

2.133 In addition to the ICO and subsidiary legislation, the OCI has also issued a variety of Guidance Notes:

- Guidance Note on Insurance Companies (General Business) (GN2)
- Guidance Note on Prevention of Money Laundering and Terrorist Financing (GN3)
- Guidance Note on 'Fit and Proper' Criteria under the ICO (GN4)
- Guidance Note on Application for Authorization to Carry on Insurance Business in or from Hong Kong (GN5)
- Guidance Note on Reserving for Mortgage Guarantee Business (GN6)
- Guidance Note on Reserving Standards for Investment Guarantees (GN7)
- Guidance Note on the Use of Internet for Insurance Activities (GN8)
- Guidance Note on Actuarial Review of Insurance Liabilities in respect of Employees' Compensation and Motor Insurance Businesses (GN9)
- Guidance Note on the Corporate Governance of Authorized Insurers (GN10)
- Guidance Note on Classification of Class C—Linked Long Term Business (GN11)
- Guidance Note on Reinsurance with Related Companies (GN12)
- Guidance Note on Asset Management by Authorized Insurers (GN13)

Details of individual Guidance Notes are discussed where relevant in the context of subsequent chapters.

Hong Kong Federation of Insurers (HKFI)

2.134 In addition to the OCI, the Hong Kong Federation of Insurers (established in 1988) plays a key self-regulatory role in respect of insurance business in Hong Kong, similar in many ways to that of the HKAB in relation to banking. Of most significance, it is responsible for the Code of Conduct for Insurers, initially adopted in May 1999.

The Code of Conduct for Insurers is divided into seven parts, addressing the **2.135** following issues: (1) introductory matters (Part I); (2) advising and selling practices (Part II); (3) claims (Part III); (4) management of insurance agents (Part IV); (5) management of staff (Part V); (6) misconduct of insurers (Part VI); and (7) inquiries, complaints, and disputes (Part VII). Details are discussed where relevant in Chapter 3.

Overall, the legal and regulatory framework for insurance in Hong Kong is **2.136** comprehensive and of an international standard, though with certain caveats discussed in the final section of this chapter as well as in subsequent chapters, especially Chapter 10.

(4) Pensions and the MPFA

The regulatory legal and regulatory framework for the pensions market in Hong **2.137** Kong consists of a statutory body called the Mandatory Provident Fund Schemes Authority (MPFA) responsible for the Mandatory Provident Fund Schemes Ordinance (MPFO) and the Occupational Retirement Schemes Ordinance (ORSO). These supplement the frameworks for securities, banking, and insurance, which are all applicable in varying contexts.

Mandatory Provident Fund Schemes Authority (MPFA)

The MPFA was established in September 1998 to regulate and monitor the **2.138** operation of privately managed provident fund schemes as part of Hong Kong's establishment of the Mandatory Provident Fund system of mandatory retirement savings. It is headed by its managing director, who is supported by six divisions responsible for supervision, enforcement, regulatory and policy issues, external affairs, corporate services, and risk management.

Its responsibilities as laid down in the MPFO include: **2.139**

- ensuring compliance with the MPFO;
- registering provident fund schemes;
- approving qualified persons as approved trustees of registered schemes;
- regulating the affairs and activities of approved trustees and ensuring that they administer the registered schemes in a prudent manner;
- making rules or guidelines for the payment of mandatory contributions and for the administration of registered schemes;
- exercising such other functions as are conferred or imposed on the Authority by or under the MPFO or any other Ordinance;

- considering and proposing reforms of the law relating to occupational retirement schemes or provident fund schemes; and
- promoting and encouraging the development of the retirement scheme industry in Hong Kong, including the adoption of a high standard of conduct and sound prudent business practices by approved trustees and other service providers.

2.140   Since January 2000, the MPFA also assumes the role of the Registrar of Occupational Retirement Schemes in administering the Occupational Retirement Schemes Ordinance (ORSO). Relevant responsibilities include:

- Processing of ORSO retirement scheme applications;
- Monitoring of ORSO registered schemes;
- Liaison with professional and industry bodies; and
- Exemption of qualified ORSO schemes from the MPF system, issuing guidelines and monitoring of MPF exempted ORSO schemes under the Mandatory Provident Fund Schemes (Exemption) Regulation.

Mandatory Provident Fund Schemes Ordinance (Cap. 485)

2.141   The MPFO comprises 49 sections and ten schedules. The Ordinance is divided into six parts, addressing: (1) preliminary matters (Part I: sections 1 to 5A); (2) Mandatory Provident Fund Schemes Authority (MPFA—Part II: sections 6 to 6W);[120] (3) contributions (Part III: sections 7 to 19); (4) Mandatory Provident Fund (MPF) schemes (Part IV: sections 20 to 34D); (5) appeals (Part V: sections 35 to 40); and (6) miscellaneous matters (Part VI: sections 41 to 49).

2.142   The ten schedules address the following: (1) exempt persons (schedule 1); (2) provisions relating to Authority (schedule 1A); (3) delegation of functions of Authority (schedule 1B); (4) minimum level of relevant income per contribution period (schedule 2); (5) maximum level of relevant income per contribution period (schedule 3); (6) covenants to be implied in governing rules (schedule 5); (7) procedure at inquiries (schedule 5A); (8) decisions which may be the subject of an appeal (schedule 6); (9) age specified for the purposes of section 15(2) (schedule 7); and (10) associates and related companies (schedule 8).

2.143   The MPFO is supported by the following subsidiary legislation:

- Mandatory Provident Fund Schemes (General) Regulation (Cap. 485A)
- Mandatory Provident Fund Schemes (Exemption) Regulation (Cap. 485B)
- Mandatory Provident Fund Schemes (Fees) Regulation (Cap. 485C)

---

[120] Part II contains the following divisions: (1) financial provisions (ss 6L–6QA); (2) Advisory Committee (ss 6R–6T); and (3) Industry Services Committee (ss 6U–6W).

- Mandatory Provident Fund Schemes (Exemption) Regulation (Specification of Date under sections 5 and 16) Notice (Cap. 485D)
- Mandatory Provident Fund Schemes (Contributions for Casual Employees) Order (Cap. 485E)
- Mandatory Provident Fund Schemes (Specification of Permitted Periods) Notice (Cap. 485F)
- Mandatory Provident Fund Schemes Rules (Cap. 485G)
- Mandatory Provident Fund Schemes (Compensation Claims) Rules (Cap. 485H)

In addition to the above, the MPFA has issued a wide range of supporting guidelines, codes, and circulars. **2.144**

Overall, the legal and regulatory framework for pensions and the MPF in Hong Kong is comprehensive and of an international standard. **2.145**

(5) Financial conglomerates

Although all four regulatory agencies are independently responsible for their respective sectors, their day-to-day supervisory work cannot be entirely separated, simply because a large number of the supervised institutions are active in banking, securities, insurance, and pensions undertakings. In addition to the Cross-Market Surveillance Committee discussed above, the HKMA and the SFC work closely in certain respects of their regulatory functions and have entered into a mutual Memorandum of Understanding (see Chapter 3), which sets out the operational details relating to the respective roles and responsibilities of the two regulators regarding the securities related activities of banking institutions. The HKMA and the SFC hold regular meetings to discuss matters of mutual interest. **2.146**

The HKMA has further entered into a Memorandum of Understanding with the OCI in 2003 to strengthen cooperation in respect of supervision of entities or financial groups in which both supervisors have a regulatory interest. **2.147**

Overall, the current legal and regulatory framework for financial conglomerates in Hong Kong, despite not having yet seen a major crisis, is in need of further strengthening, both from the standpoint of addressing risks as well as supporting competitiveness. These issues are discussed in the final section of this chapter as well as in subsequent chapters, especially Chapter 10. **2.148**

C. Conclusion

2.149   In looking at these issues a useful starting point is the Hong Kong SAR-Financial System Stability Assessment 2003.[121] The Financial System Stability Assessment (FSSA) is part of the Financial Sector Assessment Programme (FSAP), a joint International Monetary Fund (IMF) and World Bank effort introduced in 1999. It is directed at improving the effectiveness of efforts to promote the soundness of financial systems in member countries.

2.150   In respect of Hong Kong's financial markets, the FSSA established the following:

> The financial system in Hong Kong is resilient, sound and overseen by a comprehensive supervisory framework. The banking system is sufficiently well capitalized and profitable to be able to withstand the more likely macroeconomic shocks, although some pressures on banks are emerging. Weak domestic demand and shifts in global financial activity in Hong Kong are driving banks, both the internationally active large institutions and some smaller banks to expand into investment banking, brokerage, insurance and asset management services. These trends highlight the need to strengthen regulatory and insolvency procedures for financial conglomerates and for enhanced supervisory coordination among domestic and cross border regulators. The small but growing insurance sector poses some supervisory challenges, particularly as regards the risks involved in life insurance and embedded guarantees in life insurance products. Recent reforms in payments and securities settlement systems have strengthened the market infrastructure. Further strengthening is needed in the areas of transparency, accounting, and regulatory and corporate governance to help maintain Hong Kong's competitiveness as an international financial center.
>
> The financial system is facing several important challenges as economic integration with the Mainland of China deepens and efforts continue at managing the fiscal deficit. Strong macroeconomic fundamentals thus remain the key to HKSAR's prospects for continuing to grow and compete as a financial services center. In this context further strengthening of regulatory governance arrangements dealing with systemic and financial stability issues is recommended . . .[122]

2.151   In order to further strengthen Hong Kong's financial system, the FSSA makes recommendations in three key areas: banking, securities, and insurance.

2.152   According to the assessment, Hong Kong's banking sector has so far proven to be strong and flexible, specifically because of its high profitability and liquidity as well as a comparatively low level of credit delinquency and non-performing loans. It has a very high degree of compliance with the international best prac-

---

[121]   Based on information available at the time of completion of the report: 15 April 2003.
[122]   IMF, *Peoples Republic of China Hong Kong Special Administrative Region: Financial System Stability Assessment* (June 2003), p 2.

tices in banking regulation and supervision[123] and well-functioning legal, accounting, and payments and securities settlements systems are in place.

In terms of reinforcing the banking sector, the FSSA particularly suggests to: **2.153**

- improve the governance of banking regulation and supervision;
- enhance the measures for dealing with liquidity risk;
- raise supervisory attention to reputational risk and legal risks to banks; and
- strengthen the cooperation between banking and other supervisors in respect to cross-market activities.[124]

In relation to securities, according to the FSSA: **2.154**

> general preconditions for effective securities regulation are in place in Hong Kong. The securities markets are competitive and open to domestic and foreign participants. The [SFC] is a regulator with decision-making authority and a clear responsibility and accountability. It is well-resourced, professionally staffed and has sufficient surveillance, inspection and enforcement powers. Since the adoption of the [SFO] in March 2002, the SFC has been provided with a comprehensive legal framework, which covers all aspects of securities related activities. Furthermore, an adequate infrastructure for well functioning securities markets with efficient trading, clearing and settlement systems as well as appropriate listing rules is in place.[125]

In terms of improvement, the FSSA points out one primary deficiency with **2.155** respect to the responsibilities of the Financial Secretary and the Chief Executive of Hong Kong regarding a number of important regulatory decisions. Although the SFC enjoys full autonomy in daily operational practice, the Chief Executive of Hong Kong has the power to give directions to the SFC about any matter relevant to the performance of its functions.[126] In addition, in a significant number of decisions the SFC has to consult or seek the consent of various bodies, which restricts its independent functioning and hinders its ability to react quickly to any emergency situation. Those peculiarities are not in line with international best practices, namely the IOSCO principles,[127] and the FSSA suggests it is crucial to consider them.[128]

In relation to insurance, the FSSA concludes: **2.156**

> the HKSAR satisfies the prerequisites for effective insurance regulation, which include comprehensive accounting standards and strong supervision of the banking and securities sectors. In addition, the [OCI] has a range of supervisory powers to solve problems incurred by insurance companies. So far, however, the OCI is a government department subject to specific budgetary and administrative pro-

---

[123] Basel Core Principles for Effective Banking Supervision.
[124] IMF, above, pp 38–42.   [125] ibid, pp 42–50.   [126] BO s 10(1).
[127] IOSCO, *Objectives and Principles of Securities Regulation.*   [128] IMF, above.

cedures. Although it has factual independence in day-to-day operations, there is no comprehensive operational independence. This situation in particular has been pinpointed by the FSSA, as it may delay the development of a regulatory infrastructure that complies with international best practices, such as the IAIS principles.[129]

2.157 From this external review, the IMF concludes that Hong Kong largely has in place an appropriate legal and regulatory framework for financial stability, though with some weaknesses, especially in relation to financial conglomerates, the relationship between the SFC and HKEx, and independence of regulatory agencies. The FSSA, however, does not address issues of competitiveness; yet all three of these issues (discussed in subsequent chapters) also impact upon Hong Kong's competitiveness as an international financial centre. Moreover, this chapter has highlighted an additional issue of concern arising from Hong Kong's legal and regulatory framework for financial markets and relating to Hong Kong's competitiveness, namely the complexity of the current regulatory structure. Given the size of the jurisdiction and its need for competitiveness, this should be a major issue of concern and one requiring urgent attention. We return to this issue in Chapter 10.

2.158 In addition, another issue of more specific legal concern arises in relation to the constitutionality of special appeals tribunals in the context of Hong Kong's financial regulatory system. Increasingly, special tribunals are established under financial ordinances to provide means of appeal. The first major example occurred in the context of the Securities and Futures Ordinance (SFO), namely the Securities and Futures Appeals Tribunal (SFAT).[130] The operations of these tribunals attract special legal considerations. We return to related issues in Chapter 10.

---

[129] IMF, above. [130] SFO, s 216.

Part II

REGULATION OF INTERMEDIARIES, PRODUCTS, AND SERVICES

3

REGULATION OF FINANCIAL INTERMEDIARIES, PRODUCTS, AND SERVICES

As a jurisdiction which has its roots in an English common law system and one **3.01** which historically has taken a laissez-faire approach to economic matters, the regulation of financial intermediaries, products, and services in Hong Kong has been flexible and permissive rather than restrictive. Overall, this approach has supported the development of financial markets in Hong Kong into one of the world's leading financial centres. In recent years, with the enactments of the SFO, the MPFO, and changes to the regulatory framework for banking and insurance, the regulation of financial intermediaries, products, and services in Hong Kong has increased. Nonetheless, regulation continues to be largely permissive and flexible in recognition of the need to continue to foster market innovation and development.

3.02 Chapter 2 presented an overview of the legal and regulatory framework for finance in Hong Kong. This chapter progresses this discussion to focus on the business activities of financial intermediaries in relation to their customers and the wider market. In this context, the regulatory framework affects business activities at different levels:

- distinct financial products (eg bank deposits, units in mutual funds) ('financial products'),
- how such products are acted upon vis-à-vis customers and the market (eg sales and marketing activities, contracts with clients), and
- services supporting or ancillary to the foregoing, or provided as a separate business line (eg dealing investment advice, research).

3.03 Accordingly, this chapter addresses the regulatory framework applicable to each of the foregoing which, for convenience, shall collectively be referred to as 'products' as each is a discrete activity or instrument of the business endeavours of financial intermediaries. In addition, the chapter addresses the authorization and licensing of financial intermediaries (such as banks, securities firms, and so on). It also discusses the on-going compliance issues with which such institutions and the individuals acting within them, must comply with in order to retain their authorized or licensed status.

3.04 In section A, this chapter presents an overview of the legal and regulatory framework for financial products as defined above and financial intermediaries—two closely related subjects. Section B provides an overview of the legal and regulatory framework for financial products. Sections C, D, and E then discuss regulation of financial intermediaries in Hong Kong—especially banks, securities and insurance firms—in terms of, respectively, initial authorization and licensing, on-going requirements and compliance, and insolvency and exit.

A. Intermediaries, Products, and Services: Markets and Regulation

3.05 As a general matter, the regulation of financial products and services in Hong Kong focuses on the provider of the product rather than the product itself. As a result, following the UK approach, regulation of products focuses on licensing the relevant intermediary (or its agents) in most cases, although there is a growing range of product based regulation (similar to that in the US). However, as licensing of an intermediary is orientated toward products which are typically supplied by that class of financial intermediary (eg banks conduct 'banking business', securities firms engage in 'regulated activities'), this description is to some extent blurred.

A central role of the financial system is the collection of savings and their **3.06** allocation for investment. A variety of financial institutions play a key role in any such system. The nature of the functions they fulfil gives rise to risks that are present in all market economies, although dealt with in ways that reflect national, legal, and cultural characteristics as well as historical incidents of particular markets. The manner in which financial intermediation is executed creates risks for investors, as well as risks that concern the financial system in aggregate. Effective prudential regulation and supervision of financial markets and institutions (including banks, insurance companies, securities and futures intermediaries, mutual funds, and pension funds) is critical in the financial stability and efficient functioning of any economy.

Official oversight of the financial system in this regard comprises the formula- **3.07** tion and enforcement of rules and standards governing the behaviour of market participants as well as the on-going supervision of individual institutions. Such regulation and supervision play an essential role in fostering stable and robust financial systems, and should seek to support and enhance market functioning rather than displace it by establishing basic 'rules of the game' and demanding that they be observed.[1]

At the most basic level, prudential regulation and supervision serve to promote **3.08** the public confidence on which market-based financial systems are based. Further, impartial supervision and regulation are essential complements to effective management and market discipline. Whereas regulations set the standards of behaviour required, supervision acts to check such regulations have been and are being followed. However, financial market segments have different motivations and requirements. The task of such regulation and supervision is to ensure that financial institutions operate prudently, for example, in respect of the risk-related activities engaged in by a bank, that it holds capital resources sufficient for it to be self-sustaining in the event of probable periodic or episodic losses. In addition, regulations can themselves be a source of vulnerability to the extent that they are too lax, too strong, too intrusive, or provide inadequate oversight. Rules can be poorly designed, fall out of step with commercial conditions, or be inadequately implemented. The focus must therefore be on striking the right balance for regulation to be effective.

In order to achieve such goals, the pragmatic point of view requires financial **3.09**

---

[1] See C Goodhart, P Hartmann, D Llewellyn, L Rojas-Suarez, & S Weisbrod, *Financial Regulation: Why, How and Where Now?* (Routledge, 1998).

regulation to support the interests of investors, promote the efficiency of the financial markets, and thus foster the wider interests of the economy. In particular, regulation provides safeguards against instability in the financial system by imposing regulations on institutions and market systems. From an economic standpoint, financial regulation seeks to address a variety of problems ('market failures') that occur when financial transactions are left solely to market forces that can be anti-competitive and not always efficient. On the basis of this analytical framework, financial regulation should seek to address four specific issues:

- anti-competitive behaviour (competition regulation);
- market misconduct (market integrity regulation);
- information asymmetries (usually referred to as 'prudential concerns' or 'prudential regulation', also used to support consumer protection/market integrity regulation); and
- systemic instability (financial stability regulation and prudential regulation).

3.10 Regulation of financial intermediaries and products in Hong Kong focuses primarily on market integrity, prudential and system stability regulation. (As noted below, there are very few competition regulations in Hong Kong; however, authorization and change of control rules in respect of banks, securities intermediaries, and insurance companies do provide the respective regulators—HKMA, SFC, OCI—some scope to address competition issues.) Market integrity concerns are largely addressed by the framework for regulation of financial products (discussed in the following section (section C) and in Chapter 8). Prudential regulation and financial stability regulation of financial intermediaries commonly cover the following areas:

- entry requirements;
- ownership and control structures, including foreign ownership and the control of financial institutions (especially banks) by non-banking interests;
- governance requirements (for the purposes of protecting clients, ie beyond corporate governance issues as discussed in Chapter 6);
- prudential standards, including capital adequacy and liquidity requirements, risk management and control systems, and various limits on business (eg credit and positions limits);
- prevention of crime such as money laundering and the financing of terrorism;
- accounting and reporting requirements;
- special criteria for the licensing, prudential supervision and liquidation of branch and representative offices of foreign financial institutions in cooperation with foreign financial regulators;
- systems for closure and exit in connection with, for example, licence revocation, failure, compensation, or insolvency; and

- customer support schemes (such as deposit insurance and industry guarantee funds).

Following this general structure, section C addresses entry (ie licensing and authorization) including for foreign institutions, whereas section D addresses regulation of on-going activities, including prudential standards, ownership, governance, and control, reporting, as well as money laundering and related matters are covered. Section E discusses insolvency, exit, and customer support schemes. **3.11**

(1) Regulation of financial products and services

Most financial products are largely matters of private contract and therefore governed by the common law framework, with disputes adjudicated by the courts. However, in addition to this framework provided by common law, there are a variety of statutes which address an ever growing range of financial products. Similar to other jurisdictions based on English law, at the core are ordinances dealing with traditional products such as bills of exchange and cheques (Bills of Exchange Ordinance), company shares (Companies Ordinance and Listing Rules—discussed in more detail in Chapter 4), and security interests (Companies Ordinance, Bankruptcy Ordinance and other property related ordinances). These provide the essential legal framework for basic financial products. **3.12**

On top of this basic private law framework, major categories of financial products such as banking, securities, insurance, and pensions products, are largely dealt with through the regulation of financial institutions and other financial intermediaries. **3.13**

However, this framework does not catch all products. Rather, the design of product regulation through financial institution authorization and on-going requirements is limited in scope. Specifically, institutions conducting banking, securities, insurance, or pensions business must be licensed to undertake such activities. Thus, institutional regulation is largely based upon the nature of the financial product or products being provided. As a result, a major focus of product regulation via institutional regulation is a focus on the nature of the business that requires authorization. The following section of this chapter focuses in detail upon the sorts of financial business which will bring a financial services provider within the institutional regulatory framework discussed in subsequent sections. **3.14**

Finally, as a third layer, there is an increasing number of other statutory provisions addressing specific aspects of business involving financial products. The largest number and most important of these arise in the context of the SFO. **3.15**

In addition to the above framework, there are also differences in the legal and **3.16** regulatory framework for domestic and non-domestic transactions, and for wholesale markets in which retail participants are not directly involved.

International and domestic

3.17 As with most jurisdictions based on English law, regulation in Hong Kong has traditionally focused on the domestic (ie Hong Kong) market rather than extending to circumstances taking place outside of Hong Kong (eg unlike the traditionally extraterritorial approach of US financial regulation or the regional approach of EU regulation). Nonetheless, a number of recent changes have begun to erode this historical approach, largely reflecting the increasingly global-ized nature of financial markets and Hong Kong's role as an international financial centre with free movement of capital.

3.18 In the area of financial products, the territory's regulatory focus has since the early 1990s increasingly been on retail markets, especially in the qualification of market professionals dealing with the public and investor education, as well as to changes driven by the development of the internet. In the area of banking, the focus has been on electronic products and internet banking, with these now regulated largely in the same manner as other banking products offered in Hong Kong, with emphasis on the institution providing the service.

3.19 These changes are reflected in the approach to foreign banks, with an increasing emphasis on subsidiary rather than branch structures, resulting partially from experiences with the collapse of BCCI and its Hong Kong subsidiary BCC(HK). They are likely to be increasingly driven by the varying ways in which implementation of the Basel II capital accord takes place around the world.

3.20 In the area of securities, a number of changes were made in the context of the SFO to address circumstances where non-Hong Kong based securities products are marketed to the Hong Kong market. These issues are subject to special attention in the context of financial products directed at retail investors (which must meet the same standards in relation to licensing as those offered by Hong Kong based securities product providers). In addition, experiences in the Asian financial crises of 1997–8 brought a concern in Hong Kong of the risks of market manipulation from outside the borders of Hong Kong. Issues of market conduct are discussed in Chapter 8.

3.21 There has also been an effort to bring new financial products to Hong Kong, especially as regards the issuance of securities of foreign companies. As discussed in the following chapters, in addition to Hong Kong companies, companies from a limited number of other jurisdictions—namely lightly regulated off-shore centres such as the Cayman Islands—have been allowed to list equity securities on the SEHK. In the early 1990s this group was expanded to include companies from Mainland China—a group which now makes up a major portion of the capitalization of the SEHK. While important to enhance Hong Kong's competitiveness as a financial centre, especially for China, the introduction of Mainland companies to the SEHK has also brought a number of problems, especially in relation to enforcement issues.

Further, in an effort to expand its appeal as a debt market, HKEx has also **3.22** relaxed its Listing Rules for debt securities to allow companies from any jurisdiction to list such products. While this has yet to have a major impact on the market, it may highlight an opportunity for further product expansion in relation to equity securities through allowing a wider range of companies to list such securities on the SEHK. However, if this path is pursued it is likely to further highlight weaknesses in the current regulatory system in dealing with non-Hong Kong companies.

In the insurance sector, the international/domestic distinction has remained less **3.23** significant in both wholesale and retail markets. However, sales of insurance products to Mainland residents from Hong Kong insurance companies have raised certain concerns in the Mainland.

Wholesale and retail

Wholesale markets in Hong Kong largely remain lightly regulated across the **3.24** spectrum of financial products. However, reflecting a worldwide trend, regulation of retail products across the financial sector has generally increased. Nonetheless, regulation of financial products in banking and insurance remains quite light compared to other major financial jurisdictions such as the UK and the US.

In the context of wholesale markets, a number of self-regulatory regimes origin- **3.25** ating from the London markets have made their way into Hong Kong practice, including the London Rules on distressed companies (discussed in brief in the preceding chapter) and codes of practice for derivatives (discussed in Chapter 5). These practices have to a certain extent been formalized and play a significant role in Hong Kong's wholesale markets.

As noted, an increasing focus of financial regulation not only in Hong Kong but **3.26** around the world is on retail consumers. In Hong Kong, the traditional attitude of the markets, the regulatory system, and the courts has been one of caveat emptor. However, this underlying philosophy has been limited to a certain extent due to developments following the market crash of 1987 and also due to assumption for the first time of a system of self-rule under the 'one country, two systems' framework.

In the context of financial regulation, the trend away from caveat emptor and **3.27** towards retail financial services consumer protection can be seen in the SFO, limitations on the role of self-regulatory organizations such as the HKAB, HKEx, and HKICPA.

3.28 Beyond the strict context of financial law and regulation, Hong Kong still has very limited systems of consumer protection, though these are increasing to a certain extent. Most important in this context has been the creation of the Consumer Council (under the Consumer Council Ordinance (Cap. 216)), as well as the creation of an Ombudsman function. Further development of this trend can be seen through the enactment of legislation such as the Pyramid Selling Prohibition Ordinance (Cap. 355), Supply of Services (Implied Terms) Ordinance (Cap. 457), and Unconscionable Contracts Ordinance (Cap. 458), all of which place some limits on caveat emptor and increase the general level of consumer protection.

3.29 In addition, the enactment of the Personal Data (Privacy) Ordinance (Cap. 486) has improved the protection of personal information but at the same time raised new and sometimes expensive compliance concerns for financial services providers.

3.30 At the same time, Hong Kong still has no general legislation addressing false advertising (although these issues are addressed in the context of financial services specifically in the major sectoral legislation such as the SFO, Banking Ordinance, and MPFO, continuing to rely instead largely on the common law treatment of fraud.

3.31 Further, at present, there is no comprehensive competition or antitrust regulation in Hong Kong. However, in relation to certain sectors (eg telecommunications and electricity), there are sector-specific schemes. In addition, there exists a competition policy committee whose role it is to discuss competition and antitrust issues that may arise in Hong Kong. At present, it has had a limited impact. At the same time, discussions are on-going in Hong Kong (and in Mainland China) about the need for comprehensive competition or antitrust regulation. At present, no solid proposals have emerged in Hong Kong.

(2) Regulation of financial intermediaries

3.32 Within the above context, regulation of financial intermediaries therefore has much importance not only in context of the operations of the institutions themselves but more generally in the overall context of regulation of financial products. As discussed above and in Chapter 2, regulation of financial intermediaries in Hong Kong focuses on banks, securities intermediaries, and insurance companies. In addition, certain other intermediaries are also subject to institutional regulation.

Banks

All organizations engaged in banking activities or deposit-taking must be **3.33** 'authorized institutions' (AIs). Authorized institutions comprise banks, deposit-taking companies (DTCs) and restricted licence banks (RLBs), the second and third being enterprises with narrower business streams than full service banks. All are regulated by the HKMA pursuant to the Banking Ordinance (Cap. 155), subject to a significant number of exceptions. Further, all authorized institutions are regulated in all their activities, including those in other sectors, such as securities and insurance.

Hong Kong has since 1986 sought to adopt and implement international bank- **3.34** ing standards. For example, the Basel Capital Accord of 1988[2] has been applied in Hong Kong since end-1989, with its widely accepted minimum capital adequacy ratio of 8 per cent. From 31 December 1996 the HKMA implemented a reporting framework on market risks, with the revised capital adequacy regime taking statutory effect by the end of 1997, in line with Basel requirements.[3] The HKMA has also sought to follow international practice in regard to the supervision of international banking operations as embodied in the revised Basel Concordat.[4] In addition, the minimum standards for the supervision of international banking groups established by the Basel Committee in July 1992 have been taken into account in establishing the manner in which the authorization criteria are applied to overseas applicants.[5]

The approach of the HKMA, similar to that of the pre-FSA Bank of England in **3.35** the UK, is cooperative and consultative, focusing on persuasion rather than control (ie moral suasion), with ultimate responsibility lying with the institutions and their management. The function of the HKMA is not to manage banks, but rather to monitor the processes and structures for decision-making within authorized institutions.

---

[2] Basel Committee on Banking Supervision, *International Convergence of Capital Measurement and Capital Standards* (July 1988) ('1988 Basel Accord'). The Basel Accord has been periodically amended.
[3] Basel Committee, *Amendment to the Capital Accord to Incorporate Market Risks* (January 1996, rev'd September 1997).
[4] The Basel Concordat was originally agreed in 1983, following the collapse of Banco Ambrosiano. Basel Committee, *Principles for the Supervision of Banks' Foreign Establishments* (May 1983). It was supplemented in 1990. Basel Committee, *Information Flows between Banking Supervisory Authorities* (Supplement to the 'Basel Concordat' of May 1983) (April 1990).
[5] Basel Committee, *Minimum Standards for the Supervision of International Banking Groups and their Cross-border Establishments* (July 1992).

Securities intermediaries

3.36 In contrast to banks which are supervised and regulated by the HKMA, the activities of securities firms[6] are supervised and regulated primarily by the SFC under the SFO. While the core control mechanism is the licensing of intermediaries for specific regulated activities (see below), the SFC also regulates the fitness and properness of persons acting as intermediaries,[7] sets financial resources rules for intermediaries, imposes rules of conduct including for example restrictions on dealing with client assets, requirements to 'know the customer', product selling restrictions, and market activity restrictions. The sources of such regulatory measures are from both legislation (primarily the SFO and its subsidiary legislation), Codes of Conduct (referred to in primary legislation), and non-statutory rules and guidelines laid down by the SFC.

3.37 In regulating securities firms, the SFC undertakes a variety of regulatory processes, including:

- licensing and related applications;
- annual returns;
- routine audits;
- market monitoring;
- the dual filing system (see Chapter 4);
- mechanisms to deal with complaints by clients and others;
- self-reporting obligations; and
- market questionnaires (sometimes prompted by international developments).

3.38 In support of these regulatory processes, the SFC has a number of powers under the SFO, including the power to obtain records, documents, and information[8] from any person, not only licensed corporations. In this context, while professional legal privilege cannot be overridden, the right to silence and privilege against self-incrimination are abrogated. Further, it is an offence not to cooperate with an investigation of the SFC or to provide it with false or misleading information.

---

[6] In this chapter the terms 'securities intermediaries' and 'securities firms' refers to persons dealing in securities, futures or leveraged foreign exchange contracts, financial advisers, asset and fund managers, investment banks, corporate financial advisers, securities margin financiers, share registrars, financial consultants and planners, insurance brokers and agents dealing in securities or related activities, and trustees and custodians.

[7] Under SFO s 129 and guidelines issued by the SFC.

[8] Information may relate to: the affairs and management of listed companies (SFO s 179); the conduct and management of a licensed intermediary and any associated company (SFO s 180); securities, futures, and other regulated transactions (SFO s 181); breaches of the SFO or conduct contrary to the interests of the investing public (SFO s 182); and on request by an overseas regulator carrying out similar functions and subject to appropriate secrecy provisions (SFO s 186).

In general, regulations affect the ability to engage in business activities and set   **3.39**
parameters as to how it is undertaken. In terms of securities firms, the SFC
issues licences, and requires licensed persons to comply with their Codes, such
as the Code of Conduct. Licensing, conduct and related matters for securities
firms are mainly addressed by Parts V–XI of the SFO. In addition, the SFC
regulates securities market infrastructure providers, notably exchanges, clearing
houses, and share registrars.

As the regulator of the securities and futures market in Hong Kong, the SFC   **3.40**
also regulates dealings in securities, futures contracts, and leveraged foreign
exchange contracts. As already mentioned, the HKMA is the regulator and
supervisor of banking institutions and therefore governs the activities of banks
and deposit taking companies. This raises the question of the regulation of the
securities and derivatives activities of banks.

Securities activities of banks

Chapter 2 described how, in contrast to a sectoral regulatory system, banks and   **3.41**
banking activities in Hong Kong are regulated on an institutional basis by the
HKMA under the Banking Ordinance. Under the Banking Ordinance, the
HKMA undertakes consolidated supervision over all activities of 'authorized
institutions' (AIs, ie banks and quasi-banks), including securities activities.
The HKMA is thus responsible for day-to-day supervision of all securities activities of authorized institutions ('regulated activities' under the SFO). Nonetheless
regulation and supervision is, to some extent, undertaken jointly. Most importantly, all authorized institutions must register with the SFC as 'registered
institutions' (RIs) and their securities activities will be regulated and supervised
to similar regulatory standards as those applying to securities firms.

The details of the relationship between the HKMA and SFC in relation to the   **3.42**
securities activities of banks are set out in a Memorandum of Understanding
(MoU) of December 2002 signed by both the SFC and HKMA.[9] It provides a
framework for coordination and cooperation between the SFC and HKMA by
setting out the respective roles and responsibilities of the HKMA and SFC in
respect to securities activities of banks. Its stated overall goal is close cooperation
and consistent regulation. With this goal in mind, the MoU seeks to eliminate
gaps and overlapping of roles and responsibilities of the two regulators in
relation to regulating the securities business of banking institutions, and to
enhance the exchange of information. More specifically, it details the requirements applicable to 'registered' and 'authorized' institutions, and establishes the

---

[9] The memorandum replaces an earlier version from 1995 to take account of changes to the
regulatory framework that occurred with the introduction of the SFO.

division of work between the SFC and the HKMA especially with regard to the supervisory process and investigations.

3.43 Until the introduction of the SFO, certain authorized institutions were allowed to act as 'exempt dealers' and were not required to observe SFC regulations. Now, under the SFO, authorized institutions are no longer given such exemption in conducting securities activities and must seek registration with the SFC and meet its 'Fit and Proper Criteria' (see below). Only after their registration do they become 'registered institutions'. In addition, individual staff of registered institutions must now meet the same Fit and Proper Criteria applicable to staff of brokerage firms.

3.44 Registration requires authorized institutions to make application to the SFC first, which then refers the case to the HKMA for consideration. The HKMA advises on whether the applicant is fit and proper for registration under the SFO criteria. Based on the HKMA's advice, the SFC decides on whether to accept the application. The SFC is also responsible for making, publishing, and amending regulations, rules, codes, and guidelines with respect to the regulatory process applicable to the securities activities of banks.[10] However, given that the HKMA is the day-to-day supervisor of authorized institutions, the SFC must consult the HKMA before implementing new regulations. In turn, the HKMA may consult the SFC in the interpretation of rules and guidelines. This is meant to ensure consistent interpretation and approach given that the SFC is the ultimate authority in relation to the regulatory process regarding registered institutions.

Insurance firms and MPF and pensions providers

3.45 In addition to banks and securities firms, insurance companies are regulated by the OCI and Mandatory Provident Funds Schemes are regulated by the MPFA. A variety of other sorts of financial intermediaries (eg money brokers and pawnbrokers) are also regulated.

B. Financial Products and Services

(1) Banking

3.46 Any person or entity engaging in 'banking business' must become an 'authorized institution'—with requirements and consequences discussed below. However, as discussed further below, 'banking business' as defined in Hong Kong is in fact

---

[10] MoU (2002), cl 7.

quite limited in scope: namely, deposit-taking and cheque-related services. If an institution is conducting other forms of business traditionally engaged in by banks (eg lending, credit cards) but is not engaging in 'banking business' as defined, then it does not have to be an 'authorized institution' regulated by the HKMA and the HKAB. Instead, other forms of banking products may be governed by their own statutes (eg money lending) or only by the general common law framework discussed above. At the same time, all business activities of any 'authorized institution' in Hong Kong are regulated under the framework discussed in sections C, D, and E as a result of the framework of consolidated supervision under the Banking Ordinance. This extends beyond banking business, to any business in which an authorized institution is involved (eg securities, insurance, pensions, etc). Thus, financial products offered by different sorts of firms may in fact be treated differently. We would suggest that this is an odd result.

General framework

Under section 2(1) of the Banking Ordinance, 'banking business' includes either or both: (1) receiving from the general public money on current, deposit, savings, or other similar account repayable on demand or within three months or with a period of call or notice of less than that period; and (2) paying or collecting cheques drawn by or paid in by customers. Under this framework, banking products therefore include (1) deposit-taking and (2) paying or collecting cheques drawn or paid by customers. **3.47**

Under section 11(1), no banking business shall be carried on in Hong Kong except by an authorized institution, and any contravention is an offence.[11] However, given that 'banking business' excludes finance company activity (eg lending without taking deposits) and credit cards, the net effect is diluted. The principal regulatory standards applying to banking business are set by Part III of the Banking Ordinance, discussed further below. **3.48**

False advertisement

Under section 95(1) of the Banking Ordinance, where the HKMA is of the opinion that any advertisement issued in connection with the business of an authorized institution makes a statement or any representation that is false, misleading, or deceptive, it may, by notice in writing served on the institution, require the institution to withdraw or, as the circumstances require, remove, and to cease issuing such advertisements; and an authorized institution served with **3.49**

---

[11] BO s 11(2).

such a notice shall, accordingly, comply with that notice. Failure or refusal to comply is an offence for directors, chief executives, and managers.[12]

HKAB and Code of Banking Practice

3.50 As noted in Chapter 2, the HKAB once was essentially a self-regulatory banking cartel and lobby group; now it is more of normal self-regulatory organization (SRO) in the context of Hong Kong's general three-tier regulatory structure, with a defined role in relation to banking products in Hong Kong. Under section 12(1) of the HKAB Ordinance, it may set rules for the conduct of banking business, including the following:

- as to the maximum rates of interest, return, discount, or other benefit which may be paid or granted by members, or by any specified category of members, in respect of specified Hong Kong dollar deposits of their customers, and specified instruments;[13]
- as to the keeping and maintenance of clearing accounts in conformity with the terms and conditions specified by the Financial Secretary under section 3A of the Exchange Fund Ordinance;
- as to the imposition of deposit charges, and the minimum deposit charges to be so imposed;
- as to the payment of deposit charges by customers to members;
- as to the imposition of interest charges, and the rates of interest charges to be so imposed;
- as to the payment of interest charges by a member to the Financial Secretary for the account of the Exchange Fund;
- as to the conduct of foreign exchange business and the minimum commissions and charges to be applied there for;
- as to the conduct of securities and safe custody business and the minimum commissions and charges to be applied there for;
- as to the minimum charges to be applied by members for the issuance of guarantees or other documents;
- as to any other charges relating to the provision of any banking service, not being charges by way of interest or return payable on loans or advances granted by members; and
- prohibiting members from transacting any specified type of business or using any particular type of instrument.

3.51 The Code of Banking Practice (CBP) is issued under this power jointly by the

---

[12] BO s 95.
[13] Formerly, this was an important power. Now, however, all interest rate controls in Hong Kong have been abolished and are set solely by individual institutions.

HKAB and the DTC Association (DTCA) and endorsed by the HKMA.[14] It is a non-statutory code issued on a voluntary basis and is to be observed by authorized institutions in dealing with their personal customers. The CBP is issued and monitored by the HKAB and DTCA; however, the HKMA plays a very active role and the CBP is important in the context of its 'fit and proper' analysis—discussed further below. It specifically covers banking services such as current accounts, savings and other deposit accounts, loans and overdrafts, and card services, but applies generally to the overall relationship between institutions and their customers.[15] The recommendations are supplementary to and do not supplant any relevant legislation, codes, guidelines or rules applicable to institutions authorized under the Banking Ordinance.[16] HKAB and DTCA expect their respective members to comply with the CBP and the HKMA monitors compliance as part of its regular supervision.[17]

The CBP covers the following issues: **3.52**

- terms and conditions of accounts;
- fees and charges of accounts;
- use of customer information;
- compliance with the relevant ordinances for the promotion of equal opportunity;
- bank marketing;
- handling customer complaints;
- residential mortgage financing;
- card services (including credit card, debit card, and stored value card, etc);
- methods of recovery of loans and commissioning of debt collection agencies; and
- electronic banking services.

The HKAB has disciplinary powers in relation to its authority.[18] These only **3.53** extend to its members (ie authorized institutions) and not to the activities of non-banks.

Deposit-taking

As noted above, deposit-taking (and hence related products) are a key compo- **3.54** nent of 'banking business' as defined in Hong Kong. Part III of the Banking Ordinance addresses banking business, including deposit-taking. However, this Part III of the Banking Ordinance does not apply to a wide range of deposit-taking by certain businesses and entities,[19] including the taking of any deposit by:

---

[14] CBP s 1.1.   [15] CBP s 1.2.   [16] CBP s 1.3.   [17] CBP s 1.4.
[18] HKABO s 17, supported by s 21.   [19] Set out in BO s 3(1).

- a trust company registered under Part VIII of the Trustee Ordinance (Cap. 29);
- a credit union registered under the Credit Unions Ordinance (Cap. 119);
- a company, where such deposit is secured by a mortgage, or charge, registered or to be registered under the Companies Ordinance (Cap. 32);
- a person bona fide carrying on insurance business where such deposit is taken in the ordinary course of such business;
- a person bona fide operating a superannuation or provident fund where such deposit is taken for the purposes of such fund;
- a public utility company specified in Schedule 3 to the Inland Revenue Ordinance (Cap. 112) where such deposit is taken from a consumer;
- an employer where such deposit is taken from a bona fide employee;
- a solicitor, where such deposit is taken from a client, or as a stakeholder, in the ordinary course of his practice;
- a corporation who is licensed to carry on a business in dealing in securities, dealing in futures contracts, leveraged foreign exchange trading or securities margin financing under Part V of the SFO where rules made under section 149 of the SFO apply to such deposit;
- a mutual fund or unit trust authorized as a collective investment scheme under section 104 of the SFO;
- a person authorized under Part III of the SFO to provide automated trading services (ATS) as defined in Part 2 of Schedule 5 of the SFO, where such deposit is provided as security in relation to a transaction referred to in paragraph (c) of that definition;
- a recognized clearing house within the meaning of section 1 of Part 1 of Schedule 1 of the SFO, where such deposit is provided as security in relation to a market contract within the meaning of that section; or
- the Exchange Fund established by the Exchange Fund Ordinance.

3.55 In addition, the Banking Ordinance further expands the list to exclude taking of deposits from any of the following:[20]

- an authorized institution;
- a bank incorporated outside Hong Kong that is not an authorized institution;
- a money lender licensed under the Money Lenders Ordinance (Cap. 163) in the ordinary course of his business as a money lender; or
- a pawnbroker licensed under the Pawnbrokers Ordinance (Cap. 166) in the ordinary course of his business as a pawnbroker.

3.56 Further, advertising etc of deposit-taking to the public is prohibited, unless the

---

[20] BO s 3(2).

advertisement is for deposit-taking at an authorized institution[21] and to the extent that section 103(1) of the SFO (concerning offers to the public of certain investments) does not apply.[22]

Beyond these formal standards and exclusions, most regulation directed at individual deposit-taking flows from the CBP under the authority of the HKAB and to some extent the HKMA. **3.57**

Cheques and other payment products and services

Cheques

The Bills of Exchange Ordinance (Cap. 19) addresses bills of exchange, cheques, and promissory notes. It comprises 102 sections and one schedule, and addresses the following in five parts: (1) preliminary provisions (sections 1 and 2); (2) bills of exchange (sections 3 to 72); (3) cheques on a banker (sections 73 to 88); (4) promissory notes (sections 89 to 95); and (5) supplementary matters (sections 96 to 102). The schedule includes the form of protect which may be used when the services of a notary cannot be obtained. **3.58**

Stored value cards

In addition to cheques, section 14A of the Banking Ordinance addresses stored value cards, specifically limiting issuance or facilitation of the issuance of multi-purpose (not single purpose) stored value card to authorized institutions. **3.59**

Other payments services and products

Other payment services and products are generally dealt with via the rules of the relevant system (discussed in Chapter 2), established under the Clearing and Settlement Systems Ordinance and under the supervision of the HKMA. Where a product does not fall within any of the above categories, it will be governed solely by the underlying private law framework. **3.60**

Lending

Lending is not included in the definition of banking business in Hong Kong. However, lending clearly is one of the major businesses of banks and one of the major financial products available in Hong Kong. As a result, lending and loan products are available from a range of sources other than banks in Hong Kong. **3.61**

Lending by banks

While not specifically covered as banking business, lending activities of authorized institutions are nonetheless regulated or constrained in many ways, as **3.62**

---

[21] BO s 92(1).   [22] BO s 92(2).

discussed in the context of this chapter's discussion of regulation of banking intermediaries below. These include limitations of single obligor exposures to 25 per cent of the authorized institution's capital base under section 81 of the Banking Ordinance. However, specific risks are excluded including:

- any financial exposure to other authorized institutions;
- any financial exposure to the extent to which it is secured by a cash deposit, a guarantee, another undertaking which, in the opinion of the HKMA, is similar to a guarantee, securities issued, or guaranteed, by the central government or the central bank of any Tier 1 country, or covered by a letter of comfort, where such cash deposit, guarantee, other undertaking, securities, or letter of comfort, as the case may be, is accepted by the HKMA;
- any financial exposure acquired by the purchase of bills of exchange or documents of title to goods where the holder of such bills or documents is entitled to payment outside Hong Kong for goods exported from Hong Kong;
- any advances, loans, and credit facilities made against any such bills or documents;
- any financial exposure to the government;
- any financial exposure to any other government, except a government which is, in the opinion of the HKMA, one that should not be accepted for the purposes of this section;
- any financial exposure to a bank incorporated outside Hong Kong which is not an authorized institution where any such bank is, in the opinion of the HKMA, adequately supervised by the relevant banking supervisory authority;
- any share capital or debt securities held as security for facilities granted by the institution or, acquired by it in the course of the satisfaction of debts due to it;
- any financial exposure acquired under an underwriting or sub-underwriting contract;
- any indemnity given by the institution to a person to protect that person against any damages which may be incurred by the person as a result of the person registering a transfer of shares where certain requirements are met;
- any financial exposure to a multilateral development bank;
- any financial exposure to the Housing Authority, within the meaning of the Housing Ordinance (Cap. 283), arising from guarantees the Housing Authority gives for the purposes of the Home Ownership Scheme or Private Sector Participation Scheme;
- any financial exposure to the Hong Kong Mortgage Corporation Limited (HKMC) arising from the obligations placed upon it for the purposes of the Mortgage Insurance Programme;

- any financial exposure to the extent to which it has been written off, or to which specific provision has been made for it, in the books of the institution; or

- any financial exposure to the HKMC or any company that issues mortgage-backed securities in connection with or arising from the obligations placed upon the company for the purposes of the Guaranteed Mortgage-Backed Pass-Through Securitisation Programme set up by the HKMC.

This largely follows international practice.

3.63 In addition, all share capital and debt securities acquired by an authorized institution in the course of the satisfaction of debts due to it shall be disposed of at the earliest suitable opportunity, and in any event not later than 18 months after the acquisition thereof, or within such further period as the HKMA approves in writing, and subject to such conditions as it may think proper to attach thereto, in any particular case.[23]

Lending by non-banks

3.64 Under the Pawnbrokers Ordinance (Cap. 166), a 'pawnbroker' is defined as someone engaging in the business of advancing on interest or for the expectation of profit, gain, or reward, any sum of money on the security of goods taken in pawn.[24] It is an offence to carry on such business without a licence,[25] which is obtained from the Commissioner of Police.[26] However, schedule 1 of the Ordinance limits the maximum amount of any loan to which this licensing requirements applies to HK$ 50,000 (US$ 6,425), thus limiting its impact on most otherwise covered financial business in Hong Kong.

3.65 More important is money lending. Under the Money Lenders Ordinance (Cap. 163), a 'money lender' is any party whose business is that of making loans or who advertises, announces, or otherwise holds themselves out as carrying on such business.[27] Anyone engaging in such business must be licensed by the Registrar of Money Lenders[28] and is subject to a range of restrictions on the conduct of such business, including interest rates, information requirements, etc.

3.66 This Ordinance, however, does not apply to authorized institutions under the Banking Ordinance or loans to authorized institutions.[29] In addition, the following are exempted under schedule 1: (1) any subsidiary of an authorized institution under the Banking Ordinance; (2) cooperative societies under the Cooperative Societies Ordinance (Cap. 33); (3) trade unions registered under

---

[23] BO s 81(7).   [24] Pawnbrokers Ordinance, s 2.   [25] Pawnbrokers Ordinance, s 4.
[26] Pawnbrokers Ordinance, s 5.   [27] MLO s 2.   [28] MLO s 4.   [29] MLO s 3.

the Trade Unions Ordinance (Cap. 332); (4) authorized insurers under the ICO; (5) the University Grants Committee; (6) banks incorporated outside Hong Kong carrying out banking business in its own jurisdiction under the supervision of an approved supervisor by the HKMA; (7) members of the International Union of Investment Insurers ('The Berne Union') established by national governments for financing or guaranteeing exports; and (8) licensed corporations for securities margin financing or securities business under the SFO.

3.67   Further, a range of loans are also exempted under Part 2 of schedule 1, including: (1) loans by employers to employees; (2) secured lending registered under the Companies Ordinance; (3) loans made by companies under bona fide credit-card schemes; (4) loans for purchase or refinancing of real property; (5) loans made not in the ordinary course of business; (6) loans by licensed pawnbrokers; (7) loans made by statutory bodies within their powers; (7) loans made from funds established by the Legislative Council or under an Ordinance or from any superannuation or provident fund; (8) loans from companies to their subsidiaries; (9) loans for exports or imports of good or services to or from Hong Kong; (10) loans made to companies with paid up share capital of not less than HK$ 1,000,000 (US$ 128,500) or equivalent; and (11) loans involving issue of company securities registered under the Companies Ordinance or listed on an exchange.

Secured lending

3.68   As a general matter, secured lending to companies is governed by the Companies Ordinance. Secured lending on the basis of real property is governed by a variety of property related ordinances.

Other banking products and services

Credit cards

3.69   As a general matter, credit card business by authorized institutions is addressed by the Code of Banking Practice. At the same time, credit card business by non-authorized institutions is not prohibited and subject to the general regulatory framework for lending by non-banks discussed above.

Trusts and trustee services

3.70   The law relating to trusts is generally similar to that in other common law jurisdictions. In addition to common law, the major legislation dealing with trusts and trustee business is the Trustee Ordinance (Cap. 29). The Trustee Ordinance comprises 109 sections and two schedules. It is divided into nine parts, addressing the following issues: (1) preliminary matters (sections 1 to 3); (2) investments (sections 4 to 12); (3) general powers of trustees and personal representatives (sections 13 to 35); (4) appointment and discharge of trustees (sections 36 to 41); (5) powers of the court (sections 42 to 62); (6) the Judicial Trustee (sections 63 to 65); (7) the Official Trustee (sections 66 to 76); (8) trust companies (sections 77 to 108); and (9) general provisions (section 109). The schedules deal with respectively: (1) fees to be paid by trust companies to the Registrar of Companies; and (2) authorized investments. The Trustee Ordinance is supported by two pieces of subsidiary legislation: (1) Administration of Trust Funds Rules (Cap. 29A); and (2) Judicial Trustee Rules (Cap. 29B)

Money brokers

Anyone engaging in the business of money broking must be authorized by the HKMA as a 'money broker' under Part XXA of the Banking Ordinance. Money broking is carrying on the business in, to or from Hong Kong of negotiating, arranging, or facilitating agreements between other persons in respect of deposit-making, or purchase or sale of currency (whether for immediate or future delivery). The definition excludes such activities by authorized institutions under the Banking Ordinance.   **3.71**

Money changers

Money changing—the business of exchanging currencies in Hong Kong—is subject to the Money Changers Ordinance (Cap. 34). The Money Changers Ordinance comprises 11 sections and three schedules (addressing, respectively, transaction notes, permitted statements, and prescribed currencies). Money changers do not have to be licensed, registered, etc. The MCO does not apply to authorized institutions, hotel services, or transactions exceeding HK$ 100,000 (US$ 12,850) or equivalent.   **3.72**

(2) *Securities and related financial products*

Schedule 1 of the SFO defines 'financial product' as meaning any securities, futures contract, collective investment scheme, or leveraged foreign exchange contract. It also provides an extensive definition of the term 'securities' which includes not only shares, stocks, debentures, loan stocks, funds, bonds, or notes issued by a body (whether incorporated or unincorporated) but also includes any rights, options, interests in the same and any other instruments commonly known as securities. The Financial Secretary may also specify certain interests and rights, etc to be regarded as securities.[30]   **3.73**

However, the term 'securities' does not include shares or debentures of a   **3.74**

---

[30] SFO s 392.

company that is a private company within the meaning of section 29 of the Companies Ordinance (Cap. 32),[31] interests in collective investment schemes falling under the MPF regime[32] or occupational retirement regime,[33] certain classes of insurance contracts,[34] bills of exchange,[35] and various other items including certain partnership interests, negotiable certificates, non-negotiable debentures, and such rights or interests as may be specified by the Financial Secretary.[36]

3.75 Futures and leveraged foreign exchange are dealt with further in Chapter 5; collective investment schemes are dealt with below.

General framework

3.76 As a general matter, securities activities have traditionally been largely matters of private contract, subject to the regulatory requirements of the Companies Ordinance for company securities and those of the relevant exchange for listed securities. This traditional framework has been much modified in the past fifteen years to the extent that now most securities activities require licensing under the SFO. Specifically, under the SFO, any person dealing in securities or commodities in Hong Kong has to be licensed by the SFC; licensing as an intermediary by the SFC therefore is in effect a prerequisite to obtaining any trading rights to be granted by HKEx, which may impose additional requirements for persons seeking access to its markets.

3.77 The ordinance defines nine types of 'regulated activities' which are subject to licensing,[37] as follows: (1) dealing in securities (Type 1); (2) dealing in futures contracts (Type 2); (3) leveraged foreign exchange trading (Type 3); (4) advising on securities (Type 4); (5) advising on futures contracts (Type 5); (6) advising on corporate finance (Type 6); (7) providing automated trading services (Type 7); (8) securities margin financing (Type 8); and (9) asset management (Type 9).

3.78 As with banking, these activities largely comprise regulated securities and futures business in Hong Kong. In addition, schedule 5 of the SFO includes a number of exceptions to this general licensing requirement, the most relevant of which are, first, incidental services provided by certain professionals such as lawyers and accountants, and second, advice given to wholly owned group companies.

---

[31] This includes private company debentures linked to other public companies, commonly used in structured notes and thus avoiding the SFO. These issues are currently being reviewed by the SFC and are likely to be brought within the SFO in the near future.
[32] ie, registered schemes as defined in MPFO s 2(1), or its constituent fund as defined in Mandatory Provident Fund Schemes (General) Regulation (Cap. 485A), s 2.
[33] See ORSO s 2(1). [34] As specified in ICO, sch 1.
[35] As defined in Bills of Exchange Ordinance (Cap. 19), s 3.
[36] Pursuant to SFO s 392. [37] SFO, sch 5.

Each of these types of activities is significant in determining whether a given **3.79** form of securities business or product brings with it consequent licensing obligations and related requirements (discussed in detail below). If licensing is not required, then the securities product or service will generally be governed by the common law and traditional private law statutory framework.

Type 1: Dealing in securities

Under Part 1 of schedule 5 of the SFO, 'dealing in securities' is defined as **3.80** making or offering to make an agreement, or inducing or attempting to induce another to enter into or to offer to enter into an agreement for or with a view to acquiring, disposing of, subscribing for, or underwriting securities; and the purpose or pretended purpose of which is to secure a profit to any of the parties from the yield of securities or by reference to fluctuations in the value of securities.

There are a wide range of exceptions, including where the party is a recognized **3.81** exchange company operating a stock market, a recognized clearing house, an authorized ATS provider, or performs the act through a licensed or registered securities dealer, is or acts for a professional investor, enters into a contract on a recognized exchange, issues a lawful prospectus or advertisement etc, or is a trust company acting for a collective investment scheme acting lawfully.

Type 2: Dealing in futures

Under Part 1 of schedule 5 of the SFO, 'dealing in futures contracts' is defined **3.82** as making, offering, inducing or attempting to induce another to make an agreement to enter into, acquire, or dispose of a futures contract. Once again, there are a wide range of exceptions, including recognized clearing houses, acts performed through licensed or registered futures dealers, acts through recognized exchanges, or as a professional investor or agent therefor.

Type 3: Leveraged foreign exchange trading

Under Part 1 of schedule 5 of the SFO, 'leveraged foreign exchange trading' is **3.83** defined as the act of entering into, offering to enter into, or inducing or attempting to induce another to enter into or to offer to enter into, a leveraged foreign exchange contract or arrangement to enter into a leveraged foreign exchange contract. It also extends to providing financial accommodation to facilitate foreign exchange trading or arranging the same.

Again, there is a wide range of exceptions, including transactions wholly refer- **3.84** able to property other than currency or employment, corporations not in the business of dealing in currency and hedging currency exchange risks with another corporation, an exchange transaction under the Money Changers Ordinance (Cap. 34), arranged by an approved money broker and all parties are corporations or registered limited partnerships under the the Limited Partnerships Ordinance (Cap 37), for insurance business by an authorized insurer, through a recognized exchange, arranged by a central bank, as an interest in an authorized collective investment scheme, by an authorized institution, or is a transaction wholly incidental to debt securities transactions.

3.85   A 'leveraged foreign exchange contract' is a contract or arrangement the effect of which is that one party agrees or undertakes: to make an adjustment between himself and the other party or another according to whether a currency is worth more or less (as the case may be) in relation to another currency; pay an amount of money or to deliver a quantity of any commodity determined or to be determined by reference to the change in value of a currency in relation to another currency to the other party or another person; or deliver to the other party or another person at an agreed future time an agreed amount of currency at an agreed consideration.

3.86   'Foreign exchange trading' means entering into, offering to enter into, or inducing or attempting to induce another to enter into or to offer to enter into, a contract or arrangement whereby a party undertakes to exchange currency with another person, deliver an amount of foreign currency to another person, or credit the account of another person with an amount of foreign currency. It excludes generally the same categories as 'leveraged foreign exchange trading'.

3.87   These are dealt with further in Chapter 5.

Type 4: Advising on securities

3.88   Under Part 1 of schedule 5 of the SFO, 'advising on securities' is defined as giving advice on securities or issuing securities analyses or reports. In relation to analyses or reports, there are a range of exceptions including corporations giving such to its wholly owned subsidiaries or its parent holding company and sister companies, authorized institutions and their representatives, solicitors, accountants, and barristers in the context of their practice, trust companies giving advice within the context of their duties under the Trustee Ordinance (Cap. 29), and public media.

3.89   As such, this is an area where those not generally viewing themselves as needing to be licensed by the SFC may be at risk.

Type 5: Advising on futures contracts

3.90   Under Part 1 of schedule 5 of the SFO, 'advising on futures contracts' means giving advice on futures contracts or issuing analyses or reports related to futures contracts, subject to similar exceptions to Type 4 activities.

3.91   This is dealt with further in Chapter 5.

Type 6: Advising on corporate finance

Under Part 1 of schedule 5 of the SFO, 'advising on corporate finance' is defined as giving advice: **3.92**

- concerning compliance with or in respect of rules and codes made under the SFO governing the listing of securities;

- concerning any offer to acquire from or dispose of securities to the public, or acceptance of any offer given generally to holders of securities or a class of securities; and

- to a listed corporation or public company or a subsidiary of the corporation or company, or to its officers or shareholders, concerning corporate restructuring in respect of securities (including the issue, cancellation, or variation of any rights attaching to any securities).

The definition excludes advice given by a corporation to its corporate group, registered authorized institutions and their registered employees, solicitors, barristers, and accountants in the course of their practices, trust companies discharging their duties under the Trust Companies Ordinance, and public media. **3.93**

Type 7: Providing automated trading services

Under Part 1 of schedule 5 of the SFO, 'automated trading services' are defined as services provided by means of electronic facilities whereby: **3.94**

- offers to sell or purchase securities or futures contracts are regularly made or accepted in a way that forms or results in a binding transaction in accordance with established methods, including any method commonly used by a stock market or futures market;

- persons are regularly introduced, or identified to other persons in order that they may negotiate or conclude, or with the reasonable expectation that they will negotiate or conclude sales or purchases of securities or futures contracts in a way that forms or results in a binding transaction in accordance with established methods, including any method commonly used by a stock market or futures market; or

- novation, clearance, settlement, or guarantee of these transactions.

The definition excludes facilities provided by a recognized exchange companies and recognized clearing houses, and services provided by government corporations. **3.95**

Type 8: Securities margin financing

Under Part 1 of schedule 5 of the SFO, 'securities margin financing' is defined as providing financial accommodation in order to facilitate the acquisition of **3.96** securities listed on any stock market or their continued holding, whether or not those or other securities are pledged as security. The definition excludes provision of financial accommodation:

- that forms part of an arrangement to underwrite or sub-underwrite securities;
- to facilitate an acquisition of securities in accordance with the term of a prospectus, regardless of whether the offer of securities is made in Hong Kong or elsewhere;
- by a party licensed or registered for Type 1 regulated activity in order to facilitate acquisitions or holdings of securities by the person for his client;
- by an open-ended investment fund financing investments in its own funds;
- by an authorized financial institution for the purpose of facilitating acquisitions or holdings of securities by the AI's clients;
- by an individual to a company in which he holds 10 per cent or more of its issued share capital to facilitate acquisitions or holdings of securities; or
- by an intermediary by way of effecting an introduction between a person and a related corporation of the intermediary in order that the corporation may provide the person with financial accommodation.

Type 9: Asset management

3.97   Under Part 1 of schedule 5 of the SFO, 'asset management' is defined as providing a service of managing a portfolio of securities or futures contracts for another. It excludes intragroup provision of such services, registered authorized institutions and their registered employees, solicitors, barristers, and accountants in the course of their practices, and trust companies discharging their duties under the Trustee Ordinance.

Offers of investment products

3.98   Section 103(1) of the SFO contains a general prohibition on public offers of investment unless that offer is authorized by the SFC. A public offer of investment is an invitation, advertisement, or document which invites the public to enter into an agreement to acquire or dispose of securities, enter into a regulated investment agreement,[38] or acquire an interest in or participate in a collective investment scheme.[39] However, a number of exemptions are available including relating to prospectuses[40] and advertisements etc issued by or on behalf of

---

[38] *Regulated investment agreement:* an agreement whose purpose is to provide profits to the involved parties, calculated by reference to changes in the value of property, not including an interest in a collective investment scheme (SFO, sch 1).

[39] *Collective investment scheme:* a pool of several investors' funds that obtains economies of scale and spreads of investment beyond the reach of individual investors (SFO, sch 1).

[40] See Chapter 4 for the regulatory provisions concerning prospectuses.

persons licensed or registered to engage in Type 1, Type 4, or Type 6[41] regulated activities (or Type 2 or Type 5 licences in respect of futures contracts, or Type 3 in respect of leveraged foreign exchange contracts), authorized financial institutions, or by a corporation to its shareholders, creditors, or employees in respect of its securities.[42]

Authorization of offers on investment

According to section 105(1) of the SFO the SFC can authorize investment offers upon application.

3.99

Revocation of authorization

Under section 106 of the SFO, the SFC can revoke an authorization if, among others, the applicants have provided false or misleading information or the revocation is in the interest of the investing public.

3.100

Offences

Under section 107 of the SFO it is an offence to fraudulently or recklessly misrepresent any offer on investment for the purpose of inducing people to enter into any kind of investment agreement. Fraudulent and reckless misrepresentation includes false, misleading, or deceptive information with respect to the investment product and unjustified forecasts on the potential of the product. On conviction, the offender is liable to a fine of HK$ 1 million (US$ 128,500) and to imprisonment for seven years.

3.101

According to section 109 of the SFO it is also an offence to advertise unlicensed regulated activity. Such illegal advertisement consists of issuing offers of conducting regulated activity on behalf of a person who holds himself out as being properly licensed to carry out that activity.[43]

3.102

Civil liability

Section 108(1) of the SFO provides for any person who suffered material loss due to fraudulent, reckless, or negligent misrepresentation with respect to an investment product, to claim compensation from the product supplier.

3.103

Equity

Offerings of shares and listing are dealt with in Chapter 4.

3.104

---

[41] See below for a description of the different types of licences.
[42] SFO s 103(2).   [43] YK Kwan, *A Guide to the Securities and Futures Ordinance*, p 35.

Debt

3.105 Debt securities may be listed on the SEHK under the Listing Rules. As with markets elsewhere, this is largely a function of convention and has little impact on investor or issuer behaviour since issuance and trading typically take place without relation to the exchange, and issuer disclosure is almost always linked to the primary share listing.

Financial derivatives

3.106 Financial derivatives and related matters are addressed in Chapter 5.

Securitization

3.107 Currently, there are really no legal and regulatory barriers that would block the development of securitization markets in Hong Kong. The legal framework is very similar to that of the UK; the regulatory environment is quite securitization friendly; tax neutrality is achievable; and intermediaries such as rating agencies, legal counsel, and accounting firms are all experienced in securitization. The barriers, if any, are somewhat 'self imposed' by issuers and investors. Some issuers might not be willing to pay any premium or do extra work to explore securitization as an alternative source of funding to bank financing.

3.108 One issue of concern involves accounting treatment. In 2004 the HKSAR government proposed the Companies (Amendment) Bill 2004, which has stirred debate between the asset securitization professionals in the financial markets and the government. In particular the proposed Bill entrenches the definition of 'subsidiary' and that this may be detrimental to the creation of asset backed securities (ABS) in Hong Kong.

3.109 There are three accounting issues that are relevant for securitization, namely:

- IAS 27: Consolidated Financial Statements and Accounting for Investments in Subsidiaries;
- SIC 12: Standing Interpretation Committee on Consolidation of Special Purpose Entities; and
- IAS 39: Financial Instruments: Recognition and Measurement.

3.110 An important concern arising out of IAS 27 and SIC 12 in the securitization industry is the requirement to consolidate Special Purpose Entities (SPEs) into the parent company's financial statements. According to the regulations of consolidation in many jurisdictions, majority ownership such as more than 50 per cent of the voting rights of the SPE automatically implies that it should be consolidated with its parent company.

3.111 According to IAS 27 and SIC 12, however, ownership is neither sufficient nor necessary to determine the consolidation of SPEs. Rather, it is 'control' of the entity that counts. IAS 27 defines control as 'the power to govern the financial and operating policies of an enterprise so as to obtain benefits from its activities', whereas SIC 12 defines control as 'contributing to or benefiting from the risks and the rewards' of the SPE.

The Hong Kong Mortgage Corporation and the Hong Kong Capital Markets Association argued that the proposed Companies (Amendment) Bill 2004 that entrenches the definition of subsidiary by these 'control' rules will challenge the off-balance sheet objective of a typical securitization, and as a result, it will inhibit the growth of the ABS market. In particular, the UK adopted the 'linked-presentation method' for group accounts whereas the US adopted the 'carve-out' method from the definition of 'subsidiary' for asset securitization SPEs similar to the concept of the Qualification SPE available under the US accounting rules. It is argued that this will put Hong Kong in a disadvantaged position against other markets for ABS issues in the region such as Australia and Japan.[44] **3.112**

There are four fundamental questions that are being addressed, given all the opinions contained in the various submissions to the Hong Kong Legislative Council, and government's responses: **3.113**

- What is the expected impact of the meaning of 'subsidiary' in the Companies (Amendment) Bill 2004 on the asset-securitization market in Hong Kong?

- Should Hong Kong adopt instead the 'linked presentation method' for group accounts?

---

[44] It is informative to revisit here the often-stated motives for securitizing assets. The motivations for securitization include selling risks, access to cheaper funding, diversifying funding sources, optimizing balance sheets, and engaging in regulatory and or tax arbitrage. From the point of view of the ABS issuer, securitization may be viewed as a sale or a financing. Since securitization has features of both, it can reflect the many motivations of the issuer such as financial, tax, accounting, and even strategic reasons. If the ABS originator's motive for securitization is to release capital tied up in assets for re-application, it is necessary to make sure that the assets that are to be sold to the SPE represents a 'true sale' and that the ABS originator has sold the risks with the assets. In this case, consolidation of the SPE is not relevant, because ownership and control of the assets passed to the SPE. If the ABS originator, however, regards the transaction as a mechanism to release capital tied up in assets in order to turn over the capital without relinquishing control over the assets, it may be that no 'true sale' has taken place. If a jurisdiction allows these assets to be taken off-balance sheet while some of the risks still rest with the company, it is clear that such a balance sheet is not representative. For many years this 'true sale' nature of ABS has been a subject of debate, and it has cast light upon the reasons for pursuing off-balance sheet transactions. The reasons are typically seen to include (1) window-dressing a firm's balance sheet and financial ratios, (2) enhancing the firm's capital ratio so as to increase its borrowing capacity, and (3) hiding risky assets from investors who otherwise would attach a much larger discount to the firm's market value. If one accepts the modest view of the efficient markets hypothesis, all these reasons do not survive scrutiny—indeed, the common advice that no smart investor should believe a balance sheet is damning, and one that regulators should indeed lament.

- Should the Companies (Amendment) Bill 2004 be deferred until the International Accounting Standards Board (IASB) has completed its review of IAS 27 regarding whether or not the revisions to the 'control' model for subsidiaries should also be applied to SPEs?

- What is the case for providing a 'carve-out' from the definition of 'subsidiary' for asset securitization SPEs similar to the concept of the Qualification SPE available under the US accounting rules?

3.114 The questions are interrelated.[45] To commence, two aspects of the proposed amendments to company legislation seem to be in conflict, namely what 'subsidiary' means in general, on the one hand; and what the notion of a 'subsidiary' may encompass in the financial sector when SPEs and securitization may be considered on the other. The overriding context for all the questions are in the final analysis a matter of what attitudes prevail in government towards the corporate regulatory environment (including legislation that relates to corporate governance, financial reporting, etc); and then also financial sector regulation.

3.115 First, with respect to the corporate regulatory environment, few (if indeed any) arguments can be sustained which attempt to present the case that ultimately 'control' is inappropriate as a test to define what a subsidiary is and what not. In our view, any other way of treating subsidiaries would be regressive and against world opinion, because any other treatment of subsidiaries would be an attempt to misrepresent the status of the controlling business. Our position is thus entirely in accord with that of the government, which is attempting to align the Hong Kong meaning of 'subsidiary' in the Companies Ordinance more closely with that of IAS. It would seem unnecessary to present all the corporate governance reasons in support of this view again in this letter—in all, it is about disclosure, information, and a regulatory environment that attempts to facilitate information, and not obfuscation.

3.116 Second, a point of conflict arises in the Hong Kong financial sector about the meaning that the IAS treatment of 'subsidiary'. In principle, it appears if the Hong Kong Mortgage Corporation, supported by the Hong Kong Capital Markets Association, argues that the proposed requirement to consolidate subsidiaries (in this context SPEs used to create Asset Backed Securities) may create the situation where other jurisdictions, for example Singapore or Australia, may provide financial sector businesses with the opportunity to engage in regulatory arbitrage, because these jurisdictions may allow companies to move assets off-balance sheet in the creation of ABS in those jurisdictions. In this case it is

---

[45] See MKS Tse & F Pretorius, Opinions submitted to the Hong Kong Legislative Council on 'Companies (Amendment) Bill 2004—LC Paper No. CB(1) 938/04–05(06)' for more discussion regarding issues related to the four questions.

suggested that Hong Kong will lose securitization business, and so the development of its financial markets will suffer. There can be no doubt that the continued development of the Hong Kong capital markets is highly desirable, particularly with the momentum that Hong Kong has already achieved, the effort that has gone into this over the last decade or more, and the huge potential that exists for raising capital for the development of the PRC.

There is a view of financial innovation which defines it as the creation of **3.117** financial products that both suppliers and users of funds may demand, products with varying functional attributes to satisfy investment, financing, and risk management preferences. Note that this contrasts with a school of thought held in many circles (academe included) that 'financial innovation' is merely the exploitation of loopholes in legislation in a jurisdiction, or engaging in regulatory arbitrage between jurisdictions, or 'engineering' other mechanisms to take advantage of legal differences between jurisdictions.

It is here where convergence is seen between the proposed amendments to **3.118** corporate legislation and the effect it may have on SPEs in the financial sector: if Hong Kong is concerned about corporate governance matters, including financial reporting that purports to be clear and transparent, then this is to some extent contradicted by facilitating opportunities to create off-balance sheet finance opportunities.

(3) Insurance

As a general matter, insurance products (retail, wholesale, reinsurance) are governed by the common law framework, supplemented by the Marine Insurance Ordinance (Cap. 329).[46] In addition, firms engaging in insurance business must be authorized and regulated by the OCI (except authorized institutions under the Banking Ordinance, ie banks, DTCs, and RLBs). **3.119**

Under the ICO, it is an offence to engage in insurance business in or from Hong **3.120** Kong unless authorized by the OCI.[47] Importantly, any contract of insurance (except reinsurance) entered into in violation of this requirement will be void or enforceable only against the insurer.[48]

'Insurance business' is defined largely via the first schedule of the ICO. Part 2 of **3.121** the first schedule of the ICO lists the classes of 'long-term business', including: (1) life and annuity (class A); (2) marriage and birth (class B); (3) linked

---

[46] Only some insurance products such as 'investment-linked assurance schemes' and 'pooled retirement funds' have to be approved by the SFC. For details see section 104 of the SFO and the Code of Investment-Linked Assurance Schemes from April 2003.
[47] ICO s 6.   [48] ICO s 6A.

long-term (class C); (4) permanent health (class D); (5) tontines (class E); (6) capital redemption (class F); and (7) retirement scheme management (categories I–III, classes G-I). Part 3 of the first schedule of the ICO lists the classes of 'general business', including: (1) accident (class 1); (2) sickness (class 2); (3) land vehicles (class 3); (4) railway rolling stock (class 4); (5) aircraft (class 5); (6) ships (class 6); (7) goods in transit (class 7); (8) fire and natural forces (class 8); (9) damage to property (class 9); (10) motor vehicle liability (class 10); (11) aircraft liability (class 11); (12) liability for ships (class 12); (13) general liability (class 13); (14) credit (class 14); (15) suretyship (class 15); (16) miscellaneous financial loss (class 16); and (17) legal expenses (class 17).

3.122 It can be seen therefore that the coverage of insurance business (and thereby authorization and related requirements) is very broad, with the exception of reinsurance business which is generally left to contract.

(4) Funds and related products and services

3.123 The basic framework for investment funds and related products is the SFO, supplemented by subsidiary legislation, the general SFC Code on Unit Trusts and Mutual Funds, and specific codes on real estate investment trusts (REITs) and other products.

Funds: Collective investment schemes

3.124 Under section 104(1) of the SFO any public offer relating to participation in a collective investment scheme such as unit trusts and mutual funds must be individually authorized by the SFC.

3.125 This general requirement is supplemented by the SFC Code on Unit Trusts and Mutual Funds. This Code[49] provides guidance in relation to the authorization of mutual fund corporations or unit trusts as a specific form of collective investment scheme. Similar to other codes and guidelines, it does not have the force of law. The Code is divided into three Parts ((1) general matters; (2) authorization requirements; and (3) post-authorization requirements) and ten appendices. General matters address: (1) authorization procedures; (2) administrative arrangements; and (3) interpretation. Authorization requirements include: (1) trustee/custodian; (2) management company and auditor; (3) operational requirements; (4) investment: core requirements; (5) specialized schemes; and (6) additional requirements for non-Hong Kong based schemes. The post-authorization requirements include: (1) operational matters; and (2) documentation and reporting. The nine appendices address: (1) recognized

---

[49] Made under s 104(1) SFO.

jurisdiction schemes; (2) inspection regimes; (3) application form; (4) information to be disclosed in the offering document; (5) contents of the 'constitutive documents'; (6) contents of financial reports; (7) advertising guidelines; (8) guidelines for the review of internal controls and systems of trustees/custodians; (9) guidelines on hedge funds reporting requirements; and (10) guidelines for regulating index-tracking exchange-traded funds.

Further, the SFC has also issued a Guidance Note for Persons Advertising or   **3.126**
Offering Collective Investment Schemes on the Internet, which clarifies the
regulatory requirements concerning collective investment schemes (CIS) activities on the internet, reflecting the existing regulatory framework.

Hedge funds

At present, there are a number of consultations in progress concerning the   **3.127**
treatment of hedge funds that seek to raise funds from investors in Hong Kong.

Real estate investment trusts (REITs)

In order to support the development of REITs in Hong Kong, the SFC has   **3.128**
issued a Code on Real Estate Investment Trusts. This Code[50] establishes guidelines for the authorization of REITs as a specific form of collective investment scheme. Similar to other codes and guidelines, it does not have the force of law but management companies, trustees and their agents or delegates are expected to comply with the spirit of its principles. The Code is based on related principles of IOSCO, and comprises ten principles addressing respectively: (1) clarity of legal form and ownership structure; (2) effective oversight by trustee; (3) eligible management company; (4) delegation of management functions; (5) compliance with relevant requirements; (6) good governance and avoidance of conflicts of interest; (7) valuation of the scheme; (8) investment and borrowing limitations; (9) management fees and investor rights; and (10) marketing and disclosure.

MPF and ORSO products

Overall, MPF and ORSO products in Hong Kong are subject to a detailed and   **3.129**
comprehensive regulatory framework, under the MPFO and the ORSO. In fact, this is probably the most detailed and comprehensive system of product regulation in Hong Kong at present. Unfortunately, the framework may be overly comprehensive and detailed for the types of products being addressed, thereby increasing costs and decreasing attractiveness to investors.

---

[50] Made under s 104(1) SFO.

3.130 In regard to overlaps of jurisdiction between the SFC and MPFA, the SFC has issued a Code on MPF Products. This Code[51] provides guidance in relation to the authorization of MPF schemes and pooled investment funds as specific forms of collective investment schemes. While the MPFA is the primary regulator for MPF schemes, the SFC is also involved to the extent that the offering documents and marketing materials of these products are required to be authorized (along with their investment managers) by the SF prior to their issue or publication in Hong Kong. Similar to other codes and guidelines, it does not have the force of law but compliance is expected with its spirit. The Code is divided into three Parts ((1) general matters; (2) authorization requirements; and (3) post-authorization requirements) and four appendices. General matters address: (1) authorization matters; (2) administrative arrangements; and (3) interpretation. Authorization requirements include: (1) application procedures; (2) offering document; (3) investment manager; and (4) operational requirements. The four appendices address: (1) profile of new investment manager or investment management group; (2) compliance checklist; (3) acceptable inspection regimes; and (4) advertising guidelines.

(5) Money laundering and terrorist financing

3.131 Money laundering is considered to be the financial process for hiding, disguising, or transacting with the proceeds of crime as if the funds were generated by legitimate means. In Hong Kong, money laundering is a serious criminal offence with maximum punishment up to 14 years' imprisonment and a fine of HK$ 5,000,000 (US$ 643,000). Money laundering not only allows crime to continue to exist and grow; it can also undermine the entire financial system. Very often money laundering activities induce the development of a subterranean market for business and financial transactions many of which would escape the radar screen of the regulatory bodies. The financial transactions in this subterranean market may disrupt the normal operation of the legitimate financial system.

3.132 According to the statutory definition, any transaction involving the proceeds of serious crime is money laundering.[52] Table 3.1 presents some important figures on money laundering up until the end of February 2005 since the date of enactment of the money laundering and asset confiscation laws in Hong Kong.

3.133 Anyone commits the offence of money laundering if they carry out a transaction

---

[51] Made under s 104(1) SFO.
[52] Drug Trafficking (Recovery of Proceeds) Ordinance (Cap. 405), s 25; Organized and Serious Crimes Ordinance (Cap. 455), s 25.

Table 3.1 Money laundering to end-February 2005

• Number of persons convicted of 'Money Laundering'	120
• Value of assets under restraint	HK$ 1,336 million (US$ 172 million)
• Value of assets ordered by the court to be confiscated, but not yet paid to government	HK$ 113 million (US$ 14.5 million)
• Amount confiscated and paid to the government	HK$ 387 million (US$ 49.75 million)

Source: Joint Finance Intelligence Unit 2005.

involving property, including money, in circumstances in which a reasonable person would have believed that the property was the proceeds of serious crime. Whether or not there is any attempt to hide or disguise the source of the criminal proceeds is irrelevant.

In addition to the primary ordinances addressing such issues (Prevention of Bribery Ordinance (Cap. 201); Drug Trafficking (Recovery of Proceeds) Ordinance (Cap. 405); Organized and Serious Crimes Ordinance (Cap. 455); United Nations (Anti-terrorism measures) Ordinance (Cap. 575)), all of the individual regulatory agencies have published guidance on the issues in the context of their respective scopes of responsibilities. **3.134**

C. Financial Intermediaries: Licensing and Authorization

Licensing and authorization are prerequisites for financial institutions to become established in Hong Kong, participate in financial market activity, and transact in financial services. Licensing is central to the authorities' 'gate-keeping' function in respect of the quality of financial institutions. At the same time, most licensing requirements are on-going, resulting in continuing compliance obligations. As a general matter, Hong Kong is open to foreign and domestic entry to financial services business, with foreign businesses facing largely identical requirements to domestic entrants. **3.135**

In summary, deposit-taking institutions are licensed by the HKMA, securities firms (including operators of collective investment schemes) by the SFC, insurance firms by the OCI, and MPF and ORSO schemes by the MPFA. **3.136**

(1) Banks

As discussed above and in the previous chapter, banks and banking are largely regulated by the HKMA, though to some extent in conjunction with the **3.137**

HKAB. Specifically, banks and other institutions seeking to engage in banking business are licensed ('authorized') by the HKMA under the Banking Ordinance (Cap. 155). In addition, banks must also become members of the HKAB and abide by its rules. Every licensed bank, as a condition attached to its licence, is required to become and remain a member of the HKAB.[53]

3.138 It is unlawful to carry on banking business in Hong Kong except through a bank;[54] deposit-taking is restricted to authorized institutions.[55] 'Banking business' is defined in the Banking Ordinance[56] as either or both of the following:

- receiving from the general public money on current, deposit, savings or other similar account repayable on demand or within less than a three-month period[57] or with a period of call or notice of less than that period.
- paying or collecting cheques drawn by or paid in by customers.

In addition, only authorized institutions may issue multi-purpose stored value (electronic money) cards.[58]

3.139 Any institution seeking to conduct 'banking business' must be authorized by the HKMA. Part IV of the Banking Ordinance deals with authorization of banks. Under the Banking (Amendment) Ordinance 1995, the HKMA is responsible for all authorization matters, including authorization, suspension, and revocation of all three types of authorized institutions, namely licensed banks, restricted licensed banks, and deposit-taking companies.[59]

3.140 Applications for authorization are dealt with under section 15 of the Banking Ordinance. Under section 15(1), a company which proposes to carry on (a) banking business; (b) a business of taking deposits as a deposit-taking company (DTC); or (c) a business of taking deposits as a restricted licence bank (RLB), must apply to the HKMA for authorization to carry on that business.

3.141 A 'bank' means a company which holds a valid banking licence,[60] ie one issued by the HKMA under section 16 of the Banking Ordinance. Persons other than banks authorized under the Banking Ordinance are prohibited from using the term 'bank' or 'ngan-hong', 'yin-hang' or any of its derivatives, either in English or in Chinese.[61] While exemptions are in place for RLBs to use these terms, the prohibition generally means that, for example, securities houses could not incorporate into their name a term such as 'investment bank'.

3.142 This structure gives rise to a three-tier system of deposit-taking institutions, collectively known as 'authorized institutions', but each with different restrictions imposed on their banking business activities:

---

[53] HKABO s 7.   [54] BO s 11.   [55] BO s 12.   [56] BO s 2(1).
[57] Sch 1, item 1.   [58] BO s 14A.   [59] ibid.   [60] BO s 2(1).   [61] BO s 97.

- licensed banks,
- restricted licence banks (RLBs) and
- deposit-taking companies ('DTCs).

Such institutions operate in Hong Kong as either locally incorporated com- **3.143**
panies or branches of foreign banks. Only licensed banks may operate current or
savings accounts[62] and can receive deposits of any size and maturity from the
public.[63] All licensed banks must become members of the HKAB.[64] RLBs are
principally engaged in wholesale banking and capital market activities, and may
take call, notice, or time deposits of any maturity but only in amounts of at least
HK$ 500,000 (US$ 64,250). Many DTC are owned by or associated with
banks and engage in a wide range of specialized activities, including consumer
finance, trade finance, or securities businesses, and are restricted to taking
deposits of no less than HK$ 100,000 (US$ 12,850) with original terms to
maturity of at least three months.

In addition, the Banking Ordinance provides that no person shall act as a **3.144**
money broker unless that person is approved by the HKMA as a money broker
under the Banking Ordinance. The approval criteria are set out in the
eleventh schedule to the Banking Ordinance.

Minimum criteria for authorization are included in the seventh schedule to the **3.145**
Banking Ordinance.[65] The HKMA may also issue guidelines which must be
published in the Gazette.[66]

In addition to the criteria listed below, certain additional requirements must be **3.146**
met for a full banking licence to be granted to a Hong Kong company:[67]

- It is in the opinion of the HKMA closely associated and identified with Hong
  Kong;
- It has total qualifying deposits of not less than HK$ 3 billion or an equivalent
  amount and total assets (less contra items) of not less than HK$ 4 billion or
  the equivalent; and
- It has been a DTC or RLB (or any combination thereof) for not less than
  10 continuous years.

In applying for authorization, an applicant must file the following with the **3.147**
HKMA of the Banking Ordinance:[68]

- a copy of the memorandum and articles of association or other document
  constituting the company; and

---

[62] BO ss 11, 12.   [63] BO ss 12, 14 & sch 1.   [64] HKABO s 7.
[65] BO s 16; BO, sch 7.   [66] BO s 16(10).   [67] BO, sch 7, s 13(b).
[68] Pursuant to s 15(2).

- such other documents and information as may be required by the HKMA.

This is supplemented by schedule 7 which details specific requirements.

3.148 In addition, under the HKAB Ordinance,[69] a licensed bank, if required as a condition to its authorization (which is always so conditional) must become a member of the HKAB until expelled,[70] which requires the prior approval of the HKMA,[71] or it ceases to be a licensed bank.[72]

3.149 The authorization criteria for authorized institutions (licensed banks, RLBs and DTCs) seek to ensure that only fit and proper institutions are entrusted with public deposits. The HKMA conducts periodic reviews of the authorization criteria and when necessary introduces amendments with a view to reflecting the changing needs of the regulatory environment and meeting new international standards. Under the Banking Ordinance, the HKMA is the licensing authority responsible for the authorization, suspension, and revocation of all three types of authorized institutions.[73] Decisions relating to these matters are taken on the basis of transparent and clearly defined authorization and revocation criteria set out in Schedules to the Banking Ordinance. To enhance checks and balances in the authorization procedures, the HKMA is required under the Banking Ordinance to consult the Financial Secretary on important authorization decisions, such as suspension and revocation. The Chief Executive-in-Council is the appellate body for hearing appeals against decisions made by the HKMA.[74]

Ownership structure

3.150 Only a body corporate may be authorized as a bank, RLB, or DTC.[75] The HKMA must be satisfied as to the identity of each controller of a company seeking authorization.[76]

Operating plan, systems of control, and internal organization

3.151 For all applicants, the HKMA must be satisfied:

- That the company will comply with provisions respecting limitations on loans by and interests of authorized institutions in Part XV of the Banking Ordinance;[77]
- That the company maintains and will maintain adequate provisions;[78] and
- That the company has and will continue to have adequate accounting systems and systems of internal control.[79]

3.152 For a Hong Kong incorporated company, the HKMA must be satisfied that it

---

[69] s 7.   [70] s 7(1).   [71] s 7(3).   [72] s 7(2).   [73] BO s 16.
[74] BO s 132A.   [75] BO s 16(1).   [76] BO sch 7, s 2.   [77] BO sch 7, s 8.
[78] BO sch 7, s 9.   [79] BO sch 7, s 10.

presently discloses and will continue to disclose adequate information in its accounts.[80]

Fit and proper test for directors and senior managers

In addition to its other supervisory responsibilities, the HKMA is required to **3.153** vet and approve controllers, directors, and officers of authorized institutions under the Banking Ordinance under a 'fit and proper' standard. For a Hong Kong incorporated company, the HKMA must be satisfied that each person who is, or is to be, a director, controller, or chief executive of the company is a fit and proper person to hold the particular position which he holds or is to hold.[81] HKMA approval is required for appointment of the chief executive and directors of an authorized institution incorporated in Hong Kong.[82]

In addition, the HKMA must be satisfied that the business of the company **3.154** is being, and will continue to be, carried out with integrity, prudence, the appropriate degree of professional competence, and in a manner not detrimental or likely to be detrimental to the interests of depositors or potential depositors.[83]

Initial capital and financial projections

The HKMA must be satisfied that the company has, and if it is authorized will **3.155** continue to have, adequate financial resources (whether actual or contingent) for the nature and scale of its operations.[84] In addition:[85]

- Hong Kong applicants to be licensed banks must have paid-up share capital of not less than HK$ 150 million (US$ 19,280,000) or equivalent in any other approved currency;
- Any applicant to be a DTC must have paid-up share capital of not less than HK$ 25 million (US$ 3,200,000) or the equivalent; and
- Any applicant to be an RLB must have paid-up share capital of not less than HK$ 100 million (US$ 12,850,000) or the equivalent.

Further, Hong Kong incorporated companies:[86] **3.156**

- Must have and maintain an adequate capital adequacy ratio (discussed further below); and
- Must have and continue to have adequate capital to support any market risks (discussed further below).

All applicants must maintain adequate liquidity, and maintain a liquidity ratio **3.157** which complies with the requirements (discussed further below).[87]

---

[80] BO sch 7, s 11. [81] BO sch 7, s 4. [82] BO s 71. [83] BO sch 7, s 12.
[84] BO sch 7, s 6. [85] BO sch 7, s 6. [86] BO sch 7, s 6. [87] BO sch 7, s 7.

Foreign bank access

3.158 Hong Kong now places no major barriers to overseas banks operating locally in the territory. Foreign banks seeking a banking licence in Hong Kong can in practice only enter as a branch. Foreign banks licensed after 1978 were subject for some years to restrictions on the number of branches they may have and the number of buildings from which they could operate. This has, since November 2001, been fully relaxed to permit an unlimited number of offices in an unlimited number of buildings. However, as is the case with domestic institutions, the approval of the HKMA is required for the establishment of any branch.[88]

3.159 Overseas banks which do not qualify for a full banking licence can apply for authorization to operate as a RLB or DTC in Hong Kong. Whereas RLBs may enter as a branch or subsidiary, it is the HKMA's practice only to grant DTC authorization to locally incorporated subsidiaries. The HKMA nevertheless has to be satisfied that they are soundly based institutions and subject to adequate home supervision.

3.160 In addition to requirements applicable generally to all applicants (see above), certain additional requirements must be met by foreign incorporated institutions. So far as an overseas bank is concerned, the following criteria must be met for authorization to conduct banking business in Hong Kong:[89]

- it is a bank,[90]
- in respect of which the HKMA is satisfied that is adequately supervised by the relevant banking supervisory authority.

3.161 In addition, the HKMA must be satisfied that each person who is or is to be a chief executive of the business in Hong Kong of the company, or a director, controller, or chief executive of the business of the company in the place of incorporation is a fit and proper person to hold the particular position he holds or is to hold.[91]

3.162 Further, the following requirements must be met:[92]

- Either the total assets (less contra items) of the whole banking group are more than US$ 16 billion or an equivalent amount, or in the opinion of the HKMA authorization would promote the interests of Hong Kong as an international financial centre; and
- Either there is in the opinion of the HKMA an acceptable degree of reciprocity in respect of Hong Kong incorporated banks seeking to do business in

---

[88] BO s 44.   [89] BO sch 7.   [90] As defined in BO s 46(9).   [91] BO sch 7, s 5.
[92] BO sch 7, s 13(a).

the place where the applicant is incorporated, or the place where the company is incorporated is a member of the WTO.

In addition to full banking, RLB and DTC licences, the HKMA, upon application from an overseas bank, may allow it to open a representative office in Hong Kong, provided it is satisfied that the bank is adequately supervised by authorities in its home country.[93] Such offices are not empowered to transact any banking business in Hong Kong and can only act as the agent of the parent bank. The HKMA can require any information from the bank regarding the functions and activities of a representative office.[94]   **3.163**

Initial requirements for authorization are of an on-going nature.   **3.164**

Securities activities of banks

In relation to registration of authorized institutions for purposes of undertaking securities business ('registered activities'),[95] an authorized institution must be registered with the SFC as a 'registered institution' before conducting regulated activities (except for Type 3 and Type 8 activities—discussed above). An application for registration must be lodged with the SFC which refers it to the HKMA, which in turn advises on whether the authorized institution is fit and proper. The applicant must provide two Executive Officers with sufficient authority who will supervise the conduct of regulated activities and who are fit and proper. Further, any person who carries on a regulated function must register his name and details with the HKMA and must be and remain fit and proper.   **3.165**

(2) Securities firms

Unlike banks (authorized institutions under the Banking Ordinance) which are regulated comprehensively by the HKMA in conjunction to the HKAB once authorized, securities intermediaries are licensed ('registered') by the SFC for specific activities. Once licensed, securities firms are regulated for the activities for which they are registered, not all activities.   **3.166**

A key aspect of the SFO is to provide streamlined regulation of financial intermediaries. Major elements include: **3.167**

- Issuance of a single licence to each intermediary, specifying the scope of permitted business;
- All senior staff who are able to exercise significant influence over the conduct of licensed entities must be licensed and designated as responsible officers;

---

[93] BO s 46.   [94] BO s 47.   [95] Under SFO s 119.

- Licensed status is limited to corporate entities; and
- Persons dealing solely with professionals are required to have a licence, but must notify the SFC of their existence and comply with certain reporting and Code of Conduct requirements; and
- Authorized institutions under the Banking Ordinance are subject to registration under a similar framework to securities firms, albeit via the HKMA.

3.168   Securities intermediaries covered include, inter alia, persons dealing in securities, futures and leveraged foreign exchange contracts, financial advisors, asset and fund managers, investment banks, corporate financial advisors, securities margin financiers, share registrars, authorized financial institutions (AIs, as discussed above), financial consultants and planners, insurance brokers and agents dealing in securities or related activities, and trustees and custodians.

3.169   The regulation of intermediaries is addressed in the following Parts of the SFO:

- Part V—Licensing and registration
- Part VI—Capital requirements, client assets, records and audit relating to intermediaries
- Part VII—Business conduct of intermediaries
- Part VIII—Supervision and investigation
- Part IX—Discipline
- Part X—Powers of intervention and proceedings
- Part XI—Securities and Futures Appeals Tribunal

Parts V, VI, and VII will be dealt with below; Parts VIII, IX, X, and XI will be addressed in Chapter 8 dealing with market misconduct.

3.170   Part V of the SFO deals with licensing and registration. It addresses licensing of persons who conduct activities regulated by the SFC other than in relation to registered institutions (discussed above). In general, it provides for the concept of the 'single licence' for companies and the individuals accredited to them. These are termed 'licensed persons'. The legislation does not allow for sole proprietorships or partnerships or individuals (save as employed by a licensed company).[96] Transitional provisions include automatic 'deeming' of certain categories as licensed for an initial two-year period (which expired in March 2005).[97]

3.171   As discussed above, the SFO defines nine types of 'regulated activities' which are subject to licensing:[98] (1) dealing in securities (Type 1); (2) dealing in futures

---

[96] However, these were permitted under the system pre-SFO.
[97] These include corporations, dealing directors, representatives, sole proprietors, partnerships, and exempt financial institutions.
[98] SFO sch 5.

contracts (Type 2); (3) leveraged foreign exchange trading (Type 3); (4) advising on securities (Type 4); (5) advising on futures contracts (Type 5); (6) advising on corporate finance (Type 6); (7) providing automated trading services (Type 7); (8) securities margin financing (Type 8); and (9) asset management (Type 9). These licences are often referred to as a 'Type 1 licence' (referring to a licence to deal in securities), and so on.

The SFO includes a number of exceptions[99] to this general licensing require-   **3.172**
ment, the most relevant of which are, first, incidental services provided by certain professionals such as lawyers and accountants, and second, advice given to wholly-owned group companies.

Applications for a licence are subject to a number of requirements. Specifically,   **3.173**
as noted above, only companies can apply to be licensed and must have at least two 'responsible officers' for each regulated activity that it carries on. Applicants need to satisfy the SFC that they are 'fit and proper', meet financial resources requirements, and are adequately insured. Individuals can only be 'licensed representatives' and 'responsible officers' if they have sufficient authority within the licensed corporation. Finally, as discussed above, banks need to become 'registered institutions' if they wish to conduct any regulated activities.

Full details are provided in the SFC's Licensing Information Booklet, which   **3.174**
provides general information respecting licensing and registration matters under the SFO as dealt with by the SFC but excluding matters regarding registered institutions dealt with by the HKMA. It contains information in twelve parts and five appendices. The twelve parts address the following issues: (1) introduction; (2) types of regulated activity; (3) do you need a licence or registration?; (4) types of intermediary; (5) exemption from licensing requirements; (6) basic approval criteria; (7) application procedures; (8) grant of licence or registration; (9) notification of changes and other applications; (10) on-going obligations; (11) public register; and (12) disciplinary actions. The five appendices address respectively: (1) reference guide to the SFC Infoline; (2) definitions of regulated activities; (3) provision of financial information on the internet or on-line trading services; (4) application forms and supplements; and (5) licensing fees.

Temporary licences

As an international centre, it is often the case that intermediaries seek to engage   **3.175**
in regulated business activities in Hong Kong on a temporary basis. This is probably most often the case in connection with specific transactional needs or

---

[99] SFO s 5.

where an intermediary has an urgent and short-term staffing need requiring it to bring an individual from an overseas office. It could also occur where an intermediary is intending to establish a business in Hong Kong. Clearly, much transactional based activity which takes place in Hong Kong and other financial centres is 'under the radar screen' and will never be noticed. However, any regulated activity nevertheless requires the person conducting such activity to be licensed. Certain practices of the SFC in this regard have been formalized under the SFO.[100]

3.176 Temporary licences may be granted to corporations in respect of activities for which they are regulated in their home jurisdiction[101] and in respect of which the SFC considers the substantial shareholders etc to be fit and proper. However, temporary licences are not available for activities which would fall under the Type 3, 7, 8, or 9 regulated activities.

3.177 Where a temporary licence is granted, it will be for a maximum period of three months. While this can be renewed, a person may not hold a temporary licence for more than six months in any 24-month period. Temporary licence holders are not permitted to hold client assets (ie in relation to the activity for which the licence has been granted), and must identify an individual acceptable to the SFC who will be responsible for the continuing supervision of the relevant activities.

(3) Securities market infrastructure providers

3.178 Securities market infrastructure providers are dealt with under Part III of the SFO. As a general principle, the SFO provides for SFC recognition of these sorts of intermediaries. Specifically, it provides for authorization or recognition of the following types of securities market infrastructure providers:

- exchange companies
- clearing houses
- exchange controllers
- investor compensation schemes (discussed below)
- automated trading services (ATS).

It also delineates their respective duties, powers, and immunities from civil liability. In turn, these sorts of intermediaries are subject to SFC supervision of varying forms.

---

[100] s 117.
[101] Temporary licences are not available for business activities operating primarily in Hong Kong.

Exchange companies, clearing houses, and exchange Controllers

Under sections 19(1), 37(1), and 59(1) of the SFO exchange companies, **3.179** exchange controllers,[102] and clearing houses may only participate in securities and futures markets related activities when properly recognized by the SFC. The recognition may in all three cases be delivered in connection with specific conditions that the SFC finds appropriate. At the moment, only the Stock Exchange and the Futures Exchange are recognized exchange companies in Hong Kong.

Automated Trading Services (ATS)

Under the SFO, no person shall provide or offer to provide ATS, unless author- **3.180** ized (Part III) or licensed/registered (Part V). ATS are defined in Part 2 of schedule 5 of SFO as services provided by electronic facilities whereby

- offers to sell or purchase securities or futures contracts are regularly made in a way that results in a binding transaction;
- persons are regularly introduced that they may negotiate sales or purchases of securities or futures contracts in a way that results in a binding transaction; or
- transactions (referred to or resulting from the above activities or effected on a market) may be novated, cleared, settled, or guaranteed; but
- excluding facilities provided by recognized exchanges/clearing houses and services provided by or on behalf of the government.

Unlicensed/unregistered ATS providers are not permitted to deal with the retail **3.181** investing public of Hong Kong, ie financial intermediaries market only.

(4) Insurance companies

The ICO provides the licensing framework for the business of insurers and **3.182** insurance intermediaries in Hong Kong. Under the ICO starting or operating an insurance business in Hong Kong is subject to a number of conditions that must be met by the insurance company.

Authorization of insurance companies

Under section 6(1) of the ICO access to the insurance industry in Hong Kong is **3.183** restricted. According to subsection (1)(a) no person shall engage in insurance business unless it has been properly authorized by the OCI. Section 8(3)(a) to (h) of the ICO provides that an applicant must meet the following requirements to be considered for authorization:

---

[102] Exchange Controller: legal entity which owns and controls an exchange.

- the value of its assets must at minimum equal its liabilities if the applicant applies for general insurance business authorization (asset values of companies applying for long-term or combined businesses must meet additional criteria);[103]

- in case the applicant is a stock corporation, the paid-up share capital may not be less than HK$ 10 million (US$ 1,285,000), or, if the applicant wants to pursue both insurance businesses, HK$ 20 million (US$ 2,570,000) (margin solvency requirement);

- adequate reinsurance requirements must be in place;

- the applicant must be and continue to be able to meet its obligations including those not related to its insurance operations;

- relevant provisions of Part XI of the Companies Ordinance must be complied with (provisions relating to the establishment of local subsidiaries of companies incorporated outside Hong Kong);

- the provisions of the ICO must be obeyed; and

- if the applicant is carrying out business other than insurance, that business must not have an adverse effect on the interest of policy holders.

3.184 In addition, management must be 'fit and proper'. Under section 13A of the ICO the appointment of a managing director or a chief executive must be approved by the OCI. Equally, under section 13B of the ICO persons need approval of the OCI to become a controller[104] of the insurance company.

Authorization of insurance agents and brokers

3.185 The ICO recognizes two other types of insurance intermediaries: insurance agents and insurance brokers. Both types are subject to authorization by the OCI.

Insurance brokers

3.186 An insurance broker is a sales and service representative who handles insurance for clients, generally selling insurance of various kinds and of several companies.[105] According to section 65(1) of the ICO no person may deliver services as an insurance broker unless properly authorized by the OCI under section 69 of the ICO. An authorization requires the applicant to satisfy a set of minimum requirements which include:

- relevant qualifications and experience;

---

[103] ICO s 8(3)(a)(i)–(iii).
[104] ICO, s 13B(1): a *controller* is a person that is holding more than 15% of the voting power at any general meeting of the insurer.
[105] F Dearborn, *Fitzroy Dearborn Encyclopedia of Banking and Finance*, p 601.

- minimum capital and net assets of HK$ 100,000 (US$ 12,850);
- professional indemnity insurance in the minimum amount of HK$ 3 million (US$ 385,000);
- keeping of separate client accounts; and
- keeping of proper books and accounts.

The OCI keeps a register of insurance brokers which is open for public inspection.   **3.187**

Insurance agents

An insurance agent represents an insurance company and performs sales func-   **3.188** tions in relation to clients of the company. Insurance agents must be appointed by an insurance company under section 66 of the ICO. Section 66(1) of the ICO requires insurers to register their appointed insurance agents.

(5) Other intermediaries

In addition to the major categories discussed above, there are a number of other   **3.189** categories of financial intermediary subject to licensing in Hong Kong.

Asset management and MPF schemes

All providers of MPF and ORSO services are required to be licensed under the   **3.190** MPFO and ORSO and subject to monitoring by the MPFA. This is in addition to their primary licensing and monitoring regulator.

Clearing and settlement

All providers of clearance and settlement services must be registered under   **3.191** Clearing and Settlement Systems Ordinance (Cap. 584) and subject to the monitoring of the HKMA.

Money lenders

Under the Money Lenders Ordinance (Cap. 163), all money lenders must be   **3.192** licensed by the Registrar of Money Lenders. Licensing is governed by Part II (licensing of money lenders) of the MLO. In turn, Part III governs the on-going conduct of money lending business and money lenders.

Money brokers

Money brokers are regulated by Part XXA of the Banking Ordinance. Under the   **3.193** Banking Ordinance,[106] no person shall act as a money broker unless the person

---

[106] s 118A(1).

is an approved money broker. This is supplemented by schedule 11 which details specific requirements. Contravention is an offence.[107]

Pawnbrokers

3.194 Under the Pawnbrokers Ordinance (Cap. 166), all pawnbrokers must be licensed by the Commissioner of Police.[108] Licensing is based on the applicant being 'fit and proper', compliant with the provisions of the Ordinance, and that granting the licence is not contrary to the 'public interest'.[109]

D. Financial Intermediaries: On-going Requirements and Compliance

3.195 As noted above, initial licensing requirements in most cases are of an on-going nature. In addition, financial institutions in Hong Kong are subject to a variety of other on-going requirements in relation to their business operations.

(1) Banks

3.196 Hong Kong has a comprehensive system of on-going requirements for the operations of authorized institutions under the Banking Ordinance.

Transfers of authorization

3.197 Part VII of the Banking Ordinance deals with transfer of authorization. Authorization may be transferred, subject to HKMA application and approval.[110] HKMA approval also is required for sale/amalgamation/reconstruction of an authorized institution incorporated in Hong Kong.[111] For anyone to become a controller of an authorized institution incorporated in Hong Kong, due notice to and consent from the HKMA is necessary.[112] The HKMA can also object to existing controllers of authorized institutions incorporated in Hong Kong.[113] Certain persons may be prohibited from being controllers of authorized institutions (not restricted to Hong Kong incorporated authorized institutions).[114] Finally, the HKMA can restrict the use, sale, purchase, etc of shares by a controller of an authorized institution incorporated in Hong Kong and can force the sale of shares in certain circumstances.[115]

---

[107] s 118A(2) & (3).   [108] Pawnbrokers Ordinance, s 5.
[109] Pawnbrokers Ordinance, s 5.   [110] BO ss 28, 29.   [111] BO s 69.
[112] BO s 70.   [113] BO s 70A.   [114] BO s 70C.   [115] BO s 70B.

Major acquisitions or investments by a bank

An authorized institution is not allowed to acquire or hold shares in other   **3.198**
companies for sums more than 25 per cent of its own capitalization, unless it is
held as security for facilities granted or in satisfaction of debts due.[116] Certain
holdings are exempted.[117] The HKMA is also generally authorized to issue
guidelines to prevent authorized institutions from engaging in unsound
practices.[118]

In addition, there is a composite overall limit on total investments, land hold-   **3.199**
ings, and advances to directors.[119] An authorized institution is not permitted
to hold land or acquire any interest in land situated inside or outside exceeding
25 per cent of its own capitalization.[120]

Capital adequacy

Hong Kong has adopted the 1988 Basel Capital Accord and its several related   **3.200**
amendments; it is also in the process of implementing the Basel II Capital
Accord, which will have a significant impact on both the legal framework and
the actual requirements of capital and related regulation.

Under the current system based on the 1988 Capital Accord (due to be   **3.201**
replaced in the near future as a result of the Banking (Amendment) Ordinance
2005), Part XVII of the Banking Ordinance deals with capital adequacy. Under
section 98(1), an authorized institution incorporated in Hong Kong shall not,
at any time, have a capital adequacy ratio (CAR) of less than 8 per cent as
calculated in accordance with the provisions of the Third Schedule. The
HKMA may raise the requirement in relation to any locally incorporated
authorized institution and at present requires all such banks to have a CAR of
not less than 10 per cent.

For the purposes of calculating the capital adequacy ratio of an authorized   **3.202**
institution which has any subsidiary, the Monetary Authority may, by notice in
writing to the institution, require the capital adequacy ratio of the institution to
be calculated on a consolidated basis instead of on an unconsolidated basis; or
on both a consolidated basis and an unconsolidated basis.[121]

Branches of foreign banks licensed in Hong Kong are not subject to this   **3.203**
statutory capital adequacy requirement. However, in practice the HKMA will
only issue a licence where the foreign bank is subject to home regulation having
the same capital adequacy requirement (the home banking supervisor having
the primary obligation to monitor the same).

---

[116] BO s 87.   [117] BO s 87(2).   [118] BO s 82.   [119] BO s 90; see below.
[120] BO s 88.   [121] Under BO s 98(2).

3.204 This is supplemented by schedule 3 which details specific requirements.

3.205 As noted above and in Chapter 2, Hong Kong is currently in the process of implementing the Basel II framework. At present, the Banking (Amendment) Ordinance 2005 has been enacted but not yet made effective. Under the BAO 2005 framework, specific capital requirements will be moved from the Banking Ordinance and Schedules to new rules issued by the HKMA under a new rule-making power, with appeals subject to a new Capital Adequacy Review Tribunal (CART). In all likelihood, the BAO 2005 will be made effective sometime before the end of 2007, with relevant rules published for consultation in 2006.

Credit risk and liquidity

3.206 Following extensive consultation with the banking industry, the HKMA introduced on 1 August 1994 a new regime for the supervision of authorized institutions' liquidity. Under this approach, the adequacy of an institution's liquidity is assessed having regard to six factors: liquidity ratio, maturity mismatch profile, ability to borrow in the interbank market, intra-group transactions, loan to deposit ratio, and diversity and stability of the deposit base.

3.207 Part XVIII of the Banking Ordinance deals with liquidity issues. Every authorized institution shall maintain a liquidity ratio of not less than 25 per cent in each calendar month as calculated in accordance with the provisions of the Fourth Schedule and this Part.[122] The Financial Secretary may vary the percentage of the required liquidity ratio by notice in the Gazette.[123] This only applies to its principal place of business Hong Kong and its Hong Kong branches.[124] Like capital, the HKMA may require liquidity for a Hong Kong incorporated authorized institution to be calculated on a consolidated basis instead of an unconsolidated basis; or on both a consolidated basis and an unconsolidated basis.[125] The HKMA may at its discretion also vary the liquidity requirement of a particular institution by notice in writing.[126] If an institution contravenes the liquidity requirements, the HKMA may require it to take specified remedial action(s).[127]

3.208 This is supplemented by the fourth schedule of the Banking Ordinance which details specific requirements, which unusually for Hong Kong, are very much based on US practices.

Lending policies

3.209 An authorized institution is not allowed to extend any guarantee or incur any liability against the security of its own shares, subject to certain conditions.[128] Extensive limitations on lending activities to affiliates etc exist (see below).

---

122 Under s 102(1).   123 BO s 102(4).   124 Under s 102(3).
125 Under s 102(3A).   126 BO s 105.   127 BO s 104.   128 BO s 80.

Asset quality and provision

In December 1994 the HKMA introduced a loan classification system requir- **3.210**
ing authorized institutions to report on a quarterly basis their assets according to
a standardized framework. Under the system, loans are classified as Pass, Special
Mention, Substandard, Doubtful, or Loss, with the latter three categories collectively regarded as 'classified assets'. The system is supplemented by regular
reporting on provisions set aside for each category of classified loans and for
different sectors in Hong Kong.

Large exposures

An authorized institution is prohibited from lending more than 25 per cent of **3.211**
its own capitalization to:[129]

- Any one person;
- Two or more companies which are subsidiaries of the same holding company
  or controller (not being a company);
- Any holding company and one or more of its subsidiaries; or
- Any one person (not being a company) and one or more companies of which
  that person is the controller.

Connected lending

There are maximum limits imposed on an authorized institution regarding **3.212**
lending to, or incurring any liability on behalf of, the following persons
connected with it, on an unsecured basis,[130] unless such transactions are undertaken against lodgement of full acceptable securities in which case there are
no limits:

- Any director or any of his relatives;
- Any employee, who either individually or as a member of a committee, can
  determine loan applications or his relatives;
- Any controller (not being an authorized institution) of the bank or any of his
  relatives;
- Any firm, partnership, or non-listed company (not being an authorized institution), in which the institution or any of its controllers, directors, or any of
  their relatives, has an interest as director, partner, manager, or agent;
- Any firm, partnership, or non-listed company of which any controller or
  director of the institution or any of his relatives is a guarantor.

The limits are: **3.213**

---

[129] BO s 81(1).   [130] BO s 83.

- The aggregate amount of the facilities granted to all the persons listed above should not exceed 10 per cent of the capital of the institution; and
- For all persons listed minus the last two categories, the limit is 5 per cent of the capital base.

3.214 The amount of individual facilities granted for the following categories is limited to HK\$ 1 million (US\$ 128,500):

- A single director or any of his relatives as above,
- A single employee authorized to grant loans or any of his relatives as above, and
- A single controller of the bank or any of his relatives as above.

3.215 There are also limits on the advances which can be made by a bank to its own employees on an unsecured basis[131] although no restriction applies to fully secured lending. The HKMA is also empowered to impose restrictions on advances (including placing of deposits) and credit facilities granted by an authorized institution to a foreign bank.[132]

3.216 The overall limit imposed on authorized institutions regarding the aggregate of loans to/liability incurred on behalf of related persons,[133] shareholdings[134] and interests in land[135] should not exceed 80 per cent of its own capitalization.[136]

Market and other risks

3.217 As noted above, the HKMA has implemented the Basel market risk framework, which is of an on-going nature.[137]

Securities activities of banks

3.218 In regard to the supervisory process, the HKMA–SFC MoU establishes that the SFC must consult the HKMA before any exercise of its supervisory power over registered institutions (ie authorized institutions registered with the SFC).[138] Therefore, the SFC usually relies on the HKMA for supervision of RIs. In turn, the HKMA acts as frontline supervisor and initial contact point for registered institutions. In this role, it conducts on-site inspections and off-site reviews to ensure registered institutions are acting in the manner as required by the SFO.

3.219 In regard to the investigation process,[139] the SFC has limited investigation power. In fact, it can only investigate under two circumstances: first, if the investigation is for the purpose of considering whether to suspend or revoke a

---

[131] BO s 85.　　[132] BO s 86.　　[133] BO s 83.　　[134] BO s 87.　　[135] BO s 88.
[136] BO s 90.　　[137] BO sch 7.　　[138] MoU (2002), cl 7.　　[139] MoU (2002), cl 9.

registered institution's registration; or second, for the purpose of helping the HKMA to consider whether to remove someone from the register of a registered institution or becoming an Executive Officer of a registered institution. The HKMA has wide investigative powers such that it may open a case when it thinks that it is suitable to do so. After completion of the investigation, it is required to forward a copy of the report together with investigation results to the SFC.[140]

In relation to disciplinary matters, the SFC and HKMA may make recommendations to the other for its exercise of disciplinary powers, and shall let the other know how they have handled similar cases and the relevant disciplinary steps taken and consult each other before taking action. **3.220**

Finally, in order to ensure coordination, both may provide the other with necessary and relevant information to enhance transparency of work between them so that they may regulate, supervise, and investigate more effectively. **3.221**

Governance and internal controls

As a general matter, and as an on-going requirement of authorization, the HKMA must be satisfied that the business of the company presently is, and will continue to be, carried out with integrity, prudence, the appropriate degree of professional competence, and in a manner which is not detrimental or likely to be detrimental to the interests of depositors or potential depositors.[141] **3.222**

Internal controls

There is no statutory requirement for authorized institutions to have adequate systems of internal control. However, the HKMA relies on section 7(2) of the Banking Ordinance which requires that the HKMA take all reasonable steps to ensure that institutions operate in 'a responsible, honest and business-like manner' to provide the basis for a requirement of adequate control. There is also a statutory right to publish guidelines on business practices of authorized institutions.[142] These are not specifically enforceable, but failure to adhere to them could be used as part of an overall body of evidence of an institution's failure to ensure adequate control as required by the Banking Ordinance. This is supported by the HKMA's power to require auditors to report on adequacy of controls in various areas.[143] **3.223**

Ethical and professional standards

The appointment of the chief executive or any director of an authorized institution is subject to the consent of the HKMA.[144] Likewise, a controller must also **3.224**

---

[140] MoU (2002), cl 9.   [141] BO sch 7, s 12.   [142] BO s 82.   [143] BO s 63(3A).
[144] BO s 71.

be approved by the HKMA.[145] The HKMA can also prohibit certain persons from being indirect controllers and giving instructions to the directors of an institution or its parent company.[146]

Methods of on-going supervision

3.225   The supervisory approach of the HKMA is based on a policy of 'continuous supervision', through on-site examinations, off-site reviews, prudential meetings, cooperation with external auditors, and sharing information with other supervisors, which aims at detecting any problems at an early stage. The US-derived but now internationally applied CAMEL rating system (Capital, Asset quality, Management, Earnings, and Liquidity) is adopted to help identify those institutions whose weaknesses in financial condition, compliance with laws and regulations, and overall operating soundness require special supervisory attention.

3.226   Extensive requirements in relation to audits and meetings apply to all authorized institutions.[147] In addition to the regular on- and off-site processes, following the completion of the annual audit, it is possible for a meeting to be held involving the HKMA, officers of the bank, and the bank's auditors; such a meeting can be convened by any of the parties.

Off-site surveillance

3.227   On-site examinations are supplemented by ongoing off-site analysis of the financial condition of individual institutions and the assessment of the quality of their management, including the policies and systems in managing risks. The scope of off-site reviews ranges from regular analysis of statistical returns, covering various aspects of the operations of authorized institutions, to an extensive annual review of the performance and financial position of individual institutions. Annual off-site reviews are usually followed by a prudential meeting with senior management.

3.228   The off-site review, as part of the overall examination process of banking supervision, involves analysis of statistical and other information (eg statistical returns, extensive annual reviews and prudential interviews with senior management) submitted by authorized institutions to the HKMA.

On-site examination and use of internal auditors

3.229   At the core of the approach is the on-site examination of individual institutions, with coverage ranging from an investigation of specific areas to a comprehensive review of an institution's operations. They are periodic in nature. Inspection

---

[145] BO s 70.   [146] BO s 70C(2).   [147] BO ss 59, 59A, 60, 61.

of authorized institutions by bank examiners is carried out by the HKMA. This resembles a type of audit and the auditors of banking institutions have a substantial role in the examination.

The HKMA uses a combination of techniques, including a limited form of inspection, together with analytical assessment of information supplied by the institutions themselves ('off-site reviews') and supervisory responsibility of auditors.   **3.230**

Cooperation by means of discussions with both external and internal auditors is another aspect of the supervisory process, with annual tripartite discussions often held with institutions and their external auditors.   **3.231**

Consolidated supervision

Domestic banks are subject to consolidated supervision if notified by the HKMA. For example, the HKMA by notice may require any authorized institution to calculate capital on either or both a consolidated or unconsolidated basis.[148] In addition, information reporting requirements may be on a consolidated basis at the request of the HKMA.[149]   **3.232**

Information and records requirements

The HKMA collates and analyses various data from statutory returns of authorized institutions. The basis of this is the requirement of publication of annual reports by authorized institutions.[150] In addition, as a result of initiatives taken over the past few years, transparency requirements for banks in Hong Kong have been enhanced.   **3.233**

Supervisory information is subject to extensive confidentiality provisions,[151] subject to exceptions for cooperation and information sharing, both domestic and foreign.[152] Further, foreign banking supervisory authorities may examine certain aspects of local institutions' business with the approval of the HKMA.[153]   **3.234**

The HKMA has been very active in recent years in setting accounting standards for authorized institutions, which are subject to continuing reporting requirements. These are on a monthly and quarterly[154] as well as annual[155] and as required[156] basis. All authorized institutions are subject to auditing requirements,[157] and auditors are protected from liability for good faith communications with the HKMA.[158] This is supported by liability of any person who signs a document in relation to information submitted to the HKMA.[159]   **3.235**

---

[148] BO ss 98(2), (2A).   [149] BO s 63.   [150] BO s 60.   [151] BO s 120.
[152] BO s 121.   [153] BO s 68.   [154] BO s 63.   [155] BO ss 60, 63.
[156] BO ss 63, 64, 65, 66, 67.   [157] BO s 59.   [158] BO s 61.   [159] BO s 63(7).

Directors and managers are liable for false or misleading reporting in respect of information on authorized institution shareholding, affiliates, etc.[160]

(2) Securities firms

3.236 In Hong Kong, ongoing regulation of licensed securities firms focuses on three aspects:

- organizational structure (corporate responsibility, internal control, risk management, business profile, etc);
- competence of staff and ongoing training; and
- ongoing compliance both as to specific industry focused laws (SFO, subordinate legislation in the form of Rules), and as to regulatory requirements (SFC Codes, Guidelines, etc).

Capital

3.237 Part VI of the SFO deals with capital requirements for licensed firms. Most importantly, the SFO provides the SFC with the power to make subordinate legislation as regards capital.[161] The SFC in exercise of such power has promulgated the Securities and Futures (Financial Resources) Rules (Cap. 571N) (FRR). Under the FRR, licensed firms must notify the SFC if they become unable to comply with its requirements. Failure to comply with the FRR entails a number of possible consequences. First, the SFC can suspend the firm's licence or allow it to continue subject to conditions. Second, failure to comply with the FRR, to continue to trade while in breach of the FRR, or to breach a condition imposed on the licence by the SFC all constitute offences under the FRR.

3.238 The FRR set different requirements depending on the type of regulated activity, including minimum paid-up share capital (HK$ 5 million to HK$ 30 million—US$ 643,000 to US$ 3,855,000) and minimum liquid capital (HK$ 0.5 million to HK$ 15 million—US$ 64,250 to US$ 1,928,000). If a licensed firm conducts more than one regulated activity, the higher level of minimum share capital and liquid capital applies.

3.239 As discussed in the context of bank capital, capital requirements for securities firms seeks to address certain systemic risk issues, in particular, the risk that a failure of one financial institution could cause loss of investor confidence which may trigger a contagion effect or financial crisis. In fact, one of the objectives of the SFO[162] is reduction of systemic risk (in line with international practice and IOSCO standards).

---

[160] BO s 64.   [161] SFO s 145.   [162] Under s 4.

Management

The SFO also provides for requirements for the incorporation of licensed firms, **3.240** each licensed firm to have two 'responsible officers', for firms to be adequately insured, and the overall 'fit and proper' standard.

Under the 'responsible officer' concept, each licensed firm must have at least two **3.241** responsible officers to oversee licensed regulated activities and at least one of these must be an executive officer. Both must be a licensed representative of the company and meet specific 'fit and proper' requirements including as to their reputation, character, and financial integrity. The objective of the responsible office concept is to foster capable management and to provide clear accountability within the company. Responsible officers are the primary link between the SFC and the company and are responsible both for the conduct of the company and for implementing the SFC's requirements in the company's structure. It is therefore a requirement that they not only possess adequate management and industry experience[163] but also possess sufficient authority within the company to implement SFC requirements. In turn, a licensed representative must have recognized academic/industrial qualifications and regulatory knowledge.

Client assets and record keeping

A key aspect of the regulation of securities intermediaries focuses on the hand- **3.242** ling of client assets. Part VI of the SFO deals with these issues. As in other areas, the SFO provides the SFC with rule-making power in this respect,[164] which it has exercised in promulgating the Securities and Futures (Client Securities) Rules. In addition, the SFO provides rule-making power in respect to record keeping,[165] which the SFC has exercised through the promulgation of the Securities and Futures (Keeping of Records) Rules[166] and the Securities and Futures (Contract Notes, Statements of Account and Receipts) Rules.[167] Together, these provide for a detailed framework addressing client assets and records.

Location of records

Licensed persons have a number of detailed record and document retention **3.243** obligations, as highlighted above. The location of such retention must be approved by the SFC.[168] In many instances, licensed intermediaries may seek to keep certain records overseas, for example, to keep computerized records at the intermediary's IT computer centre, for example, in Singapore. In giving or withholding its approval, the SFC will consider a number of factors including

---

[163] At least 2 and 3 years respectively, subject to waiver by the SFC.
[164] SFO ss 148 & 149. [165] SFO ss 151 & 152. [166] Under SFO s 151.
[167] Under SFO s 152. [168] SFO s 130.

its ability to gain access to the records when it needs to exercise its supervisory or investigatory functions and the status of the local laws as regards the protection of personal data.

Audit

3.244 The SFO also addresses audits and related requirements, which are in turn expanded through the Securities and Futures (Accounts and Audit) Rules.

Conduct of business

3.245 Part VII of the SFO addresses business conduct of securities intermediaries. While section 168 provides a rule-making power, unlike in other areas, this has not been exercised. Instead, the SFC has relied on section 169 providing for codes of conduct, for which there is no direct liability but rather are considered as one factor in the fit and proper analysis.

3.246 The primary code is the Code of Conduct for Persons Licensed by or Registered with the Securities and Futures Commission. This Code is specifically addressed to SFC considerations in relation to fitness and properness of both licensed and registered persons. The Code includes nine general principles, derived from those of IOSCO, and addressing: (1) honesty and fairness; (2) diligence; (3) capabilities; (4) information about clients; (5) information for clients; (6) conflicts of interest; (7) compliance; (8) client assets; and (9) responsibility of senior management. The Code is divided into fifteen chapters and six schedules. The fifteen chapters address respectively: (1) interpretation and application; (2) honesty and fairness; (3) diligence; (4) capabilities; (5) information about clients; (6) client agreement; (7) discretionary accounts; (8) information for clients; (9) client priority; (10) conflicts of interest; (11) client assets; (12) compliance; (13) rebates, soft dollars, and connected transactions; (14) responsibility of senior management; and (15) professional investors. The six schedules include: (1) risk disclosure statements; (2) client identity guidance note; (3) additional requirements for licensed or registered persons dealing in securities listed or traded on the SEHK; (4) additional requirements for licensed or registered persons dealing in futures contracts and/or options traded on the HKFE; (5) additional requirements for licensed persons providing margin lending; and (6) additional requirements for licensed persons engaging in leveraged foreign exchange trading.

3.247 In addition, there are a variety of other codes and guidelines addressing conduct of more specific forms.

3.248 Further, there are specific provisions and rules on short-selling and unsolicited calls. In regard to short-selling, as a general matter covered short sales are allowed but not naked short sales.[169] This provision is expanded through the Securities and Futures (Short Selling and Securities Borrowing and Lending (Miscellaneous)) Rules. Under section 174 of the SFO, unsolicited communications in respect of certain securities or futures dealing and related matters is prohibited, breach of which is an offence. However, specific exemptions from this prohibition are provided in relation to an existing client, solicitor, or professional accountant acting in his professional capacity, licensed person, registered institution, money lender, or professional investor. Moreover, any contract entered into as a result may be rescinded by the party contacted within 28 days of entering into an arrangement pursuant to an unsolicited call or seven days of finding out about the contravention, whichever is the earlier.

Discipline

A number of alternatives are open to the SFC where a licensed intermediary **3.249** or registered institution or their relevant staff have breached applicable laws or regulations or ceases to be fit and proper.[170] Persons subject to discipline in this regard include not only licensed persons and registered institutions[171] but also their responsible officers/executive officers, individuals involved in the management of the business and, in the case of registered institutions, any individuals registered with the HKMA pursuant to the Banking Ordinance.[172] Such disciplinary actions include any or all of the following:

- revocation or suspension in part or full of any licence, registration or approval granted;
- private or public reprimand;
- prohibiting such person from applying to be licensed or registered or approved; and
- imposing a pecuniary penalty of up to HK$ 10 million (US$ 1,285,000) or three times the profit gained or loss avoided as a result of the conduct in question.

The exercise of the SFC's disciplinary powers is subject to the requirement that **3.250** guidelines be published as to the manner in which they will exercise such powers,[173] and that the person whom it is proposed to discipline is given 'a reasonable opportunity to be heard'.[174]

---

[169] SFO s 170.   [170] SFO Part XI, esp. ss 194–196.
[171] Although in respect of registered institutions the SFC is required first to consult with the HKMA–SFO s 198(2). See paragraphs 3.41–3.44 above for a discussion of the role of the HKMA in relation to registered institutions.
[172] BO s 20; SFO ss 194(7) & 196(8).
[173] SFO s 199(1). See SFC, 'Disciplinary fining guidelines' (February 2003).
[174] SFO s 198(1).

(3) Securities market infrastructure providers

3.251 Once recognized or licensed, securities market infrastructure providers become subject to a number of ongoing requirements.

Exchange companies, clearing houses, and exchange controllers

3.252 According to section 21(1) of the SFO an exchange company has the duty to ensure an orderly, informed, and fair market and to guarantee that any risks associated with its operations are managed appropriately. Under section 38(1) of the SFO clearing houses are obliged to guarantee orderly, fair, and expeditious clearing and settlement arrangements for securities and futures transactions. An exchange controller is responsible for the orderly business conduct on behalf of its controlled entity.[175]

3.253 Under sections 24(1), 41(1), and 67(1) of the SFO rules or amendments to existing rules of exchange companies, clearing houses and exchange controllers must have the written approval of the SFC in order to become effective.

3.254 In accordance with section 26 of the SFO the appointment of a chief executive of an exchange company must be approved in writing by the SFC.

3.255 Exchange companies, clearing houses, and exchange controllers all are obliged at any time to produce books, records, and any other information relevant to their respective business if the SFC requires them to do so for the performance of its functions.[176]

Automated Trading Services (ATS)

3.256 The SFC has issued guidelines as to how it will regulate ATS, which cover matters including:

- fairness, efficiency, competitiveness, transparency, orderliness in the industry
- fair and level playing field for participants
- protection of the public
- reduction of systemic risk
- core standards for ATS providers
- financial resources and risk management; operational integrity; fitness; record keeping; transparency; surveillance; and reporting
- HK's status as a competitive international finance centre
- prevention of regulatory arbitrage
- services to institutional investors only
- no direct competition with the HKEx

---

[175] SFO s 63(1)   [176] SFO ss 27(1), 42(1), & 71(1) respectively.

The SFC has stated that it 'intends to take a pragmatic approach to the regulation of ATS in Hong Kong. ATS operations are diverse and likely to grow more so. The regulatory approach will be flexible and applied on a case-by-case basis. In general, the level of regulation of an ATS will be commensurate with the functions it performs and the risks it poses. In addition, a fair and level playing field will be sought so that similar regulation is applied to similar functions.'[177]   **3.257**

(4) Insurance companies

As in other areas, Hong Kong has a comprehensive framework for on-going regulation of insurance intermediaries, under the ICO.   **3.258**

Under section 74(1) of the ICO the OCI has the power to require an insurance agent or insurance broker to provide any type of information, books, or papers. According to subsection (3) that power includes the authority to require the broker, the agent, or any auditor, director, or past director employed by either to explain the information provided.   **3.259**

Under section 75(1) of the ICO the OCI can withdraw the authorization of an insurance broker if he does not comply with the relevant provisions of the ICO or if it is in the interest of policy holders or the public to do so.   **3.260**

Under section 66(7) of the ICO the OCI has the power to deregister an insurance agent if the agent has breached the Code of Practice for the Administration of Insurance Agents.   **3.261**

Reporting requirements

Section 17 of the ICO requires insurers to submit annually their audited financial statements on global business to the OCI. Companies that conduct general insurance business additionally have to submit their Hong Kong general business returns as well as their statements of assets and liabilities. Long-term business insurers must submit annual actuarial reports to the OCI.   **3.262**

Maintenance of assets in Hong Kong

Under section 25 of the ICO a company engaging in general business insurance other than a professional reinsurer or a captive insurer is obliged to maintain assets in Hong Kong equal to not less than 80 per cent of its net liabilities in order to be able to meet claims of Hong Kong policy holders.   **3.263**

---

[177] See also the 'Guidelines for the Regulation of Automated Trading Services' from 2003, figure 12.

Insurance brokers

3.264 Under section 73 of the ICO an insurance broker is required to submit audited financial statements to the OCI annually. Additionally, in consistence with section 72 of the ICO insurance brokers must appoint an auditor who in turn is obliged to file a report with the OCI annually certifying the broker's continuing compliance with the above-mentioned minimum requirements.

Insurance agents: Code of Practice for the Administration of Insurance Agents

3.265 Under section 67 of the ICO insurers are required to comply with the Code of Practice for the Administration of Insurance Agents, which covers, among others, the rules governing the registration and deregistration of insurance agents and the 'fit and proper criteria' for insurance agents.

Discipline

3.266 Part V of the ICO contains the powers of intervention of the OCI with respect to insurers. Under section 26(1) of the ICO those powers can be exercised under the following conditions:

- the OCI considers an intervention crucial for the protection of policy holders against the risk of an insurer being unable to meet its liabilities;
- the OCI has reason to believe that an insurer did or does not comply with provisions of the ICO;
- the insurer may have provided false or misleading information to the OCI under the ICO;
- the OCI is not fully convinced that adequate reinsurance arrangements have been established by an insurer;
- there exist circumstances under which the OCI would be prohibited to authorize an insurer, if it were to apply for authorization at the time of intervention; and
- the insurer does or did not comply with requirements imposed by the OCI with respect to holding of excess of assets over liabilities.

3.267 The powers of the OCI are listed in sections 27 to 35 and 40 of the ICO. Accordingly, the OCI has the authority:

- to impose restrictions on the business of an insurer;[178]
- to prohibit the insurer to make investments of a specified class;[179]
- to require the insurer to maintain a specified amount of its assets in Hong Kong;[180]

---

[178] ICO s 27.   [179] ICO s 28.   [180] ICO s 29.

- to put assets of an insurer under its custody;[181]
- to limit premium income of an insurer;[182]
- to perform actuarial investigations of a long-term business insurer;[183]
- to set time limits for information to be provided by an insurer;[184]
- to require any type of information, records, and documents of an insurer;[185]
- to impose appropriate requirements on an insurer to take actions of any kind with respect to its business;[186] and
- to withdraw the authorization of an insurer if it ceases to carry on insurance business.[187]

E. Financial Intermediaries: Insolvency and Exit

In looking at the full spectrum of regulation of financial institutions, authoriza-   **3.268**
tion or licensing is the initial stage, followed by on-going requirements. The
final stage is the process of ceasing to be a financial institution, encompassing
exit from operations and in some cases insolvency. In general, the insolvency of
financial institutions is addressed by the general insolvency framework in Hong
Kong (addressed in Chapter 2), with no special requirements except for banks,
securities firms, and insurance companies. In addition to the general framework,
in some cases there are additional statutory provisions dealing with these issues
(eg managers and administration for banks, special provisions for winding up
of insurance companies). Further, due to concerns regarding financial system
stability, there are also a variety of consumer/institution support schemes (eg
deposit insurance for banks, investor compensation arrangements for securities
firms).

(1) Banks

The exit from operations of banks is addressed through intervention, manage-   **3.269**
ment, and revocation of authorization, deposit insurance, and provisions
addressing bank insolvency.

Hong Kong has no corporate reorganization legislation, although proposals   **3.270**
have been under discussion for a number of years, and this must be considered
a gap in the law. Likewise, there is no specific legislation governing bank
restructuring, though this is not in any way unusual. Nonetheless, the Banking
Ordinance provides a variety of tools to address these sorts of issues, including

---

[181] ICO s 30.   [182] ICO s 31.   [183] ICO s 32.
[184] ICO s 33.   [185] ICO s 34.   [186] ICO s 35.   [187] ICO s 40.

powers relating to transfers of authorization,[188] control,[189] and changes in ownership and management.[190]

3.271 In its 'Hong Kong Approach', the HKMA adapted Bank of England guidelines created in the 1990s on corporate debt restructuring practice, designed especially to assist transitions involving multiple financial creditors.[191] The scheme has been supported by Hong Kong's effective insolvency regime for recovery from debtors and through cooperation among bank lenders, but has been generally unsuccessful in major cross-border cases in which a majority of creditor claims were managed from Hong Kong.[192] Furthermore, the effectiveness of such semi-voluntary arrangements has been eroded by the growing use of loan sales and other forms of credit risk transfer.

Intervention, management, and revocation of authorization

3.272 The HKMA has broad powers to intervene in the operations of banks when necessary under the Banking Ordinance, especially as regards revocation of authorization,[193] suspension of authorization,[194] control,[195] capital adequacy,[196] liquidity,[197] and investigations.[198] There is power in Part X to appoint a manager. This power has not in fact yet been used, but is likely to feature in dealing with particularly problematic institutions in the future.

3.273 Part V of the Banking Ordinance deals with revocation of authorization. Revocation is generally addressed under section 22, under which the HKMA may, after consultation with the Financial Secretary, propose to revoke the authorization of an authorized institution on any one or more of the grounds specified in the eighth schedule applicable to or in relation to the institution; and by notice in writing served on the institution. This is supplemented by schedule 8 which details specific requirements.

Deposit insurance

3.274 Until recently, Hong Kong did not have a system of deposit insurance. However, a fair degree of depositor protection in the context of bank insolvency was provided through statutory priority for depositors in bank insolvency.[199] This meant that depositors would be paid before most other creditors up to that financial limit.

---

[188] Part VII, ss 28–31.   [189] Part X, ss 52–56 & sch 9.   [190] Part XIII, ss 69–74.
[191] The so-called 'London Rules'.
[192] HKAB and HKMA: Hong Kong approach to corporate difficulties (November 1999).
[193] Part V, ss 22–23 & sch 8.   [194] Part VI, ss 24–27.   [195] Part X, ss 52–56.
[196] Part XVII, ss 98–101.   [197] Part XIII, ss 102–106.   [198] Part XX, ss 117–118.
[199] See CO s 265(1)(db) (priority is up to HK$ 100,000 (US$ 12,850)).

The Deposit Protection Scheme Ordinance (Cap. 581), enacted in 2004, is **3.275** intended to address issues of depositor protection in Hong Kong but is not yet fully in effect. The DPSO comprises 55 sections and five schedules. It is divided into seven parts, dealing with the following issues: (1) preliminary matters (Part 1: sections 1 and 2); (2) Hong Kong Deposit Protection Board (Part 2: sections 3 to 10); (3) Deposit Protection Scheme (Part 3: sections 11 to 13); (4) Deposit Protection Scheme Fund (Part 4: sections 14 to 21);[200] (5) compensation (Part 5: sections 22 to 39);[201] (6) review by Deposit Protection Appeals Tribunal (Part 6: sections 40 to 45); and (7) miscellaneous matters (Part 7: sections 46 to 55).

The five schedules address: (1) deposits specified for purposes of definitions **3.276** of 'protected deposits' and 'relevant deposit' in section 2(1) of the DPSO (schedule 1); (2) provisions relating to Board (schedule 2); (3) provisions relating to Tribunal (schedule 3); contributions to Fund (schedule 4);[202] and (5) consequential and other amendments (schedule 5).

Bank insolvency

There has only been one case of a bank closure in recent years, that of the Hong **3.277** Kong incorporated subsidiary of BCCI in 1991. This was not a case of insolvency, since the bank was liquid and solvent, and indeed all depositors were repaid in full, with interest.

The key aspect is Hong Kong's overall legal framework for dealing with bank **3.278** insolvency (ie banks which are no longer viable), and its relationship with other financial safety nets. Bank insolvency is covered by the ordinary law of insolvency as set out in the Companies Ordinance and as modified by the Banking Ordinance. Primary responsibility lies with the HKMA, but there are other persons with public interest powers, for instance the Financial Secretary.

Similar to most common law jurisdictions, bank liquidation is handled through **3.279** the general insolvency and liquidation process, with certain modifications in the Banking Ordinance. Section 122 of the Banking Ordinance is the primary provision addressing bank insolvency. As regards specific powers, the Chief Executive in Council may direct the Financial Secretary to present a winding-up petition.[203] The Financial Secretary has an independent power on receipt of an investigator's report under section 117(5). The orders the court may make

---

[200] s 15 (contributions to Fund) is not yet in force.
[201] Part 5 is not yet in force. Part 5 is subdivided into two divisions: (1) preliminary (ss 22–26); (2) entitlement to compensation (ss 27–31); and (3) payment of compensation and related matters (ss 32–39).
[202] Sch 4 is not yet in force.   [203] BO s 53(1)(iii).

are set out in section 122(2). The provisions as regards a creditors' voluntary winding-up petition are excluded.[204] However, other creditors retain the right to petition, though the law entitles the HKMA to intervene.[205] In addition, section 122 protects dispositions made and decisions taken by appointed Managers.[206]

3.280 The system was tested by the closure and liquidation of BCC(HK) (which was a bank) and also by the failure of Peregrine (a restricted licence bank), both of which were dealt with without extreme disruption.

(2) Securities firms

3.281 In Hong Kong, procedures to deal with failure of intermediaries include civil liability of persons committing market misconduct (discussed in Chapter 8) and the Investor Compensation Fund.

Investor Compensation Fund

3.282 Under the SFO, a new company handles all compensation arrangements and provides a per client level of protection, with funding out of the then-existing Unified Exchange Compensation Fund and including a second tranche of insurance and provisions for possible market levy if necessary.

3.283 Part XII of the SFO deals with investor compensation. Specifically, it establishes the Investor Compensation Fund (ICF) to replace the Unified Exchange Compensation Fund and the Commodities Exchange Compensation Fund which limited compensation to HK$ 8 million (US$ 1.03 million) per stock broker and HK$ 2 million (US$ 2.06 million) per futures broker. Under the ICF each investor will be compensated to a limit of HK$ 150,000 (US$ 19,280) with coverage extended to include default of non-exchange participants.

Securities firm insolvency

3.284 Overall, outside the ICF and related insurance arrangements, securities firm insolvency falls under the general insolvency framework in Hong Kong.

Securities market infrastructure providers

3.285 According to sections 28(1)(4) and 43(1)(3) of the SFO the SFC has the power to withdraw a recognition under the condition that, inter alia, exchange companies or clearing houses fail to comply with the SFO or any condition attached to the recognition by the SFC. A further reason for withdrawal is the winding-up

---

[204] BO s 122(1).   [205] BO s 122(7).   [206] BO s 122(4).

of the entity. In the case of an exchange controller, the recognition can be withdrawn if it is in the interest of the investing public or crucial for the proper regulation of either exchange.[207]

Were a securities market infrastructure provider to become insolvent, in all likelihood the HKSAR government would intervene (as it did following the collapse of the market in 1987). **3.286**

(3) Insurance companies

Part VI of the ICO deals with winding-up and insolvency of insurance companies. As a general matter, the court may order a winding-up of an insurance company under the Companies Ordinance.[208] In addition, the OCI may present a petition for winding-up under the Companies Ordinance.[209] Section 45 of the ICO provides modifications to the general process under the Companies Ordinance to reflect the intricacies of insurance company insolvency, including continuing all long-term business despite the liquidation process.[210] **3.287**

F. Conclusion

As a general matter, Hong Kong's legal and regulatory framework for banks, securities intermediaries and markets, and insurance companies and business is comprehensive and of an international standard. At the same time the system's many divisions allow certain risks to be unaddressed. **3.288**

A specific area of concern applies in the context of financial conglomerates, in that there is not a clear division of responsibility between the regulatory authorities in the case of the actual or threatened insolvency of a financial conglomerate. In other words, which regulator would be obliged to act? **3.289**

At the technical legal level, the Law Reform Commission of Hong Kong Sub-Committee on Insolvency has pointed out that there are several Ordinances which allow regulatory authorities to wind up companies. In 1999 it recommended that it would be useful for a new section 177(1))(g) to be added to the Companies Ordinance to record that regulatory authorities have these powers. Such a provision would have the effect of giving notice to anyone checking the winding-up provisions that other relevant provisions exist. A further suggestion is the inclusion of a schedule containing all of the bases under which the regulatory authorities may wind up a company because, once done, this would **3.290**

---

[207] SFO s 72(1).   [208] ICO s 43. See s 42 for insolvency test.   [209] ICO s 44.
[210] ICO s 46.

be easy to maintain and the information would be helpful to anyone looking at the subject.[211]

3.291 At present, these recommendations, though highly reasonable, have not yet been implemented. Further, there is differential treatment despite efforts to bring the regulation of banks in line with that of other intermediaries, not only of institutions (eg banks conducting securities and insurance business versus securities firms and insurance companies), but also of different lines of business (advertising, etc) depending upon the nature of the financial product or service being offered. These raise both financial stability concerns as well as competitiveness issues, and are most clear in the context of offerings of company shares and listing (the subject of Chapter 4) and financial derivatives (addressed in Chapter 5).

---

[211] See *Report on the Winding-Up Provisions of the Companies Ordinance* (July 1999), para 9.3. See generally C Booth, 'When Government intervenes: winding up fraudulent companies in Hong Kong' (2000) 4:1 *Receivers, Administrators & Liquidators Quarterly* 41.

4

PUBLIC OFFERINGS AND LISTINGS
OF COMPANY SHARES

Perhaps the most high profile of transactions in Hong Kong is offering shares to **4.01**
the public and/or seeking a listing of a company's shares on HKEx's SEHK. In
general, a public offering of shares is undertaken as a means of raising funds.
Public offerings may or may not include a listing. There are many possible
reasons why a company may decide to seek a listing on an exchange, not to
mention the benefits it may gain from the standing and reputation that accom-
panies listed status. At the same time, there are many consequences and
expenses, discussed below and in Chapter 6.

As a general matter, the legal and regulatory framework addressing offering and **4.02**
listing of company shares is quite similar to the system prevalent in the UK prior
to the enactment of the Financial Services and Markets Act 2000 and the related

transfer of responsibility for listing matters from the London Stock Exchange (LSE) to the Financial Services Authority (FSA). As such, it holds few surprises for those familiar with that structure. At the same time, however, there are certain differences, mainly in relation to the 'dual-filing' system established by the SFO, under which all documents filed with the SEHK are also filed with the SFC, thereby bringing them within the liability and enforcement framework of the SFO (and especially its provisions addressing disclosure). In addition, there are continuing discussions over the need and methodologies for transferring increasing responsibilities from HKEx to the SFC.

4.03 The general framework of the Hong Kong legal and regulatory framework addressing public offerings and listings of company shares comprises laws, regulations, and market practices relating to:

- private and public companies;
- public offerings and prospectus requirements;
- admission criteria and means by which a company can become listed on the SEHK;
- preparation of prospectuses and listing documents and associated liabilities; and
- certain continuing obligations of being listed.

This chapter will address each of these aspects in turn.

A. Offering Shares to the Public

4.04 The phrase 'offering shares to the public' includes an offer to any section of the public however selected provided that an offer will not be regarded as made to the public if it can properly be regarded as not being calculated to result in the shares becoming available for subscription or purchase by persons other than those receiving the offer or invitation, or otherwise as being a domestic concern of the persons making and receiving it.[1] Where a company allots or agrees to allot any shares of the company with a view to all or any of those shares being offered for sale to the public, any document by which such offer to the public is made will be deemed a prospectus issued by the company.[2] Accordingly, all the relevant prospectus requirements of the Companies Ordinance apply together with the attendant liabilities.

4.05 In practice, well-managed companies properly advised will not accidentally trip over these provisions and generally will only be making offers to the

[1] CO s 48A.   [2] CO s 41.

public in connection with a listing process. In this context, it is worthwhile to emphasize a distinction which is not always clearly made, namely, that offering shares to the public and obtaining a listing are distinct processes involving different things.

First, one does not imply the other: it is perfectly possible to make a public **4.06** offering without involving a listing process and, conversely, it is perfectly possible to obtain a listing without involving a public offer of shares. Second, the governing context is different: whereas a public offer is primarily governed by the Companies Ordinance and involves a prospectus being produced, a listing per se is primarily governed by the Rules Governing the Listing of Securities on the SEHK[3] ('Listing Rules') and involves a 'listing document' being produced. Finally, the two are procedurally different: a prospectus must be registered under the Companies Ordinance[4] and this requires the SFC to first give its authorization to be registered. However, a listing document is the concern primarily of the SEHK, the SFC being involved as a review body with, in effect, a power of veto.

These distinctions will become clearer below where the different methods of **4.07** listing are reviewed as well as the specific role of the SFC.

(1) Private and public companies

A basic and important distinction is the one between private companies and **4.08** public companies. A private company is a company which by its articles restricts the right to transfer its shares and limits the number of its members to 50 (excluding members who are or were employees). Further, a private company must also prohibit any invitation to the public to subscribe for any shares or debentures of the company.[5] Unlike private companies, the transfer and holding of shares in public companies is not restricted. A company will lose its private status if it either alters its articles so as to be inconsistent with the foregoing requirements, or fails to comply with such requirements despite its articles being in order.[6]

Should a company cease to be a private company as a result of changing its **4.09** articles, the company will have 14 days to deliver to the Registrar for registration a prospectus complying with the prospectus requirements of the Companies Ordinance. In the event it is in default of the private company requirements despite having the correct article provision, it will lose the benefit of certain

---

[3] Or, in the case of the Growth Enterprise Market the Rules Governing the Listing of Securities on the Growth Enterprise Market of the SEHK.
[4] CO s 38D.   [5] CO s 29.   [6] CO s 30.

exemptions available to private companies (concerning accounts and annual returns).

4.10   A further distinction to note is that a public company may be either a 'listed company' or an 'unlisted company' depending on whether it has any shares listed on a recognized stock market.[7] This distinction is important in view of certain relaxations granted to unlisted companies (as regards financial assistance and purchase of its own shares), or additional requirements placed on listed companies, as indicated below.

4.11   The remainder of this chapter will be primarily concerned with public companies offering shares to the public.

(2) *Non-Hong Kong companies*

4.12   The provisions of the Companies Ordinance reviewed above are directed at companies incorporated in Hong Kong. Companies which are incorporated outside Hong Kong and which wish to offer shares in Hong Kong are subject to the provisions of Part XII of the Companies Ordinance. This distinction is relevant to note in two regards.

4.13   First, many companies operating in Hong Kong are in fact incorporated elsewhere; this includes companies established in the PRC as well as offshore jurisdictions such as Cayman Islands and Bermuda. These companies, having established places of business in Hong Kong, are known as non-Hong Kong companies.[8] Second, Hong Kong is a part of the global capital markets environment and, accordingly, it will from time to time be the case that companies established and largely operating outside Hong Kong may wish to raise capital from persons within Hong Kong.

4.14   Notwithstanding this distinction, the prospectus requirements and liability considerations applying to Hong Kong companies are broadly the same as those applying to companies subject to Part XII. These requirements and considerations are discussed below.

B. Listing of Company Shares

4.15   There are always two ways of looking at a listing process—the commercial aspect and the legal and regulatory aspect. However, one cannot happen without the other; both must necessarily be married together. The commercial process of, for example, bringing a company to the market in an initial public offering

---

[7] CO s 2.   [8] CO s 332.

(IPO), is heavily structured by legal and regulatory requirements. This can easily be seen from the following brief overview of the main stages of an IPO:

- Considering going public: becoming a public company represents an entry point into a new level of regulation as regards corporate governance and public scrutiny of one's affairs. Many changes will need to be effected, and may include the 'attitude' and organization of management, the company's accounting policies and practices, and the corporate structure of the company and its subsidiaries. In particular, it will be necessary to consider whether the company meets the basic SEHK admission criteria.

- Preparing for the IPO: before the formal application is made to SEHK, it will be necessary to engage in an extensive due diligence[9] exercise to prepare a prospectus, and a verification[10] exercise on the prospectus. Both due diligence and verification address legal liability issues. Once the prospectus has been finalized it will need to be duly registered.

- Marketing the company: the basic commercial rationale of raising capital requires investors to be sufficiently interested in the company to see it as a good investment. This will require the sponsors and certain others to 'sell' the offering to potential investors. In doing so, they will need to be aware of the means by which they are permitted to approach investors as well as the role of the prospectus in relation to any other statements or materials they may provide to investors, and the attendant liability issues.

- The offering: there is more than one way to make a public offer of shares but in general it is technically an 'invitation to treat' rather than an 'offer'[11] per se.

- After-market support of the new public company: the role of the sponsor in an offering normally will not cease once the shares have become admitted to listing. The sponsor may continue to advise the company; it is likely to engage in stabilization[12] activities to ensure a smooth opening market

---

[9] Due diligence can be defined as the process undertaken by underwriters to establish the completeness and accuracy of the information contained in the prospectus involving the collection, organization, and checking of information relevant to the company proposed to be listed, the securities themselves and such other information as an investor may need to make an informed investment decision.

[10] Verification can be defined as the process of confirming the truth or authority of statements made in a prospectus and the collection of the evidence for such a confirmation.

[11] In contract law, an offer once accepted is capable of giving rise to a binding legal contract. Offers of shares are technically invitations to treat—when a potential investor applies for shares in an offering, technically it is the potential investor which is making the offer (on the terms set out in the application form).

[12] Stabilization is a process whereby the sponsor will enter the market as a buyer or seller for up to 30 days after the company is listed. The purpose of stabilization is to stabilize the price by providing liquidity in the market on both the buy and sell sides of the market. In Hong Kong, stabilization activities must be carried out in accordance with the Securities and Futures (Price Stabilizing) Rules (Cap. 571W).

for the company's shares; and it is likely to issue research coverage of the company.

These steps and their legal and regulatory implications are addressed in detail below.

(1) The function of regulation

4.16   All exchanges have certain basic features and certain basic requirements. At the most basic level, an exchange is a forum which brings together supply and demand for fungible moveable goods or rights on a regular basis. In particular, an exchange will operate according to uniform rules which permit autonomous price discovery, facilitate order matching, and lead to the formation of binding contracts. In order for a sophisticated exchange to operate successfully, it will need to possess certain characteristics, as follows.

- Fair: there needs to be a level playing field for all market participants. Investors, being the providers of capital into the marketplace, need to have the benefit of protection, for example, against abuses of the market by its participants or issuers seeking to unfairly take advantage of its access to capital through the market.

- Efficient: a market should be efficient not only as regards the cost of participating in it but also as regards how widely and how rapidly relevant information is disseminated and is reflected in the price formation process.

- Transparent: information about trading should be publicly available on a real-time basis.

- Robust: the exchange should be relatively free of systemic risks including both (i) systems operation and (ii) the exposure of participants in the market to other participants in the market (such as to their creditworthiness).

4.17   At one level, a stock exchange regulates company listings, provides the means by which price is formed, and supervises trading matters. Many of the regulations reviewed in this chapter stem from the above characteristics, and are in place with a view to fostering and preserving a sophisticated marketplace.

4.18   The most significant of such regulations in Hong Kong are the Listing Rules, of which there are three important elements. First, the Listing Rules regulate the means by which a company may be admitted to being listed, both as regards qualification and procedural matters. Second, the Listing Rules regulate the performance of certain third parties' functions in relation to a listing (such as sponsors and accountants). Third, the Listing Rules set out the requirements and recommendations applying to companies and their management in order to remain listed. Given the importance of the Listing Rules, a key practice of the SEHK which contributes to transparency in the market is to publish, subject to any pertinent confidentiality considerations, its Listing Decisions and Rejection Letters. The foregoing provides guidance on the interpretation of the Listing Rules in an applied context.[13]

(2) Alternative market

The bulk of this chapter is concerned with companies listed on the Main **4.19** Board of the SEHK. However, the SEHK also operates an alternative stock market, the Growth Enterprise Market (GEM). The GEM is designed to accommodate companies which, although they may have good business ideas and growth potential, are unable to meet the requirements of the Main Board, especially as regards operating record and financial performance. Typically, such companies have a higher risk profile. While the overall listing process and requirements on both markets broadly follow the same principles, this chapter will also highlight some of the key differences between seeking a listing on these two markets.

(3) Methods of listing

While listing always involves securities becoming admitted to the SEHK for **4.20** trading, this may be a result of one of a number of different types of corporate and shareholder transactions. The three methods most commonly seen are offer for subscription, offer for sale, and placing. These and the other methods are set out in chapter 5 of the Listing Rules, and are summarized below. Each of the methods must be supported by a listing document (discussed below), except in the case of a placing of securities of a class already listed which does not require the publication of a prospectus.

Offer for subscription

An offer for subscription is an offer to the public by or on behalf of an issuer of **4.21** its own securities for subscription. The subscription of the securities must be fully underwritten. In the case of offers by tender, the SEHK must be satisfied as to the fairness of the basis of allotment so that every investor who applies at the same price for the same number of securities receives equal treatment.

Offer for sale

An offer for sale is an offer to the public by or on behalf of the holders or **4.22** allottees of securities already in issue or agreed to be subscribed. In the case of

---

[13] The Listing Decisions and Rejection Letters are regularly published on the SEHK's website: <http://www.hkex.com.hk>.

offers by tender, the SEHK must be satisfied as to the fairness of the basis of allotment so that every investor who applies at the same price for the same number of securities receives equal treatment.

Placing

4.23   A placing is the obtaining of subscriptions for or the sale of securities by an issuer or intermediary primarily from or to persons selected or approved by the issuer or intermediary.

4.24   Appendix 6 of the Listing Rules sets out certain criteria with which a placing must comply. This includes, for new applicants, an amount (25 per cent) to be reserved for distribution to the general public, an adequate spread of shareholders (eg not less than three holders for each HK$ 1 million (US$ 128,500) of the placing, with a minimum of 100 holders), and no allocations to certain connected persons of the lead broker. A placing by a listed issuer is normally only allowed where the placing falls within the directors' general mandate (discussed in Chapter 6) or where specifically authorized by the shareholders. In any case, the SEHK may not permit a new applicant to be listed by way of a placing if there is likely to be significant public demand for the securities.

Introduction

4.25   An introduction is an application for listing of securities already in issue where no marketing arrangements are required because the securities for which listing is sought are already of such an amount and so widely held that their adequate marketability when listed can be assumed. Introductions are usually seen where the securities are listed on another exchange (eg a company seeks dual listing or wishes to change its listing to another exchange), or in consequence of a corporate reorganization where the listed vehicle is pushed down under a new holding company.

Rights issue

4.26   A rights issue is an offer by way of rights to existing holders of securities which enables those holders to subscribe securities in proportion to their existing holdings. Rights issues are normally fully underwritten. Rights issues are subject to a number of additional detailed provisions.[14]

---

[14] See LR 7.18–7.22.

Open offer

An open offer is an offer to existing holders of securities to subscribe securities, **4.27** whether or not in proportion to their existing holdings. Open offers are normally fully underwritten.

Capitalization issue

A capitalization issue is an allotment of further securities to existing shareholders, **4.28** credited as fully paid up out of the issuer's reserves or profits, in proportion to their existing holdings, or otherwise not involving any monetary payments. A capitalization issue includes a scrip dividend scheme under which profits are capitalized.

Consideration issue

A consideration issue is an issue of securities as consideration in a transaction or **4.29** in connection with a takeover or merger or the division of an issuer.

Exchange

Securities may be listed by means of an exchange or a substitution of securities **4.30** for or a conversion of securities into other classes of securities.

Other methods

Securities may also be listed as a result of other transactions including the **4.31** exercise of options or warrants etc.

Initial public offering

'IPO' is a generic term referring to a company raising fresh capital through an **4.32** offer in connection with it first becoming listed on the SEHK. The company whose securities are listed or are to be listed is very often referred to as the 'issuer'. Whereas 'IPO' is the preferred term in some markets (eg Hong Kong, US), the terms 'flotation' and 'going public' tend to be the equivalent terms preferred in others (eg UK).

The rest of this chapter uses the IPO as the listing transaction of reference as the **4.33** IPO serves to illustrate the key points concerning admission to the SEHK. Accordingly, it is not only the IPO that incurs legal and regulatory burdens and also that securities of the company other than its shares may be listed such as options or warrants or convertibles.[15]

---

[15] See LR chapters 15, 15A, 16, & 17.

(4) Rationale for listing

4.34 While the circumstances of each company and its shareholders who seek listed status may be very different, nevertheless a number of common themes can be found as to why listing might be the right way forward. The more common reasons include:

- capital needs of company: while the initial listing normally provides the means by which a company may increase its capital for future growth, a listing also facilitates future fund-raising activities, in part due to the readily ascertainable market value of the company;

- requirements of present shareholders: the listing process provides a return on capital for founders, liquidity and readily ascertainable valuation of their shareholding, and serves to release the burden of shareholder finance, personal guarantees etc;

- a listing provides publicity to the company and raises its profile and standing in the business and investment community; and

- instead of using cash for future acquisitions, it may be possible to use the shares of the company as acquisition capital.

4.35 Gaining access to the public market brings with it not only many benefits but also many burdens, and the cost of gaining a listing should not be measured in merely monetary terms, as the following brief list illustrates:

- cost: it is expensive to obtain and maintain a listing;
- directors: duties are more onerous;
- loss of privacy: extensive disclosure required on company events and rumours in the market; analysts monitor and give commentary on corporate decisions; subject to public scrutiny;
- investor relations: time consuming for management;
- management: new committee structures etc required, increased disclosure as to business intentions, and interests of public shareholders must be considered;
- regulatory burden: company subjected to new laws and regulations, additional reporting and filing requirements, and directors subjected to restrictions on dealing;
- lock-up: controlling shareholders and interested directors subject to lock-up on shares following listing;
- management time and attention: the process of obtaining a listing requires significant time from senior management;
- mood of the market: the company's share price will in part be determined by the mood of the market and perceptions on the industry as a whole, not just the performance of the company; and
- dividend policy: may be constrained by market expectations.

(5) Listing process

Assuming one has determined an IPO to be both desirable and achievable, it will be necessary to consider the steps required and the application process. **4.36**

Preparatory steps

It is frequently the case that the company will first need to undergo some form **4.37**
of restructuring to prepare it for listing, both as regards its corporate macro
structure as well as the details of the way the company is governed and administered operationally. While the detailed reasons and methods of doing so are
outside the scope of this chapter, they include the following:

- Every company will need to ensure its constitutional documents are amended
  such that it will become a public company.
- A new holding company is often put in place as part of creating a clear
  corporate structure in which different revenue and cost units of the business
  are in separate corporate vehicles.[16]
- Certain parts of the business may be spun off into separate companies and not
  participate in the listing, for example because they may be unattractive to the
  market interested in the company's listing. PRC companies will normally
  transfer the assets to be listed into a special listing vehicle so as to segregate
  those from other assets not relevant to the business being listed.
- Excess cash in the business is likely to be distributed to existing shareholders.
- The operational divisions of the business may be reorganized so as to present a
  clearer arrangement of the company's operations. This will be particularly
  desirable where the corporate structure has evolved haphazardly without a
  clear rationale for the structure.
- Companies reorganizing may undertake a scheme of arrangement.[17]
- Companies may also need to restate their accounting policies and practices.

Qualification for admission

Leaving aside the consideration of a company's commercial marketability, the **4.38**
first step for any company to consider is whether it is qualified for listing. This
entails a consideration of the requirements of chapter 8 of the Listing Rules and
contacting the SEHK on an informal basis as to the company's eligibility. As
regards eligibility, the SEHK will in general terms consider the suitability of the
company and its business for listing.

---

[16] It is quite common for such holding company to be created in an offshore jurisdiction.
[17] CO s 166 or equivalent under their place of incorporation.

4.39 As regards qualification, the company will need to satisfy one of three quantitative tests: the profit test, the market capitalization/revenue/cash flow test, or the market capitalization/revenue test.

The profit test[18]

4.40 The company, or its group, must have an adequate trading record under substantially the same management and ownership. In quantitative terms this means satisfying all of the following:

- a trading record of not less than three financial years;
- profit attributable to shareholders in the most recent year of at least HK$ 20 million (US$ 2,570,000);
- aggregate profit attributable to shareholders in the two preceding years of at least HK$ 30 million (US$ 3,856,000);
- such profits to exclude income or loss generated by activities outside the ordinary course of its business;
- management continuity for at least the three preceding financial years; and
- ownership continuity and control for at least the most recent audited financial year.

The market capitalization/revenue/cash flow test[19]

4.41 The company must satisfy all of the following:

- a trading record of not less than three financial years;
- management continuity for at least the three preceding financial years;
- ownership continuity and control for at least the most recent audited financial year;
- a market capitalization of at least HK$ 2 billion (US$ 257 million) at the time of listing;
- revenue of at least HK$ 500 million (US$ 64.3 million) for the most recent audited financial year (revenue arising from the applicant's principal activities; revenue arising incidentally is excluded); and
- aggregate positive cash flow from operating activities of at least HK$ 100 million (US$ 12.9 million) for the three preceding financial years.

The market capitalization/revenue test[20]

4.42 The company must satisfy all of the following:

- trading record of not less than three financial years (however, see below);

---

[18] LR 8.05(1).   [19] LR 8.05(2).   [20] LR 8.05(3).

- management continuity for at least the three preceding financial years (however, see below);
- ownership continuity and control for at least the most recent audited financial year;
- market capitalization of at least HK$ 4 billion (US$ 514 million) at the time of listing;
- revenue of at least HK$ 500 million (US$ 64.3 million) for the most recent audited financial year (revenue arising from the applicant's principal activities; revenue arising incidentally is excluded); and
- at least 1,000 shareholders at the time of listing.

The SEHK's power to waive

The SEHK may accept a shorter trading record period and/or may vary or waive the above requirements where the company has a trading record of at least two financial years and it is satisfied that the listing of the company is desirable in the interests of the company and investors, and that investors have the necessary information available to arrive at an informed judgment concerning the company and the securities for which listing is sought. It may also vary the above requirements in respect of mineral companies (subject to chapter 18 of the Listing Rules) and newly formed 'project' companies (for example a company formed to construct a major infrastructure project). **4.43**

While it has not been the practice of the SEHK to date to waive the requirements of the above qualification tests, the SEHK has made exceptions in relation to the trading record and management continuity requirements of the market capitalization/revenue test. Under LR 8.05A the SEHK will accept a shorter trading record under substantially the same management where the directors have sufficient experience of at least three years in the same line of business subject to management continuity for the most recent audited financial year. **4.44**

Other requirements

Assuming the company is both eligible and qualified it must also satisfy the SEHK as to a minimum public float, sufficient initial capitalization, and a fair basis for allocating shares to investors—all discussed below. In addition, a number of other requirements need to be met, including: **4.45**

- latest financial period reported to be within six months before the date of the listing document (this will sometimes require a company to restate its financial accounts to a new date);
- sufficient management presence in Hong Kong (at least two of its executive directors must be ordinarily resident in Hong Kong) including a company secretary ordinarily resident in Hong Kong with appropriate experience;

- directors to satisfy the requirements of Chapter 3 of the Listing Rules;[21]

- the securities for which listing is sought must be freely transferable and be of a class of 'Eligible Securities';[22]

- the company must maintain in Hong Kong a register of members maintained by an approved share registrar;[23]

- where directors have a competing interest, the SEHK may require the appointment of a sufficient number of independent non-executive directors to ensure that the interests of the general body of shareholders will be adequately represented. Notwithstanding the foregoing requirements of the Listing Rules, directors continue to be subject to all the usual fiduciary and other obligations of a director (see Chapter 6); and

- the appointment of an underwriter acceptable to the SEHK as able financially to meet its underwriting commitment.

Public market and shareholding

4.46   The SEHK must be satisfied that there will be an adequate market and public interest in the business of the company and there is an open market in the securities for which listing is sought.[24] This latter requirement normally means at least 25 per cent of the company's total issued share capital to be held by the public at all times with special rules applying where the company has more than one class of shares to be listed. This is an on-going requirement and shortfalls in the public float will have consequences for the company (discussed below).

4.47   In the case of larger companies, ie with an expected market capitalization of over HK$ 10 billion (US$ 1.285 billion), the SEHK may, at its discretion, adjust the minimum percentage requirement to as low as 15 per cent subject to it being satisfied that the market will operate properly with a lower percentage.[25] In this regard the SEHK will consider the extent of distribution of the company's shareholding.

4.48   In addition to the above requirements, at the time of listing, the company must provide an adequate spread and amount of public shareholders. In general, this means:

---

[21] In brief, that they possess adequate experience, competence, and integrity, that the board is comprised of at least three independent non-executive directors, and that each director complies with the Model Code (LR Appendix 10) which sets out the required standard which the Exchange requires all listed issuers and their directors to meet.

[22] ie securities of a class eligible for deposit, clearance, and settlement in CCASS. See definition in LR 1.01.

[23] Share registrars need to be approved pursuant to SMLR s 12.

[24] LR 8.08 & 13.32–13.35.   [25] LR 8.08(1)(d).

- a minimum of 300 shareholders;
- not more than 50 per cent of the publicly held shares beneficially owned by the three largest public shareholders; and
- the public shareholding component must be at least HK$ 50 million (US$ 6.4 million).

Certain persons are regarded by the SEHK as not being part of the 'public': **4.49**

- any connected person of the company (this includes directors, any chief executive, and any substantial shareholder[26] of the company, or any of its subsidiaries or an associate of any of them);
- any person whose acquisition of the securities is financed by a connected person; or
- any person who is accustomed to take instructions from a connected person in relation to the acquisition, disposal, voting, or other disposition of the company's securities.

Basis of allocation

The SEHK imposes a requirement on the company and its underwriters to **4.50** adopt a fair basis of allocation of the securities on offer to the public and, if any securities are to be marketed contemporaneously within and outside Hong Kong that a sufficient portion (agreed with the SEHK) be offered in Hong Kong.

Initial capitalization

The expected market capitalization of a new applicant at the time of listing must **4.51** be at least HK$ 200 million (US$ 25.6 million), with each class of securities for which listing is sought being at least HK$ 50 million (US$ 6.43 million) except for options, warrants, or similar securities where the minimum is HK$ 10 million (US$ 1.285 million). Lower expected initial market capitalization may be acceptable where the SEHK is satisfied as to marketability.

Application process

Chapter 9 of the Listing Rules sets out the detailed requirements and forms **4.52** required for making an application for listing. Figure 4.1 gives an overview of this process.

The sponsor is the primary point of contact with the SEHK and accordingly is **4.53** responsible for providing the requisite documents to the SEHK in good time. The process commences with the submission of an advance booking form

---

[26] A 'substantial shareholder' is a person who holds or controls 10% or more of the voting power of the company.

```
┌─────────────────────────────────────────────────────┐
│           Apply to SEHK for advance booking           │
│                      (Form A1)                        │
└─────────────────────────────────────────────────────┘
                          ⇩
┌─────────────────────────────────────────────────────┐
│               Documentary submissions                 │
│             (at 20, 15, 10 days prior*)               │
└─────────────────────────────────────────────────────┘
                          ⇩
┌─────────────────────────────────────────────────────┐
│             Formal application for listing            │
│                   (at 4 days prior*)                  │
└─────────────────────────────────────────────────────┘
                          ⇩
┌─────────────────────────────────────────────────────┐
│       Listing Division recommends (or rejects[27])    │
│                 to Listing Committee                  │
└─────────────────────────────────────────────────────┘
                          ⇩
┌─────────────────────────────────────────────────────┐
│        Listing Committee approves (or rejects[28])    │
└─────────────────────────────────────────────────────┘
                          ⇩
┌─────────────────────────────────────────────────────┐
│           Issue of prospectus and formal notice       │
└─────────────────────────────────────────────────────┘
                          ⇩
┌─────────────────────────────────────────────────────┐
│              Dealings in shares commence              │
└─────────────────────────────────────────────────────┘
```

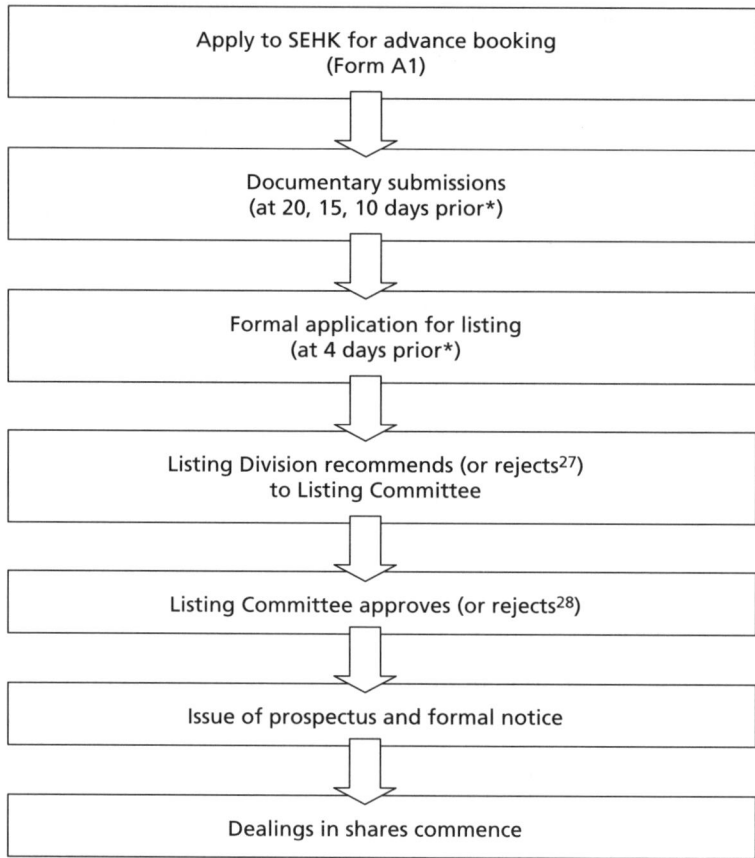

Figure 4.1 Summary of the process for a listing application
  * Refers to minimum number of clear business days before expected Listed Committee hearing. For specific requirements, see below & LR 9.11(4)–(15).

(form A1) by which the company effectively formally advises the SEHK of its intention to seek a listing and to position itself in the queue of other companies wishing to come to the market. In this latter regard, the SEHK is concerned to maintain an orderly market in new issues, ie new issues come to the market in a somewhat paced manner and not all at once. Two important features of the advance booking form are (1) the inclusion of a transaction timetable which must be agreed with the SEHK, and (2) the provision of an advanced draft prospectus constituting the listing document.

4.54 The form A1 is lodged at least 25 business days prior to the date on which the

---

[27] If rejected by the Listing Division, the Applicant may appeal to the Listing Committee.
[28] If rejected by the Listing Committee, the applicant may appeal to the Listing (Review) Committee.

Listing Committee will formally consider the application. In the intervening period of time, the SEHK will interact extensively with the sponsor and its lawyers as to the contents of the prospectus, with the SEHK normally raising many comments and questions for further clarification in the document. Chapter 9 of the Listing Rules also sets out a specific timetable as to what documents need to be submitted at what time during the process leading up to the expected hearing date. A sample list of documents required to be submitted is set out below.

During that period, the sponsor, the company, and related persons are under a **4.55** number of obligations, failure to observe which may lead to delays in or outright rejection of the listing. They include:

• no issue of publicity relating to the proposed listing except that which is reviewed and approved by the SEHK. There may be a fine line between advertising the company's business or its products (which is permitted) and advertising the forthcoming listing of the company;
• the maintenance of confidentiality prior to the announcement concerning the proposed listing; and
• a prohibition on dealing in the securities for which listing is sought by any connected person of the issuer.[29]

Documentary requirements

Many documents, in draft and final form will need to be submitted to the **4.56** SEHK at precise times during the listing process as specified in Chapter 9 of the Listing Rules. The list below is a sample list of the sorts of documents required and it is by no means a complete list of all documents required:

• a written submission on any proposed connected transactions (see the discussion on connected transactions in Chapter 6);
• a copy of every contract required by paragraph 17 of the Third Schedule of the Companies Ordinance to be stated in the prospectus;
• formal application for listing (form C1);
• a written submission to the SEHK in the form prescribed by the SEHK in support of the application for listing;
• certified copy of the certificate of incorporation or equivalent document of the issuer;
• annual report and accounts for each of the three completed financial years of the issuer or group immediately preceding the issue of the listing document;
• copies of listing agreement in the form prescribed and provided by the SEHK, duly signed for and on behalf of the issuer;

---

[29] LR 9.09 except as permitted by LR 7.11.

- certified copies of various corporate resolutions;
- specimens of the definitive certificate or other document of title;
- where the listing document is required to contain a statement by the directors as to the sufficiency of working capital, a letter from the sponsor confirming satisfaction with the statement;
- a certified copy of the memorandum and articles of association or equivalent documents and certified copies of all resolutions which are required to be registered under the Companies Ordinance;
- declarations by corporate shareholder holding over 5 per cent of the company's issued share capital;
- certified copies of every letter, report, financial statement, statement of adjustments, valuation, contract, resolution, etc referred to in the listing document;
- where the listing document constitutes a prospectus under the Companies Ordinance, an application for authorization for registration of the prospectus;[30]
- printed copies of the prospectus signed by the directors;
- copies of required announcement advertisements;
- results of allotment or, in the case of a placing, details of the placees; and
- certain declarations of the sponsor and directors of the company.

4.57 The single most important document required by the SEHK, and one which is subject to intense scrutiny, is the Listing Document. This will frequently also constitute a prospectus. The requirements for the Listing Document are discussed below.

Listing review process

4.58 The review and approval process is undertaken by the Listing Division (an organizational unit of the HKEx qua company) and the Listing Committee (a sub-committee of the Board of the HKEx). The composition of the Listing Committee is specified in the Listing Rules[31] as being 25 persons comprising exchange participants, representatives from listed companies and market practitioners and users, and the Chief Executive of HKEC (or the Chief Executive of HKEx as his alternate).

4.59 The Listing Division of the SEHK is responsible for all listing matters including the interpretation, administration, and enforcement of the Listing Rules. Every application for listing by a new applicant is required to be submitted to the Listing Division for review, and the Division is also responsible for day-to-day matters arising in relation to the listing process. However, it is the Listing

---

[30] Registration is made pursuant to CO s 38D(3) or s 342C(3).   [31] LR 2A. 17.

Committee[32] which must first grant approval in principle to list and which has the power to formally approve all applications for listing from a new applicant. The application process will therefore normally be progressed with the Listing Division until all relevant requirements under the Listing Rules are dealt with, the Listing Committee hearing being the last stage in the formal approval process just prior to the shares of the company being admitted to listing.

Filing requirements

In the case of a public company engaging in a public offer in connection with a listing on the SEHK, it is necessary to consider the filing requirements under both the Companies Ordinance (as a result of the public offer component) as well as the Securities and Futures (Stock Market Listing) Rules (Cap. 571V) ('SMLR') (as a result of the listing component). **4.60**

No prospectus shall be issued unless the prospectus complies with the require- ments of the Companies Ordinance.[33] The primary requirements are concerned with authorization, registration, and content. **4.61**

Authorization for registration under the Companies Ordinance requires appli- cation to be made to the SFC together with a copy of the prospectus signed by the directors (including proposed directors) and with certain specified endorse- ments thereon. If approved, the SFC is empowered to issue a certificate of authorization which specifies the documents which are required to be endorsed on or attached to the copy of the prospectus to be registered. However, the powers of the SFC have, where concerned with the prospectus of a company that has been approved for listing on the SEHK, been transferred to the SEHK.[34] In consequence, the SEHK vets any prospectus which relates to a listing and has the power to authorize the registration of such a prospectus by the Registrar of Companies under the provisions of the Companies Ordinance. **4.62**

Registration of a prospectus (whether or not relating to a listing) must be made with the Companies Registrar on or before the date of its publication. **4.63**

If a prospectus is issued without the appropriate endorsements the company, and every person who is knowingly a party to the issue of the prospectus, is liable to a fine and, for continued default, to a daily default fine until the required documents are endorsed or attached, as the case may be. **4.64**

---

[32] The Listing Committee is a sub-committee of the Board of the SEHK comprised of exchange participants, representatives from listed companies and market practitioners, and the Chief Executive of Hong Kong Exchanges and Clearing Limited (HKEx). The powers exercised by the Listing Division are subject to review by the Listing Committee. The details of the operations of these bodies and the review and appeal processes are set out in LR Chapters 2A & 2B.
[33] CO s 38D.   [34] Pursuant to SFO s 25.

4.65 Finally, a prospectus will need to comply with detailed content requirements of the Companies Ordinance, discussed below.[35]

4.66 The Listing Rules require a listing document which is a prospectus to comply with both the Companies Ordinance requirements as well as the requirements under the Listing Rules.

4.67 Under a relatively new dual filing regime, when the company submits its listing application to the SEHK, the company is required to file a copy of its application with the SFC within one business day thereafter.[36] Normally, the company making the application will take advantage of the ability to authorize the SEHK to file the application with the SFC on its behalf.[37]

4.68 Bearing in mind the above arrangements, the SFC is empowered[38] to require further information from the company making the filing and raise an objection to the listing. Any objection of the SFC is important as the SEHK is prohibited from listing any company to which the SFC has lodged an objection.[39] Grounds for objection would be, for example, that the prospectus does not provide sufficiently detailed information on the company and its affairs for an investor to make an informed decision,[40] or the application is false or misleading as to a material fact or omission of a material fact. Should the SFC consider it not to be in the public interest for the securities to be listed, it may also object. The SFC may also give notice that it does not object, or that it does not object subject to the satisfaction of certain conditions. An objection of the SFC is important as the SEHK is prohibited from listing the relevant company for so long as such objection is outstanding.[41]

(6) Non-Hong Kong issuers

4.69 The SEHK has created special provisions to address certain issues arising in connection with non-Hong Kong companies. While the Listing Rules apply to all issuers wherever incorporated, the Listing Rules contain additional rules applying to non-Hong Kong companies. Such rules (which provide for additional clarifications and requirements, or modifications to or exceptions from other rules) are needed either because of the nature of the legal jurisdiction in which the issuer is established (and hence the legal nature of the issuer and its securities need to be considered) or the nature of the market attaching to the securities of the issuer. An example of the latter would be where the issuer is

---

[35] Although it should be noted that certain limited exemptions are available under CO s 38A.
[36] SMLR Rule 5.   [37] SMLR Rule 5(2).   [38] SMLR Rule 6.
[39] SMLR Rule 6(4).   [40] SMLR Rule 3.   [41] SMLR Rule 6(4).

already listed (or to be listed) on another exchange in addition to its listing on the SEHK.

Non-Hong Kong issuers generally

Chapter 19 of the Listing Rules sets out the rules applying to non-Hong Kong issuers seeking either a primary or a secondary listing on the SEHK. Many of the rules in Chapter 19 reiterate the applicability of various Listing Rules to the non-Hong Kong issuer or provide for modifications in view of the issuer being other than a Hong Kong incorporated company. The three core concerns of Chapter 19 relate to shareholder protection, localization requirements, and accounting matters. **4.70**

Probably the most central requirement is that shareholders are given adequate protection, meaning protection at least equivalent to that provided in Hong Kong. This requires a consideration of the laws of the jurisdiction in which the issuer is established, or in some cases, the constitutive documents[42] of the issuer. The Listing Document prepared by the issuer will need to summarize the relevant local laws and regulations as well as the issuer's constitutive documents insofar as they concern shareholder rights, in each case highlighting any differences from that prevailing under Hong Kong laws. **4.71**

Additional requirements are concerned with localization: the presence of a person authorized to accept service of documents in Hong Kong and the establishment of a Hong Kong shareholder register. As regards the latter it is important to note that only shares registered on the Hong Kong register may be traded on the SEHK. In the context of a dual listing, shares traded on another exchange may be transferred to trading on the SEHK but only after their place of registration has been changed to the Hong Kong register. In practice, this requires some time to perform the necessary mechanics. For example, having purchased on the London Stock Exchange shares of a company listed both in London and Hong Kong, the shares may be sold on the SEHK but only after they have been withdrawn from London's clearing system, re-registered on the Hong Kong share register, and admitted into the SEHK's clearing system. **4.72**

The SEHK will also be concerned to see that the reporting accountants are properly qualified and independent of the issuer, to the standards of independence issued by the International Federation of Accountants. In addition, an audit must have been conducted at least to the standards required in Hong **4.73**

---

[42] Meaning the equivalent of the memorandum and articles of the issuer, eg its 'by-laws'.

Kong or the International Auditing and Assurance Standards Board of the International Federation of Accountants. The accounts themselves will normally be expected to be drawn up in conformity either with Hong Kong Financial Reporting Standards or International Financial Reporting Standards.

4.74   In relation to secondary listings, the SEHK will also wish to see that the primary listing is indeed the primary listing of the issuer. Accordingly, if the SEHK considers that the majority of trading will occur on the SEHK, it will require that (1) the primary listing is on a regulated market recognized by the SEHK, (2) the issuer must have an adequate connection with the primary market, and (3) the primary market and the SEHK have entered into an agreement concerning their respective roles as regards the regulation of the issuer.

PRC issuers

4.75   Chapter 19A of the Listing Rules sets out the rules applying to any 'PRC issuer', meaning an issuer incorporated in the PRC as a joint stock limited company.[43] PRC issuers require special treatment for a number of reasons. Apart from the obvious political and economic ties between Hong Kong and the PRC, PRC issuers represent a special case in view of (1) the legal system in the PRC not being based on a common law system, (2) PRC laws on foreign exchange including remittance out of the PRC, and (3) PRC laws which create different classes of domestic and foreign shares[44] of the same issuer potentially create separate markets in the shares of an issuer.

4.76   As with non-Hong Kong issuers generally, the SEHK will require the presence of a sufficient level of shareholder protection under PRC laws and the constitutive documents of the issuer. A summary of those laws and protections is required in the Listing Document. In particular, the articles of association of PRC issuers must contain provisions which reflect the different nature of domestic shares and overseas listed foreign shares (including H shares[45]) and the different rights of their respective holders. Finally, it must be provided that disputes involving holders of H shares and arising from a PRC issuer's articles of association, or from any applicable law or regulation, are to be settled by arbitration in either Hong Kong or the PRC at the election of the claimant.

---

[43] Under the Company Law of the PRC, a joint stock limited company is the equivalent of a company limited by shares: its total capital is divided into equal shares, shareholders assume liability towards the company to the extent of their respective shareholdings, and the company is liable for its debts to the extent of all its assets.

[44] Only PRC citizens and legal persons are permitted to own the domestic shares of a PRC issuer (which pay dividends in renminbi), and only foreign investors and investors from the regions of Hong Kong, Macau, and Taiwan are permitted to own the overseas listed foreign shares of a PRC issuer (which pay dividends in a foreign currency).

[45] That is, overseas foreign shares listed on the SEHK.

Where a PRC issuer is to be dual listed, an adequate 'communication arrange-   **4.77**
ment' must be in place between the SEHK and the other exchange. Given the
particular regulatory arrangements applying in the PRC, the SEHK also requires
adequate cooperation arrangements with the relevant securities regulatory
authorities in the PRC.

The SEHK is concerned with proper accounting and audit standards, auditor   **4.78**
independence, and requires PRC issuers to present their annual accounts in
accordance with Hong Kong or International Financial Reporting Standards.

A number of further Rules over and above those applying to non-Hong Kong   **4.79**
issuers generally are laid out in Chapter 19 of the Listing Rules, and these
mainly clarify matters connected with the particular status of domestic and
foreign shares, risk factors associated with PRC companies, and the status of the
issuer within the wider PRC framework.

In addition, an increased burden is placed on the sponsor to satisfy itself as to   **4.80**
the suitability for listing of the PRC issuer. In particular, the sponsor will need
to be sure that directors of the issuer understand their obligations under
the Listing Rules and applicable laws as directors of a listed company and that
they will act accordingly.

(7) Importance of the Listing Rules

It is of central concern to the SEHK in the exercise of its function as a regulator   **4.81**
that investors are properly protected and that an orderly market is maintained.
Accordingly, listing when granted is always subject to the SEHK being satisfied
as to these two concerns.

Where either of these concerns are placed in jeopardy, the SEHK has the right   **4.82**
under the Listing Rules 'at any time to suspend dealings in any securities or
cancel the listing of any securities in such circumstances and subject to such
conditions as it thinks fit, whether requested by the issuer or not'.[46] Further, the
SMLR, made pursuant to the SFO,[47] gives statutory backing to the Listing
Rules and requires applicants seeking a listing to comply with the rules and
requirements of the SEHK. In addition, where a company fails in any material
way to comply with the Listing Rules, the SEHK may suspend or cancel the
listing of the company.[48] Accordingly, compliance with the Listing Rules should
be regarded as a serious matter.

---

[46] LR 6.01.   [47] SFO s 36(1).   [48] LR 6.01(1).

(8) Growth Enterprise Market

4.83   The primary set of regulations concerning listing securities on the GEM are the Rules Governing the Listing of Securities on the Growth Enterprise Market of The Stock Exchange of Hong Kong Limited ('GEM Rules') While broadly following the same approach and structure to admission to listing and continuing obligations and so on as the main board, a number of differences are called for given the nature of the market as being 'a "buyers beware" market for informed investors'.[49] The main points of difference are summarized in Table 4.1. In general, such differences arise out of the theme of attracting a different type of company as regards track record.

4.84   In some regards, such alternative markets are seen as stepping stones to a listing on the Main Board, although this is not always the case. A company listed on GEM may after a period determine that it has outgrown GEM and that it wishes to graduate to the higher standing of a main board listing. There are no special rules which apply to graduating GEM companies. As regards their GEM listing, they will need to follow the GEM Rules concerning the withdrawal of listing. As regards gaining admission to the main board, they will need to follow the main board's Listing Rules as to admission.

C. Regulation of Sponsors and Compliance Advisers

4.85   In the next sections, which review the SEHK's requirements for the appointment of sponsors and compliance advisers, it is worth bearing in mind the nature of the transition required to be made from private to public listed company, and the ways in which the appointment of sponsors and compliance advisers may facilitate this transition to protect both the integrity of the market and the investors which participate in it.

(1) Sponsors

4.86   Every company seeking an initial listing must appoint a sponsor, that is, a corporation or authorized financial institution, licensed or registered under applicable laws to advise on corporate finance matters. The sponsor must be acceptable to the SEHK.[50] The sponsor must be both impartial and independent and the sponsor is required to make a declaration to the SEHK to this effect. For example, the sponsor or its directors may not be a shareholder holding

---

[49] Source: GEM website <http://www.hkgem.com>.
[50] LR 3A.02.

Table 4.1 Main differences between SEHK and GEM listing requirements

	MAIN BOARD	GEM
Financial requirements	Profit/ market capitalization/ revenue/ cash flow tests (LR 8.05)	No financial standards requirements
Operating history	3-year trading record (LR 8.05, 8.05A)	24-month active business pursuits or 1 year if financial thresholds met (GEMLR 11.12)
Business line etc	No requirement	Must have focused line of business and clear business objectives (GEMLR 11.12, 11.15)
Management and ownership	Substantially same management for 3-year track record period and ownership for most recent financial year (LR 8.05)	Substantially same management and ownership during period of active business pursuits (GEMLR 11.12)
Minimum market capitalization	HK$ 200m (LR 8.09(2))	No specific requirement but in practice >HK$ 120m[51]
Minimum holdings by management etc	No requirement	Management shareholders and significant shareholders to hold at least 35% of issued shares at time of listing (GEMLR 11.22)
Underwriting	Must be fully underwritten	Not compulsory but listing subject to minimum amount being raised (as set out in prospectus) (GEMLR 11.24)
Sponsors[52]	Must be acceptable to the SEHK	Sponsor must be 'qualified', ie approved by GEM (GEMLR 6.04)
Shareholder moratorium	Controlling shareholders (owning 30% of the shares in issue) may not dispose of shares for 6 months following listing (LR 10.07)	Shareholders holding >5% of the shares in issue must place their shares in escrow and not dispose of them for at least 6 months after listing (or 12 months in the case of such a shareholder who is involved in management of the company) (GEMLR 13.16–19)
Compliance officer	Must be acceptable to the SEHK	An executive director must be designated as the compliance officer for purposes of compliance with GEM Rules (GEMLR 5.19–23)

---

[51] GEMLR 11.23(2) requires at least HK$ 30m of market capitalization to be in public hands and GEMLR 11.23(1) requires the minimum public float to be 25%.

[52] The SFC are currently proposing additional licensing requirements which would specifically apply to sponsors of IPOs and which would cover initial eligibility criteria and on-going compliance requirements including as to minimum capitalization and annual self-assessments of internal controls and systems.

5 per cent or more of the applicant company, or be a significant creditor of the applicant company. In order to facilitate the sponsor's role, the Listing Rules oblige the applicant to fully cooperate with the sponsor in the performance of its roles.

4.87 The sponsor performs a number of different roles in relation to an initial listing. In its relationship with the company, it acts as an adviser in two senses. First, it advises the company as to the commercial aspects of being listed, normally including the marketing and pricing of the company's shares and leading a selling syndicate as underwriter. Second, it guides the company through the listing process as required by the Listing Rules and applicable laws.

4.88 However, the sponsor also plays another important role: as watchdog. Upon being appointed, it is required to give a signed undertaking to the SEHK. Amongst other things, the undertaking requires the sponsor to 'ensure that all information provided to the Exchange during the listing application process is true in all material respects and does not omit any material information'.[53] This is an onerous burden, particularly as it is required to inform the SEHK should it become aware of any matter casting doubt on the truth and accuracy of information so provided.

4.89 Furthering this role, once a company's application for listing has been approved, the sponsor is required to give a written declaration as to proper submission of documents and, importantly, as to having made 'reasonable due diligence enquiries' as to the truth and accuracy, and completeness and sufficiency of information in the listing document. The SEHK has set out the required standard of 'reasonable due diligence enquiries' in Practice Note 21 to the Listing Rules.

4.90 The Practice Note requires a review of documentation and interviews of management, staff, customers, suppliers, bankers, and physical inspection of assets—all quite standard for a due diligence exercise. However, it is notable that the Practice Note also requires the sponsor to assess various matters, not only as to business feasibility but also as to:

> the financial literacy, corporate governance experience and competence generally of the directors with a view to determining the extent to which the board of the new applicant as a whole has a depth and breadth of financial literacy and understanding of good corporate governance.[54]

Clearly the role of the sponsor is an onerous one as regards the requirements imposed upon it by the SEHK and every sponsor will need to ensure it is familiar with the specific expectations of the SEHK as set out in Practice Note 21.

---

[53] LR 3A.04(2).   [54] PN 21, para 11(b).

(2) Compliance advisers

Every company seeking an initial listing must also appoint a 'compliance **4.91** adviser', that is, a corporation or authorized financial institution, licensed or registered under applicable laws to advise on corporate finance matters, the identity of which is acceptable to the SEHK.[55] Such appointment must run from the initial listing of the company's securities to the date it distributes the results for its first full financial year after listing.

The function of the compliance adviser is to assist the newly listed issuer **4.92** through the early stages of its life as a listed company. Accordingly, the company will be required to consult with the compliance adviser as regards announcements, transactions which may incur regulatory consequences, or where the activities of the company deviate from those set out in the listing document or prospectus. In advising the company, the compliance adviser is required by the Listing Rules to guide the company as regards the requirements of the Listing Rules and other applicable laws and regulations.

In addition, where new directors are to be appointed, the compliance adviser **4.93** is required to assess their understanding of their fiduciary responsibilities as a director of a listed issuer and, as necessary, make recommendations to the board for appropriate remedial steps such as training.

Like the sponsor, the compliance adviser is required to fully cooperate in any **4.94** investigation of the SEHK. However, unlike the sponsor, the compliance adviser is not under any obligation to report anomalies to the SEHK.

D. Prospectuses and Related Liabilities

One of the most tangible outputs of any IPO or public offering of company **4.95** shares is the prospectus. The prospectus must give a complete and up-to-date snapshot of all aspects of the company and its group, both positive and negative. It must:

> contain such particulars and information which, having regard to the particular nature of the applicant and the securities, is necessary to enable an investor to make an informed assessment of the activities, assets and liabilities and financial position, of the applicant at the time of the application and its profits and losses and of the rights attaching to the securities.[56]

The prospectus serves three purposes. First, it is the document which constitutes **4.96** the Listing Document containing the specified information required by the

---

[55] LR 3A.19.   [56] SMLR s 3(c).

Listing Rules. Second, it is the prospectus required by the Companies Ordinance (and therefore the essential element of any public offering of shares which does not include a listing). Third, it is intended to be one of the primary selling tools containing the information the company and the sponsor consider desirable to inform and interest potential investors.

(1) Listing documents and prospectuses

4.97 Although a prospectus and a listing document are often or usually the same document, this is not always the case. For example, a listing by way of an introduction, while requiring the preparation of a listing document, does not involve any offer to the public and hence does not involve the preparation of a prospectus. This underlines the conceptual difference between the two documents: whereas the listing document is providing information to those who choose to participate in the listed securities market, the prospectus is providing information to the public generally.

4.98 To be technically correct, care should be taken as to which term to use in describing a document, although in practice when one refers to a prospectus it is assumed that this involves a listing and hence the document will also constitute a listing document. Unless otherwise indicated, this approach is followed herein. Accordingly, the listing document cum prospectus needs to comply with two sets of requirements.

Listing document requirements

4.99 Listing Rule 1.01 defines a listing document as a document issued or proposed to be issued in connection with an application of listing, and may include a prospectus, circular, or equivalent document. As already mentioned, the SMLR gives statutory backing to the Listing Rules and specifically contemplates the provision of adequate information in connection with an application (see above).[57] The SEHK's specific requirements for information are set out in Chapter 11 and Appendix 1 of the Listing Rules. Appendix 1 is divided into two parts: Part A, which is applicable to new issuers, and Part B, which is applicable to companies already listed.

Prospectus requirements

4.100 Compliance with the listing document requirements does not imply automatic compliance with prospectus requirements which are set out in the Companies Ordinance. Under the Companies Ordinance, every prospectus (unless

---

[57] SMLR s 3(c).

exempted[58]) must state the matters specified in Part I of the third schedule and set out the reports specified in Part II of that Schedule. Failure to comply with these requirements renders the company and persons a party to the issue of the prospectus liable to a fine.[59]

As already mentioned, since prospectuses normally involve a listing and there- **4.101** fore a listing document, the SEHK also performs the function of approving prospectuses for the purposes of the Companies Ordinance.

(2) Contents

Commercial parties involved in the production of the prospectus often refer to **4.102** it as having two conceptual parts, the 'front end' and the 'back end'. The former is the more commercial part, being concerned with the details of the offering (or other method of listing) and the description of the company's business. The latter is 'everything else', containing many detailed disclosures required by the Listing Rules and the Companies Ordinance.

A prospectus is normally set out in the following manner: **4.103**

The 'front end' will commence with a summary of both the offering (or what- **4.104** ever method is employed) and the company together with a timetable of events. The most critical date for all persons concerned will be the offer period and the date on which dealings are expected to commence.

A risk factors section (sometimes referred to as 'other considerations') will set **4.105** out an extensive qualification to investors as to the risks of participating in the offering. The particular risks set out will be specific to the company and its business. For example, the profitability of a company with substantial revenues denominated in a foreign currency will be subject to foreign exchange risks. A company with one or two significant individuals in management, or customers, will be subject to the risk that these people cease to be associated with the company. Other risks could include risks related to: taxation, litigation, compliance and regulatory developments, competition, conflicts of interest, and so on. One has to examine the nature of the company to understand the range of possible risks involved.

The document will then describe the share offering at length, as well as the share **4.106** capital of the company.

The business of the company will be described next. In some ways this is the **4.107** central part of the document. This section will typically cover history and

---

[58] CO s 38A.   [59] CO s 38.

development, group structure, business divisions, approach to research and development, competition, customers, management, and so on.

4.108 The business section naturally leads in to a discussion of the financial aspects of the company and sometimes one will see a section headed 'Management Discussion and Analysis', following US terminology, in which the directors consider the meaning of the financial status of the company. There are special requirements applying to comments on future performance which may amount to a profit forecast (see below).

4.109 The 'back end' of the document will provide detailed disclosure of information required to comply with regulatory requirements as well as the accountant's report, property valuations, and if the company is a non-Hong Kong company, a summary of the relevant aspects of that jurisdiction's company law. Importantly, the document will also include details of the application procedures and forms.

4.110 This layout provides the structure within which the detailed legal and regulatory requirements as to document content will be satisfied, as next described.

Formal content requirements

4.111 The specific content requirements under the Listing Rules and the Companies Ordinance are not mutually exclusive, and the requirements overlap as to content required. The following section will review the types of information required generally in the context of an IPO. Special requirements apply as regards other types of listing and in respect of special companies such as mineral companies, non-Hong Kong issuers including PRC issuers, and investment companies.[60]

4.112 The following list of information required gives an indication of the major requirements, and indicates the basis on which the contents of a listing document cum prospectus are formed.

Issuer

4.113 Information on the issuer must include:

- general information about the issuer, such as its incorporation and constitution, and its advisers;
- information about the issuer's capital including as to shareholder voting rights and any other rights affecting capital, such as options etc; and

---

[60] See LR Chapters 18, 19, 19A, & 21.

- particulars of any other stock exchange on which any securities of the issuer is listed.

Securities

Information on the securities to be listed must include: **4.114**

- information about the securities for which listing is sought and the terms and conditions of their issue and distribution including as to the total amount of the public or private issue and the number of securities offered;
- the underwriting arrangements;
- whether price stabilizing activities may be entered into in connection with an offering and the terms and duration on which the same shall be conducted; and
- the date on which dealings are expected to commence.

Directors and management

Information on the directors and management of the issuer must include: **4.115**

- information in respect of directors' emoluments as well as the five individuals whose emoluments (excluding amounts paid or payable by way of commissions on sales generated by the individual) were the highest in the issuer or the group for the year; and
- information about the issuer's management including the interests of each director and chief executive of the issuer in the securities of the company and the Model Code for Securities Transactions by Directors of Listed Companies (see Chapter 6).

Shareholders

Information on the issuer's shareholders must include details of any controlling   **4.116**
shareholder of the issuer, including a statement explaining how the issuer is satisfied that it is capable of carrying on its business independently of the controlling shareholder after listing.

Business

Information on the issuer's business must include: **4.117**

- general information about the group's business activities such as the nature of the business of the group. This is an important part of the document on which much time will be spent in due diligence and verification as it will describe not only the different aspects of the business but also comment on things affecting the business such as market conditions, new products and services introduced, market share, changes in turnover and margins, major customers and suppliers, research and development policy; and

- general information on the trend of the business of the group since the last accounts date.

Financial

4.118 Financial information on the issuer must include:

- financial information about the group and the prospects of the group including commentary on the group's liquidity and financial resources and capital structure of the group;
- auditors report for each of the three preceding years, the latest ending on a date not more than six months before the issue date of the prospectus; and
- statement by the directors as to sufficiency of working capital, any material adverse change in the financial or trading position of the group.

Other

4.119 Other information requirements include:

- the qualifications of any expert making a statement in the document and its relationship with the issuer;
- particulars of any litigation or claims of material importance pending or threatened against any member of the group;
- use of proceeds of the issue;
- material contracts (ie contracts entered into otherwise than in the ordinary course of business); and
- a list of documents for public inspection including documents such as the constitutional documents of the company, its material contracts, directors' service contracts.

4.120 Further, notwithstanding the specific requirements of Appendix 1, and in furtherance of section 3(c) of the SMLR, the SEHK may require disclosure of additional information. It may also permit reductions in information required to be provided according to the needs of the particular case.

Profit forecasts

4.121 In certain cases, a company and its sponsor may wish to include a profit or dividend forecast in the prospectus. Any reference, whether general or specific, to future profits (or losses) will be regarded as a profit forecast, as will any valuation of assets (other than land and buildings) or businesses acquired by an issuer based on discounted cash flows or projections of profits, earnings, or cash flows.

4.122 Whether to include a forecast is a matter for commercial consideration, for example, whether it makes the company appear more desirable and, conversely, the ramifications should the company not meet the forecast. It is in view of this latter concern that, normally, a forecast will only be considered if there is a relatively short period of time between the issue of the prospectus and the relevant accounting date.

Notwithstanding the commercial considerations, if a profit forecast is to be **4.123** included, it must be clearly stated and include the specific commercial assumptions on which it is based including as to the reliability of such forecast. It must also be supported by a formal profit forecast. However, dividend forecasts not based on an assumed profit are not subject to this requirement. The prospectus must also set out the report of the reporting accountants and the company's sponsor (or financial adviser) in relation to the profit forecast, the sponsor's report being additionally required to state they have satisfied themselves that the forecast has been made by the directors after due and careful enquiry.

Other requirements

Every listing document or prospectus must be in the English language together **4.124** with a Chinese translation. In addition, the listing document must contain on its front cover the SEHK's disclaimer:

> The Stock Exchange of Hong Kong Limited takes no responsibility for the contents of this document, makes no representation as to its accuracy or completeness and expressly disclaims any liability whatsoever for any loss howsoever arising from or in reliance upon the whole or any part of the contents of this document.[61]

While illustrations are permitted, the SEHK is often quite sensitive about **4.125** them as regards the potential to mislead the investor. Finally, an applicant is required to confirm in their formal application for listing[62] that the Chapter 11 requirements have been complied with.

(3) Production process

Practices vary as to who takes primary responsibility for drafting the prospectus. **4.126** Under any arrangement it will involve the coordinated efforts of company management and staff, the underwriter, their respective lawyers, and the company's accountants. The process can be divided into to phases: finding out what needs to be written (good or bad) through a process of due diligence, and checking that what has been written is justifiable through a process known as verification. Both processes are in part undertaken in consequence of various legal liabilities, which are considered below.

---

[61] LR 11.20.   [62] Form C1.

Due diligence

4.127 Due diligence can be defined as the process undertaken by underwriters to establish the completeness and accuracy of the information contained in the prospectus. It involves the collection, organization, and checking of information relevant to the company proposed to be listed, the securities themselves and such other information as an investor may need to make an informed investment decision.

4.128 Three principal purposes of due diligence are:

- information gathering—to collect up-to-date information as to the business and financial condition of the issuer;

- reduction of risk of liability—if the exercise is done properly, it significantly reduces the risk of legal liability based on the contents or omissions of the prospectus; and

- defence to liability—in the event a legal liability does arise, such as in the tort of negligence, it enables the underwriter to raise a 'reasonable care' defence. Note that such a defence is unlikely to be available for the issuer.

4.129 Due diligence is significant in terms of person-hours spent at the task. Normally an extensive list of questions will be compiled by the underwriters and its lawyers and provided to the company which will need to provide written and verbal answers as well as provide supporting documents where relevant.

4.130 The tension which sometimes arises is reluctance on the part of the company's management or staff to disclose negative information. This normally arises as a result of either pride in the achievements of the company, nervousness that any bad news may prejudice the good receipt of the company in the market, or simply a lack of understanding as to the process and the attendant legal liabilities.

4.131 As already mentioned, the SEHK has indicated in its Practice Note 21 the due diligence steps a sponsor must undertake in order for it to satisfy the SEHK. The SEHK will also play an active role in raising questions as to the contents of the prospectus and this may lead to further due diligence work being undertaken.

Verification

4.132 If one regards due diligence as the detective work, verification is the administrative end which reviews and confirms the conclusions of the detective work. Verification normally involves the production of 'verification notes' which is a document setting out, against statements made in the prospectus, the justification for such statements. The justification normally is a specific independent document or, where documentary confirmation is not available, the written confirmation of a particular management level person with a reasonable basis for such confirmation. Practices do vary as to how detailed such notes are, ranging from a line-by-line approach to only those matters which are considered to be material.

In this regard, one must also consider the context of the statements. A statement included in a prospectus shall be deemed to be untrue if it is misleading in the form and context in which it is included.[63] 'Untrue statement' includes a material omission from the prospectus. Like due diligence, verification and verification notes can assist in establishing reasonable belief after reasonable enquiry as to the accuracy of the relevant document where reasonable belief after reasonable enquiry provides an exemption from a statutory liability or to discharge some common law duty of care that is owed. Certainly, verification notes cause parties involved to test the accuracy of statements looked at in isolation as well as in context. They also identify the persons taking responsibility for statements (such persons are normally required to sign to the same). However, verification notes can be a two-edged sword. They can give the illusion of protection from liability, and in some cases can merely serve to indicate not only what was done but also to highlight what was not done. **4.133**

(4) Supplementary offering documents

It sometimes happens that, between the time the prospectus is issued and the commencement of dealings in the securities, circumstances change or new information comes to light. Where the same is significant, it will be necessary to advise the SEHK and issue a supplementary listing document or prospectus which sets out the new matter. A matter would be significant if it would have been required to be included in the prospectus had it arisen prior to the issue of the prospectus, or is significant for the purpose of making an informed investment decision. **4.134**

(5) Prospectus liability

Shortcomings in prospectuses give rise to a range of potential liabilities both criminal and civil as well as potential regulatory sanctions. This is a natural consequence of creating a document which investors rely on, and of submitting oneself to a detailed legal and regulatory process. **4.135**

In reviewing the topic of prospectus liability, it is worth bearing in mind two considerations. First, a document does not need to be called or even look **4.136**

---

[63] CO s 41A.

anything like a prospectus in order for it to be treated as one. 'Prospectus' means any document[64]

> offering any shares in or debentures of a company . . . to the public for subscription or purchase for cash or other consideration . . . or is calculated to invite offers by the public to subscribe for or purchase for cash or other consideration any shares or debentures of a company

in each case irrespective of where such company is incorporated.[65] Accordingly, any such document regarded as a prospectus would need to comply with all prospectus requirements unless exempted. Second, even if the document is not itself a prospectus, statements in it could be deemed to be part of the prospectus if circulated or issued with the prospectus. If so, such a document would need to be filed and registered as a prospectus.

4.137 Documents such as research reports commenting on the company (and possibly on its upcoming IPO) are probably the most typical examples of documents which could fall to be so treated under either of the above situations. If so treated, the potential liabilities attaching to prospectuses would also attach to the research report.

4.138 While the remainder of this section is concerned with legal liability, it is also worth bearing in mind the commercial and regulatory factors arising where prospectus preparation is poor.

4.139 Delays in finalizing the prospectus may cause the timetable to be derailed or favourable market conditions to be missed. This obviously may give rise to serious commercial consequences for the company in meeting its objectives. While delays may occur for a number of reasons beyond one's control, it should not normally occur as a result of failing to anticipate (i) the queries of the Listing Division or the SFC during the drafting stage, or (ii) the concerns of the Listing Committee at the hearing stage. As already mentioned, the Listing Division is normally very active in raising questions and seeking clarification during the drafting stage and a poorly prepared document will increase the time taken to resolve all such outstanding queries.

4.140 Further, where due diligence has been poorly undertaken resulting in a listing document not complying with the requirements of the Listing Rules, the persons involved in the document preparation[66] may be subjected to disciplinary sanctions including public censure, reporting such person to the SFC and

---

[64] This includes any prospectus, notice, circular, brochure, advertisement, or other document.
[65] CO s 2(1).
[66] This may include the company, its directors, substantial shareholders, sponsor, professional adviser. See LR 2A.10 for a complete list.

barring a professional from representing specified persons before the Listing Division or Listing Committee.[67]

Responsibility

The Listing Rules provide that each of the directors of the company (including any person proposed or named as a director in the listing document) is required to accept responsibility for the information contained in the listing document and include in the listing document a statement to that effect.[68]   **4.141**

Civil liability

Under the Companies Ordinance, civil liability is imposed on certain categories of persons to pay compensation to any person who applies for securities on the faith of the prospectus and suffers loss by reason of an untrue or misleading statement in the prospectus.[69] The following persons are potentially liable: **4.142**

- every director of the company at the time of the issue of the prospectus;
- every person who has authorized himself to be named and is named in the prospectus as a director or as having agreed to become a director either immediately or after an interval of time;
- a promoter of the company (being any person a party to the preparation of the prospectus); and
- every person who has authorized the issue of the prospectus.

A number of defences are available to each of the foregoing persons. A person will not be held liable in the following circumstances: **4.143**

- where the prospectus was issued without their consent, and that on becoming aware of its issue they forthwith gave reasonable public notice of the same;
- in relation to an untrue statement discovered after the issue of the prospectus and before allotment thereunder, such person withdrew consent thereto and gave reasonable public notice citing the reason for the same;
- in relation to any untrue statement (other than expert statements), such person had reasonable grounds to believe and did believe that the statement was true;
- in relation to an untrue statement of an expert or other report or valuation, the statement was a fair representation of the statement made by the expert, etc and that such person had reasonable grounds to believe and did believe that the person making the statement was competent to make it; or

---

[67] See LR 2A.09 for a complete list   [68] LR 11.12.
[69] CO s 40 (in relation to Hong Kong companies) & CO s 342E (in relation to non-Hong Kong companies). An untrue statement includes a material omission: CO s 41A(2) & s 343(2A).

- as regards an expert's liability in relation to the statement made by such person, that such person was competent to make the statement and had reasonable grounds to believe and did believe that the statement was true.

4.144 In the event persons are named (eg as director or expert) in a prospectus but have withdrawn their consent prior to the issue of the prospectus, the directors of the company and any other person who authorized the issue of the prospectus shall be liable to indemnify the person named as aforesaid against all damages and costs and legal liabilities which such person may incur as a result of their inclusion in the prospectus.

4.145 In addition, under the SFO, a person who makes a fraudulent, reckless, or negligent misrepresentation in a prospectus may be liable to pay compensation where a person has invested in reliance on such misrepresentation and suffers a pecuniary loss as a result.[70] Such liability attaches to each director of the company unless they can prove they did not authorize the making of the misrepresentation. This head of liability covers forecasts and omissions.

4.146 Further, market misconduct liability may arise in respect of the disclosure of false or misleading information inducing transactions.[71] A prospectus (the distribution of which involves the circulation of information likely to induce another person to subscribe for or purchase securities) issued with false or misleading information as to a material fact or the omission thereof, and the same has been issued knowingly, recklessly, or negligently as to whether such information is false or misleading, constitutes market misconduct. As such, the relevant persons would be liable to pay compensation by way of damages to any other person for any pecuniary loss sustained by the other person as a result of the market misconduct. It is not necessary to prove that the loss arises from having entered into a transaction or dealing at a price affected by the market misconduct. However, no person shall be liable to pay compensation under this provision unless it is fair, just, and reasonable in the circumstances of the case that the person should be so liable.[72]

4.147 Under Hong Kong law, as with other common law systems, liability may arise out of contract or tort law. As a general principle, where representations are made by one party which induce another to enter into a contract and those representations are deliberately, negligently, or innocently false, then rights of rescission and/or damages may be conferred on the other party.

4.148 The issue of a prospectus constitutes a bundle of representations on the basis of which moneys are offered for the shares. It is also possible that where a person has applied for shares and has been given material relating to the company,

---

[70] SFO s 108.   [71] SFO s 277.   [72] SFO s 281.

either with the prospectus or otherwise in connection with the offering, reliance has been placed on the representations contained in that material in deciding to apply for the shares and has consequently suffered loss.

All those involved in the preparation and issue of material used in connection **4.149** with the offering may be liable in negligence if they fail to exercise due care in the preparation of the material and investors relying on the material suffer losses. If the sponsor or underwriter or another party connected with the offering has circulated such material, it exposes itself to legal action. The publication of any unpublished financial information or projections obtained from the company is particularly dangerous in this context.

Finally, the agreements between the company and the underwriters may also be **4.150** a source of contractual liability as regards the prospectus. In the underwriting agreement, the company will normally warrant to the underwriters as to the accuracy and completeness of the information provided to the underwriters in their due diligence exercise and as regards the information presented in the prospectus as well as compliance with laws and regulations.

Criminal liability

Under the Companies Ordinance, criminal liability is imposed on any person **4.151** who authorizes the issue of a prospectus containing an untrue statement or a material omission.[73] Such person shall be liable to imprisonment for up to three years and a fine of up to HK$ 700,000 (US$ 90,000), unless he proves either that the statement was immaterial or that he had reasonable grounds to believe and did up to the time of the issue of the prospectus believe that the statement was true.

It is unlawful to publish any advertisement in relation to a prospectus or **4.152** proposed prospectus or to publish any extract of a prospectus by way of advertisement.[74] However, certain exemptions from this restriction are available, primarily being those which comply with the requirements of the SFC.[75]

In addition to the Companies Ordinance, a number of related provisions **4.153** under the SFO may be relevant to a prospectus. First, where a person makes a fraudulent or reckless misrepresentation in a prospectus such person is liable to imprisonment of up to seven years and a fine of up to HK$ 1 million

---

[73] CO s 40A (in relation to Hong Kong companies) & CO s 342F (in relation to non-Hong Kong companies).
[74] CO s 38B.
[75] CO s 38B(2). The SFC may, pursuant to CO s 38BA, publish guidelines in relation to the form and manner of and other matters relating to such publications.

(US$ 128,500).[76] Liability also would arise in respect of an intentional or reckless omission of a material fact. As with section 108 of the SFO, this head of liability also covers forecasts and omissions.

4.154   Second, a company is prohibited from issuing an advertisement in connection with an offer to the public unless authorized by the SFC.[77] Breach of the prohibition is an offence carrying penalties of up to three years' imprisonment and a fine of up to HK$ 500,000 (US$ 64,300).

4.155   Third, market misconduct may comprise the disclosure of false or misleading information inducing transactions.[78] A prospectus (the distribution of which involves the circulation of information likely to induce another person to subscribe for or purchase securities) issued with false or misleading, information as to a material fact or the omission thereof, and the same has been issued knowingly or recklessly as to whether such information is false or misleading, constitutes market misconduct. The commission of an offence renders the person liable to imprisonment of up to 10 years and a fine of up to HK$ 10 million (US$ 1,285,000). In addition, the courts may make certain orders against such person including disqualifying that person as a director of a listed company for up to five years. (In addition, a sponsor falling liable under this section may additionally be subject to disciplinary sanctions imposed by the SFC.)

4.156   Under common law, untrue statements in prospectuses may be misrepresentations but if it can be shown that there has been, on the part of the person responsible for the statement, intent to defraud by the deliberate or reckless making of a false statement of a material fact, then this may constitute the criminal offence of fraud.[79] This offence carries up to 14 years' imprisonment. This offence may be in addition to the offence at common law of conspiracy to defraud.

Blackout period

4.157   A blackout period is a term used to describe a period during which information about the proposed listing (and to some extent about the company itself) is not permitted to be publicly distributed. Blackout periods run from prior to the listing until after trading commences, the precise timing and length of the period being determined by a number of factors including what other jurisdictions the listing may be marketed to (and the laws in those places), and the practices of the lead underwriter. Blackout periods are important tools in

---

[76] SFO s 107.   [77] SFO s 103.   [78] SFO s 298.
[79] Theft Ordinance (Cap. 210), s 16A.

controlling potential liabilities and risks to the listing process and the parties involved.

In the Hong Kong market, the Code of Conduct for Persons Licensed by or **4.158** Registered with the SFC specifically provides for a 'quiet period' commencing upon the pricing of securities and lasting for 40 days if an IPO, or 10 days if a secondary offering. During such period a manager, sponsor, or underwriter may not issue research covering the relevant company unless it has issued research on the company with reasonable regularity in its normal course of business.[80]

Blackout periods are primarily aimed at the distribution of research reports and **4.159** the avoidance of two problems. First, there is a risk that a research report could be regarded as a prospectus and therefore become subject to the prospectus requirements of the Companies Ordinance.[81] If it is regarded as a prospectus, unless such report is duly registered and compliant as to content requirements, its issue would constitute a criminal offence by every person knowingly a party to the issue thereof. Second, even if the report is not regarded as a prospectus, statements in the report will be deemed to be part of the prospectus if circulated or issued with the prospectus and therefore will need to be registered and compliant as to content requirements.

Although research reports will often bear a legend disclaiming certain matters **4.160** including that it does not constitute an offer document, such disclaimers are unlikely to be effective where the contents of the report or other surrounding circumstances indicate otherwise.

Underlying the above problems is the concern that the contents of research **4.161** reports probably fall well short of the standard required for a prospectus (the report being unlikely to have been subjected to due diligence and verification) and consequently would give rise to additional liabilities under a number of the heads described above should it contain untrue or misleading statements.

However, a 'professionals exemption' is available as regards non-Hong Kong **4.162** issuers in that offers of shares for subscription or sale to any person whose ordinary business is to buy or sell shares, whether as principal or agent, shall not be deemed an offer to the public for the purposes of this Part of this Ordinance.[82] Accordingly, what might otherwise be regarded as a prospectus will not be if the issuer is incorporated outside Hong Kong and the reports are distributed only to professionals.

---

[80] See paragraph 16.5(g).
[81] A prospectus is defined in the Companies Ordinance to include any document calculated or likely to invite offers by the public to subscribe for or purchase shares.
[82] CO s 343(2).

4.163   A similar problem exists in relation to the offence of issuing an advertisement or invitation which is likely to lead to the public acquiring or subscribing securities.[83] The offence has various exemptions, including a professionals only exemption as described above.

4.164   Persons engaged in dealing or advising in relation to securities, or advising on corporate finance[84] are prohibited from communicating any offer to purchase or subscribe securities unless the offer contains certain details set out in the SFO.[85] Although these details will be contained in the prospectus, they are unlikely to be contained in a research report. Again, a professionals only exemption is available.

4.165   As already mentioned, the SEHK restricts the issue of publicity material relating to a proposed listing. In extreme cases, the SEHK will cancel a Listing Committee hearing if there has been inappropriate pre-listing publicity. In all cases, there is a risk that publicity could be regarded as part of the prospectus, the problem in this regard being that the level of attention paid to the content of the publicity probably falls well short of the standard required for a prospectus (the publicity may not have been subjected to due diligence and verification).

4.166   Finally, the liabilities at common law already described above may also be an issue in relation to any report issued either with or in connection with the listing if an investor relied on such report in deciding to apply for shares and subsequently suffered a loss.

E. Post-listing Events, On-going Requirements, Suspension, and De-listing

4.167   Corporate laws regulate the ways by which a company may alter its share capital and, once a company has become a listed company, it becomes subject to additional restrictions imposed by the SEHK.

(1) Stabilization

4.168   Once a company is listed, its share capital becomes subject to one very important new feature: the price of its shares as traded on the market fluctuates. As already mentioned, such fluctuation is not only in response to the financial condition and prospects of the company. In particular, in the early days of it

---

[83] SFO s 103.
[84] ie persons registered with a Type 1, 4, or 6 licence as per SFO sch 5, Part 1.
[85] SFO s 175.

being listed the company may be subject to considerable speculation as to the 'correct' level of its entry price (whether it is perceived as being over- or under-priced). Two factors which drive this perception include the extent to which the offering was over- or under-subscribed, and the amount of stagging[86] which is being done.

These factors operating in the early period of trading create potential issues for **4.169** company and investors alike. In order to address these factors, sponsors will typically engage in something called 'stabilization'. In stabilization, the stabilizing manager (typically the sponsor) will enter the market as both buyer and seller to provide a steadying balance to the price range at which the shares are trading. While the primary purpose of this activity is to maintain an orderly and liquid market, it is open to abuse and, moreover, would constitute market abuse or the commission of a criminal offence in the form of false trading,[87] or stock market manipulation.[88]

What stops such stabilizing activities from being abusive or criminal is the pres- **4.170** ence of a safe harbour provided by the Securities and Futures (Price Stabilizing) Rules (Cap. 571W). The Price Stabilizing Rules provide a framework for permitted actions for up to 30 days from the commencement of trading subject to company consent to stabilizing being undertaken, disclosure that stabilization will be undertaken and of the stabilizing trades entered into, and record keeping requirements.

The liabilities of engaging in stabilizing activities otherwise than in accordance **4.171** with the Price Stabilizing Rules are discussed further in Chapter 8.

(2) New share issues

A listed company seeking to issue new shares[89] is subject to a number of restric- **4.172** tions intended to preserve the interests of both existing shareholders and the market in the company's shares. These restrictions are discussed in Chapter 6.

(3) Share repurchases

Under Hong Kong company law, listed companies are able to purchase their own **4.173** shares, for certain stated purposes, out of distributable profits or the proceeds of

---

[86] 'Stagging' refers to the practice of persons who apply for and obtain shares in an offering with an intention to sell the shares in the first few days or weeks of the commencement of trading with the hope of obtaining a quick short-term profit. Such selling by 'stags' may exert a downward pressure on price.
[87] SFO s 274 or s 295.   [88] SFO s 278 or s 299.
[89] Or securities convertible into shares or rights (such as options or warrants) to subscribe for shares or convertible securities.

a fresh issue of shares, provided its articles so permit and the prior approval of shareholders in general meeting has been obtained.[90]

4.174 The Listing Rules require that (1) the company promptly advise the SEHK of any share repurchase it makes,[91] and (2) that it comply with the requirements of the Code on Share Repurchases.[92] The Code is issued by the SFC and sets out the permitted means by which a listed company may repurchase its own shares. The Code contemplates four means by which a repurchase may be undertaken.

4.175 First, a company which purchases shares on-market[93] is subject to no special additional requirements of the Code but continues to be subject to the requirements of its governing company law, as already mentioned above as regards Hong Kong companies.

4.176 Second, certain share repurchases are exempt from Code requirements, the most typical case of which is where shares are repurchased from employees pursuant to an approved employee share option scheme.

4.177 Third, a company may purchase shares off-market[94] provided the approval is obtained of both the company's shareholders and the Executive Director of the Corporate Finance Division of the SFC. Shareholder approval must be by a special resolution of disinterested shareholders, the shareholders having first had the benefit of being circularized with information relating to the proposed repurchase (including as to the identity and relationship with the proposed offerees), the advice of an independent financial adviser, and the recommendation of an independent committee of the board.

4.178 Finally, a company may repurchase shares via a general offer made in accordance with the Code on Takeovers and Mergers. The company will need to obtain the approval of shareholders by ordinary resolution in general meeting.[95] Such offers will need to be made pro rata to all shareholders. Occasionally, share repurchases made by general offer are conducted with a view to delisting or privatizing the company. In such cases, approval by independent shareholders by special resolution in general meeting will be required as well as meeting the requirement that not more than 10 per cent of the independent shareholder voting at the meeting vote against the resolution.

4.179 In each case (other than exempt share repurchases), on announcing a share

---

[90] CO ss 49B & 49BA.   [91] LR 13.31.   [92] LR 13.23(2).

[93] 'On-market' refers to purchases made through the facilities of an exchange (normally the SEHK).

[94] 'Off-market' refers to purchases made otherwise than on-market or through the other methods contemplated by the Code on Share Repurchases.

[95] Shareholders with a material interest different from other shareholders will normally be required by the Executive to be excluded from voting.

repurchase, the repurchasing company will be subject to a 31-day period during which it may not make any distribution of shares.

(4) *Minimum public holding*

As mentioned above, an issuer upon admission to listing must have a minimum public participation in its shareholding.[96] This is an on-going requirement of which the company must keep the SEHK advised should it fall below the required percentage. Should the percentage of shares held by the public fall below the minimum, the SEHK is empowered to suspend trading until appropriate steps have been taken to restore the minimum percentage holding. Suspension is not a necessary consequence if the SEHK is satisfied there remains an open market in the securities and that a false market does not develop. However, in the absence of an exemption, the SEHK will require the company and/or its largest shareholder to undertake to rectify the minimum percentage within an acceptable timeframe.

4.180

In some cases, the minimum percentage may be lost as a result of a shareholder who was previously regarded as part of the public float ceasing to be so regarded. However, it may be possible to continue to regard such a person as part of the public if it can be shown that such person is independent from the executive decisions of the board of the company. This situation may more commonly arise in connection with institutional investors who, although they may have a representation on the board, such representation is on a non-executive basis and such investor has widespread investment interests elsewhere.

4.181

(5) *Suspension of trading*

Suspension may arise in a number of different contexts and may be imposed by the SEHK under the Listing Rules or by the SFC under the SMLR, or it may be done at the request of the company itself.

4.182

The SEHK grants listing

4.183

> subject to the condition that where the Exchange considers it necessary for the protection of the investor or the maintenance of an orderly market, it may at any time suspend dealings in any securities or cancel the listing of any securities in such circumstances and subject to such conditions as it thinks fit.[97]

It is therefore not necessary for the company to have done anything wrong for

---

[96] LR 13.32.
[97] LR 6.01. See also LR Practice Note 11 which provides further guidance on when dealing may be suspended.

dealing in its shares to be suspended. The most typical example of this is where an unexplained or unusual change in the price or volume of trading occurs, whether due to rumours or for no apparent reason. The SEHK will normally endeavour to contact the company as to whether it has any undisclosed price sensitive information which perhaps ought to be disclosed to the market, or with a view to the company making a statement clarifying the facts from the rumours.

4.184   On the other hand, where the company is in material breach of its obligations under the Listing Rules, the SEHK may consider suspending dealings in its shares. An example of this would be where the company fails to maintain its minimum public float or fails to publish requisite periodic financial information when required to do so.

4.185   The SFC may also require the SEHK to suspend dealings in a company's shares where, inter alia, false or misleading information has been included in any document relating to the listing, or where it is necessary to maintain an orderly market or for the protection of investors.[98]

4.186   Finally, dealings in shares may also be suspended at the request of the company. This would typically occur where, for example, the company is about to announce a transaction which it expects will have a material effect on its share trading and pending a full announcement to the market of the details of such transaction. Examples would be where the company is about to launch a major new offering or repurchase, or where the board has been approached with a proposed takeover offer.

4.187   The SEHK requires the period of suspension to be kept as short as possible in order to maintain a fair and continuous market. Therefore dealings will normally recommence once a proper and full announcement has been made.

(6) Cancellation and withdrawal of listing

4.188   Cancellation and withdrawal (effectively synonymous terms) may occur voluntarily or involuntarily. In either case it poses a problem vis-à-vis the protection of investors—shareholders able to trade freely on the SEHK will have limited ability to trade if the shares are no longer listed, and of course they would not have the benefits provided by the Listing Rules.

4.189   There are two quite different contexts in which a company may seek voluntarily to withdraw its listing: where its shares are, or are to be, listed on another exchange (the 'alternative listing'); and where its shares after the withdrawal will

---

[98] SMLR s 8.

not be listed on any exchange. In making this distinction it is important to note that it is the SEHK which decides whether an alternative listing is acceptable to Hong Kong investors (for example, in terms of access and foreign exchange regulations); only if it is acceptable to the SEHK will it be regarded as an alternative listing.

In the case of an alternative listing, the company must obtain the approval of **4.190** shareholders in general meeting by ordinary resolution and provide them three months' notice of how they may transfer and trade securities to and in the new market. However, if the company's listing on the SEHK is a secondary listing, it will only be required to comply with the requirements of the SEHK of its primary listing and provide three months' notice to shareholders.

Where no alternative listing is available, approval of shareholders is again **4.191** required after circularization of the requisite information, but in this instance the approval level is by special resolution where controlling shareholders are not entitled to vote and not more than 10 per cent of the votes are cast against the resolution. A typical example is in cases where a company is being privatized in connection with a transaction governed by the Code on Takeovers and Mergers (see Chapter 7).

Cancellation may be imposed on the company by the SFC under the SMLR or **4.192** by the SEHK pursuant to the Listing Rules where the company is no longer suitable to remain listed. This may occur where the company has persistently breached Listing Rule requirements, or where necessary to maintain an orderly market. However, the most likely scenario is where the company or its business is no longer suitable for listing; for example, it has become a cash company or goes into receivership or liquidation.

F. Conclusion

Overall, Hong Kong has in place a system for public offerings of securities and **4.193** listing of companies largely based on the pre-FSMA 2000 system of the UK. As such, it is based on a combination of statutes (especially the Companies Ordinance and the SFO), regulations (especially the SMLR), self-regulation by the SEHK (mainly through the Listing Rules), and common law. Similar to other such systems past and present, it is generally effective in requiring the essential feature of such regulation: namely, disclosure of all relevant information. At the same time, however, it has been subject to criticism in relation to the essential counterpart of such regulation: namely, enforcement.

In terms of disclosure regulation for offering and listings of securities, IOSCO's **4.194** *Objectives and Principles of Securities Regulation* and *International Disclosure*

Standards for Cross-Border Offerings and Initial Listings by Foreign Issuers (IDS),[99] taken together, establish the underlying standards for the form and content of internationally acceptable offering documents. In order to build upon the general principles respecting offering and listings standards in the *Objectives and Principles*, in the IDS, IOSCO developed a framework for the minimum content of public offer prospectuses, which is intended to set a basic framework for international offering documents acceptable to regulators and stock exchanges around the world. The intention is that these standards will allow issuers to prepare a single disclosure document that will serve as an 'international passport' to capital raising and listing in more than one jurisdiction at a time. The standards have been approved by the entire membership of IOSCO, including the SFC.

4.195 Following an introduction and a glossary of terms, the Standards, in Part I, outline the contents of an acceptable document. Part II provides country specific information on areas not covered within the standards, necessary to validate the document in a given jurisdiction, which should be incorporated as a 'wrapper' to the IDS prospectus. In outline form, the cross-border prospectus is to comprise the following ten information categories: (1) identity of directors, senior management, and advisers; (2) offer statistics and expected timetable; (3) key information; (4) information on the company; (5) operating and financial review and prospects; (6) directors and employees; (7) major shareholders and related party transactions; (8) financial information; (9) the offer and listing; and (10) additional information. The Standards are to apply to listings, public offers, sales of equity securities for cash, and unless otherwise indicated, the Standards are intended to be used for prospectuses, offering and initial listing documents, and registration statements.[100] The Standards relate to non-financial statement disclosure requirements. Part II addresses disclosure issues outside of the Standards and includes 'information of a general nature and other disclosure requirements that may apply in certain countries.'[101]

4.196 In addition, IOSCO and the International Accounting Standards Board (IASB) have collaborated to produce a comprehensive set of core standards for the global listing of securities, which has been approved by the full membership of IOSCO (including the SFC) and the IASB, with a recommendation for implementation in member jurisdictions.[102] These standards essentially comprise International Financial Reporting Standards (IFRS), formerly known as International Accounting Standards (IAS).

---

[99] IOSCO, Report of the Technical Committee, International Disclosure Standards for Cross-Border Offerings and Initial Listings by Foreign Issuers (1998).
[100] IDS, p 3.   [101] IDS, p 3.
[102] See IOSCO, Resolution and List of IASC 2000 Standards (May 2000).

As a general matter, the discussion in this chapter has indicated that Hong **4.197**
Kong's offering and listing requirements are largely equivalent to the IDS of
IOSCO and the IFRS of the IASB. As noted above, the key to the effectiveness
of such requirements is enforcement, whether public, self-regulatory, or private.
In general, Hong Kong provides limited opportunities for private enforcement.
Instead, most enforcement in this context has traditionally been by the SEHK,
now operating as both regulator and profit-making entity. Not surprisingly,
there have been many calls for change, generally focusing on enhancing the role
of the SFC as a public enforcement agency for disclosure.

Some of these issues have been addressed by the double filing regime of the **4.198**
SFO. In addition, a consultation is underway on proposed amendments to the
SMLR.[103] Under this proposal, a number of Listing Rules will be removed to
form part of the SMLR. Such matters relate to disclosure, namely, as to price-
sensitive information, annual and periodic reports, and related to notifiable and
connected transactions (all discussed in Chapter 6). While the proposal would
make no substantive changes to the provisions, the effect of removing them
is that they will cease to be contractual matters between the SEHK and the
company and will instead become statutory requirements.

As such, this proposal (the implications of which are discussed further in **4.199**
Chapter 6) has the scope to enhance this area of weakness in Hong Kong's
regulation of listing and public offerings of securities. In addition, the dual filing
regime is likely to have an important impact in improving disclosure in this
context. Nonetheless, there remain strong arguments for removing the Listing
Rules from the SEHK to the SFC, as has been done in the UK through the
transfer of authority in this regard from the LSE to the FSA.

---

[103] SFC, *A consultation paper on proposed amendments to the Securities and Futures (Stock Market Listing) Rules* (January 2005); Financial Services and the Treasury Bureau, *Consultation paper on proposed amendments to the Securities and Futures Ordinance to give statutory backing to major listing requirements* (January 2005).

5

FINANCIAL DERIVATIVES

Financial derivative instruments are widely held and traded in Hong Kong, just **5.01** as in other substantial financial centres, and most of the regulatory and legal concerns that flow from the use of such contracts by financial institutions and other market participants are little different than elsewhere. Some derivative products are both comparatively new and complex in their risk management, capital adequacy, and investor protection dimensions. Regulators easily recall the scale of losses associated with derivative use in well-publicized cases since the 1980s, and share concerns that a similar new example might provoke financial collapse or contagion. How Hong Kong has responded to regulatory questions posed by these instruments is typical of the common approach now adopted by most advanced economies.

However, Hong Kong differs in one important respect from all other financial **5.02** centres, in that since the early 1990s it has housed a continuing, disproportionately high volume of retail participation in financial derivatives, mainly through exchange-traded option-based products that give leveraged exposure to Hong Kong listed equities. Growth in issuance and trading of these instruments in their present form made HKEx the world's most active single market in third party cover, or derivative, warrants in 2003–4, and Hong Kong to rank second as a domicile for such trading only to Germany, despite a population one-twelfth as large. This phenomenon gives an unusual dual focus to Hong Kong's approach to investor protection, risk management, and capital adequacy.

5.03 This chapter describes the main current types of financial derivatives, their uses and risks, and examines Hong Kong's twofold approach to their regulation. It also raises questions that may not be fully addressed in any major financial jurisdiction, for example, how the law accounts for relatively new, sophisticated contracts, especially in relation to user protection; whether related areas of law such as bankruptcy may conflict with what has become customary derivative market practice; and how credit risk transfer facilitated by derivative instruments may conflict with established precepts of financial regulation. Last, it considers whether links between the territory's regulators and the stock exchange are well-suited to the supervision of certain derivative activity and to investor protection.

A. Sources and Uses

5.04 Trends in financial globalization are commonly seen as manifested in a blurring of divisions, be they market segments or national borders. What Richard O'Brien calls the 'End of Geography' is not a finite limit, but a progression along which financial activity is increasingly less acquainted with any particular place.[1] At the same time, many financial products have begun to assume qualities of fungibility historically associated with cash. Just as two ordinary shares in a company are perfect mutual substitutes, so relatively new instruments or applications may give de facto ownership rights to the creditor, or priority of claim to the shareholder, even while debt and equity claims may wholly differ in tradition and law. All these transformations are made possible by derivative instruments. Each involves changes over time in combinations of expected risk and return for market participants, whether associated with credit risk, currencies, insurance, commodities, interest rates, shares, or financial indexes, and whether contracted singly, in combinations, or as an indistinguishable part of a structured transaction.

5.05 Certain derivatives have been known for centuries:[2] primitive commodity

---

[1] London: Royal Institute of International Affairs 1992.

[2] Writing in the fourth century BCE, Aristotle describes an option strategy involving the forward purchase of olive oil pressing capacity; *Politics* I xi: 4 (1259^{a}6–23). Contracts for the sale of goods or chattels for future delivery existed in the Middle East in the second millennium BCE and it has been claimed that a sample of such contracts closely resemble certain instruments in use today (E Swan, *Building the Global Market: a 4,000 Year History of Derivatives* (London: Kluwer, 2000), pp 31–48).

forward contracts were bought and sold in medieval Europe and organized futures or options markets existed in Japan by the late sixteenth century. Other instruments appear and vanish according to financial fashion.[3] All are more easily characterized by use or availability rather than defined as a market segment: derivatives are often evidenced by simple private law contracts but the risk management techniques that lead to their creation, aggregation, and maintenance may be immensely sophisticated. Financial derivatives draw on the language of differential calculus, and many are priced using differential mathematical functions, to imply instruments whose value is determined as a function of that of an underlying contract, security, or index, but this may not always be true, and the 'theoretical' integral may be long lost to history. For example, simple fixed-floating interest rate swaps were once priced (thus 'derived') from continuous chains of forward short-term interest rates and a comparison of the conventional borrowing costs of two dissimilar counterparties yet today's global interest rate swap markets in major currencies are so large and liquid that the swap yield curve is itself the dominant source of pricing for loans and bonds. The derived product becomes the source. In this way is seen the challenge for law and regulation in keeping pace with product development.

Although this chapter explains important aspects of derivative instruments and the risks and markets with which they are linked, its approach adheres to the central aims of this volume, and is neither technical not comprehensive as to risks or products. Hong Kong is an important centre for users of certain derivatives[4] but in most operational respects is technically indistinguishable from other financial hubs where derivatives are bought, sold, or conceived, even in respect of contracts based on HK dollar instruments or indexes. Instead, the chapter's contents reflect two aspects of derivative market activity in Hong Kong: first, the relative prominence of retail-orientated derivative products, that is, those intended for transaction by end-user individuals and companies in small nominal amounts, and second, how the Hong Kong authorities regulate derivatives activity among financial institutions operating in the territory. **5.06**

The two topics are related in that the effect of the first is to give an investor **5.07**

---

[3] Typified by structured notes with periodic coupons designed to meet the interest rate expectations of specific investor classes in particular prevailing conditions. Similar motives frequently drive issues of retail targeted warrants, a prominent feature of derivatives activity in Hong Kong.

[4] Ranked 6th by turnover in aggregate over-the-counter (OTC) foreign exchange and single currency interest rate derivatives in the 2004 Bank for International Settlements (BIS) survey of derivative market activity (albeit with a 2.6 per cent share: Britain and the US accounted for 38.1 per cent and 18.7 per cent of turnover, respectively). Report available at <http://www.bis.org/publ/rpfx05.htm>. Hong Kong is not prominent as a centre for exchange-traded derivatives other than for covered (derivative) warrants.

protection and issuer risk management focus to the second. Hong Kong's approach to wholesale market regulation is now representative of most leading financial centres. The chapter first examines instrument classifications, types and gives examples of uses to which financial derivatives are put. It describes risk features arising from the two elementary categorizations of financial derivatives, and last, focuses on important aspects of Hong Kong's approach to the regulation of these two classes of derivatives.

(1) Classification

5.08 All derivatives are evidenced by private law contracts. Some will be negotiated separately among their counterparties but most are subject to standardization of documentation that results from their either being traded on an exchange, or made to conform with the global harmonization of market practices brought about by the sector's self-regulatory organization (SRO), the International Swaps and Derivatives Association Inc. (ISDA). They can be distilled into four types according to how they are bought and sold and whether they are based on forward or option contracts.

5.09 Figure 5.1 shows how a selection of common derivative products divides among these categories.

Over-the-counter contracts		Exchange-traded contracts
FX forwards, FX swaps, forward rate agreements, interest rate swaps, basis swaps, currency swaps, cross-currency interest rate and basis swaps, commodity swaps, forward swaps, amortizing swaps, total return swaps	Forward contracts	FX futures, stock index futures, commodity futures, metal futures, shipping futures, energy futures, stock futures, interest rate futures, government bond futures, interest rate spread futures, interest rate swap futures
Interest rate caps and floors, swaptions, forward swaptions, callable swaps, credit default swaps, extendible swaps, differential swaps	Option contracts	FX options, stock index options, stock options, equity warrants, government bond options, currency warrants, debt warrants

Figure 5.1 Classification of derivatives[5]

---

[5] The figure shows examples and is not comprehensive. Note that options may exist on each instrument shown. 'Stock' refers to an equity security.

Exchange-traded derivatives

Exchange-traded products are bought and sold on a central stock or futures **5.10** exchange, which may or may not operate at a single physical location, but which will entail centralized clearing, settlement, and reporting of trades and prevailing prices. The exchange, of which the Hong Kong Futures Exchange (HKFE, part of HKEx, which also owns the the Stock Exchange of Hong Kong (SEHK)) is an example, is party to all derivatives for which it acts as a trading forum. Contracts are standardized as to commercial terms, notably their scale of interest in underlying assets from which they derive, as are the processes of dealing, settlement, and certain risk controls, most particularly the requirement that contract holders place defined settlement margins with the exchange against outstanding contract positions in the form of cash or risk-free securities. On any day, the margin demanded of a contract holder is typically the sum of fixed amounts posted upon dealing and others required to be made during the life of the contract depending upon its mark-to-market value. The exchange's rules may allow the margin to be set off in defined circumstances against the settlement obligations of the contract holder, and retained if the contract holder fails to respond to demands that it be increased. In all cases, end-users deal through exchange members.

OTC derivatives

Over-the-counter (OTC) derivative contracts are dealt and settled among finan- **5.11** cial institutions and their clients. Some banks assume the role of market makers in relatively liquid products, but all trades are entered directly between counterparties, so the nature of counterparty credit risk differs from that associated with exchange-traded contracts. OTC derivatives lack standardized margin requirements but financial institutions often require that their clients maintain liquid collateral against the mark-to-market valuation of the contract whenever it represents a net credit risk to the institution, the value established by convention as the present value of future net payments due under the instrument. OTC contracts need not be standard but tend to accord to market practice, which is more homogenous in the OTC derivatives markets than in sectors dealing in securities.

Forward contracts

Derivatives based on forward contracts require the user to buy or sell an under- **5.12** lying asset at a certain price upon expiry of the contract on a specific forthcoming date. Futures are those forward contracts that are traded on an exchange. The essence of all forward contracts is a sale or purchase struck today at a fixed price for settlement at a specific later date. It thus includes outright foreign exchange forwards, involving the future sale and purchase of currency against a second at a rate determined at the time of dealing, as well as commodity futures, by which a farmer can sell a fixed amount of produce or livestock, for example, for physical delivery at a later date at prices set upon dealing. In each case, the forward price is determined by the spot transaction price and net cost of carry, that is, the difference in receipts and expenses accruing on an asset owned today ('spot') and later ('forward').

Option-based contracts

5.13 Options contracts allow the holder to choose to sell or buy an underlying asset at a certain price on or before a specific forthcoming date. In their elemental form, options are either calls or puts, that convey the right to buy and sell, respectively, the subject asset, but in neither case the obligation so to do. Both call and put options may be bought (by the 'holder') or sold (by the 'writer'), so that it is possible for the seller of a put and the buyer of a call to face identical combinations of risk and return. Many common option based trades involve combinations of calls and puts in ways that produce a return in specified conditions, for example, if underlying asset prices move within a set range.

5.14 Thus the most obvious difference between forwards and options is the volition given to the option contract holder, that is, a contractual entitlement rather than an obligation. The distinction between forward and option based instruments is also shown in the mathematical relationship that each has with its respective underlying instrument. Forward-based derivatives are linear functions of an underlying asset, so that a price change in that asset causes a proportionately identical change in the prevailing price of the derivative. Option-based derivatives are non-linear functions of their corresponding underlying asset, so that a one per cent change in that asset's price may cause a far greater proportional change in the derivative's prevailing price.

5.15 Further, the nature of forward-based derivatives is that price losses and gains in their underlying instruments always have an equally large, or symmetrical impact on the prevailing price of the derivative, that is, it is mechanically equally possible to gain as to lose. By contrast, option-based derivatives are both non-linear and asymmetric functions of the value of the underlying instrument. First, a price change in the underlying asset will cause a disproportionate change in the price of the derivative. Second, the magnitude of price gains and losses in the derivative are unlike, given price gains or losses of equal size in the underlying instrument. Price asymmetry contributes further to the leverage associated with options of all kinds. The leverage implicit in much trading in option-based derivatives is the justification for margin requirements typical of derivative exchanges, and helps explain notorious cases such as the near-collapse of

Metallgesellschaft AG in 1993 and the fall of the Barings group in 1995, both coming quickly to crisis. In each case option-based trading losses resulted in substantial margin calls on the companies' respective US and Singapore subsidiaries, which for Barings exceeded the total financial resources of the group.[6]

Combined and embedded derivatives

Other transaction instruments, some of them commonly used by retail partici-   **5.16**
pants or financial institutions, represent either combinations of two or more of these examples, or the inclusion of a derivative element in a non-derivative setting. Thus in the first case, a forward interest rate swap is usually a combination of two conventional interest rate swaps of different tenors; a futures or options straddle is the simultaneous sale and purchase of futures or options contracts, respectively, to protect the holder against sizeable price movements in the underlying asset. In the second case, most traditional convertible bonds are simple fixed rate debt instruments with share options intrinsic in their structure. While this chapter contains examples of transactions involving embedded options, its main concern is with the regulation of exchange-traded and OTC derivatives, whether forward or option based instruments.[7]

These categories help simplify the roots of regulation in Hong Kong, given   **5.17**
that the great majority of retail derivatives are option based, exchange-traded, and often marketed broadly among non-professional participants. Here, regulation is directed through the exchange, and concentrates on rules in respect of listing, selling, and margins. In contrast, derivatives regulation for financial institutions centres on capital sustainability after transaction loss, which the Basel Accords characterize as how capital is maintained against market risks. This has entered Hong Kong law in the form of schedules to the Banking Ordinance and applies to all Authorized Institutions, as defined in the ordinance.[8] It also relies on the international harmonization of market practice standards that has accompanied the growth of the modern swap markets since the early 1980s, reflecting the central role assumed by ISDA, especially in promoting the standardization of documentation, collateral requirements, and

---

[6] Metallgesellschaft lost US$ 1.3 billion from misapplied hedging. Barings involved failures of risk management and regulation and is well-documented in 'Report of the UK Board of Banking Supervision inquiry into the circumstances of the collapse of Barings', London, HMSO 1995, and by reported English cases, eg *Re Barings plc and others (No 5), Secretary of State for Trade and Industry v Baker and others (No 5)* 1 BCLC 433. The report's findings quickly proved widely influential in legal and regulatory supervisory reform.

[7] Not considered here are asset-backed securities (ABS), which have been regarded as derivative products by some national regulators (including Hong Kong) for which practice, taxation, applicable law, and regulation are those applying to other debt securities.

[8] Cap. 155 s 2; the treatment of capital is given in sch 3. See also Chapter 3.

settlement processing, and of general acceptance of common capital equivalent risk calculations.

(2) Instrument types

5.18 This section explains the generic derivative instruments most commonly used in Hong Kong and other major financial centres, and which are examined from a legal and regulatory perspective later in the chapter. It excludes derivatives categorized by the Bank for International Settlement (BIS) as traditional foreign exchange derivatives, that is, outright forward contracts (contracts for the forward sale or purchase of foreign currency) and foreign exchange swaps (simultaneous spot sale and forward purchases of one currency for a second).

Exchange-traded derivatives

5.19 Exchange-traded derivatives are identical, fungible instruments specified according to their underlying asset, contract duration, and the settlement requirements of the exchange on which they trade, that is, HKFE for contracts offered in Hong Kong. Standard specification implies that few contracts will match the needs of all users but the same factor tends to result in greater market depth, tradability, and liquidity. Settlement of all exchange-traded derivatives was once made by physical delivery of underlying assets, the result of the markets' commodity dealing origins when physical delivery was usually desired, but the trend since the 1980s has been towards financial contracts being settled for cash. This lessens the chances of market manipulation, prevents highly leveraged contracts becoming impossible to settle for lack of deliverable assets or willing sellers of such assets, and limits distortions between the terms of contracts and underlying assets.

5.20 Typical exchange rules demand that futures and options positions are marked to market each day, with gains and losses (which sum to nil for each contract type) paid to the exchange according to formulae specified for each contract. The exchange clears these payments daily and thus eliminates all aspects of counterparty exchange risk for traders. This mark-to-market margin system means that the value of stock futures is reset on each trading day. Exchanges (including HKFE) accordingly require payment of an initial margin when a contract position is opened, together with a maintenance margin that varies with the contract price and is thus a function of the price of the underlying share. Margins may not fall below pre-set minimums.

5.21 Whenever general user demand proves commercially inadequate, contracts will fail and be withdrawn from trading unless a strategic interest requires otherwise, as has been the case with certain Hong Kong dollar interest rate contracts, which are sustained despite sporadic low usage. HKFE's contract experience is mixed:

of the 13 categories of futures and options contracts that it traded in 2004, only one generated significant volume.[9]

Stock options

Call options give the holder the right but not the obligation to buy a fixed **5.22** quantity of an underlying asset at a fixed price (the 'exercise price') on, and in some cases up to and including a given date. Put options confer to the holder the right but not the obligation to sell a fixed quantity of an underlying asset at a fixed price on, and in some cases up to and including a given date. The call seller (writer) has a corresponding obligation to deliver the underlying asset (not normally its cash equivalent) at a fixed price to the call buyer. Similarly, the put writer (seller) is obliged to buy the underlying asset at a fixed price from the put buyer. Most options will be one of two types: American-style options can be exercised at any time before expiry, while European-style options may be exercised only at expiry.[10]

The specification of stock options comprises: **5.23**

- Underlying asset, that is, the share upon which the option contract is written.
- The number of shares to which a single option relates. This is usually the minimum dealing amount (the 'board lot') of shares.
- Exercise ('strike') price, or the price at which the underlying asset may be dealt. The exercise price is said to be 'in the money' if it is below the prevailing asset's price, or 'out of the money' if it stands above that prevailing price.
- Expiry (or maturity) date; the date on which the option expires or the last date on which an American-style option may be exercised.
- Option premium; the price paid by the buyer to acquire the rights conveyed in the option.

Stock options are usually insulated from major capital changes in their under- **5.24** lying stocks to exclude the effect of rights issues, bonus issues, or unusually large dividends. This is done by adjusting the contract size and strike price to maintain the option's value. However, stock options are not protected from ordinary cash dividends.

Stock futures

Stock futures contracts are commitments to buy or sell the cash equivalent of a **5.25** number ('contract multiplier') of shares at a predetermined price ('contracted

---

[9] Hang Seng Index futures, accounting for 44% of total turnover.
[10] This distinction applies universally to all options. A small proportion of contracts known as Bermuda-style options may be exercised on a specified series of dates.

price') on a specific future date. There is no alternative of physical delivery of shares upon expiry. At expiry, profits or losses are paid to the accounts of buyers and sellers in amounts equal to the difference between the contracted price and the final settlement price multiplied by the contract multiplier.[11] Stock futures allow short positions on shares to be created or closed relatively cheaply, regardless of how costly it may be to borrow stock in the underlying cash share market. Standardized contracts allow open (uncovered) short positions to be closed (covered) at any time before expiry. Liquidity is maintained by professional market makers who post firm prices at a maximum bid-offer spread set by the exchange.

Warrants

5.26   Warrants are tradable option contracts and are issued for profit or to lessen costs by companies, banks, or investors, often as single transactions, and sometimes as part of structured or on-going financing transactions. Simple warrants convey the right but not the obligation to buy (call warrants) or sell (put warrants) an underlying asset (or its cash equivalent) at a predetermined price. Many warrants are sophisticated combinations of calls and puts intended to deliver a particular risk-return combination to the holder, for example, to produce a return if a share price or index follows a specified path during a defined period. Usually (but not always) listed and traded on an exchange, warrants are bought and sold for cash, or as part of consideration in a larger fund-raising transaction. Warrant issues have lives ranging from several months to many years but any single warrant is cancelled upon being exercised by the holder according to the warrant issue's commercial terms.

5.27   The profit ('payoff') of a call warrant on expiry is the greater of nil and the then closing price less the exercise price multiplied by the subscription ratio. The payoff of a put warrant on expiry is the larger of nil and the exercise price less the closing price multiplied by the subscription ratio. The subscription ratio (or entitlement ratio) is based on the number of warrants needed to convert into one nominal unit of the underlying asset. Closing prices are usually taken as averages over several days immediately prior to expiry. These and all other commercial terms are included as part of documents submitted at the time of listing.

5.28   Historically, warrants were first issued in the 1970s as part of financing transactions, most often bond issues, as a means to lower an issuer's borrowing costs, either before or after tax. Every ten bonds might carry one warrant, entitling the

---

[11]   HKEx's formula for final settlement price is the average of the mid-points of the best bid and offer prices quoted for the underlying stock at five-minute intervals during the last contract trading day.

holder to buy a set number of shares in the issuer at a fixed price, or the right to acquire more bonds, for example, on pre-determined commercial terms. Since investors could attribute value to the warrants when the transaction was launched, the effect of including warrants in a transaction as sweeteners in this way would be to lower the overall cost to the issuer of servicing the host bond. Moreover, the warrants could be detached ('stripped') and thereafter bought or sold separately from the host bonds so as to appeal especially to risk-preferring investors.[12] Their main appeal matches those of all option-based instruments, to offer a leveraged risk exposure compared to the underlying asset. While warrants can be linked to any asset or index for which there exists a market price, they now take two basic forms depending on whether or not the warrant is issued by the obligor of the underlying asset or by an unconnected third party, usually a bank or securities house. The latter, known as covered or derivative warrants, have become especially prominent in Hong Kong for reasons generally associated with domestic retail investors.[13]

Covered (derivative) warrants

Covered warrants are tradable option contracts issued as discrete transactions by **5.29** banks and others parties that have no ownership connection to the obligor of the underlying asset or risks. In the form most common in Hong Kong, a bank[14] will issue covered warrants for cash consideration that entitle the holder, upon exercising the warrant prior to its expiry, to receive a cash settlement determined by a formula that is a function of the prevailing price of shares in a listed company or an identified group of companies represented by an index. Other common covered warrants offer risks linked to changes in exchange rates.

Covered warrants were thought controversial by many listed companies when **5.30** first introduced in the Euromarkets in the 1980s, chiefly because of a connotation of third party control of an issue linked to shares, and its parochial implication of a lack of control for the company and its owners over the shares in issue. The same sentiment was seen with warrant issues connected with takeover activity,

---

[12] The same tactic is applied to convertible bonds by synthetically separating embedded options from the straight bond component, and selling the resulting two products as option contracts and asset swaps.

[13] Derivative terminology changes as if with the seasons. This chapter discusses warrant types currently most common in Hong Kong. It refers mainly to 'covered' or 'derivative' warrants as those issued by third parties without control of an underlying share or market risk. Previously (i) in the mid-1990s, 'covered' could refer to warrants whose issuer was also the issuer of under-lying shares; (ii) 'non-collateralized' warrants were issued by third parties unconnected to the underlying asset and were first issued and listed in 1989; and (iii) in 1994–7 'call spread' warrants were popular with local retail investors and are similar in construction to today's covered (derivative) warrants.

[14] Permissible issuers are set out in HKEx Listing Rules Chapter 15A albeit ambiguously.

for example, where a failed bidder holding a substantial shareholding in the target company might sanction the issue of warrants giving call rights over all of part of its block of shares. Such a tactic could be a favourable way of gradually disposing of share interests without suffering excessive price disruption, or of ameliorating other transaction costs through the receipt of warrant proceeds.

5.31   From this concept came the term 'covered'. In a wider contemporary sense, covered warrants are most frequently issued by banks and securities houses that then actively manage their resulting option risk exposure by hedging with trades in the underlying asset and derivatives of that asset. They constitute a second generation derivative, their creation originally made feasible by the development of derivatives as hedging instruments, prior to which they usually represented for the issuer an uneconomic or excessively risky liability. The markets for warrants now include many kinds of underlying assets and indexes, and warrants are most frequently issued independently of any other new issue. They are traditionally popular among investors in markets in Germany, Japan, and Switzerland, and in recent years in Hong Kong. The exercise of a covered warrant has no effect on the number of underlying shares in issue.

Equity warrants

5.32   By contrast, equity warrants occupy a modest corner of the main board of HKEx, whether measured by issuance or turnover: only 29 warrants of this form were listed as at end-July 2005, compared to 977 covered warrants.[15] Equity warrants are obligations of the legal entity issuing shares to which they give leveraged risk exposure, and their exercise will usually cause the issue of new shares. The rationale for issue tends to be specific to the issuer, but typically involves a device to conserve cash resources or reward shareholders in a way intended to be tax efficient.

5.33   Summary descriptions of Hong Kong's exchange-traded equity, interest rate, and fixed income futures contracts and their associated option contracts are given in section B(1).

OTC derivatives

5.34   This section describes generic examples of OTC derivatives, the majority in use of which are linked to interest rates, currencies, or credit risk, and take the form of private contracts for forwards, options, or swaps, and static or dynamic combinations taken from these three basic forms. None of the instruments in this category is peculiar to Hong Kong.

---

[15] Source HKEx at <http://www.hkex.com.hk/data/markstat/mkthl200507.htm>.

Swaps and related forward-based derivatives

Well-established, liquid money markets sustain active forward interbank trading **5.35** of deposits, from which spring both simple exchange-traded and OTC forward interest rate derivative contracts, respectively interest rate futures and forward rate agreements (FRAs), which are close commercial substitutes. Both are used extensively by non-bank and bank participants. FRAs are generally documented in a standard form but made between two counterparties according to commercial choice, and settled in cash on expiry. As an example, a 3×4 FRA represents a contract for a four-month interest rate, fixed three months forward. FRAs are more flexible in use but marginally more costly than interest rate futures; the bank that offers FRAs to clients assumes a pre-settlement credit risk not present with futures due to the exchange's mark-to-market margin requirements for futures.

Long-term swaps denominated in major currencies date from the late 1970s **5.36** in the form recognized today, beginning as single negotiated transactions but forming by the mid-1980s a series of markets whose breath and liquidity resembles those of conventional currency or short-term money markets. Interest rate swaps now exist with differing degrees of liquidity and yield curve duration in all currencies whose bond and capital markets are not subject to close direction.

Swaps may be simple in commercial definition and effect, or constructed in **5.37** tiers by a number of similar but different individual swaps; they may subsist unchanged from transaction date to maturity, or be modified and traded in portfolio as actively as any liquid security. The core model is shown in Figure 5.2.

Here, the two banks ('counterparties') agree for seven years to exchange streams **5.38** of interest based on a single notional amount, Bank A paying annually at a fixed rate calculated at *x* per cent per annum, and receiving from Bank B semi-annually a variable (floating) rate, in this case calculated at LIBOR flat.[16] There is no exchange of principal (it would be pointless to swap like amounts). Market convention influences payment frequency, day count, and settlement days, usually taken from bond market practice in the currency of the swap but payment frequency in any single swap can be entirely flexible, with cashflows (and therefore swap replacement values) always measured in present value terms. It also makes possible the netting of payments whenever they fall due

---

[16] The London interbank offered rate, LIBOR, is the benchmark short-term interest rate most frequently used in derivative contracts and by futures and options exchanges. Daily LIBOR fixings are posted by the British Bankers' Association in nine major currencies. See <http://www.bba.org.uk/bba/jsp/polopoly.jsp?d=141>.

simultaneously. Convention usually has the swap expressed as one rate (in this case, *x* per cent) against a second that is flat (free of margin) to an index (here, 6-month LIBOR).

5.39 Unless the swap in Figure 5.2 is terminated prematurely, either by agreement or due to a payment default, it will continue until the seventh anniversary of its start date (the date from which payments first accrued), at which time the mutual liability of the counterparties ceases. While the swap is extant the periodic payment liabilities of the two counterparties are usually made contingent, so that Bank A, in this case, may withhold payment if Bank B defaults, and vice versa.[17] Thus a swap is a derivative contract by which two counterparties exchange liabilities calculated with reference to an asset or index, without itself involving contractual rights over that asset or index. 'Fixed' in this context means a rate specified as a number or series of numbers at inception, so that it includes rates that step up, or down, for example, or 'off market' rates that are set at premiums or discounts to prevailing fixed-floating swap rates.

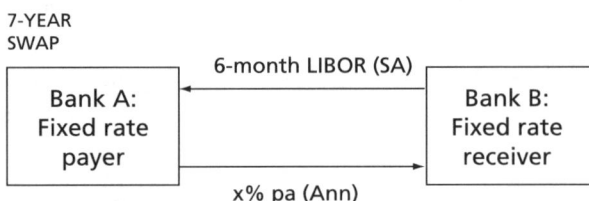

Figure 5.2 Simple single currency interest rate swap

5.40 Swaps are medium- or long-term instruments, with tenors usually of one year or more. The most substantial major currency interest rate swap markets can be broad and liquid in maturities of 10–12 years, and tradable but not broad in very long-term tenors. The market in Hong Kong dollar interest rate swaps is generally easily tradable in shorter maturities of up to five years, but not broad in longer maturities in the sense that a large number of trades could take place on a single day without major price movements.[18] Interest rate swaps account for the greatest share of global OTC derivative transactions by nominal volume, ignoring traditional foreign exchange swaps.[19] The transaction shown in Figure 5.2 is a model for trades involving a myriad of types and risks, including:

---

[17] This also assists payment netting upon termination.

[18] In minor currency or emerging swap markets fixed rate payers are often scarcer than fixed rate receivers.

[19] The BIS survey (above) reports daily average turnover in 2004 of US$ 1,292 billion and US$ 1,025 billion in foreign exchange and interest rate derivatives, respectively.

- Single currency fixed-floating swaps, including zero coupon swaps.
- Single currency basis swaps, involving the exchange of two floating rate indexes.
- Currency swaps, the majority involving the exchange of principal at inception and maturity.
- Cross-currency interest rate swaps, fixed rate versus floating rate.
- Cross-currency basis swaps, involving two floating rate indexes.
- Commodity swaps, where one or both legs of the swap are derived from a market commodity price, most commonly that of crude or refined oil.
- Forward swaps, where payments accrue from a forward date.
- Amortizing swaps.
- Differential (or quanto) swaps, which are interest rate swaps with one leg having interest determined in one currency but paid in a second.
- Constant maturity and constant duration swaps.
- Portfolio swaps.

Option-based OTC derivatives

The most widely known and used option-based OTC derivatives are banking **5.41** products sold to relatively sophisticated clients, whether corporate borrowers, institutional investors, or treasury managers within companies or financial institutions. They include:

- Interest rate caps and floors.
- Combination instruments such as interest rate collars (options spreads that consist of long call and short put options).
- Commodity options and warrants.
- Callable, puttable, and extendible swaps.
- Swap facilities and other spread hedges.
- Currency options.
- Swaptions and forward swaptions.
- Options on securities.

Issues of documentation, law and regulation with these examples are largely **5.42** identical to those affecting swaps.

Credit derivatives

Credit derivatives are an innovation of the mid-1990s that have become the **5.43** third most important aspect of the global OTC derivatives market. Used for credit risk transfer, they centre on the buying and selling of protection against single or multiple credit risks. The three elemental types of credit derivative can each be used singly, in arrays, and with other financial instruments to achieve various forms of credit risk transfer, once possible only with the sale of securities or loans.[20]

5.44 Credit derivatives are widely used in Hong Kong, and regulatory interest in their use and risk management implications is profound; first, because they are yet to be tested as volume instruments through a complete interest rate or credit cycle; second, as their use by non-bank financial institutions questions the application of regulation and the ways in which sophisticated credit risk transfer assists and impedes the functioning and stability of financial markets. All provide a means to acquire, avoid, or amend credit risk exposure to the credit protection seller without need for a direct agreement with the credit risk subject; each offers a form of protection to the buyer and a risk to the seller; some give highly leveraged credit risk exposure with a minimal deployment of capital and funding.

5.45 They divide into three main instrument types. First, the credit default swap (CDS), which most commonly relate to single credits, but also to groups of risks ('basket default swaps').

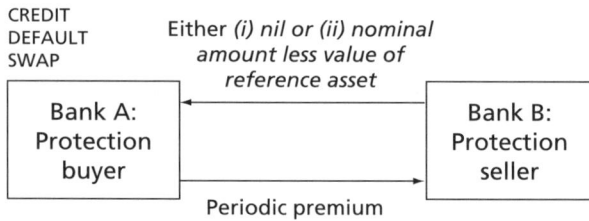

Figure 5.3 Credit default swap

5.46 The protection buyer pays a periodic premium to the protection seller as consideration for the right to compensation upon the occurrence of defined events ('credit events') on a third party's underlying reference asset. These will include payments defaults, the declaration of a debt moratorium or bankruptcy. If such a payment is triggered, the protection buyer will in return deliver the reference asset (a loan or bond in agreed form) to the protection seller in the same nominal amount as the swap. If no credit event occurs then only the premium is paid. CDSs give the protection seller leveraged exposure to credit risks, whether singly or in an array such as an industry or national group. CDSs also exist in increasing volumes on complex instruments such as collateralized debt obligations (CDOs).

---

[20] It has been argued that one or all of the instruments described in this section are not 'true' derivatives since they entail no formal mathematical relationships with underlying reference assets; indeed, this chapter takes such a view of ABS. Nowhere is there a single legal definition of derivative, and as credit derivatives are treated as such by practitioners (especially as to documentation) it is reasonable to do likewise.

CDSs make possible synthetic securitization, in which single name or multiple **5.47** name credit derivatives with the risk characteristics of a portfolio of assets can be used by a bank or other asset originator to transfer away risk without seeking balance sheet relief for an asset sale.[21]

Second, credit-linked notes (CLNs), debt securities for which repayment is **5.48** linked to the performance of a defined reference asset such as an outstanding bond or a pool of assets such as loans or receivables. If the reference asset defaults and becomes worth a fraction of its nominal value, then the noteholder receives the same proportionate payment, either in cash or as an exchange of notes for the defaulted bonds in like nominal amounts. The protection buyer is the CLN issuer, so under the simple note structure the investor (protection seller) assumes a counterparty credit risk for as long as proceeds from the reference asset are passed through the issuer.

Third, the total return swap (TRS), by which two counterparties exchange **5.49** obligations linked to the market performance of an underlying reference asset, most commonly bonds or loans.

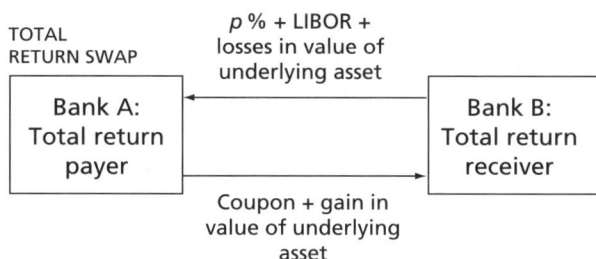

```
TOTAL              p % + LIBOR +
RETURN SWAP        losses in value of
                   underlying asset
   ┌───────────┐ ◄─────────────────  ┌───────────┐
   │ Bank A:   │                     │ Bank B:   │
   │Total return│                    │Total return│
   │  payer    │ ──────────────────► │ receiver  │
   └───────────┘                     └───────────┘
                   Coupon + gain in
                   value of underlying
                   asset
```

Figure 5.4 Generic total return swap

Bank A buys protection by entering the swap as a total return payer; Bank B is **5.50** the protection seller, or total return receiver. Either party may be the instigator of the transaction. The protection buyer's motive is to eliminate the market risk of securities issued by the subject credit risk, passing any mark-to-market losses to its counterparty protection seller in exchange for an unrelated stream of interest. If the reference asset is a fixed rate bond, for example, then the TRS functions as a fixed-floating interest rate swap but with a mark-to-market adjustment when the value of the bond changes.

All credit derivatives resemble insurance contracts, in which one counterparty **5.51** pays another a premium to ensure agreed compensation in certain circumstances,

---

[21] Such transactions could theoretically qualify for balance sheet relief if the asset originator's auditor was able to obtain in-substance defeasance based upon collateral provided by the CDS protection seller.

in this case, the default by a debtor, or a group of debtors.[22] Thus the value of these derivatives is a function of the performance of their underlying credit risks, which is indicated by the market price of cash market assets such as loans or bonds, or determined by conditions—including the events that trigger certain payments under CDSs—that form part of the derivative contract, in almost all cases a standard ISDA master agreement (the 'ISDA Master') and its annexes.

5.52 In Hong Kong as elsewhere, the market for credit derivatives is increasingly widely used but led by relatively few large international banks and insurance sector institutions. Survey data have suggested that Asia-Pacific currently accounts for around 10 per cent of global turnover, with Hong Kong and Singapore together contributing approximately 4 per cent of the total.[23] Local and foreign banks in Hong Kong began using credit derivatives in the late 1990s primarily as sellers of credit protection through CDSs and CLNs, but are thought now to engage in broader trading activity.[24]

5.53 According to one credit rating agency survey, use of CDSs dominates the two other instruments but the volume of new transactions in each has grown markedly since 2000.[25] The same report identifies the global market's most popular 25 reference credit risks in 2003, which are corporate, sovereign, public agency, and financial institution debtors, among which only Japan was Asia-domiciled. As at end-August 2005, CDSs were traded on only 30 single name risks (corresponding to the region's frequent borrowers) and three regional indexes from non-Japan Asia, according to a leading provider of index data for credit derivatives.[26] This implies that Asian banks engage heavily in credit derivatives linked to non-Asian risks.

(3) Uses

5.54 The BIS reports daily average turnover in 2004 of US$ 1,292 billion and US$ 1,025 billion in OTC foreign exchange and interest rate derivatives, respectively, with exchange-traded currency and interest rate contracts totalling US$ 4,657 billion.[27] The scale of such amounts makes interpretation meaningless

---

[22] But are distinguished in law from contracts of insurance.

[23] British Bankers' Association Credit Derivatives Report 2003–4, available at <http://www.bba.org.uk/>.

[24] HKMA 'Credit risk transfer using derivatives and implications for financial market functioning' 2003, available at <http://www.info.gov.hk/hkma/eng/research/CDS.pdf>.

[25] Fitch Ratings' Global Credit Derivatives Survey. Sept. 2004, available at <http://www.fitchratings.com.> CDS trades are thought to represent around 50–55 per cent of the current market.

[26] iTraxx, part of Deutsche Börse affiliate International Index Company (<http://www.indexco.com>).

[27] BIS Survey (above).

other than to suggest that these market segments have become sizeable and used by a variety of organizations and individuals. The total OTC turnover was 74 per cent greater than the previous survey's results from April 2001. These data are currently not unusual: other survey results show considerable on-going growth in the global volume of credit derivatives outstanding, and very substantial increases since 2002 in amounts raised by derivative-linked structured notes, especially CDOs, which are themselves both the outcome and the source of derivative activity in their internal structuring and the means by which risks associated with their collateral assets are hedged. The main components of turnover are given in Table 5.1. It shows the prominence of OTC interest rate swaps and exchange-traded currency contracts.

Every user of derivatives seeks deliberately or unconsciously to change the **5.55** expected risk-return profile of its prevailing asset or liabilities, or acquire such a profile where none previously existed. This applies to all types of market participants, be they risk-averse or risk-preferring and whether they enter a single derivative transaction on one occasion or as part of a continuous programme of trading. In several leading international cases since the 1990s involving the alleged mis-selling of derivatives the court has distinguished between the motives that appear to prompt otherwise similar transactions, for example by one

Table 5.1 Global turnover in OTC derivatives and selected exchange-traded derivatives, daily averages (US$ billion)

	Amount	Share of market segment %
Foreign exchange turnover:		
Traditional FX derivatives	1,152	89
Currency swaps	21	2
Currency options	117	9
Other currency trades	2	–
All currency derivatives	1,292	100
Interest rate turnover:		
FRAs	233	23
Interest rate swaps	621	61
Interest rate options	171	16
Other interest rate trades	–	–
All interest rate derivatives	1,025	100
Total OTC derivatives, excluding traditional FX derivatives	1,118	NA
Total OTC derivatives	2,410†	NA
Exchange-traded derivatives:		
Interest rate contracts	4,634	99
Currency contracts	23	1
Total exchange-traded derivatives:	4,657	100

(† adjusted for double counting)

Source: BIS.

borrower entering a swap to fix interest costs when contracting a new debt, and a second, that does so to seek profits.[28] A similar approach is generally reflected in the powers given to management by traditional corporate constitutions in Hong Kong and elsewhere, and in the enabling statutes of many statutory bodies. Yet today's derivative markets increasingly approach these concerns holistically, seeing their most propitious application as being to an asset or balance sheet portfolio, rather than single claims. There may be simple clarity in the effect of a derivative instrument in isolation, but not when examined against the risk-return characteristics of a complex portfolio of assets or liabilities.

5.56   Nonetheless, it is common to identify product uses with the motives of the user, which are often taken to be hedging, speculation, arbitrage, or financing, all traditional types of investment behaviour or treasury management. Those motives may be influenced by exogenous factors, such as taxation or capital controls, as well as a user's desire to shift its expected risk-return profile towards a longer duration, for example, to a higher composition of certain credit risks, or irrevocably to transfer to a third party other risks or risk classes. More traditional motives that led to the creation of commodity exchanges in Chicago or Osaka also remain important, especially in non-financial use. This would include hedging with futures, swaps, and options by commodity producers and consumers, be they farmers, food manufacturers, or airlines.

5.57   The roots of today's financial derivatives markets give clues as to their most common practical uses. Rigid market segmentation prevailed globally until after the Bretton Woods currency pact ended in the early 1970s, often making cross-border financing costly and complex. Transnational companies needing to make funding infusions into their overseas subsidiaries might face crippling local charges, tax liabilities, or the prospect of permanently locating capital beyond control. At the same time, banks and financiers might find the credit risk of a small foreign subsidiary unacceptable, even given a highly rated parent. One solution to these concerns was the parallel loan, which became a forerunner of interest rate and currency swaps. The generic model is shown in Figure 5.5

5.58   Assuming that taxation or capital controls make it preferable for the Japanese and Korean parents to fund their respective subsidiaries locally, then an exchange of roles could be an effective solution, with each bank taking direct or

---

[28] For example, the verdict of Lord Templeman in *Hazell v Hammersmith and Fulham London Borough Council and others* [1992] 2 AC 1 (England). According to Lord Ackner in the same case, swaps 'are indistinguishable from any other transaction which involves the hope of gain, which gain is intended to reduce a risk attendant on an underlying transaction. Although the phrase "debt management" may be a convenient one, swap transactions in fact leave the debt wholly unmanaged'. This approach arguably no longer accords with market practice.

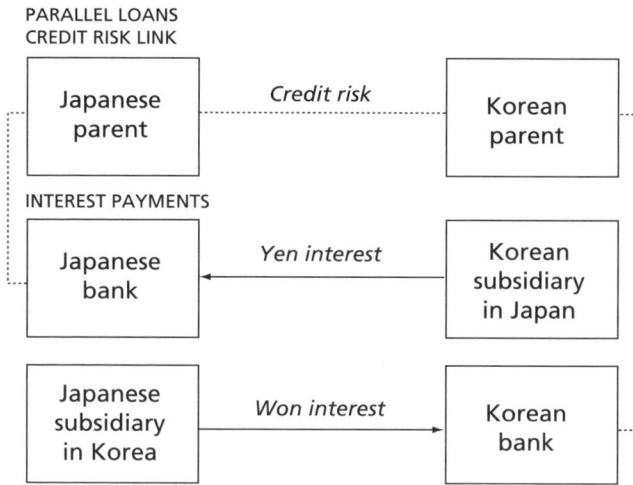

Figure 5.5 Parallel loans (interest payments shown only)

implied credit support from the domestic client, shown in the figure by broken lines. Without inducement, neither bank would lend to the local subsidiary; with inducement, each is ready to lend to insubstantive subsidiaries or to overcome cross-border capital controls. The structure still has uses for capital conservation motives.

This kind of exchange of liabilities evolved into the simple swap transaction illustrated in Figure 5.2 (above). Bank A pays a fixed rate and Bank B a floating rate for seven years. The commonest risk averse motive for Bank A to enter the swap is to hedge a fixed rate liability, for example, under a fixed rate bond issue or long-term lease agreement. Bank B may have invested in a fixed rate bond that it now wishes to fund with short-term deposits without assuming additional interest rate risks (the last example is the genesis for asset swaps and total return swaps). **5.59**

Adding a second simple swap with a different maturity gives a common transaction combination. Figure 5.6 shows Bank A receiving a fixed rate against LIBOR for three years. **5.60**

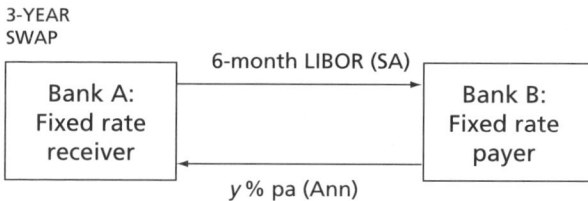

Figure 5.6 3-year reverse fixed-floating interest rate swap

5.61 Pairing the two swaps produces a forward swap, shown in Figure 5.7, where the overall effect is a four-year swap starting three years' forward, with the fixed rate determined at inception (as a function of the fixed rates on the two component swaps).

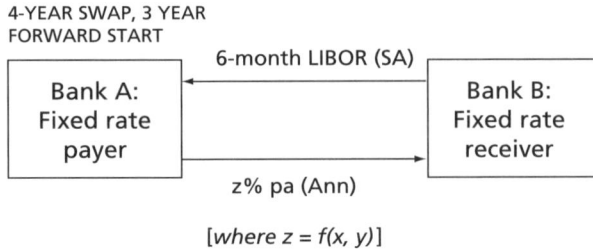

4-YEAR SWAP, 3 YEAR
FORWARD START

6-month LIBOR (SA)

| Bank A: Fixed rate payer | | Bank B: Fixed rate receiver |

z% pa (Ann)

[*where z = f(x, y)*]

Figure 5.7 Forward swap. The margins *x* and *y* are taken from Figures 5.2 and 5.6

5.62 Until the early 1980s each transaction was negotiated and administered separately, but interbank dealing practice quickly made the interest rate and currency swap markets follow more liquid markets, helped by system development and the emergence after 1987 of ISDA's imperative for standard practice and documentation. This meant the adoption of derivative instruments by brokers, electronic dealing and practices similar to market-making for liquid sectors, including warehousing.[29]

5.63 The transactions that attracted most notice and first showed the potential of swaps were arranged in 1981 for IBM and the World Bank, two identically rated AAA borrowers, each of which had suffered a deterioration in the prevailing pricing of part of its debt due to regular borrowing and credit risk segmentation. Thus IBM had over-borrowed in the domestic US bond market, and the World Bank similarly in the Swiss franc and deutschmark sectors. Each was prized in the other's preferred market but neither wanted to assume an unfamiliar currency liability. The solution was to exchange liabilities and take advantage of the opposing counterparty's more favourable new issue costs in a fresh market. One of the two main transactions appears in Figure 5.8. The aggregate cost savings were apportioned between the two issuers. These issues and swaps were heavily negotiated, but today would be seen as humdrum 'vanilla' currency swaps.

5.64 Investors in credit derivatives and synthetic asset markets are now prolific buyers of structured transactions, which began as negotiated transactions in the mid-1980s and quickly evolved into volume dealing. Asset swap transactions that combined a debt security with a swap first became popular in the 1980s among

---

[29] The retention, aggregation, and management of open swap positions by bank traders.

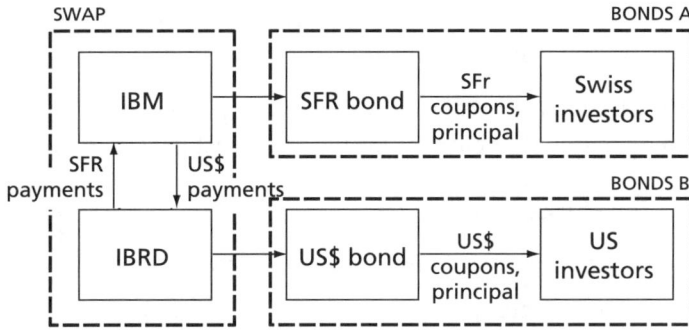

Figure 5.8 1981 IBM–World Bank US$ and SFr swapped new issues[30]

smaller commercial banks, providing a means to acquire a breadth of credit risks that were previously difficult to obtain for institutions reliant on short-term funding. All types of financial institutions now engage in simple and complex asset swap structuring, investing, and trading, including substantial non-bank institutions such as insurers, mutual funds, and hedge funds, with no real limits to the types of source assets that can be packaged with swaps and bought or sold. The generic asset swap structure is shown in Figure 5.9. Regardless of commercial terms, a typical asset swap involves the simultaneous sale of a loan or bond, often to a floating rate investor, and a swap that transforms cashflow from the asset to the investor's desired form and frequency. The arranging bank may sell the asset from inventory but will almost always take the investor as its swap counterparty, rather than the asset, but in all cases swap payments will be contingent upon payments under the asset.

Transaction structures drawn from this model have helped facilitate considerable growth in credit risk transfer, which is a contemporary regulatory concern. While the transfer of credit risks within and from the banking sector among an increasing number and diversity of investors may have systemic benefits, it also raises questions of the effects of information flows on transparency, control, and   **5.65**

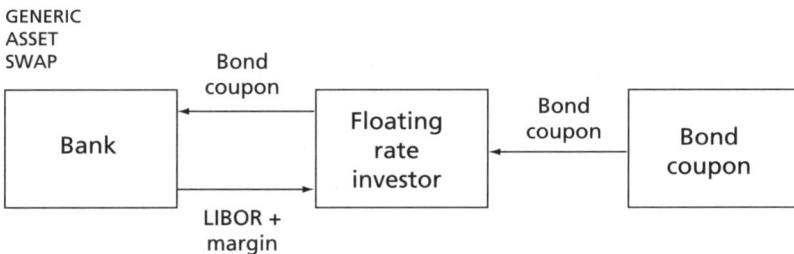

Figure 5.9 Generic asset swap structure

---

[30] Simultaneously completed US dollar and deutschmark transactions are not shown.

moral hazard[31] and illustrates how regulation has needed to adapt from its traditional institutional and segregated focus.

5.66 A second typical structure involved the repackaging of a convertible bond issue: the legal and operational impact of this kind of transformation remains valid.

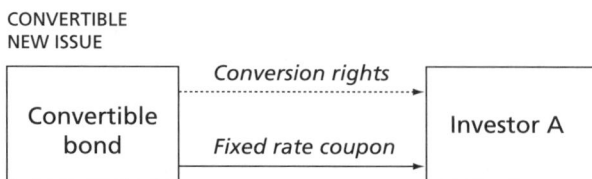

Figure 5.10 Generic convertible bond

5.67 Standard practice is to separate the two claims owned by the investor, and realign them to appeal separately to two distinct groups, shown in Figure 5.11. The only link between the two resulting instruments is contained in the terms of the warrants, which may be exercised only after the maturity of the swapped stripped bond (that is, the asset swap portion).

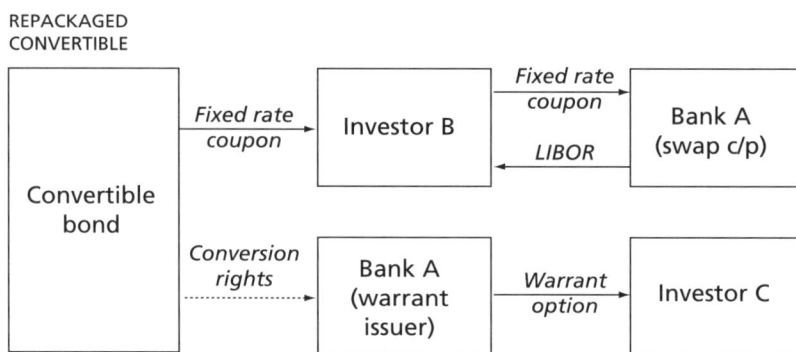

Figure 5.11 Repackaged convertible bond issue

5.68 The three current types of credit derivative have a myriad of uses and applications that spring from portfolio configurations that are for the most part private to the investor or liability manager. This phenomenon also has significant implications for risk transfer and leverage. It is not uncommon for national banking laws or regulations to set quantitative limits to aspects of bank credit exposure, for example, with single obligor limits or industry limits, usually in

---

[31] Explained in F Mishkin, 'Causes and propagation of financial instability: lessons for policy-makers', paper presented to Federal Reserve Bank of Kansas City symposium 'Maintaining Financial Stability in a Global Economy' Jackson Hole, Wyoming, August 1997, available at <http://www.kc.frb.org/>.

relation to assets or capital, real or risk-adjusted. The mechanism became instrumental to the development and widespread use of syndicated loans in the banking sector as a tool to allow substantial lending business to be captured even more broadly. If lending is the only tool available to the bank, then the amount it might advance to HK Global Garments (East Asia) Limited might be US$ 100 million, but if the same bank is able to find a derivative specialist willing to enter a CDS referenced to the company then it might place the same US$ 100 in risk-free government bonds, and gain exposure to HK Global Garments (East Asia) Limited of a far greater order than its single obligor limit would allow for conventional lending. The 1988 Basel Capital Accord and HKMA rules take notice of this issue by setting guidelines for banks in their treatment of the three current types of credit derivative, including recognition of credit protection bought, sold, or traded and its effect on capital adequacy calculations.[32]

(4) Risks and risk management

For users, employing derivative instruments can be seen as a way to influence the expected risks and returns associated with a portfolio of assets or liabilities, whether by seeking higher rewards, lower borrowing costs, a new balance of credit risks, or better to achieve an objective mix of risk and return than would be feasible with other financial instruments.[33] This section considers the main types of risk associated with financial derivatives and key aspects of current risk management practice, especially in day-to-day valuations of OTC contracts. Both topics strongly influence regulatory thinking and its application.

5.69

General considerations: types of risk

HKMA guidelines[34] for the treatment of derivative risks by banks in Hong Kong are based on a 1993 report, 'Derivatives: Practices and Principles' of the Group of Thirty consultative group of senior bankers and economists (G-30), which initiated global practice in this area of risk and regulation. The report identified seven risk categories that potentially impact upon derivative use and trading, and recommended how those risks should be measured, monitored, and mitigated. In essence this was an act of dissemination by a clutch of major banks, whose internal risk systems had been endorsed by regulators, in an effort to

5.70

---

[32] Such HKMA guidelines given effect by BO s 16(10); see also Chapter 3. Its capital adequacy provisions apply only to banks incorporated in Hong Kong.

[33] An approach common among active derivative users that originates in modern portfolio theory. H Markowitz, 'Portfolio Diversification' (1952) 1 *Journal of Finance* 77.

[34] Appearing most recently in the HKMA's policy manual (CR-G-12) for credit derivatives, 2001. Available at <http://www.info.gov.hk/hkma/eng/bank/spma/index.htm>.

stabilize industry practice. Some of the risks identified by the G-30 are now addressed systemically, for example, by exchange mark-to-market margin calls, and others by rule: they apply in all respects to OTC instruments. The G-30's recommendations successfully provoked harmonized practice among national regulators including the HKMA and SFC, and caused value-at-risk (VAR) models to be adopted as the conventional means to estimate the risk sensitivity of portfolios or entire risk-adjusted balance sheets.[35]

5.71   Table 5.2 outlines the G-30's seven risk categories.

Table 5.2 G-30's risk categories

Risk type[36]	Comments and examples
Credit	(i) Pre-settlement credit risk: pre-termination defaults. (ii) Settlement risk: default at the contract end date.
Market	Changes in the value of underlying assets.
Liquidity	(i) Market liquidity risk: a shallow market prevents trade execution. (ii) Funding liquidity risk: mismatched or unavailable funding.
Operational	Systems, human or management errors.
Legal	Unenforceability.
Regulatory	Failure to meet regulatory or legal requirements.
Reputation	Loss of confidence.

These risks apply to regulated institutions; in theory, a lightly regulated hedge fund might choose to discount certain of the risks, but in doing so would raise concerns among its bank derivative counterparties, so peer pressure insidiously requires most financial industry parties to perform in the way suggested for banks. The most closely examined category of the seven is market risks; its assessment dictates how capital is held against the derivative trading books of banks and securities firms.

5.72   The G-30 recommendation[37] in relation to market risks included the suggestion that risk takers use:

> a consistent measure to calculate daily the market risk of their derivatives positions and compare it to market risk limits.

explaining that:

> Market risk is best measured as 'value at risk' using probability analysis based upon

---

[35] This G-30 project was led by Dennis Weatherstone, who had previously instigated proprietary VAR reports as chairman of JP Morgan Inc and encouraged the practice to become an industry standard.

[36] Source: G-30, 'Derivatives: Practices and Principles' (New York: Group of Thirty, 1993).

[37] Recommendations for General Policies, 5: Measuring Market Risk.

a common confidence interval (e.g., two standard deviations) and time horizon (e.g., a one-day exposure).

Components of market risk that should be considered across the term structure include: absolute price or rate change (δ); convexity (γ); volatility (*vega*); time decay (θ); basis or correlation; and discount rate (ρ).

Since 2002 the HKMA has required that for banks: **5.73**

> the market risk associated with credit derivatives in the trading book should be managed by measuring portfolio exposures frequently—at least daily but ideally in real time—using [VAR] or other similarly robust methodology.[38]

This instruction, together with the corollary requirement to establish VAR and **5.74** other risk limits, is central to current practice in Hong Kong and in all important derivatives markets, but indirect in its regulatory focus, both by giving attention to the institution rather than the instrument, and in accepting the delegation of supervision to the institution's home regulator. It also implicitly affects the assessment of risk management performance by banks and securities houses operating in Hong Kong but outside the direct ambit of the HKMA and SFC. For example, issuers of listed covered (derivative) warrants are considered by HKEx in respect of their 'risk management systems and procedures', although this assessment may in practice be informed by other bodies.[39]

Most aspects of credit risk are dealt with systemically by exchange-traded deriva- **5.75** tives and with OTC instruments by structure and documentation. In common with other classes of financial instrument to which banks become exposed, the HKMA sets out risk concentration limits and reporting requirements for credit derivatives, couched in terms of sectoral and single obligor exposures.[40] These are defined respectively as:

> An exposure or a group of exposures with common characteristics, e.g. borrowers operating in similar or related industries, countries or loans collateralized on similar assets such as residential properties, such that any adverse changes to the common characteristics may give rise to significant losses for an [Authorized Institution].

and

> An exposure to a counterparty or a group of related counterparties which is greater than or equal to 10% of an [Authorized Institution]'s capital base.

Some case histories span several risks. Barings was broken by operational and **5.76** regulatory errors. Long-Term Capital Management (LTCM) fell after a failure of risk management: its portfolio valuation models assumed historic volatilities

---

[38] HKMA CR-G-12 manual (above) s 2.2.3.   [39] HKEx LR 15A.11.
[40] See CR-G-8 Large Exposures and Risk Concentrations, April 2004, <http://www.info.gov.hk/hkma/>.

that were irrelevant in the 1998 Russian domestic bond market collapse, to which LTCM was heavily exposed. Quantifying event risk is a perennial challenge for all current market risk models.[41] Last, derivatives induce several legal risks, especially fraud, mis-selling, and transaction enforceability.[42]

Option-related risks

5.77 The main factors affecting stock option and warrant prices are shown in the following table, together with an indication of whether the option price is positively or negatively correlated to those factors:

Table 5.3 Option price factors

	Correlation with call value	Correlation with put value
1. Price of the underlying asset	+	−
2. Price volatility of the underlying asset	+	+
3. Exercise (strike) price	−	+
4. Remaining life before expiry	−	+
5. Dividend payments on underlying assets	−	+
6. Prevailing interest rates	+	−

Thus a rise in the volatility of the underlying asset's price, that is, the amount by which the price fluctuates in any period, is correlated positively to the value of both call and put options. This forms the basis for most conventional option pricing models, which rely largely on measures of historic volatility. It also explains the need for VAR models in risk management if a portfolio is to contain option-based risks.

5.78 Regardless of structure, covered warrants confer no credit risk against an underlying asset. Despite the clear presence of transactional market risk, covered warrant holders have no contractual claim against the issuer or issuers of underlying assets, for the sole obligor under the warrants will be the bank arranging

---

[41] US General Accounting Office, Report to Congressional Requestors on Long-Term Capital Management, 1999, available at <http://www.gao.gov/new.items/gg00003.pdf>.

[42] A preponderance of 1990s cases cover fraud and mis-selling, including those involving Gibson Greetings Inc, Minmetals International Metals Trading Co, Orange County municipal authority, and Procter and Gamble Co Litigation has recently begun involving alleged mis-selling of derivative-linked CDOs, but no case has yet been decided: most prominently, HSH Nordbank AG settled a claim against Barclays Capital Ltd, having alleged mis-selling (*Financial Times* 'CDO case settled but not forgotten', 14 June 2005). The notable example of contract unenforceability is of the UK local authorities, which were prolific 1980s derivatives users. A recent example of alleged insider trading arose in the failure of China Aviation Oil (Singapore) Corp in November 2004 after oil derivative trading losses of over US$ 550 million (*Asian Wall Street Journal* 'CAO Singapore Parent Will Pay Fine as Part of Civil Settlement', 22 August 2005).

the issue, and the bank is alone responsible in however it chooses to hedge the market risk associated with the commitment to deliver proceeds according to the preset formula whenever a warrant is profitably exercised. The warrant holder may gain exposure to the price performance of an underlying share, but its claim is met by the resources of the issuing bank. This places supervisory attention on capital adequacy (regulated by the HKMA), and the quality and integrity of risk management systems to enable the bank to manage the risk exposure it acquires through issuing warrants (by HKEx).[43]

Modelling VAR

The uniform global approach to assessing the risk exposure of derivatives for capital adequacy purposes is to determine their risk equivalent amounts, comprising a general mark-to-market value and an estimate of future changes in value due to specific factors during an instrument's remaining term. Since the G-30 reported in 1993, the second component has been calculated by modelling VAR. Subject to regulator approval, banks are generally given discretion in their use of such models, both in methodology and input data, but in common with its regulatory peers the HKMA makes certain minimum demands, which are explained in its Supervisory Policy Manual.[44] More broadly, this draws on 1995 amendments to the Basel Capital Accord that require regulated banks to meet qualitative and quantitative criteria so as to demonstrate acceptable prudence, transparency, and consistency in risk management. More recently, the concept of competence has been introduced into certain of these matters, for example a screen used by HKEx in assessing warrant issuers.[45]   **5.79**

G-30 standards require that banks establish sound risk management systems that are integrated into decision making, including running regular stress testing to monitor risk model performance.[46] VAR must be calculated daily, using a 99 per cent one-tailed confidence interval,[47] input price shocks equal to a ten-day movement in historic market prices, and a minimum 12-sample period for estimations. The model must be updated quarterly. VAR methodology measures unexpected portfolio losses by probability distribution analysis, illustrated in   **5.80**

---

[43] Especially HKEx LR 15(a).

[44] See <http://www.info.gov.hk/hkma/eng/bank/spma/index.htm>, 'Use of Internal Models to Measure Market Risk' (CA-G-3) 2002.

[45] LR 15A.11.

[46] Stress testing attempts to determine model bias associated with statistical risk measures based on historic data. These tests simulate unexpected changes in market behaviour and evaluate the resulting effect on portfolio valuation.

[47] That is, the level of losses expected to occur no more than 1 per cent of the time.

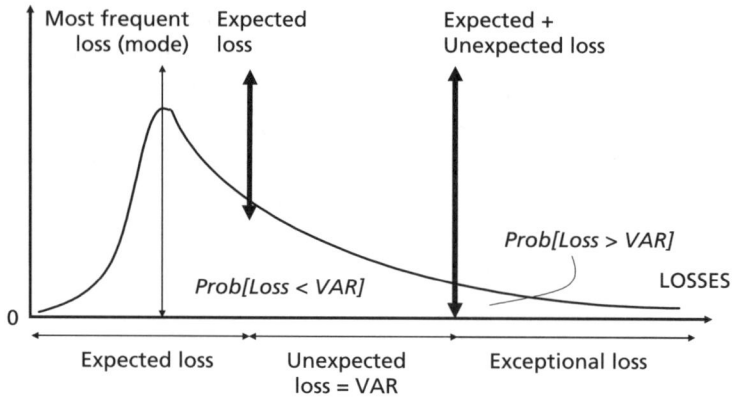

Figure 5.12 VAR loss probability distribution

Figure 5.12.[48] The distribution can be generated however the bank chooses, subject to the HKMA's satisfaction with the model's overall integrity.[49]

5.81 With the loss distribution calculated, VAR is taken to be a multiple of loss volatility, with the multiple determined by the chosen confidence level (taken in Hong Kong as 1 per cent by HKMA diktat). The capital charge against market risk (MRC) is then the higher of the previous day's VAR and a minimum of three times the average daily VAR from the preceding 60 business days. Thus:

$$MRC_t^{IMA} = \max\left(k\frac{1}{60}\sum_{i=1}^{60} VAR_{t-i}, VAR_{t-1}\right) + SRC_t$$

Here, SRC is the specific risk capital charge. The constant k is set by the HKMA to generate a further capital cushion against unpredicted extreme conditions for which history is no guide. Without this input, the typical bank's risk capital would be eliminated by losses statistically in 1 per cent of all 10 business day periods, that is, around every four years.[50] The factor k can be increased to penalize banks shown by back testing to use optimistic forecasts for earnings volatility, so that a capital incentive exists to promote sound internal risk management and accurate monitoring.[51]

---

[48] The use of standard deviations of expected returns to indicate volatility comes from Markowitz (above).

[49] Most commercial models use one of three statistical methods to estimate loss probability distributions (historic data provided by the user, Monte Carlo random simulations and the variance-covariance method).

[50] BIS Survey (above).

[51] Back testing verifies that actual losses conform to projected losses. If the model is correctly calibrated, the number of observations falling outside the prediction should be in line with the confidence level.

Note that VAR is an incomplete risk management tool, in that while it can **5.82** assess portfolio performance in certain conditions and thus provide guidance for capital adequacy, it is unable to suggest what extreme conditions may be (known as the 'fat tail' problem). In a general sense, the model helps identify the distribution's tail (the right-hand area in Figure 5.12) where probable losses exceed VAR.

Netting

One reason for the rapidity of growth in OTC derivative markets and for the **5.83** occurrence of substantial leverage in relation to the value of underlying assets that is associated with all but the most risk-averse traders is the widespread application of payment netting. This practice promotes several aspects of operational efficiency but its most powerful effect is to minimize the use of risk capital against payment defaults by financial institutions and many other OTC counterparties. Netting is used extensively in several aspects of OTC derivative risk management, chiefly in respect of settling payments under individual contracts such as swaps, where only the net amount due between counterparties is transferred whenever payment dates coincide.[52] It also takes the form of contract termination netting, counterparty netting across individual agreements, and netting for regulatory purposes. Payment and cross-agreement counterparty netting has legal consequences in the context of corporate bankruptcy and reorganization, where swap market practice may be hindered by bankruptcy law.[53]

(5) Regulatory background

The regulation of financial derivative instruments in advanced economies has **5.84** been based upon law and practice originally created to address financial products that could be comfortably regarded as discrete, and financial sector organizations that assumed easily defined roles. Loans were extended by banks, and retained until repayment as balance sheet assets on commercial terms that rarely varied; shares carried ownership rights and ranked *pari passu* within each class; protected by the courts; banks took deposits; securities dealers were commission brokers. This world view could be shared safely by lawyers, practitioners, financial economists, regulators, legislators, and the courts.

The derivative world is different: seamless, shifting, and often opaque. Its **5.85**

---

[52] Payments can be netted on a present value basis for non-coterminous payments.
[53] This question is clear under Hong Kong law, but could grow uncertain due to slow progress in bankruptcy law reform. Note that netting by novation is common foreign exchange market practice (an accumulation of periodic trades made into a regularly novating single contract) but is not associated with netting in a derivative context.

product boundaries are blurred, and participants easily assume and discard roles historically associated with other types of organization, and subject to regulation of a different order. An individual deposits cash at a regulated bank, which uses part of the liquidity to lend to a company, then enters swaps to alter entirely the nature of its ensuing interest receivables, acquires credit protection through a single name CDS from an unregulated hedge fund, issues to its depositor customer covered warrants linked through complex formulae to the trading price of the borrowing company's shares; and hedges its warrant exposure by trading in differential swaps and swaptions collateralized with shares borrowed from a second fund. Who then must the company contact when seeking an orderly reorganization of liabilities or in asking shareholders to reject a hostile takeover? If the bank fails, by what principle does the depositor recover on one unsecured claim and not the second? Only custom or path dependence offer clues.[54]

5.86   When financial institutions act as both banks and securities dealers, credit derivatives induce unregulated non-banks to engage in 'banking', and small investors become heavily involved in trading highly geared instruments that resemble traditional equity claims, it is legitimate to ask, first, whether the regulator can hope to keep pace, and second, what judgement needs to be applied to ensuing market crises. The Bank of England effectively allowed Barings to collapse, while the US Federal Reserve organized a controversial rescue of LTCM, each taking a view of the probability of the fall of one firm provoking contagion. The challenge to the law is to provide a relevant framework for such activity; the challenge to the regulator is not to abandon transparency and fairness when seeking financial stability.[55] The English courts that in the late 1990s found certain derivative contracts (mainly interest rate swaps and options) to be ultra vires British local authority borrowers[56] were examining derivative use that was then still considered novel by the markets and largely unknown to the law but which today is conducted as freely as the simplest dealings in foreign exchange. Derivative use may thus impact on claims and rights in ways not yet addressed in law or formal regulation, even though the effect is acknowledged in voluntary codes, by SROs, in takeover code practice, and by regulators such as the HKMA and SFC.

5.87   Capital requirements to address market risk were reviewed following the collapse

---

[54] The Banking Ordinance provides that claims against and premiums paid to Authorized Institutions under transactions such as covered warrants issues are not deposits.

[55] See A Crockett, 'Why is financial stability a goal of public policy?', paper presented to Federal Reserve Bank of Kansas City symposium 'Maintaining Financial Stability in a Global Economy' Jackson Hole, Wyoming, August 1997, available at <http://www.kc.frb.org/>.

[56] *Hazell v Hammersmith and Fulham London Borough Council and others*, above; [1991] 2 WLR 372; [1990] 2 QB 697, 739.

of Barings. The result was an agreed framework to address such risks for both securities firms and banks, through the 1996 market risk amendments to the 1988 Basel Capital Accord. Importantly, the Basel II Accord will leave this market risk framework largely unchanged, focusing on internal models for risk management.

Hong Kong's regulatory focus

For both OTC and exchange trade derivatives, regulatory attention is directed at **5.88** professional participants and only indirectly at products, an approach common to most aspects of Hong Kong financial market regulation.[57] OTC derivatives are unusual in this respect in that they receive similar treatment universally. This results from two factors. First, capital-regulated banks have always been the dominant users of global OTC derivatives, making regulators believe that their oversight was sufficient providing the jurisdictions under which they function could penalize fraudulent selling to non-bank clients. Second, ISDA lobbied successfully for enactment of the US Commodity Futures Modernization Act in 2000,[58] which exempted OTC derivatives from regulation by the US agency that supervises futures and commodities exchanges. ISDA's skill in promoting standardization in swap market practice, documentation, and settlement was important in this decision, and effectively ended pressure for direct regulation of OTC derivative products. Whether that harmonized stance will subsist in the event of severe market disruption cannot be known, but the prominence of lightly-regulated hedge funds in the OTC sector since the advent of credit derivatives may eventually lead to a closer watch. Hong Kong would be likely then immediately to follow any joint UK/US approach.[59] Additional pressure for a tighter regulatory regime could result from concerns of insider trading, especially where banks are taken to possess asymmetric information on corporate clients, and may use any such inside knowledge to inform decisions to trade in credit derivatives. One early analysis suggests that this is widespread practice, contrary to declared industry standards, but that it may have no deleterious impact on liquidity in the subject company's share, loan, or bond prices.[60] Again, future changes are likely to be supported by Hong Kong's regulators but

---

[57] See Chapter 3.   [58] Appendix E of P.L. 106–554, 114 Stat. 2763.

[59] The credit derivative markets performed ably in spreading risk in 2004–5 prior to bonds issued by Ford Motor Co and General Motors Corp declared sub-investment grade by Moody's Investor Services. Prolific trading in credit protection may have prevented a collapse in the corporate debt market due to forced selling by investors unable to hold sub-investment grade claims. However, mid-year problems involving CDS settlement delays would encourage those favouring tighter product supervision.

[60] V Acharya & T Johnson, 'Insider trading in credit derivatives' London Business School IFA working paper 439, 2005.

not yet seen as imperatives in view of the limited current scope of single name CDS coverage of Asian risks.

5.89 The division of responsibilities and their supporting authorities among Hong Kong regulators is little different to the contemporary pattern seen in all financial centres, and is illustrated in Figure 5.13.

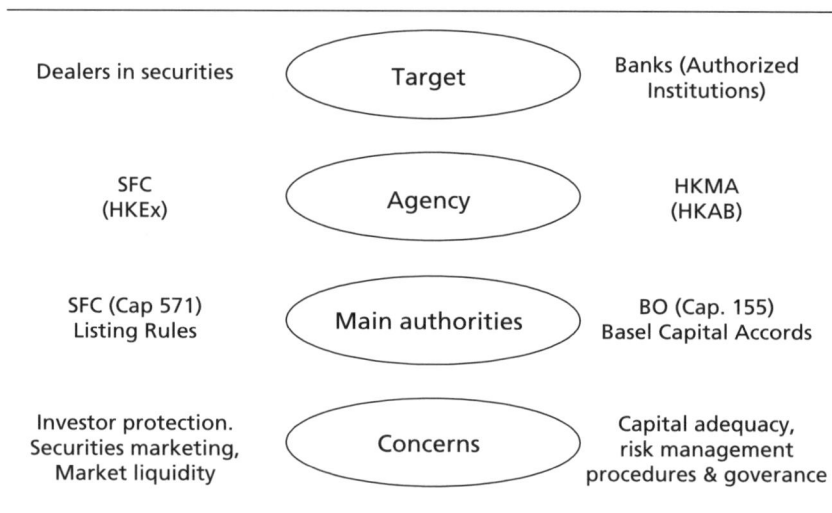

Dealers in securities	**Target**	Banks (Authorized Institutions)
SFC (HKEx)	**Agency**	HKMA (HKAB)
SFC (Cap 571) Listing Rules	**Main authorities**	BO (Cap. 155) Basel Capital Accords
Investor protection. Securities marketing, Market liquidity	**Concerns**	Capital adequacy, risk management procedures & goverance

Figure 5.13 Hong Kong's regulatory regime for derivatives

5.90 For traditional financial products, traded, sold, and managed in untroubled markets, these lines cause few difficulties. However, it is less clear that the bifurcated regime could cope fully with newer products in times of market stress, especially given Hong Kong's derivative emphasis with retail covered warrants. Banks, the main originators of covered warrants, are regulated with especial attention given to capital adequacy, and increasingly to their internal procedures for operations and risk management. The last two functions are central in covered warrant activity, given the complex dynamic hedging needed to sustain the business model. The securities dealer subsidiaries of those banks engage in selling the final product to investors, and in providing with liquidity on the exchange.

5.91 While Authorized Institutions under the Banking Ordinance engaged in securities activities are supervised as to capital adequacy and guided as to risk management by the HKMA and by fitness to deal in securities and the competence of professional staff ('recognized individuals') by the SFC,[61] it is unclear that

---

[61] The HKMA maintains a web-based register of such individuals.

HKEx has effective authority in relation to issues of securities (covered warrants but not excluding future instruments) made by such institutions, whose capital is located and supervised overseas, and for which the listing rules simply demand 'appropriate systems and skills' that HKEx cannot by itself judge. Further, the rules insist at section 15A.11 that:

> An issuer must be suitable to handle or capable of issuing and managing a structured product issue and listing. In assessing the suitability or capability of an issuer the Exchange will have regard to, inter alia, its previous experience in issuing and managing the issue of other similar instruments and whether it has satisfactory experience to manage the potential obligations under the structured product issue. Where listing of non-collateralized structured products is sought the Exchange will consider the issuer's risk management systems and procedures.

The resources to make this assessment may not lie within HKEx, and while the exchange may enjoy cordial and effective relationships with the HKMA and SFC, it remains an entity with different interests, and is not party to operational agreements with either agency in this regard. **5.92**

Figure 5.13 omits two further interests and two absent links: first, those of foreign regulators that have primary responsibility for the supervision of banks active in Hong Kong, and HKEx and the SFC in their functions under the Companies Ordinance that relate to Hong Kong listed companies; and second, how HKEx and the SFC treat bank hedging inasmuch as it arises from exchange trading with third parties, and how the SFC regards investor protection issues relating to bank risk, given that covered warrants are not primarily subject to the Banking Ordinance. These are not necessarily system flaws but rather matters of regulatory coverage that are prominent and subject to current discussion in Hong Kong, and not yet fully addressed by any leading jurisdiction. **5.93**

Hong Kong's attempts to match regulation to financial technology have centred on making more comprehensive the working arrangements and responsibilities between the HKMA and SFC. The findings of the British Board of Banking Supervision inquiry into the Barings case had a profound effect on several aspects of global financial regulation. In particular, it suggested that bank regulators lacked and needed a close understanding of non-bank activities in which the banks they supervise engage, including securities and derivatives trading.[62] In Hong Kong, this concern has led to changes and cross-references in the Banking and Securities and Futures ordinances, and the creation in 1995 of an operational memorandum of understanding between the HKMA and SFC **5.94**

---

[62] Report of the UK Board of Banking Supervision inquiry into the circumstances of the collapse of Barings (above), paras 13.56–13.70.

to encourage their mutual cooperation and allow exchanges of information on their respective charges.[63]

B. Exchange-traded Derivatives in Hong Kong

5.95 The array of products listed on HKEx or HKFE comprises:

- Covered (derivative) warrants
- Equity warrants
- Stock options
- Stock futures
- Stock index futures
- Stock index options
- Interest rate futures
- Fixed income futures

5.96 Covered (derivative) warrants are listed and traded on the main board of HKEx. This section outlines features of their treatment and regulation under the SFO, together with points relating to the principal futures and option contracts offered by the HKFE. All exchange contracts trade electronically through the HKATS order matching system and those traded on HKFE are settled and guaranteed by the HKEx clearing house, Hong Kong Securities Clearing Company (HKSCC), now the counterparty for all HKFE contracts.

(1) HKEx activity and principal contracts

Covered (derivative) warrants

5.97 Globally, warrants are usually issued for longer maturities than other forms of option contracts (usually 5–10 years) but in Hong Kong they have become prominent in relatively short maturities of up to two years due to their popularity among small investors.[64] These retail warrant issues are typically tied to Hong Kong or other prominent equities, share indexes, or foreign currencies. They have become so actively bought and sold that the trading volumes of Hong Kong warrants was the world's highest in 2004. For Hong Kong investors, the

---

[63] Available at <http://www.info.gov.hk/hkma/eng/bank/sup_coop/HKMA-SFC_MoU_eng.pdf>. The most recent version was made in 2002, and updated in March 2004. See also Chapter 3.

[64] The two-year tenor is a practice dating from stock exchange investor protection rules issued in the 1990s following the first issues of non-collateralized share warrants. Current listing rules set a maximum maturity of five years for most 'structured' products including covered warrants and a minimum of six months for all (LR 15A.38(5)).

popularity of covered warrants, known locally as derivative warrants,[65] partly reflects their low nominal purchase price and high inherent leverage compared to individual shares or baskets of shares. It may also be influenced by prevailing controls that limit the domestic channels available for gambling.[66] The most striking growth in issuance and trading volume has occurred since 2001, when changes to HKEx's listing rules made the issue of covered warrants relatively swift, simple, and inexpensive when the underlying asset or assets are themselves listed, and for the reopening of existing warrant issues.

The origin of the structure most often adopted by Hong Kong's covered warrant market since 2002 is in call spread equity warrants, where banks issue warrants tied to the performance of third party shares. In order to make the product appealing to retail investors, especially those imbided in a gambling-rich culture where lawful gambling is constrained to few channels, the arrangers often minimize the warrant premium but make leverage as high as the share's underlying volatility allows, This means that in normal circumstances the warrant's profit potential is reduced relative to the volatility of the underlying share. It also implies that the issuer's hedging performance during the life of the issue reflects a higher true share price volatility than that contained in the warrant, the difference being a source of economic rent. It is not known how covered warrant issuance might respond to a prolonged bear market in Hong Kong equities or to sustained increases in interest rates but the profitability of this sector is likely to be eroded by new entrants, which suggests that forthcoming structures will need to be novel to have appeal, or offer greater leverage to the small investor-trader. Here, perhaps is the potential for the market eventually to fail or find a different emphasis. **5.98**

HKEx listed 1,343 new covered warrant issues in the year to end-June 2005, for a total consideration of HK$ 138.3 billion (US$ 17.8 billion). The relatively short maturities of Hong Kong covered warrants partly explains the high number of issues: of the 376 warrants listed in the second quarter of 2005, only seven had expiry dates falling beyond 2006. In the first half of 2005, the amount raised by newly listed covered warrants represented 32.4 per cent of the exchange's total, and more than three times the total proceeds of listed debt **5.99**

---

[65] The change of term was deliberate. It reflects a regulatory investor protection concern, that 'covered' may imply options against which the issuer was perfectly hedged at all times. This could only be the case if the issuer always held shares or any other underlying assets equal to the volume indicated by the number of warrants outstanding, and would rarely, if ever, be profitable for the issuer.

[66] See also Chapter 9. Since 1993, instruments and transactions subject to the SFO have been excluded from the provisions of the Gambling Ordinance (Cap. 571), s 404.

securities.[67] Since April 2005, the number of covered warrants listed on HKEx has exceeded the number of listed stocks.

5.100 The factors explaining the warrant market's growth include:

- A relaxation in HKEx listing rules for this form of covered warrants in 2001.
- Declining general share price and interest rate volatility, which together tend to limit the investor's expectations of gains from share trading.
- Weakened confidence in smaller listed Hong Kong companies due to concerns over poor corporate governance, and the collapse in the market for HKEx 'penny' stocks in 2002 following rumours of mass delisting.
- Low entry prices for investors in warrants compared to those of their respective underlying shares.
- Limited lawful opportunities for domestic gambling.

5.101 Hong Kong's recent twin phenomena of prolific warrant issuance and turnover will not continue in its present form if certain market conditions alter, for example, if secular share price volatility were to rise, or if general confidence were to fall in the underlying equity market.

5.102 Earlier forms of equity-linked warrant were listed by HKEx from 1989, the majority under rules relaxed to capture issuance from overseas OTC markets and futures exchanges.

Other option products (equity warrants, equity-linked instruments, listed options)

5.103 Chapter 15 of the HKEx Listing Rules is specific to equity warrants, requiring a new issue to have a life of between one and five years. They are subject to specific shareholder approval or approval delegated to the board of directors and may not confer exercise rights over more than 20 per cent of shares in issue when the warrants are listed. The provisions allow equity warrants in respect of shares listed on 'another regulated, regularly operating, open stock market recognised by the Exchange' but none currently exist.[68] As at end-July 2005, 29 equity warrant issues were listed on the HKEx main board.

5.104 The exchange has permitted listed equity-linked instruments since 2004 in the form of structured notes of up to two years' maturity that carry option-related exposure to single stocks. These offer high coupons relative to prevailing comparable interest rates, in return for which the investor assumes (writes) a directional or range option risk on the underlying share, the payoff effect of

---

[67] But note that funds raised by share placements were exceptionally high in June 2005 at HK$ 45.6 bn (US$ 5.9 bn).
[68] LR 15.05.

which is taken to the principal amount of the note. These notes have not proven popular: only a handful are listed and trading is moribund.

Last, as of 31 July 2005, options on 39 stocks, all substantial companies, were traded on HKFE. **5.105**

Stock index products

HKFE currently trades four equity index products, described briefly in the following paragraphs. It also acts as a trading forum for 38 individual stock futures contracts on prominent Hong Kong companies and mainland groups. **5.106**

FTSE/Xinhua China 25 Index futures and options

The underlying index tracks the performance of the shares in 25 large Mainland Chinese companies listed on HKEx, with a substantial total market capitalization. The corresponding futures contract began trading in May 2005, so far with small contract volume and open interest. **5.107**

Hang Seng Index futures and options

The underlying index is HKEx's benchmark, a market capitalization-weighted index of 33 leading shares, accounting for the greater part of the market's total capitalization. The resulting futures contract was first devised in 1986 and is easily the HKFE's most consistently traded contract. Options on the index were begun by HKFE in 1993. **5.108**

H-share Index futures and options

The underlying index is the Hang Seng China Enterprises Index comprising 37 major H-share Chinese companies. **5.109**

Mini-Hang Seng Index futures and options

These contracts are retail-targeted, low margin, small denomination versions of HKFE's main Hang Seng Index contracts, using a contract multiplier that is 20 per cent of the size of the latter. **5.110**

Interest rate and fixed income contracts

HIBOR futures

The Hong Kong interbank offered rate (HIBOR) is the rate of interest offered by banks in Hong Kong on HK dollar deposits from other banks. One- and three-month HIBOR futures contracts were opened in 1997 and 1998, with contract sizes of HK$ 15 million (US$ 1.928 million) and HK$ 5 million (US$ 643,000), respectively. **5.111**

Three-year Exchange Fund Note futures

5.112 Exchange Fund Notes are quasi-sovereign fixed rate debt obligations of up to 10 years' maturity issued by the HKMA and are an important tool for it to influence money market liquidity. EFN futures are based on a notional three-year note with a 6 per cent coupon. Each contract has a HK$ 1 million nominal amount and is settled by physical delivery. Notes must have remaining maturities of 2.5–3.5 years to be eligible for delivery.

(2) Margin requirements

5.113 Exchange-traded derivatives are zero sum contracts for which one party's nominal gain equals the other's loss. The exchange's clearing system acts as central counterparty and eliminates all credit risks between users. It functions by imposing margin requirements on dealers, making automatic the daily revaluation of contract positions. In the past, these calculations could be arbitrary, and expose the exchange to unintended net risk positions. HKEx overhauled its fragmented clearing and settlement systems in 2004 by adopting a unified margin calculation model called Portfolio Risk Margining System ('PRiME'), based upon that developed for the Chicago Mercantile Exchange, which uses a conventional deconstructionist approach to option valuation.

(3) Risk management controls

5.114 Assuming that the exchange's margin systems function effectively to deal with credit risks, two issues are central in HKEx's risk management policies. First, assessment and monitoring participants whose activities it must supervise, especially when they involve the deployment of risk capital. Second, scrutiny of listing applications, and the task of ensuring that instruments that become listed conform with the exchange's rules and the requirements of law established by the SFO. The results are seen in how HKEx contributes to informing Hong Kong's banking and securities regulators as to exchange-based risk activity, and in aspects of investor protection, especially for the domestic risk-preferring retail segment.

5.115 Both aspects of the HKEx risk management focus are dealt with in its listing rules, which reflects its status as a non-statutory commercial body. Previous chapters have shown the division of regulatory and licensing responsibilities for banks and securities firms between the HKMA and SFC, together with post-Barings regulatory cooperation arrangements for information sharing on their respective charges.[69] HKEx is separate, however closely it walks with the SFC,

---

[69] Most transparently with the HKMA-SFC Memorandum of Understanding (above), and with recent legislative links in the Banking and Securities and Futures Ordinances, for example, covering the registration of individuals.

since it hosts a large number of derivative transactions arranged by banks acting primarily as securities firms, for which it requires certain functions to be performed as a condition of listing those transactions.

Issuer requirements

In particular, the listing rules for structured products contain three important **5.116** requirements of the issuer, described in the succeeding bulleted paragraphs:

- Issuers provide or arrange to provide trading liquidity through the life of **5.117** the transaction, essentially committing in normal conditions to maintain a market in the issue.[70]

Covered (derivative) warrants are issued with low premiums and dealing amounts **5.118** are often small. However, issuance has been concentrated since 2002 among a limited number of international banks: in the second quarter of 2005, 375 issues were made by 13 banks for a total consideration of HK$ 35.7 billion (US$ 4.6 billion). Committed market-making in these instruments is usually confined to a single exchange member, usually an associate of the issuer. Market-making is a qualified obligation under standard warrant terms laid down by HKEx,[71] but in a disrupted market the concentration of issuer obligors could be a concern.

- Issuers must be 'suitable to handle or capable of issuing and managing a **5.119** structured product issue and listing' and in considering a covered (derivative) warrant listing 'the Exchange will consider the issuer's risk management systems and procedures'.[72]

It is unclear whether in either case HKEx has the resources directly to do this **5.120** except by inference or a judgement as to reputation.

- While a transaction is listed, its issuer must maintain minimum capital and **5.121** reserves of HK$ 2.0 billion (US$ 258.1 million); and must either be (i) rated no lower than single-A by one credit rating agency 'recognized' by the exchange; (ii) regulated by the HKMA or a foreign counterpart 'acceptable' to the exchange; (iii) regulated by the SFC as to securities dealing in Hong Kong; or (iv) a sovereign issuer.[73] If the issuer meets none of these conditions then a listing may be granted to an issue guaranteed by a satisfactory third party.[74]

By these criteria, an unrated securities dealer could in theory become liable as **5.122**

---

[70] LR 15A.01 & 15A.22.
[71] LR, vol 2, App 1D.   [72] LR 15A.11.
[73] But 'sovereign' is looser than in contemporary bank credit risk practice and as defined by the Basel Accords.
[74] LR 15A.12–14.

obligor for an uncollateralized, structured, retail-orientated issue. The average size of issues introduced to the exchange in the first half of 2005 was only HK$ 101.5 million (US$ 13.1 million), but on average more than five began trading on each business day of the period.

5.123 HKEx performs a vetting role for which it lacks own resources, regardless of the nature of its relationships with the HKMA or SFC. In all these cases, listing approval is ultimately at the discretion of HKEx but the framework is porous. This is contrary to the intention of international standards for risk management and supervision to which the HKMA, for example, adheres. It is questionable that in a time of significant market stress, the HKMA or SFC could be confident of 'lending' compensatory resources to HKEx. Last, this section of HKEx activity contributes opaquely, if at all, to liquidity in the market for shares. Funds raised by new covered (derivative) warrants are available solely to the banks that act as their arranger and issuers. By contrast, HKEx declares as its mission:

> . . . HKEx contributes to Hong Kong's status as an international financial centre and the premier capital market for China. By servicing China's substantial long-term demand for capital and exchange services in accordance with international standards and practices, HKEx will further enhance its position as one of the world's pre-eminent exchanges.[75]

5.124 It may be inevitable that a cross-matrix oversight structure requires HKEx to be informed by others to meet the requirements set out in its listing rules. Nonetheless, it may also rely on assessments of reputation risk and presumptions as to internal system performance that have yet to be fully tested.

(4) Regulatory framework

Statutory treatment

5.125 The scope of direct SFC interest in derivatives is confined to those treated as 'securities' or 'futures contracts', and defined by the SFO to include in the case of securities:[76]

> rights, options or interests (whether described as units or otherwise) in, or in respect of, [ ] shares, stocks, debentures, loan stocks, funds, bonds or notes.

and

> certificates of interest or participation in, temporary or interim certificates for, receipts for, or warrants to subscribe for or purchase, [ ] shares, stocks, debentures, loan stocks, funds, bonds or notes.

---

[75] Source: HKEx.   [76] Sch 1.

Where such shares, stocks, debentures, loan stocks, funds, bonds, or notes are **5.126** themselves securities, and in the case of futures contracts:

a contract or an option on a contract made under the rules or conventions of a futures market.

However, the Financial Secretary may give notice that any instrument is to be **5.127** regarded for the purposes of the SFO as either a security or future.[77] This could include, for example, instruments based upon underlying claims assets that were not securities, such as foreign exchange contracts. More generally, the de facto result of the SFO is that exchange-traded derivatives can always be expected to be subject to some form of SFC oversight, regardless of underlying asset, and that OTC derivatives will not be subject to SFC supervision, even though it might appear plausible in some cases. This accords with practice in most common law jurisdictions where OTC derivatives are prominent.

Excluded by the SFO are insurance contracts specified in the Insurance Com- **5.128** panies Ordinance, even though the scope of the latter includes insurance against credit risks and certain financial losses.[78] That derivatives may be treated as insurance contracts has been an occasional concern in several jurisdictions since it raises potential problems of conflicting regulation (banking versus insurance), taxation, and contract enforceability. The uncertainty arises due to similarities among certain derivatives and insurance products, such as single name CDSs compared to financial guarantees or indemnities. A particular problem of enforceability could arise, for example, if a credit derivative was transacted between a bank and an insurer, given that as consolidated organizations each would be engaging in a business to which it was ordinarily accustomed. Counter arguments are that insurance will always involve contractual compensation for loss, and that an insured party would be expected to hold the contract's reference asset, which in neither example is the case with derivatives.[79] That today's derivatives are not insurance contracts would appear to be clear under Hong Kong law by virtue of the SFO but wholly new conflicting derivatives would need to be excluded by virtue of powers granted to the Financial Secretary by the SFO.

Market manipulation

Manipulation includes cases where an exchange-traded contract requires physi- **5.129** cal delivery. Since the 1980s it has become increasingly common for futures

---

[77] SFO s 392.
[78] Sch 1, Part 3. The SFO exclusion is at Sch 1, Part 1 under 'securities'.
[79] S Henderson, 'Credit derivatives 3: selected legal issues' (May 1999) *Journal of International Banking and Financial Law* 193; D Benton, P Devine, & P Jarvis, 'Credit derivatives are not insurance products' (1997) 16 *International Financial Law Review* 11, 29. Both articles examine statutory English insurance law, which is the basis for the Insurance Ordinance.

and options contracts to be settled in cash, and this tends to eliminate the chance of failed delivery and lessen opportunities for market manipulation. Here, manipulation is any participant's attempt to skew the market to its own advantage, and it would seem that inherent leverage and low costs of entry make exchanges amenable to such practices as squeezes, cornering, spreading false rumours, or direct price manipulation.[80]

(5) Investor protection

5.130   Covered (derivative) warrants are usually issued under a generalized 'base listing document' prepared as an umbrella for all transactions conducted by any bank through the exchange.[81] These documents, written under Hong Kong law, provide a governing framework for individual transactions and delineate the rights and duties of the issuer. Each new transaction prompts the issuer to prepare term sheets describing its main commercial conditions and that short document will form a supplement to the base listing document. Together they constitute the entire presentation to the exchange in respect of the listing of that specific transaction, subject to information on the issuer's financial condition being kept current in the base listing document.

5.131   HKEx's revised covered warrant listing rules in 2001 provided concessions to issuers and arrangers over documentary requirements, the reopening of existing issues, and aspects of disclosure, including:

- Lowering the minimum warrant launch market capitalization to HK$ 10 million (US$ 1.285 million).
- A maximum launch market capitalization of HK$ 100 million (US$ 12.85 million).
- The maximum number of a company's shares to which warrants can be linked is the lesser of 30 per cent of the public share float or 20 per cent of issued share capital.
- Further issues are freely permitted, subject to a limit for each of HK$ 100 million (US$ 12.85 million).
- There is no requirement to provide on application for listing or thereafter detailed information on the underlying company.
- The issuer is not required to disclose other outstanding warrant issues, nor of

---

[80]   These categories are acknowledged in legal analysis of US commodities market practice. See, for example, J Williams, 'Manipulation on Trial: Economic Analysis of the Hunt Silver Case' (Cambridge, 1995).
[81]   HKEx Listing Rules prescribe the information content of such documents: vol 2, App 1D. They borrow ISDA practice for OTC contracts so as to permit warrant issues to be made speedily under umbrella documents.

its dealings in the underlying shares. However, dealings by the issuer or its associates in the issuer's warrants must be reported daily to HKEx.

At the same time the exchange created a requirement favouring the investor, by making warrant issues include provision for the appointment of a 'liquidity provider', to make a market in the issue, subject to certain conditions.[82]   **5.132**

Most issuers will be authorized banks. Unsurprisingly, base listing documents provide that the warrant holder, as such, is not deemed a depositor when paying funds to the issuer, so as to avoid being granted protection over those amounts flowing from a conventional regulated bank-depositor relationship. The listing rules require that base listing documents be updated annually or upon 'a significant change affecting any matter contained in the listing document', where 'significant' is given a meaning linked to a warrant holder being able to make 'an informed assessment' of 'the assets and liabilities and financial position of the issuer and of the structured products'.[83] This is well-intentioned, and it may be both impossible and undesirable to provide otherwise. Yet this is language customary in documenting transactions between sophisticated financial organizations, and it is difficult to see how any retail investor could make an assessment of the creditworthiness of the issuer in relation to its structured product liabilities when the existence and nature of hedging is a matter of commercial confidentiality. The HKMA or SFC may be able to assess these factors, but HKEx and the warrant holder must rely largely on reputation risk and remote judgement. Issuers are required to inform potential investors that structured products are inherently risky, but the warning relates to market risk and deal structure, not to the credit risk of the issuer.   **5.133**

Investor interfaces

The intense efforts made by banks to market and distribute retail-targeted derivative instruments are subject to the legal and regulatory requirements contained in the SFO and supervised by the SFC.[84] Issuers give particular marketing emphasis to newspaper, online, and broadcast advertising and to promotional seminars, which are covered at length by the SFO, including sanctions against publicity originating from unlicensed sources.[85] HKEx listing rules for structured products allow the distribution of certain promotional material to potential investors prior to listing, which may apparently conflict with the SFC's intention to tighten regulation over the distribution of analyst material prior to share listings.   **5.134**

Licensing and registration under the Banking Ordinance[86] of individuals such as   **5.135**

---

[82] LR, sch 16.   [83] LR 15A.66.   [84] See Chapter 3.
[85] SFO s 103(1). See also more generally Chapter 3.   [86] BO s 20.

stockbrokers, securities dealers, and their agents who engage with clients in regulated financial activities and the online register of their names maintained by the HKMA are dealt in the same way for exchange-traded derivatives as all other securities, as defined by the SFO.

C. OTC Derivatives and Hong Kong Regulatory Oversight

5.136 Hong Kong is not a major hub for OTC derivative instruments on the scale of London or New York and to date the territory's OTC derivative markets are unusual neither in their use of instruments nor practice. The approach taken by the HKMA since the mid-1990s has been to support the international harmonization of practice standards and adopt an increasingly high level of sophistication in its bank supervisory activities so as to be sensitive to the needs in the territory of those major banks that deal in complex products. Thus the HKMA will allow the banks for which it is responsible to adopt the internal assessment options provided by the Basel II Capital Accord, even though the numbers able to do so are likely to be few.[87] In this way the HKMA hopes to promote the sophistication of Hong Kong as a financial hub, and makes itself a useful resource to guide the less sophisticated banks operating in the territory, a growing number of which are customers of leading derivative houses.

5.137 Thus the legal and regulatory treatment of OTC derivatives in the territory is shared with most advanced common law jurisdictions that participate in the development of global standards and practice, and as such it raises concerns and issues that are generic, rather than particular to Hong Kong. In future, this may change as a result of expanded participation in the OTC markets by a wider range of Asian companies, for which corporate governance and reporting standards are traditionally more variable. In general, OTC transactions made subject to Hong Kong law will be very similar to English law agreements.

(1) Swaps and structured transactions

5.138 OTC derivatives contracts are made by commercial agreement between two parties, and so in theory must be assessed in terms of applicable law in relation to legality, enforceability, bankruptcy or insolvency, contractual capacity and taxation, and of the transaction's place of execution for matters of regulatory

---

[87] The Banking (Amendment) Ordinance 2005, was enacted on 15 July 2005 and provides for the HKMA to implement by order the new capital adequacy regime.

oversight.[88] However, market practice and the force of global regulatory developments means that most OTC swap and structured transactions are conducted largely identically, regardless of location or the domicile of participants.[89] The reasons are fourfold:

- ISDA's success in providing reliable standard documentation includes accommodating in umbrella documents differences in jurisdictions and national practices. This can lead to protracted negotiation delays in executing documents governing the overall OTC derivative relationship between two counterparties but generally does less to disrupt trading by willing commercial counterparties, who tend to take the approach of 'agreeing to agree'. Peer pressure makes eventual execution inevitable.

- The market's international orientation encourages a majority of users to employ English or New York law to govern their dealings, even if the participants are from third and fourth domiciles and the transaction is created in a fifth. Where market custom is otherwise, for example with domestic Japanese users, the standard agreements will prevail but with certain locally framed alternative provisions, all governed by local law.

- Despite the complex nature of some instruments, the extent of leverage present in the markets for derivatives and a desire for feasible liquidity are great incentives for harmonization. Participants tend to choose a legal forum they believe to be familiar with their contemplated dealing. In some respects the newness of the markets has allowed the law to respond to their needs. (Hong Kong law is by custom employed for most public debt issues denominated in HK dollars and is generally acceptable for OTC derivative contracts involving two parties in the territory but may not be chosen ahead of a more widely used forum.)

- The general level of counterparty credit risk is high and transparent (partly due to widespread collateralization), and shared among generally sophisticated institutions. Although cases of derivative mis-selling were a feature of the first decade of the OTC swaps markets, they have become comparatively rare. Recent disputes arising from the alleged mis-sale or mismanagement of synthetic CDOs are not a direct concern in this respect, even though these may involve transactions with embedded derivatives.

---

[88] The Hague Conventions would not apply to OTC derivatives but are likely to do so for securities to which they become attached.

[89] ISDA Masters are said to document more than 90% of global OTC derivative transactions. See joint ISDA/Bond Market Association amicus brief in *Enron Corporation and others v Bear, Stearns International Ltd and others*, US Bankruptcy Court Southern district of New York, Adv No. 03–93388 (AJG), 5 July 2005.

(2) Documentation and the role of ISDA

5.139 Most of the world's OTC derivative transactions are executed under standard documents developed for ISDA, most written under English or New York law. The foundation is the umbrella ISDA Master, on which two other documents are laid, giving three main parts:

- ISDA Master. This provides the terms common to all transactions between two counterparties through a set of basic conditions and schedules, and can be written as an agreement to govern sole currency transactions confined to a single jurisdiction, or made without restriction by place or currency.

- Optional credit support annexes that deal with collateralization. To date these can be attached in several forms governed by English, Japanese, or New York law, depending on which is written into the ISDA Master.

- Either, detailed 'long form' confirmations of individual transactions; or brief 'short form' transaction confirmations that incorporate by reference a group of ISDA definitions of those market conventions that form part of any single deal.[90]

5.140 The first ISDA-inspired documents appeared in the mid-1980s; today's prevailing ISDA Master was released in 2002. It superseded a much amended predecessor from 10 years earlier and regular participants would expect to use the newer version. However, there is no reason why infrequently trading counterparties might not continue to use the 1992 ISDA Master if it suits them to renew it unchanged, however ill-advised this may seem in law. Innovations in law, regulation, practice or instruments will be met by new definitions, for example, ISDA released new commodity definitions in June 2005.[91] ISDA also provides templates for confirmations in both long and short formats. Nothing in law or regulation prevents OTC derivative transactions being documented in an alternative form by consenting counterparties, even if the work may seem wasteful, but regulatory risks associated with an unfamiliar contract may prevent banks being granted desired capital treatment.

5.141 ISDA Masters establish the principles of the two counterparties' mutual dealings,[92] and can deal with all current underlying asset classes. Financial terms deal with payment calculations and obligations; credit provisions address delivery risk by means of payment netting and conditionality, term credit risk through

---

[90] ISDA definitions cover general practice and a series of conventions for market segments, including credit derivatives, currencies, options, equities, commodities, and precious metals.
[91] See <https://www.isdadocs.org/publications/isdacommderivdefsup.html>. All current ISDA publications cited in this chapter are available at its website, which is subject to registration.
[92] Provisions exist for a counterparty to enter deals through any of its branch offices.

the status and good standing of the parties at commencement and upon new transactions, including commercial, legal, and taxation representations and warranties, and requirements for the delivery or exchange of supporting documents, corporate information, and legal opinions. Finally, the document will include commercial, legal, and taxation covenants, events of default, and provisions to address changes in prevailing law, regulation, or taxation, and enforcement by means of termination, including termination netting and the calculation of settlement payments.

Collateralization and credit support

The world's swaps markets tend always to be reclusive when faced by lesser quality credit risks. Dealing with poorly rated counterparties has been taken historically to be a hindrance to liquidity, and a function that could more properly remain with the loan or bond markets. The view was given intellectual support by the long-term nature of the market, and the general preference (after costly 1990s mis-selling litigation) to confine dealings to relatively sophisticated counterparties. Derivative trades with lesser quality credit risks, including weaker borrowers, or lightly capitalized institutional investors and hedge funds, therefore tend to form part of funding transactions, for which credit risk is inevitable and capital adequacy charges greatly exceed those attaching to the naked derivative, or be subject to collateralization. Taking collateral in the form of cash or marketable securities improves the rate of recovery from defaulted transactions, even though it can be costly to administer and subject to legal uncertainty in enforcement. **5.142**

The proportion of collateralized transactions has risen in recent years because of the growing participation of hedge funds in all instruments, so that ISDA surveys suggest that at the beginning of 2005 the share of OTC transactions secured by collateral was 55 per cent, whether measured by credit equivalent risk or trading volume. Cash deposits are the most frequently used collateral medium, and a large share of collateral tends to be re-used, that is, deployed by the holder in further transactions. In general, larger and frequent users are more inclined to recycle collateral assets in this way.[93] **5.143**

The mechanics for collateralization have three legal aspects: choice of law, form of collateral agreement, and choice of collateral. No substantive choice will exist as to the last two in single currency, single jurisdiction agreements. Otherwise, all three factors enter the ISDA framework. Choice of law is a matter for the two parties based upon the range of deals they expect to conclude. Choice of **5.144**

---

[93] ISDA Margin Survey 2005.

collateral is standardized to meet the holder's requirements for capital relief and described by ISDA in a definitions release:[94] the three options in Hong Kong are HK dollar cash and Exchange Fund bills or notes. The form of collateral agreement will follow local law in many cases. Otherwise, ISDA provides five alternative forms of collateral document based on English, Japanese, and New York laws, with a further option under English or Japanese law in the means of making collateral effective, either by pledge or title transfer. The latter is efficient but are not universally recognized, for example in the US. With its close English law roots, Hong Kong regards title transfer as enforceable, ceteris paribus. The collateral agreement will govern how collateral is to be held, used or enforced, and include representations covering the freedom to offer collateral.[95] The title transfer structure also assists in Hong Kong if a counterparty is restricted by existing contractual negative pledges that lack purchase money exceptions.

Netting

5.145 Netting is integral to risk and cost reduction in OTC derivative transactions. Contractual netting is well-established for risk management and as a general market standard. Several forms of netting are typically used in swaps transactions, including payment netting, termination (or close-out) netting, cross-agreement netting, and regulatory netting, although some forms are not universally enforceable. The concept is not unique to OTC derivatives but is highly developed in derivative markets. It takes four distinct forms:

- Payment netting takes place within single on-going transactions. On any payment date, one counterparty will make a net payment to replace two due mutually opposing gross swap payments. It may also take place across a series of swaps, so that one party makes a single net payment in place of those due across the designated series. Payment netting reduces administration, expenses, and operational risks as well as lessening credit risk.

- Termination netting produces a single net payment for the amount owed at termination prior to scheduled maturity under a swap or series of swaps. Formative transactions used a simple present value calculation of replacement costs at termination but this has evolved into a more comprehensive assessment of value that takes account of market conditions, and is captured in the 2002 ISDA Master. Termination netting affects the scale of credit, operational, and payment risks.

---

[94] ISDA Collateral Asset Definitions 2003.
[95] ISDA has expressed concern as to delays among EU members in implementing the 2002 Hague Convention No 36 on the law applicable to certain rights in respect of securities held with an intermediary, which has yet to take effect.

- Cross-agreement netting extends across two or more agreements. It seeks to reduce net credit risk exposures among two counterparties across an accumulation of transactions, and if successful will impact on credit risk mitigation by collateralization. This type of netting is unreliable in some jurisdictions.

- Regulatory netting aims to optimize mutual capital relief, especially by adjusting to requirements for large risk exposures or risk concentration.

OTC derivative documentation seeks to protect netting in a variety of contexts. **5.146** As the result of the success of ISDA documentation and related transaction support, netting is now recognized as an important risk management technique across a wide variety of jurisdictions, not least in Hong Kong. Moreover, netting receives increasing support from regulators and is acknowledged in amendments to the 1988 Basel Capital Accord and its successor Basel II, along with a range of other established credit risk mitigation techniques.[96] Most importantly, netting provisions in OTC instruments has supported the growth and widening of derivative usage by providing for efficiency in operations and in the use of risk capital. Netting has thus been the technical feature of OTC derivative structuring most responsible for the degree of leverage that the markets now support. Without near-universal netting provisions, both the market and regulatory communities would take a more severe view of leveraged risk and as a result the risk transfer and diversification benefits of many instruments, especially credit derivatives, would be eroded.

Payment and termination netting may nonetheless conflict with national bank- **5.147** ruptcy law following the default or insolvency or one or both counterparties. The most widespread prevailing standard is that netting is not prevented by any automatic stay of the recovery of payments or enforcement of collateral caused by bankruptcy provisions, and this reflects the belief that the result is less disruptive to all. This matter has been discussed in UK and US crises as notable as the collapse of Bank of Credit and Commerce International SA and LTCM, and in recent US litigation following the failure of Enron Corporation.[97] The rescue of LTCM procured by the Federal Reserve was provoked by the fear that a pre-emptive liquidation would trigger immediate termination of the fund's extensively leveraged risk portfolio, which was complex, layered, and understood by no outsider, if by LTCM, as well as a predicted frenzy by banks to seize or

---

[96] An influential positive view appears in a BIS study 'Credit Risk Transfer' 2003, at <http://www.bis.org>.

[97] In a case concerning OTC equity derivatives *Enron Corp and Enron North America Corp v Bear, Stearns International Ltd and Bear, Stearns Securities Corp* 323 BR 857 (2005) Bankr SDNY.

enforce collateral. The US bankruptcy code exempts OTC derivatives with netting provisions from automatic stay against claims that takes effect at the commencement of bankruptcy proceedings. The Fed believed in the probable integrity of netting and enforceability of collateral, and foresaw a scramble to unwind outstanding contracts and enforce collateral immediate upon the commencement of bankruptcy proceedings.

5.148 Elsewhere, concern has been expressed by ISDA and others over EU directives in the same area. For example, it is said to be 'deeply uncertain whether termination netting is threatened by set-off protection in Article 6 of the EU's Insolvency Regulation', and the 'concept of insolvency set-off in Article 6 of the [European Commission] Insolvency Regulation does not encompass the technique of insolvency close-out netting' in relation to up to nine of the pre-2005 fifteen member states.[98]

5.149 Hong Kong law is unambiguous. The Bankruptcy Ordinance allows for the automatic set off of amounts (and contingent amounts) due to and from an insolvent Hong Kong company. The courts have held that the intention of the ordinance is to 'allow for justice between the contracting parties', and treat as intact mutual claims made before the issue of a winding-up order.[99] Extensive reform of Hong Kong bankruptcy law has been awaited for some years, so that while the law is clear in permitting netting, including cross-agreement netting, there is theoretical potential for doubt given that the origin of law has no connection to modern OTC derivatives. However, the effectiveness of netting is wholly accepted by the SFC, so that eventual reform is likely to leave unchanged Hong Kong's reliable statutory protection.

Litigation

5.150 Derivatives litigation has developed in three strands. The first deals with a series of swap transactions involving UK local authorities in the 1980s,[100] the second with disputes arising from alleged mis-selling,[101] and the third addresses the validity of ISDA's documentation structure and the enforceability of its

---

[98] European Financial Market Lawyers Group 'Report on protection for bilateral insolvency set-off and netting agreements under EC law' (2004) p 21, available at <http://www.efmlg.org>.

[99] Cap. 6, s 35; *Re First Bangkok City Finance Ltd (in liquidation)* [1994] 2 HKC 735.

[100] *Hazell v Hammersmith and Fulham London Borough Council* (above).

[101] *Bankers Trust International plc v PT Dharmala Sakti Sejahtera* [1996] CLC 18, Queen's Bench Division (Commercial Court), (Transcript) 1 December 1995; *Procter & Gamble v Bankers Trust Co*, 925 F Supp 1270 (SD Ohio 1996); *Lehman Brothers v Minmetals International Metals Trading Co*, 2000 WL 1702039 (SDNY 2000).

components.[102] The UK local authority cases show the need for derivative market makers to establish the good standing and internal constitutions of new counterparties and to ensure the enforceability of applicable agreements, even in a legal setting favourable to financial innovation.

(3) Credit derivatives

Two issues of law and enforcement arise with credit derivatives in ways not encountered with other types of instruments based on financial reference assets. Both arise as examples of incomplete contracts. The first are the circumstances that prompt payment to be made by the protection seller; and second, which relates only to CDS transactions, how deliverable assets are specified and whether the protection buyer is given free choice of assets in making delivery. The concerns are not mutually exclusive: for example, a payment default on two forms of debt issued by a single reference obligor may not take an identical form, leading one bond to be valued differently to the second. This type of case has been highlighted in recent years by the tactics of 'vulture' investors, who seek to corner cheapest-to-deliver assets in expectation of credit events. It should be noted that credit events on corporate risk CDSs are not uncommon. **5.151**

Payment under credit derivatives is typically triggered by a defined credit event taking place on a reference asset, asset pool, or index. These will ordinarily include payment defaults, bankruptcy, debt restructuring, and declared moratoriums, but their specification and the requirements for agreement among counterparties or independent verification to determine whether a credit event has taken place, are in each case more complex than in relation to other classes of underlying asset. **5.152**

ISDA's far-sighted approach to standardization has resulted in its documentation model being able to adapt relatively easily to credit risk as an asset class. Nonetheless, several concerns of law may not be dealt with fully in all cases, for example, because of potential ambiguity or completeness in definitions of credit events. The ISDA Master sets out eight generic credit events: **5.153**

- Bankruptcy
- Failure to pay
- An obligation for debt acceleration
- Cross-default

---

[102] *Australia and New Zealand Banking Group Ltd v Société Générale* [1999] 1 All ER (Comm) 682; *Nuova Safim SpA v Sakura Bank Ltd* [1999] 2 All ER (Comm) 526; *Peregrine Fixed Income Ltd (in liquidation) v Robinson Department Store Public Company Ltd* [2000] CLC 1328.

- Repudiation
- Debt restructuring
- Downgrading
- Credit event upon merger.

5.154   The slightly fewer credit events recommended by ISDA to be associated with sovereign risks are:

- Failure to pay, which can be made subject to a grace period extension or a minimum payment requirement
- Debt repudiation or moratorium
- An obligation for debt acceleration
- Restructuring, which can be made subject to the involvement of multiple holder obligations
- Default requirement (as an amount).

5.155   In all cases, the need is to ensure that the credit events function properly and with as little as possible potential for dispute. Current ISDA documentation takes a more specific approach to credit event definition than its 1990s predecessor, which led to the concept of 'soft' credit events that could require outside arbitration.

(4) Regulatory framework

Capital requirements and market risk

5.156   The forthcoming Basel II Accord extends the provisions of the existing (amended) 1988 Capital Accord, including its treatment of derivatives. Provisions relating to market risk are largely unchanged but Basel II may eventually have important directional consequences on other aspects of derivative market practice, especially in regard to credit derivatives, risk transfer, and collateralization.

Questions and concerns

5.157   Three areas suggest concerns that may arise in a prolonged directional change in global credit or interest rate cycles:

- Regulatory and internal risk management. It is likely that new and more complex structured products will provoke fresh waves of litigation, especially involving transparency, information flows, and the use of models in deal pricing. Hong Kong may be vulnerable in this respect in the context of the regulation of the retail covered warrant market.
- Risk disclosure. The ease and scale of contemporary credit risk transfer is generally thought to allow for a spreading of risks among an ever-wider

community of financial institutions that is wholly beneficial. This view reflects a traditional favouring of stability in financial markets and among institutions. Yet the process by which risk is passed from one party to another may itself lack contractual completeness, and thus support new forms of improper sale, insider trading, moral hazard, and problems arising from information asymmetry. Pressure may thus build for more open standards of information to apply to OTC derivative markets.[103]

- How can the law keep up? Without debating the Hammersmith and Fulham judgment or the ultra vires issue, the case's reasoning is typical of its era and would perhaps be only part of considerations today. Market practice among frequent borrowers and banks engaged in treasury management is to examine the potential impact of single trades on asset and liability portfolios, not merely on a marginal basis, transaction by transaction. Accordingly, the example of ill-advised swaps cited in judgment by Lord Templeman could now be perfectly acceptable to a risk averse counterparty.[104] While the essence of using VAR-based models in risk management is to capture this principle, it is less clear that regulation is fully founded on the same basis, and still less sure that the law can keep pace with product development.

---

[103] A current Hong Kong example is represented by differences in SFC and ISDA views of the need for statutory disclosure of financial interests (see SFC consultative paper, 'Review of the disclosure of interests regime', January 2005).

[104] *Hazell v Hammersmith and Fulham London Borough Council and others* [1992] 2 AC 1, above.

PART III

CORPORATE AND MARKET CONDUCT

6

CORPORATE CONDUCT AND GOVERNANCE

Management is a critical element in the performance and prospects of any **6.01** company. Being in control of capital provided by others, the role of director brings with it both responsibility as well as the opportunity for negligence or even abuse. The question of how to ensure persons that manage companies do so for the benefit of the owners and are effectively accountable to them, is a perennial one and ensures that the form and function of management is always going to be subject to scrutiny.

6.02 In Hong Kong, with its tradition of family-dominated companies and groups and with its somewhat dated Companies Ordinance and non-statutory Listing Rules, corporate governance has become an increasing concern—both at the corporate level and at the level of the competitiveness of Hong Kong's financial markets generally. Further, as Hong Kong's financial system has evolved from one dominated by a very small group to one increasingly serving both Mainland China and the international financial system, Hong Kong's existing regulatory system for corporate governance (developed in a different context from that of today) appears increasingly less appropriate to the needs of the markets generally, as well as those of individual investors. These problems have been most directly highlighted by the increasing number of Mainland Chinese companies listed on the SEHK but often not subject to its effective regulatory reach.

6.03 Following an introduction to corporate governance, this chapter reviews the ways in which a company's management is regulated in Hong Kong at common law and equity, by statutory legislation, by the company's constitutional documents, and by regulatory rules. Such a framework addresses issues such as board structure and operation, the personal interests of directors, dealings between the company and directors, limiting the power of directors, disclosure of information and the question of when shareholders should be involved in decisions of the board.

A. The Topic of Corporate Governance

6.04 Over the past decade, an immense amount has been written and said about corporate governance. While corporate governance is an important issue for the functioning of any economy or financial system, it is certainly not a new issue: Adam Smith wrote of these issues in 1776, and Adolf Berle, Jr, and Gardiner Means analysed the issues in some detail in 1932. Attention once again began to crystallize around these issues in the early 1990s, with major attention arising following major corporate collapses such as Enron in the US and Parmalat in Europe.

6.05 One can engage in the corporate governance debate at different levels: at the microeconomic or corporate level and at the macroeconomic level. The discussion in this and the following sections of this chapter will look at the former.[1]

6.06 At the corporate level, corporate governance can be looked at from a variety of distances, with debate at the widest level addressing the roles and responsibilities of companies in relation to their employees, customers, and social community.

---

[1] Chapter 2 touched upon the macroeconomic level of the corporate governance topic.

For example, in the UK a change in this regard occurred with the introduction of the 1980 Companies Act in that a new provision was introduced requiring directors to have regard to the interests of the company's employees in general as well as the interests of its members. While no such changes have been or are proposed to be made in Hong Kong, it is of interest to note that further proposals are underway in the UK.[2]

Corporate governance has been defined as the set of relationships between **6.07** shareholders, board, management, and other constituencies of a company.[3] In recent years, various organizations and interest groups have been promoting corporate governance standards. For example, institutional investors have been promoting a corporate governance model focused on the interests of shareholders. These efforts were mainly focused on improving access to influence and control of management action. Other constituencies have emphasized the broader responsibilities of enterprises towards their various stakeholders in addition to shareholders, including employees, suppliers, the community in which they operate as well as local and national governments.

As a starting point, improving corporate governance seeks to improve the effi- **6.08** ciency and attractiveness of the markets for capital, following from the successful development of dispersed ownership of public corporations in the US (the 'Berle and Means corporation'), which underpins the efficiency and attractiveness of the markets for equity securities in the US.

The essential problem is well known: companies suffer from the classic agent– **6.09** principal conflict of interest between shareholders and management described by Berle and Means.[4] This conflict is most obvious in situations involving widely dispersed share-ownership and the potential conflict between the interests of management (those in control) and the shareholders (owners), most typical of markets in the US and UK (the Anglo-American model of corporate ownership, control, and governance). The focus typically is on the rights of minority shareholders. The problems in a family-controlled or state-controlled

---

[2] In March 2005 the UK government published a White Paper on Company Law Reform proposing, inter alia, a statutory statement of directors' duty to replace existing common law and equitable rules. 'The statement of duties will be drafted in a way which reflects modern business needs and wider expectations of responsible business behaviour', stating that 'the basic goal for directors should be the success of the company for the benefit of its members as a whole; but that, to reach this goal, directors would need to take a properly balanced view of the implications of decisions over time and foster effective relationships with employees, customers and suppliers, and in the community more widely'. The White Paper calls this the 'enlightened shareholder value' approach and suggests that it, is most likely to 'drive long-term company performance and maximize overall competitiveness and wealth and welfare for all'.

[3] EBRD, Sound Business Standards and Corporate Practices: A Set of Guidelines (September 1997).

[4] A Berle & G Means, *The Modern Corporation and Private Property* (Macmillan 1933).

context (both prevalent in Hong Kong), while at first glance appearing different from those in the traditional Berle and Means corporation, are in reality more pronounced, in that ownership and control are combined to a large extent, thereby reducing the capacity of non-controlling shareholders to influence management. This gives rise to a potential conflict of interest between controlling shareholders and non-controlling shareholders. So long as the interests of the controller (whether family or state) are identical to those of the corporation, these models can both be quite effective under many circumstances. Problems occur in situations in which the interests of the controllers diverge from those of the corporation, and the controller is able to use the corporation for personal benefit and to the detriment of the interests of the company as a whole. To the extent that non-controlling shareholders feel that their interests are not being served by the controllers, they will feel less inclined to invest in such companies. The end result is a potential governance problem, which may feed into lower share prices, higher costs of capital and decreased confidence, thereby reducing the potential scope and efficiency of the financial system and impacting on the rate of economic growth.

6.10 The basic significance of good corporate governance is premised on corporate performance. Investors may be willing to pay increased prices for shares in companies with good governance (a corporate governance premium). Increased share prices reduce companies' cost of capital and therefore increase competitiveness of companies across a given market. Higher share prices also increase the attractiveness of a given market to investors (both domestic and international). Further, investors will be more likely to invest in companies and markets with good governance (good governance increases confidence in the market), enhancing the transfer of funds through the financial system, thereby increasing the scale and efficiency of the financial system, which in turn enhances economic growth.

6.11 The result of this has been an increased focus over the past decade on the topic of corporate governance.

(1) Responses to a problem

6.12 One way of approaching the question 'what is corporate governance' is to see corporate governance as a response to a problem. Persons invest in companies with the expectation of financial gain. However, in large companies, such as those listed on the SEHK, most investors are not involved in management. Ownership has in the modern era become separated from control, and decisions are made by someone other than the owners.[5] While some management may

---

[5] Although in Hong Kong the presence of the controlling 'family interest' at both shareholder and board level is still reasonably prevalent as compared to, eg the UK or the US.

be shareholders with an interest that broadly corresponds to those of other investors, not all management will be shareholders.

The problem, as generally recognized in common law jurisdictions, is how   **6.13**
to ensure that the persons who manage companies do so for the benefit of the owners and are effectively accountable to them. This raises a multiplicity of related questions concerning, for example: the protections available to investors that their investment in the company will be properly managed, board powers and composition and operation, the responsibilities of directors, treatment of the personal interests of directors when they connect or conflict with those of the company, what sort of information should be provided to owners and when, and how and when should owners participate in management decisions?

To put this general problem another way, how can the function of management   **6.14**
be operated so as to best improve the chances of financial performance? And, what should be the nature and scope of the relationship between the owners of a company and those who manage it?

A cynic may look at the whole issue in a different light: the problem of corporate   **6.15**
governance is the problem of how to keep the directors 'clean', ie from abusing or improperly taking advantage of their position, such as using company assets for their own purposes, buying assets from the company at below fair value, lending money to themselves from the company on a non-commercial basis, giving favourable deals to connected persons, or simply not giving the shareholder owners of and investors in the company adequate and correct information. Unfortunately, corporate history is replete with examples of the foregoing, some of which reach the headlines of the public media, others which remain carefully undiscovered. Whether or not cynical, it is commonly recited that good corporate governance results in increased shareholder value. However, if governance is inadequately controlled, and cases of improper governance proliferate to a greater extent than they have already done so, this may lead to a lack of confidence in the system and thus weaken the corporate model.

Clearly, many cases of improper governance witnessed in the marketplace may   **6.16**
lead to civil or criminal liabilities. However, legal remedies are in general retrospective in nature, compensating or punishing rather than preventing. This gives rise to consideration of the governance topic in two regards: that which compensates or punishes governance wrongdoings, and that which seeks to prevent or make less likely governance wrongdoings. As this chapter will show, whereas the former tends to involve laws, the latter tends to involve regulations. It is in part for this reason and in part because of the more flexible and responsive nature of regulations that in contemporary times the role of regulation has assumed a certain predominance when it comes to placing

controls on corporate governance. Nevertheless, regulations necessarily assume certain laws to be in place.

6.17 Moreover, each of the foregoing imply a more fundamental judgement: what should be the normative standards of governance? And, whatever standards are agreed to be proper, how is proper governance to be monitored: how is it known when governance is being properly administered?

6.18 Under a laissez-faire model, the answer to these corporate governance problems is simple: the only relevant factor is the reputation of the individuals undertaking the management function. The competitive forces in an open and freely operating market will weed out those who do not perform and those who manage well will earn reputation and prosper.

(2) Market integrity

6.19 While the focus in much of this chapter is on the tension between the managers and the owners of a company, it should also be recognized that corporate governance plays a much wider role in relation to the integrity of the marketplace.

6.20 First, the investor marketplace in which the company participates is comprised of potential investors not merely its present investors. Companies with an established record of good corporate governance may not only be able to command greater shareholder loyalty and support, but may also be able to obtain preferable terms on future capital raising exercises.

6.21 Second, it is a core role of the marketplace to ensure investors are adequately protected. One of the means of achieving this is through the regulation of the relationship between company management and its investors, that the former do not abuse their position and take advantage of the latter.

6.22 Finally, the 'integrity of the marketplace' refers to a wide range of concepts such as the fairness, efficiency, transparency, orderliness, and robustness of the market. A successful corporate governance regime plays a role here too, in preserving and fostering not only the integrity of the market but also the general standing and reputation of the market as comprising companies which are managed in an orderly and professional manner.

6.23 With this background and analytical framework, the remainder of this chapter focuses on the laws and regulations which comprise the corporate governance framework in Hong Kong. This presently covers the relationship and obligations as between owners and companies and directors. However, as regards regulatory matters, one must also recognize the role such regulations play in the context of a company's governance within the marketplace.

B. The Corporate Governance Framework in Hong Kong

On what matters do 'corporate governance regulations' in Hong Kong bite? It is **6.24** easy to think that the sole object of corporate governance is the duties of directors and how they determine to conduct the management of a company. However, the overall framework of corporate governance is comprised of both the general and the specific. Whereas the former refers to the general duties of directors, the latter refers to certain actions required to be taken in response to specific events. Both play an important function in augmenting the quality of the management of companies and cover matters including:

- board structure and operation;
- management responsibility and accountability;
- the interests of and personal dealings of directors;
- shareholders rights, such as when shareholders should be involved in decision making;
- the making of disclosures, ie what needs to be disclosed to the market and when.

The framework for dealing with such matters is derived primarily from four **6.25** sources:

- **common law and equity** as developed and applied in the courts—primarily concerned with the fiduciary and other duties of directors;
- **statutory legislation**—in particular the Companies Ordinance, Securities and Futures Ordinance and the Securities and Futures (Stock Market Listing) Rules;
- **constitutional documents** of the company;
- **regulatory rules (ie of a non-statutory nature)** applying to publicly listed companies—the Listing Rules (and its ancillary codes and guidelines) and the Takeovers Code.

While it is obvious that not all provisions of company law and regulation **6.26** pertain to the topic of corporate governance, it could be said that the widest ambit of good corporate governance implies that directors should conduct themselves in a way which does not result in the breach of any law, article of the company's constitution or applicable regulation. Such an approach would clearly lose focus on the particular items of law, etc which make specific contributions toward the solution of the corporate governance problem. For example, a director's failure to disclose a personal interest in a proposed contract of the company has potentially quite different ramifications on the proper governance of a company as compared to his making a misrepresentation in connection with a business contract of the company. Although both give rise to liability on the part of the director, only the former specifically concerns proper governance. It can also be noted that of those provisions which do directly concern proper governance, there is a 'cut-off level' of relevance to consider when discussing corporate governance. For example, it is a basic governance requirement that directors must convene proper meetings of shareholders in accordance with the provisions of the Companies Ordinance and its constitutional documents, but it is more interesting to consider when such meetings need to be called and what information should be provided to shareholders at such meetings.

6.27   With this distinction in mind, and recognizing that there is a grey area as to what ought and ought not to be considered in a review of governance, we shall in this chapter consider the above four sources of corporate governance control under four primary headings of governance concern: directors and the board, shareholder rights, disclosure and transparency, and specific rules applying to transactions noteworthy because of their size or nature. This is done in the following sections C to F. However, before doing so, the remainder of this section shall introduce the Hong Kong context of common law and equity, statutory legislation, a company's constitutional documents and regulatory rules.

(1) Common Law and equity

6.28   As Hong Kong is a former British Crown Colony, its approach to the duties of directors has much in common with that of other Commonwealth jurisdictions, notably England, Australia, and Canada. In particular, a director of a company must consider two types of duty:

- a fiduciary duty;
- the common law duty of skill and care.

These duties are reviewed in detail below. A number of these duties have become enshrined in specific provisions in legislation and the Listing Rules.

(2) Statutory framework

6.29   The principal statutory provisions addressing corporate governance in Hong Kong arise under the Companies Ordinance and the Securities and Futures Ordinance (SFO). The Companies Ordinance in particular effects many provisions relating to the topic of the governance of a company. Many of these are very straightforward, for example, the requirement that a public company have at least two directors, that a register of directors be kept, and that directors be of at least 18 years of age.[6] Other provisions regulate the specific actions of

---

[6] Respectively, CO ss 153, 158, & 157C.

directors by setting out specific requirements, for example that notices to share-holders of meetings must set out 'such information and explanation . . . as is reasonably necessary to indicate the purpose of the resolution'.[7] In contemporary times, such provisions are 'a given'.

6.30 Although each of these 'given' provisions in some way contributes to the notion of corporate governance, the focus in this section shall be on those provisions which are generally regarded as of greater significance in maintaining a proper corporate governance regime (and not a review of the entire body of legislation concerning directors and the managing body of a company).

6.31 Statutory requirements in many respects bear a strong relationship to (or have evolved from) the director's fiduciary duties and the common law duty of care, skill, and diligence. For example, the statutory requirement concerning disclosure of interests in contracts of the company is in effect an extension and codification of the fiduciary duty not to put oneself in a position where one's own interests conflict with those of the company. Similarly, the offence of insider dealing is in some ways an extension of the fiduciary duty not to make secret profits. When reviewing the potential liabilities associated with prospectuses, it is also worth bearing in mind the implicit trust given to directors by shareholders cum investors not only as regards the general fiduciary role of the former but also as regards the specific duty of care, skill, and diligence.

6.32 Statutory provisions can be sorted into four conceptual groupings as regards corporate governance covering: the personal interests of directors; dealings between the company and directors; limits on the powers of directors and shareholder involvement; and giving of information.

6.33 An additional statutory layer was introduced in April 2003 when the Securities and Futures (Stock Market Listing) Rules (Cap. 571V) (SMLR)[8] came into effect. The SMLR established a 'dual filing' regime which gave a certain statutory backing to the Listing Rules and provides for criminal liability where companies applying for listing on the SEHK and companies already listed intentionally or recklessly disclose to the public materially false or misleading information. Although the SMLR is statutory in nature, it is further discussed below in connection with regulatory rules due to its close connection with the enforcement of the Listing Rules.

(3) Constitutional documents of the company

6.34 It should be readily apparent that provisions in the memorandum and articles of a company form a part of the corporate governance framework. While the

---

[7] CO s 155B.   [8] The SMLR have been made pursuant to SFO s 26(1).

specific provisions of such documents vary from one company to another, they normally cover such matters as how directors are appointed and removed and their general scope of power, the need to hold and notify shareholders of general meetings, and may cover basic financial matters such the amount which the company may borrow without shareholder approval and exercise some control over the dividend policy of the company. Such provisions form the basic groundwork for a director's existence and participation in the company.

6.35   While the detailed provisions of the memorandum and articles relating to directors and management will not be reviewed, certain other standard provisions are of interest, such as those which concern conflicts of interest and indemnification of directors.

(4) Regulatory rules

6.36   An important influence on maintaining the quality of corporate governance is regulatory rules, that is, rules which do not have the force of law. A core function of regulation as compared to the usual functions of common law, equity, and statute is pre-emption. Laws operate to effect restitutionary remedies or to punish when laws are broken. In contrast, regulations pertaining to corporate governance seek through a system of monitoring and supervision by regulatory authorities[9] to guide corporate governance behaviour down a path which avoids legal wrongdoings.[10]

6.37   In this regard, the Listing Rules, which apply to companies listed on the SEHK, are of primary concern. However, before discussing those rules a few preliminary comments need to be made as regards the nature of the Listing Rules.[11]

6.38   First, the Listing Rules are issued by the SEHK and are not themselves of legal binding effect. However, as mentioned above, the Listing Rules now have a certain statutory backing by virtue of the SMLR.[12] Section 3(a) of the SMLR provides that a person applying for listing on the SEHK is required to 'comply with the rules and requirements' of the SEHK. Once a company is listed it will

---

[9] We are primarily concerned with the SEHK and the SFC although other regulators play a role in relation to quality of management in their particular industries, for example, the SFC in relation to the securities and futures industry and the HKMA in relation to banking institutions.

[10] However, certain industry regulations which lay down specific rules bearing a relationship to governance topics (such as the SFC's fit and proper criteria for registered persons, codes of conduct, and guidelines for management, supervision, and internal control) nevertheless do not properly fall under the ambit of corporate governance in the sense that such regulations are primarily aimed at the relationship between the company and its customers (rather than the company and its shareholders) and, in that context, the proper operation of the financial marketplace.

[11] The Listing Rules are dealt with in Chapter 5.

[12] The SMLR have been made pursuant to SFO s 26(1).

also need to note that the SMLR grant certain rights and powers to the SFC including the right to receive on-going disclosure materials of the company[13] and the power to direct the suspension of the company's listing in certain circumstances.[14] It should equally be noted that the SMLR do not go so far as making the detailed rules comprised in the Listing Rules a statutory matter.

Second, it should be noted that a consultation is underway in which certain **6.39** portions of the Listing Rules would become absorbed into the SMLR.[15] The proposed amendments would give statutory backing to three areas of the Listing Rules concerning disclosure of price-sensitive information, disclosure, and publication of periodic financial reports, and disclosure and approval requirements for notifiable and connected transactions. While such changes if enacted would change the legal nature of the relevant rules, the consultation underway does not envisage any significant changes to the provisions of such rules.

Listing Rules

It will be noted in the following sections that a number of the Listing Rules **6.40** concerning governance issues address or reiterate issues covered by common law, equity and/or statute. This is not mere redundancy. To the extent we are dealing with mandatory rules, certain immediate and direct consequences may accrue to companies and their directors should they breach them. Unlike a legal court process, the SEHK may take very swift remedial action, without going through a full judicial process.[16]

In addition, it will be noted that the Listing Rules apply to all companies **6.41** seeking a listing on the SEHK whether or not incorporated in Hong Kong, therefore companies which may not be subject to certain governance protections of the Companies Ordinance will be subject to similar requirements found in the Listing Rules.

Although many of the provisions of the Listing Rules are directed at the **6.42** companies themselves, the rules also make clear that directors are collectively and individually responsible for ensuring the company complies with the Listing Rules.[17]

---

[13] SMLR s 7.

[14] SMLR ss 8 & 9. This topic is dealt with in more detail in Chapter 5.

[15] SFC, *A consultation paper on proposed amendments to the Securities and Futures (Stock Market Listing) Rules* (January 2005); Financial Services and the Treasury Bureau, *Consultation paper on proposed amendments to the Securities and Futures Ordinance to give statutory backing to major listing requirements* (January 2005).

[16] The organs of the Exchange making decisions and the attendant appeal processes are discussed in Chapter 5.

[17] eg LR 13.04.

6.43 In recent years, many changes in the Listing Rules have been made by the SEHK as part of a wider programme for improving the standards of corporate governance in Hong Kong. Perhaps the most significant development in recent times has been the adoption into the Listing Rules effective January 2005 of the Code on Corporate Governance (CG Code) and the Rules on the Corporate Governance Report (CG Report Rules).[18] These additions clearly set out the views of the SEHK as to good corporate governance.

6.44 Companies are expected to comply with, but may deviate from provisions of the CG Code.[19] The CG Code sets out what the SEHK considers to be the principles and practices of good corporate governance. While none of the specifics set out in the code are mandatory, a company must report on whether it has complied with the CG Code provisions and explain deviations from such provisions.[20] On the one hand, it can be said that such an approach leaves the specific standards of governance to be resolved by the commercial forces at work between a company's management, its shareholders, and the wider marketplace. While this may have a certain free market appeal about it, as the SEHK is setting terms of reference for good corporate governance (which are perceived as minimum standards), it is thereby sending out a signal to shareholders and the marketplace as to what they should be prepared to accept. It can therefore be said that compliance, though not mandatory, is 'anticipatory compliance'.

6.45 In contrast to the non-mandatory 'anticipatory' framework of the CG Code, the main body of the Listing Rules contain a number of detailed provisions of a strictly mandatory nature which implement the more specific details of corporate governance. Compliance with the mandatory provisions of the Listing Rules is a serious matter. The SEHK has the general right to suspend or cancel the listing of the company where the Exchange 'considers it necessary for the protection of the investor or the maintenance of an orderly market' and, more specifically, may do so where the Exchange considers the company has failed in any material way to comply with the Listing Rules; has an insufficient public float; operations or assets are insufficient to justify a continued listing; or is otherwise unsuitable for listing.[21]

6.46 Thus, the approach in the Listing Rules to the topic of corporate governance can be described as consisting of a general framework of 'anticipatory compliance' backed up by mandatory compliance as to specific matters.

---

[18] LR appendices 14 & 23 respectively.   [19] LR 3.25(1).
[20] LR 3.25 & CG Report Rules.   [21] LR 6.01.

CG Code and CG Report Rules

The CG Code is structured in three tiers—principles, code provisions, and **6.47** recommended best practices. The recommended best practices are expressly for guidance only. While the code provisions themselves are expected to be complied with, a company may choose to deviate from them. The CG Code expressly contemplates that a company may choose to create its own code on corporate governance practices on such terms as it considers appropriate, although the SEHK nevertheless expects due regard to be had to the principles set out in the CG Code. In any case, as explained under 'CG Report Rules' below, companies are required to report[22] on and explain deviances from the CG Code and this will in practice prove awkward if the company's own code bears little regard for the principles, provisions, and recommendations set out in the CG Code.

The CG Code is divided into five sections covering directors and their remunera- **6.48** tion (including that of senior management), accountability and audit, delegation by the board, and communication with shareholders.

The CG Report Rules sets out mandatory reporting requirements and recom- **6.49** mended disclosures. Hence, unlike the CG Code, failure to comply with manda-tory aspects of the CG Report Rules constitutes a breach of the Listing Rules. The main provisions of the CG Code and CG Report Rules are dealt with below.

(5) Other sources

A form regulation also occurs in the marketplace. The expectations of the **6.50** market are an important influence on corporate governance and undoubtedly contribute to evolving best practice. Institutional investors[23] in particular exer-cise significant influence on company management, especially as regards their expectations on management and financial performance.

As commercial practices evolve, committees such as the Committee on the **6.51** Financial Aspects of Corporate Governance (commonly known as the Cadbury Committee) articulate the developing best practices. In 1992 the Cadbury Committee produced a 'Code of Best Practice' which made certain recom-mendations in relation to the corporate governance of English public companies and companies listed on the London Stock Exchange. Although this code did not and does not have the force of law, it was in general widely supported by the

---

[22] The report is made for the relevant accounting period in the company's interim reports and annual reports (or their respective summary reports, if any).
[23] Entities such as the Investment Management Association in the UK and the Counsel of Institutional Investors in the US are industry associations representing shareholders holding many trillions of dollars worth of shares.

financial community and in consequence has a certain 'moral force'. The Cadbury Committee itself was appointed by the Financial Reporting Council, the London Stock Exchange, and the accountancy profession. Indeed, since the time of the Cadbury Report, certain of the recommendations have found their way into the Listing Rules of the SEHK. The most significant recommendations, which are addressed later in this chapter, deal with the need for and function of independent non-executive directors, and advise that directors should report on the effectiveness of a company's system of internal control.[24]

(6) Non-Hong Kong companies

6.52 On a technical point it must be noted that many of the companies operating in Hong Kong and listed on the SEHK are not incorporated in Hong Kong. In general, all the matters discussed herein apply to such companies as participants in the Hong Kong market having established a place of business in Hong Kong. However, the notable exception is that the parts of the Companies Ordinance reviewed herein apply to companies incorporated in Hong Kong, not to companies incorporated elsewhere. While this is in part ameliorated insofar as non-Hong Kong companies are incorporated in a common law jurisdiction (the laws are similar being derived and in part based on the UK Companies Act), it is of less concern as regards governance than one might at first think given the submission by such companies to the provisions of the Listing Rules. The Companies Ordinance does contain a few provisions directly concerning non-Hong Kong companies, as regards maintenance of authorized representatives in Hong Kong and delivery of annual accounts, but these are of little guidance on the question of governance.

C. Directors and the Board

6.53 As will be readily apparent, the primary subject of corporate governance is the organs and means by which a company is managed. This will include the board, any subcommittees thereof, the constitution and operation of the board, and of course the directors of the company.

(1) Ambit of 'director'

6.54 It is worth pausing for a moment to consider what we mean when we refer to a 'director'. In the simplest case, a director is the person appointed, in accordance

---

[24] There have been many other committees established for the purposes of reviewing corporate governance in Hong Kong and elsewhere since the Cadbury Committee but this is not the occasion to review the developments contributed by such other committees.

with the constitutional documents of the company, by the shareholders or by the board itself to occupy such post. However, it is worth noting the different headings under which a person may be regarded as a director in Hong Kong.

Executive versus non-executive director

Executive directors are those directors who are actively engaged in or responsible **6.55** for the running of the day-to-day business of a company. However, not all directors are so engaged and these directors, known as non-executive directors, may be involved effectively only part-time in the company. As will be reviewed in the course of this chapter, there are at law few differences in the duties and obligations owed by executive and non-executive directors.

De facto director

A person need not actually be duly appointed or be appointed at all to be **6.56** regarded as a de facto director, it being sufficient that such person 'assumes to act as director. He is held out as a director by the company and claims and purports to be a director.'[25] It is notable that section 2(1) of the Companies Ordinance defines director as including 'any person occupying the position of director by whatever name called' and therefore does not require a valid appointment to be in place for a person to be regarded as a director.

Alternate director

Under the constitutive documents of the company, the appointed director may **6.57** be entitled to nominate an alternate, such as in the absence of the appointed director. The alternate director acts in place of the appointed director and his acts are deemed the acts of the appointed director.

Shadow director

In addition, one must also be aware that certain persons may be regarded as **6.58** 'shadow directors'. Section 2(1) of the Companies Ordinance provides a widely accepted definition of a shadow director: 'a person in accordance with whose directions or instructions the directors or a majority of the directors of the company are accustomed to act.' Persons giving advice professionally will not be regarded as shadow directors merely because the directors act on advice professionally given.

The upshot for the present purposes is that there is in general no particular **6.59** distinction made between duly appointed directors, executive or non-executive

---

[25] *Re Hydrodam (Corby) Ltd* [1994] 2 BCLC 180.

directors, de facto directors, alternate directors, and shadow directors for corporate governance purposes. However, as the role of executive and non-executive directors may be distinguished (in that the former are expected to be involved in the day-to-day business of the company whereas the latter are not), so too may their liabilities should the directors collectively not fulfil their obligations.

6.60   Finally, while it is not the topic of this chapter to discuss the situation of companies in an insolvent situation, it is worth noting that the concepts discussed herein (as regards common law and fiduciary duties and the requirements of legislation) in general apply also to directors and liquidators in the receivership context. Directors and liquidators in that situation are of course subject to additional duties and legislative requirements but it is outside the scope of this chapter to cover such material.

Senior management and officers

6.61   Not all persons who are regarded as senior management or officers are directors. Such persons almost by definition have an important role in the performance of a company, and are likely to have opportunities to abuse their position within the company. Despite this, corporate governance to date has not particularly sought to broaden its ambit to senior management.

6.62   Under the Companies Ordinance, some of the controls and liabilities applicable to directors also apply to non-director officers,[26] but not all. For example, the requirement to disclose an interest in a potential contract of the company[27] applies to directors but not to officers who are not directors.

6.63   Neither the common law nor equity appears to recognize any special relationship between non-director senior management and the company (although senior management acting as directors may come to be regarded as de facto directors). The Listing Rules, however, bring within their ambit some provisions regarding senior management, for example as regards remuneration.

(2) Common Law and equity

Fiduciary duty

6.64   There are two core features of the position of director that renders him a fiduciary. First, a director is in effect an agent administering the resources of the

---

[26] For the purposes of the CO, a director is an officer but so too is the company secretary and any person who exercises management functions under the immediate authority of the board, CO s 2(1).
[27] CO s 162.

company for those who collectively own it, ie the shareholders. Second, the relationship between the directors and the shareholders is such that shareholders place their trust and confidence in the directors that they will undertake their agency properly. However, it should be clarified that the fiduciary duties owed by the directors are to the company not to the shareholders[28] and arise from the 'legal relationship between the directors and the company directed and controlled by them'.[29]

Directors may owe a fiduciary duty to shareholders where there is: 6.65

> . . . a special factual relationship between the directors and the shareholders . . . which bring the directors of the company into direct and close contact with the shareholders in a manner capable of generating fiduciary obligations.[30]

Such circumstances may arise in connection with a duty of disclosure of   6.66
material facts to shareholders, or other circumstances invoking duties of trust and confidence. In this connection, it is worth considering, for example, the directors' obligations arising in connection with a takeover (see further Chapter 7) or the raising of additional funds from shareholders (see Chapter 4). In each case, a shareholder wishing to establish such a duty would need to rely on the so-called 'special facts doctrine' and prove the relevant facts establishing the 'direct and close contact'.

As a fiduciary, the duties to the company which the directors must attend may   6.67
be described under four general categories.

Act in good faith in the best interests of the company as a whole

A director has a duty to act in good faith in the best interests of the company and   6.68
not for any collateral purpose. This implies that the directors must consider what is in the interests of the members as a class and that they may not favour one over another. However, the interests of employees are not covered by this duty.[31]

One sometimes hears the view that this duty of directors also encompasses   6.69
creditors of the company, particularly where the company is approaching insolvency or is already insolvent. Directors may certainly be held to account to the shareholders as regards entering into new credit transactions in such circumstances on the basis that to do so is not in the interests of the company as a whole. However, there is no separate duty to creditors[32] and, as it has been pointed out in two Australian cases, to give creditors a right against directors

---

[28] *Percival v Wright* [1902] 2 Ch 421.
[29] per Mummery LJ in *Peskin v Anderson* [2001] BCLC 372.   [30] ibid.
[31] The interests of employees are also not recognized under legislation.
[32] *Kuwait Bank Asia EC v National Mutual Life Nominees Ltd* [1991] AC 187.

would undermine the principle of *pari passu* participation by creditors.[33] The specific obligations owed in an insolvency situation by directors as regards creditors therefore needs to be kept distinct and under the insolvency law heading not the fiduciary duty heading.

6.70 Courts allow directors absolute discretion and do not wish to interfere in the merits of commercial decisions.[34] However, the courts will consider the question of whether no reasonable director could have believed that a course of action was in the best interests of the company. Therefore a director acting honestly but not in the best interests of the company may be in breach of this duty.

Exercise powers for proper purposes

6.71 The widest purpose of a director's appointment is to act for the benefit of the company. However, specific provisions may also be found in the contract of employment, in the constitutional documents of the company, and in the resolutions of the board. It is the duty of a director to act in accordance with such provisions.

6.72 This duty implies another, namely, that a director must exercise his powers within his own judgement and not delegate them to any other person except where he is properly authorized to do so, for example, by the constitutional documents of the company or any proper resolution of the board.

Avoid any action which would create a conflict between duties to the company and personal interest

6.73 A director must not put himself in a position where there is an actual or potential conflict between his personal interest and the interests of the company.

6.74 A director may find himself in a conflict situation in a number of different ways. He may have a personal interest as a shareholder which conflicts with his duty to the company (example: as a shareholder wanting a dividend payment but as a director considering it not in the interests of the company as a whole to declare a dividend). He may wish to engage in a transaction with the company as principle or authorize a transaction in which he has an interest (eg he owns an office furniture business and he proposes the company rent furniture from such business).

6.75 The constitutional documents of a company may provide for how to deal with such conflicts. For example, the sample articles provided in Part I, Table A,

---

[33] *Sycotex Pty Ltd v Baseler and others* (1994) 12 ACLC 494 and *Spies v The Queen* (2000) 18 ACLC 727.

[34] *Howard Smith v Ampol Petroleum Ltd* [1974] AC 821.

schedule I of the Companies Ordinance provide (in article 86) that a director who has any interest in any contract or proposed contract of the company must declare his interest and in general not vote in respect of such contract unless permitted by the company in general meeting. This topic is also addressed in section 162 of the Companies Ordinance and is dealt with below.

Not to profit from his position at the expense of the company

A concern closely related to the foregoing duty is that a director may not make a **6.76** personal profit from any opportunities that result from his directorship, even if he is acting honestly and for the good of the company. Any profit made (also known as 'secret profits') must be accounted for to the company, ie paid over to the company.

For example, a director becoming aware of a potentially lucrative business con- **6.77** tract should give the company the opportunity to undertake it before consider- ing referring it to someone else or undertaking it himself. If the company were to undertake such contract, the director would be in breach of his duty to the company if he were personally to receive a 'finder's fee' from the third party providing the business contract.

The notion of 'at the expense of the company' needs to be clarified. The loss of **6.78** an opportunity may constitute such an expense. On the finder's fee example above, the fee could have been earned by the company. Even if the fee or any other type of profit would not have accrued to the company (a finder's fee is not normally paid to a contractual principal) he must still account for it if the opportunity arose through his directorship.

Liabilities and remedies: Breach of fiduciary duty

That a director is labelled a fiduciary does not indicate the remedies **6.79** available for breach.[35] However, a number of typical remedies are nevertheless commonly seen.

Injunction

Where the breach has not yet occurred, or has occurred but is continuing, the **6.80** remedy of injunction may be available.

Ratification

It may be possible for the shareholders in general meeting to ratify the breach. **6.81** It is not entirely clear when this remedy will be available, the courts in some

---

[35] *Re Coomber* [1911] 1 Ch 723.

cases permitting ratification by majority vote[36] but not in other cases.[37] It has been suggested that ratification may be permitted where directors are making a secret profit but not where it concerns misappropriation of the company's property.[38]

Accounting for secret profits

6.82　A director will need to account for secret profits, for example, where he diverts property to his own use or makes a personal profit from his position.[39] He will also need to account where he buys company property without full disclosure of all the relevant facts and paying the fair market price[40] or sells his own property to the company irrespective of whether the price is fair.[41] In this regard, the courts are strict, it making no difference whether the company could have obtained the property on better terms or that the director was acting honestly. In the *Regal Hastings* case, it was stated that a director may obtain:

> . . . the assent of the shareholders . . . to make the profit for himself. Failing that, the only course is to let the opportunity pass. To admit of any other alternative would be to expose the principal [i.e., the company] to . . . dangers . . . The rule is an absolute, because 'the safety of mankind' requires it to be absolutely observed in the fiduciary relationship.[42]

Compensation

6.83　A director will be liable to compensate the company for any loss suffered by the company as a result of a breach of duty. For example, a director who misappropriated assets and business opportunities for his own purposes,[43] or one who charges his private expenses to the company[44] will be liable to compensate the company by way of damages or other equitable compensation.

Setting aside

6.84　The company may seek to set aside a transaction where rescission is available.[45] This remedy may be available for example where a director has sold personal property to the company in breach of his fiduciary duty. Where rescission is not available, the court may order an appropriate financial adjustment in the form of damages.

---

[36] *Regal Hastings Ltd v Gulliver* [1942] 1 All ER 378.
[37] *Cook v Deeks* [1916] 1 AC 554 PC.
[38] P Davies (ed), *Gower's Principles of Modern Company Law* (6th edn), p 647.
[39] *Boardman v Phipps* [1967] 2 AC.　　[40] *Haywood v Roadknight* [1972] VLR 512.
[41] *Gillet v Peppercorn* (1840) 3 Beav 781; *Bentley v Craven* (1853) 18 Beav 75.
[42] at p 157.　　[43] *Gencor ACP Ltd and others v Dalby and others* [2000] 2 BCLC 734.
[44] *Re Texgar Ltd* [2002] 1 HKLRD 687.
[45] *Hely-Hutchinson v Brayhead Ltd and another* [1968] 1 QB 549.

Constructive trust

Finally, in certain circumstances, for example where a director in breach of **6.85** fiduciary duty diverts the company's property to a connected company not wholly owned by him, the courts may at its discretion impose a constructive trust on the property in the hands of the connected company.[46]

Duty of skill, care, and diligence

One of the hallmarks of the development of corporate governance in modern **6.86** times has been the steady elevation of the standard of care required of directors. In earlier times, the courts tended to regard the topic as a matter between the shareholders and the director in question as it was the shareholders who appointed the director. Moreover, the role of director has not always been the one it is today—compared with the 'pleasant, if sometimes incompetent, amateurs who did not possess any particular executive skills and upon whom it would be unreasonable to impose onerous standards of care and skill',[47] the modern day director is expected to be professional and is accordingly held fully accountable.

Consistent with the approach of the courts not to interfere in the merits of **6.87** commercial or business judgments, courts have been unwilling to set out specific requirements for what constitutes due skill, care, and diligence. However, what is required of directors can be expressed in three aspects.

Degree of skill

The traditional position of the courts has been that 'a director need not exhibit **6.88** in the performance of his duties a greater degree of skill than may reasonably be expected from a person of his knowledge and experience'.[48] That is, his performance must be judged by the way he applies skills he actually possesses. Clearly there are many circumstances which may arise. Nevertheless, the courts have for a long time made it clear that all directors will be expected to exercise the level of skill which they can reasonably be expected to have in the light of their qualifications, experience, and expertise.

However, the modern tendency has been to reflect the commercial realities of **6.89** directors as being management and business professionals. In a recent English case it has been asserted that 'directors have, both collectively and individually, a continuing duty to acquire and maintain a sufficient knowledge and understanding of the company's business to enable them properly to discharge their duties as directors'.[49]

---

[46] eg as in *Cook v Deeks* [1916] 1 AC 554 PC.
[47] *Farrar's Company Law* (4th edn), pp 391–2.
[48] *Re City Equitable Fire Insurance Co* [1925] 1 Ch 407.
[49] *Re Barings plc (No 5) and others* [1999] 1 BCLC 433.

6.90   Where directors take it upon themselves to give advice to current shareholders, for example, in a takeover context, they have a duty to advise in good faith and not fraudulently, and not to mislead whether deliberately or carelessly.[50]

6.91   However, given this duty (and the two duties next discussed) is based in the law of negligence, the courts have found it difficult to enumerate the precise scope of such duty, depending as it does on the factual circumstances of the case.

Attention to the business

6.92   All directors are required to show reasonable diligence in attending to the affairs of the company. In performing his duties, he must display the 'reasonable care . . . an ordinary man may be expected to take in the same circumstance on his own behalf', although 'a director is not bound to give continuous attention to the affairs of the company. His duties are of an intermittent nature.'[51] However, a director who did not review board papers and took no other part in the management of the company would be likely to have failed to discharge his duty in this regard.[52]

Reliance on others

6.93   A director is not liable for the acts of co-directors or company officers solely by virtue of his position. A director is entitled to rely on a subordinate charged with a position for the purpose of attending to the details of management. 'In respect of duties . . . that may properly be left to some other official, a director is, in the absence of grounds for suspicion, justified in trusting that official to perform such duties honestly.'[53]

6.94   However, directors cannot completely absolve themselves of their responsibility by delegation to others but retain primary responsibility as regards the relevant matter. The exception to this is where the director has put in place proper reporting lines and other controls to enable effective supervision and for problems to be brought to the attention of the directors and/or board. That is, the director must monitor the effectiveness of the delegation on a regular basis, that those who are executing a certain function are doing so properly and within the confines of the power delegated.

6.95   Directors are generally responsible for the business of the company as a whole. However, some directors may be employed to perform a particular role in a particular area of the company's business. First, such director will be expected to exercise a high degree of skill and care in that area, perhaps higher than generally

---

[50] *Dawson International plc v Coats Paton plc and others* [1989] BCLC 233.
[51] ibid.   [52] *Dorchester Finance v Stebbing* [1989] BCLC 498.
[53] *Re City Equitable Fire Insurance Co* [1925] 1 Ch 407.

expected of directors in view of his perceived expertise. Second, it may be that the responsibility of such a director in relation to other parts of the business is correspondingly lessened to the extent that the same is outside the scope of his contractual duties.

Non-executive directors

Despite the different level of involvement in the day-to-day business affairs of a company, non-executive directors nevertheless owe the same fiduciary duties to the shareholders and a duty to exercise due skill, care, and diligence. There is no difference between the skill demanded of an executive and non-executive director.   **6.96**

However, the nature of the non-executive role as regards the duty to exercise due skill, care, and diligence is worth considering further. As with executive directors, non-executive directors are expected to exercise only that degree of care and skill which would be expected of them given their knowledge and experience in the prevailing circumstances. In practice, the nature of the non-executive role may mean (but does not necessarily imply) the non-executive will be expected to comply with a lower level of skill, care, and diligence than his executive colleagues. The level of the non-executive's remuneration may also act as a guide as to what level of involvement is expected of him in the company's affairs.   **6.97**

Nevertheless, a non-executive may not avoid involvement in the affairs of the company. The nature of the non-executive role requires him to inform himself as to the way the company is being managed, to act as a check on the decisions of the executive directors, and to take the lead where potential conflicts of interest arise.[54] As will be seen, the Listing Rules set out specific requirements for boards to include independent non-executive directors (discussed below), very much with the aforementioned functions in mind. Accordingly, non-executives clearly have a duty of skill, care, and diligence in relation to the purposes for which they were engaged.   **6.98**

Liabilities and remedies: Breach of duty of skill, care, and diligence

Breach of the duty will found an action for negligence at the suit of the company. Whether a director will be regarded as having been negligent may be a question of his actual knowledge and experience in the context of the company's business and the extent to which such director was responsible for the matters relevant to the negligence asserted. In this regard, a distinction between the duties of executive and non-executive directors may need to be made since   **6.99**

---

[54] The Committee on the Financial Aspects of Corporate Governance (commonly known as the Cadbury Committee) (UK, 1992) regarded these as key roles of non-executive directors.

the principal function of the former as compared to the latter is to be actively engaged in the business of the company. Such a distinction may lead to a different thread of liability attaching to these two types of directors[55] although the courts are likely to be slow to come to such a distinction.

6.100 The primary remedy in relation to a breach will be damages. The remedy of injunction may be available, as discussed above in relation to a breach of fiduciary duties.

Business judgment

6.101 Directors acting in the best interests of the company as a whole clearly give rise to the prospect that some decisions will disadvantage certain members. Directors are not required to obtain the approval of disadvantaged shareholders before a certain course of action is taken. Acting in the interests of the company as a whole involves business judgment. A court will only interfere with the decisions of directors if there is evidence of bad faith or if no sensible board of directors could reasonably have come to the decision which they reached.

(3) Statutory framework

6.102 The general principles governing a director's conduct as set out above are augmented by a wide range of specific duties imposed by statute. Some of these requirements are imposed not on the directors themselves but on the company per se. However, as the directors are responsible for the performance of statutory duties imposed on the company, it is the directors who must ensure compliance. As we shall see, those obligations which are imposed on directors generally take the form of either a restriction on, and/or a requirement to disclose, certain of their activities. The principal statutory duties of directors arise under the Companies Ordinance and the SFO. In many respects, these matters bear a strong relationship to the fiduciary duties and the common law duty of care, skill, and diligence discussed above. There is no distinction in the Companies Ordinance or the SFO between the roles and functions of executive and non-executive directors.[56]

Provisions concerned with the personal interests of directors

6.103 Directors often wear at least two caps—one as director of a company, another as an independent personal investor and/or businessperson. This creates a basic

---

[55] eg in *Daniels v Anderson* (1995) 13 ACLC 614 just such a distinction was applied.
[56] In the English case, *Dorchester Finance Co Ltd v Stebbing* (1989) BCLC 498, the court stated 'in the Companies Act, the duties of a director whether executive or not are the same'.

opportunity for conflict and wrongdoing. The starting point here is to know what relevant interests a director has in order that any conflict situation can be properly monitored and controlled.

Directors' shareholdings

Under Part XV of the SFO, directors of companies listed on the SEHK are **6.104** required to disclose all interests they may have in the share capital (whether or not voting shares) and debentures of the company or any of its associated companies[57] and any change in the nature or level of such interest. 'Interest' is defined widely and includes short positions and various family, trust, and corporate interests. Events giving rise to a requirement to notify would include the acquisition or disposal of shares, entering into a contract to buy or sell shares or debentures, the grant of a right to subscribe shares, and the subsequent exercise of such right. Directors have three business days in which to make the relevant disclosure.

Insider dealing

Directors need to be particularly sensitive to the risk of insider dealing as they **6.105** will regularly be in possession of confidential information which may also be price-sensitive. As discussed below, a number of provisions of the Listing Rules aimed at directors in effect seek to prevent insider dealing from occurring. Insider dealing, when entered into deliberately, clearly is a case of using confidential information of the company to the personal advantage of the director (or his associates etc). Directors dealing in securities should also note that Parts XIII and XIV of the SFO specify certain categories of market misconduct and other offences in addition to insider dealing. Insider dealing and these other forms of market misconduct are dealt with more fully in Chapter 8.

Provisions concerned with dealings between the company and directors

There clearly is nothing wrong in principle with a company entering into a **6.106** contract in which a director has a personal interest. However, given that the director is part of the management of the company making decisions about the terms of the contract and whether or not it is of benefit to the company to enter into it, the opportunity for conflict and wrongdoing arises.

Material interests in contracts

A director with a material interest in a contract or proposed contract of the **6.107** company is required to declare the nature of his interest at the earliest meeting

---

[57] An associated company includes: subsidiaries of the relevant company: a holding company of the relevant company and any subsidiaries of such holding company; companies in which the relevant company has a 20% stake in any class of shares.

of directors.[58] The contract must be 'of significance in relation to the company's business'. In place of a specific notification, a director may instead provide a general notice to the effect he is interested in a certain class of contracts.

6.108 Breach of this requirement is an offence punishable by fine unless the director is able to show he could not reasonably be expected to have knowledge of the contract and in fact did not have such knowledge.

Loans and financial accommodation

6.109 Section 157H of the Companies Ordinance generally prohibits, subject to exceptions, a public company from making any loan,[59] guarantee, or security available to a director or to any company in which a director has a controlling interest. The primary exception worth noting relates to where the company's ordinary business is to enter into such transactions (such as a bank). Any loans or quasi-loans which are entered into must be disclosed.[60]

6.110 Loans made in contravention are generally immediately repayable and guarantees etc granted are unenforceable. Directors who knowingly authorize such loans etc to be made are subject to two sources of liability. First, they are liable to indemnify the company for any loss or damage suffered by the company and account for any personal gain made from the arrangement.[61] Second, they may be guilty of an offence[62] and liable to imprisonment and a fine.

(4) Regulatory rules

6.111 Matters of regulation address a wide range of issues concerning the board, directors' duties, and behaviour of directors.

Listing Rules

6.112 The fiduciary and common law duties of directors are effectively incorporated into the Listing Rules. Directors of a company are to act in the interests of its shareholders as a whole[63] and the SEHK expects 'directors, both collectively and individually, to fulfil fiduciary duties and duties of skill, care and diligence to a standard at least commensurate with the standard established by Hong Kong law'.[64] This means that he must 'apply such degree of skill, care and diligence as may reasonably be expected of a person of his knowledge and experience and

---

[58] CO s 162.
[59] The making of 'quasi-loans' is also prohibited. A quasi-loan is an arrangement whereby the company pays off a loan payable by the director and so effectively becomes the creditor of the director.
[60] CO s 161B–161C.   [61] CO s 157I.   [62] CO s 157J.   [63] LR 2.03(5).
[64] LR 3.08.

holding his office within the listed issuer'.[65] Moreover, a director is expected to have the 'character, experience and integrity and is able to demonstrate a standard of competence commensurate with his position'.[66]

The Listing Rules in a number of places also expressly require directors to accept **6.113** responsibility in relation to the company's compliance with the Listing Rules[67] and listing and other documents produced pursuant to the Listing Rules.

The rules are also quite specific as to the composition and function of the board **6.114** and, as with the CG Code, emphasis is placed on the function of independent and other non-executive directors. For these purposes, the independence of a director is likely to be in doubt if, inter alia, he holds more than 1 per cent of the issued share capital of the issuer, is a director, partner, or principal of a professional adviser of the company, has a material interest in any principal business activity of or material business dealings with the company, or is on the board to protect the interests of an entity whose interests are not the same as those of the shareholders as a whole[68] (the recommendation under the CG Code as discussed below is that independence should also be brought into question if the director has served for more than nine years).

In summary, the requirements[69] are: **6.115**

- board must comprise at least three independent non-executive directors, one of whom must have appropriate professional qualifications or accounting or related financial management expertise;[70]
- mandatory audit committee of at least three members and comprising non-executive directors of which only independent non-executives comprise the chairperson, the majority, and at least one of whom is an independent non-executive director with appropriate professional qualifications or accounting or related financial management expertise;[71] and
- requirement to employ a qualified accountant on a full-time basis to supervise the financial reporting procedures, internal controls and Listing Rule compliance as regards financial reporting and other accounting-related issues.[72]

---

[65] LR 3.08(f).   [66] LR 3.09.   [67] LR 3.16.   [68] LR 3.13.

[69] It is worth noting that while similar requirements are in place in respect of companies listed on GEM, the GEM Listing Rules impose the additional requirement that a company designate one of its executive directors as a compliance officer responsible for compliance with the GEM Rules and other relevant laws and regulations (GEM Rules 5.19–5.23).

[70] LR 3.10–3.15 [GEM Rules 5.05–5.13].   [71] LR 3.21–3.23 [GEM Rules 5.28–5.33].
[72] LR 3.24 [GEM Rules 5.15–5.18].

Appointment of advisers

6.116 Companies are required in a number of different circumstances to appoint advisers. Such appointments are for the primary purposes of fostering compliance with the Listing Rules and applicable laws and for the protection of investors.

6.117 **Sponsors.** From the outset of a company wishing to be listed, it is required to appoint a sponsor whose role it is to assist the company through the listing process. The sponsor is required to be independent and act impartially, and, importantly, is required to give certain undertakings to the SEHK as to the proper discharge of its functions, which include using 'reasonable endeavours to ensure that all information provided to the Exchange during the listing application process is true in all material respects and does not omit any material information and, to the extent that the sponsor subsequently becomes aware of information that casts doubt on the truth, accuracy or completeness of information provided to the Exchange, it will promptly inform the Exchange of such information'.[73]

6.118 One of the wider roles of the sponsor is to assist the company prepare for life as a listed company and this includes its internal arrangements as regards governance. The SEHK's Practice Note 21 requires the sponsor to assess various matters, not only as to business feasibility but also as to the 'corporate governance experience and competence generally of the directors with a view to determining the extent to which the board of the new applicant as a whole has a depth and breadth of financial literacy and understanding of good corporate governance'.[74]

6.119 The undertaking of the sponsor to the SEHK is taken seriously by sponsors, particularly given the requirement that for any entity to act as sponsor it must be acceptable to the SEHK.[75]

6.120 **Compliance advisers.** One of the ways the SEHK seeks more specifically to foster a good governance regime is the requirement that newly listed companies appoint a compliance adviser from the time it is listed at least until it has distributed its annual reports and accounts for the first full financial year after its listing.[76] This implicitly recognizes that companies coming to the publicly listed market for the first time need to undergo a number of transitions, both as to their corporate procedures (many of which concern governance issues) and as to corporate culture.

6.121 The primary role of the compliance adviser is comprised in the obligation of the company to consult with and seek the advice of the compliance adviser as to a

---

[73] LR 3A.04(2).   [74] PN 21, para 11(b).   [75] LR 3A.02.   [76] LR 3A.19.

number of matters including the publication of any regulatory announcement, where transactions may be regarded as notifiable or connected, or where the SEHK makes an enquiry of the company.[77] As such, they are required to be licensed or authorized by the SFC to advise on corporate finance matters. The SEHK also has the right to specify particular functions the compliance adviser is to carry out as well as to require a company to maintain a compliance adviser for longer than the minimum required period.[78] Such a provision enables the SEHK to indirectly exercise some influence over companies whose standard of governance is perhaps falling short of an acceptable minimum in one or more regards.

Independent advice. In relation to specific situations, such as a corporate transaction affecting the legitimate interests of shareholders, the board will be obliged to form an independent committee of the board and appoint an external independent financial adviser. The primary purpose of such appointments is to give shareholders as a whole the benefit of independent and impartial advice. The independent committee, having considered the recommendations of the independent adviser, is required to advise shareholders whether the terms of the relevant transaction are fair and reasonable, whether the transaction is in the interests of the company and the shareholders, and how to vote.[79] Such circumstances arise in relation to notifiable and connected transactions, and takeover situations as discussed below and in Chapter 7 respectively. **6.122**

Securities transactions by directors

Inevitably, directors of listed companies will often, and sometimes must, hold shares in the company. This creates a number of governance issues. First, it creates an obvious conflict of interest between the person's role as director of the company having regard to the interests of the company as a whole, and the person's interest as an individual shareholder. Second, and not unrelated to this issue, are the potential problems regarding when the director cum shareholder may deal in the company's shares, a problem given his preferential access to information about the company, in particular that which is confidential and price-sensitive. **6.123**

These concerns are addressed under the common law, equity, and statute. However, as already mentioned, while laws may be good at specifying what constitutes a wrongdoing and the attendant consequences—effectively negative control of the problem—additional regulatory measures have developed to address the problem in a more positivistic manner. **6.124**

As regards dealing by directors in the shares of the company, they are required[80] **6.125**

---

[77] LR 3A.23.   [78] LR 3A.20.   [79] LR 13.39(6)(b).
[80] LR 3.17 & 13.67.

to comply with the 'Model Code for Securities Transactions by Directors of Listed Issuers' (the Model Code).[81] The treatment of price-sensitive information is considered below.

6.126 The Model Code sets a standard of behaviour—a company may in the alternative adopt its own version of a directors' dealing code provided such code is no less exacting than set out in the Model Code. A breach of any standard set out in the Model Code will be regarded as a breach of the Listing Rules.

6.127 The two primary principles and prohibitions of the Model Code are simple to grasp, a director privy to confidential price sensitive information:

- should not deal[82] in the relevant securities until such time as proper disclosure of the relevant information is made; and
- should caution directors not privy to such information that there is unpublished price-sensitive information in play and such other directors should not deal in the company's securities until such time as proper disclosure of the relevant information is made.[83]

6.128 While the former of these principles reflects insider dealing concerns covered by the SFO, the Model Code also specifies that knowledge of notifiable or connected transactions must also cause a director not to deal, etc. It also clarifies that where a director of one company becomes aware of price-sensitive information in another company, he should not deal.

6.129 Directors are effectively assumed to be in possession of price-sensitive information during the period starting one month prior to the date of the board meeting for approval of annual or interim financial results until disclosure of the same.[84]

6.130 Whenever a director does wish to deal, he must first notify either the chairperson of the board or the director designated by the board to receive such notifications, and receive a written, dated acknowledgement.[85] A record needs to be kept of such notifications.

6.131 The Model Code recognizes that there may be exceptional circumstances which press a director to deal, such as to meet a financial commitment. In those cases, disclosure needs to be made to the SEHK stating why the circumstances were exceptional and an announcement needs to be published to the market.[86]

---

[81] Set out in LR Appendix 10.
[82] 'Dealing' is very widely defined in the Model Code, see para 7(a) & (d).
[83] This also reflects requirements under Principle 5 of the Model Code.
[84] Or, if earlier, one month prior to the deadline to publish such results. See Model Code rule A.3.
[85] Model Code rule B.8.   [86] Model Code rule C.14.

The Model Code also recognizes that staff of the company other than directors   **6.132**
may be privy to confidential price-sensitive information and accordingly
imposes on directors an obligation to endeavour to ensure that such persons are
prohibited from dealing as if they were directors.[87]

CG Code

The first principle set out in the CG Code is worth reciting verbatim: **6.133**

> An issuer should be headed by an effective board which should assume responsibility for leadership and control of the issuer and be collectively responsible for promoting the success of the issuer by directing and supervising the issuer's affairs. Directors should take decisions objectively in the interests of the issuer.[88]

The remaining five sections of the CG Code are all relevant.

Directors

The board.   Directors should meet regularly to discuss matters, and not obtain   **6.134**
board consent merely by circularized written resolution, particularly where a
substantial shareholder or director has a conflict of interest in a matter to be
considered by the board to be material. Also, there should be a procedure to
allow directors to seek independent professional advice at the company's
expense where relevant to the discharge of their duties.

Chairman and CEO.   The chairman's role, of managing the board, and the   **6.135**
CEO's role, concerning the day-to-day management of the company's business,
should be clearly distinguished to avoid the concentration of power in any one
individual. It is also recommended that the chairman expressly take on the
responsibility for ensuring good corporate governance practices are established.
This would include the chairman facilitating the contribution of non-executive
directors and meeting with them at least annually without the executive directors
present.

Board composition.   The role of non-executive directors should in practice be   **6.136**
strengthened by the principle requiring a balanced composition of executive and
non-executive directors, the latter who should be of such calibre that their views
carry sufficient weight. This emphasizes that boards should possess a strong
independent element. It is specifically recommended that at least one-third of the
board be comprised of independent non-executive directors (note that LR 3.10
requires a board to appoint at least three independent non-executive directors).

Appointments, re-election, and removal.   The procedure should be transparent   **6.137**
and plans should be made for an orderly succession of appointments to the

---

[87] Model Code rule B.13.   [88] CG Code rule A.1.

board. All directors should be subject to re-election at regular intervals. A recommendation of interest to note is that once an independent non-executive director has served for more than nine years, the question of both his independence and his re-election should be subject to shareholder approval, the board having set out reasons why they consider such person to remain independent.

6.138 **Responsibilities of directors.** New directors should receive not only a comprehensive induction to the affairs of the company (including its business and governance policies) but also to ensure they are aware of their legal and regulatory responsibilities. Of particular interest is the emphasis lent to the role of the non-executive, for example, as to taking the lead where conflicts of interest arise, serving on various governance committees such as the audit and remuneration committees, and scrutinizing the monitoring and reporting of the company's performance.

6.139 **Supply of and access to information.** Wherever practicable, at least three days' notice should be given for board or committee meetings together with information sufficient to enable the directors to make informed decisions. However, to properly fulfil their duties, directors should not merely rely on information provided but should consider whether further enquiries are necessary and, if appropriate, make such enquiries.

Remuneration of directors and senior management

6.140 The board should establish and disclose a formal and transparent procedure for setting policy on executive director's remuneration and for fixing the remuneration package of all directors. The board should establish a remuneration committee with specific written terms of reference and comprised of a majority of independent non-executive directors. Such committee should be established with a clear ambit of authority and duties. In particular, it should have delegated responsibility to determine the remuneration packages of all executive directors and senior management. No director should be involved in the determination of his own remuneration. It is recommended that a significant portion of executive directors' remuneration should be linked to both individual and corporate performance.

Accountability and audit

6.141 **Financial reporting.** The board is to ensure its presentation of its performance, financial position and prospects, whether in its annual and interim reports and accounts or in any other price-sensitive announcements or financial disclosures, that it presents a balanced, clear, and understandable assessment of the same. In particular, where there is any reason to be concerned about the ability of the company to continue as a going concern, such uncertainties should be clearly set out and discussed at length (with supporting assumptions or qualifications as necessary). It is recommended that quarterly reports be sent out within 45 days of the end of the financial period instead of within the four-month period permitted by the Listing Rules.[89]

Internal controls.   Internal controls such as those relating to financial, oper-   **6.142** ational, compliance, and risk should be reviewed at least annually. It is recommended that the board report on the same in the CG Report.

Audit committee.   The audit committee[90] is to have clear terms of reference to   **6.143** consider the application of the CG Code principles relating to financial reporting and internal controls. The audit committee should also be charged with making recommendations to the board as regards the external auditor including its appointment and reappointment, terms of engagement and remuneration, and its removal. The audit committee should also be responsible for reviewing and monitoring the external auditor's independence and objectivity as well as the integrity of the company's reports and accounts. In addition to the internal control provisions mentioned above, the audit committee should oversee the internal control systems of the company.

Delegation by the board

As discussed above, one of the duties of a director under common law is con-   **6.144** cerned with the question of under what circumstances he may properly rely on others to discharge duties due to be undertaken by him. The CG Code fleshes out this issue, concerning itself with what manner and what controls a board may delegate. Emphasis is given to the need for clarity as to when a board must be consulted before any action is taken by management on behalf of the board.

Communication with shareholders

The principle here is to encourage dialogue with and, at general meetings, the   **6.145** participation of shareholders. There is also a specific principle and provisions dealing with making shareholders aware of the correct procedure for voting by poll.

CG Report Rules

The CG Report Rules require a company to report on a number of matters   **6.146** closely related to the CG Code and this is discussed below (in section E).

---

[89] LR 13.46.   [90] Required to be established under LR 13.21.

D. Shareholder Rights

6.147 Shareholder rights, especially minority shareholder rights, are a major focus of corporate governance and an area traditionally viewed as weak in Hong Kong.

(1) Common Law and equity

6.148 The protections afforded to shareholders by common law and equity are those provided by the director's fiduciary duties and the duty of skill, care, and diligence, as has been reviewed above. This is broadly the same in Hong Kong as in other English law-based jurisdictions. However, such law affords shareholders only limited rights in practice and the tendency has been to look to statutory and regulatory solutions.

(2) Statutory framework

Issue of shares

6.149 Notwithstanding any provision in the company's articles, directors may not exercise any power to allot shares without the prior approval of the company in general meeting unless it is an allotment made under an offer pro rata to the members of the company.[91]

Disposal of fixed assets

6.150 Directors are prohibited from disposing of any fixed asset of the company under certain circumstances unless the same is approved by the shareholders in general meeting. Such circumstances arise where the disposal, together with disposals of fixed assets made in the previous four months, would exceed 33 per cent of the value of the company's fixed assets.[92]

Disqualification of directors

6.151 As already stated, it is not generally the business of the courts to make judgments on the commercial decisions of directors. Similarly, the matter of who shareholders elect to be directors of their company is generally up to them. However, provisions of both the Companies Ordinance and SFO represent a major departure from this principle in a way that, it could be said, represents the ultimate corporate governance sanction—by removing what is perceived as the 'bad seeds' from the system of corporate governance for a prescribed period.

---

[91] CO s 57B(1).   [92] CO s 155A.

Under Part IVA of the Companies Ordinance a court may, and in certain circumstances shall, make against a person a disqualification order.[93] The effect of such an order is that the relevant person may not, inter alia, be a director of or involved in the management of a company, save with the leave of the court.

6.152

Such orders may be made in respect of any person, inter alia:

6.153

- convicted of an indictable offence in connection with the promotion, formation, management, or liquidation of a company or convicted of any other indictable offence involving proven fraud or dishonesty;[94]
- who has persistently defaulted in the requirements of the Companies Ordinance requiring returns or documents to be made or filed;[95]
- appears guilty of the offence of fraudulent trading, whether or not such person is actually convicted of such offence;[96]
- who is a director of a company which has become insolvent and, in the opinion of the court, such person's conduct as director makes him unfit to be concerned in the management of a company;[97] or
- who commits an offence under Part XIV of the SFO.[98]

Schedule 15 of the Companies Ordinance sets out the matters to which a court shall have regard concerning the question of whether a person is fit to be involved in the management of a company and include matters such as any breach of fiduciary duty or duty to the company or any misapplication of the money or property of the company.

6.154

The courts have indicated their willingness to regard persistent breaches of regulatory rules such as the Listing Rules and the Takeovers Code as evidence of breach of directors' common law duties to the company.[99]

6.155

Under section 214 of the SFO, the SFC may apply to the court for, inter alia, a director disqualification order in respect of a company which is or was listed in cases where the affairs of the company have been conducted in a manner unfairly prejudicial to the interests of its members.

6.156

Disqualification orders specify the period for which the order shall remain in force, ranging up to 15 years (five years in the case of an order made under the SFO for market misconduct) depending on the seriousness of the circumstances

6.157

---

[93] CO s 168D.   [94] CO s 168E.   [95] CO s 168F.

[96] CO s 168G. The offence of fraudulent trading is created by CO s 275.

[97] CO s 168H.

[98] SFO s 303. Such offences include: insider dealing, false trading, price rigging, disclosure of information about prohibited transactions, and stock market manipulation. These are discussed in detail in Chapter 9.

[99] *SFC v Mandarin Resources Corporation Ltd*, HCCW348/96, unreported judgment dated 19 November 1999, Burrell J (CFI).

giving rise to the order. The contravention of such orders by such person constitutes a criminal offence with liability to imprisonment and a fine[100] and, in the case of orders made under the Companies Ordinance, renders the person personally liable for all debts of the company incurred at a time when such person was involved in the management of the company.[101]

Inspection and misfeasance

6.158   A number of statutorily defined paths exist in connection with examining the actions of directors and, where relevant, bringing them to account.

6.159   The Financial Secretary is empowered under the Companies Ordinance to appoint an inspector to investigate the company's affairs.[102] In particular, shareholders may by special resolution request the Financial Secretary to appoint an inspector.[103] The powers of such inspectors extend to the production of documents and the entry and search of premises.[104]

6.160   Since the coming into effect of the Companies (Amendment) Ordinance 2004 on 15 July 2005, members of companies (whether or not incorporated in Hong Kong) have improved powers to inspect and litigate.

6.161   First, the amendment provides that members may apply to the court for an order authorizing the applicant to inspect any records of the corporation, provided such application is made in good faith and for a proper purpose.[105] 'Proper purpose' is not defined by the amendment but will presumably be restricted to cases of suspected misfeasance or for the purposes of criminal proceedings. Any information obtained as a result of such an inspection may not be disclosed other than for the proper purpose for which the court order was given or in connection with criminal proceedings or a requirement of law.[106]

6.162   Second, the amendment also introduced a new Part IVAA to the Companies Ordinance giving shareholders a statutory right to conduct a derivative action on behalf of a company[107] or to intervene in an action already commenced, in each case where a misfeasance has been committed against the company.[108] Such a provision may be relevant to the protection of shareholders where, for example, a director of the company has committed an act of misfeasance and the company fails to bring an appropriate action against such director or is dilatory in doing so. In this context, misfeasance is defined as including any fraud,

---

[100] CO s 168M; SFO s 303(7).   [101] CO s 168O.   [102] CO s 142.
[103] CO s 143(1)(b).   [104] CO ss 152A & 152B.
[105] CO s 152FA. The section specifies what members may apply.   [106] CO s 152FC.
[107] Whether or not such company is incorporated in Hong Kong.   [108] CO s 168BC.

negligence, default in compliance with any enactment or rule of law, or breach of duty.[109] The statutory provision avoids the need for shareholders to rely on the common law remedy to bring a derivative action in respect of 'fraud on the minority' and gives greater power to the courts to investigate and to award damages to shareholders where their interests have been shown to be unfairly prejudiced.

Finally, under section 37A(2) of the SFO, on a petition by the SFC, if the court **6.163** is of the opinion that the company's affairs are being or have been conducted in a manner unfairly prejudicial to the interests of its members generally or of some part of the members, the court may, with a view to bringing an end to the matters complained of, among other things:

- make an order restraining the commission of the act or conduct; and
- make any other order it thinks fit, whether for regulating the conduct of the affairs in future, or for the purchase of the shares of any members of the company, etc.[110]

(3) Constitutional documents of the company

The memorandum and articles of a company take effect as a contract under seal **6.164** as between the company and each member, and as between a member and each other member and is enforceable accordingly.[111] Where breaches of the articles infringe on the rights of a member per se, this may give rise to an enforcement action.

The memorandum and articles of a company may indemnify directors against **6.165** or exempt directors from certain liabilities, such as defending actions and damages brought against them, but this will not extend to situations where the director is guilty of negligence, default, breach of duty or breach of trust and any contrary provision in the company's articles will be void.[112]

However, a company may purchase for a director insurance against any liability **6.166** to the company or liability incurred by him in defending any proceedings (including where the director is guilty of negligence, default, breach of duty, or breach of trust) but this will not cover liability to the company for fraud.[113]

---

[109] CO s 168BB(2).
[110] See *SFC v MKI Management Services Ltd and others*, HCMP3504/94, unreported judgment dated 22 May 1995, Rogers J (High Court) where the court ordered individuals to be restrained from, inter alia, being involved in the management of the affairs of the business of MKI.
[111] CO s 23.   [112] CO s 165(1).   [113] CO s 165(3).

Further, certain sources of liability may be mitigated directly by taking specific courses of action.

(4) Regulatory rules

Listing Rules

6.167 In addition to the restrictions under applicable company law, the Listing Rules set out detailed requirements as regards the directors seeking the approval of shareholders prior to any allotment or issue of shares, securities convertible into shares or options, warrants or similar rights to subscribe for shares or such convertible securities.[114]

Approval of shareholders

6.168 Prior to any such issue, the approval of shareholders in general meeting must be obtained.[115] This will apply also to any major subsidiary of the listed company where the issue of shares by such subsidiary would materially dilute the interest of the listed company.[116] The principle here is that shareholders have waivable pre-emptive rights and it is usual for companies to obtain from shareholders in general meeting an annual waiver under something commonly known as the 'general mandate'. The Listing Rules provide that such a mandate is subject to a ceiling of 20 per cent of the existing share capital of the company. Such general mandate may be extended to include securities repurchased by the company during the year, by up to an additional 10 per cent. When such mandate is exercised, the company is required to announce the details of the issue. The general mandate may be subject to such other terms as may be proposed and approved by the shareholders.

Warrants

6.169 Prior to any issue of warrants, in addition to the approval of shareholders (unless the warrants are issued under a general mandate) the company will also need the approval of the SEHK. In order to preserve some stability of trading in the company's shares, the SEHK limits the total number of warrants which can be in issue at any one time: the aggregate of all underlying securities may not exceed 20 per cent of the issued share capital of the company, and the expiry of the warrants must be not less than one year and not more than five years from the date of issue. The company may seek a separate listing for warrants related to underlying securities which are listed.[117]

---

[114] LR 13.36.   [115] LR 13.36 & 13.28.
[116] This requirement only applies in respect of subsidiaries which are not themselves listed.
[117] See LR chapter 15.

Other

Convertible securities are securities which are convertible into the shares of, **6.170** normally, the issuer. In contrast to warrants, only the prior approval of the SEHK is required. In general, convertibles may be listed only if the underlying securities are also a class of listed securities.[118] Employee share option schemes also give rise to the issue of rights to subscribe for securities. However, because of the other considerations involved concerning management and employee remuneration, special rules cover this case.[119]

Disclosure of allotment

The company will need to consider its disclosure obligations according to the **6.171** means by which the shares are to be allotted. In the case of a public offer or open offer, the company is obliged to advise the SEHK as to the basis of such allotment. In the case of a private placing made pursuant to a general mandate, the company will need to disclose, amongst other details, the price of the shares and the names of the placees if less than six in number.[120]

Price

The directors are generally free to determine the price at which securities are **6.172** issued under the general mandate (subject to any terms imposed on the mandate by shareholders), and this is normally at a moderate discount to market price. However, where it is proposed to discount the price by 20 per cent or more, it will be necessary for the company to satisfy the SEHK as to the necessity of such discount, for example, as an urgent rescue operation in response to a serious financial situation.[121]

Finally, if newly issued shares are of a class already listed, the company must **6.173** apply for listing of those shares prior to their issue.[122]

Takeovers Code

Directors of a company approached by a potential bidder are required, with a **6.174** view to affording fair treatment to shareholders, to form an independent committee of the board as well as appoint an independent financial adviser. This reflects both the need to avoid potential conflicts of interest and the duty to act in the best interests of the company as a whole. The specific requirements of the Takeovers Code are discussed in Chapter 7.

---

[118] See LR chapter 16.   [119] See LR chapter 17.   [120] LR 13.28 & 13.29.
[121] LR 13.29.   [122] LR 13.26 & 8.20.

E. Disclosure and Transparency

6.175 Corporate disclosure and transparency of management have become important elements of corporate governance, the issue mainly being dealt with through statute and regulatory rules.

(1) Statutory framework

6.176 There is an obvious need cum right for shareholders to be provided with information about the status of the company. Information is the most basic means by which they are able to protect and/or make decisions about their investment in the company. It is also the means by which shareholders can exercise some measure of supervision over the activities of the directors.

Accounting matters

6.177 The company's annual report and accounts, and its interim reports, are the basic means by which the members gauge how well the directors have managed the company's assets entrusted to their care. It is the specific duty of the company under the Companies Ordinance to maintain proper accounting records, prepare them in a specified form, ensure that they present a true and fair view of the state of affairs of the company, and present them to its members.[123]

6.178 While such obligation is imposed on the company per se, the failure of the directors to take 'all reasonable steps' to secure compliance with these requirements renders them liable to fine and, in the case of wilful commission of the offence, imprisonment. However, it is of interest to note that a specific defence is carved out in respect of a director who can 'prove that he had reasonable grounds to believe and did believe that a competent and reliable person was charged with the duty of seeing that those requirements were complied with and was in a position to discharge that duty'.[124]

Delegation of management

6.179 Any contract of a company under which a person (other than a director in relation to the service contract) is to undertake the management and administration of any substantial part of any business of the company must be disclosed and made available for inspection.[125] The penalty for breach of this provision is a fine and a daily default fine.

---

[123] CO ss 121–123.   [124] CO ss 121(4), 122(3), & 123(6).   [125] CO s 162A.

Service contracts

Directors will normally enter into a service contract with the company relating **6.180** to their engagement as a director. The terms of this contract may be renewed from time to time while the director is engaged as such. A company must disclose in its accounts the emoluments of directors including as to pensions and any compensation for loss of office[126] but no payment by way of compensation for loss of office can be made unless disclosed and approved by the company.[127]

Prospectuses

Under the Companies Ordinance, whenever there is an offering of shares or **6.181** debentures to the public or any section thereof, a prospectus compliant with the requirements of the Companies Ordinance will be required to be issued by the company, authorized by the SFC and registered with the Companies Registry.[128]

The regulation of prospectuses is an important piece of the corporate govern- **6.182** ance framework as it represents the point of investment in a company based on information made available in the prospectus and hence is the first point of providing information transparency to shareholders. These matters are discussed in detail in Chapter 4.

A number of potential liabilities accrue to directors[129] in relation to the content **6.183** of prospectuses both civilly and criminally under both the Companies Ordinance and the SFO. In summary, the main concerns in this regard are:

- the issue of a prospectus which does not comply with the content requirements renders every person knowingly a party to its issue liable to a fine;[130]

- statements in the prospectus which are untrue or misleading give rise to both civil liability (payment of compensation to persons who have suffered loss in reliance) and criminal liability (imprisonment for up to three years and a fine of up to HK\$ 700,000 (US\$ 90,000));[131]

- statements in the prospectus which constitute fraudulent, reckless, or negligent misrepresentations give rise to both civil liability (payment of compensation to persons who have suffered loss in reliance) and criminal liability (imprisonment for up to seven years and a fine of up to HK\$ 1 million (US\$ 128,500));[132] and

- disclosure of false or misleading information inducing transactions (statements

---

[126] CO s 161(1).   [127] CO s 163.   [128] See CO ss 38D & 48A.
[129] Such liability also extends to persons named in the prospectus as proposed directors.
[130] CO s 38(1B).   [131] Civil: CO ss 40 & 342E; criminal: CO ss 40A & 342F.
[132] Civil: SFO s 108; criminal: SFO s 107.

in a prospectus could fall into this category) give rise to both civil liability (payment of compensation by way of damages) and criminal liability (imprisonment for up to 10 years and a fine of up to HK$ 10 million (US$ 1,285,000)).[133]

(2) Regulatory rules

6.184 Regulation respecting disclosure and transparency play an increasingly important role, with the SMLR, Listing Rules, CG Code, and CG Report Rules all addressing various issues.

Securities and Futures (Stock Market Listing) Rules

6.185 The SMLR is relevant to corporate governance at the level of regulating the quality of information companies provide, both on an application to list securities and in relation to on-going disclosures made under the Listing Rules.[134] All such materials are required to be copied to the SFC which has various powers under the SMLR.

6.186 Of particular relevance here is the power of the SFC to order the suspension of trading of the company's shares in certain circumstances. This will include where in the opinion of the SFC various disclosures contain 'materially false, incomplete or misleading information . . . it is in the interest of maintaining an orderly and fair market . . . [or] it is appropriate for the protection of investors' to do so.[135]

6.187 Poor corporate governance may lead to any of these problems and it is clearly a very serious matter for a company's shares to be suspended.

Listing Rules

6.188 The Listing Rules contain a number of provisions obliging companies to keep shareholders and the wider market informed, with a view to ensuring 'the maintenance of a fair and orderly market in securities and that all users of the market have simultaneous access to the same information'.[136] Failure to comply is regarded as a serious matter and could result in disciplinary action in addition to suspending the company's listing.

6.189 Given the importance of information in the marketplace, the Listing Rules are quite detailed as to the obligations of companies in this regard and list out a number of specific matters relevant to a company's business and its securities

---

[133] Civil: SFO s 277; criminal: SFO s 298.   [134] SMLR s 7.
[135] SMLR s 8(1).   [136] LR 13.03.

that would give rise to a disclosure obligation. However, the two principles underlying these obligations and different circumstances are:

- price sensitive information should be disclosed immediately it is the subject of a decision;[137] and

- any information which is necessary to enable the market to appraise the position of the company, or which might affect market activity or assist establish a false market, should be disclosed as soon as reasonably practicable.[138]

Disclosure of financial information

The timely disclosure of financial information is a key requirement of the **6.190** Listing Rules. As already mentioned, failure to comply with the timing of such disclosure requirements may lead to a suspension in the company's shares.[139] Financial disclosure can be considered in three regards: what needs to be disclosed, when, and to whom (or by what method).

The annual report and accounts must be sent to all registered shareholders **6.191** within four months of the financial year end. The Listing Rules (Appendix 16) sets out specific content requirements for the report. Companies are also required to make a preliminary announcement in the newspapers of results for the full financial year the day following the approval of the issuer's financial statements by the board. Occasionally, a company is unable to make a preliminary announcement and in such cases it is required to make an announcement as to the reasons it is unable to do so, for example, if there are uncertainties as to the valuations of certain assets, it must provide sufficient information to investors to enable them to determine the significance of the relevant assets. Failure to publish financial information when due will normally entail suspension of trading until the requisite information is published.[140]

In addition, the company must also publish and distribute (as for annual **6.192** reports) half-yearly reports within three months of the closing of that period. As with the full financial year, the company must make a preliminary announcement the day following approval of the financial statements by the board.

Transactions of the company

Certain transactions undertaken or proposed to be undertaken by a company **6.193** may be of such magnitude or of such a nature that specific information should be provided to shareholders or the prior approval of shareholders should be sought. At the level of transactions which require prior shareholder approval, rules to this effect put limits on the scope of powers of a board, and rules which

---

[137] LR 13.05.   [138] LR 13.09.
[139] See LR 13.46 & following.   [140] LR 13.50.

require specific information to be delivered to shareholders in relation to a transaction where no prior approval is required in effect raise the visibility and hence accountability of the board for actions undertaken.

6.194 These types of rules fall into two categories:

- notifiable transactions[141]—quantitative tests are applied to transactions and prospective transactions to determine the level of shareholder disclosure/involvement required;

- connected transactions[142]—those which involve persons closely connected with the company[143] and therefore require safeguards to ensure the interests of shareholders as a whole are taken into account and that such persons do not take unfair advantage of their position.

These rules are discussed in the following section, as they address both shareholder rights as well as disclosure and transparency.

CG Report Rules

6.195 Mandatory reporting is required in the annual report of the company and is required to cover the following matters:[144]

- the extent to which the company has applied the principles of the CG Code or deviated from the code provisions;
- whether the company has adopted a code of conduct concerning directors' securities transaction,[145] the details of any non-compliance and remedial steps taken;
- various details concerning the board such as how many meetings, who attended, how decisions are reached, and details of compliance with the Listing Rules pertaining to independent non-executive directors;[146]
- whether the roles of chairman and CEO are segregated;
- certain matters pertaining to the directors' remuneration policy and remuneration committee;
- certain matters pertaining to the nomination and removal of directors;
- information related to auditor's remuneration and the operation of the audit committee; and
- certain matters contemplated by the CG Code, in particular, as to the effectiveness of the systems of internal control.

---

[141] LR chapter 14.   [142] LR chapter 14A.
[143] See the definition of 'connected person' in LR 14A.11 and discussed below.
[144] CG Report Rules, rule 2.   [145] See LR appendix 10, discussed below.
[146] LR 3.10 & 3.13.

Recommended disclosures[147] cover a number of matters including the share interests of senior management, certain matters pertaining to shareholder rights and relations, and a statement as to the division of responsibilities between the board and management. The SEHK also encourages the company to include additional detail as to its internal control systems including as to how the system has been defined, how it is monitored or reviewed and how often, and how it deals with the handling of price-sensitive information.[148]   **6.196**

F. Notifiable and Connected Transactions

In the usual course of a company's business it will be engaged in many types of transactions. These may include acquiring and disposing of assets, entering into contractual or financial arrangements (such as leases and loans), forming partnerships or joint ventures with third parties, or simply earning revenue in its ordinary course of business. However, some transactions have the ability to impact on the company's share capital or even the prospect or nature of the company and its assets—for example, a company wishing to use its own shares as acquisition capital, or a significant acquisition or disposal.   **6.197**

One aspect of corporate governance is concerned with the question of what transactions of a listed company should entail shareholder involvement. Shareholder involvement could mean anything from providing specific disclosures to the shareholders about a transaction, to requiring shareholder approval before a certain transaction may be effected. Clearly, it would be inappropriate for shareholders to be involved in every transaction of a company as this would merely hinder the company and derogate from the proper role of management.   **6.198**

Accordingly, the Listing Rules in Chapters 14 and 14A identify two types of transactions which by their nature ought to involve shareholders—those which are noteworthy because of their size, and those which are noteworthy because of their nature. The application of such rules facilitates the board having proper regard to the interests of shareholders as a whole (and not just a select group). It does this by specifying clear limits on when the board may commit the company to transactions without specifically informing shareholders or, in other cases, without specifically obtaining their approval in general meeting, or conversely, when disclosure and/or approval is required.   **6.199**

Chapter 14 specifies five classes of transactions primarily defined according to the size of the transaction:[149]   **6.200**

---

[147] CG Report Rules rule 3.   [148] CG Report Rules rule 3(d).   [149] LR 14.04(7).

- share transactions;
- disclosable transactions;
- major transactions;
- very substantial acquisitions (normally referred to as 'VSAs'); and
- very substantial disposals (normally referred to as 'VSDs').

These transactions are all 'notifiable transactions' and the primary characteristic which makes them noteworthy is simply the issue of relative impact on a company: the larger the relative transaction size the greater should be the knowledge and involvement of shareholders.

6.201 The following transactions are primarily defined according to the characteristics of the transaction:

- the reverse takeover (dealt with in chapter 14 of the Listing Rules as it is also classified as a notifiable transaction—this is dealt with in Chapter 7 of this volume); and

- connected transactions (dealt with in chapter 14A of the Listing Rules).

The primary characteristic of these transactions which makes them noteworthy is that they pose the twin risks of the interests of select shareholders being taken into account rather than the interests of shareholders as a whole, and the risk of directors or substantial shareholders taking advantage of their position.[150]

6.202 It should be noted that a particular transaction may be both notifiable and connected. The classification of a transaction as a notifiable transaction and/or a connected transaction implies certain obligations on a company as regards whether it needs to make certain disclosures to shareholders or to seek the approval of shareholders in relation to the transaction. These obligations are discussed below.

(1) Transactions noteworthy due to their size: notifiable transactions

6.203 The primary point of reference for distinguishing between the five classes of notifiable transaction is a collection of five financial ratios the purpose of which is to measure the relative size or financial impact of a transaction on the business of the company. Collectively, the ratios operate as a series of tests for determining into which class of notifiable transaction a specific transaction falls to be treated. Each class of notifiable transaction sets out specific requirements to which the company must adhere, as regards disclosure and so on.

---

[150] LR 14A.01.

The ratio tests are applied as follows: **6.204**

1. for a specific transaction, calculate all five financial ratios for that transaction;
2. the largest resulting ratio so calculated determines into which particular class of notifiable transaction a transaction is to be regarded as falling; and
3. the responsibilities of the company as regards its shareholders are determined by that class of notifiable transaction.

The different percentage ratio tests and the thresholds which determine or apply to each class of notifiable transaction are given in Table 6.1 and are explained below.

Table 6.1 Notifiable transactions—applicable percentage thresholds[151]

	Assets test	Consideration test	Profits test	Revenue test	Equity capital test
Share transaction	PR < 5%	PR < 5%	PR < 5%	PR < 5%	PR < 5%
Discloseable transaction	5% ≤ PR < 25%	5% ≤ PR < 25%	5% ≤ PR < 25%	5% ≤ PR < 25%	5% ≤ PR < 25%
Major disposal	25% ≤ PR < 75%	25% ≤ PR < 75%	25% ≤ PR < 75%	25% ≤ PR < 75%	N.A.
Major acquisition	25% ≤ PR < 100%	25% ≤ PR < 100%	25% ≤ PR < 100%	25% ≤ PR < 100%	25% ≤ PR < 100%
VSD	75% ≤ PR	75% ≤ PR	75% ≤ PR	75% ≤ PR	N.A.
VSA	100% ≤ PR	100% ≤ PR	100% ≤ PR	100% ≤ PR	100% ≤ PR

A company engaging in a transaction will not know the status of the transaction   **6.205**
in this regard unless it makes the relevant calculations. The Listing Rules
expressly require companies to consider this question at an early stage of the
transaction and, if in doubt, it is required to consult the SEHK.[152]

Chapter 14 assesses transactions in a number of ways.   **6.206**

First, 'transaction' is a broadly defined term in the Listing Rules[153] and includes   **6.207**
acquisitions and disposals of assets, the formation of joint ventures, and the
entering into or termination of finance and operating leases. However, revenue
transactions in the ordinary course of the company's business are specifically
excluded.[154]

Second, transactions which form part of a series of transactions effected within a   **6.208**

---

[151] 'PR' represents the percentage ratio calculated under the relevant test.
[152] LR 14.05.   [153] LR 14.04(1).
[154] Subject to the requirements of LR 14.04(1)(g).

12-month period will normally be treated as a single transaction and aggregated for the purposes of determining the percentage ratio. Factors which will be taken into account in determining whether a transaction is part of a series of transactions include transactions with the same party (or with parties associated with one another) or in relation to the same asset or investment.[155]

6.209 Third, the share transaction is regarded slightly differently from the other notifiable transactions in that it is concerned specifically with acquisitions of assets where the consideration payable by the listed company to the seller includes securities for which listing will be sought. By comparison, the other types of notifiable transaction are not defined by reference to the nature of consideration payable.

6.210 Finally, where a listed company has a subsidiary[156] and that subsidiary issues share capital to a third person resulting in the reduction of the interest of the listed company in the subsidiary, this may be regarded as a deemed disposal and therefore regarded as a notifiable transaction.[157]

(2) Transactions noteworthy due to their nature: connected transactions

6.211 Any transaction between a company and a connected person is a connected transaction.[158] A connected person primarily refers to:

- any director (including persons who were directors within the preceding 12 months), chief executive, or substantial shareholder of the company;
- a promoter and the supervisor of a PRC company;
- any associates of the foregoing; or
- subsidiaries of the company which are not wholly owned but in which any of the foregoing persons are a substantial shareholder.[159]

6.212 The concept of the 'associate' is a relatively detailed provision necessary to deal with the often complicated family and other arrangements in place in Hong Kong. A brief list of those who fall to be regarded as associates include certain family relationships, trustees, and companies in which a controlling interest is held.[160]

6.213 However, a number of other cases are also regarded as connected transactions and include:[161]

---

[155] LR 14.22 & 14.23.
[156] Irrespective of whether or not it is consolidated in its accounts.
[157] LR 14.29.   [158] LR 14A.13.
[159] The definition of 'connected person' in LR 14A.11 is detailed and is worth a close reading. A substantial shareholder is a person who is entitled to exercise, or control the exercise of, 10% or more of the voting power at any general meeting of the company. See LR 1.01.
[160] See LR 1.01 & 14A.11(4).   [161] A complete list is provided in LR 14A.13.

- acquiring or disposing of an interest in a company where a substantial shareholder of that other company is or will become a controller[162] of the listed company;[163]
- certain transactions whereby the controller is able to subscribe, on favourable terms, for shares in a company of which the listed company is a shareholder;[164]
- the provision of financial assistance,[165] whether by the company to a connected person or by a connected person to the company;[166]
- writing, granting, exercise, etc of options involving the company and a connected person;[167] and
- entering into a joint venture, partnership, etc between a company and a connected person.[168]

Notwithstanding the foregoing rules, the SEHK may deem a person to be connected[169] and specify that certain exemptions will not apply to particular transactions.[170]   **6.214**

Connected transactions are subjected to different requirements depending on certain percentage thresholds assessing a transaction's relative size and impact on the company. The same set of financial ratios is used as for notifiable transactions except that the profits test is not used.[171] While these are calculated in the same way as for notifiable transactions, they are applied differently: the classification of the connected transaction requires all ratios to be below the relevant threshold[172] or within a boundary and less than a specified quantum. Table 6.2 sets out the relevant thresholds and requirements.   **6.215**

As with notifiable transactions, transactions which form part of a series of transactions effected within a 12-month period will normally be treated as a single transaction and aggregated for the purposes of determining the percentage ratio. Factors which will be taken into account in determining whether a transaction is part of a series of transactions include transactions with the same party (or with parties associated with one another) or in relation to the same asset or investment.[173]   **6.216**

---

[162] Meaning a director, chief executive, or controlling shareholder of the listed issuer—LR 14A.10(3).

[163] LR 14A.13(1)(b).   [164] LR 14A.13(1)(b)(iii).

[165] Financial assistance includes granting credit, lending money, providing security for, or guaranteeing, a loan—LR 14A.10(4).

[166] LR 14A.13(2)(a) & (b).   [167] LR 14A.13(5).   [168] LR 14A.13(6).

[169] LR 14A.11(4).   [170] LR 14A.30.

[171] The SEHK considers that the profits test is more likely to give rise to anomalous results, especially where a company has recorded losses in their latest accounts.

[172] For notifiable transactions, only the largest ratio is of relevance for determining class of notifiable transaction.

[173] LR 14A.25 & 14A.26.

Table 6.2 Connected transactions—size thresholds and requirements[174]

	Percentage ratio threshold[175]	Reporting	Announcement	Shareholders' approval
Fully exempt transaction (other than reporting)	each PR < 0.1% or 0.1% < = PR < 2.5% and consideration < HK$1m			
Exemption from shareholder's approval	each PR < 2.5% or 2.5% < = PR < 25% and consideration < HK$10m	•	•	
Non-exempt transaction	Fails to meet above tests	•	•	•
Continuing transactions[176] and Financial assistance transactions[177]		exempt if each PR < 0.1% or each test 0.1% < = PR < 2.5% and consideration < HK$1m[178]		exempt if each PR < 2.5% or each test 2.5% <=PR<25% and consideration < HK$10m[179]

(3) Determining percentage ratios

6.217 The percentage ratio tests comprise financial ratios which examine the relative size based on relative total assets, profit and revenue, consideration as compared to market capitalization, and relative equity capital. Where different accounting standards are used in respect of the company and the assets acquired, the company will need to perform an appropriate reconciliation.[180]

6.218 In general, the figures to be used in the calculation of each test will be derived

---

[174] 'PR' represents the percentage ratio (excluding the profits ratio) calculated under the relevant test. '•' indicates required.

[175] The same percentage ratios are used as for notifiable transactions except the profits test is not used.

[176] Note that certain other exemptions are available and these are discussed in section 6.239 below.

[177] The exemptions are available subject to other requirements, for example, whether the transaction is in the ordinary course of business or on normal commercial terms. See LR 14A.63 to 14A.66.

[178] All calculations reckoned on an annual basis.

[179] All calculations reckoned on an annual basis.

[180] LR 14.07.

from the latest published accounts. However, adjustments may be made to take into account subsequent events. Examples where this might occur include asset revaluations, further issues of shares and declared dividends (relevant to the assets ratio), and the discontinuation of a part of a business (relevant to the profits and revenue ratios).[181]

Where transactions involve both an acquisition and a disposal, the ratios need to be applied to each of these transactions separately.[182] It is occasionally the case that the application of such tests in a particular case will render an anomalous result or the ratio is not appropriate to the nature of the industry in which the company operates. In such case, the SEHK may substitute other ratios which it considers appropriate to measure the size of the transaction relevant to the company.[183] Some qualifications in the application of these tests as concern subsidiaries are discussed further below. **6.219**

Assets ratio

This ratio is defined as 'the total assets which are the subject of the transaction divided by the total assets of the listed issuer'.[184] Total assets means the aggregate of the company's tangible and intangible fixed assets, current and non-current. **6.220**

Some asset acquisitions will involve the company taking over certain liabilities. Irrespective of whether such liabilities are regarded by the parties to the transaction as affecting consideration payable, the SEHK will normally require such liabilities to be excluded from the total asset calculation.[185] **6.221**

Profits ratio

This ratio is defined as 'the profits attributable to the assets which are the subject of the transaction divided by the profits of the listed issuer'.[186] Profits means net profits after deducting all charges except taxation and before minority interests and extraordinary items. **6.222**

Revenue ratio

This ratio is defined as 'the revenue attributable to the assets which are the subject of the transaction divided by the revenue of the listed issuer'.[187] Revenue means revenue arising from the principal activities of a company but it does not include those which are of an incidental nature. **6.223**

---

[181] LR 14.16 & 14.17.   [182] LR 14.24.   [183] LR 14.20.   [184] LR 14.07(1).
[185] LR 14.19.   [186] LR 14.07(2).   [187] LR 14.07(3).

Consideration ratio

6.224 This ratio is defined as 'the consideration divided by the total market capitalization of the listed issuer'. The total market capitalization is the average closing
price of the listed issuer's securities as stated in the SEHK's daily quotations
sheets for the five business days immediately preceding the date of the transaction.[188] Consideration means the fair value of the consideration or, if higher, the
fair value of the asset the subject of the transaction.[189] In the case of joint
ventures, the consideration shall be the total capital commitment of the company save where the venture is established for a future purpose, such as a
development project, then the consideration ratio will need to be recalculated at
that point in time, ie when the purpose is carried out.[190]

Equity capital ratio

6.225 This ratio is defined as 'the nominal value of the listed issuer's equity capital
issued as consideration divided by the nominal value of the listed issuer's issued
equity capital immediately before the transaction'.[191] This test only applies to an
acquisition.

(4) Transactions concerning subsidiaries

6.226 Where transactions are effected through a subsidiary which is not wholly
owned, it is the full value of the profits or revenue attributable to the assets and
the full value of the consideration which will be used, not merely the company's
proportionate interest.[192]

6.227 Where the transaction involves an acquisition or disposal of equity capital the
numerator of the assets, profits, and revenue ratios is by reference to the assets,
profits, and revenue, respectively, attributable to the percentage interest of the
capital acquired or disposed.[193] However, if the transaction results in the subject
entity becoming or ceasing to be consolidated in the company's books, then the
full value of the entities assets, profits, and revenue will be used in determining
these ratios.[194]

6.228 Finally, where a subsidiary allots shares resulting in a reduction of the company's
percentage interest in the subsidiary, this may give rise to a deemed disposal.
This is irrespective of whether the subsidiary is consolidated in the company's
accounts.[195]

---

[188] LR 14.07(4).   [189] LR 14.15(1).   [190] LR 14.15(2).   [191] LR 14.07(5).
[192] LR 14.13, 14.14, & 14.15(5).   [193] LR 14.26.   [194] LR 14.28.
[195] See LR 14.29–14.32.

(5) Requirements for notifiable transactions

Having calculated the financial ratios and determined which class of notifiable transaction a particular transaction is to be regarded, it is then necessary to consider the obligations that are imposed on the company. In respect of less significant transactions, the making of certain announcements will be all that is required. However, as the relative size of the transaction increases, so do the obligations of the company. A summary of the requirements accompanying each class of notifiable transaction is set out in Table 6.3. Each of these requirements is summarized below. **6.229**

Announcements

In respect of every transaction regarded as a notifiable transaction, the company is required to notify the SEHK and make an announcement in a local newspaper. As with normal SEHK practice, published announcements will need to be vetted by the SEHK. The contents of the announcement will depend on the type of notifiable transaction but will include details of the transaction, **6.230**

Table 6.3 Notifiable transactions—requirements of each class of notifiable transaction[196]

	Notification to SEHK	Publication of an announcement in the newspapers	Circular to shareholders	Shareholders' approval	Accountants' report
Share transaction	•	•		[197]	
Disclosable transaction	•	•	•		
Major transaction	•	•	•	•	•
VSD	•	•	•	•	•
VSA	•	•	•	•	•
Reverse takeover[198a]	•	•	•	•[198]	•

---

[196] '•' indicates required.

[197] The company continues to be subject to the general requirement to obtain shareholder approval for an issue of shares.

[198] As a reverse takeover is treated as a new listing application, the approval of the Exchange will also be required.

[198a] Discussed in Chapter 7.

including the reasons for it being entered into.[199] Where it is not feasible to make an announcement after an agreement has been signed which gives rise to a notifiable transaction (share transaction or major or above transaction) but before the commencement of the next day's trading, the company is required to request a short suspension in trading of its shares in order to give it the opportunity to make the appropriate announcement.[200]

Circulars

6.231　Where circulars are required, they must be sent out to shareholders within 21 days of the date of the announcement.[201] The contents of the circular will depend on the type of notifiable transaction it is being sent in connection with, specific contents being specified for each class of notifiable transaction.[202] Every circular is to have regard to the general requirements of clarity, accuracy, and completeness.[203] Where shareholders' approval will be required, the circular will need to contain all information necessary to allow the holders of the securities to make a properly informed decision.[204]

6.232　For major transactions, VSAs, VSDs, and reverse takeovers (discussed in Chapter 7), an accountants' report[205] covering the preceding three financial years on the business or company being acquired (or on the company's group if a VSD) and pro forma accounts on the enlarged or remaining group will need to be prepared and provided to shareholders with the circular.[206] In the event the accountants' report can only give a qualified opinion, a shareholders' approval at a general meeting will be required.[207]

Shareholder approval

6.233　Notifiable transactions requiring shareholders' approval imply that the company must not bind itself to any such transaction, unless it is made conditional on obtaining the approval of shareholders. Shareholders must receive the circular not later than the time they receive the notice of the meeting and not less than 14 days before the date of the meeting.[208] In general, shareholders may approve a transaction by majority vote in general meeting.[209] It should be noted that shareholders and their associates who have a material interest in the transaction are required to abstain from voting.[210]

---

[199] LR 14.34 & 14.35; see LR 14.58–14.60.　　[200] LR 14.37.　　[201] LR 14.38.
[202] See LR 14.64–14.71.　　[203] LR 14.63 & 2.13.　　[204] LR 14.63(2)(a).
[205] Prepared in accordance with LR Chapter 4.　　[206] See 14.67(4), 14.69(4), & 14.68.
[207] LR 14.86.　　[208] LR 14.42.
[209] A written approval is permitted in the case of major transactions subject to certain conditions being satisfied—LR 14.44.
[210] LR 14.46.

(6) Requirements for connected transactions

A company is required to contact the SEHK whenever it proposes to enter into **6.234** a transaction which could be a connected transaction.[211] Other requirements applicable to connected transactions[212] fall into two categories concerning reporting and announcement obligations, and shareholder approval.

As a general matter, a connected transaction requires the company to report, **6.235** make announcements, and seek the approval of shareholders unless an exemption applies. The classification of connected transactions in this regard has been set out in Table 6.2 above and the more specific cases for exemption from these requirements are set out below. In addition, the SEHK has a general discretion to grant waivers from any or all of the applicable requirements.[213]

Certain transactions of a company are carried out on a continuing or recurring **6.236** basis, such as the supply of goods or services in the ordinary course of the company's business. Where this involves connected persons such transactions are known as 'continuing connected transactions'. Unless exempted, such transactions carry with it additional requirements including the need to enter into a written agreement on normal commercial terms for a period normally not exceeding three years.[214] Such transactions must be also reviewed on an annual basis by the independent non-executive directors as to the continuing fairness and commercial basis of the arrangement.[215]

A connected transaction may also be a notifiable transaction or a reverse take- **6.237** over and regard therefore must be given to the other Listing Rule requirements pertaining to those transactions.

Fully exempt transactions

Transactions which are fully exempt do not impose any reporting, announce- **6.238** ment, or shareholder approval obligations on the company although the SEHK reserves the power to specify that an exemption will not apply to a particular transaction.[216]

In addition to the exemption described in Table 6.2 for connected transactions **6.239** of a de minimis size, certain other transactions are exempted notwithstanding the involvement of a connected person in the transaction.[217] Examples of such transactions are:

---

[211] LR 14A.05.
[212] Unless waived by the SEHK pursuant to its power to do so under LR 14A.07.
[213] LR 14A.42.   [214] LR 14A.35.   [215] LR 14A.37.   [216] LR 14A.30.
[217] LR 14A.31 contains a complete list.

- intra-group transactions where any non-wholly owned subsidiary does not comprise a connected person who is a substantial shareholder of such subsidiary;
- the issue of shares to a connected person on a pro rata entitlement basis;
- certain placing and top-up transactions;
- share repurchases conducted on-exchange or under a general offer;
- directors service contracts;
- certain consumer goods and services provided on normal commercial terms and administrative services shared on a fairly allocated cost basis; and
- certain financial assistance transactions, such as where provided in the ordinary course of the company's business.[218]

Reporting and announcement

6.240   As soon as possible after the terms of the transaction have been agreed, the company must notify the SEHK and provide it with a draft announcement and make an announcement in local newspapers on the next business day. The announcement will need to contain specified information including a description of the transaction and the relationship between the parties and their interests in the transaction. Where no shareholder approval is required, the announcement must also include the views of the independent non-executive directors.[219]

6.241   The company will also need to report certain details in its next annual report and accounts including a description of the transaction and the relationship between the parties and their interests in the transaction.[220] A company subject to announcement requirements must also comply with the above reporting requirements.

Independent shareholder approval

6.242   A company may not commit itself to any transaction which requires shareholder approval unless it is made conditional on such approval.[221] In general, the approval of shareholders is to be obtained in general meeting by general resolution.[222] In addition, a company which is required to seek the approval of shareholders must also comply with the reporting and announcement requirements set out above.[223]

6.243   Prior to seeking shareholder approval, the board must establish an independent committee of the board consisting only of independent non-executive directors

---

[218] See LR 14A.65.   [219] LR 14A.56.   [220] LR 14A.45.
[221] LR 14A.18 & 14A.52.   [222] LR 14A.43.   [223] LR 14A.48.

and appoint an independent financial adviser. Both appointments are for the purpose of providing independent recommendations and advice to the shareholders as to whether the terms of the relevant transaction are fair and reasonable and whether such a transaction is in the interests of the issuer and its shareholders as a whole.[224]

Certain persons are required to abstain from voting and include connected persons with a material interest in the transaction and any shareholder with a material interest in such transaction and its associate(s).[225] Hence the approval is normally referred to as an independent shareholders' approval. However, the SEHK may permit a written approval where no shareholder would be required to abstain at a general meeting or where a written approval has been obtained from independent shareholders together holding at least 50 per cent of the voting share capital of the company.[226] Where the SEHK exercises its discretion to not require independent shareholders' approval, it will also normally require a letter from the company's auditor or financial adviser stating that in their opinion the transaction is fair and reasonable so far as the shareholders of the company are concerned.[227]   **6.244**

The circular to shareholders must contain a statement that interested persons will not vote.[228] It must also contain other specified information including an explanation of the transaction and explaining its advantages and disadvantages for the company.[229] It must be sent out within 21 days of the announcement of the connected transaction and otherwise in accordance with the requirements of Chapter 2 of the Listing Rules.[230] The circular must be accompanied by a letter from the independent board committee and the independent financial adviser.[231] The adviser's letter must set out the adviser's advice as to whether the transaction should be approved and provide the reasons for such opinion including assumptions made and factors taken into account.[232]   **6.245**

(7) Discretionary powers

The rules relating to notifiable and connected transactions in one sense may appear to be very straightforward—a transaction is classified and that leads to clear obligations being imposed on the company as regards disclosure and shareholder approval. However, there are many complexities beyond the present scope. This is particularly so where more than one group company is involved or where connected persons are involved at different levels of a group or transaction structure. Whether a straightforward or complex situation, the   **6.246**

---

[224] LR 14A.21, 13.39(6)(a) & (b).   [225] LR 14A.18 & 14A.54.
[226] LR 14A.43.   [227] LR 14A.42(1).   [228] LR 14A.18.   [229] LR 14A.58.
[230] LR 14A.49.   [231] LR 14A.58(3)(d) & 14A.21.   [232] LR 14A.22.

application of the rules may give rise to anomalous results. This is perhaps particularly so in the case of the application of the financial ratios. It is in part for these latter reasons that the SEHK reserves wide discretionary powers in applying the rules—to waive them where it is not appropriate to apply them, and to deem certain transactions as subject to the rules where they would not otherwise be subject.

G. Conclusion

6.247 The topic of corporate governance as addressed in this chapter is concerned with what form management of a company should take in order for it to be managed in the interests of its owners, and in this regard what protections need to be in place to protect those interests. The preservation of the interests of owners has long been recognized through the equitable concepts of fiduciary duty and the common law duty of care, skill, and diligence. Significant developments as to the application of these concepts have been made in the modern era.

6.248 In contrast to the broad and adaptable approach of equity and the common law, statutory law and the constitutional documents of a company provide certain points of specific reference, to matters such as the provision of information to shareholders, directors' dealings and conflicts of interest, and controls on the powers of directors.

6.249 In more recent times, probably the most significant impact on governance in public companies has been the progressive introduction of ever tougher regulatory measures. In part, the impact is undoubtedly due to the pro-active or preemptory nature of regulatory rules as compared to applicable law. However, regulatory rules have also had a major impact due to certain market realities, namely, the support often given to such rules by institutional investors, and the reality that non-compliance may have direct and immediate commercial consequences, either in the market in the company's shares or, in more serious cases, the suspension of listing.

6.250 While the governance framework is thus composed of these different approaches, that they are approaching the same problem leads to common concerns. How should a board be composed and operate? What are the responsibilities of directors and to whom? How to treat the personal interests of directors when they connect or conflict with those of the company? What are the limits of its powers and when must shareholders be consulted? What is the proper level of participation of owners in management decisions? What sort of information should be provided to owners and when?

6.251 While perhaps none of these questions are new, the way in which they have been addressed, at equity and common law, in statute and in regulation, has developed over time and in response to a changing commercial environment. Governance issues are borne out of the division between the owners of a company and those who manage it, and such a division has never been greater than in present-day publicly listed companies. Each market will have its own characteristics requiring its own particular solutions. In Hong Kong, family controlled companies are more predominant than in more highly capitalized markets. Accordingly, considerable emphasis is placed on concepts of connectedness and independence. However, there is always likely to be something very intangible about the quality of a company's governance. In the absence of good governance practices managers and owners are likely to, and even where good governance exists nevertheless can, become estranged.

Corporate governance has been receiving increasing interest, as in many other jurisdictions. The first section of this chapter outlined the reasons why this is the case, however, it is worth returning to the rationale for seeking to improve corporate governance here.

6.252

In order to investigate that actual value that investors place on corporate governance, McKinsey & Company, an international consultance, in cooperation with the World Bank and the periodical *Institutional Investor*, conducted a series of surveys to discover how shareholders perceived and valued corporate governance in both developed and emerging markets.[233] The surveys gathered responses about investment intentions from over 200 institutional investors, responsible for approximately US\$ 3.25 trillion in assets; 40 per cent of the respondents were based in the US, with the remainder drawn worldwide.

6.253

Among the key findings from the surveys are the following:[234]

6.254

- Three-quarters of investors said board practices are at least as important to them as financial performance when evaluating companies for investment.

- Over 80 per cent of investors indicated they would pay more for the shares of a well-governed company than for those of a poorly governed company with comparable financial performance. (For the purposes of the surveys, a well-governed company was defined as: (1) having a majority of outside directors on the board with no management ties; (2) holding formal evaluations of directors; and (3) being responsive to investor requests for information on governance issues. In addition, directors hold significant stockholdings in the company, and a large proportion of directors' pay is in the form of stock/options.)

---

[233] McKinsey & Co, Investor Opinion Survey on Corporate Governance (June 2000), p 1.
[234] ibid.

- The actual premium investors say they would be willing to pay for a well-governed company differs by country. Figures varied from 17.9 per cent (UK) to 27.6 per cent (Venezuela). Local investors were willing to pay on average a premium of 20.2 per cent; foreign investors were on average willing to pay a premium of 26.3 per cent.

- Based on the evidence, the size of the premium that institutional investors said they were willing to pay for good governance seems to reflect the extent to which they believe there is room for improvement. In Asia and Latin America, McKinsey concluded that the higher premia on offer reflected the need for more fundamental disclosure of information and stronger shareholder rights.

6.255   At the regulatory level, the corporate governance framework should encourage reforms or, at the very least, not hinder them.[235] Specifically, two areas were singled out as the most significant target areas: (1) improved disclosure of information, and (2) stronger shareholder rights.

6.256   In analysing the context in Hong Kong and whether the system as structured is in fact sufficient to address the needs of the market in terms of both fairness and competitiveness, it is useful to look to existing international standards, in this case the *Principles of Corporate Governance*[236] of the Organization for Economic Cooperation and Development (OECD) as a standard against which to measure the situation in Hong Kong.

6.257   The document is divided into two parts. The Principles are presented in the first part of the document and cover six areas: (1) ensuring the basis of an effective corporate governance framework; (2) the rights of shareholders and key ownership functions; (3) the equitable treatment of shareholders; (4) the role of stakeholders; (5) disclosure and transparency; and (6) the responsibilities of the board. Each of the sections is headed by a single Principle that is followed by a number of sub-principles. The second part of the document contains annotations and commentary on the Principles and their rationale, with analysis of trends and alternative models.[237]

6.258   In Hong Kong, the general requirements of the first principle (including incentive structures, legal and regulatory requirements consistent with the rule of law, transparency and enforceability, clear articulation of regulatory responsibilities, and related transparency, independence and accountability) are largely in place, though certain concerns definitely remain in relation to articulation of regulatory responsibilities, especially between the SFC and HKEx.

---

[235]   McKinsey & Co, Investor Opinion Survey on Corporate Governance (June 2000), p 1.
[236]   OECD, *OECD Principles of Corporate Governance* (2004).   [237]   ibid, p 4.

Likewise, the main requirements of the second principle (including rights to **6.259** secure ownership and registration, convey and transfer shares, obtain relevant information, share in residual profits, participate in basic decisions and at general shareholder meetings, and fair and transparent transfers of control) are all addressed by Hong Kong's regulatory system.

The third (requiring the equitable treatment of shareholders) and sixth prin- **6.260** ciples (dealing with the role of the board) is more often observed in the breach than in the affirmative. It is hoped that the dual-filing regime under the SFO and the proposals to give statutory backing to certain provisions for the Listing Rules may improve the situation. However, insider dealing, abusive self-dealing, and disclosure of material interests of directors is well covered by the SFO.

The fourth principle dealing with the role of broader stakeholder groups is **6.261** largely ignored in Hong Kong's laissez-faire economic and legal structure. At this point, the concern is protection of shareholder rights, and it is likely that only as this improves will broader issues be addressed (as has been the case in other economies around the world). The initial discussions regarding competition issues are a possible indicative start to this process.

Similar to shareholder rights, the fifth principle (disclosure and transparency) **6.262** (calling for timely and accurate disclosure on all material matters regarding the corporation including its financial situation, performance, ownership, and governance) is receiving increasing attention in Hong Kong and once again the situation has been improved by the enactment of the SFO (especially the dual-filing system and related provisions) and may be enhanced by proposed statutory backing for certain aspects of the Listing Rules. Nonetheless, given the high importance of disclosure not only in corporate governance but in market functioning and competitiveness more broadly, this is an issue deserving further attention.

7

TAKEOVERS AND MERGERS

While commercial objectives may vary considerably, at the core of any merger or **7.01** acquisition is a desire to consolidate or obtain control of another company. This Chapter reviews the regulations applying to such transactions, namely, the Code on Takeovers and Mergers (the 'Takeovers Code').[1] The Takeovers Code is a non-statutory set of rules regulating all aspects of M&A transactions as they affect public companies in Hong Kong. It affects the obligations of not only the

---

[1] References in the footnotes are to rules of the Takeovers Code unless otherwise specified.

offeror and the offeree and their respective directors but also those who may be involved as commercial parties to such transactions and their professional advisers.

7.02   Overall, Hong Kong has an effective and well-developed system addressing these sorts of activities, largely based on the UK system.

A. The Code on Takeovers and Mergers

7.03   The Takeovers Code comprises a set of non-statutory General Principles and Rules issued by the SFC. The Takeovers Code is based largely on the UK system. It is administered by the Executive Director[2] (the 'Executive') of the Corporate Finance Division of the SFC and enforced by the Takeovers and Mergers Panel (the 'Panel'). Prior to making any changes of any substance to the Takeovers Code the SFC will normally enter into a public consultation process and in all cases will consult with the Panel which is comprised of industry practitioners. As a result of the consultative process, the Takeovers Code in general is well supported by practitioners in the industry.

7.04   The Introduction to the Takeovers Code gives an excellent summary of its primary purpose:

> . . . to afford fair treatment for shareholders who are affected by takeovers [and] mergers . . . to achieve fair treatment by requiring equality of treatment of share-holders, mandating disclosure of timely and adequate information to enable shareholders to make an informed decision as to the merits of an offer and ensur-ing that there is a fair and informed market in the shares of companies affected by takeovers [and] mergers . . . [to] provide an orderly framework within which takeovers [and] mergers . . . are to be conducted.[3]

7.05   The Takeovers Code is centrally concerned with the concept of 'control' and any arrangement by one or more people to gain control or to consolidate control of a company subject to the Takeovers Code. 'Control' means 'a holding, or aggregate holdings, of 30 per cent or more of the voting rights of a company, irrespective of whether that holding or holdings gives de facto control'.[4]

7.06   In some cases, control of a company may be effectively changed in connection with the company acquiring significant assets. As regards listed companies, this is sometimes undertaken as an attempt to seek a listing for the assets so acquired without going through the lengthy listing process required under the Listing

---

[2] Or any delegate of the Executive Director.   [3] Para 1.2.
[4] Takeovers Code, Definitions.

Rules of the SEHK. This is known as a 'reverse takeover' or 'backdoor listing' and is discussed further below.

An overview of the critical points of interest arising in connection with the Takeovers Code includes: **7.07**

- the companies and transactions subject to the Takeover Code;
- offer structures;
- offers, their consequences, terms and timing, including mandatory offers and compulsory acquisitions and sales;
- obligations of the offeror and those acting in concert with it;
- responsibilities of the target company's board;
- required disclosures and restrictions applying to dealings during an offer; and
- the sanctions for non-compliance with the Takeovers Code.

In dealing with these topics, it will be apparent that, even within the confines of the procedures set down by the Takeovers Code, there are many possible commercially driven variations in the method by which a takeover is conducted. This may range from the financing aspects to the psychology of shareholders as regards accepting or not accepting an offer. It is in part due to the many possible permutations that the role of the Executive is everywhere apparent throughout the Takeovers Code. This involvement ranges from the need to seek consultation prior to action being taken, to powers given to the Executive to apply the Rules differently according the special circumstances of a particular case, to the giving of rulings on certain matters. **7.08**

The Takeovers Code is structured as General Principles and Rules. Whereas the Rules govern specific circumstances, the General Principles are intended to apply to all transactions subject to the Takeovers Code. This approach acknowledges the fact that in the course of a takeover many possible and unforeseeable circumstances may arise. Persons involved in a takeover are required to observe the spirit of the General Principles and the Rules as well as the precise wording.[5] **7.09**

(1) Scope

The Takeovers Code applies to any takeover and merger affecting 'public companies in Hong Kong and companies with a primary listing of their equity securities in Hong Kong'.[6] This definition, while clearly identifying certain companies as being subject to the Takeovers Code, is necessarily broad and so does not clearly define the full scope of companies covered by the Takeovers Code. The issue was highlighted by the high profile disagreement on this **7.10**

---

[5] Takeovers Code, Introduction, para 2.1.   [6] Takeovers Code, Introduction, para 4.1.

question in the case of the Jardine Matheson group of companies prior to the removal of its listing from the SEHK to the Singapore Exchange in December 1994/January 1995. The Introduction to the Takeovers Code[7] now clarifies (it did not previously) that the Executive will 'consider all the circumstances and will apply an economic or commercial test taking into account primarily the number of Hong Kong shareholders' as well as other (non-exhaustive) factors including the location of the company's head office and place of central management as well as the location of its business and assets, and the company's tax status. A further important factor, one which underlines the role of the SFC vis-à-vis protection of investors, is the existence or absence of protection available to Hong Kong shareholders given by any statute or code regulating takeovers and mergers outside Hong Kong. In the event a company is uncertain as to its status under the Takeovers Code in this regard it should consult the Executive at an early stage.

7.11 Persons involved in a proposed takeover are also subject to the Takeovers Code.[8] Such persons include directors of companies subject to the Takeovers Code, persons or groups of persons who seek control of companies subject to the Takeovers Code, their professional advisers, persons who are otherwise connected with transactions to which the Takeover Code applies, and those persons who are actively engaged in the securities market.

(2) General principles

7.12 As a document setting out a framework for takeovers and mergers in Hong Kong, the SFC has emphasized that circumstances may arise which are not expressly contemplated by the Takeovers Code's Rules. Accordingly, the Takeovers Code contains a statement of ten General Principles underlying the Takeovers Code and its interpretation and implementation. In summary, those principles are:

1. Equal and fair treatment of shareholders.
2. A change or consolidation of control should normally require a general offer to all other shareholders to be made.
3. When an offer is contemplated or in progress, information may not be provided to some shareholders and not others.
4. Offers, or acquisitions leading to an offer, should only be entered into after responsible consideration taking into account its financial ability to implement the offer in full.
5. Sufficient and full information, advice, and time should be given to shareholders to reach an informed decision on an offer. All documents must

---

[7] Takeovers Code, Introduction, para 4.2.   [8] ibid, para 1.5.

be prepared to prospectus standard with the highest possible degree of care, responsibility, and accuracy.

6. Prompt disclosure of all relevant information and to avoid the creation of a false market.

7. Rights of control to be exercised in good faith—the oppression of minority or non-controlling shareholders is always unacceptable.

8. Responsibility of directors, in advising shareholders, to have regard to shareholders' interests taken as a whole and not to put themselves in any situation which may give rise to conflicts of interest or result in a breach of the directors' fiduciary duties.

9. Directors of the offeree not to take any action which may frustrate a bona fide offer—it is for the shareholders to decide.

10. All concerned persons to fully cooperate with the Executive, the Panel, and the Takeovers Appeal Committee, and to provide all relevant information.

(3) Administration and enforcement

Executive

The Executive is the primary entity responsible for the monitoring and investiga-   **7.13**
tion of takeovers and mergers.[9] Insofar as the Takeovers Code is a guide as to what standards of commercial behaviour and conduct is considered acceptable in the Hong Kong market, it is an important feature of the Executive's function that it is available for consultation as to interpretation of the Takeovers Code and therefore as to what constitutes appropriate behaviour in a specific situation.

In addition to its consultative role, the Executive is also able to make rulings,   **7.14**
either on its own initiative or upon the request of concerned persons. Such rulings may serve to confirm the interpretation of a provision of the Takeovers Code in a specific situation, provide a consent to certain actions being engaged in or, where appropriate, waive compliance with a specific rule of the Takeovers Code. Unlike the consultation process, rulings are in writing and are delivered after full consideration of all the material facts. The Executive will normally publish its important rulings subject to prevailing confidentiality consider-ations. Once a ruling has been made, any disagreement may be referred to the Panel for review of the relevant ruling.

Panel

The primary functions of the Panel are to give rulings on the Takeovers Code,   **7.15**
to review rulings given by the Executive, and to hear disciplinary matters.[10]

---

[9] Takeovers Code, Introduction, paras 5–9.   [10] ibid, paras 10–13.

The Panel is established under section 8(1) of the SFO and consists of up to 30 members comprised of persons from the financial and investment community including at least one non-executive director of the SFC. While such members are appointed and removed by the SFC, SFC staff and executive directors are forbidden from themselves being Panel members. Disciplinary matters brought before the Panel are comprised of breaches of the Takeovers Code or breaches of rulings made by the Executive or the Panel. It is the policy of the Panel to publish its rulings and the reasons therefor, subject to prevailing confidentiality considerations.

Sanctions

7.16 Failure to comply with the Takeovers Code or rulings will not per se bring legal penalties. However, the administrative sanctions associated with such breaches are nevertheless effective. Companies listed on the SEHK are required to comply with the Takeovers Code—the Listing Rules expressly make any breach of the Takeovers Code a breach of the Listing Rules.[11] Non-compliance with the Takeovers Code by a listed company may therefore entail a number of potential consequences including suspension or cancellation of its listing.

7.17 All persons (whether or not listed) accessing the markets in Hong Kong are required by the SFC to comply with the Takeovers Code as a matter of market practice, and the Panel may impose any of a number of sanctions, including:

- private reprimand;
- public criticism or censure;
- reporting the offender's conduct to the SFC or other regulatory authority;
- requiring persons licensed or registered with the SFC, for a stated period, not to act for the offender; and/or
- ban an adviser from appearing before the Executive or the Panel for a stated period.

Moreover, breaches of the Takeovers Code or rulings may hamper the success of an offer, for example, if directors of the target company for this reason decide not to recommend shareholders participate in the offer. In addition, the Panel may issue a public statement to the effect that a director remaining in his post is prejudicial to the interest of investors. This would normally make it untenable for the person to retain his or her post of director and would again raise serious issues in the context of an offer. Finally, the Panel may also order compensation be paid to persons suffering loss as a result of a breach of the Takeovers Code.[12]

---

[11] LR 13.23(2) & LR 14.78.   [12] eg see Panel decision or Mr William Cheng Kai Man.

Takeovers Appeal Committee

The review of the disciplinary rulings of the Panel is undertaken by the   **7.18**
Takeovers Appeal Committee (TAC) which has been established under section
8(1) of the SFO. The TAC, as an appellate body, does not review the Panel's
finding of facts but only determines whether a sanction imposed by the Panel is
unfair or excessive.[13] The TAC is comprised of members of the Securities and
Futures Appeals Tribunal[14] and the Panel itself. As with the Panel, the rulings of
the TAC are normally published, subject to confidentiality considerations.

B. Takeover Structures

The offeror's bid to acquire control of a target company may be undertaken for   **7.19**
a variety of commercial reasons and, consequently, with a view to obtaining a
variety of outcomes. Such outcomes might range from acquiring a controlling
interest in the company to owning 100 per cent of the company and delisting
the company. Different offer structures result.

(1) Full offers

Two typical means of conducting a full offer is by the general offer or by a   **7.20**
scheme of arrangement. The former is conducted by way of contract—an offer
made by the offeror to all the shareholders of the target, and a contract being
formed when a shareholder accepts the offer. The latter is a court process governed by relevant companies legislation[15] and requiring the approval of shareholders in general meeting. A distinction should be made here between hostile
and friendly takeover situations: whereas general offers can always be used,
schemes are suitable for use only in a friendly situation as it really requires the
board of the offeree to be in agreement with the offeror.

Two key issues for any offeror in deciding between these two approaches are: **7.21**

What level of control is it seeking to obtain?

Some offerors may be satisfied with obtaining control of more than 50 per   **7.22**
cent of the target but falling short of complete control. Other offerors will be
primarily concerned with ensuring they obtain complete control with a view to
delisting the company from the SEHK.

---

[13] ibid, paras 14–16.   [14] Established under SFO Part XI.
[15] CO s 166 if the target company is incorporated in Hong Kong.

What are the prospects of success via each of these two routes?

7.23 This is a game of weighing up the votes of larger shareholders who support the bid against the likely views of other shareholders and the probability of them being either active or apathetic (ie more or less likely to take steps to accept a general offer or to attend and vote at a shareholder meeting). Apathetic shareholders may present problems for an offeror making a general offer, but may represent a benefit for an offeror pursuing a scheme of arrangement (see below). The particular objectives of an offeror and the profile of shareholders (supporting, controlling, and others) will influence the decision as to which route to take. Certainly, the mechanism of obtaining the shareholder support level required for each of these two methods is different.

General offer

7.24 Under a general offer the acceptance level is normally 50 per cent. While this level may be a lower and possibly easier threshold to meet compared to the requirements for schemes of arrangement as set out below, this approach presents issues for the bidder wishing to privatize the target. In this case, the offeror will need to rely on statutory provisions allowing for the compulsory purchase of minority shareholders. As discussed further below, this entails a 90 per cent threshold level. Accordingly, an offeror wishing to be sure of being able to privatize the target may (assuming it is making a voluntary offer) elect to set an acceptance level of 90 per cent (which in any case would normally be expressed to be waivable at the offeror's discretion).

7.25 A tactic sometimes considered to assist in this regard is for the target company to propose to its shareholders a delisting resolution—if passed it makes remaining a minority shareholder of the company less attractive. While the Listing Rules[16] require only a 75 per cent approval for such a resolution to be passed, controlling shareholders and their associates are excluded from voting. This may remove from voting shareholders backing the offeror and therefore may make such a resolution more difficult to pass.

Scheme of arrangement

7.26 A scheme of arrangement under section 166 of the Companies Ordinance is administratively more complex than an offer. First, an explanatory statement must be sent to shareholders explaining the operation of the scheme (normally either that their shares in the target will be cancelled and replaced with shares in the offeror, or that their shares will be transferred to the offeror). Such statement

---

[16] LR 6.12.

is then treated as the offer document for the purposes of both the Takeovers Code and the Listing Rules. Second, the scheme must be approved in general meeting by 75 per cent of shareholders present and voting. The Takeovers Code additionally requires a scheme to be approved by 75 per cent of the votes attaching to disinterested shares[17] voted and for the number of votes cast against the resolution to be not more than 10 per cent of the votes attaching to all disinterested shares.[18] Third, if the scheme is approved by shareholders it must be sanctioned by the court to become effective, the court's function being to determine if the scheme is reasonable in the circumstances. Finally, once the scheme has been properly registered, it will bind every shareholder of the target whether or not they attended or how they voted. Accordingly, while a scheme may present a higher threshold for obtaining approval for the takeover, it is a lower threshold as regards completing a privatization of the target (discussed below).

While schemes have greater certainty about them than a general offer, they tend **7.27** to be an 'all or nothing' bid and tend to have a longer timetable. The longer timetable and the decreased flexibility as regards being able to change the terms of the offer may be a serious disadvantage if another competing bid enters the market.

Another consideration often made in deciding to pursue a scheme is the issue of **7.28** costs. The costs associated with a court governed scheme tend to be higher than that associated with a general offer and, if the offer has not been either recommended by the offeree board or recommended by the independent financial adviser as fair and reasonable and the scheme is not passed, the costs of a scheme of arrangement incurred by the offeree will need to be borne by the offeror.[19] Although this latter scenario may seem unlikely given the friendly context, one of the problems of schemes is the longer timetable involved: the board of the target may change their mind (eg if a competing bid is made). Balancing these considerations is the potential savings made on stamp duty: whereas every share transferred under a general offer will be subject to stamp duty, shares in a scheme are normally cancelled and new shares issued, and in Hong Kong this does not attract stamp duty.

Acquisition followed by mandatory offer

In Hong Kong takeovers are sometimes structured as a private acquisition by the **7.29** offeror of shares from controlling shareholders and, assuming this takes the offeror through the 30 per cent trigger level for a mandatory bid, a mandatory bid is then made pursuant to Rule 26 (discussed below). One advantage of this

---

[17] ie shares not held or controlled by the offeror and persons acting in concert with it.
[18] Rule 2.10.   [19] Rule 2.3.

method is that the offeror may be able to negotiate warranties, representations, and undertakings from the selling shareholders, subject to the extent they are involved in the management of the target.

Privatizing and withdrawal of listing

7.30 Following a successful offer, an offeror may wish to consolidate control by seeking to privatize the target and to withdraw its listing from the SEHK. The former requires a consideration of the position of minority shareholders. Both require a consideration of the requirements of the Listing Rules and Takeovers Code.

Minority shareholders

7.31 Privatizing the company will require procuring the compulsory sale of shares held by shareholders who have not accepted the offer. This is primarily governed by the companies legislation applicable to the company.

7.32 In the case of companies established in Hong Kong,[20] the requirement is that the offeror must acquire at least 90 per cent of the target shares within a period of four months from the commencement of the offer period. If that is achieved, the offeror can then give notice that it wishes to acquire the remaining shares. Upon giving proper notice, the offeror becomes entitled and bound to acquire those shares subject to the right of the shareholder to apply to court. In the absence of the affected shareholder taking any action within the specified time limit (two months from the date of the offeror's notice), the court is entitled to execute the relevant share transfer documentation on behalf of the shareholder and deliver the same to the target company for registration.

7.33 The Takeovers Code specifies that, in addition to satisfying the requirements at law, the 90 per cent threshold test must also be passed in relation to the class of disinterested shares.[21] The same timeframe applies.

7.34 Irrespective of the offeror's intentions, where an offeror has acquired more than 90 per cent of the target's shares, each remaining shareholder may require the offeror to also acquire its shares on the same terms as the offer.[22]

Withdrawal of listing

7.35 An offeror wishing to withdraw the target's listing from the SEHK needs to comply with the relevant requirements of the Listing Rules.[23] The Listing Rules[24] permit voluntary withdrawal of the target's listing where, inter alia:

---

[20] CO s 168 & sch 9, part 1.   [21] Rule 2.11.   [22] CO sch 9, part 2.
[23] See LR Chapter 6.   [24] LR 6.15.

- all of the target's listed shares have been acquired (usually following a compulsory acquisition exercise), or
- the target is privatized following a scheme of arrangement which is governed by the Takeovers Code and relevant Takeovers Code requirements have been complied with.

In the latter case, the Takeovers Code[25] requirements broadly correspond to the **7.36** general withdrawal requirements under the Listing Rules,[26] namely: approval by at least 75 per cent of the votes cast, the number of votes cast against the resolution is not more than 10 per cent, in each case as a percentage of the disinterested shares. For these purposes 'disinterested shares' means shares in the target other than those owned by the offeror or persons acting in concert with it. In introducing the 'disinterested shares' concept, the Takeovers Code indicates that the only shareholders who may not vote at such meeting are the offeror and its concert parties. In the case of a general offer, the Takeovers Code has the additional requirement that the shareholder resolution be subject to the offeror being entitled to exercise, and exercising, its rights of compulsory acquisition.[27]

(2) Partial offers

Partial offers are unusual and the starting point for any partial offer is to seek the **7.37** consent of the Executive.[28] Consent will normally be given where the offeror and its concert parties either:

- would own less than 30 per cent of the target's shares if the partial offer were successful, or
- already own more than 50 per cent of the target's shares and would own less than 75 per cent of the target's shares if the partial offer were successful.

Such thresholds are important in the context of the mandatory bid threshold **7.38** (30 per cent) and the usual level to pass an ordinary and special resolutions of an company (50 per cent and 75 per cent respectively). If a partial offer may result in a mandatory bid obligation being triggered (see section D below), the Executive will normally not consent where the offeror or its concert parties have acquired shares in the target in the period six months prior to the commencement of the offer period. Where consent is given, a partial offer which could result in the offeror coming to hold more than 30 per cent of the target must be conditional on (1) the specified number of acceptances being received and (2) approval of the offer by shareholders holding over 50 per cent of the voting rights not held by the offeror and persons acting in concert with it.

---

[25] Rules 2.2 & 2.10.   [26] LR 6.12.   [27] Rule 2.2.   [28] Rule 28.

7.39 Partial offers must be for a precise number of shares and shareholders who accept such offer will share in it pro rata to the extent of their participation in the offer (ie unlike full offers, a shareholder may accept the partial offer in respect of all or a specified number of shares it holds).

(3) Reverse takeovers

7.40 A reverse takeover occurs where a listed company acquires assets but where such acquisition is in reality an attempt to achieve a listing of those assets.[29] As such attempts seek to avoid going through the usual process of getting listed, it is often referred to as a 'backdoor listing'.

7.41 Under a typical structure, an unlisted company which would like to be listed but desires to avoid the time-consuming and expensive process described in Chapter 4 and/or is unqualified for listing as provided in Chapter 8 of the Listing Rules, identifies a listed company experiencing very little turnover in its underlying business and/or in the market for its shares and therefore is relatively inactive. The two companies then agree along the following lines: the unlisted company sells its assets comprising the business to the listed company and, in consideration, the listed company issues shares to the unlisted company or its owners. After the transaction, a (if not the) major business of the listed company comprises the assets it has purchased from the unlisted company, and the owners of the unlisted company will have a major shareholding stake in the listed company and are likely to have a visible or perhaps governing role in the management of the listed company.

7.42 Reverse takeovers by virtue of the large relative size of the transaction will normally have two key characteristics and these are the ones the SEHK will consider as normally indicating a reverse takeover:[30]

- one or more transactions constituting a 'very substantial acquisition' (VSA— discussed in Chapter 6) have occurred, and
- there is a change in control of the listed company as a result.

For these purposes, 'control' has the meaning given to it in the Takeovers Code, namely, 'a holding, or aggregate holdings, of 30 per cent or more of the voting rights of a company, irrespective of whether that holding or holdings gives de facto control'.[31]

7.43 In some cases, a change in control may occur without any corresponding VSA. However, the SEHK is able to look at the 24-month period after such change in control and aggregate any transactions which have been entered into pursuant to

---

[29] LR 14.06(6).   [30] LR 14.06(6)(a).   [31] Takeovers Code, Definitions.

an agreement, understanding, or arrangement between the listed company and the persons who have become controllers, and regard that as a reverse takeover.[32]

Clearly, there will be a number of variations and subterfuges available to those wishing to circumvent the consequences of a transaction being treated as a reverse takeover. In this regard, the SEHK does have the discretion to exercise its 'opinion'. Further, the SEHK will treat a reverse takeover transaction as if it were a new listing applicant.[33] Accordingly, the company as enlarged by the proposed transaction must be capable of satisfying the requirements for listing set out in Chapter 8 of the Listing Rules and proceed accordingly.[34] **7.44**

In addition to the normal requirements concerning VSAs (discussed in Chapter 6), in the case of a reverse takeover, 'outgoing shareholders' also may not vote. An 'outgoing shareholder' is a person who, in connection with a change in control of the company, is selling his shares to the incoming shareholder gaining control.[35] Further, as a reverse takeover constitutes a new listing application, it will also need to comply with the procedures and requirements of Chapter 9 of the Listing Rules.[36] **7.45**

C. Offers

As can be seen from the discussion above, a central aspect to the Takeovers Code is the offer—what constitutes an offer, when it needs to be announced, what such announcement must contain to properly inform the market, what terms are and are not permitted, and under what circumstances the offer may be varied or withdrawn. The offer price is also subject to the provisions of the Takeovers Code.[36a] **7.46**

(1) Definitions

'Offeror' and 'offeree' respectively refer to the persons making the offer and the company which is the subject of the offer. That is, the offeror is seeking to gain or consolidate control of the offeree company. The offeree may also be referred to as the 'target' company and the offeror may also be referred to as the 'bidder.' Notwithstanding these common usages, it should be remembered that the offeree in any takeover bid technically is the shareholders of the offeree company, not the company itself. **7.47**

---

[32] LR 14.06(6)(b).   [33] LR 14.54.
[34] The process of obtaining a listing is discussed above.   [35] LR 14.55.
[36] LR 14.57.
[36a] 'offer' and 'offer price' as used below covers approaches to the target and its shareholders irrespective of whether structured as a general offer or scheme of arrangement, etc.

7.48 'Offer' is defined in the Takeovers Code as including takeover and merger transactions however effected, including schemes of arrangement (which may have a similar commercial effect to takeovers and mergers), partial offers, and offers by a parent company for shares in its subsidiary. The offer is also sometimes referred to as the 'bid'.

(2) When does an offer first arise?

7.49 The Takeovers Code makes it clear that any offer needs to be submitted to the board of the offeree or its advisers before it is made public.[37] Upon an offer being made, certain announcement obligations arise (discussed below).

7.50 In many cases, it will be perfectly clear when an offer is made. However, in practice, it is often the case that discussions are taking place between one or more directors of the target company and the potential offeror before any firm intention to make an offer has been formed. Depending on their relationship, these discussions may involve an exchange of information, particularly of that which assists the potential offeror in deciding whether to make an offer. In the course of such preliminary discussions, once a firm intention to make an offer is formed it is necessary to make an announcement and parties involved should not be delaying this for commercial convenience. However, even where no firm intention to make an offer has been formed, announcement obligations may arise in connection with these 'in principle' discussions.

(3) Requirements in making an offer

7.51 The first thing a potential offeror should note is that making an offer should be regarded as a point of no return as an offer once made may only be withdrawn or allowed to lapse in quite specific circumstances:[38] 'The announcement of a firm intention to make an offer should be made only when an offeror has every reason to believe that it can and will continue to be able to implement the offer. Responsibility in this connection also rests on the financial adviser to the offeror.'[39]

7.52 Accordingly, prior to making an offer, many details of the offer need to have been determined. These matters include structure of the offer including the nature of consideration payable and financial resources should the offer be fully taken up, who is the offeror (and attendant considerations, eg tax), regulatory requirements, due diligence to be undertaken, and so on.

7.53 Takeovers in certain industries perceived as being of strategic importance will

---

[37] Rule 1.1.   [38] See sections 7.81 and 7.83 below.   [39] Rule 3.5.

require the approval of a regulatory authority for a change in control to be effected without jeopardising the target company's regulatory position. Such industries (and regulatory authorities) include the banking (HKMA), financial services (SFC), insurance (OCI), and the telecommunications (Telecommunications Authority) sectors. The regulatory authority can be expected to consider the suitability of the bidder in terms of nationality, reputation, resources, and the nature of the regulatory regime in its domicile.

The approach

The approach to the offeree board will be considerably different according to whether the bid is to be regarded as hostile (ie one which the offeree board is unlikely to welcome or recommend to its shareholders) or friendly. **7.54**

In the friendly bid situation, prior to any formal offer being made, there is likely to be many meetings between the offeror and a small contingent from the board of the target, a confidentiality agreement signed, and due diligence undertaken. Care must be taken to ensure that such activities do not give rise to any announcement obligations which may arise, for example, as a result of breaches of confidentiality and leaks of information or market rumours and unusual price movements in the shares of the target. This contrasts with the hostile bid situation in which the offeror will approach the offeree board only just prior to informing the market. **7.55**

Whether hostile or friendly, any offer must disclose the identity of the person or persons making the offer.[40] No offer should be made unless the offeror can command the financial resources to complete the offer if fully accepted by all shareholders. The offeree board may in fact require to be satisfied as to the offeror's ability to fulfil this latter requirement before it is required to consider the offer a bona fide one.[41] Normally, the offeror's financial advisers or bankers would provide some form of statement of the offeror's financial backing in relation to the offer. **7.56**

Confidentiality

Discussions in connection with a possible offer generate both confidential and price-sensitive information. The Takeovers Code expressly reminds all persons privy to such information to maintain strict secrecy. Persons involved in talks should therefore make all such arrangements as are necessary to prevent leaks of such information.[42] **7.57**

---

[40] Rule 1.2.   [41] Rule 1.3.   [42] Rule 1.4.

7.58 Offers can be broadly divided into types according to the following dichotomies: voluntary versus mandatory, possible versus firm, full versus partial, conditional versus unconditional.

Voluntary versus mandatory offer

7.59 A voluntary offer is to be contrasted to the mandatory offer which is required to be made under Rule 26 (discussed further below). In the former case, the offeror is at liberty (subject to the usual regulatory and Takeovers Code considerations) to determine the timing and terms of the offer as well as control the decision-making process leading up to the making of a firm offer. In the latter case, an obligation to make a firm offer is triggered, normally by the actions (sometimes inadvertent) of the person who becomes subject to the bid obligation, and the timing and terms of the offer are then very much more controlled by the requirements of the Takeovers Code.

7.60 The Takeovers Code has recently added a new requirement that voluntary offers may not normally be made at a price 'substantially below the market price of the shares in the offeree company'. Offers at more than a 50 per cent discount to the five-day average market price of the offeree's shares will normally be regarded as 'substantially below', etc. The new requirement is intended to prevent hostile 'low ball' offers which might be used to frustrate the target's business where there is no genuine intention to acquire the target company. As such offers may create misinformed markets, the Executive will only grant a waiver of this requirement in exceptional circumstances.[42a]

Possible versus firm offer

7.61 The announcement of a firm offer fully obligates the offeror to proceed with the offer. As discussed below and elsewhere, once a firm offer has been made, in general it is not possible to avoid implementing it, subject to how the offer is phrased.

7.62 In contrast, a possible offer is not any form of offer at all but is made where the potential offeror does not want to be committed to making an offer. It is primarily an information announcement to the market that talks are taking place or that a person is considering making an offer. Such announcement may be required to be made under certain circumstances (discussed below). In contrast to a firm offer, the possible offer does not give rise to any obligation to proceed with the offer.

[42a] See Takeovers Code Definitions Note to definition of 'offer'.

Possible offers when announced are normally made in the course of determining **7.63** whether or not to make a firm offer and where information has or may leak out or as a preparatory measure when the range of persons involved in talks need to be broadened, for example in the context of discussions concerning structuring, financing, or regulatory matters.

Full versus partial offers

A full offer is an offer for all the shares of the target company. It is to be **7.64** distinguished from partial offers which are offers for a portion of the outstanding securities of the target company. Offers are normally full offers and, unless otherwise specified, references in this chapter to offers are to full offers.

Conditional versus unconditional offer

Offers made voluntarily (as compared to mandatory offers—see below) have **7.65** some latitude as to what conditions may be imposed upon the offer.[43] A condition in this context means a term which, if satisfied, renders the offer a firm offer such that any acceptance made then forms a binding contract between the offeror and the acceptor. Conversely, conditions which are not satisfied may allow the offeror the prospect of allowing the offer to lapse and hence to walk away from the offer altogether, or to waive satisfaction of the condition, or to revise the offer (see below). Not all conditions are permitted. Any condition must be clear, objective, and the satisfaction of which is not determined by subjective judgment.

In the case of conditions which are not satisfied, mention should also be made **7.66** that the Takeovers Code recommends that an offeror should only allow an offer to lapse on the non-fulfilment of a condition if the condition is 'of material significance to the offeror in the context of the offer'.[44]

An offeror is normally seeking to acquire a specific degree of control over the **7.67** target. Accordingly, a typical condition will relate to how many acceptances are required before the offer goes unconditional. This is subject to one restriction, namely, that every offer must be subject to a control condition of more than 50 per cent (meaning the aggregate of shares controlled prior to and during the offer together with acceptances received must be more than 50 per cent of the voting rights of the company).

An offeror may wish to undertake a certain amount of due diligence with a view **7.68** to finding factual data which support the terms of the offer and with a view to finding any 'skeletons in the closet' of the target company. It may elect to

---

[43] Rule 30.   [44] Rule 30.1, Note 2.

proceed on a pre-conditional possible offer basis (as discussed below), or it may wish to proceed on a conditional offer basis. In the latter case, careful thought will need to be given as to what conditions may be imposed and keep within the requirement that only objective conditions are permitted.

7.69   Every offer will contain a condition that the shares are accepted for listing and all requisite regulatory approvals are given. Other typical conditions of interest to note in this regard are:

- that the change of control of the target should the bid be successful would not trigger any contractual default or similar provisions, for example under the target's financing arrangements;
- no material adverse change in the financial condition of the target; and
- no legal proceedings which may materially and adversely affect the target.

Due diligence on the target will normally resolve these other conditions and, assuming no problems are found, the conditions will be waived.

7.70   A notable exception to the requirement for objective conditions is that a pre-conditional possible offer (see below) may provide for subjective conditions. This is appropriate given the voluntary nature of inserting a precondition to a possible offer as a means of indicating to the market under what circumstances a firm offer may be made.

Cash offer

7.71   Not all offers to acquire shares in the target will be for cash consideration. An offeror may also offer shares or convertible bonds in another listed company, normally those of the offeror.[45]

7.72   Under certain circumstances, an offeror is obliged to make a cash offer available to the target shareholders, although it may be accompanied by a non-cash offer. Such circumstances normally arise where the offeror and its concert parties have, during the offer period and the six preceding months, paid cash to acquire 10 per cent or more of the offeree's voting rights or has during the offer period paid cash to acquire any shares under offer. In such cases, the offer price contained in the cash offer must be not less than the highest price so paid.

7.73   Caution needs to be exercised where purchases have been made from directors or persons closely connected with the target. In this case, even where the amount purchased is less than 10 per cent, the Executive will examine the case closely and may require, in furtherance of General Principle 1, a cash offer to be provided.

---

[45] See rule 23.

Pre-conditional possible offer

A further twist to the possible offer discussed above is the pre-conditional **7.74** possible offer. Like possible offers, it is not really an offer at all. It occurs where a potential offeror makes a possible offer announcement which also states that it may make an offer subject to the satisfaction of certain preconditions.[46]

Although a possible offer need not be accompanied by any precondition, pre- **7.75** conditions provide a safety net for the offeror wishing to express its intent to proceed to a firm offer. Preconditions are typically used where there are due diligence concerns or regulatory matters to deal with, such as the approval of the SFC or HKMA where the target is an entity regulated by such bodies. For example, without a pre-condition as to satisfactory due diligence an offeror which finds negative information in a due diligence exercise after having made a firm offer is not generally justified by virtue of that fact to withdraw—a suitably worded pre-condition would allow an exit from proceeding.

Comparable offers

A comparable offer is required to be made where an offeror is making a bid for **7.76** voting shares in a target company which has one or more classes of equity share capital (for example, non-voting preference shares). In such a case the offeror must make a comparable offer for each such class. The conditions of the comparable offer will need to be the same as the offer although it need not be identical in view of the different rights which attach to such other classes.[47]

(5) Chain principle

The acquisition of control of one company may have as an indirect consequence **7.77** the change of control of another company to which the Takeovers Code applies. This will occur, for example, where the first company has control of a subsidiary. This does not necessarily require a bid to be made for the subsidiary company, unless the purpose of acquiring control of the first company was to acquire control of the subsidiary (the 'control test'), or if the first company's holding in the subsidiary is significant relative to the first company's assets or profits (the 'substantiality test'). As regards the latter, a relative value of 60 per cent of assets or profits would normally be considered as significant.

(6) Revising offers

An offer may be revised during the course of an offer, in which case it must be **7.78** kept open for at least 14 days.[48] In such a case, any shareholder who has

---

[46] Rule 3.5, Notes 6 & 7.   [47] Rules 14 & 28.9.   [48] Rule 16.1.

accepted the previous offer will be entitled to the revised terms. This is essential, amongst other things, to maintain the principle of equality of treatment. In making a revised offer, new conditions are normally not permitted, except where such conditions are necessary for the implementation of the new offer and with the Executive's consent.

7.79 An offer will need to be revised as to price where the offeror or its concert parties has dealt in shares at above the current offer price (see below) or where a cash offer obligation has been triggered (see above).

7.80 Because of the 14-day rule mentioned above, offerors are not permitted to revise the offer in the 14 days ending on the last day the offer is able to become unconditional as to acceptances.[49] However, this may pose a problem where the offer involves an exchange for equity in the shares of the offeror and the offeror announces any new material information (eg its trading results), which may impact on the value of the consideration offered. Where the announcement is in relation to an acquisition or disposal, the Executive will consider material any 'major transaction' as such term is defined in the Listing Rules (discussed in Chapter 6 of this book). Where such announcements are unavoidable (eg because of Listing Rule obligations), the Executive must be consulted at an early stage.[50]

(7) No withdrawal

7.81 Once an announcement of a firm intention to make an offer has been made, the offeror must proceed with the offer[51] subject to its ability to revise or improve the offer. Such requirement does not apply where the offer is subject to the fulfilment of a specific condition and that condition has not been met, or where the consent of the Executive has been given.

7.82 The consent of the Executive will not normally be given merely because there has been a change in general economic, industrial, or political circumstances. In the event an offeror discovers materially prejudicial information after the offer has been announced, this also will not normally provide any grounds to avoid going through with the offer. Accordingly, it is important that any due diligence to be conducted by the offeror is, where possible, undertaken prior to the offer being announced.

7.83 For the Executive to consent to withdrawal of an offer, circumstances of an exceptional and specific nature are required.[52] Such exceptional circumstances

---

[49] Rule 16.1   [50] Rule 16.1, Note 1.   [51] Rule 5.   [52] Rule 4.

may arise where the target contravenes the requirement not to engage in any 'frustrating action'.[53]

(8) *Offer timetables*

The Takeovers Code not only governs the timing of events, such as announce- **7.84** ments, but also other aspects of the bid process, such as the time for which an offer may remain open.[54] Consequently, the Takeovers Code generates an 'offer timetable'.

Table 7.1 Basic general offer timetable[55]

Timing[56]	Event
Pre-offer period	Preliminary discussions Appointment of financial and legal advisers Limited due diligence undertaken Irrevocable undertakings signed Commence drafting of offer document and announcement
Offer period commences (=D day)	Offeror makes formal approach to board of target Offeree announces it has received an offer Offeree establishes independent committee of board and appoints independent financial adviser
Next 3 weeks	Offer document submitted in draft to Executive and SEHK for approval
D+21 days (=P day)	Offer document sent to shareholders of target
P+21 days to P+60 days	Offer to remain open for minimum of 21 days and maximum of 60 days. During this period, offeror receives shareholder acceptances, level of acceptances watched closely
A day	Successful—announce offer becomes unconditional Unsuccessful—consider whether to extend/improve the offer
A+14 days	Earliest closing date of the offer
A+15 days	Announce level of acceptances
A+21 days	Latest date to pay accepting shareholders
Within 4 months of commencement of offer period	If 90% of target company shares acquired, consider compulsory acquisition of minority shareholders

---

[53] Frustrating action is action by the board of the target intended to stop or hinder the offer or any action taken to deny its shareholders the opportunity to decide on the merits of an offer, for example, the disposal of company assets after an offer has been announced.

[54] Rules 8 & 15.

[55] The table assumes a friendly takeover situation by way of voluntary offer.

[56] The terms 'D day', 'P day', and 'A day' are commonly used respectively to refer to the dates on which: the offer is made to commence the offer period, the offer document is dated and provided to shareholders of the target, and the announcement is made as to the outcome of the offer.

7.85 The cornerstone to the offer timetable is the 'offer period', which means the period from the time when an announcement is made of a proposed or possible offer (with or without terms) until whichever is the latest of:

- the date when the offer closes for acceptances;
- the date when the offer lapses;
- the time when a possible offeror announces that the possible offer will not proceed;
- the date when an announcement is made of the withdrawal of a proposed offer; or
- where the offer contains a possibility to elect for alternative forms of consideration, the latest date for making such election.

7.86 A basic timetable indicating the key points of reference is set out in Table 7.1.

(9) Convertible securities, warrants, and options

7.87 Where the target company has in issue, as is often the case, securities or rights convertible or exercisable into voting shares the subject of the offer[57] (in this section, collectively 'rights'), certain consequences arise. Not only is the voting share capital influenced by such other securities or rights, but also the holders of such securities or rights will clearly have an interest in the outcome of a takeover offer even though, at the time of the offer, they may not hold any shares in the subject of the offer.

7.88 The presence of such securities and rights impacts on a number of topics covered by this chapter. The most significant of which is that where an offeree has rights outstanding, the offeror is obliged also to make an offer or proposal to the holders of such rights. The offer must be 'appropriate', which means that it should be based on the offer price for the relevant underlying shares. As with the offer for the voting shares, the holders of rights are entitled to receive the advice of the independent financial adviser together with the recommendation of the board (the entitlement to receive advice etc is discussed below). Further, 'equality of treatment is required' within a class of security holders, although this concept does not apply across different classes of rights.[58]

---

[57] This could include convertible bonds, options issued under an employee share option scheme, other options to acquire shares, warrants, subscription rights, and any agreement to acquire shares or any of the foregoing securities or rights.

[58] Rule 13.1.

The existence of rights also impacts on a number of other issues which include, **7.89**
in summary, as follows:

* the offeror and its concert parties will need to disclose rights held by them;
* the restrictions and requirements in respect of dealings and disclosures apply
  also to rights; and
* a mandatory bid obligation will not normally[59] be triggered by the acquisition
  of rights, but the exercise of such rights may do so (and if it will do so, the
  Executive should be consulted prior to such exercise).

D. Mandatory Offers

As in the UK, the heart of the system of regulation of mergers, acquisitions, and **7.90**
takeovers of public companies in Hong Kong is the mandatory offer requirement. Under certain conditions, the acquisition of shares or voting rights in a
company may trigger a mandatory obligation on the acquirer to make a bid for
the entire share capital of the company, which may or may not be inadvertent.
General Principle 2 states 'If control of a company changes or is acquired or is
consolidated, a general offer to all other shareholders is normally required.' This
principle foreshadows the more specific requirements of Rule 26.

(1) Events triggering a mandatory bid obligation

Rule 26 provides that a mandatory bid obligation (ie a positive obligation to **7.91**
make a bid) will arise where:

* a person's interest in voting shares of a company crosses the 30 per cent
  trigger level: a person who has less than 30 per cent of the voting rights of a
  company acquires additional voting rights which lead to it having 30 per cent
  or more of the voting rights of a company; or
* a person's interest, having already crossed the trigger level, crosses the 2 per
  cent annual creeper: a person holds not less than 30 per cent but not more
  than 50 per cent of the voting rights of a company and increases its holding
  by more than 2 per cent from the lowest percentage holding of that person in
  the 12-month period ending on the date of the relevant acquisition.

A mandatory bid obligation will also arise where two or more persons are acting

---

[59] The Executive does have the right to look at all the circumstances of the acquisition of
rights, particularly as to whether the acquisition or issue of rights causes a de facto change of
control as regards the underlying voting rights. See Rule 26.1, Note 10.

in concert and, individually or collectively, they increase their interest in voting rights to these levels.

7.92 As indicated above, the 30 per cent level is often referred to as the 'trigger level' and the 2 per cent figure is often referred to as the 'annual creeper'. It should be noted that the trigger level under the Takeovers Code used to be 35 per cent and, accordingly, Rule 26.6 provides for transitional arrangements for persons holding 30 per cent or more but less than 35 per cent as at 19 October 2001. These transitional arrangements expire ten years after that date.

7.93 Further, an offer which starts out as a voluntary offer may subsequently become a mandatory offer if the relevant thresholds are crossed.

(2) Nature of offer required

7.94 In many cases, triggering a mandatory bid obligation results from either a poorly managed situation or an unfortunate consequence of a related transaction. As will be apparent from a comparison of what is permitted under a voluntary offer (as already described) with the requirements of a mandatory bid obligation (as next described), it will be seen that the former permits the offeror considerably greater flexibility in structuring its bid. This would include matters concerning the commercial terms, structure and progress of the offer, the ability to engage in discussions with the target board and due diligence, establishing appropriate financing arrangements, the use of pre-conditional possible offer statements, and the use of offer conditions not permitted in the mandatory context. Moreover, if the mandatory bid obligation is truly inadvertent, it is likely to be a highly undesirable situation in which to find oneself.

7.95 The following is a list of the key requirements of any mandatory offer. The Executive may in general grant dispensations from these requirements but normally would only do so in exceptional circumstances (see next section):

- The offeror shall extend offers to the holders of each class of equity share capital of the company, whether the class carries voting rights or not.
- The only condition which is both required and permitted is that the offer is conditional on the offeror's voting rights held plus acceptances amount to more than 50 per cent.
- The offer must be in cash or be accompanied by a cash alternative at not less than the highest price paid by the offeror or any person acting in concert with it for shares of that class of the offeree company during the offer period and within six months prior to its commencement.

(3) Dispensations

Given the potentially severe (and possibly unintended) consequences of a man- **7.96**
datory bid situation, Rule 26 contains a number of important qualifications to
the requirement of making a mandatory bid, although note that it should not be
assumed that the Executive will grant a dispensation. For example, although a
mandatory bid obligation may technically be triggered in the following circumstances, a mandatory bid obligation would not normally be imposed: a bank
enforcing security over shares in connection with a loan in default; corporate
rescue operations; inadvertent mistakes; placing and top-up transactions.[60] In
these cases, the Executive will normally require the relevant shares to be disposed
of to persons unconnected with the person making the disposal.[61]

(4) Whitewash

It will occasionally happen that a mandatory bid obligation would be triggered **7.97**
by the issue of new shares. This might occur for example where new shares
are being issued in consideration for an acquisition of assets, a cash subscription
or the taking up of a scrip dividend. In these circumstances, the Executive
will normally waive the bid obligation if independent shareholders[62] approve
the same.

E. Announcements

Of central importance to the Takeovers Code is specifying what needs to be **7.98**
announced to the market and when. Of primary concern is the announcement
of the offer, not only to ensure transparency of information in the market
but also because the announcement of an offer is the defining point for the
commencement of the offer period, a key reference point for a number of
obligations.

At the stage of planning an offer it is important to note General Principles 4, 5, **7.99**
and 6 which, inter alia, require an offeror to:

4. only make and announce an offer after responsible consideration;
5. provide full information to shareholders and prepare documents to
    prospectus standard; and

---

[60] A 'placing and top-up' is a transaction where a major shareholder sells part of its shareholding to an identified placee followed by a new issue of shares (in the amount of shares so sold) to
the selling shareholder. Such a transaction may cause a mandatory bid obligation to arise by virtue
of the fluctuation in the number of shares held by the selling/subscribing shareholder.
[61] See Rule 26, Notes.   [62] ie persons without any interest in the transaction in question.

6. promptly disclose all relevant information and not make statements which may mislead the shareholders or the market.

7.100 Each of these requirements places a significant onus of responsibility on any person considering making or being involved in an offer. The specific requirements as they apply to different persons involved in an offer are set out in the Rules, as next reviewed. Further, the Takeovers Code requires all documents and announcements to be filed with and normally cleared by the Executive prior to their release.

(1) Announcements prior to the offer announcement

7.101 Both the offeror and the offeree have differing responsibilities to make an announcement in relation to an offer.

Offeror responsibilities

7.102 Although a potential offeror may not yet have made an offer to the board of the offeree, it may nevertheless have announcement obligations in any of the following circumstances:[63]

- the offeree is the subject of rumour or there is undue movement in its share price or in the volume of share turnover, and there are reasonable grounds for concluding that it is the actions of the potential offeror (or its concert parties) which have led to the situation;
- when discussions are about to be extended to include more than a very restricted number of people (ie beyond the 'need to know'); or
- immediately upon triggering a mandatory offer obligation.

7.103 Accordingly, the potential offeror should keep a close watch on the offeree company's share price and volume for signs of undue movement, as well as the scope of persons whom they involve in discussions. The second of the above situations may put a potential offeror in a difficult somewhat 'premature' situation. Where the potential offeror is seeking to organize financing for the offer, irrevocable commitments or a consortium, it will be required to consult with the Executive.[64] This requirement means that the Executive may need to be informed at a very early stage in the bidder's decision-making process. For example, a bidder which is exploring the possibility of obtaining irrevocable commitments[65]

---

[63] Rule 3.1.   [64] Rule 3.1.

[65] An irrevocable commitment (also known as an irrevocable undertaking) is a contractual agreement between the offeror and the shareholder whereby the latter agrees to accept the offer (or vote in favour of a scheme of arrangement) subject to specified terms and conditions, the key condition typically being related to the offer going unconditional.

(often a precursor to it deciding its prospects for being able to consider making a bid) will need to approach the Executive before it enters any discussion with the relevant shareholder. While this clearly gives the Executive greater influence over the situation, from the potential offeror's point of view it may be perceived as restricting its ability to determine whether a takeover bid is a possibility.

What flows from this is, as already noted as regards other aspects of compliance **7.104** with the Takeovers Code, the potential offeror must very carefully control the nature of discussions as well as who participates in them.

Offeree responsibilities

Once the board of the offeree company has been approached, the primary **7.105** responsibility for making an announcement lies with the offeree company.[66] It must make an announcement in the following situations:

- when it receives a firm intention to make an offer from a serious source (note that this is regardless of whether the offer is friendly or hostile);
- an approach has been made to the offeree company (whether or not a firm intention has been expressed) and the offeree company becomes the subject of speculation about a possible offer or there is undue movement in its share price or in the volume of share turnover;
- when discussions are about to be extended to include more than a very restricted number of people (ie beyond the 'need to know'); and
- when the board (a) becomes aware of discussions between a potential offeror and persons owning shares carrying 30 per cent or more of the voting rights or (b) is seeking a potential offeror and
  — the company is the subject of speculation about a possible offer or there is undue movement in its share price or in the volume of share turnover; or
  — the number of potential persons approached is about to be increased to include more than a very restricted number of people.

As regards the last of the above points, a potential offeror will sometimes seek **7.106** irrevocable commitments from certain shareholders prior to approaching the board of the target for a number of reasons. The decision to make an offer may in some cases depend on the success in obtaining such commitments. In general, obtaining irrevocable commitments is done to improve the chances of success of the offer, to give the offeror a 'running head start' in its bid to acquire control of the company. If irrevocable commitments can be obtained from sufficiently important shareholders, or in respect of a sufficient number of

---

[66] Rule 3.2.

shares, this may lend to the offer when made a certain sense of it being a *fait accompli*.

Talks announcements

7.107 The need to make an announcement may necessitate comment on whether or not any talks are taking place. Such announcements need to be factually correct at the time of making the announcement. If an announcement states that no talks are taking place, the Executive will examine the circumstances of the announcement very closely if an offer subsequently emerges.

Undue movement

7.108 The Takeovers Code clarifies that there is no set figure for determining what constitutes an 'undue movement in share price or volume'. Rather, it is to be considered in light of all the relevant facts. The following non-exhaustive list of factors may be considered:[67]

- general market and sector movements;
- information relating to the company;
- trading activity in the company's securities; and
- the time period over which the price or volume movement has occurred.

As ever, in case of doubt the Executive should be consulted.

Suspension

7.109 When an announcement is imminent, the offeror or offeree responsible for the announcement must inform the Executive and the SEHK. The Takeovers Code requires that 'if there is any possibility that an uninformed market for shares of the offeror or the offeree company could develop prior to publication of the announcement, serious consideration should be given to requesting a suspension of trading in such shares pending publication of the announcement'.[68] This requirement again reflects the importance of preserving the integrity of the marketplace.

Potential vendor

7.110 Potential sellers of shares may also have announcement obligations. If the potential offeror is in discussions with persons owning shares carrying 30 per cent or more of the voting rights, and (a) the company is the subject of speculation about a possible offer or there is undue movement in its share price or in the

---

[67] Rule 3, Note 2.   [68] Rule 3.4.

volume of share turnover, and (b) there are reasonable grounds for concluding that it is the potential vendor's actions (whether through inadequate security or otherwise) which have led to the situation, then the potential vendor must make an announcement.[69]

Possible offer

Any of the above situations may give rise to the announcement of a possible offer. In that case, the person making the announcement (ie the potential target or offeror) will be obliged[70] to keep the market updated with one or more further announcements: **7.111**

- when a firm intention to make an offer is made;
- when talks are terminated and the potential offeror decides not to proceed; or
- in the absence of either of the foregoing within one month of the first announcement, a further announcement as to progress of the talks or possible offer. This obligation continues monthly.

The announcement of a possible offer does not necessarily involve naming the potential offeror, although the Executive will normally require it to be named where its identity is likely to be price sensitive.

Pre-conditional possible offer

Where a potential offeror intends to announce a pre-conditional possible offer it must first consult with the Executive. The concern is that such announcements may lead to confusion in the market as to the circumstances in which an offer may be made. Accordingly, it will be necessary to state whether the pre-conditions are waivable. If the announcement states that the offer will proceed if the pre-conditions are satisfied or waived, then the announcement will need to comply with the requirements as apply to the announcement of a firm offer. In order to keep shareholders and the market informed, it will be necessary to make an announcement once the pre-conditions to making an offer have been satisfied or waived.[71] In contrast to a firm offer, the Executive may permit the conditions attaching to the pre-conditional offer to be subjective in nature.   **7.112**

(2) The offer announcement

Rule 3.5 states that 'The announcement of a firm intention to make an offer should be made only when an offeror has every reason to believe that it can and will continue to be able to implement the offer.' As already mentioned, the   **7.113**

---

[69] Rule 3.3.   [70] Rule 3.7.   [71] See Rule 3.5, Note 6.

making of a firm offer announcement should be regarded by the offeror as a point of no return. It needs to carefully review its ability to implement the offer and in that regard consider many things including bid strategy and structure, financial, and regulatory matters. Before making a firm offer it should also consider its other alternatives, such as a pre-conditional possible offer. It will also need to consider what to include in the offer, especially the need for any pre-conditions or conditions.

7.114 If an offer is made it needs to be announced (sometimes referred to as a 'Rule 3.5 announcement') and contain, amongst other things, the following information:

- the terms of the offer;
- the identity of the offeror. A corporate offeror must also state the identity of its ultimate controlling shareholder and its ultimate parent company;
- details of any existing holding by the offeror of voting rights and rights over shares in the offeree;
- details of any outstanding derivative in respect of securities in the offeree company entered into by the offeror;
- all conditions (including normal conditions relating to acceptance, listing, and increase of capital) to which the offer is subject; and
- details of any arrangement (whether by way of option, indemnity, or otherwise) in relation to shares of the offeror or the offeree company and which might be material to the offer.

Where relevant, these requirements also captures the holdings or interests of any person acting in concert with the offeror.

7.115 As already mentioned, a central interest of the Takeovers Code is to create transparency of the offeror's situation in order that shareholders are fully informed. Obviously, the offeror's current interest in the share capital of the target is of considerable interest. Such interest may take a number of forms.

7.116 As discussed above, the concept of 'control' in the Takeovers Code is about the holding or control of voting rights. The offeror may have acquired voting rights without necessarily owning shares. Voting rights may be segregated from legal ownership in a number of ways. For example, a financial institution taking security over shares in connection with a lending arrangement may acquire the right to vote them (such as when the loan is in default), or parties (such as a potential offeror) may enter into a voting trust to acquire voting rights from a shareholder. Accordingly, any such interest will need to be disclosed. For the same reason, any irrevocable commitments will also need to be disclosed. Additionally, the ownership of convertible securities, warrants, or options may also give rise to control over votes (when such rights are exercised) and so ownership of these also need to be disclosed. The announcement will also need to include the financial adviser's confirmation as to sufficiency of the offeror's resources to implement the offer.

Financial adviser

The financial adviser is required to confirm the sufficiency of the offeror's **7.117** financial resources. Moreover, it is required to 'observe the highest standard of care to satisfy itself of the adequacy of resources, including performance [by the financial adviser] of due diligence'.[72] This is a more specific reflection of the general requirement placed upon the financial adviser 'to use all reasonable efforts . . . to ensure that their clients understand, and abide by' the requirements of the Takeovers Code.[73] The SFC requires a financial adviser to observe 'high standards of professionalism imposed by the [Takeovers Codes]'[74] and this undoubtedly extends to a high standard of care in satisfying itself as to the adequacy of an offeror's financial resources. However, there is doubt as to what constitutes adequacy; for example, it is arguable that this would require the use of fully funded segregated accounts. Second, how extensive is the due diligence into the affairs of the offeror to be? Third, the failure of the adviser to act responsibly and take all reasonable steps in this context may render it liable to providing the financial resources to the offeror to complete the bid.

As already mentioned, the offeror prior to making an offer must have 'every **7.118** reason to believe that it can and will continue to be able to implement the offer'. However, Rule 3.5 states that: 'Responsibility in this connection also rests on the financial adviser to the offeror.' This statement could be interpreted as requiring an implied endorsement from the financial adviser that the offeror can and will implement the offer, and would place far greater responsibility on the financial adviser beyond a mere confirmation of the offeror's financial resources. Given that the corporate decision making of the offeror is outside the control of the financial adviser, it is perhaps more likely to be regarded as sufficient that the financial adviser is not aware, having made reasonable enquiries, of any reason that may lead to the offeror not implementing the offer.

(3) Announcements during the course of an offer

Further announcements will be made during the course of the offer with a **7.119** view to keeping shareholders and the market informed as to progress. Such announcements would, amongst other things, include:

---

[72] Rule 3.5, Note 3.   [73] Introduction, para 1.7.
[74] *Goldwyn Capital Ltd. v The SFC* [1997] HKLRD 955 per Keith, J.

- when any response to an offer document is sent to shareholders;
- any extension to the offer period or revision of the terms of the offer;
- when the conditions of the offer are satisfied or waived; and
- when it is intended to carry out a compulsory acquisition of minority shareholders because the requisite number of shareholders have accepted the offer.

Standard and responsibility

7.120   'Each document issued or statement made in relation to an offer or possible offer or during an offer period must, as is the case with a prospectus, satisfy the highest standards of accuracy and the information given must be adequately and fairly presented.'[75] This rule expands more specifically on General Principle 5.

7.121   During the course of an offer, control therefore must be exercised over statements made.[76] For example, statements to the effect that the offer will or will not be improved or extended will normally have the effect of binding the offeror to those statements even if it subsequently changes its mind on these matters. This is in keeping with the principle that statements made must be certain and not mislead the market. Moreover, in interviews or discussions with the media, financial advisers must avoid making statements on sensitive areas such as future profits and prospects, asset values, and the likelihood of a revised offer.[77]

7.122   Documents issued by the offeror or offeree must state that the directors accept full responsibility, jointly and severally, for the accuracy and completeness of the information contained in the document.[78] In this regard, the rule specifically requires that all reasonable enquiries have been made and that the statements are made after due and careful consideration.

(4) No intention announcements

7.123   Under certain circumstances a person may find it necessary to make an announcement denying any intention to make an offer for a particular target company. In such cases, such person will not normally be permitted to make an offer within the next six months.[79] The exception to this is where there has been a material change in circumstances, or where the 'no intention' announcement specified an event which would permit an offer to be made and such event has occurred.

---

[75] Rule 9.1.   [76] Rule 18.   [77] Note 1 to Rule 9.1.   [78] Rule 9.3.
[79] Rule 31.1(c).

F. Involvement of Other Parties

An array of different parties will be involved in a takeover in different capacities **7.124**
and in different relationships with the offeror and offeree. The nature of their
relationship or involvement will determine their obligations under the Takeovers Code. Of particular interest are those who cooperate with the offeror in
relation to the takeover bid, the board of the offeree company, and related
service providers.

(1) Acting in concert

One of the most frequently sensitive and considered topics in the Takeovers **7.125**
Code is the concept of 'acting in concert' which the Takeovers Code defines as
meaning 'persons who, pursuant to an agreement or understanding (whether
formal or informal), actively cooperate to obtain or consolidate control of
a company through the acquisition by any of them of voting rights of the
company'. The concert party group is recognized in effect as a single person.[80]

The definition of the term provides a list of persons who will be presumed to be **7.126**
acting in concert, such as a company with its directors and its parent and
subsidiaries, an adviser with its client, members of a consortium formed for
the purposes of the bid, and individuals with their close relatives.[81] It should
be noted that these are rebuttable presumptions with the burden of proving
otherwise falling on the person allegedly a concert party.

The concert party concept is a question of fact and, as such, its composition will **7.127**
not necessarily be stagnant over time. It may change, and new concert parties
may be formed as members to a concert party act, for example in acquiring or
disposing of voting rights within or outside the original concert party. However,
it should be noted that once a concert party has been formed, 'clear evidence'
must be presented that it has broken up before the Executive will regard it as
such.[82] For example, where a vehicle has been established in connection with the
purposes of a concert party, the subsequent liquidation of such vehicle and
distribution of the shares to the members of the concert party is not of itself
sufficient to establish 'clear evidence' of the breakup of the concert party.[83]

The concert party concept is a very important one for a number of reasons **7.128**
throughout the Takeovers Code, in particular as regards mandatory offers and

---

[80] See Rule 26.1, Note 6.
[81] ie a person's spouse, de facto spouse, children, parents, and siblings.
[82] Note 3 to definition of 'acting in concert'.   [83] Panel decision of Forever Gain, 1998.

the creeper provisions, dealing, and disclosure requirements. The concert party concept means that the acts of one member of the concert party may affect the obligations of the other parties to the concert party. This may include anything from the triggering of a mandatory bid obligation to the minimum price at which an offer may be made.

7.129 Timing may be a critical element in determining whether a mandatory bid obligation is imposed.[84] For example, if party A and party B both own 20 per cent of the voting control of a company, although their forming of a concert party will result in the collective holding going through the 30 per cent threshold no bid obligation would be imposed. On the other hand, it would be imposed if they formed their concert party and either of them subsequently acquired shares which took their collective control through the 30 per cent threshold or through the 2 per cent annual creeper. On the example given, if party A acquired a 5 per cent voting block after the concert party came together, a mandatory bid obligation would arise. Persons who find themselves in a Rule 26 situation therefore need to consider carefully who are their concert parties (whether presumed or in fact) and by what means the actions of those others are to be controlled, failing which how their own obligations under Rule 26 may be affected. The risk is that any one principal member of the concert party may become subject to the obligation to extend on offer even if that person did not themselves take action to bring about that consequence.[85] Rule 26.1 provides a number of clarifications as to how the concert party concept is applied in this regard.

Fund managers

7.130 Fund managers are a frequent source of concern as regards the application of concert party rules, both as regards the shareholdings and dealing activities of its discretionary clients, and as regards its connectedness with the offer. Fund managers are regarded as acting in concert with their discretionary clients as regards the relevant investment accounts.[86] This gives rise to obvious business and legal issues for the fund manager where either (i) the fund manager's client holds or wishes to deal in the shares of a company involved in transaction subject to the Takeovers Code or is itself connected with the offeror or offeree, or (ii) the fund manager itself is a member of the same group of companies as the financial adviser to the offeror or offeree, or a member of the same group as the offeree or offeror.

---

[84] See Rule 26.1, Notes.   [85] Rule 36.
[86] The key factor determining whether an arrangement is discretionary is that the fund manager is able to make investment (buy/sell) decisions on behalf of a client within the scope of authority granted. While in general the fund manager does not take instructions from the client, this is not necessarily precluded.

First, for the purposes of the Code, a fund manager is to be regarded as the **7.131** controller of all the shares comprised in all the discretionary accounts managed by it.[87] For example, if there were 10 discretionary accounts holding shares in the offeree, and each account holding represented a 0.5 per cent stake in the offeree, the fund manager would be regarded as controlling a 5 per cent voting interest in the offeree.

Second, in the absence of anything else, where fund managers are connected **7.132** with the offeree, the offeror, or the financial advisers, they will be regarded as acting in concert with the offeree or offeror, as applicable.

However, fund managers[88] may apply to the Executive to be regarded as an **7.133** 'exempt fund manager'.[89] In broad terms, this classification enables a fund manager to continue its business as usual subject to on-going disclosure requirements and provided the fund manager is not itself connected with the offeror or offeree. This facilitates fund managers which are part of a financial services group to continue their business notwithstanding that they may be part of the same group of companies as a financial adviser involved in the offer.

(2) *Associates and associated companies*

The concept of associate and associated company is important for a number of **7.134** reasons in the Takeovers Code, primarily because it will determine the ambit of what persons are affected by the various rules and restrictions in the Takeovers Code, in particular concerning concert party issues and share dealing restrictions.

Associates include all persons acting in concert with each other but also persons **7.135** who have an interest of whatever nature in the outcome of an offer. This covers a wide range of persons including directors, professional advisers, and persons with material trading arrangements with either the target or offeror.

One company will be considered an associated company of the other if one **7.136** owns or controls 20 per cent of the voting rights of the other or if they are both associated companies of the same company. The presumption of acting in concert arises in relation to associated companies.

(3) *Responsibilities of directors and others*

The directors of the target company, the offeror, and their financial advisers are **7.137** key players in any takeover bid and have various responsibilities under the

---

[87] Rule 22, Note 10.
[88] The statements made about fund managers apply also to persons to trade as principal in securities.
[89] Takeover Code, Definitions, Rules 22 & 21.6.

Takeovers Code. Perhaps the first and most primary obligation imposed, and one which applies to all persons involved in a takeover situation, is that of confidentiality—prior to an announcement being made it is clearly of considerable importance to maintaining an orderly and fairly informed market that price-sensitive information is kept confidential on a need-to-know basis. The Note to Rule 1.4 recommends financial and legal advisers to specifically draw the attention of their clients to this requirement.

Offeree board

7.138 The Board of the offeree becomes subject to Takeovers Code obligations as soon as it receives an offer or is approached.

Announcements

7.139 At various stages of a transaction subject to the Takeovers Code, the Board will need to consider what obligations it may have as regards informing the market by way of an announcement.

Independent advice

7.140 As mentioned, one of the core concerns of the Takeovers Code is to afford fair treatment for shareholders who are affected by takeovers and mergers. Accordingly, upon receiving an approach, the Board must establish an independent committee of the Board and appoint as soon as reasonably practicable (and announce such appointment) an independent financial adviser who will be responsible for advising the independent board committee.[90] The approval of the independent board committee must be obtained prior to any such appointment. The independent board committee should comprise non-executive directors with no interest in the offer (other than as shareholder of the offeree)[91] and is charged with executing the responsibilities of the Board throughout the offer.

7.141 The primary concern of each of the independent board committee and the independent financial adviser is whether the offer is or is not fair and reasonable and as to acceptance and voting. Regard is to be had to the interests of the independent shareholders, ie those who do not have an interest in the transaction beyond their shareholding in the target.[92] The advice of the independent financial adviser (which must be given in writing and supported by reasons),

---

[90] Rule 2.1.

[91] In some cases it is not possible to form such an independent board committee and in these circumstances responsibility for representing the interests of the independent shareholders resides primarily with the independent financial adviser. See Rule 2.8.

[92] Rule 2.7.

together with the recommendation of the independent board committee (regarding acceptance of the offer), is required to be provided to shareholders by including it in the offeree board circular.[93]

It is central to its function that the adviser is independent and, accordingly, such **7.142** adviser may not be a part of the offeree's or offeror's group of companies or have had a 'significant connection' with either of them for the prior two years.[94] For example, an adviser related to the offeree's auditor would be unacceptable. The Takeovers Code not only excludes advisers who have an actual or potential conflict of interest but also considers it sufficient to exclude advisers where there is merely a perception of conflict. If the independent financial adviser is aware of anything which may impact on its independence it should consult the Executive.[95]

Schedule VII to the Takeovers Code provides some further guidance on the **7.143** issue of independence. In cases of multi-service financial organizations where one part of the organization may have material confidential information in relation to the offeror or offeree, the Takeovers Code broadly rejects using the means of information barriers (ie 'Chinese walls') to solve the problem and enable the adviser to act independently. For large organizations, this may pose considerable difficulties, to assess not only the potential conflict position but also whether information is material and confidential and gives rise to a conflict. As regards the former difficulty, the ability of a multi-service organization to be informed in this regard is in part a function of its compliance sophistication. As regards the latter difficulty, what constitutes information giving rise to a conflict is open to some debate.

Service providers

The Takeovers Code makes it clear that the financial and legal advisers involved **7.144** in an offer situation have an important role to play.[96] In particular,

> it is part of their responsibility to use all reasonable efforts . . . to ensure that their clients understand, and abide by, the requirements of the [Takeovers Code], and to cooperate to that end by responding to inquiries from the Executive, the Panel or the Takeovers Appeal Committee.[97]

Because of both the central role advisers play, and the nature of financial institutions, law firms and accounting firms in having more than one client, the Takeovers Code lays down in Schedule VII a set of guidelines for advisers as regards dealing with conflicts of interest—discussed above.

---

[93] Rule 2.1.   [94] Rule 2.6.   [95] See Panel decision of Lolliman, 1993.
[96] Takeovers Code, Introduction, para 1.7.   [97] ibid.

G. Offer Price, Dealing, and Disclosure

7.145 Central considerations in any takeover concern the offer price and related dealing and disclosure requirements.

(1) Offer price

7.146 In examining the offer price, two questions are: what type of consideration is permitted to be offered and at what value level? The answer to these questions will in part depend on whether the offer is a voluntary or mandatory offer.

Type of consideration

7.147 Mandatory offers must include a cash offer. On the other hand, the nature of consideration payable in connection with a voluntary offer is at the discretion of the offeror, unless a cash offer is required. In Hong Kong cash only are most typical, but occasionally cash and share offers do take place.[98]

Value of consideration

7.148 As a starting proposition, it may be said that an offeror may set whatever value on consideration they may choose. In a cash offer, that means any price may be offered for shares, the price level being determined purely by commercial and market forces. However, this will rarely be the case in practice.[98a]

7.149 First, in the case of mandatory offers, a minimum offer price for the cash offer will be determined by the highest price[99] at which the offeror or any of its concert parties purchased shares (or voting rights) in the target in the six months prior to the commencement of the offer period.[100] In certain cases, the mandatory bid obligation may have been triggered by the acquisition of voting rights for consideration other than cash.[101] In these cases, the non-cash consideration will need to be valued. The Executive does have the power, upon application, to adjust the price in consideration of a number of factors including, for example, where the circumstances of an earlier transaction dictated an unusually high price.

---

[98] The most notable cash and share offer of recent times being the US$ 36 bn merger of PCCW and Cable and Wireless HKT in 2000.

[98a] Note also that voluntary offers may not normally be made at a price 'substantially below the market price'—see para 7.60 above.

[99] Price paid will exclude stamp duty and dealing costs.   [100] Rule 26.3.

[101] ie no shares have been purchased but the offeror acquired control of the underlying voting rights, eg by a voting trust arrangement whereby the shareholder agrees to vote in the manner directed by the offeror.

Second, in the case of a voluntary offer, where the offeror or any of its concert **7.150** parties have in the three-month period prior to commencement of the offer period, or in the subsequent period prior to the Rule 3.5 announcement being made, purchased shares, the offer to shareholders must be on terms not less favourable than the best terms paid in that period.[102] This does not mean that if the highest price paid for shares was, say, HK$ 7.80 (US$ 1.00) that a cash offer must be made at not less than HK$ 7.80. However, it does mean that the offer must have a value at least as high as the highest relevant purchase price. How- ever, the Executive will look closely at offers where the consideration is shares, both as to the presence of any undue movements in the price of the consider- ation shares and as to the size of the market in the shares being offered. Where shares are offered as consideration, they must be either listed or the subject of an application for listing.

It should be noted that the Executive may for these purposes look beyond the **7.151** three-month period where it is necessary to give effect to General Principle 1 concerning equal and fair treatment of shareholders. This might be required where the share purchases giving rise to the reference value have been made with persons closely connected with the offeror or offeree.

Finally, irrespective of whether an offer is mandatory or voluntary, the offer **7.152** price will need to be adjusted where the offeror or any of its concert parties purchase shares in the offeree at above the current offer price. The offer price will have to be adjusted to the new highest price paid.

(2) Dealing and disclosure

Before discussing the requirements of the Takeovers Code it is worth briefly **7.153** noting certain requirements at law, namely, those concerning insider dealing and those concerning notification of interests in shares of listed companies.

Insider dealing

Where a person has knowledge of a contemplated takeover offer (or that a **7.154** takeover offer is no longer contemplated), it may constitute market mis- conduct[103] or constitute an offence[104] for such person to deal, counsel, or procure another person to deal in that company's securities, or to disclose such informa- tion to another person believing that such other person may deal, counsel, or procure a third person to deal. These issues are dealt with in Chapter 8.

In the context of a transaction subject to the Takeovers Code, it is not only the **7.155** shares in the offeree which are at issue here—knowledge of a takeover offer may

---

[102] Rule 24.   [103] SFO s 270.   [104] SFO s 291.

also constitute price-sensitive information in respect of shares of the offeror or any listed parent or subsidiary of either of them. However, any dealing etc which is conducted for the purposes of the takeover will not constitute insider dealing and this will include dealings undertaken by the offeror, its concert parties, and agents. The risk issues therefore lay with persons who have relevant information and deal, counsel, or procure dealing or pass on relevant information otherwise than for the purposes of the takeover.

Disclosures regime

7.156 As part of the drive to make the market in listed securities more transparent, Part XV of the SFO provides that persons with an interest of 5 per cent or more, and all directors, are subject to disclosure requirements in respect of their interest in shares of the relevant listed company. Changes in the relevant percentage level need to be reported within three business days as will changes in the nature of the interest. Interests in not only shares but also rights, options, and derivatives including those of associated companies are all caught by the provisions of Part XV.

Takeovers Code

7.157 The Takeovers Code extends the considerations required to be made as regards both dealing and disclosure such that certain parties involved in an offer are not only subject to additional disclosure requirements but also to restrictions and additional implications should they deal in securities of the target company. These additional requirements can be broken into three parts, namely, those which apply before, during, and after an offer.

Before an offer

7.158 The Takeovers Code in effect reiterates the restrictions on insider dealing and draws to one's attention a number of possible situations in this regard:[105]

- that information selectively provided by the target to the offeror, for example during initial discussions or a preliminary due diligence exercise, may constitute price-sensitive information;
- where a 'talks announcement' has been made and the offeror subsequently decides not to proceed, no dealing may be entered into until a clarification announcement has been made; and
- financial advisers to the target may not deal in the shares of the offeree, extend

---

[105] Rule 21.1.4.

finance to any person for such purpose, or enter into any other arrangement with any person which may affect their interest in the shares of the offeree.

This will not prohibit the offeror from dealing. However, persons acting in concert with the offeror may not deal unless there are 'no-profit' arrangements in place. **7.159**

Finally, although not a restriction but a consequence, dealings before the offer is made may set a bottom limit to the value of the consideration which may accompany any offer. **7.160**

During an offer

The offeror and its concert parties are restricted from selling securities during this period[106] although this does not apply to a sale by an offeror to members of its concert party provided the offeror retains both the risks and the benefits of the shareholding. **7.161**

Details of all dealings by the offeror or offeree or their associates in relevant securities[107] must be disclosed to the Executive, the Exchange, and to the public press prior to 10 a.m. on the business day following the transaction. **7.162**

However, where the consideration payable for an offer is securities of the offeror or its concert parties, the offeror and its concert parties are prohibited from dealing in those securities during the offer period.[108] **7.163**

After an offer

If an offer has been made and has not been successfully completed,[109] the offeror and its concert parties are prohibited from making another offer for a period of 12 months.[110] This includes not being permitted to acquire voting rights which would lead to it having a mandatory bid obligation under rule 26.[111] **7.164**

In addition, if the concert party involved in the unsuccessful offer together hold more than 50 per cent of the voting rights of the target, each person in the concert party will be prohibited, for a period of six months, from buying any shares in the company at a price higher than the offer price comprised in the unsuccessful offer. However, this does not apply to a subscription for newly issued shares. **7.165**

---

[106] Although they may do so in connection with a voluntary offer if the Executive consents, 24 hours prior public notice of such sale has been given, and the sales are at a price not less than the value of the offer. Any such sale then prohibits the seller from subsequently buying shares. Rule 21.2.

[107] Relevant securities include shares in the offeree or offeror.   [108] Rule 23.1.

[109] ie it has not gone unconditional, has lapsed or been withdrawn.   [110] Rule 31.

[111] The same will apply in respect of persons who have announced a possible offer although the period is shortened to six months.

Directors' Model Code

7.166 Directors of companies listed on the SEHK are also required to comply with the requirements of the 'Model Code for Securities Transactions by Directors of Listed Issuers' (Model Code)[112] or the company's own version of a directors dealing code provided such code is no less exacting than that set out in the Model Code. However, in the context of a takeover situation, the Model Code does not really add any additional restrictions on directors dealing although additional internal procedures will need to be followed.[113] Although the Model Code does make clear that where one director becomes aware of undisclosed price-sensitive information (eg because he is engaged in takeover talks) he should caution other directors that there is unpublished price-sensitive information in play and such other directors should not deal in the company's securities until such time as proper disclosure of the relevant information is made.

Fund managers

7.167 As already discussed a fund manager is regarded as acting in concert with its discretionary clients. Any relevant dealing for discretionary clients is subject to the same disclosure requirements during an offer as described above. However, if the relevant dealing is done by an exempt fund manager, disclosure may be made on a private basis to the Executive only provided the fund manager does not control 5 per cent or more of the shares of the offeree or offeror.[114] Whether or not the fund manager is exempt, any such dealings for non-discretionary clients will also need to be disclosed on a private basis to the Executive only.[115]

(3) Special deals

7.168 Finally, it should be noted that for the period commencing from the time an offer is 'reasonably in contemplation'[116] and ending six months after the close of an offer, the offeror and its concert parties may not enter into any transaction concerning the shares of the offeree which would involve conditions more favourable than those extended to all shareholders. However, some arrangements, such as fees paid to offeree shareholders, and arrangements made with the shareholding management of the offeree to continue their services after a successful offer will not necessarily violate this general prohibition, although the

---

[112] Set out in LR appendix 10.

[113] Such as the need to notify the Chairman or his nominated director and obtain a written consent prior to any dealing.

[114] All the account holdings of the manager will for this purpose in effect need to be regarded together, as though owned by a single person. Cf Rule 22.3; see also Rule 22.3, Note 10.

[115] Rule 22.2.   [116] Rule 25.

structure and value of such arrangements will undoubtedly be examined closely by the Executive.

H. Conclusion

An offer may arise in a number of different commercial contexts and these com- **7.169** mercial contexts are not always the same in different markets and business settings. Accordingly, a code regulating mergers and acquisitions must apply and be sensitive to the particular characteristics of the market in which it is to be applied.

Some commercial contexts are fairly universal. An offer may arise for strategic **7.170** reasons, for instance to integrate vertically (eg consolidation across the raw materials, production, and marketing aspects of a business) or horizontally (eg as a means of removing a competitor in the market through consolidation); or because the target's assets are desirable for other strategic reasons. An offer may also arise for more directly financial purposes (eg the target holds undeveloped resources—in Hong Kong these may comprise real estate assets which the target company has been unable to develop, eg through lack of resources); the target's share price is trading at a substantial discount to the net asset value (post acquisition, the acquirer then seeks to realize the undervalue); or because the company has a large cash reserve (in effect undervalued). Finally, as mentioned, listed companies which are inactively traded may also become the target for a company seeking a backdoor listing. This latter means has often been used by Mainland companies seeking quick access to the Hong Kong market.

While the Takeovers Code in general closely follows the approach taken in the **7.171** London Takeovers Code, peculiarities of the Hong Kong market require different rules and practices. One of the most distinctive characteristics of the market in Hong Kong is the predominance of family controlled companies and extensive cross holdings. Partly for this reason and partly due to cultural reasons, the friendly offer is predominant and hostile or competing offers are uncommon. These characteristics affect the roles of each of the parties involved and the way in which takeover activity is conducted in Hong Kong. It also means closer attention must be had to the role of the independent committee of the board, the position of salaried directors, and the role of the independent financial adviser.

In developing the code, sometimes the approach of the SFC is to adopt a **7.172** 'wait-and-see' approach, waiting for developments to be implemented and tested in London before making appropriate changes in Hong Kong's code. The bridge sometimes used in this regard is that the Executive may adopt practices which may to some extent reflect the approach taken in London but not codify such practices until some time later. This approach clearly has its merits and its risks.

7.173   An example of this can be seen in relation to the stock borrowing and lending market, which is quite active in certain well-traded stocks in Hong Kong. Although such transactions involve the absolute transfer of legal title and voting rights, the Executive in practice treats the lent stock as continuing to be controlled by the stock lender (as the borrower (i) normally borrows stock for the purposes of covering a short position, and (ii) is under a contractual obligation to return the stock to the lender). The Executive does not regard the stock lender and stock borrower as acting in concert and the SFC has proposed a clarification to the definition of acting in concert to clarify that when such transactions are carried out in the ordinary course of the stock lender's business this would not normally result in the stock lender being regarded as acting in concert with the stock borrower.[117] However, the absence of any clear codification of these practices leave a number of unresolved questions, such as the scope of who is to be regarded a stock lender, when is a stock lending transaction considered to be undertaken in the 'ordinary course of business', and under what circumstances (if any) should the Takeovers Code recognize the transfer of legal title in such transactions. The London Takeovers Panel has recently consulted on this matter[118] and the SFC will be engaging in further consultations on this topic before codifying its current practices.

7.174   While the possibility of competition policy reviews have been a factor in London for quite some time, the concept of competition control is in its fledgling stages in Hong Kong. In this context, the Executive has recently consulted the market concerning an appropriate framework for dealing with regulatory reviews by the Telecommunications Authority (TA).[119] The powers of the TA in this regard are relatively new and require it to consider whether a change in control of a carrier licensee would have the effect of substantially lessening competition in the telecommunications market and, if there is such a change, whether the benefit to the public outweighs any detriment to the public.[120] Such reviews may disrupt the proper progress of the offer timetable as obtaining TA approval (or rejection) of the change of control may involve lengthy delays. In this regard, the approach in Hong Kong differs from that in London. While London has adopted the concept of a 'competition reference period' which may lead to the lapse of the offer, the SFC considers such an approach to be unnecessary in the Hong Kong context on the basis that hostile offers are uncommon here. Instead,

---

[117] Consultation Conclusions on a Review of the Codes on Takeovers and Mergers and Share Repurchases, SFC, August 2005.
[118] See the London Takeover Panel's consultation paper on market issues (PCP 2004/3) and the response paper (RS 2004/3).
[119] ie where the proposed change in control of the target requires the approval of the TA, eg target is a telecom company regulated by the TA.
[120] Section 7P of the Telecommunications Ordinance (Cap. 106).

the approach of the Executive is that if the TA's enquiries are likely to exceed more than three months[121] after posting the offer document, the Executive should be consulted and it would normally be prepared to consent to the offer lapsing, and if it did consent, which provisions of the Takeovers Code would continue to apply. Further clarifications to the Takeovers Code are likely to be made on this issue in due course.

Yet another example of the particular situation of the Hong Kong context con- **7.175** cerns offerors wishing to discuss a possible offer with persons not involved in the offer. As already mentioned, where an offeror is seeking to gather irrevocable commitments it will be required to consult with the Executive. Before an announcement has been issued an offeror may approach only 'a very restricted number of sophisticated investors who have a controlling shareholding'.[122] There is a regulatory balance to be reached here, between preventing the unequal dissemination of price sensitive information[123] (as a result of too many share-holders being approached) and not unduly fettering the legitimate activities of the potential offeror in determining whether it is in a position to make an offer. In Hong Kong the balance may be more difficult to achieve as family controlled shareholders, cross shareholdings, and to some extent the culture of the city tend to encourage an unwanted spread of information. In view of these difficulties in this market, the Executive does have a discretion to allow particular shareholders to be contacted, although it will require strong reasons as to why such contact cannot be made after the offer has been announced. In some recent privatiza-tions, it has been the practice of the Executive to permit the offeror to approach a very restricted number of sophisticated investors who in aggregate held more than 10 per cent (but less than a controlling interest) of the disinterested shares. A codification of this practice is expected to be made in due course.

The operation of the Takeovers Code is well supported by the marketplace and **7.176** is in general complied with. The SFC engages in regular consultations with the market which normally lead to positive developments in the code. The independence and objectivity of the Executive and the Panel are in general respected, an essential element if the role of the Executive in exercising its discretion and in issuing rulings and interpretations is to be successfully carried out. Moreover, the Executive and Panel are active in enforcing the Takeovers Code and applying measured sanctions where appropriate.

---

[121] The three-month period is related to rule 15.4 which specifies that an offeror may not provide any material new information to the market after the 39th day following the posting of the offer document, except with the consent of the Executive.

[122] Note 4 to Rules 3.1, 3.2, and 3.3. [123] See General Principles 3, 5, and 6.

8

REGULATION OF MARKET MISCONDUCT

The integrity and efficiency of a financial market are critical in attracting both **8.01** domestic and overseas participation. While twenty years ago, the necessity of legal measures to protect the integrity of financial markets was much debated, today there is general agreement that financial markets function best in an environment of confidence in their trustworthiness. This consensus is now reflected in various international standards, including those of the International Organization of Securities Commissions (IOSCO). In looking at such issues, there are two typical approaches: disclosure regulation and market conduct regulation. Both of these have been adopted in Hong Kong through the enactment of the Securities and Futures Ordinance (SFO).

Disclosure regulation functions to provide investors with all relevant information **8.02** necessary to take informed investment decisions. Such regulation increases information available in the markets and thereby reduces the scope for misconduct based on deceit or loss of confidence—typically described as 'information asymmetries'. Likewise, disclosure regulation increases the efficiency of financial markets. Disclosure issues are considered in Chapters 3 to 7 and are further considered below. While Hong Kong has taken steps to increase the effectiveness of disclosure regulation through the SFO and other measures, problems remain, especially in regard to enforcement of disclosure by listed companies.

8.03 Market conduct regulation typically focuses on the behaviour of individual market participants, seeking to prohibit common forms of market misconduct and financial fraud. Today it is generally agreed that financial fraud and market manipulation should be prohibited and such prohibitions should be effectively enforced. In the financial markets, how best to outlaw such practices is an art, and not always a matter of objective insight, for the circumstances leading to these illegal activities are often very varied. A sound regulatory framework, however, should cover most of these circumstances. It is a tedious task to regulate market behaviour, as once legal reform becomes enacted, inevitably there will be persons who seek out the means to circumvent the rules. Nonetheless, while these issues have historically not been dealt with appropriately or effectively in Hong Kong, the SFO provides a comprehensive framework addressing these issues. Further, the system developed to address financial fraud and market manipulation is modelled on Australian legislation which in turn codifies US standards. As such, the system should hold no real surprises for those familiar with these systems or similar systems in the European Union and especially the UK.

8.04 Finally, there are certain areas of intersection between disclosure regulation and market conduct regulation, especially in the context of privileged information and its use. In ensuring that the playing field is level for all participants, insiders should not take advantage of the privileged information they possess. As a result, it is now generally agreed that such conduct is both damaging to markets generally (through reduction of confidence and therefore participation) as well as morally reprehensible. Reflecting this general understanding, through the SFO, Hong Kong now has a comprehensive framework addressing insider dealing.

8.05 This chapter first discusses the legal framework regulating market misconduct. Then, it briefly addresses the importance of mandatory disclosure in preventing market misconduct. The remaining parts of this chapter are devoted to insider dealing, market manipulation, and fraud and deception.

A. The Legal Framework Regulating Market Misconduct

8.06 The regulatory framework of finance in Hong Kong has developed on the basis of experiences in a series of crises in the financial industry, as Chapter 1 has shown. The administration and enforcement of ordinances relating to financial markets is vested in, among others, the HKMA, SFC, HKEx, OCI, and MPFA. There is a complicated separation of authority among these agencies, each with their own investigative styles and enforcement priorities. The SFC was established under the Securities and Futures Commission Ordinance (which is now consolidated into the SFO). Its main function is to administer the ordinances regulating financial markets and to take the initiative in reforming the law relating to these markets.[1] It initially had statutory powers under a number of now repealed ordinances, including the Securities Ordinance and the Securities (Insider Dealing) Ordinance. Most of the ordinances relating to financial markets have now been consolidated under the composite SFO, which consolidates ten prior ordinances covering the regulation of financial markets.[2] It also implements new measures for investor protection, requires compliance by the financial industry, seeks to foster a fair and orderly market, and enhances accountability and transparency of the regulator and in the financial markets.[3] The SFO provides a dual system of civil and criminal routes which effectively harmonize and rationalize all types of market misconduct offences.

This section first discusses what constitutes market misconduct. The mental **8.07** state of the person or persons involved is crucial, as ill-intent is the important factor distinguishing market misconduct from genuine trading. The mental element in criminal jurisprudence must therefore be examined. It then discusses the civil and criminal routes in regulating market misconduct under the SFO. The Market Misconduct Tribunal (MMT) created by the SFO is discussed including views which challenge its constitutional legitimacy. In understanding how the SFO is administered and adjudicated, there then follows a discussion of the constitutional framework and constitutionality of the tribunals established under the SFO.

(1) Market misconduct

The SFO specifies six types of market misconduct: insider dealing, false trading, **8.08** price rigging, disclosure of information about prohibited transactions, disclosure of false or misleading information inducing transactions, and stock market manipulation.[4] However, within these categories of activity, the line between legitimate conduct and market misconduct is often blurred. Therefore, the provisions in the SFO should be sufficiently clear and precise to enable market participants to function without fear of breaking the law. Unfortunately,

---

[1] SFO s 5.   [2] SFO s 407(1).
[3] Speech delivered by the Secretary for Financial Services and the Treasury at the Legislative Council meeting on 13 March 2002 (Hong Kong: Financial Services Branch, 2002).
[4] SFO s 245(1).

in many cases, this is not the case. Market misconduct is often concerned with the intentional creation of artificial or fictitious prices of securities and futures. Whether the conduct is legitimate or not, very much depends on the intention of the person entering into or carrying out his act. As intention is often difficult to establish, it is necessary to infer mens rea from the facts.[5]

8.09 A characteristic of most market misconduct is the creation of an artificial or fictitious supply or demand for securities or futures contracts, in each case affecting the price which would prevail in the absence of such misconduct. Participants in an efficient market are entitled to assume that the prices of securities and futures reflect all relevant information available in the open market.[6] If that information is tainted because of market manipulation, for example in artificially pushing up the price of a security, then the prevailing market price of the securities and any related derivatives would be affected, whether increased, reduced, or maintained and stabilized. As a result, sellers or purchasers at large of the subject securities and derivatives are misled into otherwise unintended action or inaction, whether by selling, purchasing, or retaining those securities at artificial prices.

8.10 The question in law is then whether or not a person who creates a false market or artificial price must have the intention to meddle with the financial market or the price of securities and futures. In other words, does the investing public need protection from this form of activity regardless of whether the person who enters into or carries out such activity does so intentionally, recklessly, negligently, or without fault?

8.11 Market participants are expected to take precautionary measures not to engage in market misconduct activities. If the public need protection from such activity regardless of what precautionary measures have been taken by the person committing the relevant acts, then the efficiency of the financial markets may suffer as market participants would have to pay the cost of ensuring that their act is free of risk before they carry it out. The SFO nevertheless imposes a duty of care on officers of a corporation, requiring that they take all reasonable measures to ensure that there are proper safeguards to prevent the corporation from perpetrating market misconduct.[7] It is immaterial whether the officer on whom such a duty is imposed has not engaged in market misconduct. Once the

---

[5] *Consultation Document on the Securities and Futures Bill* (Hong Kong: The Government of the Hong Kong Special Administrative Region, April 2000), p 105.
[6] There are different levels of efficiency, including weak-, semi-strong, and strong-form. Reflecting all relevant information is an element of the strong form which financial markets rarely meet. Rather, most markets have been found to reflect the semi-strong form only, under which prices do not reflect insider information.
[7] SFO s 279.

corporation is identified as having engaged in market misconduct that is attributable to a breach of such a duty, then that officer may be made liable under the ordinance.[8] Corporations licensed under the SFO are expected to take reasonable measures to prevent their clients from engaging in market misconduct, which might implicate the licensed corporation in the case of the client committing an act of market misconduct.[9]

In a financial market, all participants are dealing in securities and futures with **8.12** financial gain (or financial preservation) in mind, regardless of specific commercial objectives. They may rely on information that is publicly available or properly obtained, for example, media commentary or research analysis. There is no guarantee that their dealing activities would not affect the forces of supply and demand in the financial market, indeed, dealing activities are an integral part of the flux of supply and demand. Where trading activity does affect the prices of securities, there might be reason to suspect wrongdoing. In the event that the trader is without moral fault, the law should provide proper safeguards to protect a completely innocent trader, for example, with safe harbour defences. The SFO empowers the SFC to make rules prescribing the circumstances in which conduct shall not be regarded as constituting market misconduct after consulting the Financial Secretary.[10] The rationale behind using rules rather than primary legislation in providing safe harbour defences is to make use of the comparative flexibility of rulemaking against a background of rapidly changing financial products and technology.

(2) The mental element in market misconduct

Market manipulation can be carried out in many forms. It may be designed to **8.13** interfere with the forces of supply and demand, to induce trading, or to create artificial or fictitious prices in securities or derivatives.[11] These each create difficulties: legitimate and illegitimate demand may be hardly distinguishable; both parties may be better off in a transaction; and trading in order to effect a price change may not be harmful.[12] Therefore, there is no clear objective standard to help distinguish between manipulative and non-manipulative conduct. In overcoming these difficulties, legislation should provide statutory exceptions to the general rules, for example, through safe harbour provisions.

Academics have proposed that only a subjective test can provide a definition **8.14** for market manipulation, so that the intent of the trader would then be the

---

[8] SFO s 258(1).   [9] ibid.   [10] SFO ss 282 & 306(2).
[11] D Fischel & D Ross, 'Should the Law Prohibit "Manipulation" in Financial Markets?' (1991) 105 *Harv L Rev* 503 at p 507.
[12] ibid, pp 507–9.

determining factor.[13] Accordingly, market manipulation occurs when one or more transactions are intended to move security's price in a certain direction; the person carried on the transaction or transactions does not believe that the security's price would move in this direction but for the transaction or transactions; and this person profits from the intended price movement rather than from the possession of valuable information.[14] The person concerned here has improper motives, as he does not believe the price would move in the intended direction. In reality, the manipulative intent is not easily identifiable—it is difficult to read a person's mind. Therefore, the law has to infer manipulative intent from acts that are considered relevant.

8.15 Detecting market misconduct is a tedious task. The SFO expressly states the mental elements required in each provision dealing with market misconduct. In most cases, the prosecution must prove mens rea, that is, a guilty mind, for the commission of the offence. In market misconduct, the mens rea required normally is doing an act intentionally or recklessly. The general principle of criminal law is that a person intends to cause a result if this is the purpose of his act.[15] However, one has to determine the mental state of the defendant, ie their manipulative intent, by inferences drawn from circumstantial evidence.[16] Whether or not the defendant has the intention to commit market misconduct is a question of fact. Among the factors to be considered are the market experience and skill of the defendant, market activity before and after the commission of the alleged conduct, trading volume, exceptional circumstances, and the scheme of operation.

8.16 Reckless conduct arises when the defendant has foreseen that a particular harm might result from his act, for example a false appearance in the price of securities, but is indifferent about preventing such an outcome.[17] Such a risk must be unjustifiable.[18] What is considered to be justifiable depends on the relative value of the activity and the gravity of the harm done.[19] There are authorities suggesting an objective test in foreseeing the particular harm that might result, so that the risk that harm might result need only be obvious to a reasonably prudent person.[20] Accordingly, it is not necessary to prove that the defendant has actually foreseen the particular harm. In any event, whether the prosecution has to prove that the harm is obvious to the defendant or to a reasonable prudent person depends very much upon how the provision in the ordinance is interpreted.

---

[13] Fischel & Ross, above, p 510.   [14] ibid.
[15] J Smith & B Hogan, *Criminal Law* (London: Butterworths, 1992), p 53.
[16] Fischel & Ross, above, p 519.
[17] ibid, p 61.   [18] ibid, p 60.   [19] ibid.   [20] ibid, p 63.

The onus is on the prosecution to prove mens rea. Certain conduct is presumed **8.17** to be manipulative, for example a 'wash sale' where no change takes place in beneficial ownership. The onus is on the trader to rebut the presumption. In some cases, the presumption is made that the trader is liable without fault, or 'strict' liability. These include disclosing information about prohibited transactions in securities.

As manipulative intent is the underlying factor in criminalizing market mis- **8.18** conduct, a person should also be equally guilty of market misconduct for aiding, abetting, counselling, or procuring another person to commit a market misconduct offence. In the insider dealing provisions, a person is also guilty for counselling or procuring another person to engage in insider dealing.[21] In false trading, a person is guilty if he causes false trading.[22] In price rigging and stock market manipulation, a person is liable for entering into or carrying out market manipulation indirectly.[23] In disclosing information about prohibited transactions and false or misleading information, a person is liable for acting in concert with the person committing these offences.[24]

(3) The dual system of market misconduct: Civil and criminal

Market misconduct activities are regulated by Parts XIII and XIV of the SFO **8.19** under a dual system. Under the SFO, all market misconduct activities are criminalized. This is intended to provide adequate deterrence in punishing market misconduct. However, the burden of proof in criminal law is higher than in civil law. By lightening the heavy burden of the prosecution, the ordinance creates a civil route as an alternative to the traditional criminal route in regulating market misconduct activities. In the civil context, there is no civil offence per se, rather, the defendant is tried by the Market Misconduct Tribunal (MMT) (discussed below) under the civil standard of proof.[25] The criminal route under the ordinance, however, is intended to deter people from committing market misconduct as the court may impose harsher penalties. Prior to the enactment of the SFO, only insider dealing was considered as a civil offence and dealt with exclusively by the Insider Dealing Tribunal (IDT, now replaced by the MMT).[26]

Part XIII of the SFO provides a civil route in regulating market misconduct. **8.20** It establishes the MMT to adjudicate market misconduct, which adopts civil procedures. As market misconduct activities often involve sophisticated techniques, it can be difficult to establish the criminal standard of proving beyond

---

[21] SFO ss 270 & 291.   [22] SFO ss 274 & 295.   [23] SFO ss 275, 278, 295, & 299.
[24] SFO ss 276, 277, 297, & 298.   [25] SFO s 252(7).
[26] Now repealed: Securities (Insider Dealing) Ordinance, Cap. 395, Laws of Hong Kong.

all reasonable doubt that an offence has been committed. Therefore, a civil standard of proof is adopted. Part XIV of the SFO provides a criminal route in regulating market misconduct. It requires the criminal standard of proof, which is more rigorous, as theoretically the defendant has the benefit of the doubt. In the civil route, the standard of proof normally is 'on the balance of probabilities'. Accordingly, the penalties available under the civil route are much milder and the MMT may make civil orders but it cannot impose imprisonment. The standard of proof required to determine any question or issue before the MMT is the same standard of proof applicable to civil proceedings in a court of law.[27] The civil system in combating market misconduct has proven to be relatively more successful than the criminal system in the past.

8.21 The provisions in the SFO dealing with civil and criminal offences are generally similar. The government can choose to initiate either summary or indictable proceedings. Under the ordinance, the SFC may report and the Secretary of Justice may notify the occurrence of market misconduct to the Financial Secretary.[28] In any event, the Financial Secretary may independently refer to the Secretary for Justice that a market misconduct offence has or may have been committed.[29] The criminal route is likely to be used when the government considers it has sufficient evidence to prove that a person is guilty of market misconduct beyond all reasonable doubt. Normally, this would mean that there must be a reasonable likelihood to secure a conviction. A prima facie case is not sufficient to initiate a criminal prosecution. The Department of Justice must be satisfied that the public interest requires prosecution for the market misconduct in the circumstances.[30] In ensuring that no-one is charged twice for the same action, or substantially the same cause, the ordinance includes provisions establishing 'no double jeopardy'.[31] The government can only choose to employ either the civil or criminal route, but not both. Once a civil or criminal proceeding is commenced, it cannot be withdrawn to initiate proceedings through the alternative route.

8.22 The MMT may make civil orders against a person found to have engaged in market misconduct.[32] These orders include disqualification orders prohibiting any such person, without leave of the court, from serving as a director, liquidator, receiver, or manager of listed or other specified corporations and 'cold shoulder' orders banning any such person from acquiring, disposing, or dealing in securities for period of up to five years.[33] It may also make disgorgement orders requiring the insider to pay the government an amount not exceeding

---

[27] SFO, s 252(7).   [28] SFO s 252(8).   [29] SFO s 252(10).
[30] Para 9.1, *The Statement of Prosecution Policy and Practice* (Hong Kong: Department of Justice, 2005).
[31] SFO ss 283 & 307.   [32] SFO s 257(1).   [33] SFO s 257(1)(a) & (b).

the amount of profit gained or loss avoided and cost orders reimbursing the expenses incurred by the government and the SFC.[34] The MMT is not empowered to impose high fines as it would then risk its proceedings being considered criminal in nature.[35] Orders of the MMT are enforced through the courts as either summary or indictable offences or through punishment for contempt for failing to comply,[36] and have the same status as an order of the Court of First Instance.[37] However, penalties are much more severe under the criminal route. Both summary and indictable offences carry penalties of three and ten years' imprisonment, respectively, and fines of HK$ 1 million (US$ 128,500) and HK$ 10 million (US$ 1,285,000), respectively.[38]

In addition to their common law rights, the victims of market misconduct **8.23** can sue the wrongdoers in a court of law under the SFO by offering the determination of the MMT or the conviction of the court as evidence. The court may award damages for contravention of the SFO to a party who suffers loss as a result of the contravention whether or not the loss arises from that party having entered into or carried out a transaction or dealing at a price affected by the market misconduct.[39] The court may grant an injunction in addition to or in lieu of awarding damages.[40] However, the liability of the wrongdoer in such civil actions may be too wide. Accordingly, the SFO requires that the court must satisfy itself that it is fair, just, and reasonable for a person to pay compensation in the circumstances.[41] For contravention under the civil route, which has a lower standard of proof, the SFO makes it clear that the wrongdoer must have perpetrated, consented to, or assisted in the committing of the market misconduct.[42] Accordingly, an officer of a corporation who fails to take reasonable measures in preventing market misconduct cannot be held liable under this provision.[43] The plaintiff must also prove that the determination of the MMT or the conviction by the court is relevant to the issue in the lawsuit.[44]

(4) The Market Misconduct Tribunal (MMT)

The MMT was established by the SFO.[45] It is modelled upon the previous IDT, **8.24** which adjudicated insider dealing offences under previous legislation. It has jurisdiction to hear market misconduct cases.[46] Market misconduct under its jurisdiction includes insider dealing, false trading, price rigging, disclosure of information about prohibited transactions, disclosure of false or misleading

---

[34] SFO s 257(1)(d), (e), & (f).   [35] Goyne, above, pp 3–4.
[36] SFO ss 257(1), 258(10), & 261(2)(c).   [37] SFO s 264(1).   [38] SFO s 303.
[39] SFO ss 281 & 305.   [40] SFO ss 281(6) & 305(5).   [41] SFO ss 281(2) & 305(2).
[42] SFO s 281(3).   [43] SFO s 281(1) & (3).   [44] SFO ss 281(7) & 305(6).
[45] SFO s 251.   [46] SFO ss 245 & 252.

information, and stock market manipulation.[47] Under the SFO, the Financial Secretary may institute proceedings before the MMT on market misconduct matters.[48] The MMT has jurisdiction to determine whether any market misconduct has taken place; the identity of any person who has engaged in the market misconduct; and the amount of any resulting profit gained or loss avoided.[49] It is required to observe the hearing rules of natural justice.[50] This provision makes statutory the common law requirement to observe the requirements of natural justice. The ordinance invests the MMT with powers necessary to conduct its proceedings in a judicial manner, including the same powers as the Court of First Instance to punish for contempt.[51] The Chief Justice may make rules regulating the operation of the MMT, including taxing costs, giving notice, and service of documents etc.[52] The Secretary for Justice must appoint a Presenting Officer, who is a legal officer, counsel, or solicitor to conduct the proceedings.[53] The role of the Presenting Officer is to present available evidence, including those requested by the MMT, in enabling the tribunal to reach an informed decision.[54] In reality, the Presenting Officer's role is very much like that of a prosecutor.

8.25 The MMT has more flexibility than a court of law. It has adopted some inquisitorial powers, including the ability to consider evidence which would be non-admissible in court proceedings,[55] and requiring the attendance of any person before it and the production of materials relating to the proceedings,[56] and requiring the person to answer truthfully any question which the MMT considers appropriate.[57] In this regard, the relative success of the previous IDT is partly attributed to its power to consider non-admissible evidence and to direct further investigation. The powers of the MMT were discussed above.

8.26 Each panel of the MMT is chaired by a judge assisted by two lay members.[58] The Basic Law provides that judges must be appointed by the Chief Executive on the recommendation of an independent commission, which must consider the judicial and professional qualities of the candidates.[59] The Chairman of the MMT must be a member of the judiciary appointed by the Chief Executive on the recommendation of the Chief Justice while the lay members are appointed at the sole discretion of the Chief Executive.[60] The Chairman's appointment to the MMT does not affect his salary and tenure.[61] However, the presence of non-judicial members in the tribunal might raise doubts about their independence,

---

[47] SFO s 245(1).   [48] SFO s 252(1).   [49] SFO s 252(3).   [50] SFO s 252(6).
[51] SFO ss 253 & 261.   [52] SFO s 269.   [53] SFO s 251(4) & (5).
[54] SFO sch 9, s 21.   [55] SFO s 253(1)(a).   [56] SFO s 253(1)(b).
[57] SFO s 253(d).   [58] SFO s 251(3).
[59] Basic Law of the Hong Kong Special Administrative Region, arts 88 & 92.
[60] SFO s 251(3) & sch 9, ss 2 & 4.   [61] SFO ss 251(8)(a) & (9).

as they may be subject to commercial interests and other influences. On the other hand, the judiciary is given a number of privileges under the Basic Law to safeguard its independence, including immunity in the carrying out of their judicial functions[62] and special appointment procedures and removal safeguards.[63] Oddly, the SFO does not have any provision granting immunity to its members in the performance of their functions.

All questions before the MMT are determined by the majority of its members **8.27** except that questions of law are to be determined by its Chairman alone.[64] Collectively, the appointed judge and lay members of the MMT are exercising judicial power. Furthermore, the SFO provides that at any time prior to the hearing by the MMT, both parties may agree to have the hearing conducted by the Chairman alone.[65]

B. Minimizing Market Misconduct through Mandatory Disclosure

The market misconduct provisions under Part XIII and Part XIV of the SFO **8.28** require a sound supporting framework in properly regulating the financial market. In preventing market misconduct, transparency is important. The efficient capital markets hypothesis developed by economists over the past three decades posits that prices in an efficient market should reflect all relevant information.[66] In other words, the price of a security should fully signal all available information.[67] The investing public are entitled to timely and accurate disclosure of price-sensitive information in assessing market risks. This would maintain a level playing field in the financial markets.[68] Mandatory disclosure, of up-to-date trading/shareholding information and of other price-sensitive information, may be employed as the most powerful weapon against market manipulation.[69] In today's era of high technology, this is backed up by state-of-the-art market surveillance and tracking systems.[70] However, technological advancement can also make policing market manipulation more difficult. In

---

[62] Basic Law, art 85. For a discussion of judicial immunity under the *Basic Law*, see Y Ghai, *The Basic Law of Hong Kong* (Hong Kong: Butterworths, 1997), pp 293–5.

[63] Basic Law, arts 88–93.   [64] SFO, sch 9, s 24(c).   [65] SFO, sch 9, s 36.

[66] C Saari, 'The Efficient Capital Market Hypothesis, Economic Theory and the Regulation of the Securities Industry' (1977) 29 *Stanford L Rev* 1031.

[67] ibid, p 1035.

[68] *Overview Guide to the Proposed Securities and Futures Bill* (Hong Kong: Securities and Futures Commission, 5 July 1999), p 14.

[69] G Gilligan, *Regulation of the Financial Services Sector* (London: Kluwer Law International, 1999), p 110.

[70] ibid.

enhancing the disclosure framework in line with international standards, certain mandatory disclosure provisions were enacted into the SFO.[71]

8.29 Part XV of the ordinance provides a regulatory framework for mandatory disclosure by corporate insiders of certain interests in the capital of a company. Although the provisions therein cannot be a panacea for market misconduct, they nevertheless make the commission of market misconduct more difficult. Research has shown that public disclosure of insider information may be an alternative to policing insider dealing as the insider's informational advantage is eliminated.[72] Another advantage of mandatory disclosure is that it deters outsiders from acquiring non-public information and trading as there is less informational advantage.[73] The net effect of mandatory disclosure is improvement in the efficient pricing of securities.[74] As regulating insider dealing is costly, mandatory disclosure is more effective than prosecuting insider dealing. However, there are regulatory costs attached in compliance with the mandatory disclosure provisions.

8.30 In the absence of relevant information, individual investors cannot make informed investment decisions. In minimizing this risk, a level playing field requires that investors should be well informed before taking their investment decisions and should be periodically updated with all relevant developments. The legislative framework, however, is limited, as it can hardly foresee all circumstances. Ultimately, market forces may dictate what information should be disclosed. This may operate in a financial market where investors have significant bargaining power. However, this is seemingly impossible in Hong Kong where, according to a 2004 study, more than half of the investors surveyed relied on transaction volume rather than stock performance to guide their investment decisions, and knew nothing as to corporate governance in corporations in which they invested.[75] However, institutional investors, which have the bargaining power to demand more information from listed corporations, are increasingly important in Hong Kong, though not yet dominant to the same extent as in the US or the UK.[76]

8.31 Legislation regulating market misconduct and criminal law may be effective but not practical in protecting the investing public. In most cases where fraud has been detected, the company concerned was already close to bankruptcy.[77]

---

[71] Gilligan, above, pp 14–15.
[72] M Fishman & K Hagerty, 'Insider trading and the efficiency of stock prices' (1992) *Rand Journal of Economics* 106, p 119.
[73] ibid.   [74] ibid.
[75] E Tsoi, *Understanding Investors in the Hong Kong Listed Securities and Derivative Markets* (Hong Kong: Hong Kong Exchanges and Clearing Limited, 2004), paras 41–2.
[76] ibid, paras 7–8.
[77] J Seligman, *The SEC and the Future of Finance* (New York: Praeger, 1985), pp 240–1.

Investors should expect to be well informed of the operations and efficiency of the companies in which they propose to invest, including the underwriting costs of securities houses, and the remuneration of the directors or senior management. The interests of the ownership and management of a corporation can be in conflict, which is the classic corporate governance problem discussed in Chapter 6. For example, if management receives a stock bonus, it acquires an incentive to inflate the company's earnings.[78] According to one study, transparency will minimize the chance of conflicts of interest, self-dealing, waste, or unfair transactions.[79] This can only be carried out by mandatory disclosure. Studies show that underwriting fees are reduced when underwriters are required to disclose their fees.[80] Listed companies can then compare pricing and investors can decide whether transaction costs are reasonable.

As mandatory disclosure tends to reduce improper activities within a company, **8.32** this would enhance the corporate image and reduce the related risk premium.[81] Consequently, the company's share price will tend to be more stable and the risks of investing in its shares lessened. The 'risk aversion' theory suggests that investors choose investments with the lowest risk.[82] This would contribute to public confidence in the financial markets.[83] Furthermore, mandatory disclosure supports market efficiency by reflecting relevant information about a company in the financial markets[84] and enables financial analysts to make more accurate predictions.[85]

However, some suggest that mandatory disclosure is unnecessary and argue that **8.33** voluntary disclosure is more effective in a free market economy.[86] On this view, companies issuing securities have to compete for investors who would not purchase their shares unless the company voluntarily discloses all relevant information.[87] Theoretically, management may have an interest to avoid disclosing material information which may give rise to liability.[88] The 'signalling' theory suggests that a corporation that is reluctant to provide more information may give the markets an impression that it has financial or operational problems.[89] The attention of financial analysts, who are more interested in firms that voluntarily disclose more information, would result in higher share prices,[90] and this would benefit the company and result in greater compensation for its executives.[91] However, this may not be the case where a company adopts a voluntary regime except where information would be too damaging to release.

---

[78] ibid, p 202.   [79] ibid, pp 233–5.   [80] ibid, p 234.   [81] ibid, p 236.
[82] ibid.   [83] ibid, pp 235–7.   [84] ibid, pp 241–4.
[85] B Rosenberg & J Guy, 'Prediction of Beta from Investment Fundamentals' (May–June 1976) *Financial Analysts Journal*, pp 60–2; Seligman, above, p 244.
[86] Seligman, above, pp 197–8.
[87] ibid.   [88] ibid.   [89] ibid, pp 201–2.   [90] ibid, pp 197–8.   [91] ibid.

8.34 On the other hand, economic costs are attached to disclosure[92] and the value of the information to investors is difficult to ascertain. There is also concern that valuable information of a company issuing securities could be disclosed to competitors,[93] although the 'competitive disadvantage' of the company in disclosing its business information may be compensated by 'reciprocal disclosure' in the industry.[94] However, the situation may be aggravated when the competitors are foreign firms that do not have to provide reciprocal disclosure.[95]

8.35 Ordinary market investors do not have sufficient bargaining power to obtain certain material information to assist their portfolio investment decisions, for example, as to the controlling shareholders of listed companies or the extent of the ownership interests of directors and officers. A mandatory disclosure regime should therefore provide an optimal level of corporate disclosure as part of ensuring a level playing field.[96] The statutory framework requires two types of mandatory disclosure, related to substantial shareholdings and prospectus issuance.[97] The former is regulated by the SFO, whilst the latter is regulated by the Companies Ordinance.[98]

8.36 Part XV of the SFO replaces the now repealed Securities (Disclosure of Interests) Ordinance. Its objective is to provide investors with more comprehensive and better-quality information on a timely basis so that they may make better investment decisions.[99] The intention is to require disclosure of information that can affect the perceived value of the listed companies and securities.[100]

8.37 In Hong Kong, most companies are controlled by small numbers of shareholders and most shares are not actively traded.[101] Therefore, a small percentage of the shares outstanding, being those which are actively traded, may command a high impact on market valuation. However, for a company with a large market capitalization and wide dispersion of share ownership, a small percentage of share capital would not have a significant impact on valuation.[102] Further (and common in the context of Hong Kong), interests in shares may be held in the form of derivatives, to which different rules for disclosure may apply, if at

---

[92] Seligman, above, pp 197–8.
[93] G Foster, 'Externalities and Financial Reporting' (1980) 35:2 *Journal of Finance* 521 at pp 523–4.
[94] ibid.　[95] ibid.　[96] Seligman, above, pp 205–6.
[97] Listed companies are subject to disclosure requirements imposed by the SEHK and these are discussed in Chapter 5.
[98] Cap. 32, Laws of Hong Kong.
[99] *Outline of Part XV of the Securities and Futures Ordinance (Cap. 571)—Disclosure of Interests* (Hong Kong: Securities and Futures Commission, 2003), p 3.
[100] ibid.
[101] *Legislative Council Brief: Regulatory Reform for the Securities and Futures Market* (Hong Kong: Securities and Futures Commission, 2000), p 18.
[102] ibid.

all, thereby potentially diluting the effectiveness of any statutory disclosure framework.[103]

Part XV of the SFO requires mandatory disclosure of interests (including short **8.38** positions) from individuals or companies who have an interest in 5 per cent or more of any class of voting shares in a listed company in any shares in a listed company, including associated companies.[104] It also imposes mandatory disclosure requirements on directors and chief executives of listed companies of their interests and short positions in any shares and their interests in any debentures of the listed company, including associated companies.[105] The intention is to provide sufficient information so that investors may identify the persons who have a controlling interest in the listed company and those who may take advantage from transactions involving the associated companies of listed companies.[106] Such information should also assist the SFC to monitor insider dealing.

The Companies Ordinance[107] also provides for mandatory disclosure of infor- **8.39** mation in the form of a prospectus when a company offers securities to the public. Chapter 4 discusses the relevant disclosure requirements and other related issues in this regard.

C. Insider Dealing

Insider dealing is the trading of shares with the knowledge of information that is **8.40** not generally known to the public which, had it been generally known, is likely to affect the market price of such shares. The insider does not deal with another person in the financial markets with equal bargaining power, as the former possesses information not generally available in the market. An insider stands to gain (or avoid loss) from anticipating changes in securities prices. In the strict sense, insider dealing is a form of non-disclosure. Since it removes the fairness of the level playing field in the financial markets, investors may lose confidence in the companies and markets in which insider dealing is thought to prevail. It is sometimes considered as a breach of fiduciary duty, but the common law has not developed this area further.[108]

(1) The theoretical framework

Under the SFO, insider dealing is criminalized. As discussed above, the SFO **8.41** also enables a victim of insider dealing to commence civil action in court.

---

[103] ibid.   [104] SFO, Part XV, Division 2.   [105] SFO, Part XV, Division 7.
[106] *Outline of Part XV of the Securities and Futures Ordinance (Cap. 571)—Disclosure of Interests* (Hong Kong: Securities and Futures Commission, 2003), p 3.
[107] Cap. 32, Laws of Hong Kong.   [108] Gilligan, above, p 177.

8.42 Studies have shown that securities prices must be competitively derived for financial markets to be efficient.[109] Investors who wish to obtain relevant information on securities in which they become interested may be discouraged to do so where access to information is unequal. Therefore, if insider dealing is prevalent, financial markets may be less liquid to the extent investors believe that price movements reflect insider activity.[110] The expected return for outside investors would be reduced because they are trading against the better-informed insiders.[111] Studies also show that outsiders often own more shares when expected returns are low and fewer shares when expected returns are high.[112] On the other hand, some research suggests that insider dealing may create desirable incentives and improve economic efficiency.[113] However, if the investing public feels that insiders may take advantage of them at some point, they may never invest.[114] In any event, effective control of insider dealing would encourage the participation of outside investors from the outset.[115]

8.43 It can also be argued that insider dealing erodes the fiduciary relationship between a company and its management.[116] If insider dealing is tolerated, a company suffers in various respects.[117] First, the insiders may benefit from bad news, and, hence, they have less incentive to avoid harm.[118] Second, there is less incentive to be productive as there is a 'free-rider' problem: those who do not produce may also take advantage of inside information.[119] Third, it would influence the types of information made available to the public and the timing of announcements to the advantage of the insiders rather than the company.[120] As the shareholders of the company often may not have all the available resources, including investigative powers, to combat insider dealing effectively, an effective regulatory framework is essential.

(2) Criminalization of insider dealing

8.44 The now repealed Securities (Insider Dealing) Ordinance imposed only a civil penalty for insider dealing. The maximum fine under the old law was three

---

[109] M Fishman & K Hagerty, 'Insider trading and the efficiency of stock prices' (1992) *Rand Journal of Economics* 106, pp 118–19.

[110] H Leland, 'Insider trading: Should it be prohibited?' (1992) *Journal of Political Economy* 859 at p 883.

[111] ibid, p 884.   [112] ibid.

[113] L Ausubel, 'Insider Trading in a Rational Expectations Economy' (1990) 80:5 *The American Economic Review* 1022.

[114] ibid, p 1038.   [115] ibid.

[116] See Chapter 7 for a discussion of the fiduciary relationship between a company and its directors.

[117] J Moore, 'What is Really Unethical about Insider Trading' (1990) *Journal of Business Ethics* p 171.

[118] ibid, p 178.   [119] ibid, p 179.   [120] ibid.

times the amount of any profit gained or loss avoided plus the expenses of the inquiry and investigation.[121] As evidence against insider dealing cannot be easily produced and there was no criminal liability for such activity, the profit that could be gained by using inside information would become the opportunity cost for most culprits of insider dealing. As early as 1973, there were calls to criminalize insider dealing by the Second Report of the then Companies Law Revision Committee.[122] Commentators argued that most major financial jurisdictions had already criminalized insider dealing and the international confidence in Hong Kong as a financial centre should be enhanced.[123]

In 2002 the criminalization of the offence of insider dealing was enacted into the SFO. The legislation regulating insider dealing is Division 4, Part XIII and Division 2, Part XIV of the SFO for civil and criminal routes respectively. These provisions in the ordinance are derived from the now repealed Securities (Insider Dealing) Ordinance. The insider dealing provisions apply to both Hong Kong listed and dual listed securities. The SFO provides a definition for listed securities, covering those issued securities which are listed as well as those which are not listed but which are reasonably foreseeable to be listed and in fact become listed.[124] The latter covers trading in shares already in issue but prior to them being formally listed as well as 'grey market' trading in shares before they are formally issued and listed. **8.45**

The SFO provides a detailed definition of insider dealing in section 270, which in essence addresses trading in securities of a company by a person that has specific information not or not yet available to the general public because of his or her position with the company.[125] The present statutory definition restricts the scope of insider dealing activities, as the onus is on the prosecution to prove a connection between the person and the corporation, or that a person is contemplating to make a takeover offer for the corporation, and the use of the information. Under the ordinance, insider dealing takes place when a 'person connected' with the listed company, possessing information he knows is 'relevant information' in relation to that company, deals in the securities of that company, or counsels or procures another person to do the same.[126] The SFO expressly includes knowledge of takeover offers as insider information.[127] Thus, **8.46**

---

[121] Securities (Insider Dealing) Ordinance, Cap. 395, Laws of Hong Kong, ss 23 & 27 (now repealed).

[122] *Review of the Hong Kong Companies Ordinance* (Hong Kong: Financial Services Branch, March 1997), para 2.1.

[123] C Shum, 'Insider Dealing in Hong Kong, Part 1', December 1989 *Business Law Review* 314.

[124] SFO ss 245(2) & 285(2).

[125] F Dearborn, *Fitzroy Dearborn Encyclopedia of Banking and Finance*, p 594.

[126] SFO ss 270(1)(a) & 291(1).   [127] SFO ss 270(1)(b) & 291(2).

it deems any person who is contemplating or has contemplated making a take-over offer as an insider.

8.47   Insider dealing also takes place when a person discloses information to another person, knowing or having reasonable cause to believe that the other person will deal or counsel or procure another person likewise.[128] These provisions prohibit insiders from dealing and disclosing information, as well as counselling or procuring other persons to do the same.

8.48   As the legislative intent is to prohibit the misuse of inside information, the ordinance states that a person who receives inside information from a connected person is also liable, even though he is not a primary insider.[129] It is immaterial whether or not the information is received directly or indirectly. However, the prosecution must prove that the defendant knows or has reasonable cause to believe the information is inside information. From the above definition of insider dealing, the definitions for connected person and relevant information warrant further discussion.

Definition of connected person

8.49   Under the SFO, a person is considered to be connected with a corporation by virtue of his position. A connected person with a corporation includes any director, employee, and substantial shareholder, or its related company.[130] This covers a wide range of related persons, including very low-level employees, for example, a janitor, as they may have access to relevant information. A substantial shareholder of a corporation is a person who holds 5 per cent or more nominal value of voting shares of that corporation.[131] This class of insider owes a fiduciary duty to the corporation not to misappropriate privileged inside information for their own benefit.

8.50   The definition of connected person also extends to a person who occupies a position which may reasonably be expected to give him access to relevant information in relation to the corporation by reason of a professional or business relationship,[132] or his being a director, employee, or partner of a substantial shareholder of the corporation or a related corporation.[133] Whether there is a professional or business relationship is a question of fact in each particular case.[134] A family relationship may also involve a business relationship.[135]

---

[128] SFO ss 270(1)(c) & 291(3).   [129] SFO ss 270(1)(e) & 291(5).
[130] SFO ss 247(1), (a) & (b), & 287(1)(a) & (b).   [131] SFO ss 247(3) & 287(3).
[132] SFO ss 247(1)(c)(i) & 287(1)(c)(i).   [133] SFO ss 247(1)(c)(ii) & 287(1)(c)(ii).
[134] *Hong Kong Parkview Group Limited Inquiry Report* (Hong Kong: Report of the Insider Dealing Tribunal, 5 March 1997), p 32.
[135] ibid.

A single encounter may trigger such relationship as the relationship may exist at the time of or any time prior to the commission of the alleged insider dealing.[136]

A person may well be a connected person of the corporation if he has access to **8.51** relevant information in relation to the corporation by reason of his being a connected person with another corporation.[137] The relevant information must be related to an actual or contemplated transaction involving both corporations or between one of them or the listed securities of the other or their derivatives.[138] This class of persons are deemed as insiders because of their privileged position in possessing inside information. They should hold the information in trust for the corporation.

A person is also deemed as a connected person if the insider dealing takes place **8.52** within six months of his being a connected person as discussed above.[139] This provision intends to prevent a person from disqualifying himself as a connected person and then engaging in insider dealing with the relevant information acquired.

The provisions of the SFO require the establishment of a connection between **8.53** the 'person'[140] and the corporation to be an insider. A person is equally culpable for misusing information insofar as he knows that such information is not generally available. Therefore, the ordinance also deems a public officer or a specified person, who receives relevant information, as a connected person.[141] The ordinance provides a list of persons as specified person, including members of the Executive and Legislative Councils, public board members, and officers or employees of HKEx. However, the ordinance is silent regarding former public officers or former specified persons. In *Shum Kwok Sher v the HKSAR*,[142] the Court of Final Appeal held that the common law offence of misconduct in public office is committed when (1) a public official (2) in the course of or in relation to his public office, (3) wilfully and intentionally (4) culpably misconducts himself and the misconduct is serious. Under the conflicts of interest circular of the HKSAR Civil Service, public officers are prohibited from using any information made available to them in their capacity as a civil servant, to benefit themselves or their families, financially or otherwise, or to favour their relations or friends, or any other group of people with whom they have personal

---

[136] ibid, p 33.   [137] SFO ss 247(1)(d)(i) & 287(1)(d)(i).
[138] SFO ss 247(1)(d)(ii) & 287(1)(d)(ii).   [139] SFO ss 247(e) & 287(e).
[140] The law is not confined to physical persons only, because, a corporation also will be regarded as a person connected with another corporation so long as any of its directors or employees is a person who would be regarded as connected with that other corporation by virtue of subsection (1).
[141] SFO ss 249 & 288.   [142] Final Appeal No 1 of 2002 (Criminal).

or social ties.[143] Accordingly, this would be misconduct in public office for a public officer to use the privileged information from a company obtained in the course of their duties. The privileged information in this context could be wider in scope than relevant information. The offence may be committed by a public officer using privileged information obtained in relation to his public office.

Definition of relevant information

8.54   The SFO provides a definition for relevant information, which is 'specific' information about the company, a shareholder or officer of the company, or the listed securities of the company or their derivatives.[144] The information must be specific, that is, information must not only be precisely defined but its entire content must be precisely and unequivocally identified, expressed, and discerned.[145] The type of information the ordinance is concerned about is not the general information which insiders come across, but rather events which affect the company. There must be sufficient particulars in the information to comply with this requirement.[146] It suffices if there is a probable consequence[147] or reasonable belief[148] that the event may happen.

8.55   The ordinance does not use the phrase 'price-sensitive information'. It refers to such information that is 'not generally known' to the persons who are accustomed or would be likely to deal in the listed securities of the company but which would if it were generally known to them be, 'likely to materially affect the price of the listed securities'.[149] The question is whether or not it is likely to materially affect an ordinary reasonable investor, who is accustomed or likely to deal in those securities.[150] What is material is a question of fact to be assessed from how the general investors would have acted on the date when the insider engages in insider dealing had the general investors known the relevant information.[151] Ostensibly, the information must be authentic, and, hence, there is no insider dealing where the holder or disseminator has been misinformed.[152] As a matter of ordinary usage, the ordinance is not concerned with the use or

---

[143] *HKSAR v Chung Sim Ying Tracy*, Magistrate Appeal No 267 of 2001, para 12.

[144] SFO ss 245(2) & 285(2).

[145] *Chinese Estates Holdings Limited Inquiry Report* (Hong Kong: Report of the Insider Dealing Tribunal, 25 June 1999), p 39; *Ryan v Triguboff* [1976] ACLC 28,477 at 24,482.

[146] *Chinese Estates Holdings Limited Inquiry Report*, above, p 39.   [147] ibid.

[148] *Hong Kong Parkview Group Limited Inquiry Report*, above, p 39.

[149] SFO ss 245(2) & 285(2).

[150] *Chinese Estates Holdings Limited Inquiry*, above, p 46.

[151] *Public International Investments Limited Inquiry Report* (Hong Kong: Report of the Insider Dealing Tribunal, 5 August 1995), pp 239–40.

[152] *Chan Sing Chuk v Innovisions Ltd* [1991] 2 HKC 305 at p 308.

dissemination of information which is not genuine even though it may materially change the price of securities.[153]

The IDT took a narrow approach in interpreting 'generally known' and required **8.56** an element of specificity before the information ceased to be relevant information because it became generally known.[154] Accordingly, rumours which lacked specificity could not be said to be generally known.[155] The SFO defines the class of persons whom the relevant information is not generally known to as those 'who are accustomed or would be likely to deal in the listed securities of the corporation'.[156] What constitutes this specific class of persons is a question of fact depending on the nature of the company and the profile of expected investors.[157] In reality, the ability of the targeted investors to digest the information should be taken into account. Evidence is normally called from experts in the financial field. The more sophisticated the expected investors are, the less likely the securities are targeted to the wider investing public, and, hence, a lower threshold for 'generally known'.[158]

(3) Defences to insider dealing

The SFO provides a number of exceptions for activities which would otherwise **8.57** be regarded as insider dealing.[159] As the insider dealing provisions are general provisions, they may unintentionally catch legitimate activities which are considered morally acceptable. The onus is on the defence to establish an exception.

First, the ordinance excludes acquiring qualifying shares, performing an under- **8.58** writing agreement and where acting in the capacity of a liquidator, receiver, or trustee in bankruptcy provided the same is done in good faith.[160] An underwriter would normally possess inside information about the corporation before it agrees to the underwriting agreement to acquire and market the securities. If they are subject to the insider dealing provisions, their liberty to launch the securities for the corporation would be restricted.

Second, the SFO provides exemption for a corporation from insider dealing **8.59** activities where it has established effective information barriers (or 'Chinese walls').[161] A Chinese wall is a management tool which restricts the flow of

---

[153] ibid.

[154] *Hong Kong Worsted Mills Limited Inquiry Report* (Hong Kong: Report of the Insider Dealing Tribunal, 21 January 1998), p 45.

[155] ibid.   [156] SFO ss 245(2) & 285(2).

[157] *Chinese Estates Holdings Limited Inquiry Report*, op cit, pp 37–8; *Chevalier (OA) International Limited Inquiry Report* (Hong Kong: Report of the Insider Dealing Tribunal, 10 July 1997), pp 62–5.

[158] ibid.   [159] SFO ss 271 & 292.   [160] SFO ss 271(1) & 292(1).

[161] SFO ss 271(2) & 292(2).

confidential information between different divisions of a company. Although one or more directors or employees may possess relevant information, for the defence to be available the decision to deal must be taken by persons who are on the other side of the Chinese wall and who have not in fact had access to the relevant information.[162] More importantly, the Chinese wall arrangement must exist to secure the confidentiality of relevant information.[163] The onus is on the corporation which relies on this exemption as a defence to prove that sufficient measures have been taken to design a Chinese wall that would eliminate the prima facie real risk of abuse.[164] In other words, the question is whether or not the information barriers in place are effective in protecting the confidentiality of relevant information within a corporation.[165]

8.60 Third, the defence of not making a profit or avoiding a loss is available.[166] The onus is on the defendant to prove that such purpose exists. It suffices if the defendant can prove on a mere balance of probabilities that the decision to deal was honestly made and is unconnected with any desire to make a profit or avoid a loss.[167]

8.61 Fourth, the defence of 'innocent agent' is available under the SFO.[168] The onus is on the defendant to prove that he is an agent, who merely follows instructions from the principal, and does not know his principal is an insider or has the relevant information. The provision is intended to protect brokers and dealers who merely provide services in the course of their business. This principle is extended to trustees or personal representatives who act on advice in good faith from an appropriate person without knowledge of insider dealing.[169] The onus is on the defence to prove that reasonable measures have been taken.

8.62 Fifth, if neither the level playing field nor the investing public is affected, prohibiting insider dealing does not serve its intended purpose. Therefore, where both parties to the transaction have the relevant information and the dealing is not required to be put on record, the SFO provides a defence to a charge of insider dealing.[170] This defence is justified because both parties to the transaction are dealing off-market and are assumed to be equally sophisticated with neither party having a serious informational advantage.[171] Therefore, this

---

[162] SFO ss 271(1)(a) & (c) & 292(1)(a) & (c).   [163] SFO ss 271(1)(b) & 292(1)(b).
[164] *Supasave Retail Ltd v Coward Chance and others; David Lee & Co (Lincoln) Ltd v Coward Chance and others* [1991] 1 All ER 668 at 674
[165] *Young and others v Robson Rhodes and another* [1999] 3 All ER 524 at 539.
[166] SFO ss 271(3) & 292(3).
[167] *Chevalier (OA) International Limited Inquiry Report*, above, p 82.
[168] SFO ss 271(4) & 292(4).   [169] SFO ss 272 & 293.
[170] SFO ss 271(5) & 292(5).   [171] Goyne, above, p 12.

defence requires the defendant to establish that both parties in the transaction are dealing directly.[172]

Sixth, similarly, where a person enters into the insider dealing, otherwise than by counselling or procuring the other party to deal, and the other party knows or ought reasonably to have known that he is a connected person relating to the dealing, the activity is not regarded as illegal.[173] This defence assumes that the other party should make enquiries with the known insider before the dealing and should be able to negotiate accordingly.[174]   **8.63**

Seventh, even if he counsels or procures another person to deal in securities, but the other person does not counsel or procure the other party to deal in securities, he is not liable if the other party knows or ought reasonably to have known that the other person is a connected person relating to the dealing.[175] Under this circumstance, the level playing field is similarly maintained. This defence would protect an investment banker who advises a substantial shareholder and introduces a prospective purchaser to him.[176]   **8.64**

Eighth, in facilitating dealing in securities, a person could come across information which may be considered as relevant information. When an investment banker assists a client in building up a takeover stake and consequently hedges such activity, they run the risk of insider dealing on the knowledge of their own trading activities and those facilitating such trading.[177] A person who deals with inside information about his own trading activities should not be liable as an insider.[178] This would include a substantial shareholder who increases or reduces his shareholding.[179] Under this circumstance, the SFO provides a 'market information' defence for a person who deals with relevant information arising directly out of his involvement in the dealing.[180] It exempts certain market information from being relevant information for the purpose of insider dealing. The ordinance provides a list of information as market information, including the fact of dealing in securities and the prices at which trades have been entered into etc.[181] Under the previous law, the government would in practice not take action against a person under this circumstance.[182]   **8.65**

Ninth, there is no insider dealing if a person can prove that the dealing in question is a 'market contract'.[183] A market contract is a contract subject to the rules of HKEx entered into by the clearing house with a participant pursuant to a novation under the rules.[184] The SFO also exempts a person from engaging in   **8.66**

---

[172] SFO ss 271(5) & 292(5).   [173] SFO ss 271(6) & 292(6).
[174] Goyne, above, p 12.   [175] SFO ss 271(7) & 292(7).   [176] Goyne, above, p 12.
[177] ibid, p 11.   [178] ibid.   [179] ibid.   [180] SFO ss 271(8) & 292(8).
[181] SFO ss 271(10) & 292(10).   [182] Goyne, above, p 11.
[183] SFO ss 271(9) & 292(9).   [184] SFO, sch 1.

insider dealing activity if he can establish that he possesses the relevant information after he has been granted the option in the listed securities or the derivatives
in question.[185]

D. Market Manipulation

8.67   Market manipulation is the creation of a false or misleading market, enabling
the manipulator to buy at a lower price and sell at a higher price, thus affecting
transactions and distorting free competition in the financial markets. It meddles
with genuine market supply and demand. There are many techniques of market
manipulation, including artificially pushing up (ramping), suppressing, or stabilizing securities prices, and misleading investors by creating a false impression
of active trading in securities. These devices may be achieved by disseminating
false or misleading market information through the media, e-mails, or the
internet.

8.68   The statutory prohibition of market manipulation is not novel in common law.
This concept has its root in old common law offences, for example, forestalling
the market which is the act of buying or contracting any provision on its way to
the market, with the intention to sell it at a higher price or counselling persons
to enhance the price in the market; regrating, which is the buying at a market
any provisions with the intention of selling them in the same or nearby market
at a higher price; and ingrossing, which involves buying up so much of goods on
the market in order to monopolize the price.[186] All these common law offences
are related to the artificial interference of the fair market value of goods.

8.69   Market manipulation harms the integrity and efficiency of the financial markets
and undermines public confidence. It distorts fair market prices, damages the
hedging functions of the financial markets, and erodes the level playing field.
It damages innocent market participants most severely. Research has shown
that prices and market liquidity are higher when manipulators sell than when
they buy.[187] When manipulators sell, prices are higher when market volatility
is greater.[188] Therefore, manipulators are benefiting also at the expense of
market efficiency. Studies have shown that potentially informed parties, such
as corporate insiders, brokers, underwriters, and substantial shareholders are

---

[185] SFO ss 273 & 294.
[186] See J Girdler, *Observations on the Pernicious Consequences of Forestalling, Regrating, and
Ingrossing* (London: Baldwin & Son, 1800).
[187] R Aggarwal & G Wu, 'Stock Market Manipulation—Theory and Evidence', working paper,
2004 AFA meetings, see <http://ssrn.com/abstract=474582>, p 30.
[188] ibid.

more likely to be manipulators.[189] The opportunities to manipulate financial markets increase as sophisticated derivative products are rapidly growing. Market manipulation is often considered a white collar crime committed by well-educated criminals but likewise is one which is increasingly subject to moral and legal censure. Nonetheless, market manipulation continues because the rewards are high and because the means and opportunities to do so are evolving with new financial products, advancing financial technologies and increasing globalization.

The liquidity of stocks in the Hong Kong financial market tends to be uncertain.[190] Some securities in the Hong Kong financial market are generally liquid, but their number is restricted to a few blue chip stocks. Research shows that an illiquid stock is more vulnerable for manipulation.[191] Market manipulation in turn increases stock price volatility.[192] Studies suggest that thinly-traded securities are more prone to market manipulation than those for which there exist deep and broad markets.[193] Hong Kong has no shortage of market participants who are ready to buy securities at a moment's notice.[194]   **8.70**

In this era of globalization, market manipulation can be easily carried out cross-jurisdictionally by multi-national market participants. As most market manipulation involves the hiding of beneficial ownership, cross-border dealing makes its detection more difficult. As a result, the SFO prohibits market manipulation covering certain cross-border activity. This is intended to show that Hong Kong meets international standards in cooperation with overseas regulators to combat financial market offences.[195] The ordinance extends the market manipulation offence to trading in securities on a stock exchange out-side Hong Kong for activities entered into or carried out in Hong Kong. The market manipulation provisions apply to conduct in Hong Kong that affects the relevant overseas markets, that is, securities markets outside Hong Kong,[196] and vice versa, but, for securities traded on a relevant overseas market, the conduct of the defendant should also be unlawful.[197]   **8.71**

The most commonly used techniques in market manipulation are 'wash sales' and 'matched orders'. Wash sales (or wash trades) are the purchase and sale of   **8.72**

---

[189] ibid, p 29.

[190] W Cheung & F Song, 'Liquidity, Size and Cycle of Order Flow: Evidence from Hong Kong Stock Exchange', *Working Paper* (Hong Kong: School of Economics and Finance, University of Hong Kong, January 2005), pp 1–25.

[191] Aggrawl & Wu, above, p 29.   [192] ibid.   [193] Fischel & Ross, above, p 518.

[194] E Tsoi, *Understanding Investors in the Hong Kong Listed Securities and Derivative Markets* (Hong Kong: Hong Kong Exchanges and Clearing Limited, 2004), paras 41–42.

[195] *Consultation Document on the Securities and Futures Bill* (Hong Kong: The Government of the Hong Kong Special Administrative Region, April 2000), p 109.

[196] SFO ss 245(1) & 285(1).   [197] SFO ss 282(3) & 306(3).

securities either simultaneously or within a short period of time without changing beneficial ownership of the securities. This technique may be employed by a single investor. Where a co-manipulator is involved, two or more persons conspire to create the appearance of market activity in securities so that they may profit from the increase in price of the security. Such transactions are deceitful as they give the investing public a false impression that the securities are fairly traded at the published price, when they are not.[198] 'Matched orders' involve offsetting buy and sell orders to create a false impression of activity in a security. This technique may be employed by one or more persons making matching buy and sell orders of the same security at the same time at substantially the same price. However, the order would usually be placed through different brokers. Matched orders may also be made by more than one customer with the same broker.

8.73 Wash sales are a technique commonly employed in false trading (creating a false or misleading appearance) and price rigging (artificial or fictitious transactions without any change of beneficial ownership). False trading also employs matched orders as a device. Under the SFO, once a wash sale or matched order has been proven, the defendant has to prove that his act does not include the purpose of creating a false or misleading appearance in the market or the price of securities. The rationale is that there is no reasonable explanation for an innocent person to engage in such activities. The intention of the market participants in dealing with securities is difficult to prove. Therefore, if the defendant is innocent, he should be able to prove on a balance of probabilities that he has a legitimate reason for entering into or carrying out the wash sale or matched orders. As most market manipulation is usually established from circumstantial evidence, including the nature of the dealing, it is not unreasonable to impose a rebuttal presumption on a common-sense basis.[199]

8.74 As a matter of legal analysis, some types of market misconduct may be considered as a species of fraud.[200] For example, artificial or fictitious transactions utilising wash sales and matched orders which are calculated to mislead the investing public are fraudulent.[201] They are deceptive conducts which harm misled investors. However, many forms of market misconduct involve actual and not artificial or fictitious trading.[202] Trading itself is socially acceptable.[203] The only difference between manipulative and non-manipulative trading is the presence or absence of a manipulative intent. Fraud, however, depends not only on the intent but also other factors, for example, whether there is a false

---

[198] *United States v Brown* 79F. 2d 321 at 325   [199] Goyne, above, p 15.
[200] Fischel & Ross, above, p 510.   [201] ibid.   [202] ibid, p 511.   [203] ibid.

statement.[204] Therefore, market manipulation has to be regulated by legislation separately.

Under the SFO, market manipulation involves five specified types of market **8.75** misconduct. They are false trading, price rigging, disclosing information about transactions prohibited by the ordinance, disclosing false or misleading information inducing transactions in securities and futures, and stock market manipulation. The first four types of offence apply to both securities and futures whilst the last type of offence applies to securities transactions only. The provisions in the ordinance identify each specific market misconduct. Some of the market manipulation provisions in the ordinance will overlap and interrelate insofar as a perpetrator would be more likely to commit more than one market misconduct offence concurrently. The prosecution has the privilege to charge a person with one or more provisions in accordance to the circumstances of each case. Market manipulation is prohibited under Divisions 4 and 5 of Part XIII and Divisions 2 to 4 of Part XIV of the SFO for the civil and criminal routes respectively.

(1) False trading

False Trading is defined under the SFO[205] as creation of a false or misleading **8.76** appearance of active trading in a recognized securities market with intention of effecting artificial price levels for securities traded on a recognized market.[206] There are many forms of false trading. One of the most common is 'pooling', which comprises a pool of market participants buying and selling securities or futures successively among themselves in order to artificially increase the trading volume. Another device is 'churning', which comprises the excessive trading of a discretionary account by the trader who controls it in order to generate extra commission in disregard of the interests of the customer. This results in increasing turnover and creates a false or misleading appearance of market interest.

The SFO prohibits the creation of a false or misleading appearance of trading or **8.77** artificial pricing in securities and futures and also with respect to their market and price. There is no jurisdictional boundary for the commission of false trading or artificial pricing. Under the ordinance, it can be committed in Hong Kong or elsewhere insofar as the false or misleading appearance or artificial price is created in Hong Kong.[207] If the false or misleading appearance or artificial price is created on a relevant overseas market, then the false trading must be

---

[204] ibid.   [205] SFO s 274.
[206] YK Kwan, *A Guide to the Securities and Futures Ordinance*, p 143.
[207] SFO ss 274(1) & (3) & 295(1) & (3).

entered into or carried out in Hong Kong.[208] However, the conduct must also be illegal in that relevant overseas market.[209]

8.78 There are many activities that constitute false trading. As the list of devices or techniques for committing false trading is not exhaustive, the SFO provides a general definition for false trading. It also specifically includes wash sale, matched orders, and artificial pricing as false trading. Naturally, the ordinance is not intended to discourage genuine trading in securities even though their trading would increase in volume and so affect their price. There is always a fine line between genuine trading and false trading. False trading may be carried out by a number of transactions over a period of time, which may be difficult to trace. The test of market manipulation should be a practical test as manipulative techniques are developed over time.[210] The issue is whether conduct has been intentionally entered into or carried out resulting in a price which does not reflect the natural forces of supply and demand.[211] The present provisions regulating false trading are sections 274 and 295 of the SFO for civil and criminal offences respectively. These provisions are derived from section 135(1) and (2) of the now repealed Securities Ordinance, section 62 of the now repealed Commodities Trading Ordinance, and section 998(1) of the Corporations Act 2001 (Australia).

8.79 Under the general provisions in the SFO, false trading takes place when a person does anything, or causes anything to be done, intentionally or recklessly, which is likely to have the effect of creating a false or misleading appearance of trading in securities and futures or with respect to the market or price on a relevant recognized market (that is, HKEx) or by means of authorized automated trading services (ATS).[212] The SFC maintains a list of ATS, including the Chicago Board of Trade and London Stock Exchange, as empowered by the ordinance.[213]

8.80 A person may be liable under the provisions of the ordinance as long as he 'causes anything to be done'. The provisions cover any means in creating false or misleading appearance, including counselling and procuring another person to do so. What the ordinance requires is that the 'false or misleading appearance' is 'likely' to be effected. In other words, there must be a real and not a remote possibility that a false or misleading appearance would be effected. In determining whether there is likelihood, it is a matter of fact for the MMT or the court to decide from the evidence admitted. An objective test should be adopted. In establishing false trading, mens rea is required for the conduct that effects

---

[208] SFO ss 274 (2) & 295(2).   [209] SFO ss 282(3) & 306(3).
[210] *Cargill Inc v Hardin* [1971] 452 F.2d 1154 at 1163.
[211] ibid, p 1158.   [212] SFO ss 274(1) & (2) & 295(1) & (2).   [213] SFO s 95(2).

the false or misleading appearance. The prosecution must meet the requisite standard of proof in establishing an intention or recklessness.[214] Recklessness has to be read together with the phrase 'likely to have'. Accordingly, the prosecution has to prove that the false or misleading appearance is obvious to a reasonable prudent person rather than the defendant. This implies a lower requirement of proof.

The appearance, however, must be false or misleading. What is false and misleading is also an issue of fact based on the evidence arising from the market transactions. A single transaction in a particularly large volume undertaken for a genuine purpose may give rise to a false and misleading appearance of the financial market or price, but there is no manipulative intent. The general provisions cover all types of techniques in false trading. It suffices if a technique is likely to have the effect of creating a false or misleading appearance. The general onus is on the prosecution to prove each element of false trading, that is, the act that was likely to have the effect of creating a false or misleading appearance and the defendant possessed the relevant mens rea. **8.81**

The SFO also prohibits artificial pricing. False trading takes place when a person takes part in, is concerned in, or carries out one or more transactions which are likely to have the effect of creating or maintaining an artificial price in securities and futures or with respect to the market or price on the HKEx or an ATS.[215] It is immaterial whether or not the price is previously artificial. In establishing false trading under these provisions, the prosecution must prove that the defendant has the intention that, or being reckless as to whether, the transaction or transactions is or are likely to create an artificial price. The prosecution must meet the requisite standard of proof in establishing an intention or recklessness as in false and misleading appearance.[216] It is immaterial whether the activity is carried out directly or indirectly.[217] The provisions in the ordinance only prohibit artificial pricing. There is no artificial transaction if the trading is genuinely free from manipulation under the natural forces of supply and demand. This is also the view taken by the SFC.[218] **8.82**

It is not necessary for a false or misleading appearance to be materialized in establishing false trading. It suffices if there is an offer to sell or purchase securities or an invitation that expressly or impliedly invites a person to offer to sell or purchase securities.[219] **8.83**

Once a wash sale or matched order is proven to have taken place in the HKEx or by means of an ATS, the onus is on the defendant to prove that his act does not **8.84**

---

[214] SFO ss 274(1) & (2) & 295(1) & (2).   [215] SFO ss 274(3) & (4) & 295(3) & (4).

[216] SFO ss 274(3) & (4) & 295(3) & (4).   [217] SFO ss 274(3) & (4) & 295(3) & (4).

[218] Goyne, above, p 14.   [219] SFO ss 274(8) & 295(9).

include the purpose of creating a false or misleading appearance.[220] The SFO presumes that the defendant under these circumstances has acted intentionally or recklessly in effecting a false or misleading appearance. This statutory presumption only applies to trading in securities and not futures.[221] Such a reverse onus of proof arises when there is no change in beneficial ownership and when a person offers to sell securities at substantially the same price as an offer to purchase made for substantially the same number of securities or vice versa.[222]

8.85 The intention of the SFO is not to prohibit transactions which alter the price of securities. Rather, the relevant provisions have been enacted to protect the investing public by maintaining the determination of security prices by the natural forces of supply and demand. Dealing in securities may have many purposes and the market participants may know that it may affect the financial market or the price of the securities and futures. This does not imply that a manipulative purpose is always present. Therefore, the ordinance provides a 'no purpose' defence in cases of wash sale and matched orders. Under these 'no purpose' defence provisions, the defendant must establish that the purpose or purposes for which he commits the act does not include the purpose of creating a false or misleading appearance.[223] All the defendant need to prove is on the balance of probabilities there is no such purpose to create a false or misleading appearance.

(2) Price rigging

8.86 The SFO prohibits price rigging, defined as[224] artificial transactions of securities that do not change the beneficial ownership of the securities with the intention of causing fluctuations in their price.[225] There are two types of price rigging. The first type is the wash sale, which applies to securities only. The second type is an artificial or fictitious transaction or device. Under the ordinance, they can be committed in Hong Kong or elsewhere insofar as the price of securities or futures is affected in Hong Kong.[226] If the price of securities or futures is affected in a relevant overseas market, then the wash sale or artificial or fictitious transaction must be entered into or carried out in Hong Kong.[227] However, such activities must also be illegal in that relevant overseas market.[228] The present provisions regulating price rigging are sections 275 and 296 of the SFO for civil and criminal offences respectively. These provisions are derived from section 135(3) and (4) of the now repealed Securities Ordinance and section 998(3) of the Corporations Act 2001 (Australia).

---

[220] SFO ss 274(5) & 295(5).   [221] ibid.   [222] SFO ss 274(5) & 295(5).
[223] SFO ss 274(6) & 295(7).   [224] SFO s 275.   [225] YK Kwan, above, p 144.
[226] SFO ss 275(1) & 296(1).   [227] SFO ss 275(2) & 296(2).
[228] SFO ss 282(3) & 306(3).

In the wash sale provisions, the ordinance prohibits any sale or purchase of   **8.87**
securities that does not involve a change in their beneficial ownership and
resulting in maintaining, increasing, reducing, stabilizing, or causing fluctuations in price of securities traded on the HKEx or by means of an ATS.[229] The
activity may be carried out directly or indirectly. It is not necessary for the result
to be materialized. It suffices if there is an offer to sell or purchase securities or
an invitation that expressly or impliedly invites a person to offer to sell or
purchase securities.[230] Once a wash sale is established, the liability is strict, that
is, there is no need to establish that the defendant enters into or carries out the
transaction intentionally or recklessly. There is an implied statutory presumption that the defendant has acted intentionally or recklessly in affecting the price
of securities. The defendant has the reverse onus to prove that his act does not
include the purpose or purposes of creating a false or misleading appearance to
the securities price.[231] One such legitimate purpose is that there is no change of
beneficial ownership to facilitate tax planning. All the defendant need to prove
is on the balance of probabilities there is no such purpose to create a false or
misleading appearance.

The SFO also prohibits artificial or fictitious transactions or devices resulting in   **8.88**
maintaining, increasing, reducing, stabilizing, or causing fluctuations in price of
securities or futures traded on the HKEx or by means of an ATS.[232] Whether the
transaction is artificial or fictitious is a question of fact. This normally refers to
transactions that would not change the legal rights between the parties as it
appears to have done. The activity may be carried out directly or indirectly. The
provisions regulating artificial or fictitious transactions require a higher standard
of proof. The onus is on the prosecution to prove that the defendant has the
intention to effect, or is being reckless as to effecting, the result.

(3) *Disclosure of information about prohibited transactions*

The damage to the investing public arising from market misconduct may be   **8.89**
aggravated if the information relating to market misconduct is disseminated
to a wider audience. A person involved in market misconduct or his associates
may spread information about market misconduct in the hope that ordinary
investors may be influenced to trade, as free riders, in the targeted securities
in the direction as manipulated.[233] The SFO prohibits the dissemination of
information where the price of securities may be affected by a prohibited
transaction.

---

[229] SFO ss 275(1)(a) & 2(a) & 296(1)(a) & (2)(a).   [230] SFO ss 275(5) & 296(6).
[231] SFO ss 275(4) & 296(5).   [232] SFO ss 275(1)(b) & (2) & 296(1)(b) & (2)(b).
[233] Goyne, above, p 19.

8.90 Specifically, the SFO prohibits disclosure of information about prohibited trans-actions, defined as[234] disclosing of information about a prohibited transaction with the intention of making profit, resulting in price stagnation or fluctuation in the price of the concerned securities.[235] Under the ordinance, a prohibited transaction refers to any conduct or transaction which constitutes market mis-conduct, that is, insider dealing, all offences relating to market manipulation, and other offences relating to fraud and deception.[236] The provisions cover both securities and futures transactions. These provisions are derived from section 135(5) of the now repealed Securities Ordinance and sections 1001 and 1263 of the Corporations Act 2001 (Australia).

8.91 The SFO prohibits a person from disclosing information about prohibited transactions which affects the price of securities and futures that are traded on the HKEx or by means of an ATS, if that person, or his associate, has entered into or carried out the prohibited transaction or has received a benefit as a result.[237] Disclosure includes circulation and dissemination. A person is also liable by authorizing or being concerned with the so doing. The price is affected when it is maintained, increased, reduced, or stabilized. However, once the disclosure has taken place, it is immaterial whether or not any of the intended outcomes occur. It suffices if the disclosure is likely to cause any of these out-comes. It is irrelevant whether or not the prohibited transaction has been entered into or carried out directly or indirectly. It is not necessary for the defendant to have actually received the benefit. An expectation of receiving the benefit whether directly or indirectly suffices.

8.92 Once the defendant has committed a prohibited transaction, the mental element required to make him liable under the provisions of the ordinance in disclosing information about prohibited transaction is strict liability. There is no need for the prosecution to prove he acted intentionally, recklessly, or neg-ligently in disclosing the prohibited transaction. The intention of the ordinance is to prevent the culprit committing a prohibited transaction from inflicting further damage to the investing public by disclosing information about his wrongdoings.

8.93 However, a person such as a commentator or columnist may report or comment on the prohibited transactions innocently without knowing the manipulative intent. The provisions of the ordinance provide a statutory defence under this circumstance. When a person who is innocent to the prohibited transaction has received or expects to receive benefit from another person, but the other person is not a party to the prohibited transaction, he is not liable for disclosing

---

[234] SFO s 276.   [235] YK Kwan, above, p 145.   [236] SFO ss 276(3) & 297(4).
[237] SFO ss 276(1) & 297(1).

information about prohibited transactions.[238] Accordingly, a journalist is not liable for receiving the news as a benefit from a third-party source in writing an article in the newspaper about specific prohibited transactions.

The statutory defence is extended to a person who has received, or expects to **8.94** receive, benefit from the culprit of the prohibited transaction or his associate if he has acted in good faith.[239] An example is an investment bank engaging in market manipulation which has employees on the other side of the Chinese wall reporting the effect of market manipulation to clients in a research report in good faith.[240]

(4) Disclosure of false or misleading information inducing transactions

In *The King v De Berenger and others*,[241] the English Court of Appeal held **8.95** that spreading false or misleading information intentionally to induce others to buy securities was a common law offence. In effectively carrying out market manipulation through false trading, price rigging, and stock market manipulation, spreading rumours could hardly be omitted. Stating the obvious, such activity is fraudulent. The SFO prohibits the disclosure of false or misleading information inducing transactions.[242] Specifically, a person is liable by disclosing, circulating or disseminating, or authorizing information that is likely to 'induce': (1) another person to buy securities or deal in futures contracts in Hong Kong; (2) the sale or purchase in Hong Kong of securities by another person; (3) the maintenance, increase, reduction, or stabilization of the price of securities or futures contracts in Hong Kong. These provisions are derived from section 138 of the now repealed Securities Ordinance, section 64 of the now repealed Commodities Trading Ordinance, and sections 999 and 1261 of the Corporations Act 2001 (Australia).

Under the ordinance, the offence can be committed in Hong Kong or elsewhere **8.96** in inducing trading activities in Hong Kong.[243] The information must be false or misleading in the material fact. This includes statements omitting a material fact resulting in false or misleading information. What is a material fact is a question of fact decided on the context of the case. Trivial mistake is insufficient to establish an offence.[244] Opinion can be regarded as fact if rendered as professional opinion or construed as a representation of fact.[245] A person may be liable for rendering his opinion which he does not honestly hold or for which he has no grounds for such opinion. There is no statutory obligation for the person

---

[238] SFO ss 276(2)(a) & 297(3)(a).   [239] SFO ss 276(2)(b) & 297(3)(b).
[240] Goyne, above, p 19.   [241] 3 M & S 66–9.   [242] SFO ss 277(1) & 298(1).
[243] SFO ss 277(1) & 298(1).   [244] Goyne, above, p 17.
[245] *Aaron's Reefs Limited v Twiss* [1896] AC 273 at 281–2, 288–9, & 292.

disclosing the information to make any correction if the statement is true when made but subsequently becomes false. At common law, unless there is duty to disclose arising from limited circumstances, a person is not liable for remaining silent.

8.97 As Hong Kong is a small city where rumours can spread very rapidly, false or misleading information often has very damaging consequences. Therefore, the SFO imposes a higher standard on those people involved in the dissemination of information so they should be more careful.[246] For the civil route under Part XIII of the ordinance, proof of negligence is sufficient to secure a conviction. The prosecution must prove that the defendant knows, or is reckless or negligent as to whether, the information is false or misleading as to the material fact, or is false or misleading through the omission of a material fact.[247] In order to establish a criminal offence under Part XIV of the ordinance mens rea is required, that is, the prosecution must prove an intention or recklessness on the part of the defendant.[248]

8.98 The illegal act must be 'likely to induce' another person to deal with or to affect the price of securities or futures.[249] 'Induce' means leading by persuasion or some influence or motive that acts upon the will or leads on, moves, influences, or prevails upon something.[250] There must be a real and not a remote possibility that the other person is induced. In determining whether there is likelihood, it is a matter of fact for the MMT or the court to decide whether the information could induce an ordinary reasonable investor targeted by the information.

8.99 There is concern that the provisions prohibiting false or misleading information inducing transactions may impede the genuine supply of information from a third-party source. It would be seemingly impossible to check whether all such information is false or misleading. The SFO provides a defence if a person charged can prove that: (1) the disclosure is conducted in the ordinary course of business, the principal purpose is issuing or reproducing materials provided by others, for example, he is a mere 'conduit' such as a printer or a publisher;[251] (2) the disclosure is in the ordinary course of re-transmission business and does not devise the contents, for example, an internet hyperlink;[252] or (3) the disclosure is in the ordinary course of broadcasting business and does not devise the contents.[253] In general, the ordinance provides a due diligence defence. It is a good defence under the ordinance if the defendant can establish up to the time of the disclosure, he does not know that the information is false or misleading

---

[246] Goyne, above, p 17.   [247] SFO s 277(1)(ii).   [248] SFO s 298(1)(ii).
[249] SFO ss 277(1) & 298(1).
[250] *Oxford English Dictionary* (Oxford: Oxford University Press, 1971), p 229.
[251] SFO ss 277(2) & 298(3).   [252] SFO ss 277(3) & 298(4).
[253] SFO ss 277(4) & 298(5).

as to a material fact or is false or misleading through the omission of the material fact.[254]

(5) Stock market manipulation

At common law, it is well established that an agreement is illegal and void if **8.100** its object is to commit a crime or a tort. In *Scott v Brown, Doering, McNab & Co*,[255] the English Court of Appeal held that artificially enhancing the price of shares by entering into a contract to buy them at a fictitious premium was illegal and void. Such activity would render a contract void for illegality because its object:

> . . . was to impose upon and to deceive the public by leading the public to suppose that there were buyers of such shares at a premium on the Stock Exchange, when in fact there were none but himself. The plaintiff's purchase was an actual purchase, not a sham purchase; that is true, but is also true that the sole object of the purchase was to cheat and mislead the public.[256]

It is immaterial whether or not the purchase was a sham purchase insofar that **8.101** the sole objective was to cheat and mislead the public. This is the earlier concept of stock market manipulation dating back to 1892. Stock market manipulation creates a false and misleading impression of activity in the financial markets. The SFO provides cover-all provisions in banning such activity, but applies to transactions in securities only. The present provisions regulating stock market manipulation are sections 278 and 299 of the ordinance for civil and criminal offences respectively, which are derived from section 137 of the now repealed Securities Ordinance and section 997 of the Corporation Act 2001 (Australia).

Under the SFO, stock market manipulation is defined as entering into two or **8.102** more transactions in securities of the same corporation to increase the price of any security traded on a recognized market with the intention of inducing another person to purchase or refrain from selling securities of the corporation.[257] Under the SFO, manipulating a security's price can be committed in Hong Kong or elsewhere to induce the trading or refraining from trading.[258] If the price is affected on a relevant overseas market, then the manipulating activity must be entered into or carried out in Hong Kong.[259] However, such activity must also be illegal in that relevant overseas market.[260]

The ordinance prohibits a person from engaging in two or more transactions in **8.103** securities that are likely to have the effect of increasing, reducing, or maintaining

---

[254] SFO ss 277(2)–(4) & 298(3)–(5).   [255] [1892] 2 QB 724.   [256] ibid, 728–9.
[257] SFO s 278.   [258] SFO ss 278(1) & 299(1).   [259] SFO ss 278 (2) & 299(2).
[260] SFO ss 282(3) & 306(3).

or stabilizing their price with the intention of inducing another person to buy and sell securities, or refrain from doing so as the case may be.[261] It is immaterial whether the transaction is entered into or carried out directly or indirectly. It is not necessary for the transaction to have been entered or carried out. It suffices if there is an offer or an invitation.[262] Neither does it require the price to have been actually affected. What the ordinance requires is that the security's price is likely to be affected. In other words, there must be a real and not a remote possibility that the security's price would be affected. In determining whether there is likelihood, it is a matter of fact for the MMT or the court to decide objectively from the evidence admitted.

8.104 It usually takes two or more transactions to constitute stock market manipulation. The presumption is that a single transaction is not likely to have been intended to induce the buy and sale of securities, or refrain from doing so. However, given the right opportunity, one single transaction is capable to manipulate the security's price. There must be an 'intention of inducing another person' to deal with the securities.[263] A specific intent is required to secure a conviction. If there is no such intention, the defendant cannot be said to have manipulated the stock market. 'Inducing' means leading by persuasion or some influence or motive that acts upon the will or leading on, moving, influencing, or prevailing upon something.[264] Therefore, there is no stock market manipulation without proving the specific intent even though the transaction affects the security's price and has induced purchases or sales by others. A person who knows that his transaction would have a price effect does not necessarily have the intention of inducing another person to trade. There is a clear distinction between 'knowledge' and intention.[265]

8.105 Price stabilization is manipulative per se as it is intended to maintain or support the security's price artificially. This would distort the market price of the securities in violation of the natural forces of supply and demand in the financial markets. From time to time, a company which raises funds by issuing listed shares may encounter short-term share price fluctuations arising from the abrupt increase in supply.[266] In avoiding uncertainty of security's price in initial price offering, price stabilization may be necessary.[267] In recognition that price stabilization measures taken to stabilize the price of securities in preventing them from increasing or reducing may facilitate capital-raising, the SFC has

---

[261] SFO ss 278(1) & (2) & 299(1) & (2).   [262] SFO ss 278(3) & 299(4).
[263] SFO ss 278(1) & 299(1).
[264] *Oxford English Dictionary* (Oxford: Oxford University Press, 1971), p 229.
[265] Goyne, above, p 16.
[266] *A Consultation Paper on the Draft Securities and Futures (Price Stabilizing) Rules* (Hong Kong: Securities and Futures Commission, 2002), pp 1–3.
[267] ibid.

made safe harbour rules, as empowered by the SFO,[268] prescribing circumstances in which price stabilizing measures may be taken in public offerings.[269] These rules are discussed in Chapter 4 in connection with public offerings.

There is a contrary view about legalizing market stabilization: the argument is that stabilization artificially increases the security's price and that purchasers of the security would suffer loss once the market stabilization activity ceases. Nevertheless, there are safeguards in the price stabilizing rules, including prescribing a stabilizing period,[270] requiring mandatory disclosure of the stabilizing action,[271] and limiting the price in stabilizing action.[272] However, critics argue that disclosing stabilizing activity may cause a security's price to fall as it is signalling the security is overvalued.[273] Such a view is inconsistent with a disclosure based market. **8.106**

There may be overlapping between false trading and stock market manipulation. As the latter requires a specific intent to induce another person to trade securities, it has a higher standard of proof. In the absence of proving such specific intent, the defendant may still be liable for false trading if the prosecution can prove that he has the intention to enter into or carry out a transaction which is likely to have the effect of creating a false or misleading appearance if all other elements of the offence are present. **8.107**

E. Fraud and Deception

There are three types of market fraud offence prohibited by the SFO. They are offences involving fraudulent or deceptive devices,[274] disclosure of false or misleading information inducing others to enter into leveraged foreign exchange contracts,[275] and falsely representing dealings in futures contracts on behalf of others.[276] The former two offences are straightforward fraudulent practices. **8.108**

The ordinance creates a 'bucketing' offence, which is an offence of falsely representing that futures contracts will be executed on a futures market or ATS. This practice should be banned because the innocent party, who relies on the false information, has to assume additional risks without his knowledge. Under the ordinance, a person is prohibited from representing that futures transactions **8.109**

---

[268] SFO ss 282(2) & 306(2).
[269] Securities and Futures (Price Stabilizing) Rules, Cap. 571W, Laws of Hong Kong.
[270] Securities and Futures (Price Stabilizing) Rules, ss 2(1) & 6.
[271] Securities and Futures (Price Stabilizing) Rules, s 8.
[272] Securities and Futures (Price Stabilizing) Rules s 11.
[273] Fischel & Ross, above, p 538.   [274] SFO s 300.   [275] SFO s 301.
[276] SFO s 302.

executed on behalf of another person are executed on the HKEx or by means of an ATS if he has in fact not so executed and will not do so.[277] This provision requires mens rea, that is, the prosecution must prove beyond a reasonable doubt that the defendant has knowingly or recklessly committed the offence. The offence extends to contracts or other instruments substantially resembling a futures contract in an overseas futures market.[278]

F. Conclusion

8.110   In evaluating Hong Kong's regulation of market misconduct, it is useful to compare them in general to international standards. Unfortunately, IOSCO's *Objectives and Principles of Securities Regulation* provides limited guidance in this regard, stating only that regulation should: (1) promote transparency of trading (principle 27); and (2) be designed to detect and deter manipulation and other unfair trading practices (principle 28). While these standards provide limited guidance, there has now emerged some commonality in approaching these issues in major markets around the world.[279] As a general matter, this common approach largely follows the legislative, regulatory, and common law development in the US, in relation to insider dealing, market misconduct, and disclosure.

8.111   Overall, one can conclude that following the enactment of the SFO, Hong Kong has implemented a comprehensive system addressing market misconduct, through both disclosure regulation and market conduct regulation. While international standards do not address these sorts of issues in great detail, in general, as discussed above, much of Hong Kong's regulatory structure addressing market misconduct is derived from overseas jurisdictions (Australia and the US, and reflecting the EU and the UK) adopting international norms. This is especially the case in relation to insider dealing, market manipulation, and financial fraud and deception. Regulation addressing such issues in Hong Kong is generally of an international standard and the basic approach is common with other major financial markets.

8.112   More important, however, is the effective enforcement of such a system addressing market misconduct: specifically, Hong Kong's culture, society, and legal institutions have to support the successful implementation of such a set of international financial standards. At present, the SFC appears to be taking an

---

[277] SFO s 302(1).   [278] SFO s 302(2).
[279] See M Steinberg, *International Securities Law: A Contemporary and Comparative Analysis* (London: Kluwer, 1999), ch 2.

increasingly proactive role in this regard, though more time will be necessary to fully evaluate the effectiveness of enforcement in this regard.

In relation to disclosure, as noted throughout this volume, the SFO primarily **8.113** addresses markets and market participants but addresses listed companies and their affairs to a much lower level. As such, disclosure as a means of deterring market misconduct remains problematic in Hong Kong. Nonetheless, the dual filing requirements of the SFO as well as recent proposals to provide statutory backing for portions of the Listing Rules (see Chapter 4) should increase the effectiveness of the regulatory framework in this respect as well. However, entrenched interests continue to resist such efforts largely out of personal self-interest, despite the likelihood that such changes would benefit the quality and effectiveness (and therefore economic benefits) of Hong Kong's financial markets generally.

Finally, the provisions regulating mandatory disclosure and market misconduct **8.114** cannot operate in isolation. There are many other provisions in the SFO and Companies Ordinance which are related, as well as relevant common law rules and the Listing Rules of the HKEx. Financial technology continues to develop rapidly, and it is difficult to expect that provisions regulating financial markets can remain intact for an extended number of years.

PART IV

THE INTERNATIONAL DIMENSION

9

THE CHINA NEXUS

The economic re-emergence of China at the end of the twentieth century, after **9.01** several hundred years of relative decline, is perhaps one of the most important developments in the world economy in the past century. Hong Kong, with the exception of approximately 150 years under British rule and a short period during World War II under Japanese rule, has always been a part of China. Despite this fact, Hong Kong's economic role and significance largely developed under the British and British legal and institutional structures. Since Hong Kong's reversion to the People's Republic of China (PRC) on 1 July 1997, these British legal and institutional structures, albeit modified and developed to fit the circumstances of Hong Kong, largely continue as before July 1997. Now, however, they operate under the HKSAR Basic Law as part of two systems within the context of the one country of China.

With China's initiation of the process of transition from central planning to a **9.02** socialist market economy at the end of the 1970s, Hong Kong (while under British control) played an increasing role as an intermediary between the PRC and the rest of the world, especially as an outlet for products and as an inlet for capital. As China's process of economic liberalization accelerated in the 1990s,

Hong Kong's role and future began to be questioned, as other centres such as Shanghai, Shenzhen (a small village at the beginning of the 1990s and now a major city rivalling Hong Kong in size), Guangzhou (formerly Canton) and even Beijing, became more open to international business and finance. These concerns increased with China's accession to the World Trade Organization (WTO) in December 2001. Nonetheless, Hong Kong continues to play a major role as China's international financial centre, as well as a major trade conduit (both into and out of the Mainland).

9.03 Today, Hong Kong and its financial markets perform a number of roles in respect to China. First, since the early 1990s, Hong Kong has been the most significant centre for Mainland companies seeking to raise funds, especially through the listing of companies and sales and subsequent trading of shares. This has been supported through the introduction of H shares (discussed below and in Chapter 4) as well as the rise of so-called 'red chip' companies—often created through reverse take-overs (discussed in Chapter 7). Second, Hong Kong continues to be a major investor in the Mainland as well as an important conduit for other foreign direct investment (FDI—especially from Taiwan) due in major part to the continuity of the rule of law in the HKSAR. Third, in addition to direct business, Hong Kong serves as a major centre for companies and financial institutions doing business in China, once again largely due to institutional (as well as tax) advantages over Mainland counterparts. Fourth, an increasing number of Mainland companies and financial institutions are using Hong Kong as their base for international operations, especially those related to finance. Finally, as a result of the above factors, Hong Kong's legal and institutional system has increasingly been required to deal directly with its counterparts on the Mainland, despite their separateness under the Basic Law.

9.04 As a result, one cannot look only to the financial markets and their legal and regulatory framework in Hong Kong without also looking at their counterparts in Mainland China. Reflecting this, this chapter addresses first the opportunities presented by listings of Mainland companies in Hong Kong, as well as China's accession to the WTO and its related Closer Economic Partnership Agreement (CEPA) with the HKSAR. Second, in order to understand the opportunities presented by these three factors, it is important to have an understanding of the legal and regulatory framework for finance in Mainland China. This is addressed in the remaining sections (dealing with banking, securities, and insurance, respectively).

A. Opportunities in China Financial Services Business

In looking at opportunities for financial markets professionals in Hong Kong, **9.05**
three deserve to be highlighted. First is the development of H-shares and red
chip companies from the beginning of the 1990s. Second is China's accession to
the WTO and related financial services liberalization commitments. Third is the
CEPA between Mainland China and the HKSAR.

(1) H-shares and red chips

H-shares are renminbi-denominated shares issued by PRC issuers under PRC **9.06**
law and listed on the SEHK, the par values of which are denominated in
renminbi, and which are subscribed for and traded in Hong Kong dollars.
H-share companies raised more than HK$ 200 billion (US$ 25.7 billion) during the period from 1993 to March 2004, accounting for more than 12 per cent
of the total IPO funds raised through the HKEx securities market (Main Board
and Growth Enterprise Market). Red chips are companies with a Mainland
parent company, listed on the SEHK, or with primarily Mainland business
interests, and have often been created through reverse takeovers.

Specific rules and requirements for H-share offerings and listings are dealt with **9.07**
in Chapter 4, and Chapter 7 deals with reverse takeovers. In addition, the role
of H-shares in China's on-going economic restructuring is discussed further
below in the context of securities markets and regulation. In addition, many of
the major Mainland companies likely to be listed on the SEHK over the
coming three to five years are likely to be financial services companies, especially
banks. As such, the background of these institutions becomes quite important.
In addition, one of the key reasons for the on-going restructuring especially of
Mainland banks but also of Mainland securities and insurance companies is the
liberalization commitments made in the context of China's accession to the
WTO, as well as related commitments to HKSAR institutions under CEPA.

(2) WTO/GATS

The decision to accept China as a WTO Member was taken on 10 November **9.08**
2001 in Doha, and the legal documents relating to China's accession were
signed on that day. With respect to trade in services, the documents include the
Protocol on Accession of the People's Republic of China ('China Accession
Protocol'), Schedule of Specific Commitments on Services ('Schedule'), and the
Working Party Report. The three legal documents are interrelated and inter-
connected. The China Accession Protocol is the leading document, annexed by
the Schedule and some parts of the Working Party Report. All of the official

documents respecting China's accession are not in the Chinese language, for example, the Schedule is 'authentic only in the English language'.[1]

9.09 China's commitments respecting financial services can be divided into two main categories: horizontal and specific.

Horizontal commitments

9.10 These commitments apply to financial services, as well as all service sectors included in the Schedule. China made the following horizontal commitments:

- First, it is permitted to establish foreign capital enterprises (wholly-foreign-owned enterprises), joint venture enterprises, branches, and representative offices in China.

- Second, all land in the PRC is State-owned. Use of land by enterprises and individuals is subject to maximum term limitations, such as 50 years or 70 years.

- Third, managers, executives, and specialists as senior employees of a representative office, branch, or subsidiary in China shall be permitted entry for a period of time.

9.11 The following sections outline China's specific commitments relating to banking, insurance, and securities.

Banking

9.12 China's commitments with respect to banking services address geographic coverage, clients, licensing, and national treatment.

Geographical coverage

9.13 For foreign currency business, there are no geographical restrictions upon accession. For local currency business, the geographic restriction will be phased out as follows: Upon accession, Shanghai, Shenzhen, Tianjin, and Dalian; within one year after accession (end-2002), Guangzhou, Zhuhai, Qingdao, Nanjing, and Wuhan; within two years after accession (end-2003), Jinan, Fuzhou, Chengdu, and Chongqing; within three years after accession (end-2004), Kunming, Beijing, and Xiamen; within four years after accession (end-2005), Shantou, Ningbo, Shenyang, and Xi'an. Within five years after accession (end-2006), all geographic restrictions will be removed.

---

[1] See China Accession Protocol, Annex 9. See also China Accession Protocol, final paragraph.

Clients

For foreign currency business, foreign financial institutions are permitted to **9.14** provide services in China without restriction as to clients upon accession. For local currency business, within two years after accession (end-2003), foreign financial institutions are permitted to provide services to Chinese enterprises. Within five years after accession (end-2006), foreign financial institutions will be permitted to provide services to all Chinese clients. Foreign financial institutions licensed for local currency business in one region of China may service clients in any other region that has been opened for such business.

Licensing

Criteria for authorization to deal in China's financial services sector are to **9.15** be solely prudential (ie contain no economic needs test or quantitative limits on licences). Within five years after accession (end-2006), any existing non-prudential measures restricting ownership, operation, and juridical form of foreign financial institutions, including on internal branching and licences, shall be eliminated. Financial institutions must meet the following asset requirements in relation to form of business establishment:

- Subsidiary: total assets of more than US$ 10 billion at the end of the year prior to filing the application.
- Branch: total assets of more than US$ 20 billion at the end of the year prior to filing the application.
- Chinese-foreign joint bank or finance company: total assets of more than US$ 10 billion at the end of the year prior to filing the application.

Qualifications for foreign financial institutions to engage in local currency busi- **9.16** ness are three years' business operation in China and being profitable for two consecutive years prior to the application; otherwise, none.

National treatment

Except for geographical restrictions and client limitations on local currency **9.17** business (listed in the market access column), foreign financial institutions may do business, without restrictions or need for case-by-case approval, with foreign-invested enterprises, non-Chinese natural persons, Chinese natural persons, and Chinese enterprises. This national treatment limitation shows the relationship between market access and national treatment; ie geographical restrictions and client limitations listed in the market access column may also constitute national treatment limitations.

Insurance

China's commitments with respect to insurance services address form of estab- **9.18** lishment, geographic coverage, business scope, licences, and national treatment.

Form of establishment

9.19   Foreign non-life insurers are permitted to establish as a branch or as a joint
venture with 51 per cent foreign ownership. Within two years after China's
accession (end-2003), foreign non-life insurers are permitted to establish
wholly-owned subsidiaries, ie with no form of establishment restrictions. Upon
accession, foreign life insurers are permitted 50 per cent foreign ownership in
a joint venture with the partner of their choice. The joint venture partners can
freely agree the terms of their engagement, provided they remain within the
limits of the commitments contained in the schedule.

9.20   For brokerage of insurance of large-scale commercial risks and brokerage of
reinsurance and brokerage of international marine, aviation, and transport
insurance and reinsurance:

- upon accession, joint ventures with foreign equity no more than 50 per cent
  are permitted;
- within three years after China's accession (end-2004), maximum foreign
  equity share increased to 51 per cent; and
- within five years after China's accession (end-2006), wholly foreign owned
  subsidiaries will be permitted.

For other brokerage services, there are no such limitations.

Geographical coverage

9.21   Upon accession, foreign life and non-life insurers, and insurance brokers are
permitted to provide services in Shanghai, Guangzhou, Dalian, Shenzhen, and
Foshan. Within two years after China's accession (end-2003), foreign life and
non-life insurers, and insurance brokers are permitted to provide services in the
following additional cities: Beijing, Chengdu, Chongqing, Fuzhou, Suzhou,
Xiamen, Ningbo, Shenyang, Wuhan, and Tianjin. Within three years after
China's accession (end-2004), there will be no geographical restrictions.

Business scope

9.22   Upon accession, foreign non-life insurers will be permitted to provide 'master
policy' insurance/insurance of large-scale commercial risks, with no geographic
restrictions. In accordance with national treatment, foreign insurance brokers
will be permitted to provide 'master policy' coverage no later than Chinese
brokers, under conditions no less favourable. Foreign non-life insurers are permitted to provide insurance of enterprises abroad as well as property insurance,
related liability insurance, and credit insurance of foreign-invested enterprises in
China upon accession. Within two years (end-2003) after China's accession,
foreign non-life insurers are permitted to provide the full range of non-life
insurance services to both foreign and domestic clients.

Foreign insurers are permitted to provide individual (not group) insurance to **9.23** foreigners and Chinese citizens from accession; within three years after accession (end-2004), foreign insurers are permitted to provide health insurance, group insurance, and pension/annuities insurance to foreigners and Chinese citizens. Upon accession, foreign insurers are permitted to provide reinsurance services for life and non-life insurance as branches, joint ventures, or wholly foreign-owned subsidiaries, without geographical or quantitative restrictions on the number of licences issued.

Licences

Upon accession, licences are issued with no economic needs test or quantitative **9.24** limits on licences. Qualifications for establishing a foreign insurance institution are as follows:

- be a foreign insurance company with more than 30 years of establishment experience in a WTO member;
- have a representative office for two consecutive years in China; and
- have total assets of more than US$ 5 billion at the end of the year prior to application, except for insurance brokers.

At accession, insurance brokers must have total assets of more than US$ 500 **9.25** million this threshold amount being reduced on each anniversary of accession by US$ 100 million until the fourth anniversary (end-2005) when it is reduced to US$ 200 million.

National treatment

Foreign insurance institutions shall not engage in the statutory insurance busi- **9.26** ness. Upon accession, a 20 per cent cession of all lines of the primary risks for non-life, personal accident, and health insurance business with an appointed Chinese reinsurance company shall be required; one year after accession (end-2002), 15 per cent shall be required; two years after accession, 10 per cent shall be required (end-2003); three years after accession (end-2004), 5 per cent shall be required; and four years after accession (end-2004), no compulsory cession shall be required.

Securities

China made comparatively fewer commitments in its securities sector[2] than it **9.27** did in the banking and insurance sectors, respectively, and the securities sector

---

[2] The PRC Securities Law defines a 'securities company' as a limited liability company or limited company given approval to engage in securities business and divides securities companies into two categories: (1) comprehensive securities companies; and (2) brokerage-type securities

will open at a slower pace than either of the two aforementioned sectors. This slower pace is due, in part, to the Chinese government's desire to not have transnational capital flows potentially disrupt China's securities markets. These commitments include forms of establishment, business scope, licensing, and national treatment.

Forms of establishment

9.28 Upon WTO accession, China committed to (1) allow foreign securities firms to engage directly in B-share business without a Chinese intermediary; (2) permit the representative offices of foreign securities firms to become Special Members of all Chinese stock exchanges; and (3) allow foreign investors to establish joint venture fund management companies (FI-FMCs) provided that foreign interest in an FI-FMC does not exceed 33 per cent of the venture's registered capital. By the third anniversary of WTO accession (end-2004), China committed to (1) increase the foreign investment limit in a FI-FMC to 49 per cent of the venture's registered capital; and (2) allow foreign investors to form joint venture securities companies (JVSCs), provided that the maximum foreign interest in such entity is limited to 33 per cent of the JVSC's registered capital.[3]

Business scope

9.29 China's Schedule of Specific Commitments does not define the permitted business scope for foreign invested securities ventures as comprehensively as it does for foreign invested banking or insurance ventures. Upon accession, China committed to allow: (1) foreign securities institutions to engage directly (without a Chinese intermediary) in B-share business (brokering B-shares); (2) representative offices of foreign securities firms to become Special Members of all Chinese stock exchanges; and (3) FI-FMCs to engage in domestic securities investment fund management. By the third anniversary of WTO accession (end-2004), China committed to allow JVSCs to directly underwrite A-shares,

---

companies. Arts 118 & 120. Under Art 129, comprehensive securities companies' scope of business may include (1) securities brokerage business; (2) securities proprietary business; (3) securities underwriting business; and (4) other securities businesses as approved by the CSRC. Pursuant to Art 130, brokerage-type securities companies may only operate a brokerage business.

[3] In its services sector horizontal commitments, the Chinese government notes that foreign investment in an equity joint venture shall be no less than 25% of the venture's registered capital. This is consistent with the terms of China's Equity Joint Venture Law. However, on 30 December 2002, MOFTEC, SAT, SAIC, and SAFE jointly issued Issues Relevant to Strengthening the Administration of the Examination, Approval, Registration, Foreign Exchange Issues, and Taxation of Foreign-invested Enterprises Circular ('FIE Circular'), effective 1 January 2003. The new circular generally requires all FIEs to comply with the Equity Joint Venture Law's examination, approval, and registration requirements and reiterates the 25% foreign equity interest requirement. The FIE Circular seems to create a 'Special FIE', with less than 25%, which Special FIE, will not be eligible for any preferential tax policy. It is unclear whether 'Special FIEs' will be allowed in China's securities sector.

underwrite and broker B-shares, H-shares, and government and corporate bonds, and establish investment funds.

Licensing

As in other financial services sectors, the criteria for licensing in China's secur- **9.30** ities sector are prudential and contain no economic needs test or quantitative limit on licences.

National treatment

China placed no limitations on national treatment, apart from those national **9.31** treatment restrictions related to the presence of natural persons as provided in the Horizontal Commitments (as described above).

China's other GATS/WTO commitments concerning financial services

In addition to horizontal and specific commitments, China has made a number **9.32** of other commitments affecting trade in financial services, including specific aspects of MFN treatment, transparency, judicial review, and transitional period. Of these, those relating to transitional period are of most significance.

In China's banking commitments, there is a particular statement following the **9.33** prudential licensing requirement:

> within five years after accession, any existing non-prudential measures restricting ownership, operation, and juridical form of foreign financial institutions, including on internal branching and licenses, shall be eliminated.

This statement appears to be restrictive, but in fact it implies that any existing non-prudential measures could remain until end-2006 (five years after China's accession). What does this five-year transition period mean? Can China make new non-prudential measures after accession, and then eliminate them before end-2006? The answer depends on the meaning of 'existing non-prudential measures'. If existing non-prudential measures refer only to those measures issued before WTO entry, the answer is no. If they include new non-prudential measures issued after accession, the answer is the opposite.

The lack of clarity regarding the phase-out commitment relating to existing **9.34** non-prudential measures restricting ownership, operation, and juridical form of foreign financial institutions has resulted in interpretations that China is entitled to make new non-prudential measures during the five-year transitional period. Other interpretations (with which the authors' accord) hold that China may delay the process of elimination of 'existing non-prudential measures' to end-2006, but China cannot make any more restrictive measures, except for prudential measures or measures permitted by WTO agreements. It seems more reasonable to take the view that 'existing non-prudential measures' only includes those existing measures as of December 2001. Otherwise, the term 'existing' would be unnecessary. We would therefore argue that the particular statement should not be interpreted to entitle China to take new non-prudential measures, which is contrary to China's obligations under the WTO.

(3) CEPA

9.35 In order to promote the joint economic prosperity and development of Mainland China and the HKSAR, the Mainland and Hong Kong Closer Economic Partnership Arrangement (CEPA) was signed and took effect on 29 June 2003. In addition to the Mainland and Hong Kong CEPA, there is a similar CEPA between the Mainland and Macau, which was signed and took effect on 17 October 2003.[4] In this section, CEPA refers to the Mainland–Hong Kong CEPA. The CEPA, in essence, is a free trade agreement (FTA), which is an exception to MFN treatment.[5]

9.36 According to the CEPA, from 1 January 2004, the Mainland would apply a zero tariff rate to the import of some goods of Hong Kong origin.[6] No later than 1 January 2006, the Mainland will apply a zero tariff rate to the import of all goods of Hong Kong origin.[7] Service trade is also covered in the CEPA.[8] The core of the CEPA service trade is Mainland China's Schedule of Specific Commitments on Opening Service Trade to Hong Kong (CEPA Schedule), as Annex 4 to the CEPA, in which the financial service sector is listed.

Banking and other financial services

9.37 According to the CEPA Schedule, the categories of banking services are equivalent to those in China's WTO Schedule.[9] The fact that China did not include more categories of banking services in the CEPA indirectly indicates the scope of banking services in China's WTO commitments is sufficiently broad for the purposes of China's leadership.

9.38 As to specific market access and national treatment commitments, China provides more favoured treatment to Hong Kong (or Macau) banking service suppliers under the CEPA.[10] First, the minimum total assets requirement for a

---

[4] There is essentially no difference between the two CEPAs.
[5] See GATT Art XXIV & GATS Art V.   [6] See CEPA Art 5.2.
[7] See CEPA Art 5.3.   [8] See CEPA, chap 4.
[9] See CEPA, Annex 4, Table 1. According to a footnote in the CEPA, the 'mainland' refers to the entire customs territory of China. See WT/REG162/1, 20 January 2004.
[10] The existing schedule of specific commitments under current CEPA is unilateral. There are only service commitments made by Mainland China to Hong Kong. According to the arrangement, Mainland China and Hong Kong will negotiate service commitments to be made by Hong Kong to Mainland China, which will be contained in CEPA, Annex 4, Table 2. See CEPA, Annex 4.

Hong Kong (or Macau) bank to establish a branch or juridical person in Mainland China is reduced to US$ 6 billion. Second, there is no precondition for a Hong Kong (or Macau) bank to set up a representative office before establishing a joint equity bank or joint equity finance company. Third, the conditions for a branch of a Hong Kong (or Macau) bank located in Mainland China to apply for renminbi operations include: (1) two years' business operation in China, unlike the requirement of three years' business operation in China's WTO Schedule; and (2) comprehensive consideration of whole branches operation in order to determine whether it satisfies the profitable qualification, unlike individual consideration of a single branch operation in China's WTO Schedule.

Insurance and insurance-related services

The scope of insurance services covered in China's CEPA Schedule is the same **9.39** as that in China's WTO Schedule, ie life, health and pension/annuities insurance, non-life insurance, reinsurance, and services auxiliary to insurance. As to specific commitments, China has accorded more favourable treatment to Hong Kong financial service suppliers.

First, China has relaxed market access conditions for Hong Kong insurance **9.40** companies to enter the Mainland market. In China's CEPA Schedule, several Hong Kong insurance companies can form an insurance group to apply for entry to the Mainland insurance market and the total assets of the group can be calculated to satisfy the asset requirement of US$ 5 billion, and it is unnecessary for each insurance company in the insurance group to have 30 years' operation experience and two years of representative offices in China. If only one insurance company in the group meets the requirements of 30 years of operation experience and two years of a representative office, then it is deemed that the group meets these requirements.

Second, Hong Kong insurance companies can purchase shares of Mainland **9.41** insurance companies, albeit with a ceiling of 24.9 per cent.

Third, if a Chinese citizen who is also a Hong Kong resident obtains the **9.42** qualification of a Chinese actuary, he can engage in business in the Mainland without prior approval.

Fourth, a Hong Kong resident can engage in relevant insurance business after **9.43** obtaining a Chinese insurance business licence and being employed by a Mainland insurance institution.

Securities services

According to China's CEPA Schedule, China allows HKEx to set up a representative office in Beijing. China also simplified relevant procedures for Hong **9.44**

Kong professionals to apply for China's securities and future qualifications, such that they only need to take a legal knowledge examination, rather than a professional knowledge examination.

Opportunities for Hong Kong financial services

9.45 Generally speaking, the more favourable treatment granted to Hong Kong and Macau provide for meaningful advantages for their service providers. However, 'service supplier' in the CEPA is quite restrictive—much stricter than that in the GATS. As a result, financial services suppliers must look carefully at these requirements in order to take advantage of the opportunities offered.

9.46 On the one hand, according to GATS Article XXVIII(g), 'service supplier' means any person that supplies a service. 'Person' means either a natural person or a juridical person.[11] Since 'natural persons' are generally not allowed to supply 'banking services' (for prudential reasons), 'juridical person' is the focus for analysis. GATS Article XXVIII (m)(i) stipulates that 'juridical person of another Member' means a juridical person which is constituted or otherwise organized under the law of that other Member, and is engaged in substantive business operations in the territory of that Member or any other Member.[12] No minimum operation time is required for being a 'service supplier'.

9.47 On the other hand, according to CEPA Annex 5 'Definition of "Service Supplier" and related Rules', the standards applying to a Hong Kong service supplier providing service by way of a juridical person include: (1) establishment or registration based on HKSAR corporation regulations or other regulations, with a valid business registration certificate or licence; and (2) being engaged in substantive business operations in Hong Kong. These standards are consistent with GATS Article XXVIII(m)(i). Nevertheless, the tests to determine engagement in substantive business operation in Hong Kong include a minimum requirement of three years of registration and operation in Hong Kong.[13] To be a Hong Kong service supplier in banking and other financial services, ie a Hong Kong bank or finance company, the minimum requirement is five years of operation after obtaining a licence.[14]

9.48 From this discussion, it is useful to understand the context in which these opportunities arise, specifically Mainland China's financial markets and related law and regulation.

---

[11] See GATS Art XXVIII(j).
[12] In the case of the supply of a service through commercial presence, owned or controlled by (1) natural persons of that Member; or (2) juridical persons of that other Member. See GATS Art XXVIII(m)(ii).
[13] See CEPA, Annex 5, Art 3(1).   [14] CEPA, Annex 5, Art 3(1).

B. Financial Markets and their Regulation in Mainland China

Unlike the HKSAR, the PRC has a legal and institutional framework based on **9.49** civil law and supporting the development of a socialist-market economy. As a result, it is very different indeed. This section first presents an overview of the PRC legal system, then looks at its overall financial regulatory structure.

(1) Overview of China's legal structure

Legislative power in China does not rest exclusively in the hands of the National **9.50** People's Congress (NPC) and its Standing Committee. Rather, it depends on the level of legislation involved. According to the PRC Legislation Law of 2000, there are seven kinds of laws in the broadest meaning, including laws, administrative regulations, local regulations, autonomous regulations, separate regulations, rules of departments under the State Council, and rules of local governments.[15]

Laws

In the strict sense, laws only refer to those enacted by the NPC and its Standing **9.51** Committee. The NPC enacts and amends basic laws governing criminal offences, civil affairs, State institutions, and other basic laws, while the Standing Committee of the NPC enacts and amends laws other than those within the power of the NPC.[16] Because the NPC only holds one national conference each year, its Standing Committee enacts most laws.

Administrative regulations

Administrative regulations are formulated by the State Council in accordance **9.52** with the Constitution and laws enacted by the NPC and its Standing Committee. The main purpose of administrative regulations is to implement the laws and deal with the administrative matters within the powers of the State Council, so they are binding on the whole of the PRC, except for the HKSAR and Macau SAR.

Local regulations

China's local regions include three forms: provinces, autonomous regions, **9.53** and municipalities directly under the Central Government, each of which has its own local People's Congress and correspondent Standing Committee. These

---

[15] Legislation Law, art 2.   [16] Legislation Law, art 7.

local People's Congresses and Standing Committees may formulate local regulations, provided such regulations do not conflict with the Constitution, national laws, and/or administrative regulations.[17] In contrast to the nationally binding scope of laws and administrative regulations, local regulations are effective only within the relevant local area. The local congresses at the level of comparatively larger cities in provinces and autonomous regions may also formulate local regulations subject to approval by provincial level congresses.

Autonomous regulations and separate regulations

9.54 With respect to the political, economic, and cultural characteristics of the local nationalities, local People's Congresses in autonomous areas, including autonomous regions at provincial level and autonomous prefectures or counties at lower level, may formulate autonomous regulations and separate regulations.[18] All autonomous regulations and separate regulations must be approved by a higher People's Congress.

Rules of departments

9.55 Article 71 of the Legislation Law states:

> The ministries and commissions of the State Council, the People's Bank of China, the State Audit Administration as well as the other organs endowed with administrative functions directly under the State Council may, in accordance with the laws as well as the administrative regulations, decisions and orders of the State Council and within the limits of their power, formulate rules.

> Matters governed by the rules of departments shall be those for the enforcement of the laws or the administrative regulations, decisions and orders of the State Council.

The binding scope of the rules of departments is similar to that of administrative regulations, that is, the whole territory of China. The two terms, administrative regulations and rules of departments, are easily confused. In fact, administrative regulations (*Xingzheng Fagui* or *Xingzheng Tiaoli*) refer only to regulations issued by the State Council, while rules of departments (*Xingzheng Guizhang* or *Xingzheng Banfa*) refer only to rules issued by departments or ministries under the State Council. Therefore, all measures issued by the main financial regulatory agencies (PBOC, CBRC, CIRC, CSRC—all discussed below) should be termed 'rules', instead of 'regulations'.[19]

---

[17] Legislation Law, art 63.   [18] Legislation Law, art 66.

[19] The US Trade Representative (USTR) misused the term of 'regulations' in its report. See USTR 2003 National Trade Estimate Report on Foreign Trade Barriers, p 64. <http://www.ustr.gov/reports/nte/2003/> (18 April 2003).

Rules of local governments

The local governments of the provinces, autonomous regions, municipalities **9.56** directly under the Central Government, and the comparatively larger cities, may formulate local rules.[20]

The following chart shows the levels of legal effect for different laws (in the **9.57** broader meaning discussed above) under China's legal system.

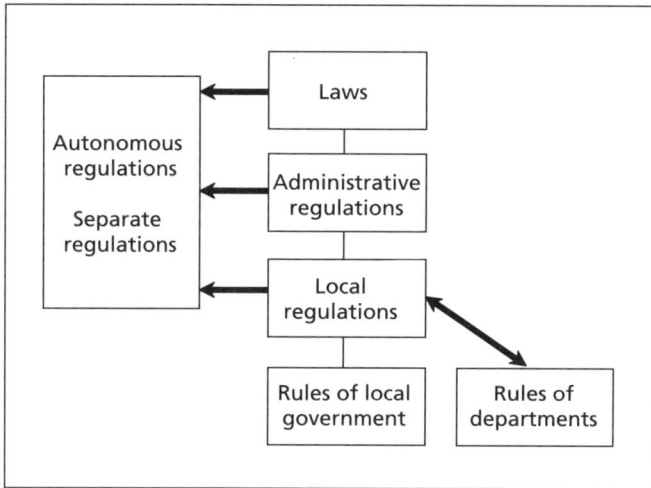

Figure 9.1 Levels of legal effect

- First, the effect of laws is higher than that of administrative regulations, local regulations, and rules of departments.[21]

- Second, the effect of administrative regulations is higher than that of local regulations and rules of departments.[22]

- Third, the effect of local regulations is higher than that of the rules of the local governments.[23]

- Fourth, the effect of the rules of departments and the effect of the rules of local governments is equal.[24] If there is inconsistency between local regulations and rules of departments, the State Council shall take the final decision.[25]

---

[20] Legislation Law, art 63.   [21] Legislation Law, art 79.
[22] Legislation Law, art 79.   [23] Legislation Law, art 80.
[24] Legislation Law, art 82.
[25] Legislation Law, art 85. If the State Council considers that local regulations should be applied, the local regulations shall be applied; if the State Council considers that rules of departments should be applied, the case shall be submitted to the NPC Standing Committee for a ruling.

- Fifth, the autonomous regulations and separate regulations shall apply in the autonomous areas concerned in accordance with the laws, administrative regulations, and local regulations.[26]

(2) Financial law and regulation in Mainland China

9.58 The above-mentioned six forms of law are not all relevant to finance. Given the uniform nature of China's financial market, China's financial laws take mainly three forms, ie financial laws, financial administrative regulations, and financial rules, and the chart is as follows:

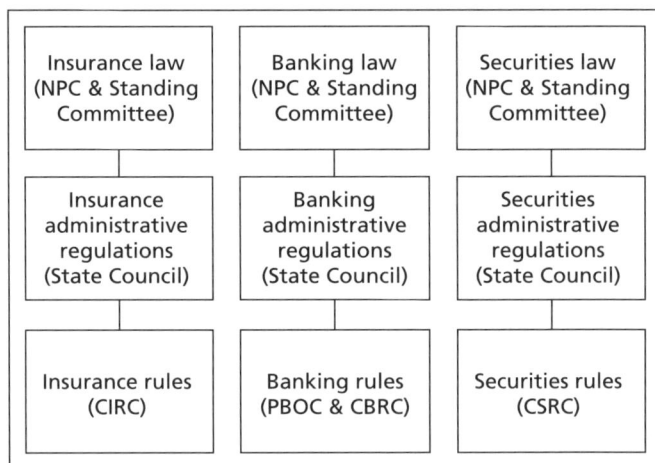

Figure 9.2 Financial law and regulation

9.59 However, following China's entry to the WTO, many laws, regulations, rules, or other measures have been abolished or amended, and this abolition and amendment process is still on-going. Therefore, it is necessary to study China's financial laws carefully in order to determine which rule is still valid.

9.60 In order to understand financial markets and related law and regulation in Mainland China, it is useful to have an overall understanding of China's regulatory structure. In essence, Mainland China has adopted a financial structure and related legal and institutional framework based on a sectoral model similar to that of the US prior to the enactment of the Graham–Leach–Bliley Financial Services Modernization Act of 1999. Under this sectoral structure, financial markets, institutions, and laws are separated into individual financial sectors, namely banking, securities, and insurance. As a result, the main financial

---

[26] Legislation Law, art 81.

regulatory agencies in Mainland China and their scope of authorities and competencies are as follows:

- People's Bank of China (PBOC): Central banking, financial stability, and monetary policy
- China Banking Regulatory Commission (CBRC): Banks and banking business
- China Securities Regulatory Commission (CSRC): Securities business
- China Insurance Regulatory Commission (CIRC): Insurance business.

At present, financial conglomerates or cross-sectoral financial services business **9.61** are not allowed in Mainland China, though this may change in the near future. In addition to the above, a number of other agencies are also often involved in different ways, including:

- National Development and Reform Commission (NDRC): Financial and development policy and planning
- Ministry of Finance (MoF): Allocation of budgetary resources, as well as some exercise of state ownership rights
- State-owned Assets Supervision and Administration Commission (SASAC): Exercise of state ownership rights.

Updated information on and from each of these agencies is available on their **9.62** respective websites.

All of these agencies, plus a range of others, together comprise the State Council, **9.63** which in many ways is the primary decision-making body respecting overall financial and economic policy and related legal and institutional issues. Based on this background, the following three sections discuss banking, securities, and insurance markets and the related legal and institutional framework in Mainland China.

C. Banking

China's banking sector is evolving from a simple and closed system in which the **9.64** government controls almost all credit allocation to an increasingly sophisticated and open system where diverse financial functions are performed by multiple institutions. Meanwhile, banking laws and regulations have paced and often led development of the banking system and banking practices. Undoubtedly, both globalization and China's transition from a planned economy to a market economy have made an overwhelming contribution to such evolution.

(1) Development of Mainland banking institutions

9.65 The banking sector plays a dominant role in China's financial market, making up more than 90 per cent of the total assets of all financial institutions.[27] Following continuous efforts directed towards transformation into a modern banking system over the last two decades, China, has developed a system in which the PBOC acts as the central bank, the state-owned commercial banks perform the dominant financial role under the primary supervision of the CBRC, and a variety of financial organizations coexist.

9.66 At the same time, China has implemented a three-tier system in its banking market. The first tier banking institutions consist of the four largest state commercial banks (the big four SOCBs), ie Agricultural Bank of China (ABC), Bank of China (BOC), China Construction Bank (CCB), and Industrial and Commercial Bank of China (ICBC). These four SOCBs still perform the most important role in the domestic financial market, accounting for more than half of deposits taken and loans granted in the entire banking system.[28] Their assets would place them among the fifty largest banking institutions in the world,[29] though there are significant problems with asset quality.

9.67 The second tier banking institutions are the policy banks. Usually, it is quite common for a transition economy to implement state policies through bank loans. In order to construct a separate commercial banking system, three policy banks were restructured in 1994, intending to alleviate the burden of the dual roles, ie policy and commercial, of state specialized banks.[30] They are the Agricultural Development Bank, China Development Bank, and Export-Import Bank of China.[31] These state development banks have to assume their own financial risks, protect their asset values, and should not compete with

[27] XH Tong et al, *Financial Services in China: The Past, Present and Future of a Changing Industry* (Singapore: China Knowledge Press Private Limited, 2005).

[28] '*Balance Sheet of Assets and Liabilities of State-Owned Commercial Banks*' [国有商业银行资产负债表], *Annual Report of People's Bank of China 2003* [中国人民银行年报2003] (Beijing: Research Institute of People's Bank of China), available at <http://www.ripbc.com.cn/yjxxw/jinrongnianbao/2003.htm>.

[29] *Top 1000 World Banks, The Banker* (London: Financial Times Business Information, July 2004), p 168.

[30] Decision of the State Council on Financial System Reform, art 2, National Distribution (*guo-fa*) 1993, No 91 [国务院关于金融体制改革的决定, 国发 [1993]第91号] (Beijing: State Council, 25 December 1993).

[31] Notice of the State Council in Restructuring the Agricultural Development Bank of China, National Distribution (*guo-fa*) 1994, No 25 [国务院关于组建中国农业发展银行的通知, 国发[1994]第25号] (Beijing: State Council, 19 April 1994); Notice of State Council in Restructuring the State Development Bank of China, National Distribution (*guo-fa*) 1994, No 22 [国务院关于组建国家开发银行的通知, 国发[1994]第22号] (Beijing: State Council, 17 March 1994).

commercially based financial institutions.[32] Their funding is mainly raised through bond issuance—large retail issues, though these are not bonds in the sense of liquid or tradable instruments.[33] Each of these banks has been assigned specific mandates in carrying out state policies.[34] In effect, they are state credit-granting agencies.

The third tier banking institutions incorporate national, regional, and local **9.68** commercial banks. As of 2004, there were eleven national and regional commercial banks—all are joint-stock.[35] One of these banks, Minsheng Bank, was incorporated in 1996 as the first private bank since the foundation of the PRC.[36] So far four of these banks have been publicly listed on the Shanghai Stock Exchange and one on the Shenzhen Stock Exchange.[37] These joint-stock banks are allowed to engage in extensive banking business, and their creation was intended to increase competition in China's domestic market.[38] Although a large bulk of their shares are still under the control of the state, they are relatively less subject to political interference, and thus, their operation appears more dynamic and performance is superior to their state-owned competitors.

In addition, urban and rural commercial banks, which have evolved from urban **9.69** and rural cooperatives respectively, are vested with specific functions relating to local development, eg for small and medium enterprises in urban areas and agricultural development in the countryside.[39] In 1995 the PBOC reorganized urban credit cooperatives into city cooperative banks in 35 pilot cities under the auspices of the respective municipal governments.[40] At the end of June 2003 there were 112 such banks,[41] and eight rural commercial and 19 cooperative banks incorporated by March 2005.[42] Their market shares are very small

---

[32] Decision of the State Council on Financial System Reform 1993, art 2.

[33] ibid.   [34] ibid.

[35] *Total Assets and Total Liabilities in 2004* [2004年总资产总负债] (Beijing: China Banking Regulatory Commission, January 2005), available at <http://www.cbrc.gov.cn/english/index.htm>.

[36] *Annual Report of People's Bank of China 2002* [中国人民银行年报 2002] (Beijing: People's Bank of China, 2002), p 68.

[37] *2003 Fact Book* (Shanghai: Shanghai Stock Exchange, 2003), available at <http://www.sse.com.cn/en_us/cs/about/factbook/factbook_us2003.pdf>; *SSE Share Information* (Shenzhen: Shenzhen Stock Exchange, September 2003), available at <http://www.szse.com.cn/sse/en/mktinfo/3-3.asp>.

[38] Decision of the State Council on Financial System Reform 1993.

[39] Decision of the State Council on Financial System Reform 1993, art 3(3).

[40] ibid.

[41] CBRC, *Fourth National Conference of Cities' Commercial Banks*, [第四次城市商业银行工作会议暨城市商业银行发展论坛] (Beijing: CBRC, August 2003), available at <http://www.cbrc.gov.cn/yaowen/detail.asp?id=129>.

[42] CBRC, 'The CBRC calls for dependent reform of rural cooperative banks and rural commercial banks' <银监会要求农村合作银行, 农村商业银行深化改革> (Beijing: CBRC, 4 April 2005), available at <http://www.cbrc.gov.cn/english/index.htm>.

because their business scope is limited to the city where they were founded, and their asset quality is rather poor due to a large amount of policy lending required by the local governments. However, urban commercial banks have become merger and acquisition targets of foreign institutions with the phased-in opening of China's financial market following its entry to the WTO.

9.70 Since the first foreign banking institution was allowed to operate in Shenzhen in 1981, foreign banks have developed rapidly. As of 2004, 62 foreign banks from 19 countries and regions had set up 204 operational institutions and 223 representative offices in Mainland China.[43] With the phase-out of geographical and business restrictions for foreign banks and full liberalization in the banking sector by 2006 under China's WTO commitments, foreign players will likely have an increasing impact on the Mainland's financial system in terms of their management expertise and diversified financial products as well as international business networks.

9.71 Although the state banks still account for the dominant part of China's financial market, private capital including foreign investment is playing an increasingly active role. Aside from traditional approaches, such as establishing wholly foreign-owned banks and joint-venture banks with domestic financial institutions, it is becoming a prevalent method for foreign players to expand their market shares in Mainland China through purchasing and holding equity stakes of domestic banks, particularly joint-stock banks and urban commercial banks.[44] Certainly, the limitations on equity holdings of overseas financial institutions in Chinese financial institutions constrain the pace of foreign business expansion in Mainland China.[45]

9.72 The central bank and the banking supervisory body have also evolved as China moves towards the creation of a market economy. During a long period from its establishment in 1948 until the late 1970s, the PBOC was the only de facto banking institution in Mainland China, assuming the dual roles of both the central and commercial bank.[46] In 1983 it was determined that the PBOC

---

[43] CBRC, 'CBRC held 2004 conference on foreign bank development in China' <银监会召开2004年在华外资银行会议> (Beijing: CBRC, 12 April 2004), available at <http://www.cbrc.gov.cn/english/index.htm>.

[44] XH Tong et al, above, p 114.

[45] Measures Governing the Equity Investment in Chinese Financial Institutions by Overseas Financial Institutions, arts 8 & 9, No 6 2003 [境外金融机构投资入股中资金融机构管理办法] (Beijing: CBRC, 8 December 2003).

[46] XL Dai (ed), *A Fifty Years History of the People's Bank of China: the Development of Central Banking System* [戴相龙主编: 中国人民银行五十年: 中央银行制度的发展历程] (Beijing, Chinese Financial Press, November 1998), p 22.

should function only as a central bank and all of its commercial business was transferred to the four commercial banks: ABC, BOC, CCB, and ICBC.[47]

The organizational reform of the PBOC in 1998 was a major step forward **9.73** towards freeing the PBOC from all the sorts of local interference common under the provincial network system.[48] In the past, the PBOC was organized into economic regions, and its provincial branches were under dual supervision of both their head office and provisional governments.[49] In strengthening the independence of the PBOC, the State Council has reorganized it and replaced the provincial network with nine trans-provincial branches.[50]

Previously, each regional office of the PBOC had supervisory power over the **9.74** banking institutions within its jurisdiction, independent from the regional governments.[51] As a result, the PBOC inevitably had conflicting roles as a regulator and central banker. A balance had to be made between maintaining rapid economic growth and prudential supervision of banking institutions. Thus, there was the risk that the PBOC might have been compelled to soften its regulatory control over risky banking institutions in accordance with State economic development policies, and that contributed to an increasing amount of non-performing loans (NPLs) in the banking system. In resolving this dilemma, the CBRC was established in April 2003 to assume the regulatory functions of the PBOC,[52] namely supervising banking and non-banking financial institutions (except insurance and securities firms), so as to ensure the stability of their operations,[53] and to help them in strengthening defences against financial risks.[54] The PBOC continues its role as a central bank with its focus on

---

[47] Decision of the State Council on the Specialization of Central Bank Functions by the People's Bank of China, para 2 [国务院关于中国人民银行专门行使中央银行职能的决定] (Beijing: State Council, 17 September 1983).

[48] *Country Finance—China* (London: Economist Intelligence Unit, August 2004), p 10.

[49] Decision of the State Council on the Specialization of Central Bank Functions by the People's Bank of China.

[50] Notice of State Council Approval of People's Bank of China Provisional Branch Restructuring, National Distribution (*guo-fa*) 1998, No 33 [<国务院批转人民银行省级机构改革实施方案的通知>, 国发[1998]第33号] (Beijing: State Council, 17 October 1998).

[51] ibid, para 2.

[52] Decision of the Standing Committee of National People's Congress on the Exercise of Regulatory and Supervisory Functions by the China Banking Regulatory Commission in Place of the People's Bank of China [全国人民代表大会常务委员会关于中国银行业监督委员会履行原由中国人民银行履
行的监督管理职责的决定] (Beijing: 26 April 2003).

[53] Banking Supervision Law, 2003, art 1.

[54] Banking Supervision Law, 2003, art 3.

formulating and implementing monetary policy and safeguarding financial stability.[55] The PBOC concentrates on regulations concerning monetary conditions and financial system liquidity with the aim of promoting economic growth and monetary stability, and the CBRC focuses on the strength of financial institutions with a focus on controlling financial risks. However, the functions of the PBOC and the CBRC seem to overlap in some areas because both have the responsibility to prevent and minimize financial risks.

9.75 It has been a task of highest priority for China's government to transform SOCBs into independent, transparent, and commercialized banking institutions. During the period in which the PBOC fulfilled both central and commercial roles, the ABC and CCB of the time, which originated through restructuring the corresponding banking institutions, merely performed specialized functions of the PBOC.[56] Through a gradual process, they became independent from the PBOC and the Ministry of Finance and took over the commercial role of the PBOC.[57] In 1984 the State Council formalized the specialized functions of the big four SOCBs.[58] Prior to the Decision of the State Council on Financial System Reform in 1993, the concept of state commercial banks was murky. Although they accepted deposits and channelled money into lending activities, they basically functioned as specialized banks under the PBOC and primarily acted as state agencies executing governmental policies in granting credit to SOEs without much regard for profitability.[59] In 1993 the socialist market economy was formally adopted by the State Council, and the big four specialized state banks were restructured as commercial banks.[60] Notwithstanding this, as well as the establishment of the policy banks to assume policy loans in 1994,[61] the SOCBs still suffer from a tremendous volume of

---

[55] Notice of the Central Committee Office on the Adjustment of Major Functions, Internal Organizations and Staff of the PBOC [中央编制委员会办公室关于中国人民银行主要职责内设机构和人员编制调整意见的通知], available at <http://www.pbc.gov.cn/detail.asp?col=100&ID=1012&keyword=国务院关于机构设置的通知>.

[56] XT Yang, et al (eds), *The General History of China's Finance* [中国金融通史] (Beijing: Chinese Finance Publishing House, 2000), pp 223–6.

[57] Decision of the State Council on the Specialization of Central Bank Functions by the People's Bank of China, para 3.

[58] Notice of the State Council on the Approving the People's Bank of China Report on the Division of Lending Functions among the Specialized Banks, para 2 [<国务院批转中国人民银行关于各专业银行发放固定贷款分工问题的报告的通知>] (Beijing: State Council, 30 May 1984).

[59] The Provisional Rules of Banking Management, arts 3 & 14, National Distribution (*guo-fa*) 1986, No 1 [<银行管理暂行条例>, 国发 [1986]第1号] (Beijing: State Council, 7 January 1986).

[60] Decision of the State Council on Financial System Reform 1993, Preface.

[61] ibid.

NPLs, to a large extent, as a result of inefficient corporate governance and excessive lending to loss-making SOEs due to the strong intervention of both central and local governments.

As mentioned above, widespread asset quality problems within China's state **9.76** banking sector can be attributed largely to the underperforming SOEs, poor banking, and directed lending. Prior to 1983 the funding of SOEs came directly from government financial grants, which have since been gradually substituted with bank loans,[62] and by 1985 loans granted by the SOCBs became the only funding source for the SOEs.[63] The SOEs relied on bank loans as an implicit financial subsidy, including low interest rate loans and defaulted principal and interest.[64] As a result, the big four SOCBs acted per se as quasi-state agencies in maintaining SOE operations and further securing social stability.[65] The central government controlled all credit allocation through strict plans implemented by the PBOC in pursuit of government economic policies, and therefore, prudential regulation was seemingly not possible for the SOCBs.[66] Despite the asset problems created among the SOCBs, this approach nonetheless supported rapid economic growth in China over the past two decades.[67]

The outbreak of Asian financial crises triggered a new round of reforms in **9.77** China's financial sector—commonly viewed as having similar potential risks, in spite of not being adversely affected by the crisis. Those reforms included strengthening prudential practices in the banking system, such as the introduction of the asset-liability management system in place of credit planning in 1998, and establishment of vertical management both in the central bank and commercial banks in order to reduce administrative intervention. Furthermore, two large bank bailouts were carried out to strengthen the reforms, ie in 1998, RMB 270 billion (US$ 33.33 billion) of capital was injected into the four SOCBs through special government bond issuance to boost their capital

---

[62] Transfer to the People's Bank of China Regarding Uniform Management of Operating Funds of State Owned Enterprise, National Distribution (*guo-fa*) 1983, No 100 [< 批转中国人民银行关于国有企业流动资金改由人民银行统一管理的报告通知>, 国发 [1983] 第100号] (Beijing: State Council, 25 June 1983).

[63] *National Budget: Infrastructure Finance will be provided by Loans [rather] than State Funds*, Budget Brief (*ji-zi*) 1984, No 2580 [<关于国家预算内基本建设投资全部由拨款改为 贷款的暂行规定>, (84) 计资2580] (Beijing: National Accounting Commission, Ministry of Finance, and Chinese Construction Bank, 14 December 1984).

[64] J Lin, F Cai, & Z Li, *The China Miracle: Development Strategy and Economic Reform* (Hong Kong: The Chinese University Press, 2003), p 221. See also *The Chinese Economy: Fighting Inflation, Deepening Reforms* (Washington, DC: World Bank, 1996), p 17.

[65] J Lin, F Cai, & Z Li, above, pp 221–2.

[66] NR Lardy, *China's Unfinished Economic Revolution* (New York: Brookings Institution Press 1998), p 83.

[67] ibid, p 220.

bases,[68] and in 1999, RMB 1.4 trillion (US$ 172.84 billion) of NPLs were transferred from the big four SOCBs to the four newly established asset management companies (AMCs).[69] Since no parallel institutional reform measures were put in place to secure the return of the capital infusion, the financial bailouts have not turned the large SOCBs into healthy institutions. As China has committed to fully liberalize its banking sector by 2006, it is has become necessary to intensify the transformation of the SOCBs in order for them to face the increasing competition and maintain national economic development.[70]

9.78 Accordingly in 2003, an all-round reform initiative featuring a three-step strategy was launched to enhance the shareholding system within the SOCBs. The first step, financial restructuring, is exemplified by the following cases: in January of 2004, BOC and CCB received US$ 45 billion in capital injections in the form of foreign reserves,[71] and in April 2005 ICBC received US$ 15 billion of fresh capital in the same form.[72] Here, the financial restructuring is intended to create favourable conditions for further shareholding restructuring and listing (likely to take place in at least Hong Kong) which are regarded respectively as the second and third steps.[73] Both CCB and BOC have completed their structural adjustment from solely state-owned institutions to limited corporations following the capital injections.[74] For the sake of thorough and fundamental

---

[68] Resolution by Standing Committee of National People's Congress on Approving the State Council's Advice that Supplementing the Capital Reserves of the Solely State-Owned Commercial Banks through Issuing Special Government Bonds, 1998 [全国人民代表大会常务委员会关于批准国务院提出的由财政部发行特别国债补充国有独资商业银行资本金的决议] (Beijing: NPC Standing Committee, 28 February 1998).

[69] Notice of the People's Bank of China, etc on Establishing China's Cinda Asset Management Company (*guoban-fa*) 1999 No 33 <国务院办公厅转发人民银行，财政部，证监会关于组建中国信达资产管理公司意见的通知，国办发1999 第33号> (Beijing: Office of the State Council, 4 April 1999); Notice of the People's Bank of China, etc on Establishing China's Huarong, Great Wall and Orient Asset Management Company (*guoban-fa*) 1999 No 66 (Bejing: Office of the State Council, 21 July 1999).

[70] PBOC News Release, 'State Council Decides to Introduce Shareholding System in Bank of China and China Construction Bank' (Beijing: PBOC, 6 January 2004). See: <http://www.pbc.gov.cn/english//detail.asp?col=6400&ID=352&keyword=sharehold-ing>.

[71] ibid.

[72] PBOC News Release, 'State Council Decided to Carry out Shareholding Reform in the Industrial and Commercial Bank of China' <国务院决定对中国工商银行实施股份制改造> (Beijing: PBOC, 21 April 2005). See <http://www.pbc.gov.cn/english/detail.asp?col=6400&id=517>.

[73] ibid.

[74] PBOC News Release, 'Bank of China Co Ltd Inaugurated' <中国银行股份有限公司创立大会召开> <http://www.pbc.gov.cn/english//detail.asp?col=6400&ID=419&keyword=Huijin>; PBOC News Release, 'Speech by Mr Xie Ping, General Manager of Central Huijin Investment Company at the Inauguration Ceremony of China Construction Bank Co Ltd.' <中央汇金投资有限责任公司总经理谢平在中国建设银行股份有限公司成立大会上的致辞>, see <http://www.pbc.gov.cn/ detail.asp?col=4200&ID=128>.

transformation, China's policymakers have imposed a stiffer regime of corporate governance and a set of strict assessment indicators on the SOCBs benefiting from these pilot recapitalizations.[75] However, these measures have not yet removed the fundamental problems of the SOCBs, and concerns about corporate governance and substantial transformation in the entities mean further steps are expected to propel full commercialization.

(2) Development of banking laws and regulations

The main banking laws, the Law on the People's Bank of China ('PBOC Law'—the central bank law) and the Law on Commercial Banks ('Commercial Banking Law'), were enacted by the NPC and its Standing Committee, respectively, in 1995, and both were amended in 2003.

China's legal framework for banking mainly takes three forms, ie banking laws, banking administrative regulations, and banking rules. Prior to the enactment of the PBOC Law and the Commercial Banking Law in 1995, there was no substantial banking law in China and the legal system regulating the banking market in China was mainly comprised of administrative regulations stipulated by the State Council and a variety of rules or measures by the PBOC and other government departments. The Provisional Regulations on Banking Management, issued by the State Council in 1986, was the first comprehensive legislation in China to regulate the banking sector.[76] However, it was relatively rough and simple due to the immature markets of the time. The promulgation of the two banking laws alongside the Law on Security and the Law on Bills was a milestone for China's banking legislation, marking the formation of a modern banking legal system in China.

The 1995 PBOC Law was enacted to provide supervision and administration of banking operations, as well as the making and implementation of currency policy.[77] The PBOC of the time had very wide supervisory powers, including authorization, auditing deposits and loans, settlement of accounts, addressing bad debts and business affairs of banking institutions, and taking appropriate

9.79

9.80

9.81

---

[75] PBOC News Release, 'State Council Decides to Introduce Shareholding System in Bank of China and China Construction Bank' <国务院决定中国银行和中国建设银行实施股份制改造> (Beijing: PBOC, 6 January 2004). See <http://www.pbc.gov.cn/english//detail.asp?col=6400&ID=352&keyword=share-holding>. Also CBRC, *Guidelines on Corporate Governance Reforms and Supervision of Bank of China and Construction Bank of China* <中国银行业监督管理委员会关于中国银行、中国建设银行公司治理改革与监管指引> (Beijing: CBRC, 11 March 2004). See <http://www.cbrc. gov.cn/english/index.html>.

[76] Regulations on Banking Management (ineffective) [银行管理暂行条例] (Beijing: State Council, 7 January 1986).

[77] PBOC Law 1995, art 2.

supervisory actions including suspension, termination, and takeovers of banking institutions as necessary.[78] Notwithstanding this, the detail of day-to-day supervision of banking institutions was implemented through administrative guidelines issued by the PBOC.[79] These guidelines have the force of law, as the PBOC has legal capacity to make administrative rules or measures.[80] In order to formulate monetary policy, a monetary policy committee was set up within the PBOC in 1997. Additionally, the PBOC is granted a series of market-oriented instruments to realize monetary policy and adjust financial markets, ie deposit reserve system, basic interest rates, rediscounting business, re-lending, and open market operations.[81] Corresponding to the creation of the CBRC, the amendment to the PBOC Law was enacted in December 2003 to refocus and refine the independent role of the PBOC as a central bank in making and implementing monetary policy and in safeguarding overall financial stability.[82] As a part of those amendments, anti-money-laundering was added on the list of responsibilities of the PBOC.[83] The amended PBOC law has also expanded the powers of the PBOC in imposing monetary as well as other administrative penalties on wrongdoers.

9.82 The operation of the CBRC is legally based on the Law on Banking Regulation and Supervision ('Banking Supervision Law'), promulgated in 2003. The CBRC has assumed many functions and authorities previously exercised by the PBOC. The Law provides the CBRC with unambiguous powers to approve or revoke banking licences, to supervize the operations and to take over administration of banks in distress, and to dismiss or restrict the authority of directors and senior managers. A remarkable provision in this law is the clear establishment of prudential operation as the core principle for banking business.[84] Reducing NPLs, restructuring state banks, and implementing prudential practices in accordance with international standards are set as top tasks for the CBRC.[85]

9.83 The Commercial Banking Law was passed in 1995 and amended in December 2003, providing a legal foundation for the construction of China's commercial banking system. The law formulates a series of provisions governing the establishment and organizational structure of commercial banks, banking business rules as well as relevant legal liabilities in view of developing a market-oriented

---

[78] PBOC Law 1995, arts 31, 32, & 64. [79] PBOC Law 1995, art 31.
[80] Legislation Law, arts 71 & 82. [81] Legislation Law, art 23.
[82] PBOC Law 2003, art 2. [83] PBOC Law 2003, art 4(10).
[84] Banking Supervision Law 2003, art 21.
[85] *The CBRC identified supervisory priorities for the coming years for the wholly state-owned commercial banks and joint shareholding commercial banks* (Beijing, CBRC, 4 September 2003), available at <http://www.cbrc.gov.cn/english/module/viewinfo.jsp?infoID=472>.

commercial banking system. In the 1995 version the independence of SOCBs in granting loans was highlighted.[86] However, the law required commercial banks to develop their lending business under the guidance of state industry policies supporting the national economy and social development,[87] which left ample opportunities to local governments to meddle with the affairs of the commercial banks under the guise of providing direction on industrial policies. A major change in the 2003 amendment is that the power of the State Council to direct commercial banks to grant specific loans is abolished,[88] which is one step forward toward autonomy of banking institutions. Also, the 2003 amendment has strengthened corporate governance by imposing stiffer penalties on corporate wrongdoers of banking institutions.[89] The amendment puts safety as the top priority for banking operations whereas efficiency was stationed as the first principle in the 1995 version.[90] The most extensive revisions are seen in relation to legal responsibilities. Essentially, the revisions lay out in detail the monetary penalties for negligence or malfeasance by banks.

9.84 The revised PBOC Law and Commercial Banking Law do not change the overall sectoral structure of the Mainland financial system and related legal framework.[91]

9.85 An effective banking legal framework should protect banking institutions from problematic borrowers. However, China's banking sector is still facing legal barriers in protecting creditor rights. First, the banking law does not in substance prohibit political interference in the banking system. Although both the PBOC Law and Commercial Banking Law prohibit political interference in the loan granting process,[92] they leave ample opportunity for such interference as no provision imposes any penalty for breach of this prohibition. Moreover, the policy-directed supervision and arrangement of branches based on administrative regions enable local governments to exert profound influence over business decisions of the commercial banks. Secondly, the law of bankruptcy and mortgage in China does not provide adequate protection for creditors, especially in that China's outdated Enterprise Bankruptcy Law gives limited powers to creditors in the bankruptcy process. Severe political meddling in SOE bankruptcies

---

[86] Commercial Banking Law 1995, arts 4 & 41.
[87] Commercial Banking Law 1995, art 34.
[88] Commercial Banking Law (Amendment) Decision, art 11 (Beijing: NPC Standing Committee, 27 December 2003) deleting Commercial Banking Law 1995, art 41(2).
[89] Commercial Banking Law (Amendment) Decision, arts 27 & 34, amending Commercial Banking Law, arts 76 & 78 and adding art 89.
[90] Commercial Banking Law (Amendment) Decision, art 2 (Beijing: NPC Standing Committee, 27 December 2003).
[91] Commercial Banking Law 1995, art 43.
[92] PBOC Law 1995, art 7; Commercial Banking Law 1995, art 41.

leaves little protection for the interests of banking institutions since local authorities put stability in their jurisdictions as the top priority and clearly one which may be affected by the failure of regional SOEs in maintaining employment. The costly procedure to realize mortgaged assets is also a barrier to protecting the interests of banking institutions as creditors. In order to protect local interests, local governments always try to prevent the foreclosure of mortgaged property by interfering with the valuators, auctioneers, courts, and other administrative agencies involved in the valuation and sale of mortgaged property.[93] Thirdly, the Mainland banking institutions have limited powers to supervise the operation of problematic debtors. Under the current legal framework banking institutions cannot invest in non-banking financial industries and other enterprises. Further legislative authority is required to improve this situation.

9.86 China's banking supervisory system is undergoing fundamental transformation from a simple credit control model to a sophisticated risk-based model. Credit planning had previously been the most important approach for the PBOC to implement monetary policies through controlling the loan limits of the banking institutions. As a significant instrument to realize national economic policies, it was not completely abolished until 1998 when a management system based on the asset–liability ratio was formally put in practice.[94] The asset–liability ratio management system, to a large extent, was a major step in liberalizing the operations of the banking sector and implementing a sound supervisory mechanism. Credit and asset quality were usually ignored under the previous system supervision when the ratio of credit to deposits within a banking institution did not exceed 75 per cent.[95] The newly launched risk-based supervisory approach puts more emphasis on banking risk through strengthening capital requirements and tightening credit risk management rather than just controlling the growth of credit lending.

9.87 Non-transparent operational systems are more vulnerable to risks of underestimating and hiding banking problems, and therefore transparency is a major issue for the Mainland banking sector to address. Mainland China's banking sector has been rife with transparency problems resulting from an inaccurate loan classification system, incomplete financial reporting requirements, unauthentic auditing reports, and unreasonable taxation standards. In order to control the expansion of financial risks, in 2002, the PBOC enacted Interim Measures for the Information Disclosure of Commercial Banks, which

---

[93] F Zhou (ed), *The Debt Work-Out for SOEs in China* [国企债务重组] (Beijing: Peking University Press, 2003), pp 239–40.
[94] *Almanac of China's Finance and Banking* [中国金融年鉴] (Beijing: Editorial Board of Almanac of China's Finance and Banking, 1999), p 7.
[95] Commercial Banking Law 2003, art 39(2).

set the minimum requirements for commercial banks in terms of information disclosure and also the principles of authenticity, accuracy, integrity, and comparability when disclosing information.[96] Financial reports, various kinds of risk management, corporate governance, and major events must be disclosed in order to meet the minimal requirements of this measure.[97] Also, penalties can be imposed on relevant responsible persons who provide false financial statements or false auditing reports.[98] This was emphasized further under the Banking Supervision Law.[99] As the pilots of financial reform, the BOC and CCB are charged with stricter responsibility in keeping transparent operations.[100]

9.88 Following the creation of the CBRC, a series of supportive administrative regulations, which cover risk management, internal controls, capital adequacy, asset quality, loan loss provisioning, risk concentrations, connected transactions, and liquidity management, were formulated in line with international standards to ensure the implementation of the prudential rules.[101]

9.89 The Regulation Governing Capital Adequacy of Commercial Banks was claimed to incorporate a number of recommendations of the proposed Basel II Capital Accord,[102] including supervisory review and information disclosure.[103] Under the Regulation all commercial banks are required to meet the international standard of 8 per cent capital adequacy ratio and 4 per cent for core capital adequacy ratio by 2007,[104] and the risk weight is stipulated as 100 per cent for all types of business enterprises and individuals, including SOEs.[105] The CBRC is provided extensive powers to take corrective actions in relation to inadequately capitalized institutions[106] and to exert penalties on senior

[96] Interim Measures for the Information Disclosure of Commercial Banks, arts 3 & 5 (Beijing: PBOC, 21 May 2002).
[97] Interim Measures for the Information Disclosure of Commercial Banks, art 8.
[98] Interim Measures for the Information Disclosure of Commercial Banks, arts 27 & 28.
[99] Banking Supervision Law 2003, arts 33, 35, 36, 45, & 46
[100] CBRC, *Guidelines on Corporate Governance Reforms and Supervision of Bank of China and Construction Bank of China* <中国银行业监督管理委员会关于中国银行、中国建设银行公司治理改革与监管指引> (Beijing: CBRC, 11 March 2004). See <http://www.cbrc.gov.cn/english/index.htm>.
[101] Banking Supervision Law 2003, art 21.
[102] Regulation Governing Capital Adequacy of Commercial Banks, No 2 2004 <商业银行资本充足率管理办法, 中国银行业监督管理委员会令2004 第2号> (Beijing: CBRC, 23 February 2004); *The New Basel Capital Accord* (Basel: Bank for International Settlements, 11 October 2003), available at <http://www.bis.org/publ/bcbsca.htm#pgtop>.
[103] *The responses to the press by the senior official of the China Banking Regulatory Commission on issues relating to the New Capital Accord* (Beijing: CBRC, 14 September 2003), available at <http://www.cbrc.gov.cn/english/module/viewinfo.jsp?infoID=468>.
[104] Regulation Governing Capital Adequacy of Commercial Banks, arts 7 & 53.
[105] Regulation Governing Capital Adequacy of Commercial Banks, art 23.
[106] Regulation Governing Capital Adequacy of Commercial Banks, art 40(3).

management members if the capital reserve is significantly below the threshold.[107]

9.90 To ensure that commercial banks will develop their risk-taking activities on the basis of risk management capacity and capital strength, credit risk management plays an important part in the new supervisory system. Larger banking institutions have already begun implementing the two-dimensional rating system as recommended by Basel II.[108] In 2004 the Guidelines on Market Risk Management of Commercial Banks was issued by the CBRC, which require commercial banks to enhance market risk management by identifying, measuring, monitoring, and controlling the market risks arising from all their activities.[109] To ensure the capture of risks and adjustment to the changing environment, another important measure, the Provisional Rules on Assessment of Internal Controls of Commercial Banks, was issued to encourage commercial banks to establish systematic, transparent, and documented internal control systems.[110] Connected transactions between commercial banks and their insiders or shareholders are also strictly regulated.[111] In addition, on an experimental basis, the old four-category loan system based on payment experience has been replaced with a five-category system in accord with international standards,[112] and banking institutions are required to draw adequate loss reserve funds according to the Guidelines on Banking Loan Loss Provisioning[113] before computing reliable profit-reporting and capital.[114]

9.91 Constructing sound corporate governance structures within China's banking institutions is set as a crucial point to ensure the success of China's banking

---

[107] Regulation Governing Capital Adequacy of Commercial Banks, art 41(1).

[108] *The responses to the press by the senior official of the China Banking Regulatory Commission on issues relating to the New Capital Accord* (Beijing: CBRC, 14 September 2003), available at <http://www.cbrc.gov.cn/english/module/viewinfo.jsp?infoID=468>.

[109] Guidelines on Market Risk Management of Commercial Banks, art 1, No 10 2004 <商业银行市场风险管理指引, 中国银行业监督管理委员会令2004 第10号> (Beijing: CBRC, 16 December 2004).

[110] Provisional Rules on Assessment of Internal Controls of Commercial Banks, arts 4 & 7, No 9 2004 <商业银行内部控制风险评价, 中国银行业监督管理委员会令2004 第9号> (Beijing: CBRC, 20 August 2004).

[111] The Administrative Measures for the connected transactions between commercial banks and their insiders or shareholders <商业银行与内部人和股东关联交易管理办法> (Beijing: CBRC, 2 April 2004).

[112] Notices of People's Bank of China on the Full Implementation of the Five-grade Loan Classification System, Bank Distribution (*yin-fa*) No 263 1999 & No 416 2001 [中国人民银行关于全面推行贷款五级分类工作的通知,银发[1999]第263号暨银发[2001]第416号](Beijing: PBOC, 15 September 1999 and 31 December 2001).

[113] PBOC, Guidelines on Banking Loan Loss Provisioning (*yin-fa*) No 98 2002 <银行贷款损失准备计提指引,银发2002 第98号> (Beijing: PBOC, 2 April 2002).

[114] Provisional Measures for Monitoring and Assessing the Distressed Assets of Commercial Banks, art 4 <商业银行不良资产监测和考核暂行办法> (Beijing: CBRC, 25 March 2004).

reform. In 2002 Guidelines on Corporate Governance in Joint-Stock Commercial Banks, as well as Guidelines on Independent Directors and Outside Supervisors of Joint-Stock Commercial Banks, were released to provide a legal basis for the establishment of effective governance mechanisms within joint-stock commercial banks.[115] Establishing modern corporate governance has always been a top goal in reforming China's state banking sector. However, state ownership itself makes this task rather difficult. After receiving capital infusions, three pilot banks, namely BOC, CCB, and ICBC, were requested to implement a shareholding system with strict corporate governance at its centre.[116]

Foreign banks in Mainland China have benefited considerably from the improving legal environment. China's entry to the WTO accelerates the openness of the legal system for foreign participants. As a result, the major legislation regulating the operations of foreign financial institutions in China, ie Regulations on the Administration of Foreign-Funded Financial Institutions as well as its detailed implementation rules, were much revised, so as to be more compliant with GATS/WTO rules and more favourable to foreign participants.[117] The Rules Governing the Equity Investment in Chinese Financial Institutions by Overseas Financial Institutions issued by the CBRC,[118] which raised the maximum foreign equity holding in Chinese financial institutions, encourages foreign counterparts to participate in the reforms of domestic banks through helping them improve service quality and competitiveness. However, a series of prudential

9.92

---

[115] PBOC, Guidelines on Corporate Governance of Joint-Stock Commercial Banks, No 15 2002 <公司治理指引> (Beijing: PBOC, 4 June 2002); PBOC, Guidelines on Independent Directors and Outside Supervisors of Joint-Stock Commercial Banks, No 15 2002 <股份制商业银行独立董事和外部监事制度指引 (Beijing: PBOC, 4 June 2002).

[116] PBOC News Release, 'State Council Decides to Introduce Shareholding System in Bank of China and China Construction Bank' <国务院决定中国银行和中国建设银行实施股份制改造> (Beijing: PBOC, 6 January 2004). See <http://www.pbc.gov.cn/english//detail.asp?col=-6400&ID=352&keyword=shareholding>; PBOC News Release, 'State Council Decided to Carry out Shareholding Reform in the Industrial and Commercial Bank of China'<国务院决定对中国工商银行实施股份制改造> (Beijing: PBOC, 21 April 2005). See <http://www.pbc.gov.cn/english/detail.asp?col=6400&id=517>; Also CBRC, *Guidelines on Corporate Governance Reforms and Supervision Bank of China and Construction Bank of China*中国银行业监督管理委员会关于中国银行、中国建设银行公司治理改革与监管指引> (Beijing: CBRC, 11 March 2004). See <http://www.cbrc.gov.cn/english/index.htm>.

[117] State Council, Regulation on the Administration of Foreign-Funded Financial Institutions, No 340 2001<外资金融机构管理条例, 国务院令第340号> (Beijing: State Council, 20 November 2001); CBRC, Detailed Rules on the Implementation of the Regulation on the Administration of Foreign-Funded Financial Institutions, No 4 2004 <外资金融机构管理条例实施细则, 中国银行业监督管理委员会2004第4号> (Beijing: CBRC, 26 July 2004).

[118] CBRC, Measures Governing the Equity Investment in Chinese Financial Institutions by Overseas Financial Institutions, No 6 2003 <境外金融机构投资入股中资金融机构管理办法> (Beijing: CBRC, 8 December 2003).

requirements and limits on foreign equity participation in Chinese banks are set to prevent possible risks and market monopoly associated with foreign investment.[119] The promulgation of these regulations and rules has significantly improved the transparency and efficiency of the legal framework, making China's policy more encouraging and attractive for foreign involvement with domestic financial institutions.

9.93 Also, the participation of foreign investors in the restructuring of China's SOEs and SOCBs has received strong legal support from the government. In 2003 the Interim Provision on Restructuring State-owned Enterprises with Foreign Investment was issued by the SETC providing a basic framework for foreign capital to enter into the strategic restructuring of SOEs.[120] The legal framework addressing NPL problems through absorbing foreign capital began to take shape in 2001 when the Provisional Rules on Drawing Foreign Capital into the Asset Restructuring and Disposal by Financial Asset Management Companies was enacted as an administrative regulation.[121] It expressly states that all AMCs may receive foreign capital in the restructuring and disposing of NPLs. However, it only offers limited guidance to foreign investors in disposing of NPLs, and the relating legal and regulatory problems have yet to be resolved.[122] Furthermore, settlements for redundant employees of SOEs is still a delicate and problematic issue for foreign investors as the government still puts top priority on such issues as resettling employees, guaranteeing their lawful rights and interests, and maintaining social stability.[123]

9.94 The system dealing with banking exit is inadequate in China. So far, there is no specific legal regime governing the exit of financial institutions, though the legal basis for closure of financial institutions can be found in the Bankruptcy Law for general enterprises, the PBOC Law, Banking Supervision Law, Commercial Banking Law, and Company Law as well as some administrative regulations. Nonetheless, Regulations on the Cancellation of Financial Institutions, enacted by the State Council and taking effect in 2001, is currently the most comprehensive legal document providing the administrative resolution for financial

---

[119] Measures Governing the Equity Investment in Chinese Financial Institutions by Overseas Financial Institutions, arts 8 & 9.

[120] Provisional Rules on Reorganization of SOEs by Using Foreign Fund (sic), No 42 2002 [利用外资改组国有企业暂行规定, 国家工商行政管理总局, 国家外汇管理局第42号] (Beijing: State Economic & Trade Commission, 8 November 2002).

[121] The Provisional Rules of Attracting Foreign Capital into Asset Restructuring and Disposition of Asset Management Companies, No 6 2001 [金融资产管理公司吸收外资参与资产重组与处置的暂行规定, 外经贸部, 财政部等令 [2001] 6 号] (Beijing: Ministry of Foreign Trade & Economic Cooperation, 26 October 2001).

[122] D Liu, 'Foreign Investment in NPL Assets: Is China's Legal Environment Up to the Task?', *China Law & Practice* (May 2003), pp 27–8.

[123] Provisional Rules on Reorganization of SOEs by Using Foreign Fund (sic), art 4(3).

institutions in distress in Mainland China.[124] In practice, one regional joint-stock bank, several trust and investment companies, and some deposit-taking credit cooperatives were closed during 1997–2001,[125] with more closures in the following two years. Apparently, China's banking supervision has been more focused on market entrance. A robust exit policy, however, should be clearly defined in legal measures, under which the failed bank must be removed from the market. A set of rules in detail should also be established to classify the standards and procedures regarding the exit of financial institutions.

In conclusion, the creation of the CBRC, together with the revised commercial **9.95** banking and central bank laws marked a big and firm step forward not only for the effective bank regulation in China, but also for the reform of the whole system. Hopefully, the introduction of such prudential measures will assist China's banking institutions to operate in line with international practices, improve asset quality, and address NPLs. As all Chinese banks will gradually adopt the corporate system and offer shares to the public, including foreign strategic investors, the regulatory authority will have to take more robust measures to maintain greater transparency in banks' operations and ensure their ultimate accountability for the interests of investors as well as the State.

D. Securities

Mainland China's securities market and related legal framework have evolved **9.96** gradually, though not always smoothly, alongside the country's liberalization and economic reform. Nonetheless, both the market and its regulation have now achieved some level of maturity.

(1) Development of Mainland securities markets

Mainland China's securities markets have been developing since the 1980s, in **9.97** tandem with the market reforms and the liberalization of the country's economy. In July 1981 issuance of treasury bonds began in Mainland China. Six years later, a secondary market for the trading of treasury bonds was established, though not entirely successfully. By the mid-1980s, state enterprises had begun to issue both shares and corporate bonds.[126]

---

[124] Regulations on the Cancellation of Financial Institutions, State Council Decree No 324, 2001<金融机构撤销条例, 国务院令324号> (Beijing: State Council, 23 November 2001).
[125] *Almanac of China's Finance and Banking* [中国金融年鉴] (Beijing: Editorial Board of Almanac of China's Finance & Banking, 2002), p 9.
[126] CSRC, 'China's Securities and Futures Markets' April 2004, available at <http://www.csrc.gov.cn>.

9.98 China's securities markets formally took shape with the establishment of the two domestic stock exchanges: the Shanghai Stock Exchange and Shenzhen Stock Exchange in December 1990 and June 1991 respectively. The two stock exchanges were initially only regional markets. At that time, only 14 joint stock companies were listed in China with a total equity capital of RMB 600 million (US$ 74 million), and a total market value of around RMB 11 billion (US$ 1.36 billion).[127] The small-scale market had little effect on the country's economic life. Most enterprises preferred bank loans to share issuance in the securities market despite the low availability of bank loans. China's securities market was at its experimental stage, and was regarded as a capitalist phenomenon and thus contradicting the country's socialist ideology.

9.99 In the process of China's liberalization and economic reform, the Communist Party of China gradually evolved its ideology of socialism to one supporting development of a socialist market economy, which greatly benefited the development of the country's securities markets. In 1992 the first governmental regulatory agency for the securities market, namely the Securities Commission of the State Council, was established. In April 1993 the State Council promulgated the first influential legislation concerning market regulation: the Provisional Regulations for the Administration of the Issuance and Trading of Stock (ITS).[128] In December 1993 the Company Law was enacted. At the same time, many normative documents relating to the regulation of those markets were promulgated. The development in legislation inspired market growth. As a result, the securities market experienced rapid expansion in 1993 and 1994. By the end of 1994, the number of listed companies on the Shanghai and Shenzhen Stock Exchanges rose to 181 and 291 respectively, with respective equity capitalization of RMB 35.8 billion (US$ 4.42 billion) and RMB 63.8 billion (US$ 7.88 billion). The total market value of China's securities market amounted to RMB 354.2 billion (US$ 43.73 billion).[129] Enterprises gradually realized the advantages of raising capital through stock issuance.[130]

9.100 However, new problems occurred in the development of the market. The rapid expansion of the market generated a big gap between the demand for and supply of capital. Consequently, the secondary market experienced adjustment. Taking market volume and scale into consideration, the Chinese government

---

[127] See Zhang Huoqi, 'How About the Publicly-held Corporations: a Comment on the Development of the Publicly-held Corporations', *People's Daily*, 6 February 1999, at p 5.

[128] This statute is still valid even after the Securities Law of China came into force in July 1999 (though the major part of the ITS has been replaced by the Securities Law).

[129] See Zhang Huoqi, above, at p 5.

[130] The most apparent advantage is that enterprises are free from the pressure of returning the principal, not to say paying interest as will take place with bank loans. This makes equity financing less risky than debt financing.

became more cautions in approving applications for stock issuance from 1994. By the end of 1995 the number of listed companies only increased by 32 on the two domestic stock exchanges. Compared to the previous year, the market value even dropped by RMB 2 billion (US$ 246.9 million).[131]

The second period of marked growth of the Chinese securities market occurred **9.101** from 1996 to 1998. By the end of 1998 the number of listed companies in the Chinese market had risen to 745, and the market capitalization had increased to RMB 2 trillion (US$ 246.9 billion). The Shanghai and Shenzhen Stock Exchanges had by then grown into national markets.[132]

In December 1998 the most important statute for China's securities markets, **9.102** the Securities Law, was promulgated, which greatly promoted the development and the regulation of the market. Since then, the CSRC has established its status as the competent authority for the Chinese securities market. The accumulation of the government's experience in market regulation and the development of the legal system support the development of Chinese securities markets. From that time, these markets have entered a period of standardization and steady development.

At present, China's securities market offers seven types of financial instruments, **9.103** including: 'A' shares,[133] 'B' shares,[134] treasury bonds, treasury bond repurchase agreements ('repos'), corporate bonds, convertible bonds, and securities investment funds (closed and open-ended). The offering and trading of shares and close-end investment fund units are dematerialized, with trading and settlement procedures standardized across the market for all participants. Insurance companies are allowed to invest in the securities market indirectly via purchasing securities investment funds. The Social Security Fund can entrust approved asset management institutions to invest in the securities market on its behalf.

As of September 2005, 1,381 companies were listed on the Shanghai and **9.104** Shenzhen Stock Exchanges with a total market capitalization and float value of RMB 3.34 trillion (US$ 429.63 billion) and RMB 1.07 trillion (US$ 135.8 billion) respectively. The number of investor accounts totalled 73.13 million.[135] As China developed domestic securities markets, it also encouraged domestic companies to enter international capital markets. By the end of 2003, 93 domestic companies had listed overseas.[136]

---

[131] See Zhang Huoqi, above, at p 6.   [132] See Zhang Huoqi, above, at p 3.
[133] Common shares denominated in RMB.
[134] Domestically listed common shares quoted in US dollars or HK dollars.
[135] Statistics available at <http://www.csrc.gov.cn>.
[136] CSRC, 'China's Securities and Futures Markets' April 2004, available at <http://www.csrc.gov.cn>.

9.105 By the end of April 2004 there were 34 fund management companies running more than 100 funds (including both close-end and open-end funds) in China. The scale of investment funds totalled 256.3 billion shares with net assets of RMB 267.9 billion (US$ 33.1 billion). The market value of shares held by funds amounted to 11 per cent of the float market value of 'A' shares.[137] By the end of 2003 China had issued RMB 628 billion (US$ 77.5 billion) of treasury bonds and RMB 35.8 billion (US$ 4.42 billion) of corporate bonds. The turnover for treasury bonds trading in the spot market and bond repurchases were RMB 575.6 billion (US$ 71.1 billion) and RMB 5.3 trillion (US$ 654.32 billion) respectively.[138]

9.106 Conventional debt issuance by central and state government and financial institutions began in the early 1980s, but has suffered hiatuses caused by economic, institutional, or irregular shocks. Its contemporary form has evolved only since 1994. While issuance by central government and state organizations has become substantial, a true market for notes and bonds has always been modest, with only peripheral trading liquidity available to investors of all types. Corporate bonds have an irregular history: state organizations were permitted to issue bonds in a semi-regulated fashion in the mid-1980s and the results became chaotic.[139] Similarly, in the early 1990s markets in exchange-traded and OTC interest rate and bond futures and options were wholly speculative in use, became discredited and were prohibited by 1995. Issuance by SOEs is now modest, non-state enterprise issuance trivial and secondary trading virtually non-existent. New interest rate and exchange rate derivatives will be permitted with the eventual implementation of reform guidelines announced in 2004.

9.107 The growing breadth of financial intermediation in China means that professional and investor interest in issuance and trading is profound, and a limited number of approved investment firms now engage in trading state sector debt issues with the considerable sophistication known in major markets, despite general illiquidity.[140] Their success on an observable scale requires the loosening of symbiotic links between state banks and government typical of Asia's

---

[137] 'Muqian Zhongguo Zhengquan Shichang Xiangzhuang [Current Situation of the Chinese Securities Market]', 7 June 2004, available at <http://news1.jrj.com.cn/new>.

[138] CSRC, 'China's Securities and Futures Markets' April 2004, available at <http://www.csrc.gov.cn>.

[139] Scott & Ho identify four separate phases of issuance of non-government, non-financial bonds since 1980, encouraged by two competing sets of laws and at least three waves of regulation. D Scott & I Ho, *China's Corporate Bond Market* (Washington: World Bank, 2004).

[140] An early and influential example is described in Li Huaizhong, 'Challenges to and opportunities for investing in China bond markets' (November 2003), mimeo presentation to Asian Bond Market Forum, University of Hong Kong, available at <http://www.aiifl.com>.

domestic money markets, where banks and their regulators form a circle that restricts the use of debt instruments by other parties.[141]

Since 2002–3 China's central authorities[142] have accumulated a strong under- **9.108**
standing of the practicalities of building robust market and issuance infra-
structures for debt instruments of all kinds, not least due to massing attention of
foreign and multinational organizations and transaction-seeking private sector
banks. However, there is a profound need for commensurate legal and regulatory reform, both enabling in nature and specific to markets or instruments.
The speed at which implementation can occur is limited by competing political
interests, the outcomes of past quasi-market developments, the need for policy
sequencing, and by the timetable for China's service sector WTO obligations,
which set more demanding and hasty agendas for banking and insurance reform
than for changes in the securities industry. CSRC and PBOC policy heads are
also aware that time pressure may be subsumed to the tactics needed to secure
new legislation.

The solution adopted by agencies such as CSRC and PBOC is twofold. First, to **9.109**
use a problem-solving approach, seeking legislative support in the NPC for pilot
projects or single transactions so as to demonstrate their value and to make clear
the need for overarching reform that accords with prior declarations of intent by
the State Council. Second, to prevent reform leading to shocks and uncertainty
by combining the creation of modern debt markets with the pressing need for a
market structure to recycle impaired assets from the balance sheets of state
banks.

Outstanding debt securities market capitalization was US$ 483.3 billion as at **9.110**
end-2004, of which 63.3 per cent and 33.6 per cent were central government
and financial issues, respectively. Net issuance in 2004 was US$ 42.9 billion
(2003 US$ 63.2 billion), ignoring non-negotiable retail targeted bonds (around
one-third of the gross amount in issue). Annual gross treasury bond issuance
since 2001 exceeds US$ 70.0 billion. Central government issues fixed and float-
ing rate treasury bills (2–5 years) and bonds (since 2002 of up to 30 years' tenor)
and sanctions financial institution bonds. Most of this debt is bought by
commercial banks for liquidity requirements or under a system of mandatory
allocation. A growing non-bank financial institutional sector has a lesser
investment and trading role.

---

[141] A problem addressed by M Mohanty, 'Improving liquidity in government bond markets:
what can be done?', Basel: BIS papers 11 (2002).
[142] Especially CSRC, PBOC, Ministry of Finance, and NDRC, which until 1995 was the lead
bond regulator, then losing status after market failures. Early in 2004 the State Council endorsed
the principle of modern markets for government and corporate debt, and in the regulated use of
commodity, interest rate, and equity derivatives. All initiatives required new legislation.

9.111 During their development, Mainland China's securities markets are becoming more open to the outside world. After its accession to the WTO in December 2001, China has been actively fulfilling its commitments through allowing the establishment of foreign-invested securities companies and fund management companies. Furthermore, China is making efforts to attract foreign investment to its securities market by launching the Qualified Foreign Institutional Investor (QFII) scheme, which opens up China's domestic 'A' share market to overseas investors.

9.112 To sum up, Mainland China's securities markets have been developing rapidly since 1992 with remarkable progress in market size, infrastructure development, legal framework, and market maturity. It is now the third largest in Asia after Tokyo and Hong Kong.[143] Further, the securities markets have become key components of China's socialist market economy and play an important role in the reform of SOEs, improving resource allocation, facilitating structural adjustment, and propelling economic growth. The Mainland government is continuing its efforts to develop a modern financial system and build effective and efficient securities markets.

(2) Structure of the Mainland securities legal system

9.113 Markets and legislation always interact with each other. On the one hand, markets are influenced and guided by legislation; on the other hand, legislation is made to meet the needs of reality and evolves with the development of markets. This is also the case in China. The development of a sound regulatory framework has been a key cornerstone in the development of Mainland China's securities markets. Its aim is to ensure that the development of the market is orderly and fair.

Share classification system in the Chinese securities market

9.114 Before introducing the legal framework for the Mainland China's securities market, it is necessary to explain a crucial background to this framework: the share classification system in China's securities market and related ownership structure in listed companies. As the entire legal system is divided into pieces in the light of the classification of shares, it is reasonable to say that this structure stems from the share classification system in Mainland China's stock market, which is mainly based on the legal status of shareholders.

---

[143] *Doing business with China*, in association with the China Association of International Trade, Ministry of Foreign Trade & Economic Cooperation, China Link, London; Sterling VA: Kogan Page, 2003, p 282.

Interests traded on China's securities market are divided into several share **9.115**
categories. Two of the principal share categories are 'A' shares and 'B' shares.
Generally speaking, 'A' shares are initially designed for domestic investors and
'B' shares are for overseas investors. Based on the identity of investors, 'A' shares
are further classified as state shares, legal person shares, and individual shares.

According to statistics, among all the domestic listed companies, 65 per cent **9.116**
have the state as their largest shareholder, and 31 per cent have a legal person as
their largest shareholder.[144] As state shares and legal person shares are under the
division of 'A' share market, obviously the scale of the 'B' share market is much
smaller than that of the 'A' share market. According to the CSRC statistics in
September 2005, among the 1,381 companies listed in the domestic stock
market, 1,326 issued 'A' shares, while only 109 issued 'B' shares.[145] In general,
the state accounts for an average of two-thirds of the ownership of listed companies, in the form of either state shares (directly) or legal person shares
(indirectly).[146]

The implication of this classification system is that different classes of shares are **9.117**
governed by different issuing and trading rules, and markets for different categories of shares are isolated from each other. In Mainland China's stock markets, different categories of shares are not convertible between each other. First,
'A' shares and 'B' shares are not allowed to convert to each other. Second,
different classes of shares under the 'A' share category are also not convertible to
each other. Finally, the transfer within the same class of share may also be
limited. Usually, the only category of 'A' shares which can be publicly transferred are individual shares,[147] while state shares and legal person shares that
consist of the major part of ownership in most Chinese listed companies are not
allowed to convert and trade freely on the stock market.[148] In a word, the
scheme of issuing categories of shares by one company, with state shares and
legal person shares essentially non-publicly tradable, results in the artificial
segregation of the securities market and its low liquidity.

Fortunately, the negative effects of the classification of ordinary shares and the **9.118**
segregation of the securities market have been commonly recognized in the PRC

---

[144] Li Maosheng & Yuan Dejun (chief editors), *Zhongguo Zhengquan Shichang Wenti Baogao*,
[Report on the Problems of the Chinese Securities Market] Shehui Kexue Chubanshe (Social
Science Publishing House, 2003) p 79.
[145] The data are available at <http://www.csrc.gov.cn>.
[146] See Zhang Xin, 'Regulating Chinese M&A', 29 August 2002 available at <http://www.
financeasia.com>.
[147] Fang Liufang, 'China's Corporatization Experiment', 5 Duke J Comp. & Int'l L 149
(1995), p 212.
[148] Tingting Tao, 'The Burgeoning Securities Investment Fund Industry in China: Its Development and Regulation', 13 *Colum. J Asian L* 203 (1999), p 229.

and the country is working to eliminate the classification of shares based on the nationality and identity of shareholders during the process of China's extension of its interconnection with the outside world. China has unveiled legislation that tends to dismantle the dichotomy between shares reserved for citizens and those reserved for foreigners. Foreign investors have been able to participate in China's 'A' share market as well as 'B' share market, and are able to improve their position in relation to the majority.[149] At the same time, the CSRC announced in February 2001 that domestic individual investors in the PRC could open trading accounts for 'B' shares which were previously reserved only for overseas investors since its debut.[150]

9.119 As a bigger step, the Chinese government is prudently carrying out experimental reform by selling down part of shares held by the state and legal persons and gradually allowing these shares to be freely traded in the secondary market[151] for the purpose of appropriate settlement of the long-existing problem in the securities market which is regarded as the key obstacle for the development of this market. As the reform is at its very early stage, its result remains to be seen.

Overview

9.120 Along with the development of its securities market, Mainland China's regulatory mechanism concerning the market has also been gradually improved. Initially, the regulatory authority was dispersed among a number of central governmental departments and local governments. A dual regulatory system evolved later, with the Securities Commission of the State Council being responsible for macro control and the CSRC exercising specific regulatory functions. The promulgation of the Securities Law (1998) then firmly and clearly established China's securities regulatory regime with centralized and unified regulation and supervision of the securities market by the CSRC at the core, supported by self-disciplinary regulation by the stock exchanges and the Securities Industry Association.

---

[149] This statement refers to the implementation of such rules as the Administration of Securities Investments in China by Qualified Foreign Institutional Investors Tentative Procedures (2002) and the Notice on Relevant Issues Concerning the Transfer to Foreign Investors of Listed Company State-owned Shares and Legal Person Shares (2002).

[150] See ' "B" share Opens to Domestic Investors', *China Daily*, 20 February 2001, available at <http://www.china.org.cn>.

[151] The experiment was launched in April 2005 symbolized by the CSRC Notice on the Issues Concerning the Reform of the Split Share Structure among Listed Companies promulgated on and effective as of 29 April 2005. On 4 September 2005 the CSRC promulgated the *Administrative Measures on the Split Share Structure Reform of Listed Companies*. 'The split share structure' refers to the phenomenon that state shares and legal person shares are not allowed to be freely traded in the Mainland's secondary stock market, hence are segregated from publicly tradable shares such as individual shares and foreign capital shares.

Meanwhile, under the principle of 'rule of law, regulation and supervision, **9.121**
self-discipline and standardization', a legal system regulating the securities
markets has gradually taken shape.[152] Since 1992 Mainland China has promulgated numerous normative documents in relation to the regulation of its
securities markets. Legislation in this field includes securities issuance
rules, securities listing and trading rules, information disclosure rules, rules
regulating securities organizations and specialized organizations, legal
responsibility system governing securities activities, etc.

Within this framework, there are generally three categories of normative docu- **9.122**
ments: national laws, administrative regulations, and departmental rules mainly
by the CSRC as well as operational rules by the stock exchanges. The Company
Law, the Securities Law, and the Securities Investment Fund Law are the three
basic national laws governing Mainland China's securities market. The administrative regulations by the State Council either fill in the legislative blanks in
related areas or provide specific details on related legal regimes. The departmental rules issued by the CSRC in accordance with relevant laws and administrative regulations are to provide necessary particulars and supplements for
relevant laws and regulations, thereby constituting the important elements and
major part of the PRCs legal system governing the securities market. By the end
of 2003 there were over 300 such rules in force.[153]

National laws

As mentioned above, there are three laws highly relevant to the regulation of the **9.123**
securities market in Mainland China.

Company Law

On 29 December 1993 the Standing Committee of the NPC adopted the **9.124**
Company Law, which came into effect on 1 July 1994 and was amended on
25 December 1999 and 27 October 2005.[154]

The Company Law promotes a fundamental change in the organizational struc- **9.125**
ture of enterprises in China. It seeks to provide a nationwide standard of establishing and operating limited liability companies and companies limited by
shares in this country. By doing so, the Company Law aims to provide a part of
the overall legal framework that will be essential to transforming China's SOEs

---

[152] See *Doing business with China*, above, p 283.
[153] CSRC, 'China's Securities and Futures Markets' April 2004, available at <http://
www.csrc.gov.cn>.
[154] Effective 1 January 2006.

into independent entities, hence fostering overall domestic economic growth.[155] This law stipulates the establishment and the organization of limited liability companies and companies limited by shares, as well as the responsibilities of corporate management. Part V of the law provides the issuance and assignment of shares by companies limited by shares. This law also includes provisions on the issuance of company bonds (Part VII). All these contents make the law vital to the regulation of the securities market.

9.126   The amendment made in 2005 aims to encourage investment and promote the establishment of companies and the development of domestic capital markets through granting greater autonomy to companies.

Securities Law

9.127   On 29 December 1998 the Securities Law was promulgated by the Standing Committee of the NPC and became effective on 1 July 1999. This is the first national securities law in Mainland China and is the fundamental law comprehensively regulating activities on the securities market.

9.128   The Securities Law applies to the issuance and trading in the PRC of shares, corporate bonds, and other securities designated by the State Council.[156] It contains provisions governing various aspects of the securities market such as the issuance of securities, securities trading, takeovers by listed companies, administration of stock exchanges, securities companies, securities registration and settlement organizations, securities trading services organizations, securities industry associations, and securities regulatory bodies.

9.129   The Securities Law is vital to the development of China's securities market, as it endeavours to 'standardize the issuance and trading of securities, protect the lawful rights and interests of investors, safeguard the economic order and public interests of society and promote the development of the socialist market economy'.[157] For this purpose, the law establishes the principles of securities related activities as 'openness, fairness and equitability'.[158] In addition, it serves to enhance the objectivity and transparency in China's securities regulatory process.

9.130   On 27 October 2005 the PRC revised the Securities Law with the purposes of promoting the healthy growth of the securities markets, strengthening the regulation of the markets, and improving the protection for investors. The amendment came into force as of 1 January 2006.

---

[155] S Huo, 'Comment: the Company Law of the People's Republic of China', 13 *UCLA Pac Basin LJ* 373 (1995), p 376.
[156] Securities Law, art 2.   [157] Securities Law, art 1.   [158] Securities Law, art 3.

Securities Investment Funds Law

On 28 October 2003 the Standing Committee of the NPC enacted the **9.131**
Securities Investment Fund Law, effective as of 1 February 2004. This law is
formulated in order to regulate securities investment funds, to safeguard the
lawful rights and interests of investors and other parties involved, and to promote the healthy development of securities investment funds and the securities
market.[159]

This law is applicable to investment fund activities within China carried out **9.132**
through the public sale of shares of funds to raise securities investment funds
that are administered by fund managers and held by custodians, and that
engage in securities investment using a portfolio of assets for the profits of
fund shareholders.[160] Fund operating methods may be close-end, open-end, or
otherwise.[161]

The law stipulates the provisions regarding fund managers, custodians, the **9.133**
placement and trading of funds, subscription and redemption of funds, operations and information disclosure, modification and termination of contracts,
liquidation of funds, rights, and interests of fund holders and their exercising,
supervision, and administration of funds, and legal liabilities, etc.

Administrative regulations

In this category, the following four normative documents are mainly under the **9.134**
enforcement by the CSRC in their regulation of Mainland securities markets.

Provisional regulations for the administration of the Issuance and Trading of
Stock (ITS)

On 22 April 1993 the State Council promulgated the ITS, which came into **9.135**
force on the same day, with a purpose to further China's goal of majority state
ownership and minority private equity participation in the stock market.[162]
Issued just after the formal establishment of China's securities market, it is the
first comprehensive statute for the regulation of this market. The ITS deals with
the application and approval procedures for public offerings of and trading in
stock, takeovers of listed companies, deposit, settlement and transfer of listed
stock, disclosure of information with respect to a listed company, enforcement
of law, and penalties and dispute settlement.

---

[159] Securities Investment Fund Law, art 1.   [160] Securities Investment Fund Law, art 2.
[161] Securities Investment Fund Law, art 5.
[162] B Chun, 'A Brief Comparison of the Chinese and United States Securities Regulations
Governing Corporate Takeovers', 12 *Colum J Asian L* 105 (1998).

9.136 Due to limited knowledge about securities markets and the government's persistent vigilance towards capitalism, this statute took a conservative attitude towards this new market. The ITS has been predominantly superseded by the Securities Law when the latter came into force in 1999.

Special regulations concerning offering and listing of shares overseas by companies limited by shares (Overseas Offering and Listing Regulations)

9.137 On 4 July 1994 the State Council promulgated the Overseas Offering and Listing Regulations to meet the requirements of raising funds overseas by joint stock companies. These regulations deal mainly with the issuance, subscription, trading, and declaration of dividends and other distributions of foreign capital stock listed abroad and disclosure of information, articles of association of companies limited by shares having foreign capital stock listed abroad.

Regulations concerning the domestic listed foreign shares of joint stock limited companies (Domestic Listed Foreign Shares Regulations)

9.138 On 25 December 1995 the State Council promulgated the Regulations. These regulations apply to the issuance, subscription and trading of, and declaration of dividends and other distributions of domestic listed foreign shares, and disclosure of information by companies limited by shares having domestic listed foreign capital shares.

Provisional Regulations Concerning the Trading of Futures

9.139 On 2 June 1999 the State Council promulgated the Provisional Regulations Concerning the Trading of Futures, which came into force on 1 September 1999. These regulations aim to regulate futures transactions, strengthen the supervision and regulation of the futures market, guarantee normal market order, control market risk, and protect lawful rights and interests of participants and public interests.

Departmental rules

9.140 As has been mentioned earlier in this section, departmental rules are the major components of the PRC's securities legal system, and the number of rules amounts to hundreds. Therefore, it is impossible to list and introduce all of them here. For the purpose of clarification, the table opposite chooses 23 relatively important rules issued by the CSRC as examples.

9.141 Following China's accession to the WTO, the CSRC has rectified and amended all the rules and administrative approval procedures in order to comply with relevant securities commitments. Some new rules have also been promulgated by the CSRC for this purpose. At the same time, both the Shanghai and

Table 9.1 Mainland China's securities rules

Securities rule title (English)	Issuing date	Effective date
Provisional Measures on the Administration of Securities and Futures Investment Consultation	25 Dec. 1997	1 Apr. 1998
Interim Rules on the Administration of Qualification of Senior Officials in Securities Operation Institutions	11 Nov. 1998	11 Nov. 1998
Rules on the Administration of Representative Offices of Foreign Securities Institutions in China	21 Apr. 1999	21 Apr. 1999
Implementing Measures for Convertible Bonds of Listed Companies	26 Apr. 2001	26 Apr. 2001
Guidelines for Establishing the System of Independent Director among Listed Companies	16 Aug. 2001	
Code of Corporate Governance for Listed Companies in China	7 Jan. 2002	7 Jan. 2002
Standards for the Content and Format of Information Disclosure by Listed Companies (Nos 1 to 22).	15 Mar. 2001– 8 Oct. 2003	15 Mar. 2001– 8 Oct. 2003
Opinions on Several Issues concerning Foreign Investment in Listed Companies	5 Nov. 2001	
Administration of Stock Exchange Procedures	12 Dec. 2001	12 Dec. 2001
Rules for the Administration of Securities Companies	28 Dec. 2001	1 Mar. 2002
Code of Corporate Governance for Listed Companies in China	7 Jan. 2002	7 Jan. 2002
Administration of Futures Broker Companies Procedures	17 May 2002	1 July 2002
Administration of Futures Exchange Procedures	17 May 2002	1 July 2002
Rules for Establishing Foreign-invested Securities Companies	1 June 2002	1 July 2002
Rules for Establishing Foreign-invested Fund Management Companies	1 June 2002	1 July 2002
Administration of the Takeover of Listed Companies Procedures	28 Sept. 2002	1 Dec. 2002
Notice on Relevant Issues Concerning the Transfer to Foreign Investors of Listed Company State-Owned Shares and Legal Person Shares	1 Nov. 2002	1 Jan. 2003
Interim Rules on Administration of Securities Investment of Qualified Foreign Institutional Investors in China	5 Nov. 2002	1 Dec. 2002
Administration Measures on the Qualifications of Personnel Engaged in the Securities Industry	16 Dec. 2002	1 Feb. 2003
Interim Measures on the Sponsor System for Securities Public Offerings	9 Oct. 2003	1 Feb. 2004
Interim Measures on the Public Offering Review Committee of the CSRC	5 Dec. 2003	5 Dec. 2003

[Continued overleaf]

459

Table 9.1 continued

Securities rule title (English)	Issuing date	Effective date
Administration of Securities Investment Funds Operations Procedures	29 June 2004	1 July 2004
Administration of the Sale of Securities Investment Funds Procedures	25 June 2004	1 July 2004
Several Regulations Concerning Strengthening the Protection for the Lawful Rights and Interests of Public Shareholders	7 Dec. 2004	7 Dec. 2004
Rules on Administration of the Qualification of Custody of Securities Investment Funds	29 Nov. 2004	1 Jan. 2005
Special Rules on Information Disclosure of Money Market Funds	25 Mar. 2005	1 Apr. 2005
Administrative Measures on the Split Share Structure Reform of Listed Companies	4 Sept. 2005	4 Sept. 2005

Shenzhen Stock Exchanges have revised their rules of management on membership and on 'B' share trading seats, in compliance with China's WTO commitments.

(3) Mergers, acquisitions, and takeovers

9.142 As the result of Mainland China's continuous efforts in legislation, its legal system concerning the securities market has been improved to a great extent. Many important aspects are becoming complete and practical. The regulation of takeovers is a good example. Major statutes in this category include the ITS (Chapter IV: on Takeover of Listed Companies), the Securities Law (rules for securities transactions: Articles 38, 39, 40, and 43; provisions in reference to forbidden transactions: Articles 73 to 84 of the Securities Law; substantial shareholding and corporate acquisition under Chapter IV—mainly Articles 67, 85 to 101), and the Administration of the Takeover of Listed Companies Procedures and the Disclosure of Information on the Change of Shareholdings in Listed Companies Procedures (2002).

9.143 The Administration of the Takeover of Listed Companies Procedures is the latest and most specific statute addressing takeovers of listed companies in the PRC. On the same day when the Takeover Procedures was published, the CSRC issued the Disclosure of Information on the Change of Shareholdings in Listed Companies Procedures, requiring public disclosure of certain shareholding activities. With the Takeover Procedures and the Disclosure of Information Procedures which set up a regime governing the acquisition of a substantial or controlling stake in Chinese listed companies and the associated disclosure requirements, China has taken a signficant step in bringing its regulatory framework for M&A closer to international norms.[163] Together with the ITS, the Securities Law, and some related and more detailed department rules, the Takeover Procedures and the Disclosure of Information Procedures create a comprehensive and solid legal basis for the Mainland securities market, which should stimulate M&A development, and trigger a wave of corporate consolidation in China.[164]

E. Insurance

Development of insurance markets and the related legal and institutional framework has been more straightforward than that of banking or securities, largely as a result of the lack of any such market and related framework in the context of a centrally planned economy. Markets and their framework thus have developed in parallel with the move towards a socialist market economy in Mainland China.
9.144

In 1995 the Standing Committee of the NPC enacted China's first Insurance Law. At that time, insurance regulation rested with the PBOC. (For example, the PBOC issued the Interim Rules of Administration of Insurance in 1996, stating that the PBOC was in charge of insurance regulation.)[165] In 1998 the CIRC was established and the insurance regulatory function was transferred from the PBOC to the CIRC.[166]
9.145

Article 148 of the Insurance Law 1995 is similar to Article 92 of the Law on Commercial Banks 2003, stipulating that the establishment of foreign-fund-participated insurance companies or branches of foreign insurance companies shall be subject to this insurance law, but the laws and regulations specifically related to foreign related insurance companies, if any, shall prevail. In October 2002 the Standing Committee of the NPC amended the Insurance Law 1995 (hereinafter referred to as the Insurance Law 2002),[167] at least partially to make the law consistent with China's WTO commitments.[168] For instance, Article
9.146

---

[163] T Ng, 'M&A in Asia—China in the spotlight', 7 February 2003.
[164] See Zhang Xin, 'Regulating Chinese M&A', 29 August 2002 available at <http://www.financeasia.com>.
[165] See Interim Rules of Administration of Insurance, art 65. This interim rule was abolished after the CIRC issued the Rules of Administration of Insurance Companies in 2000.
[166] See Notification on the Establishment of the CIRC [*Guowuyuan Guanyu Chengli Zhongguo Baoxian Jiandu Guanli Weiyuanhui de Tongzhi*], *Guofa* [1998], No 37.
[167] The amended Insurance Law came into force from 1 January 2003.
[168] See CIRC's chairman's statement, Wu Dingfu, available at <http//www.circ.gov.cn/news/wudingfu.htm>.

154 of the Insurance Law 2002 replaced Article 148 of the Insurance Law 1995, adding wholly-foreign-funded insurance companies as one of the forms of foreign-invested insurance companies.[169]

9.147 In accordance with Article 2 of the Rules on Administration of Insurance Companies,[170] the CIRC is entitled to supervise insurance companies by the authorization of the State Council.[171] The first duty of the CIRC granted by the State Council is 'to formulate policies and rules concerning commercial insurance'.[172] For the purpose of formulating insurance rules, that is, the CIRC formulated a special rule on how to formulate insurance administrative rules, Rules on the Formulation Procedures of Insurance Administration Rules[173] by which such rules generally take the name of 'rule' or 'detailed rules of implementation'.[174] The most relevant CIRC insurance rules are shown in Table 9.2 opposite.

F. Conclusion

9.148 As China is advancing towards a socialist market, its financial sector has been transformed, opening many opportunities and challenges, not only on the Mainland but also in Hong Kong.

9.149 The preference of the Chinese government for strictly controlling financial resources, in spite of its necessity at this stage of transition, is one of the major obstacles for financial institutions and markets to function independently and efficiently. However, reforming China's financial architecture in line with international standards does not necessarily enhance the functioning of its financial system as China is experiencing a radical transformation from a planned economy to a socialist market economy. Notwithstanding this, restructuring Mainland China's financial sector into an independent, transparent, and commercialized system is essential both for a sound financial market and sustainable economic development.

9.150 China's developing legal system has been facilitating the transformation of its financial sector, and the rapid economic growth in China is correlated with the

---

[169] According to China's insurance commitments, within two years after China's accession, foreign non-life insurers will be permitted to establish as a wholly-owned subsidiary.

[170] This rule was published by CIRC in January 2000.

[171] See Organic Law of the State Council 1982, art 10.

[172] See Notification on the Establishment of CIRC.   [173] *Baojianfa* [1999] No 111.

[174] '*Guiding*' is suitable for insurance regulation or insurance activities in part, while '*Banfa*' is suitable for detailed rules on insurance regulation or insurance activities; Detailed Implementation Rule is suitable for a complete and detailed rules for the enforcement or operation of one particular law or regulation. See art 3 of Rules on the Formulation Procedures of Insurance Administration Rules.

Table 9.2 CIRC insurance rules

Insurance rule title (English)	Issue date	Effective date	Document number
Interim Rules on Administration of Investment in Securities Investment Fund by Insurance Companies	29 Oct. 1999	29 Oct. 1999	*Baojianfa* [1999] No 206. This rule was slightly amended in 2000, *Baojianfa* [2000] No 96
Interim Rules on Investment in Insurance Companies	1 Apr. 2000	1 Apr. 2000	*Baojianfa* [2000] No 49. This rule amended *Baojianfa* [1999] No 270
Rules on Administration of Insurance Assessors	16 Nov. 2001	1 Jan. 2002	CIRC Order [2001] No 3 Some articles of this rule were amended in 2002 in order to be consistent with WTO accession demands
Rules on Establishment of Reinsurance Companies	17 Sept. 2002	17 Sept. 2002	CIRC Order [2002] No 4
Provisions on the Administration of Marketing Departments of Insurance Companies	1 Feb. 2002	1 Mar. 2002	Joint order by CIRC and State Administration on Industry and Commerce
Provisions on the Administration of the Amount of Solvency and Relevant Regulatory Index of Insurance Companies	24 Mar. 2003	24 Mar. 2003	CIRC Order [2003] No 1
Rules on Administration of Representative Offices of Foreign Insurance Companies	15 Jan. 2004	1 Mar. 2004	CIRC Order [2004] No 1
Rules on Administration of Insurance Companies	15 Mar. 2004	15 June 2004	CIRC Order [2004] No 3
Detailed Rules for Implementation of Regulations of the PRC on Administration of Foreign-funded Insurance Companies	13 Mar. 2004	15 June 2004	CIRC Order [2004] No 4
Rules on Administration of Insurance Agencies	11 Nov. 2004	1 Jan. 2005	CIRC Order [2004] No 14
Rules on Administration of Insurance Brokers	11 Nov. 2004	1 Jan. 2005	CIRC Order [2004] No 15
Rules on Administration of Reinsurance	14 Oct. 2005	1 Dec. 2005	CIRC Order [2005] No 2

progression in its legal development.[175] As a transition country, however, China's efforts to reform its financial system under a rule-based framework is

---

[175] R Peerenboom, *China's Long March toward Rule of Law* (Cambridge: Cambridge University Press, 2002), pp 463–4.

far from perfect. Therefore, the measures adopted to resolve problems must proceed through trial and error, and this can hardly be achieved in strict compliance with a formal legislative process. The need for flexibility and expediency must be balanced against the costs of 'legislative forbearance', ie relaxing the strict rule of law. The reform of China's corporate and financial law is very challenging because it has to keep a balance between global competition and maintaining social stability in post-WTO China. However, a well-functioning legal framework with efficient judicial system, credible supervisory authorities with sufficient enforcement capacity, and an efficient administrative structure with less corruption, are crucial for constructing and maintaining a healthy financial system. Although the special environments of the transition process, including social, political, and economic aspects, constrain the legal regime, good legal mechanisms should and can be adopted to provide adequate restrictions on the power of the government and sufficient incentives for market participants.

9.151 Effective legal infrastructure serving to establish and enforce property rights and contracts, as well as creditor and shareholder rights, underpins a sound and stable financial system.[176] However, disparity between extensive legislation and insufficient compliance is a problematic issue for China, in common with other transition economies.[177] Therefore, it is very important to cultivate a credit culture through improving legal enforceability.

9.152 In compliance with the WTO Agreement, China's legal system has to be transparent and consistent across the entire country.[178] A process is on-going to abolish or amend many financial laws, regulations, and rules which are not in accordance with the WTO commitments. But, uniformity in the implementation of laws and the WTO Agreement cannot be realized insofar as China's legal system is still taking an ad hoc piecemeal approach in the context of transition. Regulations, rules, decisions, and orders comprise the large part of China's legal system with their advantage of adapting rapidly to the developing economy, but they are often lacking in clarity, certainty, universality, and stability. Moreover, legislative competition among government agencies seeking rents through issuance of regulations, orders, and complex procedures further complicates market participation.

9.153 Besides the previously mentioned problem caused by the basic systematic flaws of China's securities market, there are some other pitfalls in the legal system that are worthy of attention.

---

[176] European Bank for Reconstruction and Development (EBRD), *Transition Report 1998* (London: EBRD, 1998), p 116.
[177] ibid, pp 108–9.
[178] D Blumental, 'Reform or Opening? Reform of China's State-owned Enterprises and WTO Accession—The Dilemma of Applying GATT To Marketizing Economies', 16 *UCLA Pacific Basin Law Journal* 198, at 234.

First, an overly administrative approach is adopted in financial market regula- **9.154**
tion. Government intervention is still much wider and deeper than necessary.
Market participants have not enjoyed sufficient freedom and power to take
decisions. This problem originated in the centrally planned economic system
adopted by China before its reform towards a socialist market economy, and it
commonly exists in the regulation of economic activities, including financial
activities. Though China has acted to change this situation, there remains a long
way to go.

Second, many statutes are imprecise and lack detail. Though the legal system **9.155**
seems to be comprehensive, there is insufficient detail available for practice in
some normative documents. The major components of the legal system contain
many basic principles, which are too general to apply in practice. Not all of the
normative documents contain applicable procedures or arrangements. Specific
implementing rules have to be improved gradually.

Third, the protections for public investors and minority shareholders are rela- **9.156**
tively weak. Due to the dominance of the State and legal persons as the major
shareholders among Chinese listed companies, minority shareholders (in most
cases, public investors) need better protection from the abuse of majority ownership. However, many legal mechanisms necessary for this protection have not
been established or recognized in the Chinese legal system. Investors cannot find
proper weapons to safeguard their lawful rights and interests.

Fourth, many issues that have arisen or are arising in China's financial markets **9.157**
during their development and liberalization remain unaddressed. Securitization,
management buy-outs, stock options, and other activities and objects that are
common in well-developed markets and mature legal systems worldwide need
to be addressed by regulation in China. This is an urgent need for the further
development of the Chinese market.

In short, the Chinese legal system is far from perfect. If we summarize all the **9.158**
defects in this system, the most critical defects are the lack of a full legal foundation for the functioning of the market and an artificial separation between the
regulations for investors with different statuses.

As a result of its reform programme, China has produced an economy with one **9.159**
of the most rapid growth rates in the world and is regarded as a miracle. In this
process, the financial markets must contribute more to the national economy
and performing functions such as raising capital, optimizing resource allocation,
and improving corporate governance. This can be achieved with the improvement of the legal system. Besides improvement in the legal system, it is also
important (or even more important) that all the normative rules are observed
and implemented strictly.

9.160 In conclusion, this chapter has focused on the financial markets and related legal and institutional frameworks in Mainland China, in the context of China's liberalization commitments under the WTO and CEPA. As part of the PRC, Hong Kong increasingly must deal directly with resulting issues and questions, both as a result of the increasing use by Mainland companies of Hong Kong's financial markets (eg listing on the SEHK) as well as supporting business in China (eg through CEPA and/or WTO commitments). At the same time, the resulting interconnection between the two economies and financial systems brings challenges for Hong Kong. This is especially true of questions relating to Mainland companies raising money in Hong Kong and resulting issues of disclosure, corporate governance, and related enforcement problems.

9.161 These issues are addressed further in the final chapter.

10

GLOBALIZATION AND FINANCIAL REGULATION IN HONG KONG

This book has reviewed the legal and regulatory framework for financial markets **10.01** in Hong Kong in the context of their development, and local characteristics and practices. Part I provided an overview of financial markets and their legal and regulatory foundations in Hong Kong covering their historical development along with some of the unique or unusual features of those markets (Chapter 1) and the overall legal and regulatory framework supporting those markets and developed in tandem with and in response to their characteristics (Chapter 2). Part II discussed the regulation of financial intermediaries, products, and services generally (Chapter 3), and specifically that relating to public offerings and listings of company shares (Chapter 4) and financial derivatives (Chapter 5). Part III then looked to the framework governing corporate and market conduct in Hong Kong, focusing on corporate governance (Chapter 6), takeovers and mergers (Chapter 7), and market misconduct (Chapter 8). Finally, Part IV looks to the wider context in which those markets operate, especially their interconnection with the financial, legal, and economic systems of Mainland China (Chapter 9) and the global context.

In addition to describing financial market law and practice in Hong Kong, this **10.02** volume has sought to point out related major issues, whether legal, economic, or cultural. Each chapter has concluded with an evaluation of specific features of Hong Kong's markets and legal and regulatory framework, identifying weaknesses and where reform is most needed.

10.03 This final chapter takes the analysis further: rather than highlighting issues within the context of specific areas of reference, it seeks to present an overview of major concerns for the future of Hong Kong's financial markets and their legal and regulatory systems. These arise in two main respects: first, risks to be addressed out of concern for financial stability and the continued economic development of Hong Kong; and second, opportunities to enhance Hong Kong's competitiveness as a financial centre, especially in the context of prospects for China and East Asia.

10.04 An important consequence of the globalization of financial services is that strengthened linkages across the world's major financial markets have intensified competition among financial centres. Three fundamental technological shifts will shape the competitive landscape of financial markets.

10.05 First, virtualization implies that financial services can be provided over a much larger and dispersed geographical area, bypassing certain cultural barriers that impede face-to-face interaction.[1] Virtualization of financial services has begun to reduce the necessity of direct contact between financial services providers and their clients. This is particularly true for certain retail products: large-scale transactions tend to be slower to shed attachment to a physical location. Many regular transactions are capable of being handled through the internet or by telecommunications technology, although national barriers continue to pervade conventional consumer banking.

10.06 Second, technological progress has also produced more powerful and efficient management information systems for companies. Different offices and departments of the same company are connected not only in one particular location, but also across branch offices and headquarters scattered across different parts of the world. Hence the costs of communication and information channelling within the same company are greatly reduced. Virtualization and the development of information technology have spurred the growth of international financial services, which also requires that regulatory frameworks of different jurisdictions be able to communicate with one another. At the same time, competition between financial services centres is made evident.

10.07 Third, financial engineering in the form of product innovation, especially involving the use of derivatives, has been a major precursor of growth in financial service usage around the world. For example, credit derivatives now enable investors and other financial creditors freely to acquire or shed counterparty credit risks, gain exposure to risks that were hitherto unavailable, and in

---

[1] R Grosse, *The Future of Global Financial Services: Global Dimensions in Business* (Malden Ma: Blackwell, 2004), p 35.

some cases allow a more aggressive approach to marketing complex credit products to borrowers and investors. One contribution of financial engineering is in providing more complete tools for assessing, altering, or transferring hedging risks, which has been the broad assessment of the BIS committee on financial stability. However, it is blamed by some for inducing speculative risk-taking behaviour that may lead to financial losses and failures of prominent corporations.[2]

This chapter does not purport to answer all the regulatory issues and questions raised in previous chapters. Rather, its main objective is to raise concerns that highlight the shortcomings and deficiencies of the current regulatory framework and indicate opportunities for future growth and development. It is hoped that it will provide guidance as to the current state of the regulatory system and a vision for its improvement. **10.08**

Section A presents a framework for analysing key risks and competitiveness issues in Hong Kong's financial regulatory system. From this framework, Section B presents suggestions for regulatory reform in Hong Kong to enhance both financial stability and its competitiveness as an international financial centre. The following sections then look to specific areas of concern. Section C examines corporate governance, in particular, issues of corporate ethics and the value system pertinent to Chinese society. Section D discusses the role of product innovation and the possible role of the government in supporting financial market development. Section E discusses financial fraud and misconduct, including in the corporate context. **10.09**

A. Financial Stability and International Competitiveness

As discussed in Chapter 2, Hong Kong has in place a legal and regulatory framework sufficient to support financial stability. Nonetheless, as emphasized by the IMF there are certain weaknesses, especially in relation to the independence of regulatory authorities, and gaps in regulation (both of financial institutions, especially financial conglomerates, and financial markets more generally, especially in regard to differential treatment of similar behaviour and products in different financial segments) that raise concerns as to financial stability. These issues should be addressed not only out of concern for financial risk and stability, but also as part of a broader pattern to support the competitiveness of Hong Kong as an international financial centre. **10.10**

---

[2] See A Steinherr, *Derivatives: The Wild Beast of Finance* (Chichester: John Wiley, 1998). The BIS findings are explained more fully in Chapter 5.

10.11   Hong Kong is perhaps the only jurisdiction in the world that is legally required to maintain its status as an international financial centre (under Article 109 of the Basic Law). However, compared to other international financial jurisdictions; Hong Kong has not placed significant attention at a high level to its overall competitiveness. Nonetheless, individual regulatory agencies in Hong Kong (especially the HKMA in the area of banking and the SFC in relation to securities) have expended and continue to expend significant efforts to enhance the efficacy (especially in regard to financial stability concerns) and also the attractiveness of their respective regimes.

10.12   One traditional view[3] holds that Hong Kong became a financial hub only in the 1970s but others[4] have noted earlier events and characteristics that helped create Hong Kong's financial sector platform since the 1960s, and the many overseas factors that inadvertently assisted Hong Kong's growth (including rules or omissions by other centres).

10.13   The issues raised in this section concern two well-known and unresolved issues: what most influences economic growth; and the relationship of financial systems to economic development, including links between legal systems and financial structure. Both questions have interested theoretical and empirical scholars for some years, but attention has only recently focused on institutional aspects of aggregate or sectoral financial markets and systems. Except among historians, little of the work has paid close regard to Asian economies or institutions, partly for lack of sufficient conventional data.[5]

10.14   The related work includes a considerable body of empirical studies seeking evidence of causal relationships between financial market or institutional sophistication or structure, including legal origins and conditions, and economic development, commonly measured by growth in national output.[6] While not

---

[3] YC Jao, 'Shanghai and Hong Kong as international financial centres: historical perspective and contemporary analysis' Hong Kong Institute for Economics and Business Strategy wp1071 (2003).

[4] C Schenk, 'Banks and the emergence of Hong Kong as an international financial centre' (2002) *Journal of International Financial Markets, Institutions and Money* 12; 'Closing the Hong Kong gap; the Hong Kong free dollar market in the 1950s' (1994) *Economic History Review*, XLVII(2).

[5] A recent exception in cross-country empirical studies is B Eichengreen & P Luengnaruemitchai, 'Why doesn't Asia have bigger bond markets?' National Bureau of Economic Research wp10576 (2004).

[6] In the style established by Goldsmith and following the statistical methods begun by King & Levine and later La Porta, Lopez-de-Silanes, Shleifer & Vishny (LLSV): R Goldsmith, 'Financial structure and development' (New Haven CT: Yale UP, 1969); R King & R Levine, 'Finance & growth: Schumpeter might be right' (1993) *Quarterly Journal of Economics* 108; R La Porta, F Lopez-de-Silanes, A Shleifer, & R Vishny, 'Legal determinants of external finance' (1997) *Journal of Finance* 52(3), and 'Law and finance' (1998) *Journal of Political Economy* 106(6).

unanimous, these studies generally suggest that finance often has a positive effect on growth, although (contrary to popular belief) there is no accepted theoretical school that asserts the contrary, that the primary causal flow is from economic growth to financial development. Detailed aspects of that analysis have been criticized on grounds of statistical methodology[7] and qualitatively in the selection or specification of explanatory variables.[8]

Until the 1970s economic or finance theory gave little attention to the nature of financial systems or how they may affect economic development. Similarly, the importance and influence of the characteristics of financial markets and institutions has been accepted only since the late-1980s, with the growth of the law and finance and institutional economics schools. As an example, Hong Kong is an acknowledged financial hub that developed in part due to financial policy decisions made by itself and elsewhere over a lengthy period, yet Edward Szczepanik makes scarcely any mention of finance in his 1958 account of Hong Kong's economy, generally acknowledged as the first definitive study. **10.15**

One reason for the newness of the study of financial markets and institutions may be that both neo-classical economic theory and post-1940s growth theory either dismissed or assumed away the nature of financial systems. A similar pattern persisted until recently in finance theory: Allen suggests that to ignore the existence of financial institutions in particular relation to intermediation is to contradict the asset pricing tenets of finance theory and the agency problem of corporate finance theory, but in so doing he states the importance of financial intermediaries only in a limited way.[9] Thus while modern finance and corporate finance theory began long ago to examine the creation of commercial organizations from a contractual or cost perspective,[10] a similar approach has been considered for financial institutions only recently, especially examining how transaction costs influence the development of single institutions such as banks, the formation and evolution of financial systems, and the relative importance of different institutional models within advanced economies and some developing economies. **10.16**

Economic history repeatedly shows how legal and regulatory reforms have **10.17**

---

[7] D Blum, K Federmair, G Fink, & P Haiss, 'The financial-real sector nexus: theory & empirical evidence' Research Institute for European Affairs working papers 43 (2002); M Thiel, 'Finance & economic growth—a review of theory & the available evidence' European Commission economic paper 158 (2001); P Wachtel, 'How much do we really know about growth & finance?' (2003) *Federal Reserve Bank of Atlanta Economic Review* Q1.

[8] D Berkowitz, K Pistor, & J-F Richard, 'The transplant effect' (2003) 51 *Am J Comp L* 163.

[9] F Allen, 'Do financial institutions matter?' (2001) *Journal of Finance* LVI(4).

[10] R Coase, 'The nature of the firm' (1937) *Economica* 4(6); 'The problem of social cost' (1960) III *Journal of Law & Economics*.

produced significant effects in financial systems.[11] However, the most distinguished historians have often failed to identify generic, non-time specific lessons in their analysis and thus drawn only temporary conclusions as to financial sector prospects.[12]

10.18 North[13] and Roe[14] respectively use path dependence to explain the creation of single financial institutions and the development of critical aspects of financial and corporate governance in the US and certain other advanced economies: this approach will strongly inform this chapter. The life cycles of financial hubs, market clusters and collected institutions have been examined for 20 years in economic geography[15] and for a considerably longer period by historians[16] but most recent theoretical work has used an institutional economic perspective.[17] Factors affecting change in the financial sector may vary by place and time (as the economic history of hubs shows).

10.19 Thus while the subject of this section is therefore new (especially in an Asian context), it is closely linked to voluminous work in related or adjacent fields, including economic history, economic geography and finance theory, but most particularly from institutional economics, and law and finance analysis.

---

[11] Including Baskin in assessing how financial institutions first dealt with information asymmetry; Cameron & others on the development of banking laws (Pollard & Ziegler); Kindleberger in describing the effects of regulatory change, and many authors in relation to the emergence of eurocurrency markets in the 1960s): J Baskin, 'The development of corporate financial markets in Britain and the United States, 1600–1914: overcoming asymmetric information' (1988) *Business History Review* 62(2); S Pollard & D Ziegler, 'Banking & industrialisation: Rondo Cameron twenty years on' in Y Cassis (ed), *Finance & financiers in European history 1880–1960* (Cambridge: CUP, 1992); C Kindleberger, *A financial history of Western Europe* (New York: Oxford University Press, 1984).

[12] Thus Kindleberger, who predicted Brussels becoming Europe's leading financial hub well before 2000; Gurley suggested that bank intermediaries were not essential to the growth process: C Kindleberger, 'The formation of financial centres: a study in comparative economic history' *Studies in International Finance* 36, Princeton (1974); J Gurley, 'Banking in the early stages of industrialization: a study in comparative economic history' (1967) *American Economic Review* 57(4).

[13] D North, 'Institutions' (1991) *Journal of Economic Perspectives* 5(1); 'Some fundamental puzzles in economic history/ development' Economics working paper archive at WUSTL 1995.

[14] M Roe, *Strong managers, weak owners: the political roots of American corporate finance* (Princeton, NJ, Princeton UP, 1994).

[15] L Budd, 'Globalization, territory & strategic alliances in different financial centres' (1995) 32(2) *Urban Studies*; I McCarthy 'Offshore banking centers: benefits and costs' (1979) *Finance and Development* 16(4); S Sassen, *The global city: New York, London, Tokyo* (Princeton: Princeton University Press, 1991).

[16] Including A Gerschenkron, 'Reflections on the concept of "prerequisites of modern industrialization"', in *Economic backwardness in historical perspective* (Cambridge MA: Belknap Press, 1962); M Porter, *The competitive advantage of nations* (New York: The Free Press, 1990).

[17] Williamson; Matthews; Roe—all recognizing the work of Coase and North: O Williamson 'The new institutional economics: taking stock, looking ahead' (2000) *Journal of Economic Literature* 38(3); R Matthews, 'The economics of institutions and the sources of growth' (1986) *Economic Journal* 96 (384).

Law and finance scholars have emphasized the primacy of the legal system in   **10.20**
financial development but this can be a hazardous conclusion. Issues and
questions raised by the law and finance school include:

- institutional development and its relationship to economic welfare shown
  by growth, and the narrower relationship between legal origins and the
  effectiveness of legal systems;
- whether legal origin (or the nature of its introduction) is a significant
  determinant of the effectiveness of a legal system;
- whether common law is more effective in encouraging financial development
  than other forms of law.

Clearly, from the perspectives of practice, history, and theory, Hong Kong's legal   **10.21**
and regulatory system for financial markets has played a key role in its development as an international financial centre and likewise will play a key role in its
future development.

This suggests a framework to evaluate the competitiveness of Hong Kong as an   **10.22**
international financial centre focusing on five crucial elements, namely: (1)
range of financial products and quality of service; (2) management expertise;
(3) policy, regulatory and cultural environment conducive to attracting the
best human resources; (4) business toolkit for finance, including risk management, valuation, and financial engineering; and (5) corporate governance,
social responsibility, and education. Table 10.1 overleaf indicates the main
components for each element.

Management and business toolkit issues have little legal content, so are beyond   **10.23**
the scope of the present analysis. Of more direct concern are issues of financial
product coverage and innovation, regulatory environment, and corporate
governance.

In relation to financial products and services, as a general matter, Hong Kong   **10.24**
has a full range of financial products and services and a legal system that supports innovation and development. Nevertheless, the system could be more
supportive of development while at the same time addressing resulting risks.
These issues are discussed in Section E below.

The regulatory environment and corporate governance are of direct com-   **10.25**
petitiveness concern and are addressed in the following sections.

B. Financial Regulatory Structure and Reform

As noted above, a crucial factor to Hong Kong's success has been its underlying   **10.26**
legal and institutional framework, based largely on nineteenth-century English

Table 10.1 Hong Kong as an international financial centre

Financial products and services	• Mutual funds • Hedge funds • Fixed income • Insurance • Reinsurance • Derivatives • Financial advisory • Customer services • Capital raising • Trust & estate management • Mergers & acquisitions • Risk management • Restructuring
Management	• Shared vision and mission • Market positioning • Penetration • Brand management • Competitive strategies • Supply chain strategies • Alliance strategies • Mergers & acquisitions • Restructuring
Regulatory environment & culture	• Immigration policy • Language • Financial regulations • Ethics and conduct • Government policy
Business toolkit	• Valuation • Internet • Management information systems • Marketing • Financial engineering • Risk management • Research & development • Analysis • Asset-liability management
Corporate governance system, social responsibility & education	• OECD Principles • Personal operating system • Higher & professional education • Continuing education • Training and support

prototypes. These antecedents have increasingly been remodelled over the past fifteen years to better address Hong Kong's domestic characteristics.

10.27 Hong Kong's success in many ways is based on its common law system (and the Basic Law provides that the common law system shall be maintained until

2047).[18] In seeking to enhance competitiveness, Hong Kong in general looks to models and experiences from certain Commonwealth jurisdictions, especially the UK, Canada, and Australia. However, a blind adoption of international financial architecture without considering the local factors may have adverse effects on the legal development of Hong Kong. Studies have shown that the successful operation of a legal system very much depends on the legal culture of the jurisdiction,[19] and the nature of how the system comes to be transplanted.[20] The common law was first imported to Hong Kong in 1841 and has undergone its own development, although it has been deeply influenced by the precedents and legislation of the UK prior to 1 July 1997.

Reforms in Hong Kong in relation to international financial architecture may **10.28** distort rather than enhance the regulatory framework unless its legal infrastructure is prepared for change.[21] There is a concern that international standards have not been put to the test of functionality in individual jurisdictions.[22] The effect is that lay members of the investing public may be misled into believing that those international standards are properly implemented and rely upon perceived protection. Moreover, the regulatory mechanism has to ensure full compliance with these standards. When conflicts of interest are the prevailing norm in the political culture, as in Hong Kong, it raises doubts about the merit of adopting international standards, at least not without appropriate modification.

There is often no single correct approach to a regulatory issue. Legislation and **10.29** regulatory structures vary between jurisdictions and reflect local market conditions and historical development. The particular manner in which a jurisdiction implements the various international standards reflected in Chapter 2 and in the IMF evaluation discussed therein must have regard to the entire domestic context, including the relevant legal and commercial framework.

Based on the requirements of Article 109 of the Basic Law, it may be advanta- **10.30** geous for Hong Kong to undertake a comprehensive analysis of the competitiveness and efficacy of its financial regulatory system with the express objective of improving its competitive attractiveness and effectiveness and in addressing financial stability concerns.

---

[18] Basic Law, art 8.
[19] See B Hsu, *The Common Law in Chinese Context* (Hong Kong: Hong Kong University Press, 1992).
[20] D Berkowitz, K Pistor, & J-F Richard 'Economic development, legality, and the transplant effect' (2003) 47 *European Economic Review* 165.
[21] K Pistor, 'The Standardization of Law and Its Effect on Developing Economies' (2002) 40 *American Journal of Comparative Law* 97, at p 99.
[22] ibid, p 102.

10.31 As one possible model for reform, the government could alter the structure of financial regulation in Hong Kong to match today's needs and opportunities. Hong Kong's existing system developed largely through trial and error and is now a confusing matrix of sectoral laws and agencies with many gaps and inconsistencies. The need is clear for a coherent system based upon specific objectives and roles, that is, a more functional than sectoral or institutional framework. Such a framework would resemble systems adopted in Australia, France, and the Netherlands.

10.32 Under such an approach, two regulatory bodies would have mutually exclusive functions—one being primarily responsible for the regulation of financial institutions themselves (such as licensing, capital adequacy, supervision, and enforcement of both banks and securities houses), the other primarily responsible for product and market regulation. HKEx would remain responsible for listing matters beyond the remit of the product and market regulator (similar to the role of the New York Stock Exchange vis-à-vis the Securities and Exchange Commission in the US or the London Stock Exchange vis-à-vis the FSA in the UK). As a result, there should be greater harmonization and consistency of treatment across, on the one hand, financial institutions and, on the other hand, products and markets.

10.33 This reform would also address issues including the complexity and expense of dealing with Hong Kong's existing regulatory framework and with respect to compliance costs. However, this would be a major change and in all likelihood would not appeal to the various regulatory agencies (which are comfortable with their current roles), local business interests (which may prefer the complexity and opportunities for regulatory arbitrage and the advantage it presents) or the government (which would have a difficult task in managing the process). However, most consumers (whether individuals or non-local companies and financial firms) would prefer a simpler, clearer, more effective framework. As a result, the following sections address issues of more direct concern which could be addressed readily.

C. Corporate Governance

10.34 Another theme of this volume has been corporate conduct and governance issues in Hong Kong and the role of the legal and regulatory system, both in terms of market quality and competitiveness.

10.35 Laws, regulations, and market forces are necessary but insufficient to safeguard ethical behaviour in the financial markets. Other than providing a return to shareholders, business nowadays is charged with other tasks as well: acting lawfully, producing safe products and services at costs commensurate with quality, minimizing negative social and environmental impacts, and being socially responsible.[23]

In the wake of recent business scandals, corporate governance is no longer a phrase heard mainly inside academia. The epidemic effect threatened by the fall of Enron, Barings, and WorldCom is that investor confidence worldwide is seriously undermined and the development of capital markets and economic growth thus damaged.

10.36

All over the world, many reforms and practices have been proposed to improve corporate governance standards, to establish new measures to strengthen corporate governance in an effort to prevent Enron-style accounting scandals and high-profile bankruptcies, to make complex corporate structures such as holding companies and 'pyramid' shareholdings more transparent, to prohibit holding companies whose main assets are their shareholdings in another listed company from having a stock market listing of their own, to allow shareholders more say in setting management pay, particularly in the award of stock options, and to make the chief executive and the chief financial officer individually, or even the whole management board, responsible for the accuracy of financial statements.

10.37

However, it is arguable that an 'epidemic effect' is ephemeral in a systemic sense so that investor sentiment is only temporarily undermined. On the other hand, there is evidence that corporate governance has become an important decision element in the investment process following the scandalous events in recent years.[24] The implication is straightforward. Corporate governance practices can change investors views of a company and hence their portfolio choice, and therefore will affect the performance and the long-term survivability of a company.

10.38

The impact of corporate governance as a business strategy in improving a firm's competitiveness in the marketplace has also been examined in a recent study that examined the fashion retailing sector, a highly competitive market sector in Hong Kong.[25] Through questionnaires to companies and surveys of

10.39

---

[23] David Vogel bears the view that there is not much basis for the claim that corporate social responsibility systematically pays and that for almost all firms corporate social responsibility is largely irrelevant to their profitability. For details see D Vogel, 'Social Responsibility: The Low Value of Virtue' (June 2005) 83:6 *Harvard Business Review* 26.

[24] D Baum, 'Corporate Governance: The Implications of Recent Events on Investor and Corporate Decision Making', Goldman Sachs, 4 April 2003. An investor survey by Goldman Sachs on the importance of corporate governance showed that more than 70% of the respondents indicate that corporate governance issues matter in making investment decisions.

[25] JCK Lam, S Salahuddin, & CSJ Tsoi, 'Corporate Governance as a Competitive Necessity', The University of Hong Kong (Team: LP/HKU/02), Corporate Governance for the New Generation, organized by Hong Kong ICAC, 2003.

consumers, the study investigated the way in which corporate governance was perceived by business and consumers to affect the competitiveness of a firm. The survey of consumers focused on how consumers would rank a particular brand name among others based on the perceived obligation and responsibility of the companies towards society, and how consumers made their purchasing decisions. The questionnaire to companies enquired about the companies' understanding of corporate governance, competition within the retail sector, consumer demands, knowledge of environmental issues and corporate social responsibility, and the role of corporate governance in elevating their competitiveness.

10.40 The analysis of the data collected from the survey and the questionnaire revealed interesting implications for the retail sector in Hong Kong. First, corporate governance was not yet perceived as a necessary component of a business strategy in Hong Kong, contrary to findings for the European and the US markets. However, both consumers and the companies believed that corporate governance was gaining importance in terms of enhancing corporate competitiveness. Second, consumers seemed to value social and ethical responsibility and environmental management of firms more than the firms had realized. Also, consumers were looking for more transparency in the disclosure of corporate information. Although this study focused on the retail fashion sector, the results shed light more broadly on corporate governance issues in Hong Kong.

10.41 There are different approaches to defining corporate governance, all with some variations in detail but the subject matter is largely the same.[26] The better known and adopted is the OECD Principles of Corporate Governance developed in 1998 and revised in 2004, discussed in Chapter 6.

10.42 In recent years, significant research has studied the relationship between corporate governance and corporate performance and on how sound corporate governance can further enhance the good performance of a firm. The research supports the following observations:[27]

- Companies with good and strong corporate governance have much more resilient share prices during market downturns.

- Companies with good corporate governance outperform others with poorer corporate governance standards.

- Bad market environments host companies with exceptional governance standards, and forward-looking management will strive harder to surpass the poor levels of governance in their market to attract a larger pool of investors.

---

[26] Examples are APEC, OECD, and CLSA.
[27] 'Corporate Governance-Emerging Markets Equities Research' CLSA Ltd, October 2000.

- Good corporate governance can help bring down the cost of capital of a company as the demand by large and sophisticated investors for its shares will increase.

However, the same report also points out that strong economies with sound macro-economic management, such as Hong Kong and Singapore, that have good governance standards with strict enforcement of rules and regulations provide no guarantee for widespread compliance with good corporate governance standards. In fact, surprisingly few companies in these markets have outstanding governance, with most only meeting mandatory requirements.[28] Despite the seemingly high ranking Hong Kong has achieved in corporate governance, the perception of Hong Kong's governance is found to be better than it really is.

10.43

One recent corporate governance survey of 168 listed companies confirms this view. The authors found that the level and quality of corporate governance vary widely across firms in Hong Kong, with H-shares performing more poorly than the thirty-three Hang Seng constituent stocks.[29] A major finding was that management generally ignores the interests of minority shareholders by not consulting their views in decisions on stock repurchases, dividend policy, and executive compensation.

10.44

The survey may adopt an international perspective that does not agree with the characteristics of Hong Kong's commercial environment: family-controlled local businesses are more predominant than in other major markets. Concentrated ownership allows minority shareholders little scope to oppose management, as in most parts of Asia. So-called independent directors are rarely independent at all; a number of them tend to be friends of the controlling shareholders. Investors at large are mostly speculative and are uninterested in governance issues. As a consequence, listed companies disregard corporate governance unless they have substantial relationships with foreign or institutional shareholders, or meeting the minimum standards required by regulation. This picture shows that Hong Kong is far from representing a model of corporate governance.

10.45

In view of these problems, Hong Kong regulatory and professional agencies and SROs such as the ICAC, SFC, HKEx, and HKICPA all have taken a strong pro-active role in promoting the value of corporate governance to the general public and different business sectors in Hong Kong and Mainland China. However,

10.46

---

[28] ibid, p 1.
[29] SYL Cheung, JT Connelly, P Limpaphayom, & L Zhou, 'Do Investors Really Care About Corporate Governance? Evidence from the Hong Kong Market', available at <http://webb-site.com/codocs/dircacghk.pdf>, a website maintained by David Webb, a well-known investor and corporate governance activist.

challenges still lie ahead. An important issue arises from Hong Kong's recent achievement as the most important overseas capital raising centre for Mainland China's state-owned and private enterprises. As the financial relationship between Hong Kong and China develops further in this respect, one immediate concern is whether Hong Kong's governance system will deteriorate as a result of trying to attract even more China enterprises to raise capital or set up overseas operations in Hong Kong. Currently, the risk management and corporate governance systems of the Hong Kong financial markets are generally rated higher than those in Mainland China. The concern is justified by a recent study which discovered that pairs of economically interdependent countries—especially if the countries are both economically developed—appear to adopt common corporate governance standards even after accounting for the effects of common legal origin.[30] As China becomes more economically developed, the governance systems of Hong Kong and China may converge to a common set of standards. It is therefore imperative that Hong Kong continues to reform its own governance system and share its experiences with the regulatory bodies in China in order to come up with a common set of standards which stand above where Hong Kong and China are today.

10.47 Overdependence on market forces and the regulatory bodies to monitor and control the management behaviour of a firm can lead to a costly corporate governance process. What is of concern from the regulatory perspective is not about prohibiting a particular firm getting into a high-profile financial scandal. But rather it is the extent and the scale of abuse across businesses that is the practical issue, for it may trigger rounds of regulatory campaigns to fight the war against fraud. As the war machinery against fraud improves, it is likely to generate more complex regulation and accounting rules which lack transparency and inherently encourage regulatory arbitrage.

10.48 Many professional bodies have codes of conduct to maintain the professional and ethical conduct of their members and to protect the best interests of the society.[31] It is only by means of promoting professional integrity, ethics, and social responsibility, that corporate governance can add value by saving cost to the firm and to the society at large.

10.49 The standard corporate governance mechanisms that are the focus of much of the literature in finance and economics do not appear to work very effectively. According to two authoritative writers:

---

[30] T Kahnna, J Kogan, & K Palepu, 'Globalization and Similarities in Corporate Governance: A Cross-Country Analysis', working paper, 9 August 2002.
[31] Examples include estate agents, insurance, bankers, accountants, lawyers, medical practitioners, and engineers.

... despite this lack of outside discipline and monitoring, most firms seem to operate fairly efficiently. In all the countries considered there are many firms that compete effectively in international markets and their shareholders have historically received high rates of return. ... How can firms operate efficiently and generate returns for shareholders when standard corporate governance mechanisms are ineffective? We have argued that a broader perspective than the standard agency view of governance is necessary.[32]

This point is particularly true for Asian cities such as Hong Kong where the **10.50** listed companies on the main board of the SEHK tend to meet just the minimum requirements for corporate governance and yet their performance has been satisfactory.

The same authors went on to suggest that the crucial driving force is the **10.51** dynamic competition in product markets:

In order for firms to survive in competitive markets in constantly changing environments, they must have entrepreneurial management teams that do more than cost minimize. They must make good decisions about the future direction of the firm should move in.

This view is well shared by Po Chung and Saimond Yip in *The Five Dynamics of Entrepreneurship*.[33] They reason that no corporate governance system and regulatory framework can function if the 'Personal Operating System' and the 'Root Qualities' of the executives in charge or the entrepreneur should falter.[34] Here, the personal operating system is the set of values that a person should abide by in life in order to be able to contribute to the overall good of the society.

In Chinese society, the most highly regarded set of virtues is the famous **10.52** list of the thirteen Confucian virtues, namely;[35] 仁(*ren*)—kindness; 義(*yi*)—righteousness; 禮(*li*)—respect; 智(*zhi*)—wisdom; 信(*xin*)—trustworthiness; 忠(*zhong*)—loyalty; 勇(*yong*)—courage; 廉(*lian*)—uncorruptedness; 恥(*chi*)—shame; 孝(*xiao*)—care for the old; 悌(*ti*)—care for the young; 改(*gai*)—self-correction; and 恕(*shu*)—forgiveness.

The virtues were recorded more than two thousand years ago for civil adminis- **10.53** trators who assumed responsibility for all social, political, economic, and legal

---

[32] F Allen & D Gale, 'Corporate Governance and Competition', in X Vives (ed), *Corporate Governance: Theoretical and Empirical Perspectives* (Cambridge University Press 2000), pp 77–8.

[33] *The Five Dynamics of Entrepreneurship* is a forthcoming book by Po Chung and Saimond Yip, 2006. An article on *The Five Dynamics of Entrepreneurship* can be downloaded from <http://www.casebv.com>.

[34] Some minimum 'root qualities' defined by Po and Yip are: (1) Minimum passion, focus, and dedication, (2) minimum luck/blessing factor and health, (3) minimum risk tolerance and sleep factor, (4) minimum guts and stamina; and (5) minimum IQ and EQ.

[35] *Pin-yin* is put in brackets.

matters in China.[36] This perspective has a bearing on the governance of businesses in Hong Kong. Most of the big businesses in Hong Kong are family-controlled and their corporate governance systems are less than impressive. What counts towards their success is really the personal operating system of the dominant shareholders.

10.54 A series of studies sponsored by the Hong Kong ICAC in 2003 led to the following conclusions: (1) corporate governance can enhance the competitive advantage of the firm by means of retaining and attracting human capital to the firm;[37] (2) corporate governance can enable the firm to accumulate both internal and external social capital which is essential for the long-term success of the firm;[38] and (3) good and sound corporate governance promotes integrity, ethical conduct, and social responsibility.[39] When good corporate governance practices are in place, they attract human capital and increase the social value of a firm. The drivers for value creation are corporate governance and integrity, honesty, and social responsibility rather than the traditional finance notion of maximization of shareholders' value. Although government regulations can help prevent misconduct by corporate executives, the implementation and enforcement process may be costly to the tax payers and to the society as a whole.

D. Product Innovation

10.55 Although Hong Kong has well-developed financial product markets, its government may also wish to influence certain financial parameters such as market volatility or liquidity, or at times to affect prevailing prices by means of regulation. The regulatory environment may have a deterrent effect on illegal trading and transaction behaviour but the state's ability to influence market prices has

---

[36] Po Chung and S Yip, above.

[37] WN Chua, 'Corporate Governance as a Competitive Necessity', National University of Singapore, Singapore (Team: S/NUS14/P), Corporate Governance for the New Generation, organized by Hong Kong ICAC, 2003.

[38] Huang Yuanjiang & Liu Yang, 'Corporate Governance as a Competitive Necessity', Zhongshan University, Guangzhou, China (Team: C/ZSU14/P), Corporate Governance for the New Generation, organized by Hong Kong ICAC, 2003.

[39] Yu Lingyan & Tian Xiangwen, 'Corporate Governance and the Promotion of Integrity, Ethical Conduct and Social Responsibility', Zhongshan University, Guangzhou, China (Team: C/ZSU08/P); Zheng Yang & Zhu Jingping, 'Corporate Governance and the Promotion of Integrity, Ethical Conduct and Social Responsibility', Zhongshan University, Guangzhou, China (Team: C/ZSU15/P), Corporate Governance for the New Generation, organized by Hong Kong ICAC, 2003.

been found to be inconclusive.[40] However, one example of a field where government may be able to support product innovation may be in using securitization as a form of structured finance, especially through the use of the debt capital markets to securitize revenue from public works and projects. One recent example was a series of 2004 securitized transactions arranged for the Hong Kong government that raised over HK$ 8.0 billion (US$ 1.28 billion) using transport toll revenues.

Securitization has certain advantages for government compared to outright pri-   **10.56**
vatization and other similar ways to deploy public assets to raise funds. These include creating a customized capital structure that can deconstruct market and credit risks to suit the risk-return preferences of varying classes of investor. It also provides a true revenue-based operational and valuation mechanism that increases commercial transparency. Hong Kong is likely to be able to attract considerable investor support by securitizing revenue from public assets, including housing, retail space, car parks, and transport infrastructure. The process may also offer an incentive for efficiency in public project management because securitization allows the delineation of duties among operators, capital providers (investors), regulators, servicing and reporting agencies, and account administrators. Accordingly, it may increase the transparency of business operations and create a more accountable mechanism for professional managers.

A wider economic benefit that Hong Kong may generate from a large-scale   **10.57**
securitization programme is that a more balanced and developed capital market would provide broader and comprehensive investment products in terms of risk-spectrum and capital structure, which are beneficial to both issuers (government or private sector) and investors (institutional and retail). It could certainly bring more financial stability to Hong Kong's economy in the long run. The development of securitization and other similar debt strategies could also lessen the risk of contagion and instability in the event of a financial crisis.

There are several steps that the Hong Kong government should take to facilitate   **10.58**
the growing use of securitization. First, it can continue to foster a market-friendly regulatory environment with an investor-supportive legal securities framework. The SFC should also ensure the transparency and independence of the securities markets, encourage the general awareness of securitization techniques, and support accounting reforms that do not unreasonably penalize the use of the technique by financial institutions. One approach is for the government to continue its asset utilization efforts, for example through the HK

---

[40] eg S Pruitt & M KS Tse, 'Federal Reserve Margin Changes and OTC Stocks', in A Lo (ed), *The Industrial Organization and Regulations of the Securities Industry* (Chicago: National Bureau of Economic Research, 1996).

Link transactions, and begin to establish long-term investor confidence. A by-product of this strategy may be that Hong Kong will see activity expand in this specialized transaction area as a fund-raising capital market hub for non-Chinese corporate entities. While this has long been the case for multilateral bond issuers in the local HK dollar sector and in the international banking markets, where Hong Kong and Singapore are the dominant centres for regional syndicated lending in East Asia, a similar pattern has not been established for debt or equity market instruments, in part due to prevailing HKEx listing requirements that generally favour local and Mainland entities to the prejudice of well-rated foreign companies.

10.59 Limits to the development of a flourishing securitization market stem from both issuers and investors, in terms of unfamiliarity with transaction mechanics, worries as to poor secondary market liquidity, and the costs of competing sources of funds. High local banking and equity sector liquidity has long tended to make borrowers rely on traditional funding methods, but failing to diversify in funding sources is risky in times of potential market stress. Furthermore, the transactions expenses associated with securitization deals are relatively high, especially in a new market where both the frequency and volume of securitization transactions are low. Securitization involves many third party intermediaries and requires more resources in due diligence, including iterative credit rating processes and the intensive modelling of collateral asset performance data. These factors can burden both issuers and investors.

E. Financial Fraud and Misconduct

10.60 Financial fraud and misconduct is a theme highlighted throughout this volume. One objective of financial regulation is to help prevent and to deter crime and unethical decisions in financial and economic transactions.

10.61 In relation to criminalization of money-laundering and the financing of terrorism, Hong Kong is in line with international standards.[41] However, according to a recent IMF report on Hong Kong,

> Statistics reveal a disparity between the large number of investigations initiated and the relatively small number of resulting prosecutions and even smaller number of convictions, suggesting either that there are too many investigations or that there is some impediment to effectively prosecuting and securing convictions.[42]

10.62 In this respect, one method to evaluate the efficiency of regulation of financial misconduct is to look to the number of investigations initiated, the rate of

---

[41] IMF, HKSAR Report, above, p 79.   [42] ibid, p 33.

prosecutions out of investigations, and the rate of consequential successful convictions. The number of investigations initiated may suffer from inadequate oversight of remittance agents and money changers and inadequate resources of the Joint Financial Intelligence Unit. The rate of prosecutions may be reduced by difficulties in ascertaining customer identification in the case of shell companies and problems in the quality of reports on suspicious transactions. By these criteria, Hong Kong ostensibly scores poorly in terms of sound infrastructure for fighting money-laundering and financing of terrorism.[43]

The efficiency of regulation depends significantly on the effectiveness of the enforcement and prosecution process. For example, consider corruption. The whole process starts with how individuals are to report suspected corruption cases to the ICAC. The willingness to report depends on the general public's awareness of the sorts of corrupt activities taking place around them and how well-protected they feel they are if they proceed to make a report to the ICAC. Further, out of cases reported to the ICAC, what percentage is really related to corruption? This percentage can only improve by educating the public on what constitutes corruption. Out of those apparently corruption related, what percentage is perusable? Out of those cases that are perusable, the prosecution ratio depends in part on whether investigators have the ability to collect adequate evidence and facts to initiate prosecution. It also depends on the investigators' understanding of intricate business and financial transactions and their expertise in forensic accounting. **10.63**

Two critical elements for achieving the regulatory goal of deterring fraud and financial misconduct are: to maximize the probability of catching those who have committed an offence against the law and, to those who have been caught, impart a punitive judgment severe enough to have a deterrent effect on others who intend to commit similar acts. In order to enhance the chance of a successful catch, the law-enforcing bodies must be knowledgeable about or at least be aware of the possible means for committing financial crimes or unethical acts under various adverse business conditions. This also requires good coordination and communication of key market practice information between the different professional bodies such as accounting, law, and finance, the corresponding regulatory bodies, and the law enforcement body. On the other hand, the degree of punishment depends on the extent to which the courts are empowered to take actions against suspects such as freezing of assets, or to give judgment on the convicted such as confiscation of relevant assets. **10.64**

Overall, despite frequent efforts to try to set up a more effective regulatory framework to deter financial crimes, they will continue to exist and grow in **10.65**

---

[43] ibid.

complexity, articulation, and scope. This is part of the nature of any financial market in the world.

10.66 This is particularly true in a world in which information is the dominant factor that drives market movements and especially when information, raw or analysed, may not be equally accessible to all parties concerned. The world is dynamic and messy. Very often information, electronic or not, is incomplete. The general public can hardly identify and discriminate relevant and useful information from gossip and tell the difference between rumours and insider information until it is too late.[44] As Robert J Shiller puts it in *Irrational Exuberance*, 'Investors are striving to do the right thing, but they have limited abilities and certain natural modes of behaviour that decide their actions when an unambiguous prescription for action is lacking.'[45] This allows room for the creation and proliferation of success stories. 'Get on quick, Get off soon' has therefore become a formula for making a fortune for some in the financial markets and a tombstone for many others.

10.67 Financial disasters often begin with excessive greed.[46] Greed easily ensues from seeing one's neighbour who seems to be able to do all the right things to make a lot of money effortlessly. When compounded with a basic human interest in gambling seen in all cultures,[47] greed can transpire into all sorts of risk-taking behaviour in the speculative markets. As losses mount, the gambler would perhaps more readily render his decision based on instinct and emotion. As long as things develop by human instinct and emotion, mistakes will be made, and to salvage from the financial crisis caused by those mistakes, crimes will likely be committed.

10.68 As a result, while no regulatory framework for financial fraud and misconduct is perfect, in Hong Kong, the gaps between the new SFO framework and that available outside its context is a clear issue and one that could be addressed more thoroughly (see section B above).

10.69 In addition, there is clearly a link between corporate governance (discussed in the previous section) and financial fraud and misconduct, in that many cases of financial fraud and misconduct occur in the context of corporate environments. Common fraudulent business practices of firms operating in financial markets (especially financial firms) can be generally classified into: (1) diversion of cash and asset misappropriations, (2) deception about earnings, (3) deception about

---

[44] KS Tse, 'The Lines between Bull and Bear Markets in the New Economy', 22 *Sun Magazine* (17 June–14 July 2000), pp 18–20.
[45] R Shiller, *Irrational Exuberance* (Princeton University Press, 2000), p 136.
[46] Examples are Barings and Enron.   [47] Shiller, above, p 140.

positions, and (4) deliberate misreporting of positions.[48] Most of the business frauds committed are, by nature, an operational risk, often being associated with the weak management and ineffective internal control process within the firm.

Understanding the motives behind such fraudulent practices is perhaps a factor **10.70** in establishing an effective regulatory framework and management system for internal control and self-monitoring purposes. What is the psychology of fraud? An individual's decision on unethical or even criminal choice can be better understood from the economics and finance theory on an individual's attitude towards risk aversion, loss aversion, and risk-taking and how individuals make important financial choices when faced with uncertainty.

Economic downturns are more likely to give rise to imminent losses and the **10.71** visibility of fraudulent acts will be greater because it is more likely that corporate problems will be exposed.

Fraudulent business practices are not unique to bad economic conditions. Even **10.72** during good economic times, frauds do not go away either. Essentially, a manager having to meet a demanding financial objective within a relatively short time horizon would have to take on high-risk investments, which is the case especially when the manager is concerned about being unable to meet the target by the end of the time period.[49] By taking on high-risk alternatives, the manager is more likely to be faced with an imminent loss so big that he could not but push his luck to the limit by taking on even more risky endeavours.

Because of these reasons, regulation of corporate governance practices can also **10.73** have an important effect on financial fraud and misconduct in the corporate context.

F. Conclusion

The future of Hong Kong's financial markets hinges on how well Hong Kong **10.74** can play out its role as a financial hub in the region and as a capital raising and risk management centre for China and other leading economies, and how well connected Hong Kong is to other major financial centres in the world.

Hong Kong's financial markets at present comprise a number of different seg- **10.75** ments, namely domestic finance, Mainland China finance, Asian finance, and global finance. Each of these segments has different characteristics and their

[48] S Allen, *Financial Risk Management* (John Wiley, 2003), ch 3 on Operational Risk.
[49] MKS Tse, M White, & J Uppal, 'Downside Risk and Investment Planning' (1993) 28:4 *Financial Review* 585–605.

respective development will have an important role in Hong Kong's future as a financial centre in Asia. Further, while certain policy, institutional, legal and regulatory matters are under the control of Hong Kong itself, others are not. These relate especially to the interaction between Hong Kong and Mainland China on the one hand, and between Hong Kong and other countries in Asia on the other.

10.76 In this picture, the 'China effect' on international financial markets cannot be ignored. On the one hand, Hong Kong as the gateway to China has been enjoying the benefits of the fast economic growth of China. On the other hand, problems are developing and surfacing. While China has emerged in recent years as the largest recipient of foreign direct investment, research has also raised concerns as to whether China is taking direct investment away from other Asian economies and hence whether China's fast growth will hamper their growth.[50]

10.77 Although research indicates that China's effect on other Asian countries' shares of world inward FDI is mixed, minimal, and not significant and that the China effect is not the most important determinant of inward direct investment to these economies, it also opens up other concerns. First, the high rate of flow of foreign direct investment into China also may amount to overinvestment leading not to high returns on capital but waste of resources. If this is the case and China experiences similar problems to those experienced by other Asian economies during the financial crises of 1997–8, this will have a severe adverse impact on the Hong Kong economy. Second, Hong Kong has been playing a key role in channelling foreign investment into China in recent years. If the flow slows due to increasing perceptions of investment and regulatory risk in China coupled with lower rates of return on capital, the development of Hong Kong as a financial hub for China and Asia will be slowed dramatically.

10.78 How well Hong Kong can achieve its objectives and weather difficulties hinges on its financial infrastructure. In particular, Hong Kong needs to provide and offer a range of quality financial products and services, to have in place a sound and effective regulatory system that ensures fairness to all market participants, to have the expertise in financial engineering, valuation, and research and development in business and finance, and to have good corporate governance and culture.

10.79 International financial centres provide a platform for large values of foreign exchange, cross-border securities issuance and trading, international bank deposits and lending, and other international financial transactions to take

---

[50] B Chantasasawat, KC Fung, H Lizaka, & A Siu, 'International Competition for Foreign Direct Investment: The Case of China', HIEBS Working Paper No 1134, The University of Hong Kong, December 2003.

place, and to allow and facilitate a wide range of financial services to take place internationally from various locations. From this perspective, Hong Kong as an international financial centre serves a multi-faceted role. First, financial services in Hong Kong serve to channel surplus funds from net savers in Hong Kong and to end-users in Hong Kong, Mainland China, and other economies. Second, Hong Kong's financial markets help channel to end-users in Hong Kong the surplus funds of net savers in China and other foreign countries. A third role that Hong Kong's financial services can play is to help channel net savings generated in other economies to end-users scattered across economies outside Hong Kong. Finally, Hong Kong can continue to serve as a centre of resource excellence for transaction-seeking financial institutions, investors, and multi-national companies, in fund-raising, fund management, and financial services not involving flows of capital.

Rankings of international financial centres vary according to whether more importance is attached to international banking activities such as cross-border deposits, lending, foreign exchange, or to international investment activities such as stock and bond issuance and trading, or to insurance such as underwriting and brokerage, or to derivatives and financial innovation for risk management.[51] Hong Kong ranks highly in some of these surveys in recent years, especially in foreign exchange transactions, insurance underwriting, and stock issuance.[52] **10.80**

At the same time, it faces competition from other centres in the region, including Tokyo, Singapore, and Shanghai. **10.81**

Tokyo is by far the largest financial centre in Asia. The key advantage of Tokyo derives from the expansion of the Japanese economy since World War II and its growth to become the second largest economy in the world. Although Tokyo serves as the base for yen-based financing and asset-holding in the global setting of financial services, it is largely a domestic market by nature, servicing Japan's trading activities with other countries. **10.82**

In some respects, Singapore is similar to Hong Kong as a financial centre. However, there are some important differences as well. For example, Singapore remains an independent, sovereign jurisdiction whereas Hong Kong is a part of China under the formulation of 'one-country two systems'; and traditionally has a different regulatory orientation to Hong Kong (emphasizing the role of the government in the economy) and relatively little incursion into domestic **10.83**

---

[51] eg the WFE Report 2004 gives a comprehensive set of cross-countries statistics on fixed-income market, equity market, foreign exchange market, derivatives, and market activity. See <http://world-exchanges.org>.

[52] See Chapter 1 of this volume.

banking business by foreign participants. Singapore has been successful mainly in fund management, forex-related trading, and derivatives. In many areas such as IPOs, debt capital markets, and financial engineering and innovation, Singapore has been competing aggressively against Hong Kong to become the major financial hub serving China and the Asian region. Over the last twenty years, the political uncertainty in countries such as Indonesia, Philippines, and even Malaysia, have helped transform Singapore into a 'safety-box' centre for capital in that part of the region. At the same time, however, it lacks two key advantages of Hong Kong: first, it is not part of China; and second, it lacks the traditional free-market culture of Hong Kong, thereby reducing scope for financial and economic innovation in Singapore.

10.84 Shanghai is the largest financial centre in Mainland China. It has often been compared to Hong Kong in terms of when Shanghai would overtake Hong Kong and assume the position of being the country's premier capital-raising centre. In terms of stock market capitalization, amount of domestic bonds outstanding, and size of international reserves, Shanghai has already caught up with, if not overtaken, Hong Kong.[53] Moreover, the City Government of Shanghai and the Central Government of China have over and again indicated that Shanghai be designated as the international financial centre in China to help bring capital to the needs of China's economic reforms and growth. In 1992 the central government designated Shanghai 'an international financial centre' and said the city's financial sector should account for 18 per cent of municipal GDP by 2005 (though this has not been achieved and has been quietly dropped).[54] On the other hand, between 2002 and 2005, the Shanghai stock market was declining by about 20 per cent a year, despite the injection of funds into the stock market was by the central government as an attempt to salvage market confidence.[55]

10.85 Although Shanghai has certainly made tremendous progress to establish itself as the financial centre in China, the role of Hong Kong as an international financial centre in China cannot be replaced overnight. Hong Kong has been functioning as a regional financial centre for more than half a generation. Its financial and regulatory infrastructure, open-market system, expertise, and experience are among the finest in the world. Most especially, its legal system based on the rule of law will not be matched anytime soon by Shanghai; this is likely to remain Hong Kong's key competitive advantage in the years to come.

---

[53] IMF, 2003 Report on Hong Kong Special Administrative Region.
[54] 'Hong Kong still the belle of the ball', *South China Morning Post*, 11 June 2005.
[55] ibid.

Moreover, with China having a huge and growing economic system, there is   **10.86**
no reason why China should have only one financial centre, especially with
the recent competitive economic development between the Pearl River Delta
(nine southern provinces plus Hong Kong and Macau) and Yangtzee River
Delta which includes Shanghai. Recently, Shanghai officials are more inclined
to talk of Shanghai as 'an international transportation centre' with a new
deep-water port, an expanded international airport and road and rail links at
the top of their priority list. Overall, Hong Kong and Shanghai will definitely play different roles as capital formation centres for their respective
regions.

With globalization as the on-going trend for the future growth and develop-   **10.87**
ment of financial markets, capital flows across different borders and countries
will be freer. The Hong Kong SAR government will be under pressure to attract
both local and foreign capital to support financial market growth and development. In order to do this, the government must maintain Hong Kong as a stable
and growing economy with transparent financial and other government regulations and minimize possible shocks due to regulatory risk or uncertain shifts in
government policies that would undermine the confidence of capital. In order
for Hong Kong to have a unique and significant role to play in the globalized
financial markets, Hong Kong will have to continue its traditional neo-liberal
monetary and fiscal policies, open borders, low inflation, and balanced-budget
or low-deficit growth paths, all operating within the context of a rule of law
system operating under the framework of 'one country, two systems'.

At the same time, Hong Kong will have to pursue a regulatory framework   **10.88**
compatible with the needs of Hong Kong, China, and global financial market
trends. However, as discussed above and throughout this volume, this will not
be easy as challenges will always arise which undermine regulatory efforts.

At present, a key challenge facing the regulatory bodies in Hong Kong is the   **10.89**
recent divergence on the regulatory framework between the US and the EU in
areas such as the Basel II Capital Accord on capital reserves and International
Accounting Standard 27 (IAS 27) on Consolidated Financial Statements and
Accounting for Investments in Subsidiaries (discussed in Chapter 3).

In relation to Basel II, in April 2005, the US bank regulatory agencies   **10.90**
announced that they would delay the release of a proposal to implement Basel II,
which was originally targeted for mid-2005.[56] The decision is based on a recent
industry survey by the regulators focusing on the quantitative impact of the

---

[56] The US bank regulatory agencies are the Federal Reserve, the Office of the Comptroller of
the Currency (OCC), the Federal Deposit Insurance Corporation (FDIC), and the Office of
Thrift Supervision (OTS).

accord on banks and financial institutions. Their initial analysis of the results raised more questions than expected and showed that there were material reductions in the aggregate minimum capital reserves required for the participant population and significant dispersion of results across institutions and portfolio types.[57] The bank regulators further suggest that additional work is necessary to determine whether these results reflect differences in risk, reveal limitations of the study, identify variations in the stages of bank implementation efforts (particularly related to data availability), and/or suggest the need for adjustments to the Basel II framework. Although the US bank agencies remain committed to the implementation of Basel II, they intend to retain other measures affecting bank reserves which include prompt corrective action and leverage requirements.

10.91 By contrast, the European Commission is rapidly progressing towards the finalization of a Directive implementing Basel II in the EU. In the EU, Basel II will extend not only to banks but to all financial services firms.

10.92 The result will be an interesting conflict between the goals of financial liberalization and market access and those of financial stability and especially regulation of internationally active banks and other financial firms. This conflict will be very evident in the context in Hong Kong, where banks and other financial services firms from the US, EU, and many other jurisdictions are active. In all likelihood, Hong Kong will address this through requiring foreign banks to incorporate locally capitalized subsidiaries subject to local rules in order to access its markets. However, the issue of differing capital requirements for different financial institutions (ie banks, securities firms, insurance companies) will remain. This is a competitiveness issue which will need to be addressed.

---

[57] 'US Bank Regulators Delay Basel II Proposal', *Wall Street Journal*, 29 April 2005. Previously, US regulators have set January 2008 to be the target date for the implementation of Basel II, which is expected to allow large, well-capitalized banks and others that can show adequate risk management to hold less regulatory capital for loans.

INDEX